Lecture Notes in Artificial Intell

Subseries of Lecture Notes in Computer Scien
Edited by J. G. Carbonell and J. Siekmann

Lecture Notes in Computer Science

Edited by G. Goos, J. Hartmanis and J. van Leeuwen

Springer
Berlin
Heidelberg
New York
Barcelona
Hong Kong
London
Milan
Paris
Singapore
Tokyo

Harald Ganzinger   David McAllester
Andrei Voronkov (Eds.)

Logic for Programming and Automated Reasoning

6th International Conference, LPAR'99
Tbilisi, Georgia, September 6-10, 1999
Proceedings

 Springer

Series Editors

Jaime G. Carbonell, Carnegie Mellon University, Pittsburgh, PA, USA
Jörg Siekmann, University of Saarland, Saarbrücken, Germany

Volume Editors

Harald Ganzinger
Max-Planck-Institut für Informatik
Im Stadtwald, D-66123 Saarbrücken, Germany
E-mail: harald.ganzinger@mpi-sb.mpg.de

David McAllester
AT&T Labs Research
180 Park Ave, Florham Park, NJ 07932-0971, USA
E-mail: dmac@research.att.com

Andrei Voronkov
University of Manchester, Department of Computer Science
Oxford Road, M13 9PL Manchester, UK
E-mail: voronkov@cs.man.ac.uk

Cataloging-in-Publication data applied for

Die Deutsche Bibliothek - CIP-Einheitsaufnahme

Logic programming and automated reasoning : 6th international conference ;
proceedings / LPAR '99, Tbilisi, Georgia, September 6 - 10, 1999. Harald
Ganzinger ... (ed.). - Berlin ; Heidelberg ; New York ; Barcelona ; Hong Kong ;
London ; Milan ; Paris ; Singapore ; Tokyo : Springer, 1999
 (Lecture notes in computer science ; Vol. 1705 : Lecture notes in artificial
intelligence)
 ISBN 3-540-66492-0

CR Subject Classification (1998): I.2.3, F.3, D.1, F.4.1

ISBN 3-540-66492-0 Springer-Verlag Berlin Heidelberg New York

© Springer-Verlag Berlin Heidelberg 1999
Printed in Germany

Typesetting: Camera-ready by author
SPIN 10704915   06/3142 – 5 4 3 2 1 0   Printed on acid-free paper

Preface

This volume contains the papers presented at the Sixth International Conference on Logic for Programming and Automated Reasoning (LPAR'99), held in Tbilisi, Georgia, September 6–10, 1999, and hosted by the University of Tbilisi.

Forty-four papers were submitted to LPAR'99. Each of the submissions was reviewed by three program committee members and an electronic program committee meeting was held via the Internet. Twenty-three papers were accepted.

We would like to thank the many people who have made LPAR'99 possible. We are grateful to the following groups and individuals: to the program committee and the additional referees for reviewing the papers in a very short time, to the organizing committee, and to the local organizers of the INTAS workshop in Tbilisi in April 1994 (Khimuri Rukhaia, Konstantin Pkhakadze, and Gela Chankvetadze). And last but not least, we would like to thank Konstantin Korovin, who maintained the program committee Web page; Uwe Waldmann, who supplied macros for these proceedings and helped us to install some programs for the electronic management of the program committee work; and Bill McCune, who implemented these programs.

July 1999

Harald Ganzinger
David McAllester
Andrei Voronkov
LPAR'99 Program Chairs

Conference Organization

Program Chairs

Harald Ganzinger (MPI Informatik, Saarbrücken)
David McAllester (AT&T Labs Research)
Andrei Voronkov (University of Manchester)

Assistant to Program Chairs

Konstantin Korovin

Program Committee

Arnon Avron (Tel-Aviv University)
Leo Bachmair (SUNY at Stony Brook)
Franz Baader (RWTH Aachen)
Howard Barringer (University of Manchester)
Manfred Broy (Munich University of Technology)
Maurice Bruynooghe (Catholic University of Leuven)
Alan Bundy (University of Edinburgh)
Harald Ganzinger (MPI Informatik, Saarbrücken)
Jürgen Giesl (Darmstadt University of Technology)
Georg Gottlob (Vienna Technical University)
Ryuzo Hasegawa (Kyushu University)
Neil Jones (DIKU University of Copenhagen)
Jean-Pierre Jouannaud (CNRS)
Maurizio Lenzerini (Università di Roma "La Sapienza")
Giorgio Levi (Pisa University)
Leonid Libkin (Bell Laboratories)
Patrick Lincoln (SRI International)
Yuri Matiyasevich (Steklov Institute of Mathematics, St.Petersburg)
David McAllester (AT&T Labs Research)
Robert Nieuwenhuis (Technical University of Catalonia)
Catuscia Palamidessi (Pennsylvania State University)
Frank Pfenning (Carnegie Mellon University)
Vladimir Sazonov (Program Systems Institute, Pereslavl-Zalesski)
Helmut Schwichtenberg (Ludwig-Maximilian University, Munich)
Andrzej Tarlecki (Warsaw University)
Yoshihito Toyama (Japan Advanced Institute of Science and Technology)
Moshe Vardi (Rice University)
Andrei Voronkov (University of Manchester)
Michael Zakharyashev (Keldysh Institute of Applied Mathematics, Moscow)

Local Organization

Rusiko Asatiani (Tbilisi University)
Nani Chanishvili (Tbilisi University)
Gela Chankvetadze (Tbilisi University)
Georgi Chikoidze (Tbilisi University)
Temur Khurodze (Tbilisi University), Chair
Temur Kutsia (Tbilisi University)
Khimuri Rukhaia (Tbilisi University)
Konstantin Pkhakadze (Tbilisi University)

List of Referees

Gianluca Amato
Frederic Blanqui
Gerd Brewka
Judicael Courant
Ludwik Czaja
Anatoli Degtyarev
Alessandra Di Pierro
Hans de Nivelle
Jacques Fleuriot
Hiroshi Fujita
Maurizio Gabbrielli
Roberta Gori
Jeremy Gow
Bernhard Gramlich
Katsumi Inoue
Andrew Ireland
Beata Konikowska
Miyuki Koshimura

Martin Kübler
Alexei Lisitsa
Dale Miller
Juan José Moreno Navarro
Rodrigo Readi Nasser
Yoshihiko Ohta
Jeff Polakow
Francesco Scarcello
Alexander B. Schmidt
Peter H. Schmitt
Carsten Schuermann
Gerd Stumme
Margus Veanes
Michael von der Beeck
Toby Walsh
Kevin Watkins
Klaus Weich
Markus Wenzel

Conferences preceding LPAR'99

RCLP'90, Irkutsk, Soviet Union, 1990
RCLP'91, Leningrad, Soviet Union, aboard the ship "Mikhail Lomonosov," 1991
LPAR'92, St. Petersburg, Russia, aboard the ship "Mikhail Lomonosov," 1992
LPAR'93, St. Petersburg, Russia, 1993
LPAR'94, Kiev, Ukraine, aboard the ship "Marshal Koshevoi," 1994

Table of Contents

Proofs About Lists Using Ellipsis

Alan Bundy and Julian Richardson*

Institute for Representation and Reasoning
University of Edinburgh
80 South Bridge, Edinburgh EH1 1HN, Scotland.
a.bundy@ed.ac.uk,julian.richardson@ed.ac.uk

Abstract. In this paper we explore the use of *ellipsis* in proofs about lists. We present a higher-order formulation of elliptic formulae, and describe its implementation in the λ*Clam* proof planner. We use an unambiguous higher-order formulation of lists which is amenable to formal proofs without using induction, and to display using the familiar ... notation.

1 Introduction

A notation often used in informal mathematical proofs is ellipsis (the dots in $a_1 + ... + a_n$). Not only does the use of ellipsis make many proofs much easier to understand, but it also naturally lends itself to theories where induction has been replaced by suitable axioms.

Ellipsis can be used to abbreviate many different kinds of formulae; in this paper, we explore the use of ellipsis in proofs about lists. This allows us to address important issues in the automatic treatment of ellipsis and, while we do not extensively consider it here, can be extended by applying fold functions (see for example equation (2) below and §11) to reasoning about elliptic formulae in which the main connective is not list cons. We present a higher-order formulation of elliptic formulae, and describe its implementation in the λ*Clam* proof planner [8]. To resolve the ambiguities inherent in elliptic representation, we use an underlying unambiguous representation which is portrayed by ellipsis. We define a higher-order function $\square$ which represents a list by the length of the list and a function which takes a natural number n and returns the nth member of the list.

Displaying proofs in elliptic notation poses interesting challenges. One step of a proof in the elliptic notation may require several steps in the implementation. The display mechanism can itself perform quite sophisticated rewriting in order to get a useful portrayal of a formula. The portrayal system cannot just be bolted on top of the theorem prover but must itself influence the way in which proofs are carried out; ensuring that formulae are in a form for which elliptic portrayal is effective imposes restrictions on the order in which proof steps are applied.

---

* The authors gratefully acknowledge the support of EPSRC grants GR/L/11724 and GR/M/45030, and the comments of their colleagues in the Mathematical Reasoning Group. We would also like to thank the referees for their insightful comments.

2   A Motivating Example

We consider two alternative definitions of a *foldl* function, one a recursive definition, the other an elliptic definition. The recursive definition is given in (1).

$$foldl(\otimes, A, []) = A$$
$$foldl(\otimes, A, [H|T]) = foldl(\otimes, A \otimes H, T) \tag{1}$$

How quickly can you spot what this function does? Compare this with an elliptic definition:

$$foldl(\otimes, A, [E_1, E_2, \ldots, E_n]) = (\ldots(A \otimes E_1) \otimes E_2) \otimes \ldots \otimes E_n) \tag{2}$$

Do you find that easier to understand?

If you are like us, you find (2) much easier to understand than (1). In fact, one can argue that (2) is the *real* meaning of *foldl*, and (1) is merely the best way to represent this meaning in most logics. Unfortunately, (2) is not normally available because ellipsis is not usually a legal part of the syntax.

We will call formulae like (2) *schematic*, because we can think of it as a schema standing for an infinite number of formulae: one for each n. Imagine we had a logic in which schematic formulae were legal syntax and in which (2) was the *definition* of *foldl*. We will call this a *schematic logic*. Such a logic was used in [1] to represent generalised proofs. From time to time other people propose such logics, e.g. [6].

We can use definition (2) to prove the following theorem:

$$foldl(\otimes, A, [E_1, \ldots, E_{n-1}, E_n]) = foldl(\otimes, A, [E_1, \ldots, E_{n-1}]) \otimes E_n$$

This is a trivial theorem in the schematic logic. It requires just two applications of definition (2). We must only be careful to insert the condition that $1 \leq n$, so that the right hand side is meaningful. By contrast the usual inductive proof using (1) is less immediately understandable as it requires induction and choosing an appropriate instantiation for the A in the induction hypothesis.[1]

It seems that schematic definitions and proofs that use them can be easier to understand than their regular counterparts. It is often possible to avoid induction by using a generalised schematic proof, i.e. one in which ellipsis is used in the proof as well as the formulae.

There are several problems which must be solved to make this possible:

1. Ellipsis can be ambiguous. There has to be a mechanism for deciding what is elided in the .... For example, what is meant by $[E_2, ..., E_{16}]$? Does the list have 15, 8, 4 or some other number of elements? In the preceding examples, the meaning of the ellipsis is clear, but in general it may be necessary to restrict the use of ellipsis to those cases that are unambiguous, if we can decide what those are.

---

[1] If A is not universally quantified in the conjecture, then an additional generalisation step is required in the inductive proof.

2. It is necessary to keep track of conditions, like $1 \leq n$ in the proof above, which are needed to ensure that schematic formulae are well formed. This can get quite hard.

3. We might want to translate the resulting schematic proof into a proof in a regular logic. Writing the tactics for this would be a challenge.

In the sections which follow, we present a representation of lists which lends itself both to formal proof and to elliptic proof and portrayal. To address (1) above, we do not consider the *input* of formulae which contain ellipsis, but aim instead merely to portray formulae using ellipsis in a predictable way which is unambiguous to the reader. We address (2) by disregarding well-formedness conditions in our initial implementation and checking manually to ensure that ill-formed formulae do not appear in the proof. The proofs we construct are proofs in a higher-order logic, so no translation is necessary to satisfy (3) above.

3   The Representation of Ellipsis

3.1   The Ambiguity of Ellipsis

The first problem in formalising ellipsis is its inherent ambiguity. The reader of a formula containing ellipsis has to induce a pattern from the expressions on either side of the dots. For instance, it is necessary to induce that $a_1 + \ldots + a_n$ means $\sum_{i=1}^{n} a_i$ and not $\sum_{i=1/2}^{n/2} a_{2.i}$, say, *i.e.* that the numbers go up in ones not twos — or threes — or in some more complicated pattern. One can try to disambiguate ellipsis by putting in more context, *e.g.* $a_1 + a_2 + \ldots + a_n$, but some ambiguity will always remain.

More importantly, it is hard to see how we can ensure that a "proof" is in fact a **proof** unless it can be expressed in an *unambiguous* internal representation.

3.2   An Unambiguous Representation

If an unambiguous internal representation is needed anyway, then why not use this instead of ellipsis? Ellipsis can be used as an external 'portray' form of this unambiguous representation. This will avoid the need for constant pattern recognition to figure out what is going on, but externally can be indistinguishable. Pattern recognition would be needed only if ellipsis is used when *inputting* formulae. This is the view we adopt here.

For n-ary sums and products we already have such an unambiguous notation in $\sum$ and $\prod$. However, we don't have such a notation for lists, sequences or other n-ary operations. The main focus of this paper is to introduce a similar notation for lists. This notation is then used for representing sequences and any other use of ellipsis. We will use the notation $\square$ in a similar way to $\sum$ or $\prod$.

$\square$ is a polymorphic, second order function of type:

$$\square : (nat \rightarrow (nat \rightarrow \tau)) \rightarrow list(\tau)$$

Its first argument is the length of the list. It applies the function to each of the natural numbers 1, 2, *etc.* up to this length and returns a list of the results, *i.e.*

$$\Box(n, f) = [f(1), \ldots, f(n)]$$

Note that we use function application instead of subscripts, so a subscribed term a_i is represented by a function application $a(i)$.

4   The Axiomatisation of $\Box$

$\Box$ can be defined recursively as follows (where :: and <> are infix *cons* and *append* respectively):

$$\Box(0, F) = nil$$
$$\Box(s(N), F) = \Box(N, F) <> (F(s(N)) :: nil)$$

Or, alternatively, as:

$$\Box(0, F) = nil$$
$$\Box(s(N), F) = F(1) :: \Box(N, \lambda i.\ F(s(i)))$$

Armed with $\Box$ we can avoid much of the need for recursion in defining new functions (*cf.* the work of Bird [2]). All we need is an axiom that says that all lists can be put in $\Box$ form, *i.e.*

$$\forall L{:}list(\tau), \exists n{:}nat, \exists f : (nat \to \tau).\ L = \Box(n, f)$$

Then we can define *len*, <> (infix *append*) and *rev* as:

$$len(\Box(N, F)) = N$$
$$rev(\Box(N, F)) = \Box(N, \lambda i.\ F(s(N) - i))$$
$$\Box(M, F) <> \Box(N, G) = \Box(M + N, comb(M, F, G))$$

where *comb* is defined by:

$$comb(M, F, G)(i) = \begin{cases} F(i) & \text{if } i \leq M \\ G(i - M) & \text{if } i > M \end{cases} \tag{3}$$

These definitions should be portrayed, in elliptic notation, as:

$$len([F(1), \ldots, F(N)]) = N$$
$$rev([F(1), \ldots, F(N)]) = [F(N), \ldots, F(1)]$$
$$[F(1), \ldots, F(M)] <> [G(1), \ldots, G(N)] =$$
$$[F(1), \ldots, F(M), G(1), \ldots, G(N)]$$

5   Proofs Using Ellipsis

As so many of the definitions are non-recursive, the proofs can be non-inductive. In this section we present an example.

5.1   Rotate Length

Consider the classic rotate-length conjecture:

$$rot(len(L), L) = L$$

Informally, $rot(N, L)$ returns a list with the same length as the list L but with the first N elements removed from the front and appended to the end. Here is a definition of rot using ellipsis:

$$M \leq N \rightarrow rot(M, \square(N, F)) = \square(N - M, \lambda i . F(M + i)) <> \square(M, F)$$

In elliptic notation, this definition translates to:

$$rot(M, [F(1), ..., F(N)]) = [F(M + 1), ..., F(N)] <> [F(1), ..., F(M)]$$

Then the $\square$ proof is:

$$
\begin{aligned}
rot(len(\square(N, F)), \square(N, F)) &= rot(N, \square(N, F)) \\
&= \square(N - N, \lambda i.\ F(N + i)) <> \square(N, F) \\
&= \square(0, \lambda i.\ F(N + i)) <> \square(N, F) \\
&= \square(0 + N, comb(0, \lambda i.\ F(N + i), F)) \quad (4) \\
&= \square(N, F)
\end{aligned}
$$

or in elliptic notation:

$$
\begin{aligned}
rot(len([F(1), \dots , F(N)]), [F(1), \dots , F(N)]) \\
= rot(N, [F(1), \dots , F(N)]) \\
= [] <> [F(1), \dots , F(N)] \\
= [F(1), \dots , F(N)]
\end{aligned}
$$

For comparison, $\lambda Clam$ cannot prove this theorem using its standard inductive strategy. The $Clam$ proof planner [4] is unable to prove this theorem without using critics [5]. Both $Clam$ and $\lambda Clam$ are able to prove the generalised theorem $rot(len(l), l <> m) = (m <> l)$.

6   Elliptic Portrayal

The key to the success of this technique is that the internal $\square$ notation can be portrayed in an intuitively satisfying external elliptic notation. A comparison of the number of steps in the formal (four steps), versus the informal (two steps), proofs above indicates that there need not be a 1-1 correspondence between proof steps in the formal and informal proofs, and conversion between the two representations may not be entirely straightforward. Rewriting is often required to process the internal representation into a portrayable form. For example, correct portrayal of (4) above requires two rewrites: $0 + N \Rightarrow N$, and $comb(0, \lambda i.\ F(N + i), F) \Rightarrow F$. Sometimes internal proof steps cannot be portrayed at all and must be omitted, leading to a mismatch between internal and external proof steps.

Consider, for instance, the definition of append:

$$\Box(M, F) <> \Box(N, G) = \Box(M + N, comb(M, F, G))$$

which we would like to portray as:

$$[F(1), \dots, F(M)] <> [G(1), \dots, G(N)]) =$$
$$[F(1), \dots, F(M), G(1), \dots, G(N)]$$

Firstly, note that we do not want the internal function *comb* to appear at all. We want to evaluate expressions like $comb(M, F, G)(M + N)$ to $G(N)$, which requires the rewriting:

$$comb(M, F, G)(M + N) \Rightarrow G(M + N - M)$$
$$\Rightarrow G(N)$$

In general, there is no limit to the amount of rewriting that might be required here. A lot of conjectures can be proved, however, by normalising arithmetic expressions when possible, and applying a few rewrite rules concerning *comb* and similar functions.

Secondly, note that which elements of the list we portray is very context sensitive. We do not always want to portray just the first and last elements, but also the elements either side of significant boundaries. In general, detecting such critical boundaries involves solving inequalities over the natural numbers modulo some domain theory. Inequality reasoning is not implemented in the current system. This limits both portrayal and proof to a small but interesting class of examples.

7   Implementation

We have implemented a system for reasoning about ellipsis in lists in the higher-order proof planner, $\lambda Clam$ [8]. $\lambda Clam$ provides a convenient basis for our implementation because we need to reason carefully about higher-order functions and variable scope; correct reasoning about functions and variable scope is built into $\lambda Clam$'s underlying meta-theory.

The implementation consists of a number of proof planning methods [3] and some code for portraying elliptic formulae.

7.1 Portrayal

The bulk of the work which is necessary during portrayal is normalisation of arithmetic expressions. For example, portraying $\Box(n - (m + (n - 1)) + (m + 1 + n), F)$ as the elliptic term $[F(1), ..., F(n - (m + (n - 1)) + (m + 1 + n))]$ is both ugly and destroys the simplicity of presentation which is the main point of the exercise. The first step in elliptic portrayal is therefore to simplify the first argument as much as possible using a procedure which normalises expressions built from positive integer constants, variables, $+$ and $-$. The above example is correctly portrayed by our implementation as $[(F\ 1), ..., (F\ (n + 2))]$.

7.2 Methods

$\lambda Clam$ was extended with a new proof planning method: boxintro, which converts conjectures about lists in the standard notation to conjectures about lists in the $\Box$ notation. Every universal quantifier $\forall l : list(\tau)$ is replaced by two quantifiers $\forall n : nat\ \forall f : nat \to \tau$, and the occurrences of l which are in this quantifier's scope are replaced by $\Box(n, f)$. Occurrences of nil in the conjecture are replaced by $\Box(zero, (\lambda x\,.\,x))$.

In addition, $\lambda Clam$'s symbolic evaluation (exhaustive rewriting) method has been modified to apply equations which simplify expressions involving natural numbers before other equations.[2] This is necessary in order to help the portrayal code simplify arithmetic expressions as soon as possible and thereby avoid portrayals such as $[F_1(s(len([F_1(1), ...F_1(V_0)]))), ..., F_1(V_0)]$, which was produced by an early version of the system (and in fact turned out to be $[\,]$, a fact which is only apparent after equation (length3) (see below) has been applied).

In the following sections we give some example output from the system, and discuss the issues it raises.

8 An Example: The Rotate Length Theorem

The rotate-length example of §5.1 cannot be proved by the standard version of $\lambda Clam$.[3] Using ellipsis, it is proved automatically by $\lambda Clam$ using only repeated rewriting. For clarity, in the presentation below, we have removed quantifiers, written equality in infix form, and written function applications as $f(x)$ instead of $f\ x$. The elliptic parts of the presentation are however as produced by the system.

The following rewrite rules are used:

---

[2] $\lambda Clam$ applies the equations exhaustively but does not currently try to reduce arithmetic expressions to a normal form.

[3] $Clam$ can prove it but only with the aid of a critic.

$$len([F(1), ..., F(N)]) \Rightarrow N \qquad \text{(length3)}$$
$$rot(M, [F(1), ..., F(N)]) \Rightarrow$$
$$[F(M+1), ..., F(N)] <> [F(1), ..., F(M)] \qquad \text{(rot1)}$$
$$N - N \Rightarrow 0 \qquad \text{(minus4)}$$
$$[F(1), ..., F(N)] <> [G(1), ..., G(M)] \Rightarrow$$
$$[F(1), ..., F(N), G(1), ..., G(M)] \qquad \text{(box3)}$$
$$0 + X \Rightarrow X \qquad \text{(pluszeroleft)}$$
$$\Box(N, (comb(0, F, G))) \Rightarrow \Box(N, G) \qquad \text{(combdef2)}$$
$$X = X \Rightarrow trueP \qquad \text{(idty)}$$

$\lambda Clam$ automatically constructs the proof below. In this presentation, we use the notation $\Downarrow$ *name* to indicate application of a rewrite rule (*name*).

$$\vdash rot(len([F_1(1), ...F_1(V_0)]), [F_1(1), ...F_1(V_0)] = [F_1(1), ...F_1(V_0)])$$
$$\Downarrow length3$$
$$\vdash rot(V_0, [F_1(1), ...F_1(V_0)]) = [F_1(1), ...F_1(V_0)]$$
$$\Downarrow rot1$$
$$\vdash [] <> [F_1(1), ...F_1(V_0)] = [F_1(1), ...F_1(V_0)]$$
$$\Downarrow minus4$$
$$\vdash [] <> [F_1(1), ...F_1(V_0)] = [F_1(1), ...F_1(V_0)]$$
$$\Downarrow box3$$
$$\vdash [F_1(1), ...F_1(V_0)] = [F_1(1), ...F_1(V_0)]$$
$$\Downarrow pluszeroleft$$
$$\vdash [F_1(1), ...F_1(V_0)] = [F_1(1), ...F_1(V_0)]$$
$$\Downarrow combdef2$$
$$\vdash [F_1(1), ...F_1(V_0)] = [F_1(1), ...F_1(V_0)]$$
$$\Downarrow idty$$
$$\vdash trueP$$

Three proof steps — application of equations *minus4*, *pluszeroleft*, and *combdef2* — do not change the portrayed form of the proof. They should therefore be completely suppressed, or only reported briefly.[4]

9   Results

All of the theorems about lists in the standard corpus of *Clam* were imported into $\lambda Clam$. Systematic tests showed that our initial implementation of ellipsis proves, without list induction, 50% of the test theorems which $\lambda Clam$ proves with list induction. The results are tabulated in figure 1. One additional theorem (the last one in figure 1) was added to the test set; the ungeneralised form which was presented in §5.1 of the rotate-length conjecture.

The tested version of $\lambda Clam$ was unable to prove the *member* examples because of a problem using the definition of *member* which is suitable for elliptic

---

[4] It is interesting to ponder to what extent there is a correspondence between these "null" proof steps and proof steps which would be considered "trivial" by a human.

proofs — $member(x, \Box(n, F)) \leftrightarrow \exists i \leq n \,.\, x = F(i)$. We expect to fix this problem soon.

We plan to increase this 50% figure in three steps:

1. Fixing the problem which prevented the application of the elliptic definition of *member*.
2. Implementation of a method for normalising arithmetic expressions in $\lambda Clam$. Currently, the portrayal code is able to normalise arithmetic expressions but $\lambda Clam$ is not.
3. Implementation of conditional rewriting and methods for solving simple inequalities. This third step should enable the system to prove using ellipsis all of the theorems that $\lambda Clam$ can prove using induction, and more besides.

Conjecture	Ellipsis	List Induction
$l <> nil = l$	Y	Y
$reverse(l) <> reverse(m) = reverse(m <> l)$		Y
$l <> (m <> n) = (l <> m) <> n$		Y
$l = m \rightarrow (x <> l) = (x <> m)$		Y
$len(l <> m) = len(m <> l)$	Y	Y
$len(l) = len(reverse(l))$	Y	Y
$len(l <> m) = len(l) + len(m)$	Y	Y
$member(x, l) \rightarrow member(x, l <> m)$		Y
$member(x, m) \rightarrow member(x, l <> m)$		Y
$member(x, l) \lor member(x, m) \rightarrow member(x, l <> m)$		Y
$nth(n, nil) = nil$	Y	Y
$qrev(l, nil) = rev(l)$	Y	
$qrev(l, m) = rev(l) <> rev(m)$	Y	Y
$reverse(x :: nil) = x :: nil$	Y	Y
$reverse(l <> (x :: nil)) = x :: reverse(l)$		Y
$reverse(l) <> (x :: nil) = reverse(x :: l)$		Y
$rot(len(l), l) = l$	Y	

Fig. 1. Performance of $\lambda Clam$ with ellipsis versus list induction proof strategies on a subset of *Clam*'s list theory. Conjectures which are proved are marked with a Y in the relevant column. For space reasons, we omit quantifiers. In the conjectures above, all free variables are universally quantified (l, m, and n are quantified over $list(nat)$ and x is quantified over nat).

Note that some of the elliptic proofs still use induction over the natural numbers. For example, the proof that $len(l <> r) = len(r) + len(l)$ uses induction over natural numbers after the use of ellipsis in order to prove the commutativity of addition.

An interesting failed proof attempt is *appreverse*:

$$\forall l, m \, list \,.\, reverse(l) <> reverse(m) = reverse(m <> l)$$

The proof attempt stumbles when it is unable to prove:

$$\Box(n + m, comb(n, (\lambda i.F(n - i + 1)), (\lambda i.G(m - i + 1)))) =$$
$$\Box(m + n, (\lambda i.(comb(m, G, F)(m + n - i + 1))))$$

Proof of this goal is difficult because to make the two sides of the equality syntactically equal, we must rewrite the application term $(\lambda i.(comb(m, G, F)))\,(m + n - i + 1)$ to a *comb* term. This involves reasoning about inequalities to decide the values of i which cause the application term to fall into either the first or the second case of the definition of *comb* (3).

10   Discussion

As noted in §7.2, the need for a clear elliptic presentation of a proof can affect the order in which proof steps are carried out. If the set of rewrite rules which is applied during the proof is not confluent, then the changes caused by reordering the application of rewrite rules in the proof can be significant, and can lead for example to different lemmas being applied or to failure of the proof. This possibility of causing fundamental changes in the proof indicates that proof portrayal cannot be relegated to a "pretty-printing" role but must instead be considered at the time the conjecture is proved.

Some functions do not easily lend themselves to representation in the $\Box$ formulation, for example *flatten* over arbitrarily nested lists. There may be a correspondence between such difficult examples and recursive definitions which are difficult to understand.

11   Related Work

We briefly mentioned in (§1) that our approach can be extended by means of the higher-order fold function to the representation and manipulation of formulae involving ellipsis where the main connective is not list cons. If the function $\otimes$ is associative, then the portrayal in equation (2) can be simplified by removing the brackets — $foldl(\otimes, a, \Box(n, F))$ is portrayed as $a \otimes F(1) \otimes ... \otimes F(n)$. Such an approach produces a similar formulation to the "Three Dots Language" (TDL) presented in [7], in which (following the terminology of [7]) the iteration star "*" is essentially a higher-order *fold* function (compare the equations (1) defining *foldl* above with the expansion equations in [7, p.231]), and the iteration counter "$\hat{c}$" represents lambda abstraction. For example, the elliptic formula $\forall x^* \exists d.\,(x_1 \cdot x_1 + ... + x_1 \cdot x_n \le a_{b+k} \cdot ... \cdot a_{d+k})$ is represented in TDL by equation (5) below (equation 13 of [7, p.237]) and in our formalism by (6).

$$\forall x^* \exists d.\,(((x_1 \cdot x_{\hat{c}})\ +^*\ \hat{c}, 1..n) \le (a_{\hat{c}+k}\ \cdot^*\ \hat{c}, b..d)) \qquad (5)$$
$$\forall^F x \exists d.\,foldl(\lambda z \lambda w.x(1) \cdot z + w, 0, \Box(n, (\lambda i.x(i)))) \le \qquad (6)$$
$$foldl(\lambda z \lambda w.z \cdot w, 1, \Box(d - b + 1, (\lambda i.a(b + k - 1 + i))))$$

Since TDL concentrates on defining a small mathematical language in which terms can be reduced to a normal form, it is quite restrictive. Our approach allows us to represent and manipulate quite general kinds of elliptic formulae (for example subscripts can be nonconsecutive because of the presence of a *comb* operator (which has no equivalent in TDL)). We have tested our formalism in an automated theorem proving system (λ *Clam*).

12   Conclusion

In this paper we have proposed a mechanism for allowing ellipsis in automatic proofs. The key idea is to use an internal notation in which the ambiguity inherent in elliptic notation is resolved. This uses a second-order functional $\square$, which is similar to $\sum$ and $\prod$. Ellipsis is recovered from this notation by portray-like print routines which hide the internal notation and replace it with ellipsis.

With this notation many functions which normally require recursive definitions can be given explicit ones. As a result induction and generalisation can be eliminated from many proofs which normally require them. The result is proofs which seem closer to ordinary mathematical intuitions, in fact, we might describe these as more 'informal' proofs. Axiomatisation of lists using $\square$ has a similar flavour to the work described in [2], but the representation and its use for proofs using ellipsis that we present are new.

A heavy burden is transferred to the portray routines. To present intuitively satisfying formulae and proofs they must carry out significant rewriting to transform the internal representation into a printable form. They must also make subtle decisions about which elements of an elliptic sequence are portrayed and which suppressed. It also may be necessary to rearrange the order in which rewrite rules are applied. This indicates that in general we need to consider how to present proofs clearly at the time the proof is constructed; we cannot leave it to a post-processing step.

References

1. S. Baker. *Aspects of the Constructive Omega Rule within Automated Deduction.* PhD thesis, Edinburgh, 1993.
2. R. S. Bird. An introduction to the theory of lists. In M. Broy, editor, *Logic of Programming and Calculi of Discrete Design*, pages 5–42. Springer-Verlag, 1987. International Summer School. Proceedings of the NATO Advanced Study Institute, Marktoberdorf.
3. A. Bundy. The use of explicit plans to guide inductive proofs. In R. Lusk and R. Overbeek, editors, *9th International Conference on Automated Deduction*, pages 111–120. Springer-Verlag, 1988. Longer version available from Edinburgh as DAI Research Paper No. 349.
4. A. Bundy, F. van Harmelen, C. Horn, and A. Smaill. The Oyster-Clam system. In M. E. Stickel, editor, *10th International Conference on Automated Deduction*, pages 647–648. Springer-Verlag, 1990. Lecture Notes in Artificial Intelligence No. 449. Also available from Edinburgh as DAI Research Paper 507.

5. A. Ireland and A. Bundy. Productive use of failure in inductive proof. *Journal of Automated Reasoning*, 16(1–2):79–111, 1996. Also available as DAI Research Paper No 716, Dept. of Artificial Intelligence, Edinburgh.
6. E. B. Kinber and A. N. Brazma. Models of inductive synthesis. *Journal of Logic Programming*, 9:221–233, 1990.
7. Leon Łukaszewicz. Triple dots in a formal language. *Journal of Automated Reasoning*, 22(3):223–239, March 1999.
8. J. D. C Richardson, A. Smaill, and I. M. Green. System description: proof planning in higher-order logic with λ*Clam*. In C. Kirchner and H. Kirchner, editors, *Proceedings of CADE-15*, volume 1421 of *Lecture Notes in Computer Science*. Springer Verlag, 1998.

On the Complexity of Counting the Hilbert Basis of a Linear Diophantine System

Miki Hermann[1], Laurent Juban[1], and Phokion G. Kolaitis[2]*

[1] LORIA (CNRS and Université Henri Poincaré Nancy 1), BP 239, 54506
Vandœuvre-lès-Nancy, France. {hermann,juban}@loria.fr
[2] Computer Science Department, University of California, Santa Cruz, CA 95064,
U.S.A., kolaitis@cse.ucsc.edu

Abstract. We investigate the computational complexity of counting the
Hilbert basis of a homogeneous system of linear Diophantine equations.
We establish lower and upper bounds on the complexity of this problem
by showing that counting the Hilbert basis is #P-hard and belongs to the
class #NP. Moreover, we investigate the complexity of variants obtained
by restricting the number of occurrences of the variables in the system.

1 Introduction and Summary of Results

The Hilbert basis of a homogeneous system of linear Diophantine equations over
the non-negative integers is the set of all non-zero vectors that are *minimal* solutions with respect to the pointwise order. This set forms indeed a basis of the
space of solutions of the system, that is, every solution can be written as a positive linear combination of vectors from the Hilbert basis, and no member of the
Hilbert basis can be expressed as a positive linear combination of other members. Moreover, this basis is essentially unique. The concept of a Hilbert basis
was studied as early as the second half of the 19th century by Gordan [Gor73]
and Hilbert [Hil90]. Since that time, it has received considerable attention in
linear algebra and integer programming (see Schrijver [Sch86]).

Computing the Hilbert basis of a homogeneous system of linear Diophantine
equations over non-negative integers has turned out to be one of the key problems
in automated deduction. Its importance in this area emerged through the work
of Stickel [Sti75,Sti81], who designed the first algorithm for unification in the
presence of associative-commutative (AC) function symbols. Stickel showed that
the minimal complete set of unifiers of a simultaneous elementary AC-unification
problem can be obtained from the Hilbert basis of an associated homogeneous
system of linear Diophantine equations over non-negative integers. Indeed, the
minimal complete set of AC-unifiers is the set of all *compatible* subsets of the
Hilbert basis of that system, where compatible in this context means that every
variable can be instantiated by a non-zero linear combination of the members
of the compatible subset. Other AC-unification algorithms were presented afterwards, including algorithms by Fages [Fag87], Herold and Siekmann [HS87],

---

* Research partially supported by NSF grants CCR-9610257 and CCR-9732041.

Boudet [Bou93], and Boudet, Contejean, and Devie [BCD90]. Although these AC-unification algorithms differ from each other in several aspects, they all rely on computing the Hilbert basis of the associated homogeneous system.

Following the publication of Stickel's algorithm [Sti75], researchers became interested in algorithms for computing the Hilbert basis. Huet [Hue78] described a conceptually simple algorithm for a single equation. Clausen and Fortenbacher presented in [CF89] a more sophisticated algorithm for a single equation based on automata theory. These papers assume that the computation of the Hilbert basis of a system can be reduced to successive computations of the Hilbert basis of single equations, interlaced with substitutions of the result into the rest of the system. Aggregation is a different method for transforming a system of equations into a single equation with the same space of solutions [EE85]. Both methods entail an exponential blow-up during the transformation. Several researchers, including Contejean and Devie [CD94], Lankford [Lan89], Domenjoud [Dom91a,Dom91b], have also developed direct algorithms for computing the Hilbert basis of systems with an arbitrary number of equations.

Every algorithm for computing the Hilbert basis of a system can also be used to count at the same time the number of elements of the Hilbert basis. Lankford [Lan89] derived an exponential lower bound on the cardinality of the Hilbert basis of a particularly challenging homogeneous Diophantine equation. In the present paper, we investigate the problem of counting the Hilbert basis of a system from a complexity-theoretic perspective. Our results imply that this counting problem is highly intractable and, thus, they shed light on the inherent complexity of algorithms for computing the Hilbert basis. According to Lankford [Lan89], "a complete description of the complexity of non-negative basis algorithms seems to be a difficult open problem".

The computational complexity theory of counting problems was developed by Valiant [Val79a,Val79b], who introduced and studied the class #P of functions that count the number of accepting paths of nondeterministic polynomial-time Turing machines, as well as the larger class #NP of functions that count the number of accepting paths of nondeterministic polynomial-time Turing machines with access to NP oracles. Valiant [Val79a,Val79b] demonstrated that these classes possess natural complete problems under suitable polynomial-time reductions. In particular, there is a large variety of #P-complete problems that arise in graph theory, logic, algebra, and combinatorics. Furthermore, #P-complete problems are encountered in the context of counting the number of minimal complete matchers modulo an equational theory, as shown in [HK95a,HK95b]. It should be noted that #P-complete and #P-hard problems are considered to be highly intractable, since, as established by Toda [Tod89], they dominate in an exact technical sense all problems in the polynomial hierarchy PH (the bottom level of which is NP).

We show that the problem of counting the Hilbert basis is #P-hard and is a member of the class #NP. These two results provide reasonably tight lower and upper bounds on the complexity of counting the Hilbert basis, even though they do not decisively pin down its exact complexity. We also analyze variants of this counting problem for restricted systems of homogeneous linear Diophantine equations; to this effect, we show that if every variable has at most two occurrences in the system, then the problem of counting the Hilbert basis is a member of the class #P. Finally, we establish that it is a #P-complete problem to count the number of compatible subsets of a given set of linearly independent and pairwise incomparable vectors. This result quantifies in a precise manner the inherent complexity of an important step in most AC-unification algorithms.

2   Counting Problems and Computational Complexity

This section contains the definitions of basic concepts, as well as some background material on counting problems and computational complexity. We assume some familiarity with the fundamentals of associative-commutative unification and computational complexity. Additional material on these topics can be found in the survey article [JK91] and in the monographs [BN98,Pap94,Sch86].

A homogeneous linear Diophantine system over non-negative integers is a system of equations $S: Ax = 0$, where $A = (a_i^j)_k^n$ is a $k \times n$ integer matrix and $x = (x_1, \ldots, x_n)$ is a vector of variables ranging over non-negative integers. We say that a solution s of S is *nontrivial* if it is different from the all-zero solution $(0, \ldots, 0)$. We say that a solution $s = (s_1, \ldots, s_n)$ of S is *smaller* than a solution $s' = (s_1', \ldots, s_n')$, and write $s < s'$, if $s \neq s'$ and, for all $i = 1, \ldots, n$, it is the case that $s_i \leq s_i'$. The relation $<$ is called the *pointwise order* on solutions. A solution s is *minimal* if it is nontrivial and there is no smaller nontrivial solution s'', that is, $s'' < s$ is false for every nontrivial solution s'' of S. The i-th coordinate s_i of a solution s, corresponding to the variable x_i, is alternatively denoted by $s(x_i)$.

The *Hilbert basis* $H(S)$ of the system S is the set of all minimal solutions of S. This set is indeed a *basis* for the space of nontrivial solutions of S, which means that no minimal solution can be expressed as a positive linear combination of the other minimal solutions, whereas every nontrivial solution can be expressed as a positive linear combination of minimal solutions. The Hilbert basis $H(S)$ is finite and it is the unique basis of the space of nontrivial solutions of S.

It is well known that Hilbert bases can be used to compute minimal complete sets of AC-unifiers. Indeed, let $AX \doteq_{AC} A'X'$ be a simultaneous elementary AC-unification problem, where A and A' are matrices over non-negative integers, $X = (X_1, \ldots, X_j)$ and $X' = (X_{j+1}, \ldots, X_n)$ are not necessarily disjunctive vectors of formal variables, and $+$ is the unique AC-symbol. With this AC-unification problem, associate the homogeneous linear Diophantine system $S: (A - A')x = 0$, where the arithmetic variable x_i corresponds to the formal variable X_i for $i = 1, \ldots, n$. Consider the Hilbert basis $H(S)$ of the system S over the variables $x_1, \ldots, x_n$. Let $\{\alpha_1, \ldots, \alpha_m\}$ be a subset of $H(S)$ and $v = (v_1, \ldots, v_m)$ be a vector of new variables. For each $i = 1, \ldots, n$, assign the linear expression $\alpha_1^i v_1 + \cdots + \alpha_m^i v_m$ to the variable x_i, where α_j^i is the i-th coordinate of the vector α_j. We say that $\{\alpha_1, \ldots, \alpha_m\}$ is a *compatible subset* of $H(S)$ if, for each variable x_i, there exists a vector α_j such that $\alpha_j^i \neq 0$, that is, the variable x_i is not assigned the value 0. The minimal complete set of unifiers of the AC-unification problem $AX \doteq_{AC} A'X'$ turns out to be the set of all compatible subsets of $H(S)$ of the system S above, where $x_i \mapsto \alpha_1^i v_1 + \cdots + \alpha_m^i v_m$ is the substitution of the variable x_i, when $\{\alpha_1, \ldots, \alpha_m\}$ is the chosen compatible subset.

In this paper, we are mainly concerned with the computational complexity of finding the cardinality of the Hilbert basis $H(S)$ of a given homogeneous linear Diophantine system $S: Ax = 0$, that is, counting the number of minimal solutions of S.

Valiant [Val79a,Val79b] was the first to investigate the computational complexity of counting problems. To this effect, he introduced the class #P of functions that count the number of accepting paths of nondeterministic polynomial-time Turing machines. The prototypical problem in this class is #SAT, which is the counting version of Boolean satisfiability.

#SAT

Input: Set V of Boolean variables and Boolean formula ϕ over V in conjunctive normal form.

Output: The number of truth assignments for the variables in V that satisfy ϕ.

In addition to initiating the study of #P, Valiant [Val79a,Val79b] developed a machine-based framework for introducing higher classes of counting problems. Specifically, for every complexity class $\mathcal{C}$ of decision problems, he defined #$\mathcal{C}$ to be the union $\bigcup_{A \in \mathcal{C}}(\#P)^A$, where $(\#P)^A$ is the collection of all functions that count the accepting paths of nondeterministic polynomial-time Turing machines having A as their oracle. Thus, in this framework, #NP is the class of functions that count the number of accepting paths of NP^{NP} machines, that is, nondeterministic polynomial-time Turing machines that have access to NP oracles. More recently, however, researchers have introduced complexity classes of counting problems using the framework of *witness functions* and *witness sets*. In this framework, a counting problem is viewed as a *witness function* w such that if x is an input, then $w(x)$ is a set of succinct certificates (witnesses) for x, and the goal is to compute the cardinality $|w(x)|$ of this *witness set* $w(x)$. Different classes of counting problems can then be obtained by considering the computational complexity of deciding membership in the witness set. Specifically, if C is a complexity class of decision problems, then Hemaspaandra and Vollmer [HV95] define $\# \cdot C$ to be the class of all witness functions w that satisfy the following conditions:

(1) There is a polynomial p such that for every x and every $y \in w(x)$, we have that $|y| \leq p(|x|)$, where $|x|$ is the size of x and $|y|$ is the size of y;

(2) The decision problem "given x and y, is $y \in w(x)$?" is in C.

It is easy to verify that $\#P = \# \cdot P$, that is, Valiant's class #P coincides with the class of witness functions for which membership in the witness set can be tested in polynomial time. For complexity classes C beyond P, however, the corresponding classes $\#C$ and $\# \cdot C$ may differ, unless unlikely collapses of complexity classes occur (see [HV95]); in general, finer-grained complexity classes can be obtained using the witness-based framework. For our purposes here, we are interested in a result from Toda's Ph.D. thesis [Tod91] that reveals a rather surprising connection between the two different approaches.

Theorem 1 (Toda). $\#NP = \# \cdot coNP$.

Thus, the above result asserts that Valiant's class $\#NP$ coincides with the class of witness functions for which membership in the witness set is in coNP. A proof of this theorem can also be found in [HV95]. It is clear that $\#P$ is contained in $\#NP$. Moreover, $\#P$ contains the class FP of counting functions that can be computed in deterministic polynomial time. Therefore, we have the inclusions: $FP \subseteq \#P \subseteq \#NP$; note that it is not known whether these inclusions are proper.

As a general principle, what makes a complexity class C interesting is the existence of natural *complete* problems for C, that is, members of C such that every problem in C can be reduced to them via a suitable reduction. As regards classes of counting problems, these reductions are polynomial-time reductions that allow us to efficiently compute the number of solutions of one problem from the number of solutions of another. Let v and w be two witness functions with domain Π^* and Σ^* respectively, where Π and Σ are finite alphabets. The counting problem v is *polynomial-time Turing reducible* to the counting problem w if there exists a polynomial-time deterministic Turing machine M that computes v by making calls to an oracle for w. Restricted notions of polynomial-time Turing reductions between counting problems have also been considered. In particular, a *polynomial-time 1-Turing reduction* is a polynomial-time Turing reduction in which the Turing machine M is allowed to make at most one call to the oracle for w [Val79a,TW92]. *Parsimonious reductions* constitute the most restricted notion of reducibility. These are the special case of polynomial-time 1-Turing reductions in which $v = w \circ g$, for some polynomial-time computable total function g. In other words, the oracle for w is queried once and no computation is performed after the answer of the oracle is received. Thus, parsimonious reductions preserve the number of solutions between counting problems.

Let $\#C$ be a counting complexity class, such as $\#P$ or $\#NP$. A counting problem w is $\#C$-*hard* if, for each counting problem v in $\#C$, there is a polynomial-time Turing reduction from v to w. If, in addition, w is a member of $\#C$, then we say that w is $\#C$-*complete*. If restricted notions of reductions are considered, then analogous concepts of hardness and completeness can be defined. For example, it is easy to show that $\#SAT$ is $\#P$-complete under parsimonious reductions.

It should be pointed out that $\#P$-hard problems are considered to be truly intractable. As a matter of fact, establishing $\#P$-hardness implies in a precise technical sense that the problem at hand is substantially more intractable than an NP-complete problem (see [Joh90, page 109]). Valiant's [Val79a,Val79b] seminal discovery was that there are $\#P$-complete counting problems such that, unlike SAT, their underlying decision problem is solvable in polynomial time. In fact, there are $\#P$-complete problems having a trivial decision problem. The following two counting problems manifest these phenomena.

#PERFECT MATCHINGS [Val79b]
Input: Bipartite graph G with $2n$ nodes.

Output: The number of *perfect matchings* of G, i.e., sets of n edges such that no two edges share a common node.

#POSITIVE 2SAT [Val79b]

Input: Set V of Boolean variables and Boolean formula ϕ over V in conjunctive normal form, such that each clause of ϕ consists of exactly two positive literals.

Output: The number of truth assignments for the variables in V that satisfy ϕ.

Since the decision problem for positive 2CNF formulas is trivial, #POSITIVE 2SAT cannot be #P-complete under parsimonious reductions. Similarly, since there is a polynomial-time algorithm that tells whether a perfect matching exists, #PERFECT MATCHINGS cannot be #P-complete under parsimonious reductions, unless P = NP. It is known, however, that #PERFECT MATCHINGS is #P-complete under polynomial-time 1-Turing reductions (see [Pap94,Zan91]).

Both #PERFECT MATCHINGS and #POSITIVE 2SAT will be of use to us in establishing lower bounds for the complexity of the counting problems that we will study in the sequel. It is now time to formally introduce these problems.

#HILBERT

Input: A system of homogeneous linear Diophantine equations $S: Ax = 0$ over non-negative integers.

Output: The cardinality of the Hilbert basis $H(S)$ of S.

We mentioned earlier that Hilbert bases are used in computing minimal complete sets of unifiers of elementary AC-unification problems. As an intermediate step in this computation, one has to produce the set of all compatible subsets of a Hilbert basis $H(S)$ of a homogeneous linear Diophantine system $S: Ax = 0$ with n variables, where a set $\{\alpha_1, \ldots \alpha_m\}$ of n-dimensional vectors is *compatible* if for every $i \leq n$ there is a $j \leq m$ such that $\alpha_j^i \neq 0$. Note also that the members of a Hilbert basis are pairwise incomparable in the pointwise order and linearly independent with respect to linear combinations with nonnegative coefficients. This motivates the following counting problem.

#COMPATIBLE SUBSETS

Input: A set T of vectors of non-negative integers that are pairwise incomparable in the pointwise order and linearly independent with respect to linear combinations with nonnegative coefficients.

Output: The cardinality of the set of all compatible subsets of T.

3   The Complexity of Counting the Hilbert Basis

In this section, we obtain upper and lower bounds for the computational complexity of counting the Hilbert basis. Before stating and proving the main results, we address the issue of how the inputs are encoded.

If the input of a decision problem involves integers, then the complexity of that problem may depend on whether these integers are encoded in binary or in unary. For instance, KNAPSACK is NP-complete when the coefficients of the input are given in binary, but is solvable in polynomial time, when these coefficients are given in unary. In contrast, 3-PARTITION remains NP-complete, even if the coefficients of the input are given in unary (see [GJ79]). Note that typically the inputs of an AC-unification problem are given in unary, that is, each monomial ax is encoded by $|a|$ bits (instead of $\log|a|$ bits), because ax represents $|a|$ occurrences of the variable x and the inputs are terms over the alphabet of variables and function symbols. Since #HILBERT originates in elementary AC-unification, it would be natural to assume that the coefficients of linear Diophantine systems are written in unary. In linear algebra and integer programming, however, coefficients of linear systems are usually given in binary. As it turns out, however, the complexity of #HILBERT does not depend on whether the coefficients are encoded in binary or in unary, because there is a polynomial-time reduction that reduces #HILBERT in binary to #HILBERT in unary. Specifically, each system $S\colon Ax = 0$ can be transformed in polynomial time to a system $S'\colon A'x' = 0$ such that the coefficients of the matrix A' are 0, 1 or -1, there is a one-to-one mapping from the variables x to the variables x', and there is a one-to-one and onto mapping between the Hilbert bases of S and S'. For every monomial ax with $|a| > 2$ occurring in the system $S\colon Ax = 0$, let $p = \lceil \log_2 |a| \rceil$ and let $|a| = \sum_{i=0}^{p} a_i 2^i$ be the binary expansion of the absolute value of the coefficient a. Introduce p new variables $z_0, \ldots, z_{p-1}$, and add the equations $z_0 = x$ and $z_i = 2z_{i-1}$ for each $i = 1, \ldots, p-1$. Furthermore, introduce a new variable v and add the equation $v = a_0 z_0 + \cdots + a_p z_p$. If $a > 0$, then replace the monomial ax by the variable v; otherwise, replace ax by $-v$. By applying this transformation repeatedly, we obtain a system with coefficients from $\{-2, -1, 0, 1, 2\}$. Now, replace each monomial $2x$ (respectively, $-2x$) by the expression $v_1 + v_2$ (respectively, $-v_1 - v_2$), and add the equation $v_1 = v_2$ for the new variables v_1 and v_2. This completes the transformation of S to a system S' with the desired properties. Moreover, the entire transformation can be carried out in polynomial time, since for each monomial ax with $|a| > 2$ we add $\mathcal{O}(\log_2 |a|)$ new variables and equations, i.e., polynomially many in the size of the system S in binary.

Theorem 2. *The counting problem* #HILBERT *is in the class* #NP.

Proof. We first show that #HILBERT belongs to the class $\#\cdot\mathrm{coNP}$, and then use Theorem 1 to conclude that it is in #NP.

Suppose we are given a homogeneous linear Diophantine system $S\colon Ax = 0$, where A is a $k \times n$ integer matrix. As the witness set for S, we take the set of all minimal solutions of S. We have to verify that the size of each minimal solution is polynomially bounded in the size of S, and that testing for minimality is in coNP. Papadimitriou [Pap81] proved that INTEGER PROGRAMMING is in NP by establishing that if a system of Diophantine equations has a non-negative integer solution, then it has a "short" nonnegative integer solution. Several different researchers, including Domenjoud [Dom91a], Lambert [Lam87], and Pottier [Pot91] have shown that Papadimitriou's [Pap81] argument can be adapted to yield the stronger result that every minimal solution is "short" (see also [BN98]). Specifically, if $(s_1, \ldots, s_n)$ is an arbitrary minimal solution of $S\colon Ax = 0$, then $s_i \leq n(ka)^{2k+1}$ holds for all $1 \leq i \leq n$, where a is the maximum

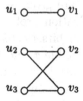

Fig. 1. A bipartite graph with two perfect matchings

of the coefficients of the matrix A. It follows that the size of every minimal solution is at most $n \log n + n(2k+1)(\log a + \log k)$, which implies that it is bounded by a polynomial in the size of the system S.

Finally, we have to show that the following decision problem is in coNP: given a system S as above and a vector s, is s a minimal solution of S? Since testing that s is a solution of S can be checked in polynomial time, we may as well assume that the given vector s is a solution of S. The complement of the aforementioned decision problem is in NP: to show that s is *not* a minimal solution, simply guess a nontrivial solution s' that is smaller than s in the pointwise order. $\Box$

For the lower bound, we show that #HILBERT is #P-hard. For this, we produce a parsimonious reduction from #PERFECT MATCHINGS to #HILBERT.

Let $G = (U, V, E)$ be a bipartite graph with $2n$ nodes, where $|U| = |V| = n$. For every edge $e_i^j = (u_i, v_j) \in E$, introduce a variable x_i^j. In addition, introduce a variable y. For every node u_i in U, form the equation $x_i^{i_1} + \cdots + x_i^{i_l} = y$, where $e_i^{i_1}, \ldots, e_i^{i_l}$ is the list of all edges adjacent to u_i. Similarly, for each $v_j \in V$, form the equation $x_{j_1}^j + \cdots + x_{j_m}^j = y$, where $e_{j_1}^j, \ldots, e_{j_m}^j$ is the list of all edges adjacent to the node v_j. Let S be the homogeneous linear Diophantine system consisting of the above equations for all nodes $u_i \in U$ and $v_j \in V$. Thus, S consists of $2n$ equations; note that the left hand side of each equation contains occurrences of the variables x_i^j, whereas the right-hand of each equation is always y. Note also that each variable x_i^j occurs exactly twice in the system: once in the equation for node u_i and once in the equation for node v_j. We illustrate this construction with an example.

Example 1. Let $G = (\{u_1, u_2, u_3\}, \{v_1, v_2, v_3\}, E)$ be the bipartite graph depicted in Figure 1, having (u_1, v_1), (u_2, v_2), (u_2, v_3), (u_3, v_2), and (u_3, v_3) as edges. Then the system S consists of the following equations in the variables $x_1^1, x_2^2, x_2^3, x_3^2, x_3^3, y$:

$$
\begin{array}{ll}
u_1: & x_1^1 = y \\
u_2: x_2^2 + x_2^3 = y \\
u_3: x_3^2 + x_3^3 = y
\end{array}
\qquad
\begin{array}{ll}
v_1: & x_1^1 = y \\
v_2: x_2^2 + x_3^2 = y \\
v_3: x_2^3 + x_3^3 = y
\end{array}
$$

The Hilbert basis of the preceding system S is $H(S) = \{110011, 101101\}$. Note that the bipartite graph G has two perfect matchings and that the Hilbert basis $H(S)$ has two vectors. It turns out that this is not accidental. Indeed, in a sequence of three lemmas we establish that there exists a one-to-one correspondence between the perfect matchings of an arbitrary bipartite graph G and the minimal solutions of the associated system S.

The first lemma is proved using the well-known Hall's theorem.

Theorem 3 (Hall). *Let $G = (U, V, E)$ be a bipartite graph, where $|U| = |V|$. Then G has a perfect matching if and only if for every subset $A \subseteq U$, we have that $|A| \leq |R(A)|$, where $R(A) = \{v \in V \mid \exists u \in A, (u, v) \in E\}$.*

Lemma 1. *If a bipartite graph G has no perfect matching, then the only solution of S is the trivial all-zero solution $y = 0$, $x_i^j = 0$, where $1 \leq i, j \leq n$.*

Proof. If G has no perfect matching, then, by Hall's theorem, there exists a set of nodes $A \subseteq U$ such that $|A| > |R(A)|$ holds. Let E_A be the set of edges between the nodes of A and of $R(A)$ in the graph G. Let X_A be the variables corresponding to the edges E_A. By summing up the equations for the nodes $u_i \in A$, we obtain the equation $\sum_{x_i^j \in X_A} x_i^j = |A| y$. Similarly, by summing up the equations for the nodes $v_j \in R(A)$, we obtain the relation $\sum_{x_i^j \in X_A} x_i^j \leq |R(A)| y$, since the edges E_A are a subset of the edges incident to $R(A)$. The left-hand sides of these two expressions are equal, therefore we can derive the relation $|A| y \leq |R(A)| y$. Since $|A| > |R(A)|$ holds, the only solution of the last inequation is $y = 0$. The right-hand side of each equation in S is equal to 0, therefore each variable x_i^j must also be 0. □

The proof of the next lemma is quite straightforward.

Lemma 2. *For every perfect matching M in G, there exists a solution of the system S such that $y = 1$, $x_i^j \in \{0, 1\}$, and $x_i^j = 1$ if and only if $e_i^j \in M$. Conversely, for every solution of S with $y = 1$ there exists a perfect matching in the bipartite graph G. Moreover, every solution of S with $y = 1$ is minimal.*

The last lemma implies that all minimal solutions of S must have $y = 1$.

Lemma 3. *If a solution of S is such that $y \geq 2$, then it is not minimal.*

Proof. Let $(s_1, \ldots, s_n, t)$ be a solution of $S(x_1, \ldots, x_n, y)$ such that $t \geq 2$. Transform the system S to a system S^* by eliminating all variables x_i for which $s_i = 0$. We obtain the system $S^*(x_1^*, \ldots, x_m^*, y)$ with the solution $(s_1^*, \ldots, s_m^*, t)$, where $s_i^* > 0$ for each $i = 1, \ldots, m$. Note that the system S^* corresponds to a bipartite graph $G^* = (U, V, E^*)$ that is a subgraph of G.

Since $t > 0$, Lemma 1 implies that there exists a perfect matching in G^*. From Lemma 2, it follows that there exists a solution $(s_1', \ldots, s_m', 1)$ of S^* such that $s_i' \in \{0, 1\}$. Clearly, $(s_1^*, \ldots, s_m^*, t) > (s_1', \ldots, s_m', 1)$ in the pointwise order. Therefore, also $(s_1, \ldots, s_n, t) > (s_1'', \ldots, s_n'', 1)$ holds, where $s_i'' = s_i'$ if $s_i = s_i^*$ and $s_i'' = 0$ if $s_i = 0$. Moreover, $(s_1'', \ldots, s_n'', 1)$ is a solution of S. Consequently, $(s_1, \ldots, s_n, t)$ is not a minimal solution of S. □

Lemmas 1,2, and 3 show that there is a reduction from #PERFECT MATCH-INGS to #HILBERT. Thus, we have just completed the proof of the following theorem.

Theorem 4. *The counting problem* #HILBERT *is* #P*-hard.*

The preceding Theorems 2 and 4 yield upper and lower bounds for the complexity of counting the Hilbert basis. We now discuss some of the difficulties that arise if one attempts to narrow the gap between #P-hardness and membership in #NP. An inspection of the proof of Theorem 2 reveals that #HILBERT would be in #P, if testing a solution for minimality were solvable in polynomial time. Durand, Hermann, and Juban [DHJ99], however, have shown that it is a coNP-complete problem to tell whether a given solution of a homogeneous linear Diophantine system is minimal for a homogeneous linear Diophantine system. Thus, assuming P $\neq$ NP, to prove that #HILBERT is in #P would require one to come up with a very different set of witnesses for #HILBERT and show that membership in that witness set is in polynomial time. We believe that this is not possible and conjecture that #HILBERT is *not* in #P. Note that this conjecture implies that #P $\neq$ #NP, which, in turn, implies that P $\neq$ NP. As regards the lower bound, we showed that #PERFECT MATCHINGS has a parsimonious reduction to #HILBERT. Since, as mentioned earlier, #PERFECT MATCHINGS is #P-hard under polynomial-time 1-Turing reductions (see [Pap94,Zan91]), it follows that #HILBERT is also #P-hard under polynomial-time 1-Turing reductions. In a breakthrough paper [TW92], however, Toda and Watanabe proved that if a counting problem is #P-hard under polynomial-time 1-Turing reductions, then it is also #·C-hard under such reductions for every level $C = \Sigma_i$P or $C = \Pi_i$P, $i \geq 1$, of the polynomial hierarchy PH (note that, by definition Σ_1P = NP and Π_1P = coNP). In particular, it follows that #HILBERT is #NP-complete under polynomial-time 1-Turing reductions. Thus, at first sight it appears that the exact complexity of #HILBERT has been pinpointed. A moment's reflection, however, reveals that there is something quite unsatisfactory with this conclusion. Indeed, Toda and Watanabe's [TW92] result suggests that polynomial-time 1-Turing reductions cannot help us differentiate between problems that are #·C-complete for different levels C of the polynomial hierarchy PH. Moreover, Toda and Watanabe's [TW92] result provides strong evidence that #P, #NP and other higher counting complexity classes #·Σ_iP and #·Π_iP, $i \geq 1$, are not closed under polynomial-time 1-Turing reductions. Consequently, to draw distinctions between complete problems for different counting classes, one has to consider more restricted reductions under which the classes at hand are closed. Clearly, the counting complexity classes #·Σ_iP and #·Π_iP, $i \geq 1$, are closed under parsimonious reductions. Moreover, for every $i \geq 1$ both #·Σ_iP and #·Π_iP contain natural problems that are complete for them under parsimonious reductions. For instance, Valiant [Val79a] considered a counting satisfiability problem called NSAT, which turns out to be #·NP-complete (#·Σ_1P-complete) under parsimonious reductions. Here, we are interested in the following counting problem #Π_1SAT, which is a "dual" version of NSAT.

#Π_1SAT

Input: A Boolean formula ϕ in disjunctive normal form and a partition of its variables into two sets X and Y.

Output: The number of truth assignments s to the variables in X so that the resulting formula $\phi(X/s)$ is a tautology (i.e., for every truth assignment t to the variables of Y, the concatenation st satisfies ϕ).

It is clear that #Π_1SAT is in #·coNP = #NP. Moreover, Durand [Dur99] has showed that Π_1SAT is #NP-complete under parsimonious reductions. We now show that, unless P = NP, no parsimonious reduction from #Π_1SAT to #HILBERT exists.

Proposition 1. *If #Π_1SAT has a parsimonious reduction to #HILBERT, then P = NP. Consequently, #HILBERT is not #NP-complete under parsimonious reductions, unless P = NP.*

Proof. Using the hypothesis, we will show that one can decide in polynomial time whether a Boolean formula ψ in disjunctive normal form is a tautology, which implies that coNP = P = NP. Let ψ be a Boolean formula in disjunctive normal form with $D_1, \ldots, D_m$ as disjuncts, and $Y = \{y_1, \ldots, y_n\}$ as variables. Let x be a new variable and let ϕ be the formula $(D_1 \wedge x) \vee \cdots \vee (D_m \wedge x)$. Observe that if ψ is a tautology, then there is exactly one truth assignment to x (namely, $x = true$) such that $\phi(x/true)$ is a tautology. Furthermore, if ψ is not a tautology, then no truth assignment s to x turns $\phi(x/s)$ to a tautology. Let g be a parsimonious reduction of #Π_1SAT to #HILBERT. It follows that ψ is a tautology if and only if the homogeneous linear Diophantive system $g(\phi(x, Y))$ has at least one minimal solution. Clearly, a homogeneous linear Diophantine system has at least one minimal solution if and only if it has a non-trivial solution over the non-negative integers. The latter condition, however, can be checked in polynomial time, because it is easily reducible to linear programming. Indeed, it is clear that the system $S \colon Az = 0$ has a non-trivial solution over the non-negative integers if and only if the system $Az = 0, z_1 + \cdots + z_n \geq 1, z_1 \geq 0, \ldots, z_n \geq 0$ has a solution over the rationals. □

Thus, we are left with the intriguing question: are there polynomial-time reductions under which #NP is closed and #HILBERT is #NP-complete? To appreciate this question, we note that it is not known whether polynomial-time reductions exist under which #P is closed and #PERFECT MATCHINGS is #P-hard.

4 Restricted Systems of Diophantine Equations

To understand further the sources of intractability of #HILBERT, in this section we examine the complexity of counting the Hilbert basis for systems of homogeneous linear Diophantine equations that obey certain structural restrictions. As regards systems of equations, a natural restriction is to impose bounds on the number of occurrences of the variables in the system. In fact, this type of restriction has been studied in the context of elementary AC-matching and in many cases has helped in delineating the boundary between tractability and intractability [BKN87,HK95b]. In what follows, we investigate the impact of this structural restriction on the complexity of #HILBERT.

For every positive integer m, let #HILBERT(m) be the restriction of #HILBERT to systems of equations, such that for every variable x the sum of the occurrences of x in the equations of the system is at most m, where a monomial ax accounts for $|a|$ occurrences of the variable x. We first observe that #HILBERT(m), with $m > 3$, has a parsimonious reduction to #HILBERT(3). As seen earlier, each system $S: Ax = 0$ can be transformed to an essentially equivalent system $S': A'x' = 0$, where the coefficients of the integer matrix A' are from $\{-1, 0, 1\}$. Let x be a variable with $m > 3$ occurrences. Introduce m new variables u_1, ..., u_m. Replace the i-th occurrence of the variable x by u_i and obtain a new system S'' by adding the equations $u_1 = u_2, u_2 = u_3, \ldots, u_m = u_1$. It is clear that each variable in S'' has at most three occurrences and that the coefficients of the system are from $\{-1, 0, 1\}$. It is also clear that there is a one-to-one and onto correspondence between the solutions of the systems S and S''. Furthermore, only a polynomial number of new equations is added. Thus, there exists a parsimonious reduction from the general problem #HILBERT to the restricted problem #HILBERT(3).

In view of the above, we focus our attention on the computational complexity of #HILBERT(1) and #HILBERT(2). Lincoln and Christian [LC89] pointed out that the Hilbert basis of a homogeneous linear Diophantine equation of the form $x_1 + \cdots + x_k = y_1 + \cdots + y_n$ consists of kn solutions. Specifically, it consists of all vectors satisfying the condition that there exist two indices i and j such that $x_i = 1, x_l = 0$ for all $l \neq i$, and $y_j = 1, y_m = 0$ for all $m \neq j$. Since there are k independent choices for i, and n independent choices for j, we have a total of kn minimal solutions. Suppose now we are given a system of homogeneous linear Diophantine equations in which each variable occurs exactly once. Thus, each variable occurs in exactly one equation and every equation of the system is of the form $x_1 + \cdots + x_k = y_1 + \cdots + y_n$. Note that each minimal solution of a single equation can be extended to exactly one minimal solution of the system by setting the variables of all other equations to zero. Conversely, it is easy to see that each minimal solution of the system consists of a minimal solution of a single equation and a zero-assignment to the variables of all other equations. Consequently, the cardinality of the Hilbert basis of such a system can be computed in polynomial time by first finding the number of minimal solutions for each equation separately, and then add these numbers. This argument shows that the counting problem #HILBERT(1) is in the class FP of functions computable in deterministic polynomial time.

It remains to consider the computational complexity of #HILBERT(2), that is, counting the Hilbert basis of systems of homogeneous linear Diophantine equations in which each variable has at most two occurrences. Our main result in this section is that #HILBERT(2) is in the class #P and, thus, appears to have lower complexity than #HILBERT(3). The proof of this theorem is based on the following two lemmas.

Lemma 4. *Let S be a homogeneous linear Diophantine system over non-negative integers such that each variable has at most two occurrences. Then there exists a homogeneous linear Diophantine system S', called the reduced form of S, that is equivalent to S and has the following properties:*

- *Each variable has at most two occurrences;*
- *Each equation is of type $x_1 + x_2 = x_3$ (type A) or of type $x_1 = x_2$ (type B);*
- *Each variable having exactly two occurrences appears in two distinct equations, once in an equation of type A and once in an equation of type B.*

Proof. (Hint) Let $S: Ax = 0$ be a homogeneous linear Diophantine system with at most two occurrences of each variable. Eliminate from S all variables that can only take 0 as value, e.g., the equation $2x_1 + x_3 + 2x_5 = 0$ forces $x_1 = x_3 = x_5 = 0$. Eliminate all trivial equations $0 = 0$. Move the variables with negative coefficients to the right-hand side of the equations. Replace each monomial of the form $2x$ by $x_1 + x_2$, where x_1 and x_2 are new variables, and add the equation $x_1 = x_2$. Now, every variable occurs with coefficient 1. After these transformations, each equation has the form $\alpha x = \alpha' x$, where α, α' are vectors over $\{0, 1\}$. Split each equation of the form $\alpha x = \alpha' x$ into $\alpha x = x'$, $\alpha' x = x''$, and $x' = x''$, where x', x'' are new variables. Split each equation of the form $x_1 + x_2 + \cdots + x_n = x_{n+1}$, where $n > 2$, into the three equations $x_1 + x'_1 = x_{n+1}$, $x_2 + \cdots x_n = x''_1$, and $x'_1 = x''_1$. Repeat this last step until there are no more equations with more than two variables on the left-hand sides. Finally, if there are two equations of the type $x_1 = x_2$ and $x_2 = x_3$, then contract these equations to a single equation $x_1 = x_3$ and delete the variable x_2. □

We saw earlier that the size of every minimal solution of an arbitrary homogeneous linear Diophantine equations is bounded by a polynomial in the size of the system. The second lemma shows that this bound can be dramatically improved, if every variable has at most two occurrences in the system.

Lemma 5. *Let S be a homogeneous linear Diophantine system over non-negative integers such that every variable has at most two occurrences. Then every minimal solution $(s_1, \ldots, s_n)$ of S has the property that the value of each coefficient s_i is at most 2.*

Proof. (Hint) The main idea of the proof is to transform the system S and a given solution s into a graph having the following property: each cycle in the graph represents a new solution s' such that s' is either the trivial all-zero solution or it is a solution that is pointwise smaller than or equal to the original solution s. After this, using properties of the graph, it can be shown that each variable with value 3 can be decremented by 1 or 2, and the result is still a solution of the original system. This is established via an analysis of 16 cases, the details of which can be found at http://www.loria.fr/~juban/16cases.ps.gz. It follows that in every minimal solution each variable must have value at most 2 [Jub98]. □

Theorem 5. *The counting problem* #HILBERT(2) *is in the class* #P.

Proof. In order to establish that the problem #HILBERT(2) belongs to #P, we need to show that the following conditions hold for systems S of homogeneous linear Diophantine equations in reduced form (we use here Lemma 4): (1) the size of every minimal solution of S is bounded by a fixed polynomial in the size of S; (2) there is a polynomial-time algorithm to test whether, given a vector s and a system S in reduced form, s is a minimal solution of S. The first condition clearly holds (for instance, by Lemma 5). Thus, it remains to show that we can verify in polynomial time that a vector s is a minimal solution of a system S. It is straightforward to verify in polynomial time that the vector s is a solution of S and that it satisfies the bounds stated in Lemma 5. To verify minimality, we give a polynomial-time reduction to the problem of finding an *alternating circuit* or an *augmenting path* in a graph, a problem that is well known to be solvable in polynomial time. Before proceeding with the rest of the proof, we define the necessary graph-theoretic concepts.

Let $G = (V, E)$ be a graph. A *matching* of G is a set $M \subseteq E$ of edges, such that no pair of edges in M share a common vertex. A vertex $v \in V$ is called *matched* by a matching M if there is an edge $e \in M$ adjacent to v. Otherwise, the vertex v is called *exposed* or *free* for M. An *alternating path* p for a matching M is a simple path in G (without repeated vertices), joining two distinct vertices, such that edges from M alternate in p with edges from $E \setminus M$. Similarly, an *alternating circuit* c for M is a simple circuit in G (without repeated vertices except the first and the last one), that alternates edges from M and from $E \setminus M$. An alternating path for a matching M that joins two exposed vertices is called an *augmenting path*.

Given a homogeneous linear Diophantine system S over non-negative integers with each variable occurring at most twice and a solution s, we will construct a graph $G = (V, E)$ and a matching $M \subseteq E$ having the property that the solution s is *not* minimal if and only if there exists an alternating circuit or an augmenting path for M not including all vertices V.

In the first stage, we eliminate from S each variable that takes the value 0 in the solution s, and we construct a system S' in the reduced form (cf. Lemma 4) equivalent to the original system S. For each solution s of S, there exists a solution s' of S' such that s is minimal for S if and only if s' is minimal for S'. The system S' has the property that each variable occurs at most twice, once in a type A equation and once in a type B equation. Moreover, the solution s' has the property that the constraint $1 \leq s'_i \leq 2$ holds for each of its coefficients.

We will restrict further the system S', so that each variable with one occurrence appears in a type A equation. We will see later, during the transformation of the system S' to the graph G, why this restriction is necessary. Before performing this restriction, let us analyze the possible situations for a variable with one occurrence. Assume first, that a variable x with one occurrence appears in a type B equation $x = x'$. We perform a case analysis on the number of occurrences of x'. If the variable x' has one occurrence and the system S' contains also other equations, then the solution s' is *not* minimal, since a vector s^*, where we set $s^*(x) = x^*(x') = 0$ and $s^*(y) = s'(y)$ for the variables y different from both x and x', is a smaller solution of S' than s'. If the variable x' has one occurrence and $x = x'$ is the unique equation in the system S', then s' is minimal if and only if $s'(x) = s'(x') = 1$. Otherwise, if $s'(x) = s'(x') = 2$, then the solution s' is obviously not minimal. If the variable x' has two occurrences, then we can delete the equation $x = x'$ from the system S'. This can be done, since the value of the variable x is fully determined by the value of x' and the variable x' is determined by the remaining system $S \setminus \{x = x'\}$. In the last case, the systems S' and $S' \setminus \{x = x'\}$ have the same number of solutions. Hence, we get a new system $S'' = S' \setminus \{x = x'\}$ and a new solution s'', restricted to the variables of S'', such that s is a minimal solution of the system S if and only if s'' is a minimal solution of the system S''.

We construct a graph $G = (V, E)$ and a matching M form the system S'', such that s is a minimal solution of S if and only if there is no augmenting path and no alternating circuit in G. The vertices V are constructed from the solution $s'' = (s''_1, \ldots, s''_n)$. For each coefficient $s_i = 1$ we add the vertex v_i to V. Similarly, for each coefficient $s_i = 2$ we add the vertices v_i^1 and v_i^2 to V. The edges E correspond to the equations of the system S''. The set of edges E is the union $E_A \cup E_B$ of two disjoint sets, corresponding respectively to the type A and the type B equations. For each type A equation $x_i + x_k = x_j$ we add the four edges $(x_i, x_j^1), (x_i, x_j^2), (x_k, x_j^1), (x_k, x_j^2)$ to E_A. For each type B equation $x_i = x_j$, such that $s_i = s_j = 1$, we add the edge (v_i, v_j) to E_B. For each type B equation, such that $s_i = s_j = 2$, we add the two edges $(v_i^1, v_j^1), (v_i^2, v_j^2)$ to E_B. Note that the degree of each vertex $v \in V$ is at most 3 and that the set of edges E_B is a matching M of the graph G. Indeed, each vertex is incident to at most one edge from E_B, since each variable occurs at most once in a type B equation.

An augmenting path p in the graph G for a matching M has the property that the vertices on the extremities of p are exposed. We will show that each augmenting path in G for a matching M allows us to construct a new solution s^* smaller than s. In fact, the augmenting path p corresponds to a traversal of equations, alternating type A and type B equations. Moreover, the vertices on the extremities of p correspond to variables with one occurrence. Thus, we can construct a new solution s^* from s by decrementing by 1 every variable corresponding to a vertex in the path p. The variables x_i with value $s_i = 2$ are represented by two vertices v_i^1 and v_i^2, hence they can be decremented twice. An alternating circuit c of even length in the graph G for a matching M alternates edges from M with edges from $E \setminus M$. Similarly, as for augmenting paths, each alternating circuit of even length in G for a matching M allows us to construct a new solution s^* smaller than s. Once more, we decrement by 1 every variable corresponding to a vertex in the circuit c.

Note that the fact of having deleted the type A equations $x = y$ when one of the variables occurs only once, allows us to find a 1-to-1 correspondence between a new smaller solution of the system and the existence of an augmenting path or an alternating circuit in the corresponding graph. If we did not delete these equations, we would have alternating paths that are neither augmenting paths nor alternating circuits not corresponding to any solution of the system.

After the construction of the graph G with the matching M, we make correspond to each solution s^*, such that $s^* < s''$, an augmenting path or an alternating circuit of even length. Indeed, if $r_i = s_i'' - s_i^*$ for each $i = 1, \ldots, n$, then there exists an augmenting path or an alternating circuit containing the vertices corresponding to the non-zero coefficients $r_i \neq 0$. If $r_i = 2$ then both vertices v_i^1 and v_i^2 are in the path or circuit. Otherwise, either v_i is present, when $s_i = 1$, or one of the vertices v_i^1, v_i^2 is present, when $s_i = 2$. We know that finding an augmenting path or an alternating circuit in a graph G for a matching M is a polynomial-time problem. Therefore we can detect the existence of a smaller solution $s^* < s$ in polynomial time. The only drawback is that s^* can be the trivial all-zero solution, when the found augmenting path or alternating circuit contains all vertices of the graph G. We must avoid this situation by deleting some edges from E, constructing a new graph G'. We cannot delete a vertex and all its adjacent edges, since then another vertex, that was matched before, can become exposed. Instead, to assure that a vertex v is *not* included into an augmenting path or an alternating circuit, it is sufficient to delete all edges from $E \setminus M$ that are adjacent to v. In this case, since no edge from the matching M is deleted, the augmenting paths and the alternating circuits of the graph G' are those also in the original graph G. Moreover, it is sufficient to choose only matched vertices v for deleting the adjacent edges from $E \setminus M$, since each exposed vertex is connected by an edge from $E \setminus M$ to a matched vertex. This is a direct consequence of alternating edges from E_A and E_B.

Let v be a matched vertex in the graph G with the matching M. Construct the graph G_v from G by deleting the edges from $E \setminus M$ adjacent to v. If there exists an augmenting path or an alternating circuit in G_v for M, then the solution s of the system S is *not* minimal. Since there are only polynomially many possibilities to choose a matched vertex in the graph G and an augmenting path or an alternating circuit can be found in polynomial time with respect to the size of the graph, we can check in polynomial time whether a vector s is a minimal solution of a homogeneous linear Diophantine system S in which every variable has at most two occurrences. This completes the proof of the theorem.   □

It is an interesting open problem to determine whether this upper bound is tight or it can be lowered even further. We conjecture that #HILBERT(2) is actually a #P-complete problem.

5   The Complexity of Counting the Compatible Subsets

Stickel's algorithm [Sti75] for simultaneous elementary AC-unification proceeds by first finding the Hilbert basis of the associated homogeneous linear Diophantine system, and then producing the set of all compatible subsets of that basis. To gain insight into the inherent complexity of this algorithm, we examine the computational complexity of counting the number of compatible subsets of a given set T of linearly independent and pairwise incomparable vectors of non-negative integers. We identify the complexity of this problem by showing that #COMPATIBLE SUBSETS is #P-complete and, thus, highly intractable. Before embarking on the proof of this result, we remind the reader that, when we speak about linear combinations, we always restrict ourselves to linear combinations with non-negative coefficients. By the same token, when we speak about linearly independent vectors, we mean independence with respect to linear combinations with nonnegative coefficients.

Theorem 6. *The counting problem* #COMPATIBLE SUBSETS *is* #P*-complete.*

Proof. Since membership in #P is quite obvious, we focus on the #P-hardness of this problem. This will be achieved by showing that #POSITIVE 2SAT has a polynomial-time 1-Turing reduction to #COMPATIBLE SUBSETS. Let $X = \{x_1, \ldots, x_k\}$ be the set of variables and let $C = \{c_1, \ldots c_m\}$ be the set of clauses of a positive 2CNF formula φ. Consider the $k \times m$ matrix $A = (a_i^j)_k^m$ such that $a_i^j = 1$, if the variable x_i appears in the clause c_j, and $a_i^j = 0$, otherwise. Without loss of generality, we can assume that no two rows of the matrix A are equal. Indeed, assume that x and y are two variables such that the corresponding rows of A are equal. If each of the variables x and y has at least two occurrences in φ, say in the clauses c_i and c_j, then we must have $c_i = c_j = x \vee y$, which is impossible, since C consists of different clauses. If each of the variables x and y has only one occurrence in φ, say in the clause c, then we can delete the clause c from the set C and consider instead the positive 2CNF formula ψ with clauses $C \setminus \{c\}$. Note that the number of satisfying assignments of φ is equal to three times the number of satisfying assignments of ψ. The reason for this is that the variables x and y do not occur in ψ, whereas the clause $c = x \vee y$ has three satisfying assignments.

Our goal is to transform A into another matrix A^* such that the rows of A^* form an instance of #COMPATIBLE SUBSETS. For this, we augment the matrix A with an additional column vector $\beta = (\beta_1, \ldots, \beta_k)$ such that each β_i is equal to one plus the number of zeros in the i-th row of A. We claim that the resulting matrix A^* has the property that all rows are pairwise incomparable in the pointwise order and that no row can be written as a linear combination with non-negative coefficients of the remaining rows.

Since no two rows of A are equal, it follows that the same property holds for the rows of A^*. Suppose that A^* has two comparable rows $a_i^* < a_j^*$. Then the relation $a_i < a_j$ must hold for the corresponding rows a_i and a_j of A. Consequently, the number of the zero entries of row a_i must be bigger than the number of zero entries of row a_j. In turn, this implies that $\beta_i > \beta_j$, which contradicts the inequality $a_i^* < a_j^*$. Suppose now that A^* has a row a_i^* that is a linear combination with non-negative coefficients of the remaining rows. This implies that the corresponding row a_i of A is a nonnegative linear combination of the remaining rows in A. It follows that there exists a row a_j of A for some $j \neq i$ that occurs with a positive coefficient in the linear combination producing row a_i. Consequently, the inequality $a_j < a_i$ must hold. As before, this implies

Counting Problem	Lower Bound	Upper Bound
#HILBERT	#P-hard	#NP
#HILBERT(3)	#P-hard	#NP
#HILBERT(2)	???	#P
#HILBERT(1)	—	FP

Table 1. The complexity of counting the Hilbert basis

that $\beta_j > \beta_i$, hence the rows a_j^* and a_i^* of A^* must be incomparable. This, however, contradicts the assumption that a_i^* is a nonnegative linear combination in which a_j^* occurs with a positive coefficient.

We now claim that there is a one-to-one correspondence between satisfying truth assignments of the given 2CNF formula and compatible subsets of the set of rows of A^*. A truth assignment to the variables of φ can be identified with the set of variables that are assigned value *true*. Consequently, such a truth assignment can be identified with the subset of the rows of A^* whose corresponding variables are assigned value *true*. A truth assignment satisfies the positive 2CNF formula φ if and only if for each clause c_i there exists at least one variable x_j in c_i such that x_j is assigned value *true*. This means that the set of rows identified with the truth assignment is a compatible subset of the set of all rows of A^* (note that the last row of A^* consists entirely of positive entries). Vice versa, every compatible subset of A^* gives rise to exactly one satisfying assignment of φ. Thus, we have produced a polynomial-time 1-Turing reduction of #POSITIVE 2SAT to #COMPATIBLE SUBSETS.   □

6   Concluding Remarks

In this paper, we initiated a study of the computational complexity of counting the Hilbert basis of a homogeneous system of linear Diophantine equations. We established that #HILBERT is in #NP and also that it is #P-hard under polynomial-time 1-Turing reductions. Admittedly, these results yield only upper and lower bounds on the complexity of this problem. Nonetheless, they appear to be the first results on the complexity of counting the Hilbert basis. Furthermore, we argued that, in view of Toda and Watanabe's work [TW92], it appears unlikely that the bounds obtained here can be made tighter without significant advances in computational complexity.

We also examined restricted variants of #HILBERT obtained by taking into account the number of occurrences of the variables in the system. In particular, we showed that if each variable has at most two occurrences, then the problem of counting the Hilbert basis is a member of the class #P (see also Table 1). Finally, we established that it is a #P-complete problem to count the number of compatible subsets of a given set of pairwise incomparable and linearly independent set of vectors.

Acknowledgement: We wish to thank Lane A. Hemaspaandra and Heribert Vollmer for many helpful email exchanges in which they provided us with pointers to references and valuable information about polynomial-time 1-Turing reductions.

References

[BCD90] A. Boudet, E. Contejean, and H. Devie. A new AC unification algorithm with a new algorithm for solving Diophantine equations. In *Proceedings 5th LICS, Philadelphia (PA, USA)*, pages 289–299, June 1990.

[BKN87] D. Benanav, D. Kapur, and P. Narendran. Complexity of matching problems. *Journal of Symbolic Computation*, 3:203–216, 1987.

[BN98] F. Baader and T. Nipkow. *Term rewriting and all that*. Cambridge University Press, 1998.

[Bou93] A. Boudet. Competing for the AC-unification race. *Journal of Automated Reasoning*, 11(2):185–212, 1993.

[CD94] E. Contejean and H. Devie. An efficient incremental algorithm for solving systems of linear Diophantine equations. *Information and Computation*, 113(1):143–172, 1994.

[CF89] M. Clausen and A. Fortenbacher. Efficient solution of linear Diophantine equations. *Journal of Symbolic Computation*, 8(1-2):201–216, 1989.

[DHJ99] A. Durand, M. Hermann, and L. Juban. On the complexity of recognizing the Hilbert basis of a linear Diophantine system. In L. Pacholski, editor, *Proceedings 24th MFCS, Szklarska Poreba (Poland)*, LNCS, Springer-Verlag, September 1999.

[Dom91a] E. Domenjoud. *Outils pour la déduction automatique dans les théories associative-commutatives*. PhD thesis, Université Henri Poincaré, Nancy, France, September 1991.

[Dom91b] E. Domenjoud. Solving systems of linear Diophantine equations: An algebraic approach. In A. Tarlecki, editor, *Proceedings 16th MFCS, Kazimierz Dolny (Poland)*, LNCS 520, pages 141–150. Springer-Verlag, September 1991.

[Dur99] A. Durand. Personal communication, June 1999.

[EE85] A. A. Elimam and S. E. Elmaghraby. On the reduction method for integer linear programs II. *Discrete Applied Mathematics*, 12(3):241–260, 1985.

[Fag87] F. Fages. Associative commutative unification. *Journal of Symbolic Computation*, 3(3):257–275, 1987.

[GJ79] M. R. Garey and D. S. Johnson. *Computers and intractability: A guide to the theory of NP-completeness*. W.H. Freeman and Co, 1979.

[Gor73] P. Gordan. Ueber die Auflösung linearen Gleichungen mit reellen Coefficienten. *Mathematische Annalen*, 6:23–28, 1873.

[Hil90] D. Hilbert. Ueber die Theorie der algebraischen Formen. *Mathematische Annalen*, 36:473–534, 1890.

[HK95a] M. Hermann and P. G. Kolaitis. The complexity of counting problems in equational matching. *Journal of Symbolic Computation*, 20(3):343–362, 1995.

[HK95b] M. Hermann and P. G. Kolaitis. Computational complexity of simultaneous elementary matching problems. In J. Wiedermann and P. Hájek, editors, *Proceedings 20th MFCS, Prague (Czech Republic)*, LNCS 969, pages 359–370. Springer-Verlag, August 1995.

[HS87]   A. Herold and J. H. Siekmann. Unification in Abelian semigroups. *Journal of Automated Reasoning*, 3(3):247–283, 1987.

[Hue78] G. Huet. An algorithm to generate the basis of solutions to homogeneous linear Diophantine equations. *Information Processing Letters*, 7(3):144–147, 1978.

[HV95]   L. A. Hemaspaandra and H. Vollmer. The satanic notations: Counting classes beyond #P and other definitional adventures. *SIGACT News*, 26(1):2–13, March 1995.

[JK91]   J.-P. Jouannaud and C. Kirchner. Solving equations in abstract algebras: A rule-based survey of unification. In J.-L. Lassez and G. Plotkin, editors, *Computational Logic. Essays in honor of Alan Robinson*, chapter 8, pages 257–321. MIT Press, Cambridge (MA, USA), 1991.

[Joh90] D. S. Johnson. A catalog of complexity classes. In J. van Leeuwen, editor, *Handbook of Theoretical Computer Science, Volume A: Algorithms and Complexity*, chapter 2, pages 67–161. North-Holland, Amsterdam, 1990.

[Jub98] L. Juban. Comptage de l'ensemble des éléments de la base de Hilbert d'un système d'équations diophantiennes linéaires. Technical Report 98-R-066, LORIA, 1998.

[Lam87] J.-L. Lambert. Une borne pour les générateurs des solutions entières positives d'une équation diophantienne linéaire. *Compte-rendus de l'Académie des Sciences de Paris*, 305(1):39–40, 1987.

[Lan89] D. Lankford. Non-negative integer basis algorithms for linear equations with integer coefficients. *Journal of Automated Reasoning*, 5(1):25–35, 1989.

[LC89]   P. Lincoln and J. Christian. Adventures in associative-commutative unification. *Journal of Symbolic Computation*, 8(1-2):217–240, 1989.

[Pap81] C. H. Papadimitriou. On the complexity of integer programming. *Journal of the Association for Computing Machinery*, 28(4):765–768, 1981.

[Pap94] C. H. Papadimitriou. *Computational complexity*. Addison-Wesley, 1994.

[Pot91] L. Pottier. Minimal solutions of linear Diophantine systems: bounds and algorithms. In R.V. Book, editor, *Proceedings 4th RTA, Como (Italy), LNCS 488*, pages 162–173. Springer-Verlag, April 1991.

[Sch86] A. Schrijver. *Theory of linear and integer programming*. John Wiley & Sons, 1986.

[Sti75] M. Stickel. A complete unification algorithm for associative-commutative functions. In *Proceedings 4th IJCAI, Tbilisi (USSR)*, pages 71–82, 1975.

[Sti81] M. Stickel. A unification algorithm for associative-commutative functions. *Journal of the Association for Computing Machinery*, 28(3):423–434, 1981.

[Tod89] S. Toda. On the computational power of PP and ⊕P. In *Proceedings 30th FOCS, Research Triangle Park (NC, USA)*, pages 514–519, 1989.

[Tod91] S. Toda. *Computational complexity of counting complexity classes*. PhD thesis, Tokyo Institute of Technology, Department of Computer Science, Tokyo, Japan, 1991.

[TW92]   S. Toda and O. Watanabe. Polynomial-time 1-Turing reductions from #PH to #P. *Theoretical Computer Science*, 100(1):205–221, 1992.

[Val79a] L. G. Valiant. The complexity of computing the permanent. *Theoretical Computer Science*, 8(2):189–201, 1979.

[Val79b] L. G. Valiant. The complexity of enumeration and reliability problems. *SIAM Journal on Computing*, 8(3):410–421, 1979.

[Zan91] V. Zankó. #P-completeness via many-one reductions. *International Journal of Foundations of Computer Science*, 2(1):77–82, 1991.

Solving Combinatorial Problems with Regular Local Search Algorithms*

Ramón Béjar and Felip Manyà

Departament d'Informàtica
Universitat de Lleida
Jaume II, 69, E-25001 Lleida, Spain
{ramon,felip}@eup.udl.es

Abstract In this paper we describe new local search algorithms for regular CNF formulas and investigate their suitability for solving problems from the domains of graph coloring and sports scheduling. First, we define suitable encodings for such problems in the logic of regular CNF formulas. Second, we describe Regular-GSAT and Regular-WSAT, as well as some variants, which are a natural generalization of two prominent local search algorithms – GSAT and WSAT – used to solve the propositional satisfiability (SAT) problem in classical logic. Third, we report on experimental results that demonstrate that encoding graph coloring and sports scheduling problems as instances of the SAT problem in regular CNF formulas and then solving these instances with local search algorithms can outperform or compete with state-of-the-art approaches to solving hard combinatorial problems.

1 Introduction

In recent years, regular CNF formulas (defined in Section 2) have received increasing interest in the community working on automated theorem proving in multiple-valued logics. This interest is due to the fact that an instance of the propositional satisfiability (SAT) problem in any finitely-valued logic is polynomially reducible to an instance of the SAT problem in regular CNF formulas [7]. Moreover, the computational properties of such formulas have been studied and efficient algorithms for solving the regular SAT problem have been designed and implemented. See [1,2,3,5,8,9,12,13] for further details.

Motivated by the success of propositional satisfiability algorithms for solving real-world problems encoded as instances of the classical SAT problem (e.g. [4,11]), we will investigate the suitability of local search algorithms for solving graph coloring and sports scheduling problems encoded as instances of the SAT problem in regular CNF formulas. The algorithms we will use to conduct our experiments are Regular-GSAT and Regular-WSAT, as well as some variants,

---
* Research partially supported by the project CICYT TIC96-1038-C04-03. The first author is supported by a doctoral fellowship of the Comissionat per a Universitats i Recerca (1998FI00326).

which are a natural generalization of two prominent local search algorithms – GSAT [17] and WSAT [16] – used to solve the SAT problem in classical logic.

We believe that encoding combinatorial problems as instances of the regular SAT problem, instead of the classical SAT problem, is a promising approach due to several reasons:

- Classical CNF formulas are a subclass of regular CNF formulas. As the latter are a more expressive representation formalism, some problems encoded as regular SAT instances give raise to more compact encodings. There are combinatorial problems encoded as classical SAT instances that cannot be practically solved because the CNF formulas obtained are too large. It is expected that regular CNF formulas will extend the range and size of problems that can be solved using SAT encodings.
- Problems encoded as regular SAT instances usually need a smaller number of propositional variables. For instance, an encoding of the k-colorability problem for an undirected graph with V vertices as a regular SAT instance only needs V propositional variables. It is expected that this could have positive effects in the search for a solution.
- Algorithms and heuristics for classical CNF formulas can be generalized to regular CNF formulas naturally. The good properties of the classical algorithms remain in regular algorithms [2]. This can be observed in the algorithms Regular-GSAT and Regular-WSAT described in Section 4. This implies that for designing new algorithms for regular CNF formulas we do not have to start from scratch, we can take advantage of the techniques that have proven to be successful in the classical setting.

In this paper we report on the first experimental investigation conducted for showing that regular local search algorithms used to solve real-world problems encoded as regular SAT instances can outperform or compete with state-of-the-art approaches to solving hard combinatorial problems. This claim is confirmed by the experimental results reported here from the domains of graph coloring and sports scheduling. We expect to find a similar behaviour in other problem domains.

This paper is organized as follows. In Section 2 we define the logic of regular CNF formulas. In Section 3 we define how to encode graph coloring and sports scheduling problems as regular SAT instances. In Section 4 we describe Regular-GSAT and Regular-WSAT. In Section 5 we report on our experimental investigation. We finish the paper with some concluding remarks.

2 Regular CNF formulas

Definition 1. *A truth value set N is a finite set $\{i_1, i_2, \ldots, i_n\}$, where $n \in \mathbb{N}$. Any subset S of N is a sign.*

Definition 2. *Let $\uparrow i$ denote the set $\{j \in N \mid j \geq i\}$ and let $\downarrow i$ denote the set $\{j \in N \mid j \leq i\}$, where $\leq$ is a total order on the truth value set N and $i \in N$. If a sign S is equal to either $\uparrow i$ or $\downarrow i$, for some i, then it is a regular sign.*

Definition 3. *Let S be a regular sign and let p be a propositional variable. An expression of the form $S\!:\!p$ is a* regular literal *and S is its* sign. *The* complement *of the regular literal $L = S\!:\!p$, denoted by $\overline{L} = \overline{S}\!:\!p$, is $(N \setminus S)\!:\!p$. A* regular clause *is a finite set of regular literals. A* regular CNF formula *is a finite set of regular clauses. The* length *of a regular CNF formula Γ is the total number of occurrences of regular literals in Γ.*

Definition 4. *An* interpretation *is a mapping that assigns to every propositional variable an element of the truth value set. An interpretation I* satisfies *a regular literal $S\!:\!p$ iff $I(p) \in S$. An interpretation* satisfies *a regular clause iff it satisfies at least one of its regular literals. A regular CNF formula Γ is* satisfiable *iff there exists at least one interpretation that satisfies all the regular clauses in Γ. A regular CNF formula that is not satisfiable is* unsatisfiable. *The regular empty clause is always unsatisfiable and the regular empty CNF formula is always satisfiable.*

3 Encodings using regular CNF formulas

In this section we present the encodings used to formalize the k-colorability problem of graphs and the round robin problem of sports scheduling as instances of the regular SAT problem.

3.1 The k-colorability problem of graphs

In the k-colorability problem we are given an undirected graph $G = (V, E)$, where V is the set of vertices and E is the set of edges, and we are asked whether there is a function $c : V \rightarrow \{1, \dots, k\}$ such that for each edge $[u, v] \in E$ we have $c(u) \neq c(v)$. Given such a graph we construct an instance of the regular SAT problem as follows: for each edge $[u, v] \in E$, we define k regular clauses:

$$
\begin{array}{ll}
(C_1) & \{\uparrow 2 : u, \uparrow 2 : v\} \\
(C_2) & \{\downarrow 1 : u, \uparrow 3 : u, \downarrow 1 : v, \uparrow 3 : v\} \\
\vdots & \qquad \vdots \\
(C_i) & \{\downarrow (i-1) : u, \uparrow (i+1) : u, \downarrow (i-1) : v, \uparrow (i+1) : v\} \\
\vdots & \qquad \vdots \\
(C_{k-1}) & \{\downarrow (k-2) : u, \uparrow k : u, \downarrow (k-2) : v, \uparrow k : v\} \\
(C_k) & \{\downarrow (k-1) : u, \downarrow (k-1) : v\}
\end{array}
$$

and we take as truth value set $N = \{1, \dots, k\}$. The intended meaning of the previous regular clauses is that vertex u and vertex v do not have the same color. For each $i \in \{1, \dots, k\}$, the intended meaning of regular clause C_i is that vertex u and vertex v are not both colored with color i. Observe that from the definition of interpretation we can ensure that every vertex is colored with only one color. Also observe that the length of the regular CNF formula obtained is in $\mathcal{O}(|N| \cdot |E|)$, where $|N|$ is the number of colors and $|E|$ is the number of edges.

3.2 The round robin problem

In this section we first introduce the round robin problem and then its formalization using the logic of regular CNF formulas. In the below description of the round robin problem we follow the presentation of [6].

In sports scheduling problems one of the issues is timetabling, where by timetabling we mean determining the existence of a feasible schedule that takes into consideration constraints on how the competing teams can be paired, as well as how each team's games are distributed in the entire schedule. The round robin problem for n teams (n-team round robin problem) is formally defined as follows:

1. There are n teams (n even) and every two teams play each other exactly once.
2. The season lasts $n - 1$ weeks.
3. Every team plays one game in each week of the season.
4. There are $n/2$ periods and, each week, every period is scheduled for one game.
5. No team plays more than twice in the same period over the course of the season.

Table 1 shows a solution that we have obtained in our experiments for the 10-team round robin problem; teams are named $1, \ldots, 10$. An n-team round robin timetable contains $n(n-1)/2$ slots and each slot is filled in with a game. A game is represented by a pair of teams (t_1, t_2) such that $t_1 < n$ and $t_1 < t_2$.

	Week 1	Week 2	Week 3	Week 4	Week 5	Week 6	Week 7	Week 8	Week 9
Period 1	$(6,9)$	$(4,6)$	$(1,8)$	$(4,10)$	$(2,8)$	$(7,9)$	$(5,7)$	$(1,2)$	$(3,5)$
Period 2	$(2,3)$	$(1,5)$	$(2,4)$	$(1,7)$	$(9,10)$	$(8,10)$	$(3,6)$	$(4,9)$	$(6,8)$
Period 3	$(5,10)$	$(2,7)$	$(3,9)$	$(5,9)$	$(1,3)$	$(1,6)$	$(4,8)$	$(6,10)$	$(4,7)$
Period 4	$(1,4)$	$(8,9)$	$(5,6)$	$(3,8)$	$(6,7)$	$(2,5)$	$(1,10)$	$(3,7)$	$(2,10)$
Period 5	$(7,8)$	$(3,10)$	$(7,10)$	$(2,6)$	$(4,5)$	$(3,4)$	$(2,9)$	$(5,8)$	$(1,9)$

Table1. A 10-team round robin timetable

The n-team round robin problem is encoded as an instance of the regular SAT problem as follows:

1. The truth value set N is $\{1, 2, \ldots, n\}$. Each truth value represents a team.
2. The set of propositional variables is

$$\{p_{ij}^r \mid 1 \le r \le 2, 1 \le i \le n/2, 1 \le j \le n-1\}$$

and its cardinality is $n(n-1)$.

Each slot in the timetable is represented by a pair of variables. The pair (p_{ij}^1, p_{ij}^2) refers to the slot corresponding to period i and week j. Since the total number of slots is $n(n-1)/2$, we use $n(n-1)$ variables. Given a satisfying interpretation I, the intended meaning of (p_{ij}^1, p_{ij}^2) is that team $I(p_{ij}^1)$ will play against team $I(p_{ij}^2)$ in period i and week j.

3. For each slot (p_{ij}^1, p_{ij}^2), we define the regular clause

$$\{\downarrow(n-1) : p_{ij}^1\}$$

in order to ensure that $I(p_{ij}^1) < n$.

4. For each team t and for each slot (p_{ij}^1, p_{ij}^2), we define the regular clause

$$\{\downarrow(t-1) : p_{ij}^1, \uparrow(t+1) : p_{ij}^1, \uparrow(t+1) : p_{ij}^2\}$$

in order to ensure that $I(p_{ij}^1) < I(p_{ij}^2)$. We assume in all the steps that regular literals either of the form $\downarrow 0 : p$ or of the form $\uparrow(n+1) : p$ appearing in a regular clause are removed.

5. For each two different slots $(p_{i_1 j_1}^1, p_{i_1 j_1}^2)$ and $(p_{i_2 j_2}^1, p_{i_2 j_2}^2)$, and for each possible game (t_1, t_2), we define the regular clause

$$\{ \downarrow(t_1-1) : p_{i_1 j_1}^1, \uparrow(t_1+1) : p_{i_1 j_1}^1, \downarrow(t_2-1) : p_{i_1 j_1}^2, \uparrow(t_2+1) : p_{i_1 j_1}^2,$$
$$\downarrow(t_1-1) : p_{i_2 j_2}^1, \uparrow(t_1+1) : p_{i_2 j_2}^1, \downarrow(t_2-1) : p_{i_2 j_2}^2, \uparrow(t_2+1) : p_{i_2 j_2}^2 \}$$

in order to ensure that every two teams play each other exactly once. Since the total number of slots coincides with the total number of possible games, the above regular clauses not only ensure that each possible game appears at most in one slot, but exactly once.

6. For each team t and for each two different variables $p_{i_1 j}^{r_1}$ and $p_{i_2 j}^{r_2}$ such that $i_1 \neq i_2$, we define the regular clause

$$\{\downarrow(t-1) : p_{i_1,j}^{r_1}, \uparrow(t+1) : p_{i_1,j}^{r_1}, \downarrow(t-1) : p_{i_2,j}^{r_2}, \uparrow(t+1) : p_{i_2,j}^{r_2}\}$$

in order to ensure that every team plays one game in each week of the season.

7. For each team t, for each period i, and for each three different weeks j_1, j_2 and j_3, we define the regular clauses

$$\bigwedge_{1 \leq r_1 \leq 2} \bigwedge_{1 \leq r_2 \leq 2} \bigwedge_{1 \leq r_3 \leq 2} \begin{cases} \downarrow(t-1) : p_{ij_1}^{r_1}, \uparrow(t+1) : p_{ij_1}^{r_1}, \\ \downarrow(t-1) : p_{ij_2}^{r_2}, \uparrow(t+1) : p_{ij_2}^{r_2}, \\ \downarrow(t-1) : p_{ij_3}^{r_3}, \uparrow(t+1) : p_{ij_3}^{r_3} \end{cases}$$

in order to ensure that no team plays more than twice in the same period over the course of the season.

The length of the regular CNF formula obtained for the n-team round robin problem is in $\mathcal{O}(n^6)$. If we use additional variables, we can reduce the length of the regular CNF formula derived. We solved the n-team round robin problem using additional variables, but the running times obtained were worse.

4 Regular local search algorithms

In this section we describe a number of regular local search algorithms that we have designed and implemented in C++ in order to conduct our experimental investigation. First, we describe Regular-GSAT and Regular-WSAT, which are a natural generalization of GSAT [17] and WSAT [16] (also called walksat) to the framework of regular CNF formulas. We then describe Regular-WSAT/G, which is a generalization of WSAT/G [14] (a variant of WSAT often used in the literature). Finally, we describe the averaging strategy of [15] that we have extended to the regular setting and incorporated into the previous algorithms. Each algorithm differs from the others in the strategy employed to escape from local minima.

Regular-GSAT, whose pseudo-code is shown in Figure 1, tries to find a satisfying interpretation for a regular CNF formula Γ performing a greedy local search through the space of possible interpretations. It starts with a randomly generated interpretation I. If I does not satisfy Γ, it creates a set S formed by the variable-value pairs (p, k) that, when the truth value that assigns I to p is changed to k, give the largest decrease (it may be zero or negative) in the total number of unsatisfied clauses of Γ. Then, it randomly chooses a propositional variable p' that appears in S. Once p' is selected, it randomly chooses a truth value k' from those that appear in variable-value pairs of S that contain p'. Next, it changes the assignment of the propositional variable p' to the truth value k'. Such changes are repeated until either a satisfying interpretation is found or a pre-set maximum number of changes (MaxChanges) is reached. This process is repeated as needed, up to a maximum of MaxTries times.

The pseudo-code of Regular-WSAT is shown in Figure 2. The way of making changes in Regular-WSAT and Regular-GSAT is different. Regular-WSAT proceeds as follows: (i) it randomly chooses an unsatisfied clause C, (ii) it chooses – using function select-WSAT – a variable-value pair (p', k') from the set S of pairs (p, k) such that C is satisfied by the current interpretation I if the truth value that I assigns to p is changed to k, and (iii) it creates a new interpretation I' that is identical to I except that $I'(p') = k'$. Function select-WSAT calculates, for each pair (p, k) in S, the number of broken clauses; i.e. the number of clauses that are satisfied by I but that would become unsatisfied if the assignment of p is changed to k. If the minimum number of broken clauses found (u) is greater than zero then either it randomly chooses, with probability ω, a pair (p', k') from S or it randomly chooses, with probability $1 - \omega$, a pair (p', k') from those pairs for which the number of broken clauses is u. If $u = 0$, then it randomly chooses a pair from those pairs for which $u = 0$.

Regular-WSAT/G differs from Regular-WSAT in the function that chooses the variable-value pair (p', k') that gives raise to a new interpretation. The pseudo-code of such a function, called select-WSAT/G, is shown in Figure 3. Function select-WSAT/G calculates, for each pair (p, k) in S, the decrease in the number of unsatisfied clauses when the truth value of p is changed to k. If the maximum decrease found is u' then either it randomly chooses, with proba-

procedure Regular-GSAT

Input: a regular CNF formula Γ, MaxChanges and MaxTries
Output: a satisfying interpretation of Γ, if found
```
begin
  for i := 1 to MaxTries
    I := a randomly generated interpretation for Γ;
    for j := 1 to MaxChanges
      if I satisfies Γ then return I;
      Let S be the set of variable-value pairs of the form (p, k) that, when
      the truth value that assigns I to p is changed to k, give the largest
      decrease in the total number of clauses of Γ that are unsatisfied;
      Pick one variable p' from the set {p | (p, k) ∈ S};
      Pick one value k' from the set {k | (p', k) ∈ S};
      I := I with the truth assignment of p' changed to k';
    end for
  end for
  return "no satisfying interpretation found";
end
```

Figure1. The Regular-GSAT procedure

bility ω, a pair (p', k') from S or it randomly chooses, with probability $1 - \omega$, a pair (p', k') from those pairs whose decrease is u'.

The averaging strategy [15] modifies the way in which the procedure generates a new interpretation at the beginning of each try. The idea behind this strategy is to profit from the interpretations found in previous tries. We have generalized this strategy as follows. Let I_i^{init} and I_i^{final} be the interpretation at the beginning and at the end, respectively, of the i-th try. In the first try, the procedure randomly generates I_1^{init}. In the second try, it generates I_2^{init} from I_1^{init} and I_1^{final} as follows: the value assigned to a variable is v if v is the value that both I_1^{init} and I_1^{final} assign to the variable; otherwise (the values assigned to the variable are different), the value is randomly chosen either from I_1^{init} or from I_1^{final} with equal probability. The initial interpretation I_i^{init} for the remaining tries is generated as above but using interpretations I_{i-2}^{final} and I_{i-1}^{final}. We reset the initial interpretation to a new randomly generated interpretation after a pre-set number of tries. We will refer to Regular-GSAT, Regular-WSAT and Regular-WSAT/G incorporating this strategy as Regular-GSAT+A, Regular-WSAT+A and Regular-WSAT/G+A, respectively.

5   Experimental results

In this section we report on a series of experiments performed in order to compare the performance of the above algorithms in graph coloring and sports scheduling

procedure Regular-WSAT

Input: a regular CNF formula Γ, MaxChanges, MaxTries and ω
Output: a satisfying interpretation of Γ, if found

```
begin
  for i := 1 to MaxTries
    I := a randomly generated interpretation for Γ;
    for j := 1 to MaxChanges
      if I satisfies Γ then return I;
      Pick one unsatisfied clause C from Γ;
      S := { (p, k) | S' : p ∈ C, k ∈ S' };
      (p', k') := select-WSAT( S, Γ, ω );
      I := I with the truth assignment of p' changed to k';
    end for
  end for
  return "no satisfying interpretation found";
end
```

function select-WSAT(S, Γ, ω) : (propositional_variable,truth_value)

```
begin
  u := min( {broken((p, k), Γ) | (p, k) ∈ S} );
  if (u > 0) then
    with probability ω
      Pick one variable p' from the set {p | (p, k) ∈ S};
      Pick one value k' from the set {k | (p', k) ∈ S};
      return (p', k');
    end with
  end if
  Pick one variable p' from the set {p | broken((p, k), Γ) = u, (p, k) ∈ S};
  Pick one value k' from the set {k | broken((p', k), Γ) = u, (p', k) ∈ S};
  return (p', k');
end
```

Figure 2. The Regular-WSAT procedure

function select-WSAT/G(S, Γ, ω) : (propositional_variable,truth_value)

```
begin
  u' := max ( {decrease((p, k), Γ) | (p, k) ∈ S} );
  with probability ω
    Pick one variable p' from the set {p | (p, k) ∈ S};
    Pick one value k' from the set {k | (p', k) ∈ S};
    return (p', k');
  end with
  Pick one variable p' from the set {p | decrease((p, k), Γ) = u', (p, k) ∈ S};
  Pick one value k' from the set {k | decrease((p', k), Γ) = u', (p', k) ∈ S};
  return (p', k');
end
```

Figure3. The selection function for the Regular-WSAT/G procedure

problems. Such experiments were performed on a Sun Sparc Ultra-4 with 384 MB of memory. In the below tables, we give the setting of MaxChanges (MC), and the best time and the median time obtained for each one of the instances considered. Each graph coloring instance was run nine times with each algorithm. The cutoff time for each instance was 9 hours. Each sports scheduling instance was run nine times with each algorithm. The cutoff time for each instance was 12 hours. If the median is *, it means that there was at least one run that did not finish within the cutoff time. If the best time is *, it means that the algorithm was unable to solve that instance within the cutoff time.

Table 2 shows the experimental results obtained for some graph coloring instances considered in [10] and in [15]. Our results indicate that the performance of our algorithms is competitive with the results of [10,15]. It is difficult to provide a more accurate comparison because the hardware used in the experiments was different and the results reported in [15] are not very detailed.

Table 3 shows the experimental results obtained for some instances of the n-team round robin problem considered in [6]. Using an integer programming formulation, Gomes et al. [6] were unable to find a solution for this problem for $n = 14$ and they last 14 hours to find a solution for $n = 12$. Using a constraint programming formulation, they did not find a solution for $n = 16$ with a deterministic algorithm. Using the same constraint programming formulation, they found a solution for $n = 16$ with a randomized constraint programming algorithm in 2 hours on average, which is competitive with our results. It is worth mentioning that the algorithm of [6] was executed 100 times and found a solution in 6 runs; with Regular-WSAT/G we found a solution in each run. These results suggest that Regular-WSAT/G is a good candidate to solve the round robin problem. As far as we know, it is the first time that the round robin problem has been solved with a propositional satisfiability algorithm.

Instance	Colors	MC	Regular-GSAT time (h:m:s)		Regular-WSAT time (h:m:s)		Regular-WSAT+A time (h:m:s)	
			minimum	median	minimum	median	minimum	median
DSJC125.5.col	18	30000	0:00:20	0:04:40	0:00:15	0:00:26	0:00:07	0:00:34
DSJC125.5.col	17	110000	*	*	0:12:35	0:53:12	0:09:40	0:34:42
C250.5x.col	15	30000	0:00:03	0:00:05	0:00:06	0:00:11	0:00:07	0:00:10
DSJC250.5.col	29	90000	*	*	1:19:50	*	0:08:26	1:33:53

Table2. Experimental results for instances of the k-colorability problem

Instance	MC	Regular-WSAT/G time (h:m:s)		Regular-WSAT/G+A time (h:m:s)	
		minimum	median	minimum	median
6-team	20000	0:00:01	0:00:01	0:00:01	0:00:01
8-team	25000	0:00:01	0:00:03	0:00:01	0:00:04
10-team	30000	0:00:03	0:01:33	0:00:02	0:00:39
12-team	40000	0:01:09	0:06:10	0:02:00	0:16:17
14-team	80000	0:11:05	1:18:34	0:29:02	1:16:43
16-team	90000	0:18:46	2:21:14	*	*

Table3. Experimental results for instances of the n-team round robin problem

6 Concluding remarks

In this paper we have described a number of new local search algorithms for regular CNF formulas and reported on an experimental investigation that provides evidence that regular CNF formulas are a suitable formalism for representing and solving combinatorial problems. The approach presented here can outperform or compete with state-of-the-art approaches to solving hard combinatorial problems. As case studies we have considered graph coloring and sports scheduling problems. We plan to investigate other problem domains in the near future.

References

1. B. Beckert, R. Hähnle, and F. Manyà. Transformations between signed and classical clause logic. In *Proc. International Symposium on Multiple-Valued Logics, ISMVL'99, Freiburg, Germany*, pages 248–255. IEEE Press, Los Alamitos, 1999.
2. R. Béjar and F. Manyà. A comparison of systematic and local search algorithms for regular CNF formulas. In *Proceedings of the Fifth European Conference on Symbolic and Quantitative Approaches to Reasoning with Uncertainty, ECSQARU'99, London, England*, pages 22–31. Springer LNAI 1638, 1999.
3. R. Béjar and F. Manyà. Phase transitions in the regular random 3-SAT problem. In *Proceedings of the International Symposium on Methodologies for Intelligent Systems, ISMIS'99, Warsaw, Poland*, pages 292–300. Springer LNAI 1609, 1999.

4. J. M. Crawford and A. B. Baker. Experimental results on the application of satisfiability algorithms to scheduling problems. In *Proceedings of the 12th National Conference on Artificial Intelligence, AAAI'94, Seattle, WA, USA*, pages 1092–1097, 1994.

5. G. Escalada-Imaz and F. Manyà. The satisfiability problem for multiple-valued Horn formulæ. In *Proceedings of the International Symposium on Multiple-Valued Logics, ISMVL'94, Boston, MA, USA*, pages 250–256. IEEE Press, Los Alamitos, 1994.

6. C. P. Gomes, B. Selman, K. McAloon, and C. Tretkoff. Randomization in backtrack search: Exploiting heavy-tailed profiles for solving hard scheduling problems. In *Proceedings AIPS'98, Pittsburg, PA, USA*, 1998.

7. R. Hähnle. Short conjunctive normal forms in finitely-valued logics. *Journal of Logic and Computation*, 4(6):905–927, 1994.

8. R. Hähnle. Exploiting data dependencies in many-valued logics. *Journal of Applied Non-Classical Logics*, 6:49–69, 1996.

9. R. Hähnle and G. Escalada-Imaz. Deduction in many-valued logics: A survey. *Mathware and Soft Computing*, 4(2):69–97, 1997.

10. D. S. Johnson, C. R. Aragon, L. A. McGeoch, and C. Schevon. Optimization by simulated annealing: An experimental evaluation; part II, graph coloring and number partitioning. *Operations Research*, 39(3):378–406, 1991.

11. H. A. Kautz and B. Selman. Pushing the envelope: Planning, propositional logic, and stochastic search. In *Proceedings of the 14th National Conference on Artificial Intelligence, AAAI'96, Portland, OR, USA*, pages 1194–1201, 1996.

12. F. Manyà. The 2-SAT problem in signed CNF formulas. *Multiple-Valued Logic, An International Journal*, 1999. In press.

13. F. Manyà, R. Béjar, and G. Escalada-Imaz. The satisfiability problem in regular CNF-formulas. *Soft Computing: A Fusion of Foundations, Methodologies and Applications*, 2(3):116–123, 1998.

14. D. McAllester, B. Selman, and H. Kautz. Evidence for invariants in local search. In *Proceedings of the 14th National Conference on Artificial Intelligence, AAAI'97, Providence, RI, USA*, pages 321–326, 1997.

15. B. Selman and H. A. Kautz. Domain-independent extensions of GSAT: Solving large structured satisfiability problems. In *Proceedings of the International Joint Conference on Artificial Intelligence, IJCAI'93, Chambery, France*, pages 290–295, 1993.

16. B. Selman, H. A. Kautz, and B. Cohen. Noise strategies for improving local search. In *Proceedings of the 12th National Conference on Artificial Intelligence, AAAI'94, Seattle, WA, USA*, pages 337–343, 1994.

17. B. Selman, H. Levesque, and D. Mitchell. A new method for solving hard satisfiability problems. In *Proceedings of the 10th National Conference on Artificial Intelligence, AAAI'92, San Jose, CA, USA*, pages 440–446, 1992.

Evidence Algorithm and Sequent Logical Inference Search

Anatoli I. Degtyarev[1]*, Alexander V. Lyaletski[2], and Marina K. Morokhovets[3]

[1] Manchester Metropolitan University, Department of Computing and Mathematics,
Chester Street, Manchester M1 5GD
e-mail: A.Degtiarev@doc.mmu.ac.uk
[2] Taras Shevchenko Kyiv University, Cybernetics Department,
6, Glushkov avenue, 252127 Kyiv, Ukraine
e-mail: lav@tk.cyb.univ.kiev.ua
[3] Glushkov Institute of Cybernetics, Digital Automata Theory Department,
40, Glushkov avenue, 252187 Kyiv, Ukraine
e-mail: mmk@d105.icyb.kiev.ua

Abstract. In this paper we continue to develop the approach to automated search for theorem proofs started in Kyiv in 1960-1970s. This approach presupposes the development of deductive techniques used for the processing of mathematical texts, written in a formal first-order language, close to the natural language used in mathematical papers. We construct two logical calculi, gS and mS, satisfying the following requirements: the syntactical form of the initial problem should be preserved; the proof search should be goal-oriented; preliminary skolemization is not obligatory; equality handling should be separated from the deduction process. The calculus gS is a machine-oriented sequent-type calculus with "large-block" inference rules for first-order classical logic. The calculus mS is a further development of the calculus gS, enriched with formal analogs of the natural proof search techniques such as definition handling and application of auxiliary propositions. The results on soundness and completeness of gS and mS are given.

1 Introduction

Investigations in automated reasoning gave rise to the appearance of various computer-oriented calculi for the proof search in classical 1st-order logic. In practical applications preference is usually given to the methods based on the results of Skolem and Herbrand (for instance, resolution-type methods, Maslov's inverse method, tableau methods, connection graph methods, etc.). The possibilities given by Gentzen-type calculi are less investigated. This happens due to higher efficiency of first-kind methods as compared to sequent-type calculi. This is mainly connected with various orders of the quantifier rule applications and formula duplications in Gentzen calculi while the first-kind methods, due to skolemization, are free from this deficiency.

---

* On leave from Glushkov Institute of Cybernetics

At the same time, the deduction process in Gentzen calculi reflects natural theorem-proving methods which, as a rule, do not include preliminary formula skolemization, so that logical inference is made within the scope of the signature of the initial theory. This feature of Gentzen calculi becomes important when the proof is found in an interactive mode since it is preferable to present the output data in the form usual for a user. This is how the problem of the efficient quantifier manipulation makes its appearance.

The desire to overcome the lack of efficiency of standard Gentzen-type calculi has resulted in the appearance of the sound and complete 1st-order calculus of a-sequents [1] (denoted by S below), which uses the original notion of an admissible substitution to optimize enumaration connected with the possibilities of different orders of elimination of quantifiers (without obligatory carrying out preliminary skolemization). It has been shown later that this notion of an admissible substitution can be easily introduced into standard Gentzen calculi [2]. The S calculus was constructed to meet the following requirements: the syntactical form of an initial problem should be preserved; preliminary skolemization is not obligatory; proof search should be goal-oriented; equality handling should be separated from the deduction process.

In this paper such approach to automated theorem proving is realized by means of constructing certain modifications of S, denoted by gS and mS.

The calculus gS is a Gentzen modification of the calculus S for classical first-order logic; the main results on gS are presented.

The calculus mS is a modification of the calculus gS "enriched" with rules for application of definitions and auxiliary propositions for machine-oriented logical inference search in the environment of a self-contained mathematical text written in the so-called first-order TL-language (TL1-language).

2   Historical Notes

The calculus S was developed in the framework of the complex programme of automated theorem proving. This programme was initiated by V.M.Glushkov at the beginning of 1960s and called Algoritm Ochevidnosti (Evidence Algorithm), or AO. The exposition of the idea of AO can be found in [3].

In fact, in the frame of the programme it was proposed to conduct in parallel the following main lines of investigations:

1) construction a formalized language (languages) for writing down mathematical texts from different substantial sections of mathematics in the form which is as much as possible close to the form of natural-language mathematical publications;

2) formalization and consecutive development of the concept of machine evidence of a proof: every proof step in a formalized text has to be properly substantiated by computer with the use of formal proof search methods and mathematical facts already known to AO;

3) construction and development (by means of AO) of information base containing descriptions of mathematical concepts, their connections and properties, and having an influence on the concept of evidence of a proof step;

4) implementation of interface which enables a user to understand a proof search process and control it in an interactive mode.

The first paper about the development (in Kyiv) of a procedure for theorem proof search appeared in 1966 [4]. Its further improvement resulted in construction of a machine-oriented inference search procedure for logical calculi [5].

In 1970 a new period in realization of the AO programme began. The main characteristic feature of the works held during that period was their orientation towards forming an integral mathematical text processing system as a single whole.

During that period, research of language support of the system was carried out and the input language TL (Theory Language) of the system was developed [6], that was similar to the natural mathematical one and convenient, from the practical point of view, for use in man-machine systems. Also, various logical inference search methods were proposed and investigated (a machine-oriented sequent-type calculus without skolemization [1], resolution-type methods with a possibility to attach various techniques for equality handling [7], heuristic methods of proof searching based on using auxiliary propositions, or lemmas [8]).

After a number of experiments with the system [9], the system was improved and extended in various directions. As a result, in 1980 the first implemented version of the system called SAD (Systema Avtomatizatsiyi Dokazatel'stv) was described in [10].

After 1980 SAD was developed in the following directions: formulation of admissible inference rules for resolution-type procedures to reduce enumaration during inference searching; development of equality handling techniques; investigation of natural theorem proving techniques and their combination with resolution procedures [11, 12]. Note, that proof search procedures of SAD could function both in automatic and interactive modes.

At the beginning of 1990s, when ES computers went out of use, the experiments with SAD were curtailed.

In more detail, the history of investigation on AO is given in [13].

This paper reflects present efforts to attack problems in automated theorem proving in the AO-style.

3   Logical Inference Search in the AO-style

In this section, we give a formal description of the calculus gS, the main results on the calculus, and exemplify its peculiarities.

As for mS, we shall restrict ourselves to the consideration of the substantial interpretation of mS, drawing the analogy to the calculus gS, and to an example of constructing the proof of a certain theorem. To make this proof transparent we comment every proof step in detail. We hope that the example will make up a good background for understanding the approach to ATP in the AO-style.

3.1   The Calculus gS

We treat here classical first-order logic in the form of the sequent calculus G given in [14]. We use the name *Gal* instead of G.

We treat the notion of a substitution as in [15]. Any substitutional component is considered to be of the form t/x, where x is a variable and t is a term of a substitution.

Let L be a literal, then $\sim L$ denotes its complement. We use the expression $L(t_1, \ldots, t_n)$ to denote that $t_1,...,t_n$ is a list of all the terms (possibly, with repetitions) occupying the argument places in the literal L in the order of their occurrences in L. If x, y are variables and F is a formula then $F|_y^x$ denotes the result of replacing x with y.

We also assume that besides usual variables there are two countable sets of special variables, namely unknown variables and fixed variables (sequences of "dummies" and "parameters" in the terminology of [16]).

Note, that the basic object of gS (as of S [1]) is an a-sequent. An a-sequent may be considered as a special generalization of the standard notion of a sequent. We consider a-sequents having one object (goal) in its succedent only.

An ordered triple $< w, F, E >$ is called *an ensemble* iff w is a sequence (a word) of unknown and fixed variables, F is a 1st-order formula, and E is a set of pairs of terms t_1, t_2 (equations of the form $t_1 = t_2$).

An a-sequent is an expression of the form $[B], < w_1, P_1, E_1 >,...,< w_n, P_n, E_n > \Rightarrow < w, F, E >$, where $< w_1, P_1, E_1 >,...,< w_n, P_n, E_n >,< w, F, E >$ are ensembles, $[B]$ is a list of literals, possibly empty.

Ensembles in the antecedent of an a-sequent are called premises, and an ensemble in the succedent of an a-sequent is called a goal of this a-sequent. The collection of the premises is thought as a set. So, the order of the premises is immaterial.

Let W be a set of sequences of unknown and fixed variables, and s be a substitution. Put $A(W, s) = \{< z, t, w >:$ z is a variable of s, t is a term of s, $w \in W$, and z lies in w to the left of some fixed variable from $t\}$. Then s is said to be *admissible* for W iff (1) the variables of s are unknown variables only, and (2) there are not elements $< z_1, t_1, w_1 >,...,< z_n, t_n, w_n >$ in $A(W, s)$ such that $t_2/z_1 \in s,...,t_n/z_{n-1} \in s, t_1/z_n \in s$ $(n > 0)$.

Decomposition of some formula F by its principal logical connective and possible interaction with P_i results in generating new a-sequents. The sets $E_1,...,E_n,$ E define the terms to be substituted for the unknown variables in order to transform every equation $t_1 = t_2$ from $E_1,...,E_n, E$ to identity $t = t$ after applying to $E_1,...,E_n, E$ a substitution chosen in a certain way. The sets $w_1,...,w_n, w$ serve to check whether the substitutions generated during proof searching are admissible. Note, that in any a-sequent some (or all) sequences from $w_1,...,w_n, w$ and some (or all) sets from $E_1,...,E_n, E$ may be empty.

An initial a-sequent is constructed as follows. Suppose that we want to establish deducibility of a sequence $P_1, \ldots, P_n \Rightarrow F$ (in the terms of the calculus Gal). Then an a-sequent $[\,], <, P_1, >, \ldots, <, P_n, > \Rightarrow <, F, >$ will be considered as an initial a-sequent (w.r.t. $P_1, \ldots, P_n \Rightarrow F$).

During proof searching in gS an inference tree is constructed. At the beginning of a search process it consists of an initial a-sequent. The subsequent nodes of the inference tree are generated in accordance with the rules described below. Inference trees grow "from top to bottom".

Goal Splitting Rules (GS-rules). These rules are used for elimination of the principal logical connective from the formula in the goal of an a-sequent processed. Application of any rule results in generation of a new a-sequent (a-sequents) with only one goal (and, possibly, with new premises). Elimination of the propositional connectives is done according to the rules of 1st-order classical logic. It can be easily expressed in the terms of derivative rules of standard Gentzen-type calculi, and $w_1, \ldots, w_n, w, E_1, \ldots, E_n, E$ therewith are not changed. Essential deviation from traditional Gentzen techniques of inference search is observed in quantifier processing. This deviation reflects specific quantifier handling techniques when variables of eliminated quantifiers are replaced by unknown or fixed variables depending on an eliminated quantifier. Therewith w, but not $w_1, \ldots, w_n, E_1, \ldots, E_n, E$, is changed, and new premises can be generated.

In formulation of rules below, M denotes a set of premises.

Propositional Rules

$(\Rightarrow \supset_1)$-rule:

$$\frac{[B], M \Rightarrow < w, F \supset F_1, E >}{[B], M, < w, F, E > \Rightarrow < w, F_1, E >}$$

$(\Rightarrow \supset_2)$-rule:

$$\frac{[B], M \Rightarrow < w, F \supset F_1, E >}{[B], M, < w, \neg F_1, E > \Rightarrow < w, \neg F, E >}$$

$(\Rightarrow \wedge)$-rule:

$$\frac{[B], M \Rightarrow < w, F \wedge F_1, E >}{[B], M \Rightarrow < w, F, E > \quad [B], M \Rightarrow < w, F_1, E >}$$

$(\Rightarrow \vee_1)$-rule:

$$\frac{[B], M \Rightarrow < w, F \vee F_1, E >}{[B], M, < w, \neg F, E > \Rightarrow < w, F_1, E >}$$

$(\Rightarrow \vee_2)$-rule:

$$\frac{[B], M \Rightarrow < w, F \vee F_1, E >}{[B], M, < w, \neg F_1, E > \Rightarrow < w, F, E >}$$

$(\Rightarrow \neg)$-rule:

$$\frac{[B], M \Rightarrow < w, \neg F, E >}{[B], M \Rightarrow < w, F', E >}$$

where F' is the result of one-step transferring "$\neg$" into F.

Quantifier Rules

($\Rightarrow \forall$)-rule:

$$\frac{[B], M \Rightarrow < w, \forall x F, E >}{[B], M \Rightarrow < w\overline{x}, F|_{\overline{x}}^{x}, E >}$$

where $\overline{x}$ is a new fixed variable.

($\Rightarrow \exists$)-rule:

$$\frac{[B], M \Rightarrow < w, \exists x F, E >}{[B], M, < w, \forall x \neg F, E > \Rightarrow < w x', F|_{x'}^{x}, E >}$$

where x' is a new unknown variable.

Auxiliary Goal Rules (AG-rules). These rules are "extracted" from [1] and applied when formula F in the goal of an input (for AG) a-sequent is **a literal**. Applying AG-rules, we begin with some premise $< w_i, P_i, E_i >$, s.t. the literal F from the goal of the input (for AG) a-sequent has a positive occurrence (modulo equations) in P_i. Denote this occurrence by F'. Then we generate a-sequents deterministically eliminating the principal logical connective from P_i and so on until we get the literal F'.

Such series of eliminations of connectives in premises done deterministically can be viewed as an application of a "large-block" inference rule. (The phrase "modulo equations" means informally that the occurrence F' extracted from P_i can be transformed into F by replacing simultaneously terms occupying the argument places in F' with some terms from F. Below the phrase "modulo equations" will be often omitted.) As for elimination of principal logical connectives in premises, the remarks referring to the GS-rules are true excluding, naturally, remarks on $w_1,...,w_n, w, E_1,...,E_n, E$. An application of a AG-rule results in generation of m ($m > 0$) a-sequents with new goals and, possibly, some new (w.r.t. an input for AG a-sequent) premises.

Let us introduce inductively a notion of *a positive (negative) occurrence of a literal L in a formula F (denoted by $F\lfloor L^+ \rfloor$ and $F\lfloor L^- \rfloor$, respectively) modulo equations* in a rigorous way:

(I) suppose that a literal F ($\sim F$) can be obtained from $L(t_1,\ldots,t_n)$ by means of replacing $t_1,...,t_n$ with some terms $t'_1,...,t'_n$. Then L is said to have a positive (negative) occurrence in F modulo the equations $t_1 = t'_1,...,t_n = t'_n$;

(II.1) if $F\lfloor L^+ \rfloor$ ($F\lfloor L^- \rfloor$) modulo the equations $t_1 = t'_1,...,t_n = t'_n$ and F_1 is a formula then L has a positive (negative) occurrence (modulo the equations $t_1 = t'_1,...,t_n = t'_n$) in the following formulas: $F \wedge F_1$, $F_1 \wedge F$, $F \vee F_1$, $F_1 \vee F$, $F_1 \supset F$, $\forall x F$, $\exists x F$;

(II.2) if $F\lfloor L^+ \rfloor$ ($F\lfloor L^- \rfloor$) modulo the equations $t_1 = t'_1,...,t_n = t'_n$ and F_1 is a formula then L has a negative (positive) occurrence (modulo the equations $t_1 = t'_1,...,t_n = t'_n$) in the following formulas: $F \supset F_1$, $\neg F$;

(III) there are no other cases of positive (negative) occurrences of L in F.

Propositional Rules

$(\supset_1 \Rightarrow)$-rule:

$$\frac{[B], <w, F\lfloor L^-\rfloor \supset F_1, E' >, M \Rightarrow <w', L, E >}{[B], <w, (\neg F)\lfloor L^+\rfloor, E' >, M \Rightarrow <w', L, E > \quad [B, \sim L], M \Rightarrow <w, \neg F_1, E' >}$$

$(\supset_2 \Rightarrow)$-rule:

$$\frac{[B], <w, F \supset F_1\lfloor L^+\rfloor, E' >, M \Rightarrow <w', L, E >}{[B], <w, F_1\lfloor L^+\rfloor, E' >, M \Rightarrow <w', L, E > \quad [B, \sim L], M \Rightarrow <w, F, E' >}$$

$(\vee_1 \Rightarrow)$-rule:

$$\frac{[B], <w, F \vee F_1\lfloor L^+\rfloor, E' >, M \Rightarrow <w', L, E >}{[B], <w, F_1\lfloor L^+\rfloor, E' >, M \Rightarrow <w', L, E > \quad [B, \sim L], M \Rightarrow <w, \neg F, E' >}$$

$(\vee_2 \Rightarrow)$-rule:

$$\frac{[B], <w, F\lfloor L^+\rfloor \vee F_1, E' >, M \Rightarrow <w', L, E >}{[B], <w, F\lfloor L^+\rfloor, E' >, M \Rightarrow <w', L, E > \quad [B, \sim L], M \Rightarrow <w, \neg F_1, E' >}$$

$(\wedge_1 \Rightarrow)$-rule:

$$\frac{[B], <w, F\lfloor L^+\rfloor \wedge F_1, E' >, M \Rightarrow <w', L, E >}{[B], <w, F\lfloor L^+\rfloor, E' >, <w, F_1, E' >, M \Rightarrow <w', L, E >}$$

$(\wedge_2 \Rightarrow)$-rule:

$$\frac{[B], <w, F \wedge F_1\lfloor L^+\rfloor, E' >, M \Rightarrow <w', L, E >}{[B], <w, F, E' >, <w, F_1\lfloor L^+\rfloor, E' >, M \Rightarrow <w', L, E >}$$

$(\neg \Rightarrow)$-rule:

$$\frac{[B], <w, \neg(F\lfloor L^-\rfloor), E' >, M \Rightarrow <w', L, E >}{[B], <w, F'\lfloor L^+\rfloor, E' >, M \Rightarrow <w', L, E >}$$

where F' is the result of one-step transferring "$\neg$" into F.

Termination Rules

$(\Rightarrow \natural_1)$-rule:

$$\frac{[B], <w, L(t_1, \ldots, t_n), E' >, M \Rightarrow <w', L(t'_1, \ldots, t'_n), E >}{M \Rightarrow <w, \natural, E'' >}$$

(Here $E'' = E' \cup E \cup \{t_1 = t'_1, \ldots, t_n = t'_n\}$; $L(t_1, \ldots, t_n)$, $L(t'_1, \ldots, t'_n)$ are literals.)

$(\Rightarrow \natural_2)$-rule:

$$\frac{[B_1, L(t_1, \ldots, t_n), B_2], M \Rightarrow <w', L(t'_1, \ldots, t'_n), E >}{[B_1, L(t_1, \ldots, t_n), B_2], M \Rightarrow <w', \natural, E' >}$$

(Here $E' = E \cup \{t_1 = t'_1, \ldots, t_n = t'_n\}$; $L(t_1, \ldots, t_n)$, $L(t'_1, \ldots, t'_n)$ are literals.)

Quantifier Rules

($\forall \Rightarrow$)-rule:

$$\frac{[B], < w, \forall x(F\lfloor L^+\rfloor), E' >, M \Rightarrow < w', L, E >}{[B], < wx', F|_{x'}^x \lfloor L^+\rfloor, E' >, < w, \forall x F, E' >, M \Rightarrow < w', L, E >}$$

where x' is a new unknown variable.

($\exists \Rightarrow$)-rule:

$$\frac{[B], < w, \exists x(F\lfloor L^+\rfloor), E' >, M \Rightarrow < w', L, E >}{[B], < w\bar{x}, F|_{\bar{x}}^x \lfloor L^+\rfloor, E' >, M \Rightarrow < w', L, E >}$$

where $\bar{x}$ is a new fixed variable.

Premise Addition Rule (PA-rule). This rule affects the whole proof search tree. After every application of ($\forall \Rightarrow$)-rule (($\exists \Rightarrow$)-rule) the new premise $< wx'$, $F|_{x'}^x \lfloor L^+\rfloor, E' > (< w\bar{x}, F|_{\bar{x}}^x\lfloor L^+\rfloor, E' >)$ is added to antecedents of all a-sequents containing the premise $< w, \forall x(F\lfloor L^+\rfloor), E' > (< w, \exists x(F\lfloor L^+\rfloor), E' >)$ through the current tree.

Axioms. Axioms are a-sequents of the form $[B], M \Rightarrow < w, \natural, E >$, where $\natural$ denotes an empty formula.

Applying the rules "from top to bottom" to an input a-sequent and afterwards to its "heirs", and so on, we finally obtain an inference tree. An inference tree Tr is called *a proof tree* for an input a-sequent (in gS) if and only if (1) every leaf of Tr is an axiom; (2) there exists the most general simultaneous unifier (mgsu) s of all sets of equations from Tr; (3) s is admissible for the set of all sequences of fixed and unknown variables from Tr.

Remark 1. The formulation of the calculus gS shows that the order of quantifier rule applications is immaterial, i.e. it does not influence the final result. In the calculus gS, the quantifier rules are needed to determine a quantifier structure of formulas from an input sequent $P_1, \ldots, P_n \Rightarrow F$. Also, note that generating the most general simultaneous unifier and checking the admissibility of the mgsu can be done in arbitrary moment of constructing an inference tree (in particular, this moment can be determined by a user).

Main Results on gS. Below we give main results on gS. Remember that we consider 1st-order classical logic in a sequent form.

Proposition 1 (soundness and completeness of gS). *Let $F_1, \ldots, F_n \Rightarrow F$ be a sequent (with its usual meaning) and the set $\{F_1, \ldots, F_n\}$ be consistent. The sequent $F_1, \ldots, F_n \Rightarrow F$ is deducible in the calculus Gal if and only if there exists a proof tree for the input a-sequent $[\ ], < , F_1, >, \ldots, < , F_n, > \Rightarrow < , F, >$ in gS.*

A Proof Scheme. It can be shown that having a proof tree Tr in gS it is possible to construct a proof tree Tr' in the calculus mG [2] and vice versa. In [2], it is shown (using some results from [17]) that Tr' can be transformed into a proof tree in *Gal* and vice versa.

Corollary 1. *A formula F is valid if and only if there exists a proof tree for the input a-sequent $[\,] \Rightarrow <, F, >$ in the calculus gS.*

An Example on gS. A simple example given below demonstrates the peculiarities of quantifier handling in the calculus gS and proof tree generation techniques.

Suppose, we would like to establish the deducibility of the following sequent in the calculus *Gal*: $\forall y_1 \exists z_1 \forall x_1 (F_1 \lor F_2) \Rightarrow \forall x_2 \exists y_2 F$, where F_1 is $R(f(z_1, y_1), x_1)$, F_2 is $R(f(z_1, x_1), x_1)$, and F is $R(y_2, f(x_2, c))$ (R is a predicate symbol, f is a functional symbol, c is a constant symbol). To follow a proof search process, Figure 1 is given. The corresponding initial a-sequent in the calculus gS is:

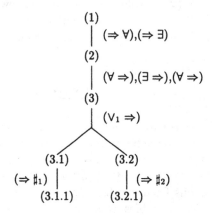

Fig. 1. The proof tree constructed in gS

(1) $[\,], <, \forall y_1 \exists z_1 \forall x_1 (F_1 \lor F_2), > \Rightarrow <, \forall x_2 \exists y_2 F, >$
Applying subsequently to (1) the rules $(\Rightarrow \forall)$ and $(\Rightarrow \exists)$ we obtain:
(2) $[\,], <, \forall y_1 \exists z_1 \forall x_1 (F_1 \lor F_2), >, P \Rightarrow < \bar{x}_2 y_2', F', >,$
where P is $< \bar{x}_2, \forall y_2 \neg R(y_2, f(\bar{x}_2, c)), >$ and F' is $R(y_2', f(\bar{x}_2, c))$. There is a positive occurrence of F' into F_2 $(F_2 \lfloor F'^+ \rfloor)$, so AG-rules, namely, $(\forall \Rightarrow)$, $(\exists \Rightarrow)$, $(\forall \Rightarrow)$, are applicable to (2). As a result, we have:
(3) $[\,], < y_1' \bar{z}_1 x_1', F_1' \lor F_2' \lfloor F'^+ \rfloor, >, P_1, P_2, P \Rightarrow < \bar{x}_2 y_2', F', >,$
where F_1' is $R(f(\bar{z}_1, y_1'), x_1')$, F_2' is $R(f(\bar{z}_1, x_1'), x_1')$, P_1 is $<, \forall y_1 \exists z_1 \forall x_1 (F_1 \lor F_2), >$, and P_2 is $< y_1' \bar{z}_1, \forall x_1 (F_1'' \lor F_2''), >$, with $R(f(\bar{z}_1, y_1'), x_1)$ for F_1'' and $R(f(\bar{z}_1, x_1), x_1)$ for F_2''.
From (3) by $(\lor_1 \Rightarrow)$, we obtain two a-sequents:
(3.1) $[\,], < y_1' \bar{z}_1 x_1', F_2' \lfloor F'^+ \rfloor, >, P_1, P_2, P \Rightarrow < \bar{x}_2 y_2', F', >$
(3.2) $[\neg F'], P_1, P_2, P \Rightarrow < y_1' \bar{z}_1 x_1', \neg F_1', >.$

Note, that

1) GS-rules are applied until the formula in the succedent of the a-sequent is a literal;

2) AG-rules are applied "to shell" a positive occurrence of the goal in the antecedent. So, transition from the a-sequent (1) to the a-sequent (2) and, then, from the a-sequent (2) to the a-sequents (3.1) and (3.2) can be thought as the results of application of two "large-block" inference rules. Moreover, these transitions are strongly directed by the goal formula.

As F_2' is $R(f(\overline{z}_1, x_1'), x_1')$ and F' is $R(y_2', f(\overline{x}_2, c))$, so $(\Rightarrow \natural_1)$-rule is applicable to (3.1) yielding

(3.1.1) $[\ ], P_1, P_2, P \Rightarrow < y_1' \overline{z}_1 x_1', \natural, E_1 >$,

where $E_1 = \{y_2' = f(\overline{z}_1, x_1'), f(\overline{x}_2, c) = x_1'\}$.

As F_1' is $R(f(\overline{z}_1, y_1'), x_1')$ so $(\Rightarrow \natural_2)$-rule is applicable to (3.2), and the result is

(3.2.1) $[\neg F'], P_1, P_2, P \Rightarrow < y_1' \overline{z}_1 x_1', \natural, E_2 >$,

where $E_2 = \{y_2' = f(\overline{z}_1, x_1'), f(\overline{x}_2, c) = x_1'\}$.

We have obtained the tree Tr in which every leaf has an a-sequent with the empty formula in a goal. The set $E_1 \cup E_2$ is unifiable with mgsu $\sigma = \{f(\overline{x}_2, c)/x_1', f(\overline{z}_1, f(\overline{x}_2, c))/y_2', f(\overline{x}_2, c)/y_1'\}$.

For the tree Tr, we have the following set W of all sequences of fixed and unknown variables: $W = \{\overline{x}_2, \overline{x}_2 y_2', y_1', y_1' \overline{z}_1, y_1' \overline{z}_1 x_1'\}$. So, $A(W, \sigma) = \{< y_1', f(\overline{z}_1, f(\overline{x}_2, c)), y_1' \overline{z}_1 >, < y_1', f(\overline{z}_1, f(\overline{x}_2, c)), y_1' \overline{z}_1 x_1' >\}$. As $f(\overline{z}_1, f(\overline{x}_2, c))/y_1' \notin \sigma$, so σ is admissible for W. Then Tr is a proof tree, and by proposition 1 the initial sequent is deducible in Gal.

Remark 2. If we would take $\exists y_2 \forall x_2 F$ as a goal formula in the initial sequent, then "repeating" construction of Tr we would obtain the "copy" Tr' of Tr with the same mgsu σ and with the following set W' of all sequences of fixed and unknown variables: $W' = \{y_2', y_2' \overline{x}_2, y_1', y_1' \overline{z}_1, y_1' \overline{z}_1 x_1'\}$. For W' and σ, we have: $A(W', \sigma) = \{< y_1', f(\overline{z}_1, f(\overline{x}_2, c)), y_1' \overline{z}_1 >, < y_1', f(\overline{z}_1, f(\overline{x}_2, c)), y_1' \overline{z}_1 x_1' >, < y_2', f(\overline{z}_1, f(\overline{x}_2, c)), y_2' \overline{x}_2 >\}$. As $f(\overline{z}_1, f(\overline{x}_2, c))/y_2' \in \sigma$, so σ is not admissible for W', and then Tr' is not a proof tree in gS. If we choose other positive occurrences of F in premises, we shall obtain the same result. (Note, that special techniques for checking the admissibility of substitutions have been proposed in [2].)

Remark 3. This example illustrates that both $(\Rightarrow \natural_1)$-rule and $(\Rightarrow \natural_2)$-rule are substantive for gS completeness. Really, if we refuse from any of the rules, we shall not get a proof tree.

Remark 4. There is no application of PA-rule in the above example. However, it is not difficult to see, that PA-rule is necessary to prove the following sequent: $\exists x R(x) \Rightarrow \exists y (R(y) \wedge R(y))$.

3.2   A Brief Description of mS

The calculus mS permits to present an initial problem as a text in a certain 1st-order formal language containing definitions and auxiliary propositions, and to use analogs of such natural theorem proving techniques as application of definitions and auxiliary propositions. The peculiarity of mS is that needed definitions and auxiliary propositions are extracted from a self-contained mathematical text written in the formal language TL [6] approximated to languages of usual mathematical papers. A self-contained mathematical text is a text that, in addition to a proposition to be proved, also includes assumptions, propositions, and definitions that can be used when the proof of a given assertion (theorem) is searching.

Processing a self-contained mathematical text for the purpose of proving a given theorem is divided into two parts:

1. Translating an original TL-text into so-called 1st-order TL-text ($TL1$-text). $TL1$-sentences, on the one hand, are analogs of 1st-order logic formulas, and, on the other hand, preserve the signature of an original TL-text, its syntax and structure (i.e. partitioning into definition sections, auxiliary proposition sections and theorem to be proved). Notice, that translation of a TL-text (which satisfies certain restrictions) into a $TL1$-text can be done automatically (see, for example, [18]). A $TL1$-text is a source for the inference search procedure in the calculus mS. Note, that to use an inference search procedure in the calculus gS a $TL1$-text should be translated into a set of 1st-order formulas.

2. Searching for a proof in the calculus mS.

After the text has been written in TL-language and converted into a $TL1$-text, a theorem proof search is carried out using the inference rules of mS.

The assertion T to be proved is represented as a substantive $TL1$-section "theorem", in which conditions and a conclusion are separated, and an initial a-sequent (with respect to T) is constructed with the conditions and conclusion in its antecedent and succedent, respectively. (The remaining part of the $TL1$-text is given as the set of definitions and auxiliary propositions.)

The basic object of mS (as of gS) is an a-sequent.

As in gS, an a-sequent of mS is an expression of the form $[B], < w_1, P_1, E_1 >,$ $..., < w_n, P_n, E_n > \Rightarrow < w, F, E >$, where $w_1,...,w_n, w, E_1,...,E_n, E, B$ are the same as in gS-sequents, but $P_1,...,P_n, F$ are $TL1$-sentences.

As $TL1$-sentences can be viewed as first-order formulas, GS-rules, AG-rules, and PA-rule are extended to mS-sequents in obvious way. In this connection, we omit the formulation of the rules here and use the same names for these rules in mS.

Structuring $TL1$-texts according to substantive sections (i.e. definitions, propositions, etc.) enables introducing in mS the *definition application rule* (DA) and *auxiliary proposition rule* (AP) in a natural way. These rules can be viewed as specific variants of AG. A definition or auxiliary proposition being a substantive section of a $TL1$-text is treated as a premise for the goal under consideration. As in the case with AG, the DA and AP rules can be applied depending on the existence in the premise of a positive occurrence (modulo equations) of the $TL1$-sentence from the goal of an input (for DA or AP) a-sequent. DA and AP represent analogs of natural theorem-proving techniques for application of definitions and auxiliary propositions.

As in gS, during proof search in mS an inference tree Tr is being constructed (w.r.t. the theorem T to be proved and "environmental" $TL1$-text Txt). The a-sequent in the root of Tr is uniquely defined by T. A notion of a proof tree in mS has the same meaning as in gS.

In any moment during inference search, it is possible to test whether a current inference tree can be transformed into a proof tree. When construction of a proof tree is made in an interactive mode, a user may initiate this test.

Remark 5. Let Tr be a current inference tree, s be an admissible substitution for Tr (in the sense of [1, 2]). Let $Tr * s$ denotes a result of application of s to every $TL1$-sentence from a-sequents occurring in Tr. It is possible to search for a proof in mS in such a way that enables to continue a proof search with $Tr * s$, when Tr is not a proof tree, and then backtrack if necessary. The example given below is exactly the case of using a search technique of this type, with an admissible substitution generated after every AG, or DA, or AP application.

Main Results on mS. It was noted above that any $TL1$-sentence can be treated as an analog of some 1st-order classical logic formula. It enables constructing formula patterns of such units of a $TL1$-text as the theorem to be proved, a definition, an auxiliary proposition and to treat a self-contained $TL1$-text as a set of 1st-order formulas. So, it is possible to understand unambiguosly the terms "$TL1$-text consistency", "logical consequence of a theorem from a given $TL1$-text", and "validity" (of the theorem to be proved) without special defining the semantics of the $TL1$-language. With this in mind, we state main results about mS as follows.

Proposition 2 (soundness and completeness of mS). *$TL1$-theorem T is a logical consequence of a consistent $TL1$-text Txt if and only if a proof tree w.r.t. T and Txt can be constructed in mS.*

A Proof Scheme. As $TL1$-sentences can be viewed as analogs of first-order formulas, and DA and AP are special variants of AG, so Proposition 1 guarantees validity of Proposition 2.

Corollary 2. *A $TL1$-theorem T is valid if and only if a proof tree w.r.t. T only can be constructed in mS.*

We note, as a side-result, that rather rich collection of rules in mS enables to construct various proof search strategies which model proofs from usual mathematical texts, and, by maintaining the interactive mode of proof search, to allow a user to influence a proof process actively. If such a strategy (with or without the participation of a human) ensures an exhaustive search, then Proposition 2 and corollary 2 guarantee the soundness and completeness of the strategy.

An Example on mS. As we present below a proof (but not a proof search), we use a standard Gentzen notation for sequents instead of the a-sequent notation, "hiding" equation handling and variable sequence processing into comments. Below, we regard a sequent to be proved if it is of the form: $[B], P_1, \ldots, P_{i-1}, F, P_{i+1}, \ldots, P_n \Rightarrow F$, because it is obvious that subsequent AG-rule application transforms this sequent into the axiom.

Let us consider the proof of the following assertion: "If M is a subset of any set then M is empty". We treat this assertion as a part of the self-contained mathematical TL-text. Note that we use English version of TL and $TL1$ to which [19] is dedicated.

The corresponding TL-text is as follows.

The TL-text "Sets".

Definition 1. Let X be a_set. Let Y be a_set. Y is a_subset_of X IFF any element_of Y is an_element_of X.

Definition 2. Let Z be a_set. Z is empty IFF it_is_not_true_that there_exists an_element_of Z.

Proposition 1. Any subset_of any set is a_set.

Proposition 2. There_exists the empty set.

Theorem. If M is a_subset_of any set then M is empty.

As a result of the syntactical transformation of the above TL-text, we get the following $TL1$-text.

The $TL1$-text "Sets".

Definition 1. Let X be a_set. Let Y be a_set. Y is a_subset_of X IFF for_any e it_is_true_that if e is an_element_of Y then e is an_element_of X.

Definition 2. Let Z be a_set. Z is empty IFF it_is_not_true_that there_exists e such_that e is an_element_of Z.

Proposition 1. For_any X, Y it_is_true_that if Y is a_set and X is a_subset_of Y then X is a_set.

Proposition 2. There_exists u such_that u is empty and u is a_set.

Theorem. Let for_any X it_is_true_that if X is a_set then M is a_subset_of X. Then M is empty.

Note, that both in $TL1$-text and in the proof given below usual names for mathematical notions are preserved. It is suitable for a user while searching for a proof in an interactive mode. To make a proof search process more transparent, the proof tree constructed in mS is shown in Figure 2.

Proof. The following initial sequent corresponds to the theorem:
For_any X it_is_true_that if X is a_set then $\overline{M}$ is a_subset_of $X \Rightarrow \overline{M}$ is empty, where $\overline{M}$ is a fixed variable. Denote the formula in the antecedent of this sequent by Π. Then we have:

1. $\Pi \Rightarrow \overline{M}$ is empty.

First of all, AG is to be tried. It is not applicable in this case, because there are no occurrences of the goal in the premises. GS-rules are not applicable, too, as the current goal does not include logical connectives. The rule DA is applied to the goal. Note, that when DA is applied, a definition is copied and then those variables which belong to the copy are renamed. In the text below, each renamed variable has a superscript which is equal to the number of a particular definition. In this case DA is applicable to Definition 2. As a result, we have:

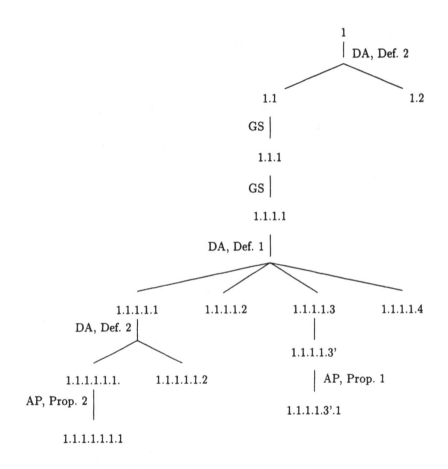

Fig. 2. The proof tree constructed in mS

1.1. $\Pi \Rightarrow$ it_is_not_true_that there_exists e such_that e is an_element_of $\overline{M}$.

1.2. $\Pi \Rightarrow \overline{M}$ is a_set.

So, inferencing the sequent 1 reduces to inferencing the sequents 1.1 and 1.2. Consider 1.1. Applying GS, we obtain:

1.1.1. $\Pi \Rightarrow$ for_any e it_is_true_that (it_is_not_true_that e is an_element_of $\overline{M}$).

1.1.1.1. $\Pi \Rightarrow$ it_is_not_true_that $\overline{e}$ is an_element_of $\overline{M}$.

Here $\overline{e}$ is a fixed variable; it cannot be substituted by terms. Now 1.1.1.1 is a current sequent. As there are no occurrences of the current goal in the premise, DA is applied to Definition 1:

1.1.1.1.1. $\Pi \Rightarrow$ it_is_not_true_that $\overline{e}$ is an_element_of X_1^1.

1.1.1.1.2. $\Pi \Rightarrow \overline{M}$ is a_subset_of X_1^1.

1.1.1.1.3. $\Pi \Rightarrow \overline{M}$ is a_set.

1.1.1.1.4. $\Pi \Rightarrow X_1^1$ is a_set.

X_1^1 is a new unknown variable; it can be replaced by terms.

Note that Definition 2 is also applicable to 1.1.1.1. However, as we demonstrate the proof, and not the protocol of proof search, so we show only "successful" steps. Choose 1.1.1.1.1 to process. There are no occurrences of the goal in the premise. The rule DA is applicable to Definition 2. The application with appropriate substitution $\{Z_1^2/X_1^1\}$ results in two sequents:

1.1.1.1.1.1. $\Pi \Rightarrow Z_1^2$ is empty.

1.1.1.1.1.2. $\Pi \Rightarrow Z_1^2$ is a_set.

Here Z_1^2 is an unknown variable. One more point needs to be made. A unifier produced when a particular inference rule is applied to the current goal should be used in every node of the inference tree.

Both Definition 2 and Proposition 2 are applicable to 1.1.1.1.1.1. We choose to apply Proposition 2. As a result, the set of premises for the current goal is extended and the substitution $\{\overline{u}/Z_1^2\}$ is generated. New premises can be added to the antecedent of any sequent in the inference tree and can participate in further inference steps. Then we have:

1.1.1.1.1.1.1. Π, $\overline{u}$ is empty, $\overline{u}$ is a_set $\Rightarrow \overline{u}$ is empty.

As there is an occurrence of the current goal in the premises, so this goal is proven. The sequent 1.1.1.1.1.2 is now of the form: Π, $\overline{u}$ is empty, $\overline{u}$ is a_set $\Rightarrow Z_1^2$ is a_set.

There is an occurrence of the goal in the premises (the corresponding unifier is $\overline{u}/Z_1^2$). So, the goal "Z_1^2 is a_set" is also proven. The next sequent is 1.1.1.1.2. It is provable, because there is an occurrence of its goal in the premises (the corresponding substitution is X_1^1/X_1^0, where X_1^0 ia a new variable which substitutes X in Π when searching for an occurrence of the goal of the sequent in Π). Consider sequent 1.1.1.1.3 taking into account the additional premises:

1.1.1.1.3'. Π, $\overline{u}$ is a_set, $\overline{u}$ is empty $\Rightarrow \overline{M}$ is a_set.

There are no occurrences of the current goal in the premises. The rule AP is applicable to Proposition 1. Notice that the assumptions of Proposition 1 are true under the premises of the current sequent. It is particularly transparent if Π is transformed into "M is a_subset_of set_ X", and the premise of Proposition 1 is transformed into "X is a_subset_of set_ Y". (Note that, in general, representation of assumptions of propositions and premises of sequents in such a form makes a part of a proof environment along with definitions and auxiliary propositions.) In that way, we obtain:

1.1.1.1.3'.1. Π, $\overline{u}$ is a_set, $\overline{u}$ is empty, $\overline{M}$ is a_set $\Rightarrow \overline{M}$ is a_set.

So, the goal "$\overline{M}$ is a_set" is proven. Then the sequents 1.1.1.1.3 and 1.2 are proven, too. In respect that the additional premises have been introduced and the substitution has been generated, the sequent 1.1.1.1.4 is now of the form:

Π, $\overline{u}$ is empty, $\overline{u}$ is a_set $\Rightarrow \overline{u}$ is a_set.

Now, AG is applicable. The sequent is proven. There is not any more sequents to prove. So, the initial theorem is proven.

4   Related Work

In this paper we mainly focused on theorem proving in the AO-style but the AO programme also concerns issues other than theorem proving.

By now, a lot of various ATP systems have been developed (see, for example, [20]). They differ in the types of calculi underlying inference search procedures, search methods used, ranges of problems tackled. Of course, historical relationship between AO and the other systems which are well-known in the world and the relationship between the calculi presented here and the systems in use today are worth of special discussion. But here we would like to mention some of the works (both projects and functioning systems) which are mostly congenial to the ideas underlying the AO programme, i.e. those supporting an integrated environment for "doing mathematics" and concerning the following issues:

- source data language is rich enough to support communication with a user in the terms of a given application domain;

- different computer mathematical tools, such as theorem provers, computer algebra systems, numerical computation procedures, proof editors, etc., are integrated to assist in solving mathematical problems;

- a base of mathematical knowledge is used during problem solving, and it evolves and increases as new knowledge is obtained;

- problem solving can be done in an interactive mode, enabling a user to influence search processes.

The system MIZAR [21] is oriented to theorem proof checking within a mathematical environment. Its input data language is closer syntactically to the usual mathematical one than a first-order logic language.

The system THEOREMA [22] is being built as an integrate environment for solving mathematical problems. So, the issues of interaction between a user and the system, enriching an input data language, the development of natural-like proof search procedures, natural language formulation of proofs are dealt with as the system progresses.

The system OMEGA [23] supports theorem proving in mathematics and mathematical education in which different units for "doing mathematics", namely deductive procedures, both well-known general-purpose theorem provers and specialized reasoners, and a computer algebra system are integrated. It provides a structured knowledge base of mathematical theories and supports theorem proving as a human-oriented interactive process.

The system ISABELLE [24] is an environment for interactive theorem proving. It contains a mathematical knowledge base: a library of concrete mathematics and various packages for advanced mathematical concepts. It also attempts to support the kind of proving usual for mathematicians by reasoning "in the terms" of a given application domain.

As the final goal of the QED project [25] is computer supported integration of existing mathematical knowledge, the problems of adequate representation of mathematical data, particularly, of the development of appropriate languages for mathematical theories description, and efficient mathematical theorem validation techniques arise.

5   Conclusion

Nowadays, there is observed a tendency of integration of various systems for representing and processing mathematical knowledge. Taking this fact into consideration, the authors hope that this paper and some theses on the AO programme can be helpful in attacking such problems as distributed automated theorem proving, checking self-contained mathematical texts for correctness, remote training in mathematical disciplines, extracting knowledge from mathematical papers, and constructing data bases for mathematical theories.

6   Acknowledgements

This research was supported by projects INTAS 96-0760 and INTAS-RFBR 95-0095, and the EPSRS grant GR/M46631 given to the first author. The authors thank all the participants of these projects.

The authors would also like to thank anonymous referees whose comments and useful remarks made it possible to improve the quality of this paper.

References

1. Degtyarev, A., Lyaletski, A.: Logical inference in SAD (In Russian). In: Kapitonova, Yu. (ed.): Matematicheskie osnovy sistem iskusstvennogo intellekta. Institute of Cybernetics, Kiev (1981) 3–11
2. Lyaletski, A.: Gentzen calculi and admissible substitutions. In: Actes preliminaries, du Simposium Franco-Sovetique "Informatika-91". Grenoble, France (1991) 99–111
3. Glushkov, V.: Some problems of automata theory and artificial intelligence (in Russian). Kibernetika 2 (1970) 3–13
4. Anufriyev, F., Fediurko, V., Letichevski, A., Asel'derov, Z., Didukh I.: On one algorithm of theorem proof search in Group Theory (in Russian). Kibernetika 1 (1966) 23–29

5. Anufriyev, F.: An algorithm of theorem proof search in logical calculi (in Russian). In: Teoriya avtomatov 5. Institute of Cybernetics, Kiev (1969) 3-26
6. Glushkov, V, Vershinin, K., Kapitonova, Yu., Letichevski, A., Malevanniy, N., Kostyrko, V.: On a formal language for description of mathematical texts (in Russian). In: Avtomatizatsiya poiska dokazatel'stv teorem v matematike. Institute of Cybernetics, Kiev (1974) 3-36
7. Degtyarev, A.: The strategy of monotone paramodulation (in Russian). In: Proc.of 5th All Soviet Union conf.on mathematical logic. Novosibirsk (1979) 39
8. Atayan, V., Vershinin, K.: On formalization of some inference search methods (in Russian). In: Avtomatizatsiya obrabotki matematicheskikh tekstov. Institute of Cybernetics, Kiev (1980) 36-52
9. Kapitonova, Yu., Vershinin, K., Degtyarev, A., Zhezherun, A., Lyaletski, A.: On a system for mathematical texts processing (in Russian). Kibernetika 2 (1979) 48
10. Glushkov, V.: The System for Proving Automation (in Russian). In: Avtomatizatsiya obrabotki matematicheskikh tekstov. Institute of Cybernetics, Kiev (1980) 3-30
11. Degtyarev, A.: Equality handling techniques in theories with a full set of reductions (in Russian). In: Matematicheskoye obespecheniye sistem logicheskogo vyvoda i deduktivnych postroyeniy na EVM. Institute of Cybernetics, Kiev (1983) 42-55
12. Atayan, V., Morokhovets, M.: Combining formal derivation search procedures and natural theorem proving techniques in an automated theorem proving system. Cybernetics and System Analysis 32 (1996) 442-465
13. Degtyarev, A., Kapitonova, Yu., Letichevski, A., Lyaletski, A., Morokhovets, M.: A brief historical sketch on Kiev school of automated theorem proving. In: Buchberger, B., Jebelean, T. (eds.): Proc. Second International THEOREMA Workshop. RISC, Linz, Austria (1998) 151-155
14. Gallier, J. : Logic for computer science: foundations of Automatic Theorem Proving. Harper and Row, Inc. New York (1986) 513 p.
15. Robinson, J.: A Machine-Oriented Logic Based on Resolution Principle. JACM (1965) 23-41
16. Kanger, S.: Simplified proof method for elementary logic. In: Comp. Program. and Form. Sys.: Stud. in Logic. Amsterdam, North-Holland, Publ. Co. (1963) 87-93
17. Lyaletski, A.V.: Variant of Herbrand Theorem for Formulas in Prefix Form (in Russian). Kibernetika 1 (1981) 112-116
18. Atayan, V., Vershinin, K., Zhezherun, A.: On structural processing of mathematical texts (in Russian). In: Raspoznavaniye obrazov. Institute of Cybernetics, Kiev (1978) 43-54
19. Morokhovets, M., Luzhnykh, A.: Representing mathematical texts in a formalized natural-like language. In: Buchberger, B., Jebelean, T. (eds.): Proc. Second International THEOREMA Workshop. RISC, Linz, Austria (1998) 157-160
20. http://www-formal.stanford.edu/clt/ARS/systems.html
21. http://mizar.uw.bialostok.pl/
22. Buchberger, B., Jebelean, T., Kriftner, F., Marin, M., Tomuta, E., Vasaru, D.: A survey of the *Theorema* project. In: Kuechlin, W. (ed.): Proc. ISSAC'97, Maui, Hawaii (1997) 384-391
23. http://www.ags.uni-sb.de/projects/deduktion/projects/omega/
24. http://www.cl.cam.ac.uk/Research/HVG/Isabelle/
25. http://www.Cybercom.net/~rbjones/rbjpub/logic/qedres00.htm

First Order Linear Temporal Logic over Finite Time Structures

Serenella Cerrito[1], Marta Cialdea Mayer[2*], and Sébastien Praud[1]

[1] Université de Paris-Sud, L.R.I., e-mail: {serena, praud}@lri.fr
[2] Università di Roma Tre, e-mail: cialdea@dia.uniroma3.it

Abstract. In this work, the notion of provability for first order linear temporal logic over *finite* time structures, $FO\text{-}LTL^{fin}$, is studied. We show that the validity problem for such a logic is not recursively enumerable, hence $FO\text{-}LTL^{fin}$ is not recursively axiomatizable.

This negative result however does not hold in the case of *bounded* validity, that is truth in all temporal models where the object domain is possibly infinite, but the underlying sequence of time points does not exceed a given size. A formula is defined to be k-valid if it is true in all temporal models whose underlying time frame is not greater than k, where k is any fixed positive integer. In this work a tableau calculus is defined, that is sound and complete with respect to k-validity, when given as input the initial formula and the bound k on the size of the temporal models. The main feature of the system, extending the propositional calculus defined in [7], is that of explicitly denoting time points and having tableau nodes labelled by either expressions intuitively stating that a formula holds in a given temporal interval, or "temporal constraints", i.e. linear inequalities on time points. Branch closure is reduced to unsatisfiability over the integers of the set of temporal constraints in the branch.

1 Introduction

The model of time underlying Linear Temporal Logic (LTL) is a discrete, linear sequence of states, usually taken to be bounded in the past and infinite in the future. In other words, the set of time points is isomorphic to $\mathbb{N}$. Different sets of temporal operators may be considered: mainly, future time operators ($\Box$: always, $\Diamond$: eventually, $\bigcirc$: next, $\mathcal{U}$: until), possibly restricting to the fragment with $\Box$ and $\Diamond$ only, or both past and future time ones ("full" LTL). In the propositional case, several sound, complete and terminating proof-systems for LTL have been provided; see for instance [19, 18, 4, 2]. As far as first order LTL, equipped with the infinite semantics, is concerned, it has been proved that no complete recursive axiomatization can exist (see [14, 1, 16]). This explains why relatively little work has been done on the proof theory of first order LTL. An exception is [2], where a first order non-clausal resolution system is defined, which is complete w.r.t. the class of the so called "formulae provable with a clock".

* This work has been partially supported by Agenzia Spaziale Italiana (ASI) and CNR.

In this work, we consider first order LTL with a *finite* semantics, $FO\text{-}LTL^{fin}$, where time is assumed to be finite both in the past and in the future, while the object domain can be infinite. Its interest is due to the fact that there are problems in Computer Science and Artificial Intelligence where only a finite fragment of the time sequence is of interest. For instance, in the case of a database evolving through time by means of updates, queries involving several states of the database, as well as dynamic integrity constraints, may be expressed by first order temporal formulae and the database history, from the initial state up to the current state, can be modeled by a finite time temporal interpretation [11, 3, 6]. Similarly, the specification of a planning problem may be expressed by means of a set of temporal logic formulae; since a plan is a finite sequence of actions, leading from the initial situation to the desired goal, it can be modeled by a finite time temporal interpretation [7, 8].

In [7] the propositional version of LTL over finite time frames is studied and a labelled tableau calculus is defined and proved sound, complete and terminating. Obviously, however, propositional logic is expressively too poor for the above mentioned applications. In the case of $FO\text{-}LTL^{fin}$, decidability is clearly lost, but what about semi-decidability? In both [1] and [16], the kernel of the proof techniques used to get the intrinsic incompleteness result for first order LTL with the infinite semantics is the possibility of encoding arithmetic into such a logic. It is apparent that such proofs cannot be adapted to the case of $FO\text{-}LTL^{fin}$, where a time frame is isomorphic to a *finite* initial segment of the natural numbers. In this work, however, we show that the validity problem for $FO\text{-}LTL^{fin}$ is still not recursively enumerable, by use of a different, and quite natural, technique. As a consequence, no effective proof system for $FO\text{-}LTL^{fin}$ may exist.

In the case of $FO\text{-}LTL^{fin}$, a weaker notion than validity can be considered. If k is any given positive integer, the notion of k-validity of a formula is defined as follows: F is k-valid iff it is true in any finite interpretation whose underlying time frame is not greater than k. Such a notion of *bounded validity* is still a useful one in several applications, for instance, in databases, where the question of the preservation of an integrity constraint after a given number k of updates is important [5], and in planning, where the searched plan can be reasonably required not to exceed a given length.

In this work we propose a labelled tableau calculus which is sound and complete w.r.t. the notion of bounded $FO\text{-}LTL^{fin}$-validity. The main difference of our approach, w.r.t. to "traditional" tableaux for LTL, is the use of *labels* on formulae, making it possible to embed semantical information in the calculus itself, namely the fact that a temporal frame is isomorphic to $\mathbb{N}$. Tableaux rules introduce linear constraints on world variables, so that specific algorithms for solving integer constraints may be used in order to check satisfiability. The idea of using linear constraints over integers in proof systems for propositional linear temporal logic (with the infinite semantics) first appeared in [13] and [18, 17], and it has been revisited in the calculus proposed in [7, 8]. In the present work, we extend the calculus of [7] to the first order case, obtaining a system that is sound and complete w.r.t. bounded validity (albeit sound, modulo a minor modification, but obviously incomplete, w.r.t. validity in finite time frames *tout court*).

2   Syntax and Semantics of *FO-LTL^{fin}*

The language of linear temporal logic we consider includes the classical operators $\neg, \wedge, \vee, \perp$ (always false), $\top$ (always true), $\forall$ and $\exists$, the unary modal operators $\square$ (always in the future),   and $\boxminus$ (always in the past), and the binary ones $\mathcal{U}$ (until) and $\mathcal{S}$ (since). The alphabet contains a set P of predicate symbols and a set F of function symbols; all the function symbols in F are *rigid*.[1] When the distinguished equality predicate $=$ is considered, it is also taken to be rigid, in the sense that its interpretation (identity) does not change over time.

The semantics of the language with predicate symbols in P and function symbols in F is defined as follows. A *temporal frame* T is a finite initial segment of the natural numbers, $\langle 0, \cdots, k \rangle$; its elements are called *time points*. A temporal interpretation $\mathcal{M}$ is a quadruple $\langle T, D, \delta_P, \delta_F \rangle$ where T is a temporal frame, D is a non-empty set (the object domain, possibly infinite), δ_P is a mapping from $P \times \{0, ..., k\}$ to the set of relations on D such that, for any n-ary predicate symbol p with $n > 0$ and any $i \in T$, $\delta_P(p, i)$ is a subset of D^n, and δ_F is a mapping from F to the set of (total) functions on D such that, for any n-ary function symbol f with $n \geq 0$, $\delta_F(f)$ is a function from D^n to D.

Let σ be a variable assignment, i.e. a function from the set of variables Var to the domain D. Given any term t, its value $[t]_{\mathcal{M},\sigma}$ w.r.t. the interpretation $\mathcal{M}$ and the variable assignment σ, is defined like in the classical case. Note that, since the language is assumed to have only rigid functional symbols, the interpretation of a term is the same at any time point.

If A is a formula, the satisfiability relation $\mathcal{M}_{\sigma,i} \models A$ (to be read: A is satisfied by $\mathcal{M}$ w.r.t. the variable assignment σ at the time point i) extends the classical definition – with base cases $\mathcal{M}_{\sigma,i} \models p(t_1, ..., t_n)$ iff $\langle [t_1]_{\mathcal{M},\sigma}, ..., [t_n]_{\mathcal{M},\sigma} \rangle \in \delta_P(p, i)$, and a similar one treating equality – as follows:

1. $\mathcal{M}_{\sigma,i} \models \square A$ iff for all j such that $i < j$, $\mathcal{M}_{\sigma,j} \models A$.
2. $\mathcal{M}_{\sigma,i} \models A\mathcal{U}B$ iff $\exists j \in T$ such that $i < j$ and $\mathcal{M}_{\sigma,j} \models B$, and for any k with $i < k < j$ $\mathcal{M}_{\sigma,k} \models A$.
3. $\mathcal{M}_{\sigma,i} \models \boxminus A$ iff for all $j < i$, $\mathcal{M}_{\sigma,j} \models A$.
4. $\mathcal{M}_{\sigma,i} \models A\mathcal{S}B$ iff $\exists j \in T$ such that $j < i$ and $\mathcal{M}_{\sigma,j} \models B$ and for any k with $j < k < i$ $\mathcal{M}_{\sigma,k} \models A$.

Note that, due to the "strict" interpretation of the modal operators (excluding the present time point in both cases of future and past time operators), the weak and strong "Next" and "Last" operators are definable. The $\diamondsuit$ (eventually) and $\overleftarrow{\diamondsuit}$ (sometimes in the past) operators are also definable in terms of,

---

[1] Note that non-rigid function symbols may always be simulated via predicates. Thus, considering only rigid function symbols does not affect the expressive power of the considered logic.

respectively, $\mathcal{U}$ and $\mathcal{S}$, as well as all the other standard temporal operators. The operators taken as primitive are all necessary in order to have a negation normal form property, that is exploited in Section 4.

When A is closed, we omit σ and we just write $\mathcal{M}_j \models A$ to mean that A is satisfied by the structure $\mathcal{M}$ at the time point j. Truth of a formula A is satisfiability of its universal closure in the initial state: a formula A is true in $\mathcal{M}$ (and $\mathcal{M}$ is a model of A) iff $\mathcal{M}_0 \models \forall x_1, ..., \forall x_n A$, where $x_1, \cdots, x_n$ are all the free variables in A. Truth of sets of formulae is defined as usual. Satisfiability of a closed formula is truth in at least one model, validity is truth in all models.[2] If k is a positive integer and A a closed formula, A is said to be k-satisfiable if it is true in some model whose temporal frame $\langle 0, ..., m \rangle$ is such that $m \leq k$. A is k-valid iff it is true in any model whose temporal frame $\langle 0, ..., m \rangle$ is such that $m \leq k$.

A formula is in *negation normal form* (nnf) iff no logical operator is in the scope of a negation. Two formulae A and B are equivalent iff for all $\mathcal{M}$ and i, $\mathcal{M}_i \models A$ iff $\mathcal{M}_i \models B$. It can easily be shown that, under this strong notion of equivalence, every formula can be transformed into an equivalent formula in nnf.

3   *FO-LTL^{fin}* Is Not Semi-decidable

In [1] it is proved that a complete recursive axiomatization for first order LTL, equipped with the infinite semantics, cannot exist, by exploiting the power of the future time temporal operators $\bar{\Box}$ (*non strict always*, whose semantics includes the present time point) and $\bigcirc$ (next). The proof makes use of the notion of Π_1^1 formulae, that is formulae having the form $\forall R_1 ... \forall R_k \forall F_1 ... \forall F_{k'} B$, where B is some classical first order formula and $0, s, \leq, +, \times, R_1, ..., R_k, F_1, ..., F_{k'}$ are all the predicate and function symbols in B. The complexity class Π_1^1 includes all problems no harder than the truth problem for Π_1^1 formulae. What is shown is that the LTL validity problem is Π_1^1-complete. The kernel of the proof consists in exhibiting a recursive embedding E of Π_1^1 formulae in LTL formulae, such that, given any Π_1^1 formula F, F is true if and only if $E(F)$ is LTL valid. The definition of the mapping E uses the equality predicate $=$, one non-rigid constant a and only the (future) temporal operators $\bar{\Box}$, the corresponding "non strict eventually" operator and $\bigcirc$ (next) – of course, the use of a may be actually simulated by an appropriate use of predicate symbols. In [16] some interpretability results of classical arithmetical theories in temporal theories are proved and, as a corollary, two versions of the incompleteness result for first order LTL with the future time operators are obtained. Since, as it has been afterwards shown in [15], validity of first order LTL formulae containing $\bar{\Box}$ and $\bigcirc$ may be reduced to validity of formulae containing only $\bar{\Box}$ as a temporal

---

[2] A different definition of validity can also be found in the literature: A is valid iff for any temporal interpretation $\mathcal{M}$ and for any time point i, $\mathcal{M}_i \models A$. However, it is easy to see that the two notions of validity are interdefinable.

operator, it follows that validity for first order LTL with equality and $\bar{\Box}$ is not recursively enumerable.

In both [1] and [16], the kernel of the proof techniques used to get the incompleteness result is the possibility of encoding arithmetic into LTL. Thus, such proofs cannot be adapted to the case of $FO\text{-}LTL^{fin}$, where a time frame is isomorphic to a *finite* initial segment of the natural numbers.

However, it can be shown that the set of $FO\text{-}LTL^{fin}$ valid formulae is not recursively enumerable by reducing the complement of the halting problem for Turing Machines to the validity problem for $FO\text{-}LTL^{fin}$.

Theorem 1. *Given any Turing machine M and word w, a temporal formula $F_{M,w}$ can be constructed, such that $F_{M,w}$ is $FO\text{-}LTL^{fin}$-valid iff M never halts when given w as an input.*

Proof. The proof, whose details can be found in [9], bears some similarities with the proof of the fact that validity in finite domains of classical predicate calculus formulae is not recursively enumerable. However, in the case of classical logic, the set of finitely satisfiable formulae is trivially recursively enumerable, so that in order to conclude that "finite validity" is not so it suffices to show that finite satisfiability is not recursive, by exhibiting a formula, for each Turing Machine M and input word w, which is finitely satisfiable if and only if M halts on w. In the case of LTL^{fin}, the class of satisfiable formulae is not recursively enumerable either (since classical first order satisfiability can trivially be reduced to LTL^{fin} satisfiability), hence an explicit construction of a LTL^{fin} formula which is *valid* if and only if M does *not* halt on w must be accomplished.

The proof can be sketched as follows. Given a deterministic Turing machine :

$$M = \langle Q, \Sigma, \Delta, q_0, q_f \rangle$$

(where Q is the set of states, Σ the alphabet, Δ the transition table, q_0 the initial state and q_f the final state of the machine) and a word w in the alphabet of M, the language $\mathcal{L}_{M,w}$ of $F_{M,w}$ contains: a constant symbol 0 and a unary functional symbol s, the equality predicate and the binary relation symbol $<$, for each state $q_i \in Q$, the unary predicate symbol Q_i, and, for each symbol $s_i \in \Sigma$, the unary predicate symbol S_i.

We say that M halts before time k if for some time $n < k$, M is in state q_f at time n. We define a set of "intended interpretations" $\mathcal{M}^k$ of the language $\mathcal{L}_{M,w}$, for each $k \geq 0$ such that the machine M does not halt before time k, when given the word w as an input. The time structure in $\mathcal{M}^k$ is $\langle 0, ..., k \rangle$. The domain is $\mathbb{N}$. $\mathcal{M}^k$ assigns zero to 0 and the successor function to s. Moreover, if σ is a variable assignment and $t \in T$:

1. $\mathcal{M}^k{}_{\sigma,t} \models Q_i(x)$ iff at time t the machine is in state q_i, scanning square number $\sigma(x)$
2. $\mathcal{M}^k{}_{\sigma,t} \models S_i(x)$ iff at time t the symbol s_i is in square number $\sigma(x)$
3. $\mathcal{M}^k{}_{\sigma,t} \models x < y$ iff $\sigma(x)$ is less than $\sigma(y)$

Given a Turing machine M with input w, the formula $G_{M,w}$ is the conjunction of a set of formulae describing the behaviour of M (i.e. the initial state, the transition table of M, standard properties of s and $<$, the fact that the machine can be in at most one state at a time and that time ends when the final state is reached). The only temporal operators needed in the encoding are $\bar{\Box}$ (non strict always, including the present time point), defined as $\bar{\Box}F \equiv_{def} F \wedge \Box F$, and $\bigcirc$ (weak next), defined as $\bigcirc A \equiv_{def} \Box \bot \vee \bot \mathcal{U} A$.

The formula $\overline{H}_{M,w}$ is $\bar{\Box}\forall x \neg Q_f(x)$, intuitively stating, in the intended interpretations, that the machine never halts, and $F_{M,w}$ is $G_{M,w} \rightarrow \overline{H}_{M,w}$.

It can be proved that the formula $G_{M,w}$ logically implies a description D_t of time t, for each time point t such that the machine M has not halted before time t (i.e. for any $n = 0, ..., t-1$, M is not in the final state). Such formulae have the form $\bigcirc^{(t)} A$, where $\bigcirc^{(t)}$ is a t-length sequence of $\bigcirc$ operators and A describes the symbols on the tape and which the state of the machine and the scanned square are at time t.

The fact that if $F_{M,w}$ is valid then M never halts when given w as an input is straightforward. For the converse, let us assume that M never halts when given w as an input and however there exists a model $\mathcal{M}$ of $G_{M,w} \wedge \neg \overline{H}_{M,w}$. Let m be the size of its temporal frame. Since $\mathcal{M} \models \neg \bar{\Box} \forall x \neg Q_f(x)$, there is a time point $k \leq m$ such that $\mathcal{M}_k \models \exists x Q_f(x)$ (note that, if the usual encoding of Turing Machines in classical logic is considered, in the corresponding (classical) model, the time point k could be a non standard number). By using the fact that, if M never halts when given w as an input, $G_{M,w}$ logically implies some description D_k of state k, it can be proved that $G_{M,w}$ logically implies a closed formula of the form $\bigcirc^{(k)} Q_f(\bar{p})$, where $\bar{p}$ is some term of the form $s(s(...(0)...))$. Therefore $\mathcal{M}^k \models \bigcirc^{(k)} Q_f(\bar{p})$, where $\mathcal{M}^k$ is the intended interpretation of size k. It follows that at time k the machine M, when given w as an input, is in the final state q_f. I.e. M halts on w: contradiction.   ∎

Such a result has an impact also on first order LTL with the *infinite* semantics. Consider the first order fragment LTL_{past}, containing only unary past time operators, and say that A is valid iff A holds at each time point of each temporal interpretation (in this case, the notion of validity defined in Section 2 is not interesting). A rather straightforward application of Theorem 1 enables us to prove the following result:

Theorem 2. *First order LTL_{past} is not recursively axiomatizable.*

4   First Order Bounded Tableaux

In this section, we propose a labelled tableau system to check k-satisfiability of $FO\text{-}LTL^{fin}$ formulae. It extends the system introduced in [7] for the propositional case, whose purpose is to verify whether a set of formulae in nnf is finitely satisfiable (the restriction to nnf formulae is introduced only to simplify the presentation of the rules). The main feature of the system, that is inspired by [13] and [18], is that of explicitly denoting time points and having tableau nodes labelled either by expressions intuitively stating that a formula holds in a given temporal interval, or "temporal constraints", i.e. linear inequalities on time points. Branch closure is reduced to unsatisfiability over the integers of the set of temporal constraints in the branch.

Let $C = \{start, finish, d_1, d_2, d_3, ...\}$ be a set of *time constants* (intuitively denoting time points, where *start* is the initial time point and *finish* the last one). A *state* is any expression of the form $c + n$, for $c \in C$ and $n \in \mathbb{Z}$. The set of states is denoted by Σ. It is intended that $C \subset \Sigma$ (c can be rewritten as $c + 0$). If $s, t \in \Sigma$, then $s \leq t$ is a *temporal constraint*. A *labelled formula* is an expression of the form $[s, t]A$, where $s, t \in \Sigma$ and A is a closed LTL formula in nnf (intuitively meaning that A holds at each point in the closed interval $[s, t]$). $[s, s]A$ will be abbreviated by $[s]A$.

Tableau nodes are labelled either by temporal constraints or labelled formulae (in this last case they are called *logical nodes*). If S is a finite set of formulae in nnf and K is the singleton $\{finish \leq start + k\}$ for some integer $k \geq 0$ (representing the maximal size of the searched models), then tableaux for $S \cup K$ are initialized with the set $\{[start]A \mid A \in S\} \cup K$. Nodes are expanded by application of the rules in Table 1, where the expressions $s, t, s', t', ..$ are elements of Σ, C is a set of time constants and $P = \{a_1, a_2, a_3, ...\}$ is a set of "fresh" parameters (whose role is to "give names" to elements of the object domain), treated as individual constants. Rules for the equality predicate may be added to the rules in Table 1, in a standard way. The set of nodes occurring above the line of a rule is called the *premise* of the rule, while the sets of nodes occurring below are the *expansions* of the premise.

In the δ-rule, c is a fresh element of C and a is a fresh element of P. In the γ-rule, u is any ground term occurring in the branch. Note that a sort of contraction is implicit in the β-rule and in the δ-rule: in both cases, the rightmost expansion of the rule contains a node with the same formula already occurring in the premise, even though the labels (intervals) of the nodes are different. Moreover, logical formulae are in general not automatically "consumed" by expanding them; in particular, one may need to expand a universal formula several times by means of the γ-rule, as usual.

The intuition behind the β-rule is the following: either A is true in the whole interval (leftmost branch), or there exists a smallest time point c in the interval where A is false, hence B is true; since c is chosen to be the first of such points, A is true in the (possibly empty) subinterval before it. Similarly, the δ-rules can be read as stating that if $\exists x A(x)$ holds in the non empty interval $[s, t]$, then either $A(a)$ holds at each point of the interval for the same object a (leftmost branch), or $A(a)$ holds for the same object A in a first segment $[s, c]$ of the interval (possibly with $c = s$), and in the remaining part $\exists x A(x)$ holds again.

The interval and conflict resolution rules augment the set of temporal constraints in the tableau. When the interval rule is applied to expand $[s, t]A$, we say that it is applied to the interval $[s, t]$, independently of the formula A. This rule distinguishes the cases where an interval is empty or not. Its role is to provide the preconditions for the application of the logical and resolution rules. Intuitively, it is useless – and sometimes incorrect – to expand a node $[s,t]A$ when the interval is empty and, given two nodes $[s,t]p$, $[s',t']\neg p$, there is no conflict to be solved if either $[s,t]$ or $[s',t']$ (or both) are empty. Note that such a rule could be dispensed with, and a corresponding branching added to most of the other rules, handling the case where the considered interval is empty.

When the leftmost conflict resolution rule is applied, we say that it is applied to the intervals $[s,t]$ and $[s',t']$.

Logical rules			
α-rule	**β-rule**	**$\mathcal{U}$-rule**	**$\Box$-rule**
$\dfrac{\begin{array}{c}[s,t]A \wedge B \\ s \leq t\end{array}}{\begin{array}{c}[s,t]A \\ [s,t]B\end{array}}$	$\dfrac{\begin{array}{c}[s,t]A \vee B \\ s \leq t\end{array}}{[s,t]A \qquad \begin{array}{c} s \leq c \\ c \leq t \\ \hline [s,c-1]A \\ [c]B \\ [c+1,t]A \vee B \\ c \in C \text{ fresh}\end{array}}$	$\dfrac{\begin{array}{c}[s,t]A\mathcal{U}B \\ s \leq t\end{array}}{\begin{array}{c}[c]B \\ t+1 \leq c \\ [t+1,c-1]A \\ [s+1,t]A \vee B \\ c \in C \text{ fresh}\end{array}}$	$\dfrac{\begin{array}{c}[s,t]\Box A \\ s \leq t\end{array}}{[s+1,finish]A}$
γ-rule	**δ-rule**	**S-rule**	**$\overline{\Box}$-rule**
$\dfrac{\begin{array}{c}[s,t]\forall x A(x) \\ s \leq t\end{array}}{[s,t]A(u)}$	$\dfrac{\begin{array}{c}[s,t]\exists x A(x) \\ s \leq t\end{array}}{[s,t]A(a) \qquad \begin{array}{c} s \leq c \\ c \leq t \\ \hline [s,c]A(a) \\ [c+1,t]\exists x A(x) \\ c \in C \text{ fresh} \\ a \in P \text{ fresh}\end{array}}$	$\dfrac{\begin{array}{c}[s,t]ASB \\ s \leq t\end{array}}{\begin{array}{c}[c]B \\ c \leq s-1 \\ [c+1,s-1]A \\ [s,t-1]A \vee B \\ c \in C \text{ fresh}\end{array}}$	$\dfrac{\begin{array}{c}[s,t]\overline{\Box}A \\ s \leq t\end{array}}{[start,t-1]A}$

Interval rule	Conflict resolution rules		
$\dfrac{\begin{array}{c}[s,t]A\end{array}}{t \leq s-1 \qquad s \leq t}$	$\begin{array}{c} s \leq t \\ s' \leq t' \\ \ [s,t]p \\ [s',t']\neg p \end{array}$	$\dfrac{}{t \leq s'-1 \qquad t' \leq s-1}$	$\dfrac{[s,t]\bot}{t \leq s-1}$

Table 1. Tableau expansion rules

In the following, if $\mathcal{B}$ is a tableau branch, $const(\mathcal{B})$ denotes the set of temporal constants (elements of C) occurring in $\mathcal{B}$, including $start$ and $finish$.

Definition 1. *Let C be a set of constants (including start and finish) and $\mathcal{I}$ a mapping from C to the natural numbers. The notation $\mathcal{I}^*$ is used to denote the extension of $\mathcal{I}$ from states to the integers such that $\mathcal{I}^*(c+n) = \mathcal{I}(c) + n$ for every $c \in C, n \in \mathbb{Z}$.*

1. *Let $T = \langle 0, ..., k \rangle$ be a finite sequence of integers starting at 0. $\mathcal{I}$ is a temporal mapping for C with range T if $min\{\mathcal{I}(c) \mid c \in C\} = \mathcal{I}(start) = 0$ and $max\{\mathcal{I}(c) \mid c \in C\} = \mathcal{I}(finish) = k$. Hence, in particular, the range of a temporal mapping is always finite.*
2. *If K is a set of temporal constraints over C, then $\mathcal{I}$ is a solution to K iff:*
   (a) *$\mathcal{I}$ is a temporal mapping for C;*
   (b) *if $s \leq t \in K$, then $\mathcal{I}^*(s) \leq \mathcal{I}^*(t)$.*
3. *Let B be a tableau branch, $C = const(B)$ and $\mathcal{M}$ a temporal interpretation with domain T.*
   (a) *If $\mathcal{I}$ is a temporal mapping for C with range T, then $\langle \mathcal{M}, \mathcal{I} \rangle$ satisfies B ($\langle \mathcal{M}, \mathcal{I} \rangle \models B$) iff:*
      i. *$\mathcal{I}$ is a solution to the set of temporal constraints occurring in B;*
      ii. *if $[s, t]A$ occurs in B, then for every integer i, if $i \in T$ and $\mathcal{I}^*(s) \leq i \leq \mathcal{I}^*(t)$, then $\mathcal{M}_i \models A$.*
   (b) *B is satisfiable in $\mathcal{M}$ iff there exists a temporal mapping $\mathcal{I}$ for C such that $\langle \mathcal{M}, \mathcal{I} \rangle \models B$.*

Definition 2. *Let B be a tableau branch and K the set of temporal constraints occurring in B. B is open iff there exists a solution to K. Otherwise it is closed.*

The following definition captures the intuitive idea of tableaux where no wasteful expansions are ever performed. In particular, closed branches are never expanded.

Definition 3. *A tableau branch B is canonical iff:*

- *The interval rule is applied at most once to each interval.*
- *Every logical node is expanded at most once by means of a logical rule, but for nodes of the form $[s, t]\forall x A$, that can be expanded more than once.*
- *If a node $[s, t]\forall x A$ is expanded twice to, respectively, $[s, t]A(u)$ and $[s, t]A(u')$, via two applications of the γ-rule, then the ground terms u and u' are syntactically different.*
- *Each conflict resolution rule is applied at most once to each interval (second conflict resolution rule) or pair of intervals (first conflict resolution rule)*
- *No proper initial subsegment of B is closed.*

A tableau is canonical iff all its branches are canonical.

Definition 4. *If B is a tableau branch, then B is complete iff there exists no canonical expansion of B. A tableau is complete if all its branches are complete.*

Obviously, like in classical tableau systems, a canonical open branch may be infinite, because of the possible reapplication of the γ rule to a same node. More important, a priori, nothing ensures that a canonical *closed* branch is finite. In fact, an infinite branch may be closed (i.e. unsatisfiable) because its infinite set K of constraints is unsatisfiable, yet any finite subset of K has a (finite) solution. As an example, consider $K = \bigcup_{i \in \mathbb{N}} \{c_i \leq c_{i+1} - 1\}$: each finite subset of K has a solution, however K is not finitely satisfiable. Hence, in principle, a canonical tableau might be closed (all its branches being closed) and yet infinite (at least one branch being infinite). However, in the next section, we show that, thanks to the presence of the initial constraint $finish \leq start + k$ (setting a bound on the size of the searched models), closed tableaux are always finite.

5   Properties of the Bounded Tableau Calculus

In this section we establish the key properties of the calculus defined above. For space reasons, we do not give the full proofs here, which can however be found in [10]. The system can easily be proved to be sound:

Theorem 3 (Soundness w.r.t. k-Unsatisfiability). *Let S be a set of closed formulae. If there exists a closed tableau for $S \cup \{finish \leq start + k\}$ then S is k-unsatisfiable. A fortiori, if there exists a finite closed tableau for $S \cup \{finish \leq start + k\}$, then S is k-unsatisfiable.*

Conversely, any complete open branch describes some model of its initial formulae. Such a result needs some preliminary lemmas and definitions. First of all, the invertibility of all the logical rules with respect to their logical nodes can be established, in the following form:

Lemma 1.   *1. Let $\mathcal{M} = \langle T, \sigma \rangle$ be a temporal interpretation and $\mathcal{I}$ a temporal mapping with range T. For every logical rule but the γ-rule*

$$\frac{[s,t]\,F}{\quad s \leq t \quad} \qquad or \qquad \frac{[s,t]\,F}{\quad s \leq t \quad}$$
$$\frac{}{\mathcal{B}_1 \qquad \mathcal{B}_2} \qquad\qquad \frac{}{\mathcal{B}_1}$$

if $\langle \mathcal{M}, \mathcal{I} \rangle \models \mathcal{B}_i$ (for some $i = 1, 2$), then $\langle \mathcal{M}, \mathcal{I} \rangle \models [s,t]F$.
2. Let $\mathcal{B}$ be an open and complete branch of a tableau and let $[s,t]\forall x A(x)$ be a node in $\mathcal{B}$, expanded via a γ-rule. Let $\mathcal{M}$ be a temporal interpretation such that its object domain is exactly the set of ground terms in the branch, and $\mathcal{M}(u) = u$ for any ground term u in $\mathcal{B}$. Suppose that, for any labelled node $[s,t]A(u)$, where u is a ground term, for each i in $[\mathcal{I}^*(s), \mathcal{I}^*(t)]$, $\mathcal{M}_i \models A(u)$. Then, for any such i, $\mathcal{M}_i \models \forall x A(x)$.

The following definition captures the idea of a sequence of applications of the β-rule, each of them expanding an expansion of the previous one, and the similar notion for the case of the δ-rule.

Definition 5. *Let $\mathcal{B}$ be a tableau branch. A β-node in $\mathcal{B}$ is a node of the form $[s,t]A \vee B$. A δ-node in $\mathcal{B}$ is a node of the form $[s,t]\exists x A(x)$. A β-chain in $\mathcal{B}$ is a sequence of β-nodes $X_0, X_1, ...$ such that, for every $i \geq 1$, X_{i-1} is expanded in $\mathcal{B}$ by application of the β-rule and X_i is the β-node in the corresponding rightmost expansion. A k-length-β-chain is a finite β-chain $X_0, X_1, ..., X_{k+1}$, constituted by $k + 2$ nodes.*

A node X in B is the root node of a β-chain if it is the first node in a β-chain and it is not itself obtained by an application of the β-rule, i.e. there exists a maximal length β-chain in B having X as its first node.

The corresponding notions of δ-chain, k-length-δ-chain and root node of a δ-chain are defined similarly.

A tableau branch may contain an infinite number of β-chains or δ-chains. Moreover, in principle, each chain might be of unbounded length. However, if the branch is satisfiable by a model $\mathcal{M}$ whose temporal frame is $\langle 0, ..., k \rangle$, each chain has at most $k+1$ elements. This fact is stated by the next lemma, whose proof is similar to the corresponding one in [7].

Lemma 2. *If B is a canonical open branch and its constraints have a solution $\mathcal{I}$ whose range is $\langle 0, ..., n \rangle$, then B contains no k-length-β-chain or k-length-δ-chain with $k > n$.*

The previous lemmas enable us to prove the following result:

Lemma 3. *If B is a complete and open tableau branch and $\mathcal{I}$ is a solution of the set of temporal constraints occurring in B, then there is an interpretation $\mathcal{M}$ such that $\langle \mathcal{M}, \mathcal{I} \rangle \models B$.*

Proof. Suppose that $\mathcal{I}$ is a solution for the constraints in B and let $T = \langle 0, ..., n \rangle$ be the range of $\mathcal{I}$. Let $\mathcal{M}$ be $\langle T, D, \delta_P, \delta_F \rangle$ where D is the set of ground terms in B; for each i in T, sequence $t_1, .., t_n \in D^n$, and n-ary predicate p: $t_1, ..., t_n \in \delta_P(p)$ iff there is a node $[s,t]p(t_1, ..., t_n)$ in B such that $\mathcal{I}^*(s) \le i \le \mathcal{I}^*(t)$; for any n-ary function symbol f and i in T: $\delta_F(f)(t_1, ..., t_n) = f(t_1, ..., t_n)$.

We need to prove that, for any labelled formula $[s,t]F \in B$ such that $[I^*(s), I^*(t)] \neq \emptyset$, and for any $i \in [I^*(s), I^*(t)]$: $\mathcal{M}_i \models F$ (the case of an empty interval being trivial). In order to do that, we define an order $<$ on the labelled formulae in B as follows. Given $[s,t]F \in B$ and $[s',t']F' \in B$, we set $[s,t]F < [s',t']F'$ iff either F is a strict subformula of F', or else $[s,t]F$ is obtained by applying either a β-rule or a δ-rule or a $\mathcal{S}$-rule or an $\mathcal{U}$-rule to $[s',t']F'$.

Note that the order $<$ is partial and all the labelled formulae $[s,t]L$ in B where L is a literal are minimal for it. *The order $<$ is well founded*; in order to prove it, the only delicate point is the second item in the definition of $<$. In fact, a priori, there might be an infinite decreasing $<$-chain, whose starting point is either a β-formula or a δ-formula or a $\mathcal{S}$-formula or a $\mathcal{U}$-formula. However, since $\mathcal{I}$ is a solution to the constraints in B (with at most $n+1$ time points), Lemma 2 rules out such a possibility.

Thus, it suffices to prove by induction on $<$, that if $[s,t]F \in B$ then, for any $i \in [\mathcal{I}^*(s), \mathcal{I}^*(t)]$, $\mathcal{M}_i \models F$. The inductive step uses Lemma 1.

The proof may be slightly modified so as to hold also in the case where equality rules are present. Of course, in order to define the domain of the model $\mathcal{M}$, the set of ground terms needs to be quotiented w.r.t. equality. ∎

As a consequence, we have the following result:

Theorem 4 (Quasi-Completeness w.r.t. k-unsatisfiability). *Let S be a set of formulae and k a natural number. If S is k-unsatisfiable, then there exists a closed tableau for $S \cup \{finish \leq start + k\}$*

The reason why we call such a result *quasi-completeness*, rather than completeness, is the following. As we have already remarked, a priori a closed branch might be infinite, because, in principle, we could have an infinite set K of temporal constraints in the branch, such that any finite subset of K has a (finite) solution but K itself has no solution. Thus, in principle, we could have an infinite tableau for a formula A that is indeed closed without being able to finitely recognize this fact. Such an infinite closed tableau would not be a "refutation" since "being a refutation" is meant to be a recursive predicate. Thus, if infinite closed tableaux might exists, Theorem 4 would not imply that the tableau calculus is an effective complete proof system, enabling us to semidecide the k-validity problem for $FO\text{-}LTL^{fin}$.

However, thanks to the presence of the initial constraint $finish \leq start + k$, any closed branch is indeed finite. In fact, if a branch contains an infinite set of constraints K and K has no solution, some finite subset of K has no solution. This property holds because:

1. Since the constraint $finish \leq start + k$ belongs to K, and, for each temporal constant c, the constraint $c \leq finish$ (implicitly) belongs to K, any solution for K is necessarily upper bounded by k.
2. If each finite subset of a denumerable set of constraints K has a solution that is upper bounded by k, then K itself has a solution upper bounded by k.

The second fact is a corollary of a more general property:
Let K be a denumerable set of constraints and k a function from the set of constants C occurring in K to the natural numbers. If any finite subset K' of K has a solution $\mathcal{I}$ such that, for any constant $c \in K'$ $\mathcal{I}(c) \leq k(c)$, then K has a solution $\mathcal{I}^+$ such that, for each constant $c \in K$, $\mathcal{I}^+(c) \leq k(c)$.

Proof. This property can be proved by standard combinatorial techniques. Let $c_1, c_2, \ldots$ be an enumeration of the set C of constants appearing in K. Let $e_1, e_2, \ldots$ be an enumeration of the elements of K; such an enumeration induces an enumeration $K_1, K_2, \ldots$ of finite subsets of K, where $K_i = \{e_1, \ldots, e_i\}$. Say that the finite set of constants appearing in S_i is C_i. For each $i \geq 1$, by hypothesis there is some solution $\mathcal{I}_i$ of K_i such that $\mathcal{I}(c) \leq k(c)$ for any constant $c \in C_i$; let us extend such a solution $\mathcal{I}_i$ to a function $\mathcal{I}'_i$ from C to the natural numbers, by assigning any value to the constants in $C - C_i$. This operation can be visualized like the construction of a table, possibly having an infinite number of lines and an infinite numbers of columns:

	c_1	c_2	c_3	$\cdots$
K_1	$\mathcal{I}'_1(c_1)$	$\mathcal{I}'_1(c_2)$	$\mathcal{I}'_1(c_3)$	$\cdots$
K_2	$\mathcal{I}'_2(c_1)$	$\mathcal{I}'_2(c_2)$	$\mathcal{I}'_2(c_3)$	$\cdots$
$\vdots$	$\vdots$	$\vdots$	$\vdots$	$\cdots$

where the labels of the columns are the constants in C and the labels of the lines are the finite subsets K_i. Any line labelled by K_i corresponds to the codomain of the function $\mathcal{I}'_i$ and, for each j such that $c_j \in C_i$, the case (i,j) actually contains the value $\mathcal{I}_i(c_j)$, where $\mathcal{I}_i$ is a "local" solution for K_i. Given any j, let us call "OK cases" of the column j those cases (i,j) in the column such that (i,j) contains $\mathcal{I}_i(c_j)$. In order to obtain the required global solution $\mathcal{I}^+$, its values $\mathcal{I}^+(j)$ are defined by induction on j, as follows.

For $j = 1$, since the values appearing in all the OK cases of the first column are bounded by $k(c_1)$, and there are infinitely many such OK cases, there is at least a number n_1 which appears infinitely often in these cases. Set $\mathcal{I}^+(c_1) = n_1$, then update the table by erasing each line i such that the content of the case $(i,1) \neq n_1$. (Note that an infinite numbers of lines is left).

For $j > 1$, the table updated at the previous stage is considered. Again, there is at least a number n_j which appears in all the infinitely many OK cases of the j-th column. Set $\mathcal{I}^+(c_j) = n_j$, then "erase" each line i such that the content of the case $(i,j) \neq n_j$. By construction, $\mathcal{I}^+$ satisfies each constraint in C, and, for any $c \in C$, $I^+(c) \leq k(c)$. ■

Hence, as a consequence of Theorems 3 and 4 we obtain:

Theorem 5. *Let S be a set of $FO\text{-}LTL^{fin}$ formulae, k be any positive integer and $K = \{finish \leq start + k\}$.*

1. *If there exists a closed tableau for $S \cup K$, such a tableau is necessarily finite and S is k-unsatisfiable. (Soundness with respect to k-unsatisfiability)*
2. *If S is k-unsatisfiable, then there exists a finite closed tableau for $S \cup K$. (Completeness with respect to k-unsatisfiability)*

The tableau system defined in this work is not sound w.r.t. validity *tout court*: obviously, a formula A might be true in all the temporal interpretations whose time structure is bounded by a given number k without being valid. However, we can slightly modify the tableau definition, simply removing the initial constraint $finish \leq start + k$, to obtain a calculus that is indeed sound w.r.t. validity: if a closed tableau for $\neg A$ exists, then $\neg A$ is unsatisfiable, i.e. A is valid.

However, in the unbounded calculus, a closed tableau for S may contain an infinite branch. For instance, take S to be the unsatisfiable set of formulae $\{\Box \exists x p(x)), \ \Diamond \forall y \neg p(y)\}$. Because of the implicit contraction in the δ-rule, the rightmost branch of any tableau for S will contain an infinite set of constraints of the form $\{c_1 + 1 \leq c_2 \leq finish, c_2 + 1 \leq c_3 \leq finish, ...\}$: the absence of the initial constraint on the size of the searched model enables us to continue the construction of a δ-chain *ad libitum*. Each finite subset of such a set of constraints has a solution, but the set itself has no (finite) solution at all. Thus, although the tableau for S is closed, such a tableau is not a *refutation* of S.

Hence the unbounded calculus is *incomplete* w.r.t. to validity. Note that the analogous of Theorem 4 holds for the unbounded calculus: given any set S of unsatisfiable formulae, a closed tableau for S does exist. Yet, this does not provide a semidecision procedure for validity.

6 Conclusions

The contribution of this paper is twofold: we report a negative result on $FO\text{-}LTL^{fin}$, i.e. first order linear temporal logic over finite temporal frames, and prove a positive one. The negative result shows the impossibility of defining an effective proof system that is complete with respect to $FO\text{-}LTL^{fin}$ validity. The analogous result for "standard" LTL equipped with *future* time operators had been proven in [1] and [16]; however, such proofs are not immediately exploitable in the case of LTL^{fin}, since they essentially depend on the possibility of encoding arithmetical formulae in LTL. As a byproduct of our negative result for LTL^{fin}, first order LTL-validity of formulae containing only *past* time operators is not recursively enumerable either. As far as $FO\text{-}LTL^{fin}$ with the $\square$ operator only is concerned, it would be interesting to check whether a result analogous to [15] holds (at a first check, the answer seems to be positive, but the details of the proofs are still to be worked out).

On the positive side, we have defined a labelled tableau calculus which is sound and complete w.r.t. bounded validity, that can be the basis for the construction of theorem provers for applications where information is needed about the validity of a temporal formula in all models where the number of time points does not exceed a given bound. This is the case, for instance, of dynamic constraint management in databases, where the question of the "safety" of a given sequence of updates - of a fixed length - with respect to a given constraint is important, as well as of the search of bounded length plans. The tableau calculus we propose makes use of annotations on formulae, indicating the time intervals in which formulae are taken to hold, hence it is formulated in a *labelled deduction* style, similarly to [13, 18]. In the case of linear temporal logic, the use of labels enables us to encode, inside the proof system itself, the information that time points "behave" as natural numbers. With respect to non labelled calculi (see for example [19]), such an approach presents, in principle, the following main advantages: the possibility of "immediately executing" *eventualities* (i.e. formulae with an existential commitment), without the need to systematically choose the specific point where the considered formula must hold, and a symmetric treatment of past and future time operators, without the need of a preliminary transformation of formulae into a "separated" form (see [12] and [4]).

Acknowledgments. The authors wish to thank Laurent Rosaz for useful discussions and suggestions.

References

1. M. Abadi. The power of temporal proofs. *Theoretical Computer Science*, 65:35–83, 1989.
2. M. Abadi and Z. Manna. Nonclausal deduction in first-order temporal logic. *Journal of the Association for Computing Machinery*, 37:279–317, 1990.
3. S. Abiteboul, L. Herr, and J. Van den Bussche. Temporal versus first-order logic to query temporal databases. In *Proc. of the 15th Int. Conf. on Principles of Databases (PODS'96)*, 1996.

76   Serenella Cerrito, Marta Cialdea Mayer, and Sébastien Praud

4. H. Barringer, M. Fisher, D. Gabbay, G. Gough, and R. Owens. METATEM: a framework for programming in temporal logic. In *Proc. of REX Workshop on Stepwise
Refinement of Distributed Systems: Models, Formalisms, Correctness*, volume 430
of *LNCS*. Springer, 1989.
5. V. Benzaken, S. Cerrito, and S. Praud. Vérification statique de contraintes
d'intégrité dynamiques. In *Proc. of 15èmes Journées Bases de Données Avancées
(BDA99)*, Bordeaux, France, October 1999. To appear.
6. N Bidoit and S. De Amo. A first step towards implementing dynamic algebraic
dependencies. *Theoretical Computer Science*, 2(190):115–149, january 1998.
7. S. Cerrito and M. Cialdea Mayer. Bounded model search in linear temporal logic
and its application to planning. In H. De Swart, editor, *International Conference
on Automated Reasoning with Analytical Tableaux and Related Methods*, pages 124–
140. Springer, 1998.
8. S. Cerrito and M. Cialdea Mayer. Using linear temporal logic to model and solve
planning problems. In F. Giunghiglia, editor, *Proceedings of the 8th International Conference on Artificial Intelligence: Methodology, Systems, Applications
(AIMSA'98)*, pages 141–152. Springer Verlag, 1998.
9. S. Cerrito, M. Cialdea Mayer, and S. Praud. First order linear temporal logic over
finite time structures is not semi-decidable. Tecnical Report LRI n. 1208, available
at http://www.dia.uniroma3.it/~cialdea/papers/nonre.ps. Presented at the
Workshop Methods for Modalities 1 (M4M) (Amsterdam, May 1999).
10. S. Cerrito, M. Cialdea Mayer, and S. Praud. A tableau calculus for first order
linear temporal logic over bounded time structures. Technical Report LRI n. 1207,
available at http://www.dia.uniroma3.it/~cialdea/papers/foltl.ps.
11. J. Chomicki. Temporal query languages: a survey. In D.M. Gabbay and H.J.
Ohlbach, editors, *Temporal Logic: ICTL'94*, volume 827 of *Lecture Notes in Computer Science*, pages 506–534. Springer-Verlag, 1994.
12. D. Gabbay. Declarative past and imperative future: Executable temporal logic for
interactive systems. In B. Banieqbal, H. Barringer, and A. Pnueli, editors, *Proc.
of Colloquium on Temporal Logic in Specification*, number 398 in LNCS, pages
409–448. Sprinber-Verlag, 1989.
13. R. Hähnle and O. Ibens. Improving temporal logic tableaux using integer constraints. In D. M. Gabbay and H. J. Ohlbach, editors, *Proceedings of the First
International Conference on Temporal Logic (ICTL 94)*, volume 827 of *LNCS*,
pages 535–539. Springer, 1994.
14. D. Harel. Recurring dominoes: Making the higly undecidable higly understandable.
Annals of Discrete Mathematics, 24:51–72, 1985.
15. M Kaminski and C.K. Wong. The power of the "always" operator in first-order
temporal logic. *Theoretical Computer Science*, pages 271–281, 1996.
16. F. Kröger. On the interpretability of arithmetic in temporal logic. *Theoretical
Computer Science*, 73:47–61, 1990.
17. P.H. Schmitt and J. Goubault-Larrecq. A tableau system for full linear temporal
logic. Draft, available at: http://www.dyade.fr/fr/actions/vip/jgl/ltl2.ps.gz.
18. P.H. Schmitt and J. Goubault-Larrecq. A tableau system for linear-time temporal
logic. In E. Brinksma, editor, *3rd Workshop on Tools and Algorithms for the
Construction and Analysis of Systems (TACAS'97)*, LNCS. Springer Verlag, 1997.
19. P. Wolper. The tableau method for temporal logic: an overview. *Logique et Analyse*,
28:119–152, 1985.

Model Checking Games
for the Alternation-Free μ-Calculus and
Alternating Automata

Martin Leucker

Lehrstuhl für Informatik II
Aachen University of Technology, Germany
leucker@i2.informatik.rwth-aachen.de

Abstract. We relate game-based model checking and model checking via *1-letter simple weak alternating Büchi automata* (1SWABA) for the *alternation-free μ-calculus*. Game-based algorithms have the advantage that in addition to checking whether a formula is valid or not they determine a winning strategy which can be employed for explaining to the user why the formula is valid or not. 1SWABA are a restricted class of alternating Büchi automata and were defined in [BVW94]. They admit efficient automata-based model checking for CTL and the alternation-free μ-calculus. We give an interpretation for these automata in terms of game theory and show that this interpretation coincides with the notion of model checking games for CTL and the μ-calculus. Then we explain that the efficient non-emptiness procedure for 1SWABA presented in [BVW94] can also be understood as a game-based model checking procedure. Furthermore, we show that this algorithm is not only useful for checking the validity of a formula but also for determining a *winning strategy* for the winner of the underlying model checking game. In this way we obtain a linear time algorithm for model checking games.

1 Introduction

Verification of concurrent systems is one of the main research issues in Computer Science. However, more important than a correctness statement about a system is a hint why a certain feature is not satisfied. Hence, instead of *verifying*, *debugging* is more important in developing concurrent systems ([CW96]). Model Checking has been proven to be a powerful tool for verifying systems. Given a system M and a property expressed as a logical formula φ, model checking answers the question whether M is a model for φ. While every model checking algorithm answers this question, an algorithm suitable for practical applications has to have additional characteristics:

- it must be *local*, i.e., the algorithm must construct the system, usually specified by some equation system over some process algebra, on demand. In this way, even bugs in an infinite state system may be found
- it must support *debugging*

The first item is well understood and supported by several model checking algorithms. Especially automata-theoretic based model checking algorithms admit a local implementation. Translating *linear temporal logic* formulas to automata has proven to be an effective approach for implementing linear-time model-checking ([VW86,DGV99]). On the other hand, for *branching time temporal logic*, automata-theoretic techniques have long been thought to introduce an exponential blow-up for the model checking procedure. However, in [BVW94,KVW98] *1-letter simple weak alternating Büchi automata* (1SWABA) were introduced which are suitable for model-checking the logic CTL ([Eme90]) and the alternation free fragment of the μ-calculus in linear time ([Koz83,Sti92]).

Regarding the second requirement for practical model checking algorithms, it is not clear how to support a user with debugging information in general . In case of a linear time logic, there is always one run violating a property φ if φ does not hold. However, for branching time logics or the well known μ-calculus one single counterexample may not exist since you can express properties like *"there is a run such that ..."* and if such a property is not satisfied, the set of all runs of the system is a counterexample. It is obvious that a set of runs is difficult to be visualized to the user.

Stirling ([Sti95]) introduced game based model checking as a technique suitable for debugging. He related model checking to games of two players, $\exists$loise and $\forall$belard, and showed that a formula φ is valid if and only if $\exists$loise has a winning strategy, i.e., she has a chance to win the corresponding game regardless how $\forall$belard plays. A game based model checking algorithm determines a winning strategy for either $\exists$loise or $\forall$belard (depending on the validity of φ). Suppose the model checker determines that φ does not hold. If you try to find this error in your design you can play a game against a verification tool in which you are $\forall$belard and the tool is $\exists$loise. If it is your turn you can move the system into a successor state which you think will validate the formula. If it is $\exists$loise turn the system will pass into a state falsifying φ. In this way you interactively pass through the states of your system. Given the strategy, the tool wins and shows you in this way why your design is not correct.

In this paper, we argue that the notion of games and 1SWABA have strong similarities. We explain how 1SWABA can be interpreted in terms of games. It turns out that a run of a 1SWABA corresponds to plays of a corresponding game from $\exists$loise's point of view. We introduce the notion of a *co-run* of an alternating Büchi automaton representing $\forall$belard's point of view. We show that a 1SWABA has either accepting runs or co-runs. We show that a 1SWABA has an accepting run iff $\exists$loise has a winning strategy and that it has an accepting co-run iff $\forall$belard has a winning strategy for the corresponding game. Furthermore, we rephrase the algorithm for checking non-emptiness of 1SWABA from [KVW98] and show that it can also be used to determine a winning strategy for the winner of the game.

Furthermore, we show that the notion of model checking games introduced by Stirling for the alternation free fragment of Kozen's μ-calculus corresponds to the game interpretation of 1SWABA. Given a transition system and a property, we define a corresponding 1SWABA such that an accepting run (co-run) of the automaton can directly be interpreted as winning strategy for ∃loise (∀belard, resp.) of the corresponding model checking game. In this way, we obtain a 1SWABA-based, linear-time algorithm for model checking games for the alternation free fragment of the μ-calculus. Hence, it meets the best known bounds for model checking this fragment ([CS92]) and is more efficient than the game-based algorithm for the full μ-calculus by Stirling and Stevens ([SS98]) which is quadratic for the alternation-free part of the logic.

In the next section, we recall the definition of the μ-calculus and explain game based model checking. Section 3 introduces alternating Büchi automata, 1SWABA and gives their interpretation in terms of game theory. Furthermore, we explain how the algorithm presented in [KVW98] can be used to determine winning strategies. 1SWABA for the alternation free μ-calculus are introduced in Section 4 and it is shown that the notion of model checking games and games for 1SWABA coincide. Finally, we summarize the paper.

2   The μ-Calculus

This section recalls the syntax and semantics of the μ-calculus and introduces corresponding model checking games. The definitions cover the full μ-calculus. In the next section, we restrict ourselves to its alternation-free fragment.

2.1   Syntax and Semantics

Let *Var* be a set of propositional variables and $\mathcal{A}$ a set of actions. Formulae of the modal μ-calculus over *Var* in positive form as introduced by [Koz83] are defined as follows:

$$\varphi ::= \mathtt{true} \mid \mathtt{false} \mid K \mid \varphi_1 \wedge \varphi_2 \mid \varphi_1 \vee \varphi_2 \mid [K]\varphi \mid \langle K \rangle \varphi \mid \nu X.\varphi \mid \mu X.\varphi$$

where $X \in$ *Var* and K ranges over subsets of actions $\mathcal{A}$. [1]

A formula φ is *normal* if every occurrence of a binder μX or νX in φ binds a distinct variable, and no free variable X in φ is also used in a binder μX or νX. It is obvious that every formula can easily be converted into an equivalent normal formula by renaming bound variables. If a formula φ is normal, every variable X of φ *identifies* a unique subformula $\mu X.\psi$ or $\nu X.\psi$ of φ where X is a free variable of ψ.

Let $\mathcal{T} = (S, T, K, s_0)$ be a *labeled transition system* where S is a finite set of states, K a set of actions and $T \subseteq S \times K \times S$ denotes the transitions. As usual, we write $s \xrightarrow{a} t$ instead of $(s, a, t) \in T$. Furthermore, let $s_0 \in S$ be the initial state of the transition system. We employ valuations $\mathcal{V}$ mapping a variable X to a set of states $\mathcal{V}(X) \subseteq S$. Let $\mathcal{V}[X/E]$ be the valuation which is the same as

---

[1] Note that we defined a slightly generalization of Kozen's logic as sets of actions instead of single actions appear in modalities ([Sti96]). $\langle - \rangle \varphi$ is an abbreveation for $\langle \mathcal{A} \rangle \varphi$

$\mathcal{V}$ except for X when $\mathcal{V}(X) = E$. Then the satisfaction of a formula wrt. to a transition system $\mathcal{T}$ and a state $s \in S$ is inductively defined as follows:

$(\mathcal{T}, s) \models_{\mathcal{V}}$ true

$(\mathcal{T}, s) \models_{\mathcal{V}} X \quad$ iff $s \in \mathcal{V}(X)$

$(\mathcal{T}, s) \models_{\mathcal{V}} \varphi \wedge \psi$ iff $(\mathcal{T}, s) \models_{\mathcal{V}} \varphi$ and $(\mathcal{T}, s) \models_{\mathcal{V}} \psi$

$(\mathcal{T}, s) \models_{\mathcal{V}} \varphi \vee \psi$ iff $(\mathcal{T}, s) \models_{\mathcal{V}} \varphi$ or $(\mathcal{T}, s) \models_{\mathcal{V}} \psi$

$(\mathcal{T}, s) \models_{\mathcal{V}} [K]\varphi$ iff $\forall a \in K$ if $s \xrightarrow{a} t$ then $(\mathcal{T}, t) \models_{\mathcal{V}} \varphi$

$(\mathcal{T}, s) \models_{\mathcal{V}} \langle K \rangle \varphi$ iff $\exists a \in K \ s \xrightarrow{a} t$ and $(\mathcal{T}, t) \models_{\mathcal{V}} \varphi$

$(\mathcal{T}, s) \models_{\mathcal{V}} \mu X.\varphi$ iff $\exists E \subseteq 2^S, s \in E$ and $\forall t \in E : (\mathcal{T}, t) \models_{\mathcal{V}[X/E]} \varphi$

$(\mathcal{T}, s) \models_{\mathcal{V}} \nu X.\varphi$ iff $\forall E \subseteq 2^S$ if $s \notin E$ then $\exists t \in S : t \notin E$

$\qquad\qquad$ and $(\mathcal{T}, t) \models_{\mathcal{V}[X/E]} \varphi$

In the following, we abbreviate $(\mathcal{T}, s_o) \models_{\mathcal{V}} \mu X.\varphi$ by $\mathcal{T} \models \varphi$ for a formula φ without any free variables. We will use variables like $\varphi, \psi, \ldots$ for formulae, $s, t, \ldots$ for states and $a, b, \ldots$ for actions of the transition system under consideration. K will denote a set of actions. A σ is used for either μ or ν whenever the sort of the fixed point does not matter.

2.2   Games for the μ-calculus

Given a transition system $\mathcal{T} = (S, T, K)$ and a formula φ we are able to define the model checking game. Its board is the Cartesian product of the set of states and of the set of subformulae $S \times Sub(\varphi)$. The latter is defined by:

$$
\begin{aligned}
Sub(\text{true}) &:= \{\text{true}\} \\
Sub(\text{false}) &:= \{\text{false}\} \\
Sub(X) &:= \{X\} \\
Sub(\varphi \vee \psi) &:= \{\varphi \vee \psi\} \cup Sub(\varphi) \cup Sub(\psi) \\
Sub(\varphi \wedge \psi) &:= \{\varphi \wedge \psi\} \cup Sub(\varphi) \cup Sub(\psi) \\
Sub([K]\varphi) &:= \{[K]\varphi\} \cup Sub(\varphi) \\
Sub(\langle K \rangle \varphi) &:= \{\langle K \rangle \varphi\} \cup Sub(\varphi) \\
Sub(\sigma X.\varphi) &:= \{\sigma X.\varphi\} \cup Sub(\varphi)
\end{aligned}
$$

The game is played by two players, namely ∀belard (the pessimist), who wants to show that $\mathcal{T} \models \varphi$ does **not** hold, whereas ∃loise (the optimist) wants to show the opposite.

The game can be viewed as moving pebbles on both components of the game board. The idea of the playing rules is already given by the semantics of the μ-calculus. The question whether a state fulfills a formula can be answered by inspecting its successors and/or the subformulae. Therefore the model checking game is a (possibly infinite) sequence $G(s, \varphi) = C_0 \rightarrow_{p_0} C_1 \rightarrow_{p_1} C_2 \rightarrow_{p_2} \cdots$ of configurations, where $C_i \in S \times Sub(\varphi)$ for all i. The second component of a configuration C_i determines the player p_i who is to choose the next move. ∀belard does universal $\rightarrow_{\forall}$-moves, ∃loise does existential $\rightarrow_{\exists}$-moves. That means, whenever

1. $C_i = (s, \text{false})$, then the game is finished.

2. $C_i = (s, \psi_1 \wedge \psi_2)$, then $\forall$belard chooses either $\varphi = \psi_1$ or $\varphi = \psi_2$ and $C_{i+1} = (s, \varphi)$.
3. $C_i = (s, [K]\psi)$, then $\forall$belard chooses a transition $s \xrightarrow{a} t$ with an action $a \in K$ and $C_{i+1} = (t, \psi)$.
4. $C_i = (s, \nu X.\psi)$, then $C_{i+1} = (s, \psi)$. [2]
5. $C_i = (s, \text{true})$, then the game is finished.
6. $C_i = (s, \psi_1 \vee \psi_2)$, then $\exists$loise chooses either $\varphi = \psi_1$ or $\varphi = \psi_2$ and $C_{i+1} = (s, \varphi)$.
7. $C_i = (s, \langle K \rangle \psi)$, then $\exists$loise chooses a transition $s \xrightarrow{a} t$ with an action $a \in K$ and $C_{i+1} = (t, \psi)$.
8. $C_i = (s, \mu X.\psi)$, then $C_{i+1} = (s, \psi)$. [2]
9. $C_i = (s, X)$ and $\varphi = \sigma X.\psi$ is the fixed point formula belonging to X, then $C_{i+1} = (s, \varphi)$.

As the moves 1,4,5,8 and 9 are deterministic no player needs to be charged with them. With regard to the winning strategies and the algorithm we will speak of $\forall$belard-moves in cases 1–4 and 9 if $\sigma = \mu$, and $\exists$loise-moves in all other cases.

Unlike traditional Ehrenfeucht-Fraïssé games the players need not move alternately. The next turn is not determined by the player, but by the current subformula φ.

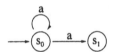

Fig. 1. A small transition system

Let us consider an example. We present three possible plays for the game given by the transition system in Figure 1 and the formula $\varphi = \mu X.\langle - \rangle X \vee \langle a \rangle \text{true}$:[3]

- $G_1(s_0, \varphi) = (s_0, \varphi) \rightarrow_\exists (s_0, \langle - \rangle X \vee \langle a \rangle \text{true})$
  $\rightarrow_\exists (s_0, \langle a \rangle \text{true})$
  $\rightarrow_\exists (s_1, \text{true})$
- $G_2(s_0, \varphi) = (s_0, \varphi) \rightarrow_\exists (s_0, \langle - \rangle X \vee \langle a \rangle \text{true})$
  $\rightarrow_\exists (s_0, \langle - \rangle X)$
  $\rightarrow_\exists (s_1, X)$
  $\rightarrow_\forall (s_1, \varphi)$
  $\rightarrow_\forall (s_1, \langle - \rangle X \vee \langle a \rangle \text{true})$
  $\rightarrow_\exists (s_1, \langle a \rangle \text{true})$

---

[2] Note that in [Sti97] Stirling uses slightly different rules for the unwinding of the fixed point formulae.

[3] φ expresses the possibility to do an a-action somewhen.

$$
\begin{aligned}
- \; G_3(s_0,\varphi) = (s_0,\varphi) \;\;\; &\to_\exists \;\; (s_0, \langle - \rangle X \vee \langle a \rangle \mathtt{true}) \\
&\to_\exists \;\; (s_0, \langle - \rangle X) \\
&\to_\exists \;\; (s_0, X) \\
&\to_\forall \;\; (s_0, \varphi) \\
&\to_\exists \;\; \ldots .
\end{aligned}
$$

It is clear that the first play is won by ∃loise because she forced it to end in a true-configuration. It is also clear that ∀belard wins G_2, because ∃loise became stuck as there is no a-action possible in state s_1.

The question is now: Who wins the third game that has an infinite loop? As the game contains infinitely many X-configurations it is equivalent to an infinite unfolding of a least fixed point formula. That means the fixed point could not be computed (otherwise the game should be of finite length). Least fixed points are special (second order) ∃-quantifiers. So ∃loise—who should do correct existential moves—failed. Therefore ∀belard wins G_3.

In general, ∀belard wins a game G iff

- $G = C_0, \ldots, C_n$ and $C_n = (s, \mathtt{false})$ for any state s.
- $G = C_0, \ldots, C_n$ and $C_n = (s, \langle K \rangle \varphi)$ and $\not\exists t \; : \; s \xrightarrow{a} t$ for any $a \in K$.
- $G = C_0, \ldots$ has infinite length and the outermost fixed point which is un-wound infinitely often is a μ-fixed point.

Dually, ∃loise wins a game G, iff

- $G = C_0, \ldots, C_n$ and $C_n = (s, \mathtt{true})$ for any state s.
- $G = C_0, \ldots, C_n$ and $C_n = (s, [K] \varphi)$ and $\not\exists t \; : \; s \xrightarrow{a} t$ for any $a \in K$.
- $G = C_0, \ldots$ has infinite length and the outermost fixed point which is un-wound infinitely often is a ν-fixed point.

The example showed that a game given by a transition system and a formula can have several plays and these need not have the same winner. In order to use the games for model checking we must avoid such variant plays. (Note that ∃loise can always win every game for our example if she moves as it was done in G_1.) That leads to the notion of a winning strategy. A *strategy* is a set of rules for a Player p telling her or him how to move in the current configuration. A *winning strategy* is a set of rules allowing p to win every game if she/he plays regarding the rules. The relation between winning strategies and model checking is expressed by the following theorem. It means that the model checking problem for the μ-calculus is equivalent to finding a winning strategy for one of the players.

Theorem 1 ([Sti96]). *Let T be a transition system with starting state s and let φ be a μ-calculus formula.*

1. $(T,s) \models \varphi \Rightarrow$ *∃loise has a winning strategy for every game starting at (s,φ).*
2. $(T,s) \not\models \varphi \Rightarrow$ *∀belard has a winning strategy for every game starting at (s,φ).*

In Section 4 we will present an algorithm for determining a winning strategy for either ∃loise or ∀belard for model checking games for the alternation free μ-calculus. As a corollary, we obtain a proof for the last theorem (restricted to formulas of the alternation free fragment).

All possible plays of a game are captured in the *game graph*. It is the graph which nodes are the elements of the game board and which arrows are the possible moves of the players. A game graph is shown in Figure 2 (Section 4).

In the following, we restrict ourselves to the alternation free μ-calculus which is the sublogic of the μ-calculus such that no subformula ψ of a formula φ contains both a free variable X bound by a μ in φ as well as a free variable Y bound by a ν in φ.

3 Alternating Büchi Automata

Nondeterminism gives an automaton the power of existential choices: A word w is accepted by an automaton iff there exists an accepting run on w. Alternation gives a machine the power of universal choices and was studied in [BL80,CKS81] (in the context of automata). In this section we recall the notion of alternating automata along the lines of [Var96] where alternating Büchi automata are used for model checking LTL. For an introduction to Büchi automata we refer to [Tho90].

For a finite set X of variables let $\mathcal{B}^+(X)$ be the set of *positive Boolean formulas* over X, i.e., the smallest set such that

- $X \subseteq \mathcal{B}^+(X)$
- $\texttt{true}, \texttt{false} \in \mathcal{B}^+(X)$
- $\varphi, \psi \in \mathcal{B}^+(X) \Rightarrow \varphi \wedge \psi \in \mathcal{B}^+(X), \varphi \vee \psi \in \mathcal{B}^+(X)$

The dual of a formula $\varphi \in \mathcal{B}^+(X)$ denoted by $\overline{\varphi}$ is the formula where $\texttt{false}$ is replaced by $\texttt{true}$, $\texttt{true}$ by $\texttt{false}$, $\vee$ by $\wedge$ and $\wedge$ by $\vee$.

We say that a set $Y \subseteq X$ *satisfies* a formula $\varphi \in \mathcal{B}^+(X)$ ($Y \models \varphi$) iff φ evaluates to *true* when the variables in Y are assigned to *true* and the members of $X \backslash Y$ are assigned to *false*. For example, $\{q_1, q_3\}$ as well as $\{q_1, q_4\}$ satisfy the formula $(q_1 \vee q_2) \wedge (q_3 \vee q_4)$.

Let us consider a Büchi automaton (BA). For a state q and an action a let $\{q_1, \ldots, q_k\} = \{q' \mid q \xrightarrow{a} q'\}$ be the set of possible next states for (q, a). The key idea for alternation is to describe the nondeterminism by the formula $q_1 \vee \cdots \vee q_k \in \mathcal{B}^+(Q)$. Hence, we write $q \xrightarrow{a} q_1 \vee \cdots \vee q_k$. If $k = 0$ we write $q \xrightarrow{a} \texttt{false}$. An alternation is introduced by allowing an arbitrary formula of $\mathcal{B}^+(Q)$. Let us be more precise:

Definition 1. *An* Alternating Büchi Automaton *(ABA) over an alphabet Σ is a tuple $\mathcal{A} = (Q, \delta, q_0, \mathcal{F})$ such that Q is a finite nonempty set of states, $q_0 \in Q$ is the initial state, $\mathcal{F} \subseteq Q$ is a set of accepting states and $\delta : Q \times \Sigma \to \mathcal{B}^+(Q)$ is the transition function.*

Because of universal quantification a run is no longer a sequence but a tree. A Q-*labeled tree* τ is a pair (t, T) such that t is a tree and $T : nodes(t) \to Q$. As T is not necessarily one to one we identify nodes in the following canonical way: The root is marked with ε, if a node s is marked with w then a child s' labeled with q is marked with wq.

For a node s let $|s|$ denote its *height*, i.e., $|\varepsilon| = 0$, $|wq| = |w| + 1$. A branch of τ is a maximal sequence $\beta = s_0, s_1, \ldots$ of nodes of τ such that s_0 is the root of τ and s_i is the father of s_{i+1}, $i \in \mathbb{N}$. The *word induced by* β (for short β's word) is the sequence of labels of β, i.e., the sequence $T(s_0), T(s_1), \ldots$

A *run* of an alternating BA $\mathcal{A} = (Q, \delta, q_0, \mathcal{F})$ on a word $w = a_0 a_1 \ldots$ is a (possibly infinite) Q-labeled tree τ such that $T(\varepsilon) = q_0$ and the following holds:

if x is a node with $|x| = i$, $T(x) = q$ and $\delta(q, a_i) = \varphi$ then either $\varphi \in \{\texttt{true}, \texttt{false}\}$ and x has no children or x has k children $x_1, \ldots, x_k$ for some $k \leq |Q|$ and $\{T(x_1), \ldots, T(x_k)\}$ satisfies φ.

The run τ is *accepting* if every finite branch ends on $\texttt{true}$ (i.e., $\delta(T(x), a_i) = \texttt{true}$ where x denotes the maximum element of the branch wrt. the height and i denotes its height) and every infinite branch of τ hits an element of $\mathcal{F}$ infinitely often.

It is obvious that every Büchi automaton can be turned into an equivalent (wrt. to the accepted language) alternating Büchi automaton in the way described above. The converse is also true and is described for example in [Var96]. However, the construction involves an exponential blow up. Hence, checking for the emptiness of the language of an ABA by transforming it into an equivalent BA is not feasible for real world model checking applications. However, for a subclass of ABAs suitable for our needs a linear non-emptiness decision procedure can be given.

An ABA $\mathcal{A} = (Q, \delta, q_0, \mathcal{F})$ over an alphabet Σ is called *1-letter* iff the alphabet contains just one letter, i.e., $|\Sigma| = 1$. A formula $\varphi \in \mathcal{B}^+(X)$ is *simple* if it is either atomic, $\texttt{true}$, $\texttt{false}$ or is either a conjunction or disjunction of the variables of X. That means it has the form $x_1 * \cdots * x_k$ where $* \in \{\vee, \wedge\}$ and $x_i \in X$. An ABA is *simple* if all its transitions are simple.

An ABA is called *weak* iff there exists a partition of Q into disjoint sets $Q_1, \ldots, Q_m$ such that for each set Q_i, either $Q_i \subseteq \mathcal{F}$, in which case Q_i is an *accepting set*, or $Q_i \cap \mathcal{F} = \emptyset$, in which case Q_i is a *rejecting* set. In addition, there exists a partial order $\leq$ on the collection of the Q_i's such that for every $q \in Q_i$ and $q' \in Q_j$ for which q' occurs in $\delta(q, a)$ for some $a \in \Sigma$, we have $Q_j \leq Q_i$. Thus, transitions from a state in Q_i lead to states in either the same Q_i or a lower one. It follows that every infinite path of a run of a weak ABA ultimately gets "trapped" within some Q_i. The path then satisfies the acceptance condition if and only if Q_i is an accepting set. Indeed, a run visits infinitely many states in $\mathcal{F}$ iff it gets trapped in an accepting set.

In the following, we will take a closer look on 1-letter simple weak alternating Büchi automata (1SWABA) which were first considered in [BVW94]. While on the first sight, they seem to be a quite unnatural restriction of ABA, they have a nice interpretation in terms of games. Before we come to this, we need a few basic insights of 1SWABA.

A *co-run* of an ABA $\mathcal{A} = (Q, \delta, q_0, \mathcal{F})$ on a word $w = a_0 a_1 \ldots$ is a (possibly infinite) Q-labeled tree τ such that $T(\varepsilon) = q_0$ and the following holds:

if $|x| = i$, $T(x) = q$ and $\delta(q, a_i) = \varphi$ then either $\varphi \in \{\text{true}, \text{false}\}$ and x has no children or x has k children $x_1, \ldots, x_k$ for some $k \leq |Q|$ and $\{T(x_1), \ldots, T(x_k)\}$ satisfies $\overline{\varphi}$ (the dual of φ).

The co-run is *accepting* if every finite branch ends on false (i.e., $\delta(T(x), a_i) = \text{false}$ where x denotes the maximum element of the branch and i denotes its height) and every infinite branch of τ does *not* hit an element of $\mathcal{F}$ infinitively often.

Let $\Sigma = \{a\}$. We will show in the following that a 1SWABA has an accepting run if and only if has no accepting co-run. Then it is obvious that the language accepted by a 1SWABA is either empty or $\{a^\omega\}$ and the co-language is $\{a^\omega\}$ or empty (resp.) where the *co-language* of a 1SWABA consists of the words of Σ^ω for which an accepting co-run exists. Hence, the most interesting question for 1SWABA is whether it accepts a word or not, i.e., whether is has an accepting run or an accepting co-run on a^ω.

However, before we will present an algorithm for checking the emptiness we are going to interpret 1SWABA $\mathcal{A} = (Q, \delta, q_0, \mathcal{F})$ over $\{a\}$ in terms of games. As in the last section, let ∃loise be the optimist and ∀belard the pessimist. ∃loise wants to show that $\mathcal{A}$ accepts a^ω while ∀belard wants to show the contrary. Hence, ∀belard wants to show that there is an accepting co-run. What are the rules of the game? The *board* consists of Q. A *configuration* is a state $q \in Q$. Consider $\varphi = \delta(q, a)$. If $\varphi = \text{true}$ then ∃loise has won. Dually, if $\varphi = \text{false}$ ∀belard has won. If $\varphi = q_1 \vee \cdots \vee q_k$ ∃loise must pass the pebble to one of the q_i. Dually, if $\varphi = q_1 \wedge \cdots \wedge q_k$ then ∀belard has to pass the pebble to one of the q_i.[4] If the play is going on forever, then ∃loise wins if she passes infinitively many $q \in \mathcal{F}$. Otherwise, ∀belard wins.

Now we are going to show that accepting runs (co-runs) "capture" winning strategies for ∃loise (∀belard). Suppose that there is an accepting run for a^ω. Then, every branch of the run can be understood as a play which ∃loise wins. It is obvious that every sequence of configurations of every branch of an accepting run is a play according to the rules. Furthermore, if the branch is finite, it corresponds to a finite play. Since the run was accepting it ends on true. Hence, ∃loise has won. If the branch is infinite, the run is accepting only if infinitively many final states are visited. So again ∃loise wins. If there is an accepting co-run, every branch can also be understood as a play. However, these plays are won by ∀belard. Either the branch is finite in which case it ends on false. Then ∀belard wins. If the branch is infinite, the accepting condition requires to visit states from $\mathcal{F}$ only finitely often. Hence, ∀belard wins also these plays.

More specifically, a run on a^ω can be understood as a winning tree for ∃loise and a co-run can be understood as a winning tree for ∀belard. A *winning tree*

---

[4] We do not bother ourselves with discussing who has to move for the case $k = 1$

for a player P is a tree, such that the nodes are labeled by configurations of the game and every configuration q is a parent of q' only if there is a possible move from q to q'. Furthermore, the root is labeled by the initial configuration of the game. In addition, if q is a configuration and $q_1, \ldots, q_k$ are all possible moves of the opponent then q has at least k children labeled by $q_1, \ldots, q_k$ (and every label occurs). Hence, a winning tree for player P subsumes all possible moves of the opponent.

Suppose that there is an accepting run on a^ω. Then ∀belard has the possibility to choose in a configuration q with $\delta(q,a) = q_1 \wedge \cdots \wedge q_k$ how to proceed. However, due to the definition of a run there are at least k successors labeled by $q_1, \ldots, q_k$ and for every successor it either ends by true or it is a branch visiting a final state infinitely often. Hence, given an accepting run for a^ω ∃loise has a winning strategy by playing according to an arbitrary branch of the tree. Dually, suppose that there is an accepting co-run for a^ω. Then ∃loise has the possibility to choose in a configuration q with $\delta(q,a) = \varphi$ with $\varphi = q_1 \vee \cdots \vee q_k$ how to proceed. However, due to the definition of a co-run, there are at least k successors labeled by $q_1, \ldots, q_k$ and for every successor it either ends by false or it is a branch visiting every final state only finitely often. Hence, ∀belard has a winning strategy by playing according to an arbitrary branch of the tree.

On the other hand, a winning strategy for ∃loise (∀belard) gives rise to an accepting run (co-run) on a^ω. Suppose that ∃loise has a winning strategy for the game starting in the initial configuration q_0. By considering the possible moves of ∀belard and ∃loise a run can be defined inductively. If the game ends in a configuration q then $\delta(q,a) =$ true. Then a new node labeled by true is added as a child for q in the run tree. If it is ∀belard's turn in the configuration q let $\{q_1, \ldots, q_k\}$ be the possible moves. This means that $\delta(q,a) = q_1 \wedge \cdots \wedge q_k$. New nodes labeled by q_1 to q_k can be added as children for q in the run and the configurations $q_1 \ldots q_k$ are considered inductively. Note that $\{q_1, \ldots, q_k\}$ satisfies $\delta(q,a)$. If it is ∃loise's turn in the configuration q then her winning strategy identifies a move q'. Add the new node labeled by q' as a child for q. Because of the rules of the game, this includes that $\{q'\}$ satisfies $\delta(q,a)$. Note that the run defined in this way is well-defined. Furthermore, it is accepting. Every finite branch ends on true. Every infinite branch captures a possible game where ∃loise plays according to her winning strategy. So she wins which means that a final state is passed infinitely often. The dual argumentation shows that a winning strategy for ∀belard gives rise to a co-run for the automaton.

Now we are going to give a sketch of an algorithm which decides whether the language of a 1SWABA $\mathcal{A}$ is empty or not. Hence, it determines whether there is a run or a co-run for a^ω. More specifically, it will construct a graph whose nodes are the states of $\mathcal{A}$ (or in terms of games, the possible configurations of the game). It labels a state q by *green* or *red* depending on whether there is a winning strategy for ∃loise or ∀belard for a game beginning in q. In terms of automata, this means that there is an accepting run or co-run for the automaton starting in q. Furthermore, if the initial configuration of the graph is labeled by *green* then unwinding (certain) green nodes of the graph yields an accepting run (or in terms of games a winning tree for ∃loise). Dually, if the initial node is labeled by *red* then unwinding of (certain) red nodes of the graph yield an accepting co-run (or in terms of games a winning tree for ∀belard). Checking whether there is either an accepting run or an accepting co-run is reduced to checking whether the initial state is labeled by *green* or *red*.

Furthermore, the labeling can be determined in linear time wrt. to the number of states of the automaton ([BVW94]). However, we restrict ourself to showing the idea of the algorithm. We refer to [BVW94] where the emptiness problem for 1SWABA is solved by such a labeling algorithm.

Let (Q, E, l) be the graph where the nodes are the states of the automaton $\mathcal{A}$ and $(q, q') \in E \subseteq Q \times Q$ iff q to q' is a possible move of the game. Furthermore, let $l : Q \to \{\exists\text{loise}, \forall\text{belard}\}$ be the mapping telling whether in configuration q it is ∃loise's turn or ∀belard's, i.e., $\delta(q, a)$ is a disjunction or a conjunction, resp.

As $\mathcal{A}$ is weak, there exists a partition of Q into disjoint sets Q_i such that for each set Q_i, either $Q_i \subseteq \mathcal{F}$, in which case Q_i is an *accepting set*, or $Q_i \cap \mathcal{F} = \emptyset$, in which case Q_i is a *rejecting* set. Furthermore there exists a partial order $\leq$ on the Q_i such that for every $q \in Q_i$ and $q' \in Q_j$ for which q' occurs in $\delta(q, a)$, we have that $Q_j \leq Q_i$. Thus, transitions from a state in Q_i lead to states in either the same Q_i or a lower one. Without loss of generality, states q for which $\delta(q, a) = \text{true}$ ($\delta(q, a) = \text{false}$) form a singleton set which is accepting (rejecting, resp.) and least elements wrt. the partial order.

The graph can be colored by processing the Q_i up according to the partial order. To make the algorithm deterministic, enlarge the partial order on the Q_i to a total order. Let Q_i be minimal wrt. to $\leq$. Hence, every transition for every state of Q_i leads to Q_i. If Q_i is accepting its nodes are labeled by *green* otherwise by *red*. In particular, if Q_i only consists of a state q with $\delta(q, a) = \text{true}$ (false) it is labeled by *green* (*red*).

Let Q_j be the next set of states wrt. to the total order. Then all states in $Q_i \leq Q_j$ are already colored by either *red* or *green*. Now we distinguish two cases. Suppose Q_j is a rejecting set. If there is a node x in which it is ∃loise's turn leading to a smaller component Q_i which is labeled by *green* then all the nodes are labeled by *green*. Otherwise ∃loise has no possibility to successfully leave the rejecting set and all the nodes are colored by *red*. If Q_j is an accepting set, one has to look for a node leading to a smaller, *red*-colored component for which it is ∀belard's turn. Then the component is colored by *red*, otherwise by *green*.

In this way, all nodes can be colored by either *green* or *red*. Furthermore, it is obvious that a node q is labeled by *green* iff ∃loise has a winning strategy for the play beginning in q. Dually, a node is labeled by *red* if and only if ∀belard has a winning strategy for the play beginning in q. Hence, we have shown that a 1SWABA has either an accepting run or an accepting co-run. If the initial node of the colored graph is labeled by *green* then the automaton has an accepting run otherwise an accepting co-run. Furthermore, suppose the automaton has an accepting run. Then one run can be obtained employing the colored graph in the following way. We start with the initial node which is labeled by *green*. Given a node x in the run tree of the graph we add all successors of x iff it is Vbelard's turn. If it Vbelard's turn, then $\delta(x,a)$ is a conjunction and we have to add all successors of x to satisfy this conjunction. Since all the successors are labeled by *green* (otherwise x wouldn't be *green*), ∃loise has still the chance to win the play. In other words, every branch still can be augmented to an accepting branch. Now, suppose it is ∃loise's turn in a node x. Hence $\delta(x,a) = \varphi$ is a disjunction and every successor satisfies φ. Now it is ∃loise's duty to choose a suitable successor. Of course, she has to take a child labeled by *green*. If x is a member of a rejecting set, then ∃loise must not take a successor of the same component but one x' of a smaller component. Note that because of the labeling algorithm such a node must exist. Hence, every branch of the subtree beginning at x' ends in an accepting set. That means, either is contains a node labeled by true or the nodes are a subset of $\mathcal{F}$. Hence, the run is accepting. The dual procedure identifies a co-run, if the initial node is labeled by *red*.

In the next section we are going to define a 1SWABA for a given transition system and a formula of the alternation free fragment of the μ-calculus.

4   1SWABA for Model Checking the Alternation Free μ-Calculus

In this section, we will show that model checking games can be understood as 1-letter weak simple alternating Büchi automata. Given a transition system $\mathcal{T} = (S, T, K, s_0)$ and a formula φ of the alternation free μ-calculus, we define by employing the rules of the corresponding model checking game a 1SWABA $\mathcal{A}$ such that the language of this automaton is empty if and only if Vbelard has a winning strategy for $G(s_0, \varphi)$. Furthermore, a corresponding co-run is a winning tree for Vbelard. Dually, if the language of the automaton is non-empty then ∃loise has a winning strategy and a corresponding run is a winning tree for her. As a corollary, this shows Theorem 1 restricted to the alternation free fragment of the μ-calculus.

Let the states of $\mathcal{A}$ be the Cartesian product of S and $Sub(\varphi)$. Let $\Sigma = \{a\}$ for an arbitrary a. Let δ be defined in the following way:[5]

- $\delta(s, \text{false}) = \text{false}$
- $\delta(s, \psi_1 \wedge \psi_2) = (s, \psi_1) \wedge (s, \psi_2)$
- $\delta(s, [K]\psi) = (s_1, \psi) \wedge \cdots \wedge (s_k, \psi)$ where $\{s_1, \ldots, s_k\} = \{t \mid s \xrightarrow{a} t$ with an action $a \in K\}$
- $\delta(s, \nu X.\psi) = (s, \psi)$
- $\delta(s, \text{true}) = \text{true}$
- $\delta(s, \psi_1 \vee \psi_2) = (s, \psi_1) \vee (s, \psi_2)$
- $\delta(s, \langle K \rangle \psi) = (s_1, \psi) \vee \cdots \vee (s_k, \psi)$ where $\{s_1, \ldots, s_k\} = \{t \mid s \xrightarrow{a} t$ with an action $a \in K\}$
- $\delta(s, \mu X.\psi) = (s, \psi)$

---
[5] For notational convenience we write $\delta(s, \varphi) = \psi$ instead of $\delta((s, \varphi), a) = \psi$

- $\delta(s, X) = (s, \psi')$ where $\psi' = \sigma X.\psi$ is the fixed point formula belonging to X[6]

Note that we identify an empty conjunction with **true** and an empty disjunction with **false**.

It is obvious that $\mathcal{A}$ is a 1-letter and simple alternating automaton. To show that $\mathcal{A}$ is also weak, we define a partition of the states Q into disjoint sets Q_i and a partial order over these sets. Therefore, we first define a quasi ordering $\leq_q$ on $S \times Sub(\varphi)$ which is the reflexive and transitive closure of the edge relation in the game graph. More formally: Let $\leq_e \subseteq S \times Sub(\varphi)$ be defined by $(s, \psi) \leq_e (s', \psi')$ iff

- $s = s'$ and $\psi \in Sub(\psi')$[7] or
- $s \overset{a}{\to} s'$ for an $a \in K$ and $\psi = \langle K \rangle \psi'$ or $\psi = [K]\psi'$.

Furthermore, let $\leq_q$ be the quasi ordering obtained as the reflexive and transitive closure of $\leq_e$. Let $\equiv \subseteq S \times Sub(\varphi)$ be defined in a natural way by $(s, \varphi) \equiv (s', \varphi')$ iff $(s, \varphi) \leq_q (s', \varphi')$ and $(s', \varphi') \leq_q (s, \varphi)$. Then the Q_i are given by the equivalence classes of $S \times Sub(\varphi)$ wrt. $\equiv$ and the partial order $\leq$ can be defined as $\leq_q / \equiv$.

We define $\mathcal{F}$ to be the set of states $\{q \in S \times Sub(\varphi) \mid q \equiv (s, \nu X.\psi)$ for suitable $s \in S$ and $\psi \in Sub(\varphi)\}$. Then in particular, each set is either contained in $\mathcal{F}$ or is disjoint from $\mathcal{F}$.

Hence, we have constructed a 1SWABA. Furthermore, it is obvious that the game interpretation of this automaton coincides with model checking games introduced in Section 2. This allows us to employ the algorithm of the last section for obtaining a winning strategy and a winning tree for either $\exists$loise or $\forall$belard.

Note that the same construction can also be carried out for formulas of the full μ-calculus. However, for the full μ-calculus the plays obtained by considering the accepting runs of the corresponding automaton differ from the games won be $\exists$loise.

Figure 2 shows the graph constructed by the non-emptiness algorithm from the last section for the transition system in Figure 1 and the formula $\varphi = \mu X. \langle - \rangle X \vee \langle a \rangle \mathbf{true}$. The nodes framed with a box are colored by *green* while the nodes framed with a circle are colored by *red*.

5   Conclusion

In this paper, we argued for the need of game based model checking algorithms for practical verification tools since they admit a suitable form for debugging concurrent systems. We presented an interpretation of 1-letter simple weak alternating Büchi automata (1SWABA) in terms of games. We explained that

---

[6] Remember that we restricted ourselves to *normal* formulas. So every variable X identifies a unique subformula $\sigma X.\psi$ of φ.

[7] here let $\sigma X.\psi$ be an element of $Sub(X)$ where $\sigma X.\psi$ is the formula identified by X

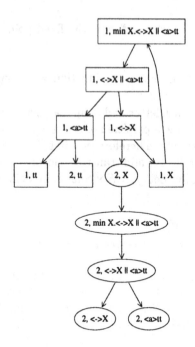

Fig. 2. A colored game graph

model checking games for the alternation free fragment of the μ-calculus coincide with the game interpretation of 1SWABA. In this way, the well explained non-emptiness proof for 1SWABA given in [KVW98] can be used to check whether either ∃loise or ∀belard has a winning strategy for the model checking game. Furthermore, we showed that the algorithm from [KVW98] is not only suitable for checking which player has a winning strategy but can easily be extended to obtain a winning strategy.

The algorithm is integrated in the verification platform TRUTH ([LLNT99]) with a text-based possibility to play model checking games. Truth is designed to be a test-bed for new algorithms and model checking techniques as well as a tool to be used for educating students in the area of formal verification. The algorithm has proven to be useful for debugging concurrent systems. At the moment, we are also working on a graphical front end for playing model-checking games.

References

[BL80]   J.A. Brzozowski and E. Leiss. On equations for regular languages, finite automata, and sequential networks. *Theoret. Comp. Sci.*, 10:19–35, 1980.

[BVW94] O. Bernholtz, M.Y. Vardi, and P. Wolper. An automata–theoretic approach to branching–time model checking. In D.L. Dill, editor, *Proceedings of the 6th International Conference on Computer–Aided Verification (CAV'94)*, volume 818 of *LNCS*, pages 142–155. Springer–Verlag, 1994.

[CKS81]   Ashok K. Chandra, Dexter C. Kozen, and Larry J. Stockmeyer. Alternation. *Journal of the ACM*, 28(1):114–133, January 1981.

[CS92]   R. Cleaveland and B. Steffen. A linear–time model–checking algorithm for the alternation–free modal mu–calculus. In Kim G. Larsen and Arne Skou, editors, *Proceedings of Computer Aided Verification (CAV '91)*, volume 575 of *LNCS*, pages 48–58, Berlin, Germany, July 1992. Springer.

[CW96]   E. M. Clarke and J. M. Wing. Formal methods: State of the art and future directions. Technical Report CMU-CS-96-178, Carnegie Mellon University (CMU), September 1996. URL: ftp://reports.adm.cs.cmu.edu/usr/anon/1996/CMU-CS-96-178.ps.

[DGV99]   M. Daniele, F. Giunchiglia, and M. Y. Vardi. Improved automata generation for linear temporal logic. In *Proc. of 11th Inter. Conf. on Computer Aided Verification, CAV '99*, 1999.

[Eme90]   E. A. Emerson. Temporal and modal logic. In J. van Leeuwen, editor, *Handbook of Theoretical Computer Science*, volume B: Formal Models and Semantics, chapter 14, pages 996–1072. Elsevier Science Publishers B.V.: Amsterdam, The Netherlands, New York, N.Y., 1990.

[Koz83]   Dexter Kozen. Results on the propositional mu-calculus. *Theoretical Computer Science*, 27:333–354, December 1983.

[KVW98]   O. Kupferman, M.Y. Vardi, and P. Wolper. An automata–theoretic approach to branching–time model checking. Full version of CAV'94 paper, 1998, URL: http://www.cs.rice.edu/~vardi/papers/cav94rj.ps.gz.

[LLNT99] M. Lange, M. Leucker, T. Noll, and S. Tobies. Truth – a verification platform for concurrent systems. In *Tool Support for System Specification, Development, and Verification*, Advances in Computing Science. Springer-Verlag Wien New York, 1999.

[SS98]   Perdita Stevens and Colin Stirling. Practical model-checking using games. In B. Steffen, editor, *Proceedings of 4th International Conference on Tools and algorithms for the construction and analysis of systems (TACAS'98)*, volume 1384 of *LNCS*, pages 85–101, New York, NY, USA, 1998. Springer.

[Sti92]   Stirling, C. Modal and temporal logics. In *Handbook of Logic in Computer Science*, volume 2, pages 477–563. Clarendon Press, Oxford, 1992.

[Sti95]   C. Stirling. Local model checking games. In Insup Lee and Scott A. Smolka, editors, *Proceedings of the 6th International Conference on Concurrency Theory (CONCUR'95)*, volume 962 of *LNCS*, pages 1–11, Berlin, GER, August 1995. Springer.

[Sti96]   C. Stirling. Games for bisimulation and model checking, July 1996. Notes for Mathfit Workshop on finite model theory, University of Wales, Swansea,, URL: http://www.dcs.ed.ac.uk/home/cps/mfit.ps.

[Sti97]   C. Stirling. Games for bisimulation and model checking, June 1997. Notes for Mathfit instructional meeting on games and computation, Edinburgh, URL: http://www.dcs.ed.ac.uk/home/cps/mathfit.ps.

[Tho90]   Wolfgang Thomas. Automata on infinite objects. In J. van Leeuwen, editor, *Handbook of Theoretical Computer Science*, chapter 4, pages 133–191. Elsevier Science Publishers B. V., 1990.

[Var96]   Moshe Y. Vardi. *An Automata-Theoretic Approach to Linear Temporal Logic*, volume 1043 of *LNCS*, pages 238–266. Springer, 1996.

[VW86]   M. Y. Vardi and P. Wolper. An automata-theoretic approach to automatic program verification. In *Symposium on Logic in Computer Science (LICS '86)*, pages 332–345, Washington, D.C., USA, June 1986. IEEE Computer Society Press.

Animating TLA Specifications *

Yassine Mokhtari[1] and Stephan Merz[2]

[1] LORIA-UMR n°7503, Université Henri Poincaré, Nancy, France
[2] Institut für Informatik, Universität München, Germany
mokhtari@loria.fr, merz@informatik.uni-muenchen.de

Abstract. TLA (the Temporal Logic of Actions) is a linear temporal logic for specifying and reasoning about reactive systems. We define a subset of TLA whose formulas are amenable to validation by animation, with the intent to facilitate the communication between domain and solution experts in the design of reactive systems.

1 Introduction

The Temporal Logic of Actions (TLA) has been proposed by Lamport [21] for the specification and verification of reactive and concurrent systems. TLA models describe infinite sequences of states, called behaviors, that correspond to the execution of the system being specified. System specifications in TLA are usually written in a canonical form, which consists of specifying the initial states, the possible moves of the system, and supplementary fairness properties. Because such specifications are akin to the descriptions of automata and often have a strongly operational flavor, it is tempting to take such a formula and "let it run". In this paper, we define an interpreter algorithm for a suitable subset of TLA. The interpreter generates (finite) runs of the system described by the specification, which can thus be validated by the user.

For reasons of complexity, it is impossible to animate an arbitrary first-order TLA specification; even the satisfiability problem for that logic is Σ_1^1-complete. Our restrictions concern the syntactic form of specifications, which ensure that finite models can be generated incrementally. They do not constrain the domains of system variables or restrict the non-determinism inherent in a specification, which is important in the realm of reactive systems.

In contrast, model checking techniques allow to exhaustively analyse the (infinite) runs of finite-state systems. It is generally agreed that the development of reactive systems benefits from the use of both animation for the initial modelling phase, complemented by model checking of system abstractions for the verification of crucial system components.

The organization of the paper is as follows: in sections 2 and 3 we discuss the overall role of animation for system development, illustrating its purpose at the hand of a simple example, and discuss executable temporal logics. Section 4 constitutes the main body of this paper; we there define the syntax and semantics of an executable

---

* This work was partly supported by a grant from DAAD and APAPE under the PROCOPE program.

subset of TLA, give the interpreter algorithm, and prove it sound and complete with respect to the logical semantics. Section 5 shows how fairness conditions can be taken into account and briefly describes our current prototype implementation, which also contains a model checking component. Finally, section 6 concludes by summarizing our results and comparing them to related work.

2   The role of animation

Requirements capture and analysis is the first step in typical lifecycle models of software engineering. It is the process of identifying and recording the needs of a customer. It fulfills two different roles:

- The customer must be convinced that the requirements are completely understood and recorded.
- The designer must be able to use the requirements to produce a structure around which formal reasoning and an implementation can be developed.

The success of this step depends on the communication between customer and designer. In general, the analysis and requirements document constitutes the interface between *problem domain experts* with little knowledge of computers and *solution domain professionals* with little knowledge of the problem and a large understanding of computer systems and techniques. Thus, the communication should be oriented towards the customer: the formal model of requirements should be understood and communicated to the customer. Validation is the key technique that supports this communication.

In the formal methods community, the validation of formal specifications is mainly based on either (automatic or computer-supported interactive) proof or on animation, that is, execution. The verification of TLA specifications has been amply studied; we focus here on validation by animation. Hoare [16] has studied the feasibility of animating specifications. Emphasizing the tradeoff between expressiveness of the formal notations and their animation, he has initiated a lively debate in the community. Hayes and Jones [17] represent one side of this debate; they explain that specifications need not be executable by considering various problems involving different formal notations. They argue that the expressiveness should not be sacrificed in favor of animation since a formal specification is intended for "human consumption", whereas the additional requirements of executability may easily lead to over-specification. Consequently, the implementor may be tempted to follow the algorithmic structure of the executable specification. Moreover, Hayes and Jones argue that validation is achieved by proof rather than by animation, and that animation techniques should be restricted to particular problems such as the design of user interfaces [15]. As an exponent of the other side, Fuchs [11] argues that the specifications are (preferably) executable. He considers the same problems stated by Hayes and Jones and translates them into a logic specification language (LSL), which is more expressive than Prolog. He emphasizes the value of animation as the primary vehicle of communication between the client and the designer.

The limitations in expressiveness can be overcome by appropriate specification languages. For example, the B-Toolkit [3, 4] supports type-checking, animation, and proofs. When there is non-determinism, the user is referred to as an oracle. In DisCo [7], the concept of external functions is used to extend the notations.

Of course, animation should not be thought of as a panacea; it certainly does not exclude formal proofs. Rather, proofs and tests are complementary and should be used in conjunction. As an example, Rushby [26] considers the problem of sorting a sequence. The question whether a sorting function is idempotent can be addressed by proof or by animation. The latter can examine the property for a few representative values. Most importantly, animation can help us to ask the right questions. As with model-checking, the goal is to find a counter-example. When we have gained confidence in both the specification and the property then we can use a theorem-prover to attempt a formal proof.

Related to implementation, Zave and Yeh [31, 32] argue that the border between implementations and executable specifications is resource management. Implementations have to meet performance goals by an optimal use of resources while executable specifications should only specify the functional properties of the system. There is also a distinction between prototypes and executable specifications. Prototypes are mainly used to explore only part of the functionality of the system. On the other hand, executable specifications form the basis of the implementation [11].

3   Validating specifications by animation

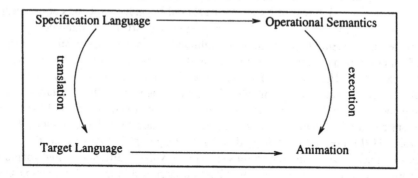

Fig. 1. Overall approach to animation [27]

Figure 1 illustrates two approaches to animate formal specifications. The first approach consists of (automatically) translating specifications into a target language, which is immediately executable. In the second approach, one defines an operational semantics for the specification language, perhaps using a standard SOS format, which can then be interpreted by a custom-built interpreter or even using a standard tool. Theoretically, the two approaches are equivalent: in both cases we must preserve correctness (and completeness if possible). Technically, the definition of the animation by the translation is a programming activity, and proving properties of the translation is often nontrivial.

The second approach favors compositionality of the translation, which simplifies formal reasoning.

3.1 Criteria for animation systems

Breuer and Bowen [6] identify three qualitative measures that can be used to compare animation systems: coverage, efficiency and sophistication. Utting [28] suggests three additional evaluation criteria: interactivity, transparency and operational equivalence. Among these criteria, we have chosen the following requirements which allow us to classify the different techniques of animation:

- the expressiveness of the animation language,
- efficiency, measured as the time and space requirements for execution,
- correctness: every outcome of the execution conforms to the original specification, and
- completeness: every model of the original specification is a possible outcome of the animation.

3.2 Using animation to validate systems

We illustrate what kinds of specification errors the animation may help to detect, and why it is useful to combine animation and proof. Figure 2 shows an example due to Gravell [15], but reformulated in TLA$^+$, a specification language introduced by Lamport [19, 20] and based on top of TLA. The specification should be easy to understand even without detailed knowledge of TLA$^+$.

---

module *Counter*

VARIABLE
$\quad x$

$Init \quad \triangleq \quad x = 0$

$Next \quad \triangleq \quad \land x \leq 995$
$\qquad\qquad\qquad \land x' = x + 5$

$Fair \quad \triangleq \quad \text{WF}_x(Next)$

$Spec \quad \triangleq \quad \land Init$
$\qquad\qquad\quad \land \Box[Next]_x$
$\qquad\qquad\quad \land Fair$

THEOREM
$\quad Invariant \quad \triangleq \quad \Box(x \in Nat \land x < 1000)$

Fig. 2. Specification of a counter.

As explained by Gravell, there are two problems with this specification. The first one concerns the test $x \leq 995$. When $x = 995$, the action *Next* is enabled and can thus be executed. But, the invariant is not preserved. This kind of errors can be found easily by animation. The validation of the invariant can be done by first checking that the predicate *Init* satisfies the invariant and secondly by checking that the execution of actions are closed with respect to the invariant. This is done by checking the validity of the invariant at the initial state, and again after the execution of any action.

On the other hand, the animation points out that the invariant, when corrected, could be strengthened by asserting that $x \bmod 5 = 0$. For example, this stronger invariant implies that an implementation of the counter could internally use an 8 bit representation of integers. On the other hand, it could be the case that this invariant holds just "by accident" and is not actually desired by the client.

Although this example is trivial, it illustrates what we expect from using animation. As a realistic example, Gravell [15] has discovered an error in a specification which had been published in a book about Modula-3.

3.3   Executable Temporal Logic

Temporal logic [18, 23] is a standard framework for specifying and reasoning about reactive systems. It combines classical logic for assertions concerning single states with temporal operators expressing assertions that relate several states. The behaviors of reactive systems are modelled as infinite sequences of states. Temporal logic can be used to model reactive systems at a high level of expressiveness. If we can directly execute (a reasonable subset of) temporal logic specifications, they can be validated early on, without constructing and verifying intermediate refinements of the original specification. For this reason, there has been some interest in executing temporal logic specifications [9], and we review the central points.

The "execution" of a temporal formula F aims to build a model for F. The outcome is therefore a model $\mathcal{M}$ such that $\mathcal{M} \models F$ holds. In general, an animator will only produce finite prefixes of infinite behaviors. It should be the case that any finite sequence of states produced by the animator can be extended to a model of the input specification. Moreover, the animator should be able in principle to produce prefixes of every model, possibly with some guidance by the user in the case of non-determinism.

The construction of models for propositional temporal logic specifications is usually based on automata-theoretic techniques [30, 8]. The satisfiability problem is decidable in the propositional case, but it is rather complex (PSPACE-complete). For first-order temporal logics, the satisfiability problem is highly undecidable (Σ_1^1-complete), and it is not in general possible to incrementally construct models. Faced with these problems, Merz [24] suggests to find a tradeoff between expressiveness and efficient implementability.

We have chosen a subset of first-order TLA as our specification language. As opposed to model checking, we want to be able to animate specifications that involve complex, unbounded data structures, while we are prepared to give up on full coverage of the state space. Compared to other temporal logics, TLA differs in that it emphasizes automata-like descriptions of reactive systems, which have proven to be scalable to specifications of realistic size. It provides a simple logical language to describe both systems and their properties, an important point when one is interested in refinement, and thereby simplifies the interface between the domain and solution experts.

4   Animating TLA specifications

4.1   Overview

TLA specifications are usually written in the canonical form [21]

$$Init \wedge \Box[N]_x \wedge L$$

where $Init$ describes the initial states of the machine, N is the next-state relation, written as a disjunction of possible moves, x is a tuple of all variables of interest and L is a formula that describes the fairness requirements. A TLA specification thus defines an *abstract machine* whose state space is defined by the variables of the specification and whose transition relation is described by actions (transition predicates). An *execution* is modelled as an infinite sequence of states, called *behavior*, where a terminating execution is modelled as repeating the final state.

As a first step, we ignore fairness conditions, which will be considered in section 5.1, and concentrate on the safety part of specifications, written as

$$Init \wedge \Box[N]_x$$

Such a formula is satisfied by a behavior whose initial state satisfies the predicate $Init$ and where every pair of successive states satisfies N, or else doesn't change x. Thus, the key requirement for animation is the ability to generate a *finitely representable* set of successors of each state. We can now state this idea more formally:

Definition 1. *A specification in TLA can be characterized by a triple (St, I, A) where St is a set of all possible states, $I \subseteq St$ is the set of initial states, and A is a set of actions.*

The interpretation of a state predicate p, written $[p]$, is a mapping from states to the booleans. The interpretation of an action a, written $[a]$, is a boolean valued function on steps, where a step is a pair of states. For each action $a \in A$, we can define its *enabling condition*, written ENABLED (a) as the state predicate that is true precisely in those states where a may be executed. Semantically, ENABLED (a) is defined by

$$s[\text{ENABLED}\,(a)] \triangleq \exists\, t \in St : s[a]t$$

A necessary condition for a specification to be executable is that for every (reachable) state s and every action $a \in A$, the set

$$\{t \in St : s[a]t\}$$

of legal successor states of s w.r.t. a be recursively enumerable. We will restrict the action syntax in order to ensure this condition:

- Atomic actions are of the form $x' = v$ where v is a (computable) state function.
- Conjunctions and disjunctions of actions are again actions.
- Implications are allowed only if the formula on the left-hand side is a (computable) state predicate; this restriction in particular ensures that the negation of an action cannot in general be expressed.

The following sections formally define the syntax and semantics of our executable subset of TLA and describe an algorithm that generates (finite) models of such specifications. We show that our interpreter algorithm is both correct and complete as explained in section 3.1.

One may argue that our restrictions on executable formulas are too severe and result in a specification language of insufficient expressivity. On the other hand, it is clear that for fundamental reasons of computability theory, it is impossible to syntactically characterize the full set of specifications such that the set of legal successor states is recursively enumerable. We expect to extend the class of allowed specifications given more experience with our present prototype animator.

4.2   The logic of transitions

Like TLA, the subset of TLA has two tiers, with the temporal formulas defined on top of nontemporal transition formulas. We now define the syntax and semantics of transition formulas.

Syntax We assume given a denumerable set of variables $\mathcal{V}$. These are partitioned into denumerable sets $\mathcal{V}_R$ of rigid variables and $\mathcal{V}_F$ of flexible variables.

We also assume given a sequence $\mathcal{L}$ of symbols, partitioned into a sequence $\mathcal{L}_P$ of predicate symbols and a sequence $\mathcal{L}_F$ of function symbols. To each of the symbols in $\mathcal{L}$ is assigned a natural number, its arity.

The syntax of nontemporal transition formulas has three tiers:

1. The first tier concerns the *constant formulas* whose meaning is state-independent. Rigid variables may occur in these formulas.
2. The second tier concerns the *state formulas* whose meaning is state-dependent. State formulas comprise *state functions* and *state predicates*. Both *rigid variables* and *flexible variables*, whose value is state-dependent, may occur in state formulas.
3. The third tier concerns the *transition formulas*; they comprise only *transition predicates* called *actions*. Transition formulas may contain primed occurrences of flexible variables.

We will explicitly define state and transition formulas. Constant formulas are state formulas that do not contain flexible variables.

State Functions. The set of state functions is the smallest set such that:

- If $x \in \mathcal{V}_F \cup \mathcal{V}_R$ then x is a state function.
- If $f \in \mathcal{L}_F$ is a function symbol of arity n and $v_1, \ldots, v_n$ are state functions then $f(v_1, \ldots, v_n)$ is a state function.

State Predicates. The set of state predicates is the smallest set such that:

- If $p \in \mathcal{L}_P$ is a predicate symbol of arity n and $v_1, \ldots, v_n$ are state functions then $p(v_1, \ldots, v_n)$ is a state predicate.
- If v_1 and v_2 are state functions then $v_1 = v_2$ is a state predicate.
- If P is a state predicate then $\neg P$ is a state predicate.
- If P and Q are state predicates then $P \wedge Q$ is a state predicate.

Further connectives like $\vee, \Rightarrow$ and $\equiv$ are defined as standard abbreviations.

Actions. The set of actions (transition predicates) is the smallest set such that:

- If P is a state predicate then P is an action.
- If $x \in V_F$ and v is a state function then $x' = v$ is an action.
- If A and B are actions then $A \wedge B$ and $A \vee B$ are actions.
- If P is a state predicate and A is an action then $P \Rightarrow A$ is an action.

We sometimes write $x' = x$ where x is a finite list $\langle x_1, \ldots, x_n \rangle$ of flexible variables to denote the conjunction of all actions $x_i' = x_i$.

Logical semantics The basic semantical concept of $\mathcal{L}$ is a structure $\mathcal{M}$ that consists of:

- a non-empty domain $\mathcal{U}$ called a *universe.*
- an n-ary function $\mathcal{M}(f) : \mathcal{U}^n \to \mathcal{U}$ for every n-ary function symbol f.
- an n-ary predicate $\mathcal{M}(p) \subseteq \mathcal{U}^n$ for every n-ary predicate symbol p.

A *rigid variable valuation* (with respect to $\mathcal{U}$) assigns some $\xi(x) \in \mathcal{U}$ to every $x \in V_R$. In this paper, we assume given a fixed structure $\mathcal{M}$ and valuation ξ of the rigid variables.

The semantics is defined in terms of *states.* A *state* is a mapping from flexible variables V_F to *values* from $\mathcal{U}$. Thus, a state $s \in St$ assigns a value $s(x)$ to every flexible variable $x \in V_F$.

State functions. The meaning $[v]$ of a state function v is a mapping from states to values in $\mathcal{U}$. For every state s, we define $s[v]$ by induction as follows:

- If $x \in V_F$ then $s[x]$ is $s(x)$.
- If $x \in V_R$ then $s[x]$ is $\xi(x)$
- $s[f(v_1, \ldots, v_n)]$ is $\mathcal{M}(f)(s[v_1], \ldots, s[v_n])$

State Predicates. The meaning $[P]$ of a state predicate P is a mapping from states to booleans, so $s[P]$ equals true or false for every state s. We say that a state s *satisfies* a predicate P iff $s[P]$ equals true. The semantics of state predicates is inductively defined as follows:

- $s[v_1 = v_2]$ is true iff $s[v_1]$ and $s[v_2]$ are equal.
- $s[p(v_1, \ldots, v_n)]$ is true iff $(s[v_1], \ldots, s[v_n]) \in \mathcal{M}(p)$.
- $s[\neg P]$ is true iff $s[P]$ is false.
- $s[P \wedge Q]$ is true iff both $s[P]$ and $s[Q]$ are true.

Actions. An action (transition predicate) represents a relation between states, where the unprimed variables refer to the state before the transition and the primed variables refer to the state thereafter.

Formally, we say that a pair (s, t) of states *satisfies* an action $\mathcal{A}$, and we write $s[\![\mathcal{A}]\!]t$ iff:

- If $\mathcal{A}$ is a state predicate P then $s[\![\mathcal{A}]\!]t$ is true iff $s[\![P]\!]$ is true.
- If $\mathcal{A}$ is $x' = v$ then $s[\![\mathcal{A}]\!]t$ is true iff $t[\![x]\!]$ and $s[\![v]\!]$ are equal.
- If $\mathcal{A}$ is $A \wedge B$ then $s[\![\mathcal{A}]\!]t$ is true iff $s[\![A]\!]t$ and $s[\![B]\!]t$ are true.
- If $\mathcal{A}$ is $A \vee B$ then $s[\![\mathcal{A}]\!]t$ is true iff $s[\![A]\!]t$ or $s[\![B]\!]t$ is true.
- If $\mathcal{A}$ is $P \Rightarrow A$ then $s[\![\mathcal{A}]\!]t$ is true iff $s[\![P]\!]$ is false or $s[\![A]\!]t$ is true.

Operational semantics We now complement the traditional, logical semantics of TLA defined above with an operational semantics that allows us to effectively evaluate actions. This operational semantics is based on the first-order structure $\mathcal{M}$, which we assume to be effectively presented. We are not concerned with how exactly $\mathcal{M}$ is defined; in practice, it will be provided by a host language, possibly extended with algebraic data types [14].

Informally, if $s[\![\mathcal{A}]\!]t$ holds for a pair (s, t) of states then the execution of $\mathcal{A}$ in state s can produce the new state t. We effectively construct t with the help of an operational semantics of actions that allow us to build the state t incrementally. At each step of the construction, we have partial information about the state t. This partial information is represented by a *valuation*. Operationally, we define the meaning of an action in a state s as a set of valuations with finite domains. For example, $s[\![x' = x + 1]\!]$ is the set that contains just the valuation $[x \leftarrow \mathcal{M}(+)(s[\![x]\!], \mathcal{M}(1))]$. We need two fundamental notions. The first one ensures that two valuations τ_1 and τ_2 are compatible, that is, they agree on the value of all variables they both determine. The second notion is the operation JOIN that allows us to compose sets of valuations.

Definition 2. *A valuation τ is a (possibly partial) mapping from $\mathcal{V}_F$ to $\mathcal{U}$ .i.e.*

$$\tau : \mathcal{V}_F \to \mathcal{U}$$

Note that a state s can be regarded as a valuation with $\text{dom}(s) = \mathcal{V}_F$. However, in the following the domain of τ will often be finite. We write $[x_1 \leftarrow v_1, \ldots, x_n \leftarrow v_n]$ for the valuation τ with $\text{dom}(\tau) = \{x_1, \ldots, x_n\}$ and $\tau(x_i) = v_i$. In particular $[\,]$ denotes the trivial valuation that is nowhere defined.

Definition 3. *Let τ_1 and τ_2 be two valuations. We say that τ_1 and τ_2 are compatible, written $\tau_1 \simeq \tau_2$, iff $\tau_1(x) = \tau_2(x)$ for every $x \in \text{dom}(\tau_1) \cap \text{dom}(\tau_2)$.*

Definition 4. *The composition of two compatible valuations τ_1 and τ_2, written $\tau_1 \bullet \tau_2$, is the valuation such that:*

- *$\text{dom}(\tau_1 \bullet \tau_2) = \text{dom}(\tau_1) \cup \text{dom}(\tau_2)$ and*
- *for every variable $x \in \text{dom}(\tau_1 \bullet \tau_2)$:*

$$(\tau_1 \bullet \tau_2)(x) = \begin{cases} \tau_1(x) \text{ if } x \in \text{dom}(\tau_1) \\ \tau_2(x) \text{ if } x \in \text{dom}(\tau_2) \end{cases}$$

Definition 5. *The operation* JOIN *is defined by*

$$S \text{ JOIN } T = \{\rho \bullet \tau : \rho \in S, \tau \in T, \rho \simeq \tau\}$$

for any two sets S and T of valuations.

We note the following properties of these definitions, which are later used to establish the soundness and completeness of our semantics.

Lemma 6. *If $\tau \in \text{JOIN}_{i=1}^{n}\{[x_i \leftarrow c_i]\}$ then $dom(\tau) = \{x_1, \ldots, x_n\}$ and $\tau(x_i) = c_i$ for every $x_i \in dom(\tau)$.*

Lemma 7. *Let S, T be two sets of valuations and t be a state. There exists some $\tau \in (S \text{ JOIN } T)$ such that $t \simeq \tau$ iff there exist $\tau_1 \in S$ and $\tau_2 \in T$ such that $t \simeq \tau_1$ and $t \simeq \tau_2$.*

Now, we can define the meaning of an action as a mapping from states to sets of valuations. The semantics of actions is defined by structural induction as follows:

- $s[x' = v] = \{[x \leftarrow s[v]]\}$.
- If P is a state predicate and $s[P]$ is true then $s[P] = \{[]\}$.
- If P is a state predicate and $s[P]$ is false then $s[P] = \{\}$.
- $s[A \wedge B]$ is $s[A]$ JOIN $s[B]$.
- $s[A \vee B]$ is $s[A] \cup s[B]$ where $\cup$ is set union.
- If $s[P]$ is true then $s[P \Rightarrow A]$ is $s[A]$.
- If $s[P]$ is false then $s[P \Rightarrow A]$ is $\{[]\}$.

4.3   Temporal formulas

Temporal formulas are built on the basis of transition formulas as defined above. We now define their syntax and semantics.

Syntax The only form of temporal formulas is

$$Init \wedge \Box[N]_x$$

where:

- *Init* is a state predicate describing the initial values of x. We restrict *Init* to be of the form $\bigvee_{i=1}^{m} \bigwedge_{j=1}^{n} x_{ij} = c_{ij}$ where c_{ij} is a constant and x_{ij} is a variable.
- N is an action describing the next-state relation.
- x is a tuple of flexible variables that appear in N. We require each step to satisfy N or else leave all variables in x unchanged. We may consider such steps as being performed by the environment.

Semantics The semantics of temporal formulas is defined on behaviors, that is, infinite sequences of states. If $\sigma = \langle s_0, s_1, \ldots \rangle$ is a behavior then $\sigma_{|n}$ is its prefix $\langle s_0, \ldots, s_n \rangle$. Let St^∞ denote the set of all behaviors.

Definition 8. *Let* $\sigma = \langle s_0, s_1, \ldots \rangle \in St^\infty$ *be a behavior. We say that* σ *satisfies the temporal formula* $Init \wedge \Box[N]_x$*, written* $\sigma[Init \wedge \Box[N]_x]$ *iff* $s_0[Init]$ *is true and for all* $n \in Nat$, $s_n[N \vee x' = x]s_{n+1}$ *is true.*

A fundamental result about TLA asserts that all formulas are invariant under stuttering, that is, finite repetitions of identical states. Formally, *stuttering equivalence* is the finest equivalence relation on behaviors such that any two behaviors $\pi \circ \langle s, s \rangle \circ \sigma$ and $\pi \circ \langle s \rangle \circ \sigma$ are stuttering equivalent. Invariance under stuttering allows refinement to be represented by logical implication. All formulas written in our restricted logic are therefore also stuttering invariant. The proof of the following proposition appears in [2].

Proposition 9. *Let* $F \equiv Init \wedge \Box[A]_x$.
If σ *and* τ *are two stuttering equivalent behaviors, then* $\sigma[F]$ *holds iff* $\tau[F]$ *holds.*

4.4   Soundness and completeness of our semantics

We now define an operational semantics for temporal formulas, based on the operational semantics for actions, and relate it to the logical semantics by proving soundness and completeness theorems.

Let $F \equiv Init / \Box[A]_x$ be a temporal formula. We write TRACES(F) to denote the set of finite behaviors that satisfy F. Formally, TRACES(F) is defined by induction as follows:

Definition 10. TRACES(F) *is the smallest set such that:*

– *If* $Init \equiv \bigvee_{i=1}^{m} \bigwedge_{j=1}^{n} x_{ij} = c_{ij}$ *then* $\langle s_0 \rangle \in$ TRACES(F) *iff* $s_0 \simeq \tau$ *for some* $\tau \in \bigcup_{i=1}^{m}$ JOIN$_{j=1}^{n}\{[x_{ij} \leftarrow c_{ij}]\}$.
– *If* $\langle s_0, \ldots, s_n \rangle \in$ TRACES(F) *then* $\langle s_0, \ldots, s_{n+1} \rangle \in$ TRACES(F) *iff* $s_{n+1} \simeq \tau$ *for some* $\tau \in s_n[Ax' = x]$.

TRACES(F) is therefore the set of finite behaviors that can be constructed by repeatedly applying the operational semantics for actions from section 4.2. It defines the operational semantics of temporal formulas.

Lemmas 11 and 12 establish the soundness and completeness of our semantics for the initial predicate and for actions.

Lemma 11. $s_0[\bigwedge_{i=1}^{n} x_i = c_i]$ *is true iff* $s_0 \simeq \tau$ *for some* $\tau \in$ JOIN$_{i=1}^{n}\{[x_i \leftarrow c_i]\}$.

Lemma 12. *Let* A *be an action and* s, t *be states.* $s[A]t$ *is true iff* $t \simeq \tau$ *holds for some* $\tau \in s[A]$.

These lemmas are the essential steps in proving the following theorems 13 and 14, which assert the soundness and completeness of the operational semantics with respect to the logical semantics.

Theorem 13 (Soundness). *Let $F \equiv Init \wedge \Box[N]_x$ and $\sigma \in St^\infty$ be a behavior. If $\sigma_{|n} \in \text{TRACES}(F)$ holds for all $n \in \mathbb{N}$ then $\sigma[F]$ is true.*

Theorem 14 (Completeness). *Let $F \equiv Init \wedge \Box[N]_x$ and $\sigma \in St^\infty$ be a behavior. If $\sigma[F]$ is true then $\sigma_{|n} \in \text{TRACES}(F)$ holds for all $n \in \mathbb{N}$.*

4.5   The interpreter algorithm

The interpreter algorithm iteratively constructs a set of finite behaviors that are prefixes of models of an executable specification F. Let $F \equiv Init / \Box[A]_x$ be a temporal formula and $W = FV_{temp}(F)$ be the free flexible variables of F. Intuitively, W constitutes the space state. A *configuration* $\mathcal{K}$ is a mapping from W to values, i.e.

$$\mathcal{K} : W \to \mathcal{U}$$

In fact, the algorithm constructs a forest of simulation trees whose roots correspond to the initial states and whose nodes are configurations. This tree represents the set of finite behaviors allowed by the formula F.

For each state under construction, we want to generate a set $\mathcal{C}$ of configurations, based on valuations τ produced by the operational semantics defined above. It only remains to assign values to any variables in W that are not in the domain of τ. Uninitialized variables typically correspond to environment inputs; their values have to be provided by the user or be randomly generated by the animator. If τ is a valuation with $\text{dom}(\tau) \subseteq W$, we let $\text{CONFIGURATIONS}(\tau)$ denote the valuation $\tau \bullet input$ where $input$ is some valuation with domain $W \setminus \text{dom}(\tau)$. We extend CONFIGURATIONS to sets of valuations in the obvious way. Figure 3 illustrates the algorithm.

Input Let $F \equiv Init \wedge \Box[A]_z$ where $Init \equiv \bigvee_{i=1}^{m} \bigwedge_{j=1}^{n} x_{ij} = c_{ij}$.
Output simulation tree

Initialization $C_0 = \text{CONFIGURATIONS}\left(\bigcup_{i=1}^{m} \text{JOIN}_{j=1}^{n} \{[x_{ij} \leftarrow c_{ij}]\} \right).$

Construction
  1. choose any subaction of A, say B.
  2. $C_{i+1} = \bigcup_{s \in C_i} \text{CONFIGURATIONS}(s[Bx' = x]).$

Fig. 3. The interpreter algorithm.

Example. To illustrate the algorithm, consider the following example. Let

$$F \equiv x = 0 \wedge \Box[y > 0 \wedge x' = x + 1 \wedge y' = y + 1]_{\langle x, y \rangle}$$

where x and y are flexible variables. At time 0, we may have by initialization:

$$C_0 = \{[x \leftarrow 0, y \leftarrow 3]\}$$

We assume that the user has chosen to instantiate y with 3. At time 1, we have by the construction of configurations:

$$C_1 = C_0 \cup \{[x \leftarrow 1, y \leftarrow 4]\}$$

The construction continues in a similar way. Figure 4 illustrates the simulation tree.

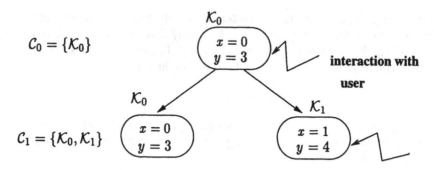

Fig. 4. Simulation tree

5 Extensions

We extend the basic set of executable TLA formulas considered so far by fairness conditions and give a brief indication of the current implementation, which complements the animator with a simple model checker for the analysis of finite-state specifications.

5.1 Fairness requirements

Fairness conditions are used to constrain the nondeterministic choices present in the specifications of concurrent systems at an abstract level of description. For example, consider the specification of the manager of a shared resource. We may use a fairness condition to require that every request must be eventually served. A typical implementation may queue the waiting requests. But, including a queue in the specification of the resource manager has at least two drawbacks. On one hand, this solution over-specifies the requirements and on the other hand it enforces implementation decisions at the requirements level. Observe moreover that without fairness requirements, a TLA component specified by a canonical formula $Init \wedge \Box[N]_v$ may at some point simply stop operating, since every stuttering action satisfies the safety requirement.

In general, fairness conditions assert that an action that is enabled often enough will eventually be executed. Standard interpretations of "often enough" are either "forever from some point onwards" (*weak fairness*) or "infinitely often" (*strong fairness*). Clearly, strong fairness implies weak fairness. In TLA, these fairness conditions can be defined as

$$\mathrm{WF}_f(A) \triangleq (\Box\Diamond\langle A\rangle_f) \vee (\Box\Diamond\neg\mathrm{ENABLED}\,\langle A\rangle_f)$$
$$\mathrm{SF}_f(A) \triangleq (\Box\Diamond\langle A\rangle_f) \vee (\Diamond\Box\neg\mathrm{ENABLED}\,\langle A\rangle_f)$$

We allow conjunctions of weak and strong fairness conditions to appear in executable formulas. They are implemented with the help of *schedulers*, ensuring that every infinite behavior that is a limit of the finite behaviors produced by the animator satisfies the fairness conditions as well as the safety part of the given specification. Of course, the choice of a fixed scheduler destroys the completeness property, since the nondeterminism of the original specification is constrained. In our implementation, the user has the freedom to override the scheduler's choice of which action to execute next.

For the sake of clarity, we separately define schedulers for specifications that contain either weak or strong fairness conditions. It is easy to combine the algorithms to obtain a scheduler for specifications that contain both types of fairness requirements.

Weak Fairness. The scheduling algorithm for weak fairness is a simple round robin scheduler that cycles through the list of actions that have associated fairness conditions. In particular, an action that is continuously enabled from some point on will eventually be chosen for execution, thus satisfying the weak fairness condition.

Formally, let $F \equiv Init \wedge \Box[\bigvee_{i=1}^{l} A_i]_x \wedge \bigwedge_{i=1}^{m} \mathrm{WF}_x(A_i)$. We adapt the definition of $\mathrm{TRACES}(F)$ as follows:

Initialization If $Init \equiv \bigvee_{i=1}^{p} \bigwedge_{j=1}^{q} x_{ij} = c_{ij}$ then $\langle s_0\rangle \in \mathrm{TRACES}(F)$ iff $s_0 \simeq \tau$ for
some $\tau \in \bigcup_{i=1}^{p} \mathrm{JOIN}_{j=1}^{q}\{[x_{ij} \leftarrow c_{ij}]\}$.
Body Assume that $\langle s_0, \ldots, s_n\rangle \in \mathrm{TRACES}(F)$.
1. If $s_n[\langle A_{(n \bmod l)}\rangle_x] \neq \emptyset$ then $\langle s_0, \ldots, s_{n+1}\rangle \in \mathrm{TRACES}(F)$ iff $s_{n+1} \simeq \tau$ for
   some $\tau \in s_n[\langle A_{(n \bmod l)}\rangle_x]$.
2. If $s_n[\langle A_{(n \bmod l)}\rangle_x] = \emptyset$ then $\langle s_0, \ldots, s_{n+1}\rangle \in \mathrm{TRACES}(F)$ iff $s_{n+1} \simeq \tau$ for
   some $\tau \in s_n[(\bigvee_{i=1}^{l} A_i) \vee x' = x]$.

Theorem 15 (Soundness). *Let* $F \equiv Init \wedge \Box[\bigwedge_{i=1}^{l} A_i]_x \wedge \bigwedge_{i=1}^{m} \mathrm{WF}_x(A_i)$. *For any behavior* $\sigma \in St^\infty$, *if* $\sigma_{|n} \in \mathrm{TRACES}(F)$ *holds for all* $n \in \mathbb{N}$ *then* $\sigma[F]$ *is true.*

Strong Fairness. The scheduling algorithm for strong fairness maintains a list of actions with associated fairness conditions and at every step tries to execute the first enabled action from that list, which is then moved to the end of the list. Intuitively, this corresponds to a priority scheduler where actions that cannot be executed move towards the beginning of the list. If the action is infinitely often enabled without being executed, it will eventually be the first enabled action in the list, and thus be executed by the scheduler.

Formally, let $F \equiv Init \wedge \Box[\bigwedge_{i=1}^{l} A_i]_x \wedge \bigwedge_{i=1}^{m} \mathrm{SF}_x(A_i)$. We adapt the definition of $\mathrm{TRACES}(F)$ as follows, simultaneously defining a sequence $P_0, P_1, \ldots$ of lists of actions with fairness conditions (we use superscripts to refer to the element of a list at a given position):

Initialization

1. If $Init \equiv \bigvee_{i=1}^{p} \bigwedge_{j=1}^{q} x_{ij} = c_{ij}$ then $\langle s_0 \rangle \in \text{TRACES}(F)$ iff $s_0 \simeq \tau$ for some $\tau \in \bigcup_{i=1}^{p} \text{JOIN}_{j=1}^{q}\{[x_{ij} \leftarrow c_{ij}]\}$.

2. $P_0 = \langle 1, \ldots, m \rangle$

Body Assume that $\langle s_0, \ldots, s_n \rangle \in \text{TRACES}(F)$.

1. If $\text{SCHED}(P_n, s_n) = i \neq 0$ then $\langle s_0, \ldots, s_{n+1} \rangle \in \text{TRACES}(F)$ iff $s_{n+1} \simeq \tau$ for some $\tau \in s_n[\langle A_i \rangle_x]$, and $P_{n+1} = \langle P_n^1, \ldots, P_n^{i-1}, P_n^{i+1}, \ldots, P_n^m, P_n^i \rangle$.

2. If $\text{SCHED}(P_n, s_n) = 0$ then $\langle s_0, \ldots, s_{n+1} \rangle \in \text{TRACES}(F)$ iff $s_{n+1} \simeq \tau$ for some $\tau \in s_n[(\bigvee_{i=1}^{l} A_i) \vee x' = x]$ and $P_{n+1} = P_n$.

Here, $\text{SCHED}(P, s) = \begin{cases} 0 & \text{if } s[\langle A_{P^j} \rangle_x] = \emptyset \text{ for all } j \\ \min\{j : s[\langle A_{P^j} \rangle_x] \neq \emptyset\} & \text{otherwise} \end{cases}$

Theorem 16 (Soundness). *Let* $F \equiv Init \wedge \Box[\bigwedge_{i=1}^{l} A_i]_x \wedge \bigwedge_{i=1}^{m} \text{SF}_x(A_i)$. *For any behavior* $\sigma \in St^\infty$, *if* $\sigma_{|n} \in \text{TRACES}(F)$ *holds for all* $n \in \mathbb{N}$ *then* $\sigma[F]$ *is true.*

5.2   Model checker

The animator is complemented by a model checker for finite-state TLA$^+$ specifications. The model checker is based on our subset of TLA and uses an explicit state enumeration algorithm to check the properties of the system and produce counterexamples to those properties that do not hold of the system. It uses an on-the-fly algorithm, which interleaves the generation of the state space and the search for errors, avoiding the construction of the complete state space. The states are stored in a hash-table, so that is that it can be decided efficiently whether or not a newly-reached state is old (has been examined already) or new.

There are two kinds of properties that designers check with model checking tools: *safety properties* and *liveness properties*. Checking safety properties can be reduced to reachability analysis, whereas checking liveness properties amounts to searching for cycles in the state graph. More precisely, the procedure of verification is described in the following.

Given an executable TLA specification G and a property f expressed in propositional TLA, the verification procedure [12] is defined as follows:

1. Build a Büchi automaton $B_{\neg f}$ for the negation of the formula f.
2. Compute the product $B_G \otimes B_{\neg f}$ of the transition system that corresponds to the specification G and the automaton $B_{\neg f}$; the accepting runs of this automaton correspond to infinite computations of G accepted by $B_{\neg f}$
3. Check whether the language accepted by $B_G \otimes B_{\neg f}$ is empty or not.

The first step is based on the relation between Büchi automata and LTL. Vardi and Wolper [29] showed that any LTL formula can be translated into a Büchi automaton which *accepts* precisely those (infinite) system executions that satisfy the LTL formula. The algorithm [12] is based on a tableau procedure and computes the states of the Büchi automaton by computing the set of subformulas that must hold in each reachable state and in each of its successor states. Liveness conditions give rise to the set of accepting states of $B_{\neg f}$.

The language of $B_G \otimes B_{\neg f}$ is nonempty iff the automaton contains an acceptance cycle. The search for acceptance cycles can be interleaved with the construction of the product automaton [13].

5.3   Implementation

We have implemented the tools outlined in our paper in Java. The figure 5 illustrates a screen-shot of our environment for TLA$^+$. The tools include the following components:

Source Editor Edit source files using a point-and-click editor. The Source Editor also
   serves integrated display mechanism for the other TLA$^+$ tools component.
Compiler Manager Build all TLA$^+$ modules.
Animator Animate a TLA$^+$ specification.
Model checker Model checker for TLA$^+$ specifications.

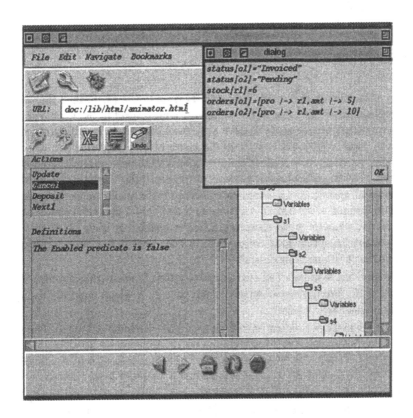

Fig. 5. An example of a scenario

Figure 5 illustrates the animation of the invoice system specification. It consists of a system which is composed of the following components: *set of orders, stock,* and *entry flows.* An order contains one reference to a product of a certain quantity. It may change its state from the state *pending* to *invoiced* if and only if the ordered quantity of the product is less than or equal to the quantity of this product in stock. The same reference of the product may occur in different orders. The entry flows allow us to change the state of the set of orders and the stock: (i) entries in the set of orders : new orders (**receive operation**) or cancelled orders (**cancel operation**). (ii) entry in stock : new entry of quantities of products in stock at warehouse (**deposit operation**).

Further, the figure shows an example of a user's interaction with the animator. We assume that the user initializes the system with two orders, namely o_1 and o_2 and one reference, namely r_1. Then the user chooses the scenario which consists in carrying out the sequence of actions: $Receive(o_1, r_1, 5), Receive(o_2, r_1, 10), Deposit(r_1, 11)$, $Update(o_1)$. Next, we reach a state depicted by the figure in which the first order o_1 is invoiced and the stock is updated. Finally, we can try to cancel the order o_1. The animator displays the following message "The Enabled predicate is false" which means that we cannot change the status of the order which is already invoiced. Thus, the execution of the action $Cancel(o_1)$ is not authorized. For futher explanations, the reader may refer to [33].

6   Conclusion

We have presented an executable subset of TLA and have established the soundness and completeness of our operational semantics with respect to the logical semantics. The interpreter algorithm needs to store only the current state in order to compute its successors; there is no need to refer to the entire history. Nevertheless, we store the choices present at each step so that the user can backtrack and explore different branches of the tree. Note in particular that because of the possibility of taking stuttering steps, and because all specifications in the subset defined in this paper are machine closed [1], a temporal formula in our subset is satisfiable if and only if the initial condition is. The user is alerted when only the stuttering action is enabled at some point; he can then decide whether the system state corresponds to a deadlock or to a quiescent state where all activity has terminated successfully.

We intend this work as a first step towards the development of an animator for TLA and TLA$^+$ [19]. We have developed a prototype in Java which faithfully incorporates the ideas outlined in this paper.

We are not alone in studying animation techniques for temporal logics. The classical approach for finite-state systems is based on the correspondence between propositional temporal logic (PTL) and finite-state automata on ω-words such as Büchi automata. Wolper [30] shows that for a given propositional temporal logic formula ϕ, one can construct an ω-automaton which accepts precisely those models that satisfy ϕ. This automaton can be taken as the basis of a PTL animator. While fully general for propositional logics, this approach is inherently restricted to finite-state systems. Moreover, the resulting automaton can be prohibitively large.

Other approaches are based on symbolic manipulation to ensure that each step in the execution obeys the specification. For example, METATEM [10] is based on full linear-time temporal logic, where formulas are restricted to the form

past time antecedent $\Rightarrow$ future time consequent

which means "on the basis of the past do the future". Given a program consisting of a set of rules R_i of the above form, the interpreter attempts to construct a model of the formula $\Box \bigwedge_i R_i$. It proceeds informally in the following manner:

1. find those rules whose past-time antecedents evaluate to true in the current history;
2. "jointly execute" the consequents of applicable rules with any commitments carried forward. This will result in the current state being completed and the construction of a set of commitments to be carried out in the future;
3. repeat the execution process from the new commitments and the new history resulting from 2 above.

METATEM is more general in that it has an input language equivalent in expressiveness to full first-order temporal logic. The interpreter can therefore not ensure that finite behaviors constructed up to a certain point are in fact prefixes of models. Besides, it has to store the complete history of each run in order to evaluate past-time formulas in the antecedents of rules.

Finally, there have been extensions of PROLOG to incorporate temporal modalities [5, 25]. However, these approaches are based on sets of rules that may involve temporal logic, and answer queries for such historical databases; they are not intended for the construction of behaviors of reactive systems.

References

[1] M. Abadi and L. Lamport. The Existence of Refinement Mappings. Theoretical Computer Science 81(2):253–284, 1991.
[2] M. Abadi and S. Merz. On TLA as as logic. in M. Broy (ed.): Deductive Program Design. Springer-Verlag, NATO ASI series F, 1996.
[3] J.-R Abrial. The B-Book. Cambridge University Press, 1996.
[4] B-core. B-Toolkit. User's Manual, Release 3.2. Technical Report, B-core, 1996
[5] M. Baudinet. Temporal Logic Programming is Complete and Expressive. In Proc. ACM Conf. on Princinples of Programming Languages, pp. 267–280 (1989)
[6] P. Breuer and J. Bowen. Towards Correct Executable Semantics for Z. In J. Bowen and J. Hall, editors, Proc. 8th Z Users Workshop (ZUM94), Workshops in Computing, pages 185-212. Cambridge, Springer-Verlag, Berlin, 1994.
[7] http://www.cs.tut.fi/laitos/DisCo/DisCo-english.fm.html
[8] E.A. Emerson and E.M. Clarke. Using branching-time temporal logic to synthesize synchronization skeletons. Science of Computer Programming 2 (1982), pages 241–266.
[9] M. Fisher and R. Owens. An introduction to Executable Modal and Temporal Logics. In Michael Fisher and Richards Owens editors, Executable Modal and Temporal Logics, volume 897 of Lecture Notes in Computer Science , pages 1–20, Springer-Verlag, 1993.
[10] M. Fisher. Concurrent METATEM—The Language and its Applications. In Michael Fisher and Richards Owens editors, Executable Modal and Temporal Logics, volume 897 of Lecture Notes in Computer Science , Springer-Verlag, 1993.

[11] N. E. Fuchs. Specifications are (preferably) executable. Software Engineering Journal,7(5),pages 323-334,1992

[12] R. Gerth, D. Peled, M. Vardi and P. Wolper Simple on-the-fly automatic verification of linear temporal logic PSTV, XIII, pages 3-18, 1995

[13] P. Godefroid and G. J. Holzmann On the verification of temporal properties PSTV, XIII, pages 109-124, 1993

[14] J. Goguen and G. Malcolm. Algebraic Semantics of Imperative Programs. MIT Press, 1997.

[15] A. Gravell. Executing Formal Specifications Need Not Be Harmful. Available on the WWW at URL http://dsse.ecs.soton.ac.uk/ amg/papers.html.

[16] C.A. Hoare. An Overview of Some Formal Methods for Program Design. IEEE Computer, pages 85-91, 1987.

[17] I. J. Hayes and C. B. Jones Specifications are not (necessarily) executable. Software Engineering Journal,4(6),pages 320-338,1989

[18] F. Kröger Temporal Logic of Programs. EATCS Monographs on Theoretical Computer Science 8. Berlin, Springer-Verlag, 1987

[19] L. Lamport. The module structure of TLA$^+$ Research Report 1996–002, Digital Equipment Corporation, Systems Research Center.

[20] L. Lamport. The operators of TLA$^+$ Research Report 1997–006a, Digital Equipment Corporation, Systems Research Center.

[21] L. Lamport. The temporal logic of actions. ACM Transactions on Programming Languages and Systems, 16(3):872–923, May 1994.

[22] A. C. Leisenring. Mathematical Logic and Hilbert's ε-Symbol. Gordon and Breach, New York, 1969.

[23] Z. Manna and A. Pnueli The Temporal Logic of Reactive and Concurrent Systems - Specifications New-York etc.: Springer-Verlag, 1992

[24] S. Merz. Efficiently Executable Temporal Logic Programs. In Michael Fisher and Richards Owens editors, Executable Modal and Temporal Logics, IJCAI'93 Workshop, volume 897 of Lecture Notes in Computer Science , pages 69–85, France, 1993, Springer.

[25] M.A. Orgun and W.W. Wadge. Towards a unified theory of intensional logic programming. Journal of Logic Programming 13(4), pp. 413ff (1992)

[26] J. Rushby. Formal Methods and their Role in the Certification of Critical Systems. SRI Technical Report CSL-95-1, March 1995.

[27] L. Sterling, P. Ciancarini and T. Turnidge. On the animation of "not executable" specifications by Prolog. International Journal of Software Engineering and Knowledge Engineering, 6(1):63-87.

[28] M. Utting. Animating Z: Interactivity, transparency and equivalence. Technical Report 94-40. Software Verification Research Center.

[29] M. Vardi and P. Wolper An automata-theoretic approach to automatic program verification Proceedings on the First Symposium on Logic in Computer Science, pages 322-331,1986

[30] P. Wolper. Temporal Logic Can Be More Expressive. Information and Control 56. pages 71–99, 1983

[31] P. Zave and R. T. Yeh. Executable requirement specification for embedded system. Proc. 5th Int. Conf. on Software Engineering, San Diego, California, pages 295-304, 1981.

[32] P. Zave An operational approach to requirements specifications. IEEE Trans. SE-8(3), pages 250-269, 1982.

[33] Y. Mokhtari The invoice system problem in TLA+ Proc. International Workshop on Comparing Systems Specification Techniques, University of Nantes, France March 1998.

Transforming Conditional Rewrite Systems with Extra Variables into Unconditional Systems

Enno Ohlebusch

University of Bielefeld, Faculty of Technology, P.O. Box 10 01 31, 33501 Bielefeld, Germany, email: enno@TechFak.Uni-Bielefeld.DE

Abstract. Deterministic conditional rewrite systems are interesting because they permit extra variables on the right-hand sides of the rules. If such a system is quasi-reductive, then it is terminating and has a computable rewrite relation. It will be shown that every deterministic CTRS $\mathcal{R}$ can be transformed into an unconditional TRS $U(\mathcal{R})$ such that termination of $U(\mathcal{R})$ implies quasi-reductivity of $\mathcal{R}$. The main theorem states that quasi-reductivity of $\mathcal{R}$ implies innermost termination of $U(\mathcal{R})$. These results have interesting applications in two different areas: modularity in term rewriting and termination proofs of well-moded logic programs.

1 Introduction

Conditional term rewriting systems (CTRSs) are the basis of functional logic programming; see [Han94] for an overview of this field. In CTRSs variables on the right-hand side of a rewrite rule which do not occur on the left-hand side are often forbidden. This is because it is in general not clear how to instantiate them. On the other hand, a restricted use of these extra variables enables a more natural and efficient way of writing programs in a functional logic programming language. For instance the Haskell *quicksort* program

```
split x []      = ([],[])
split x (y:ys) | x <= y       = (xs,y:zs)
               | otherwise    = (y:xs,zs)
                        where (xs,zs) = split x ys

qsort []      = []
qsort (x:xs)  = qsort ys ++ (x:qsort zs)
                 where (ys,zs) = split x xs
```

corresponds to the CTRS

$$split(x, []) \rightarrow ([], [])$$
$$split(x, y : ys) \rightarrow (xs, y : zs) \Leftarrow split(x, ys) \rightarrow (xs, zs), x \le y \rightarrow true$$
$$split(x, y : ys) \rightarrow (y : xs, zs) \Leftarrow split(x, ys) \rightarrow (xs, zs), x \le y \rightarrow false$$
$$qsort([]) \rightarrow []$$
$$qsort(x : xs) \rightarrow qsort(ys) \mathbin{+\!\!+} (x : qsort(zs)) \Leftarrow split(x, xs) \rightarrow (ys, zs)$$

which has extra variables on the right-hand side of every conditional rule. The rewrite relation induced by the above CTRS is effectively terminating (that is, computable and terminating) because the system is a *quasi-reductive deterministic* CTRS. This class of CTRSs was introduced by Ganzinger [Gan91] in order to efficiently translate order-sorted specifications into conditional many-sorted equations. Quasi-reductivity is in general undecidable but sufficient criteria to check quasi-reductivity have been proposed in [Gan91,ALS94].

Similar to the approach of Marchiori [Mar96], we will show how every deterministic CTRS $\mathcal{R}$ can be transformed into an unconditional TRS $U(\mathcal{R})$ such that termination of $U(\mathcal{R})$ implies quasi-reductivity of $\mathcal{R}$. This result is interesting because standard methods for proving termination of TRSs can be employed to infer quasi-reductivity automatically; see [AG97a]. On the one hand, an example in [Mar95] shows that quasi-reductivity of $\mathcal{R}$ does not imply termination of $U(\mathcal{R})$ but on the other hand the main theorem of this paper states that it does imply *innermost* termination of $U(\mathcal{R})$. (The proof of this theorem is non-trivial.) This has two striking consequences.

Firstly, Gramlich [Gra95] showed that for non-overlapping TRSs innermost termination coincides with termination. Since $U(\mathcal{R})$ inherits non-overlappingness from a syntactically deterministic CTRS $\mathcal{R}$, termination of $U(\mathcal{R})$ and quasi-reductivity of $\mathcal{R}$ are equivalent for this class of CTRSs. Consequently, quasi-reductivity is modular for non-overlapping syntactically deterministic composable CTRSs.

Secondly, Ganzinger and Waldmann [GW93] proved that a translation of a well-moded logic program $\mathcal{P}$ into a quasi-reductive deterministic CTRS $R_{\mathcal{P}}$ yields a termination proof for $\mathcal{P}$. Using an imperative procedure, Arts and Zantema [AZ95,AZ96] transformed a logic program $\mathcal{P}$ directly into an *unconditional* TRS (which in essence coincides with $U(R_{\mathcal{P}})$) and showed that innermost termination of this system ensures termination of $\mathcal{P}$. Consequently, it is remarked in [AZ95] that the suggested method "is applicable to a wider class of logic programs" and hence it is "stronger than the other results". Although $U(R_{\mathcal{P}})$ is not necessarily non-overlapping, it can be shown that in this particular case innermost termination and termination are equivalent. A consequence is the surprising fact that the methods of Ganzinger & Waldmann and Arts & Zantema are equally powerful, in the sense that every logic program which can be shown as terminating by one of the methods can be shown as terminating by both methods. Our new two-stage transformation approach to proving termination of an LR-well-moded logic program can be automated and moreover it has certain advantages over the direct transformation. These advantages are discussed at the end of the paper.

2   Preliminaries

The reader is assumed to be familiar with the basic concepts of term rewriting which can for instance be found in the textbook of Baader and Nipkow [BN98]. Here we will only recall the definitions which are crucial to this paper.

In a CTRS $(\mathcal{F}, \mathcal{R})$ rules have the form $l \to r \Leftarrow s_1 = t_1, \ldots, s_k = t_k$ with $l, r, s_1, \ldots, s_k, t_1, \ldots, t_k \in \mathcal{T}(\mathcal{F}, \mathcal{V})$. l may not be a variable. We frequently abbreviate the conditional part of the rule by c. If a rule has no conditions, we write $l \to r$, demand that $Var(r) \subseteq Var(l)$, and call $l \to r$ an unconditional rule. The $=$ symbol in the conditions can be interpreted in different ways, leading to different rewrite relations associated with $\mathcal{R}$. For instance, in a *join* CTRS the $=$ symbol stands for joinability ($\downarrow_{\mathcal{R}}$). This paper deals with *oriented* CTRSs in which the equality signs are interpreted as reachability ($\to^*_{\mathcal{R}}$). A *normal* CTRS $(\mathcal{F}, \mathcal{R})$ is an oriented CTRS in which the rewrite rules are subject to the additional constraint that every t_j is a ground normal form with respect to $\mathcal{R}_u$, where $\mathcal{R}_u = \{l \to r \mid l \to r \Leftarrow c \in \mathcal{R}\}$.

For every rule $\rho : l \to r \Leftarrow c$, the set of variables occurring in ρ is denoted by $Var(\rho)$ and the set of extra variables in ρ is $\mathcal{E}Var(\rho) = Var(\rho) \setminus Var(l)$. A 1-CTRS has no extra variables, a 2-CTRS has no extra variables on the right-hand sides of the rules, and a 3-CTRS may contain extra variables on the right-hand sides of the rules provided that these also occur in the corresponding conditional part (i.e., $Var(r) \subseteq Var(l) \cup Var(c)$).

3   Quasi-Reductive Deterministic 3-CTRSs

First of all, we will review the definition of deterministic systems from [Gan91].

Definition 1. *An oriented 3-CTRS $\mathcal{R}$ is called* deterministic *if (after appropriately changing the order of the conditions in the rewrite rules) for every $l \to r \Leftarrow s_1 \to t_1, \ldots, s_k \to t_k$ in $\mathcal{R}$ and every $1 \le i \le k$, we have $Var(s_i) \subseteq Var(l) \cup \bigcup_{j=1}^{i-1} Var(t_j)$. In the following, we will frequently use the notation $\mathcal{E}Var(t_i) = Var(t_i) \setminus (Var(l) \cup \bigcup_{j=1}^{i-1} Var(t_j))$.*

The rewrite relation $\to_{\mathcal{R}}$ associated with an oriented deterministic 3-CTRS $\mathcal{R}$ is defined by: $s \to_{\mathcal{R}} t$ if and only if there exists a rewrite rule $\rho : l \to r \Leftarrow s_1 \to t_1, \ldots, s_k \to t_k$ in $\mathcal{R}$, a substitution $\sigma : Var(\rho) \to \mathcal{T}(\mathcal{F}, \mathcal{V})$, and a context $C[]$ such that $s = C[l\sigma], t = C[r\sigma]$, and $s_i\sigma \to^*_{\mathcal{R}} t_i\sigma$ for all $1 \le i \le k$. We would like to stress the fact that σ instantiates every variable in ρ and not only those variables occurring in l; for an extra variable x, $x\sigma$ is determined as follows. The conditions are evaluated from left-to-right. Since s_1 contains only variables from $Var(l)$, the variables in $Var(s_1)$ have a binding. Then $s_1\sigma$ is rewritten until $t_1\sigma$ matches a reduct. The term $t_1\sigma$ may contain extra variables but all of these are bound during the match. Now s_2 contains only variables which already occurred to its left (in l and t_1) and are thus bound. The instantiated term s_2 is then reduced until the (partially) instantiated term t_2 matches a reduct and so on. If all the conditions are satisfied, then all variables in the conditions are bound in the process of evaluating the conditions. Hence the reduct of $l\sigma$ is well-defined (but in general not unique) because r contains only variables which also appear in the conditions.

The proper subterm relation is denoted by $\rhd$. The next definition is based on the well-known fact that if $\succ$ is a well-founded partial order which is closed under contexts, then the order $\succ_{st} = (\succ \cup \rhd)^+$ is also well-founded.

Definition 2. *A deterministic 3-CTRS $(\mathcal{F}, \mathcal{R})$ is called* quasi-reductive *if there is an extension $\mathcal{F}'$ of the signature $\mathcal{F}$ (so $\mathcal{F} \subseteq \mathcal{F}'$) and a reduction order $\succ$ on $\mathcal{T}(\mathcal{F}', \mathcal{V})$ which, for every rule $l \rightarrow r \Leftarrow s_1 \rightarrow t_1, \ldots, s_k \rightarrow t_k \in \mathcal{R}$, every substitution $\sigma : \mathcal{V} \rightarrow \mathcal{T}(\mathcal{F}', \mathcal{V})$, and every $0 \leq i < k$ satisfies:*

1. *if $s_j \sigma \succeq t_j \sigma$ for every $1 \leq j \leq i$, then $l\sigma \succ_{st} s_{i+1}\sigma$,*
2. *if $s_j \sigma \succeq t_j \sigma$ for every $1 \leq j \leq k$, then $l\sigma \succ r\sigma$.*

Quasi-reductive deterministic 3-CTRSs were introduced by Ganzinger [Gan91, Def. 4.2] without mentioning that the original signature can be extended. This, however, is crucial because otherwise Propositions 4.3 and 4.4 in [Gan91] would be incorrect. For instance, [Gan91, Prop. 4.3] states the following sufficient condition for quasi-reductivity (cf. [BG89]): Let $\mathcal{F}'$ be an enrichment of the original signature $\mathcal{F}$ such that the order $\succ$ can be extended to a reduction order over $\mathcal{T}(\mathcal{F}', \mathcal{V})$. A deterministic rule $l \rightarrow r \Leftarrow s_1 \rightarrow t_1, \ldots, s_k \rightarrow t_k$ is quasi-reductive if there exists a sequence $h_i(x)$ of terms in $\mathcal{T}(\mathcal{F}', \mathcal{V})$, $x \in \mathcal{V}$, such that $l \succ h_1(s_1), h_i(t_i) \succeq h_{i+1}(s_{i+1}), 1 \leq i < k$, and $h_k(t_k) \succeq r$.

In order to show that [Gan91, Prop. 4.3] would be incorrect if signature extensions are not allowed, consider the 1-CTRS from [DOS88]

$$\mathcal{R} = \begin{cases} b \rightarrow c \\ f(b) \rightarrow f(a) \\ a \rightarrow c \quad \Leftarrow b \rightarrow c \end{cases}$$

over the signature $\mathcal{F} = \{a, b, c, f\}$. Note that no reduction order on $\mathcal{T}(\mathcal{F}, \mathcal{V})$ can prove quasi-reductivity of $\mathcal{R}$ because no partial order $\succ$ on $\mathcal{T}(\mathcal{F}, \mathcal{V})$ which is closed under contexts and has $f(b) \succ f(a)$ can have $a \succ b$. However, [Gan91, Prop. 4.3] is applicable with $\mathcal{F}' = \mathcal{F} \cup \{h\}$ and $\succ = \rightarrow^+_{\mathcal{R}'}$, where

$$\mathcal{R}' = \begin{cases} b \rightarrow c \\ f(b) \rightarrow f(a) \\ a \rightarrow h(b) \\ h(c) \rightarrow c \end{cases}$$

The relation $\succ$ is a reduction order on $\mathcal{T}(\mathcal{F}', \mathcal{V})$ because $\mathcal{R}'$ is terminating.

Next, we will introduce the new notion of quasi-decreasingness.

Definition 3. *A deterministic 3-CTRS $(\mathcal{F}, \mathcal{R})$ is called* quasi-decreasing *if there is a well-founded partial order $\succ$ on $\mathcal{T}(\mathcal{F}, \mathcal{V})$ satisfying:*

1. $\rightarrow_{\mathcal{R}} \subseteq \succ$,
2. *$\succ$ has the subterm property (hence $\succ = \succ_{st}$),*
3. *for every rule $l \rightarrow r \Leftarrow s_1 \rightarrow t_1, \ldots, s_k \rightarrow t_k \in \mathcal{R}$, every substitution σ, and $0 \leq i < k$: if $s_j \sigma \rightarrow^*_{\mathcal{R}} t_j \sigma$ for every $1 \leq j \leq i$, then $l\sigma \succ s_{i+1}\sigma$.*

Lemma 4. *Every quasi-reductive deterministic 3-CTRS is quasi-decreasing.*

Proof. If $(\mathcal{F}, \mathcal{R})$ is quasi-reductive, then there is an extension $\mathcal{F}'$ of the signature $\mathcal{F}$ and a reduction order $>$ on $\mathcal{T}(\mathcal{F}', \mathcal{V})$ which meets the requirements of Definition 2. It follows that the relation $\to_{\mathcal{R}}$ on $\mathcal{T}(\mathcal{F}', \mathcal{V})$ is a subset of $>$; see [Gan91, Lemma 4.5]. Let $\succ$ denote the restriction of $>_{st}$ to $\mathcal{T}(\mathcal{F}, \mathcal{V})$. Clearly, $\succ$ is a well-founded order on $\mathcal{T}(\mathcal{F}, \mathcal{V})$ such that $\to_{\mathcal{R}} \subseteq \succ$ and $\rhd \subseteq \succ$. Thus $\mathcal{R}$ is quasi-decreasing w.r.t. $\succ$ provided that for every rule $l \to r \Leftarrow s_1 \to t_1, \ldots, s_k \to t_k \in \mathcal{R}$, every substitution $\sigma : \mathcal{V} \to \mathcal{T}(\mathcal{F}, \mathcal{V})$, and $0 \le i < k$ we have: $s_j\sigma \to_{\mathcal{R}}^* t_j\sigma$ for every $1 \le j \le i$ implies $l\sigma \succ s_{i+1}\sigma$. Obviously $s_j\sigma \ge t_j\sigma$ is a consequence of $s_j\sigma \to_{\mathcal{R}}^* t_j\sigma$, where $1 \le j \le i$. Since $(\mathcal{F}, \mathcal{R})$ is quasi-reductive, it follows $l\sigma >_{st} s_{i+1}\sigma$. Finally, we obtain $l\sigma \succ s_{i+1}\sigma$ from $l\sigma, s_{i+1}\sigma \in \mathcal{T}(\mathcal{F}, \mathcal{V})$.

We do not know whether or not quasi-decreasingness implies quasi-reductivity. It is favorable, however, to handle quasi-decreasingness because it has two advantages over quasi-reductivity: (i) It does not depend on signature extensions and (ii) in requirement (3) of Definition 3, $l\sigma \succ_{st} s_{i+1}\sigma$ must hold only if $s_j\sigma \to_{\mathcal{R}}^* t_j\sigma$ whereas it must hold for all $s_j\sigma \succeq t_j\sigma$ according to Definition 2(1).

Finite quasi-reductive deterministic 3-CTRSs have a terminating and computable rewrite relation [Gan91,ALS94] and the same holds for quasi-decreasing systems. Our next goal is to provide a systematic way of showing quasi-reductivity. To this end, we transform every deterministic 3-CTRS $\mathcal{R}$ into an unconditional TRS $U(\mathcal{R})$. For normal 1-CTRSs, a similar transformation was already given in [BK86, Def. 2.5.1]. Marchiori [Mar96,Mar95] studied such transformations of 1-CTRSs (which he called *unravelings*) in detail.

Definition 5. *Let $\mathcal{R}$ be a deterministic 3-CTRS over the signature $\mathcal{F}$. For every rewrite rule $\rho : l \to r \Leftarrow c \in \mathcal{R}$, let $|\rho|$ denote the number of conditions in ρ. In the transformation, we need $|\rho|$ fresh function symbols $U_1^\rho, \ldots, U_{|\rho|}^\rho$ for every conditional rule $\rho \in \mathcal{R}$. Moreover, by abuse of notation, Var (resp. $\mathcal{E}Var$) denotes a function which assigns the sequence of the variables (in some fixed order) in the set $Var(t)$ (resp. $\mathcal{E}Var(t)$; cf. Def. 1) to a term t. We transform $\rho : l \to r \Leftarrow s_1 \to t_1, \ldots, s_{|\rho|} \to t_{|\rho|}$ into a set $U(\rho)$ of $|\rho| + 1$ unconditional rewrite rules as follows:*

$$l \to U_1^\rho(s_1, Var(l))$$
$$U_1^\rho(t_1, Var(l)) \to U_2^\rho(s_2, Var(l), \mathcal{E}Var(t_1))$$
$$U_2^\rho(t_2, Var(l), \mathcal{E}Var(t_1)) \to U_3^\rho(s_3, Var(l), \mathcal{E}Var(t_1), \mathcal{E}Var(t_2))$$
$$\cdots$$
$$U_{|\rho|}^\rho(t_{|\rho|}, Var(l), \mathcal{E}Var(t_1), \ldots, \mathcal{E}Var(t_{|\rho|-1})) \to r$$

Since $\mathcal{R}$ is deterministic, the system $U(\mathcal{R}) = \bigcup_{\rho \in \mathcal{R}} U(\rho)$ is an unconditional TRS over the extended signature $\mathcal{F}' = \mathcal{F} \cup \bigcup_{\rho \in \mathcal{R}, 1 \le i \le |\rho|} \{U_i^\rho\}$ (that is, $Var(r') \subseteq Var(l')$ holds for every rewrite rule $l' \to r' \in U(\mathcal{R})$). In the following, the symbols from $\mathcal{F}' \setminus \mathcal{F}$ are called U-symbols.

For example, the transformation of the *quicksort* system is

$$split(x, []) \rightarrow ([], [])$$
$$split(x, y : ys) \rightarrow U_1'(split(x, ys), x, y, ys)$$
$$U_1'((xs, zs), x, y, ys) \rightarrow U_2'(x \leq y, x, y, ys, xs, zs)$$
$$U_2'(true, x, y, ys, xs, zs) \rightarrow (xs, y : zs)$$
$$split(x, y : ys) \rightarrow U_1''(split(x, ys), x, y, ys)$$
$$U_1''((xs, zs), x, y, ys) \rightarrow U_2''(x \leq y, x, y, ys, xs, zs)$$
$$U_2''(false, x, y, ys, xs, zs) \rightarrow (y : xs, zs)$$
$$qsort([]) \rightarrow []$$
$$qsort(x : xs) \rightarrow U_1'''(split(x, xs), x, xs)$$
$$U_1'''((ys, zs), x, xs) \rightarrow qsort(ys) +\!\!+ (x : qsort(zs))$$

If functions are specified via distinct cases as in the *split* function (that is, the left-hand sides of two or more rules and a prefix of the sequences of their conditions coincide), then the transformation can be "optimized" as follows:

$$split(x, y : ys) \rightarrow U_1'(split(x, ys), x, y, ys)$$
$$U_1'((xs, zs), x, y, ys) \rightarrow U_2'(x \leq y, x, y, ys, xs, zs)$$
$$U_2'(true, x, y, ys, xs, zs) \rightarrow (xs, y : zs)$$
$$U_2'(false, x, y, ys, xs, zs) \rightarrow (y : xs, zs)$$

We omit the formal definition of this obvious optimization of the transformation U. It turns out that termination of $U(\mathcal{R})$ is a sufficient but not a necessary condition for quasi-reductivity of $\mathcal{R}$.

Proposition 6. *If $U(\mathcal{R})$ is terminating, then $\mathcal{R}$ is quasi-reductive.*

Proof. Let $\succ = \rightarrow_{U(\mathcal{R})}^+$ and note that $\succ$ is a reduction order on $\mathcal{T}(\mathcal{F}', \mathcal{V})$. For every rule $l \rightarrow r \Leftarrow s_1 \rightarrow t_1, \ldots, s_k \rightarrow t_k$ in $\mathcal{R}$, we show that $s_j\sigma \succeq t_j\sigma$ for every $1 \leq j \leq i < k$ implies $l\sigma \succ_{st} s_{i+1}\sigma$. We have the following derivation

$$
\begin{aligned}
l\sigma &\rightarrow_{U(\mathcal{R})} U_1^\rho(s_1, Var(l))\sigma \\
&\rightarrow_{U(\mathcal{R})}^* U_1^\rho(t_1, Var(l))\sigma \\
&\rightarrow_{U(\mathcal{R})} U_2^\rho(s_2, Var(l), \mathcal{E}Var(t_1))\sigma \\
&\rightarrow_{U(\mathcal{R})}^* U_i^\rho(t_i, Var(l), \mathcal{E}Var(t_1), \ldots, \mathcal{E}Var(t_{i-1}))\sigma \\
&\rightarrow_{U(\mathcal{R})} U_{i+1}^\rho(s_{i+1}, Var(l), \mathcal{E}Var(t_1), \ldots, \mathcal{E}Var(t_i))\sigma
\end{aligned}
$$

because $s_j\sigma \rightarrow_{U(\mathcal{R})}^* t_j\sigma$. Thus $l\sigma \succ_{st} s_{i+1}\sigma$. Requirement (2) of Definition 2 can be shown similarly.

A similar result for normal 1-CTRSs and a surprising counterexample to the converse of Proposition 6 can be found in [Mar96, Mar95]. In our *quicksort* example, termination of the transformed system can be shown automatically by the dependency pair method of Arts and Giesl [AG97a]. Thus the *quicksort* system is quasi-reductive.

4   The Main Theorem

Although quasi-decreasingness of a deterministic 3-CTRS $\mathcal{R}$ does not imply termination of $U(\mathcal{R})$, it does imply innermost termination of $U(\mathcal{R})$. This entire section is dedicated to a proof of this non-trivial fact.

Definition 7. *Let $\mathcal{R}$ be a deterministic 3-CTRS and $U(\mathcal{R})$ its transformed TRS. We define a transformation $\nabla \colon \mathcal{T}(\mathcal{F}', V) \to \mathcal{T}(\mathcal{F}, V)$ by*

$$\nabla(t) = \begin{cases} t & \text{if } t \in V \cup \mathcal{F}^{(0)} \\ f(\nabla(t_1), \ldots, \nabla(t_n)) & \text{if } t = f(t_1, \ldots, t_n), f \in \mathcal{F}^{(n)} \\ l\tau & \text{if } t = U_i^\rho(u, t_1, \ldots, t_n, \ldots) \end{cases}$$

where l is the left-hand side of the rule ρ, $Var(l) = x_1, \ldots, x_n$ (that is to say, $U_i^\rho(u, Var(l), \ldots) = U_i^\rho(u, x_1, \ldots, x_n, \ldots)$), and $\tau \colon Var(l) \to \mathcal{T}(\mathcal{F}, V)$ is defined by $\tau(x_j) = \nabla(t_j)$. For any σ, we define σ_∇ by $x\sigma_\nabla = \nabla(x\sigma)$.

For instance, if $\mathcal{R} = \{\rho_1 : f(x, y) \to z \Leftarrow x \to z, \rho_2 : a \to b \Leftarrow g(c) \to d\}$, then $U(\mathcal{R}) = \{f(x, y) \to U_1^{\rho_1}(x, x, y), U_1^{\rho_1}(z, x, y) \to z, a \to U_1^{\rho_2}(g(c)), U_1^{\rho_2}(d) \to b\}$ and for the term $t = g(U_1^{\rho_1}(U_1^{\rho_2}(d), U_1^{\rho_2}(b), U_1^{\rho_1}(a, b, U_1^{\rho_2}(d))))$, we have $\nabla(t) = g(f(a, f(b, a)))$.

Informally, in a derivation $D : s \xrightarrow{i}{}^*_{U(\mathcal{R})} t$, where $s \in \mathcal{T}(\mathcal{F}, V)$, ∇ replaces every maximal U-subterm u (a *U-subterm* is a subterm with a U-symbol at the root) by $\nabla(u) \in \mathcal{T}(\mathcal{F}, V)$ – the term which created u in D.

Lemma 8. *Let $s \in \mathcal{T}(\mathcal{F}, V)$. If $s \xrightarrow{i}{}^*_{U(\mathcal{R})} t$, then $s \to^*_{\mathcal{R}} \nabla(t) \xrightarrow{i}{}^*_{U(\mathcal{R})} t$.*

Proof. By induction on the length ℓ of the derivation $D : s \xrightarrow{i}{}^*_{U(\mathcal{R})} t$. The base case $\ell = 0$ is obviously true. So suppose $D\colon s \xrightarrow{i\ell}{}_{U(\mathcal{R})} t' \xrightarrow{i}{}_{U(\mathcal{R})} t$. According to the inductive hypothesis, we have $s \to^*_{\mathcal{R}} \nabla(t') \xrightarrow{i}{}^*_{U(\mathcal{R})} t'$. We show $\nabla(t') \to^*_{\mathcal{R}} \nabla(t) \xrightarrow{i}{}^*_{U(\mathcal{R})} t$ by case analysis. Suppose first that the redex contracted in the step $t' \xrightarrow{i}{}_{U(\mathcal{R})} t$ is below a U-symbol. Note that $l\sigma \xrightarrow{i}{}_{U(\mathcal{R})} U_1^\rho(s_1, Var(l))\sigma$ or $U_i^\rho(t_i, Var(l), \ldots)\sigma \xrightarrow{i}{}_{U(\mathcal{R})} U_{i+1}^\rho(s_{i+1}, Var(l), \ldots)\sigma$ imply that every argument in the terms $U_1^\rho(s_1, Var(l))\sigma$ and $U_{i+1}^\rho(s_{i+1}, Var(l), \ldots)\sigma$ is in normal form except for (possibly) the first one. This means that the redex contracted in $t' \xrightarrow{i}{}_{U(\mathcal{R})} t$ is a subterm of the first argument of some U-subterm of t'. So

$$\nabla(t) = \nabla(t') \xrightarrow{i}{}^*_{U(\mathcal{R})} t' \xrightarrow{i}{}_{U(\mathcal{R})} t$$

because the definition of $\nabla(t)$ is independent of the first argument of U-subterms of t. Next, we assume that there is no U-symbol above the contracted redex. Note that if $t' = C[l'\sigma] \in \mathcal{T}(\mathcal{F}', V)$ with $l' \to r' \in U(\mathcal{R})$ and there is no U-symbol above $l'\sigma$ in C, then $\nabla(t') = \nabla(C)[\nabla(l'\sigma)]$. Thus, it suffices to show the claim for the following cases:

1. $t' = l\sigma \xrightarrow{i}_{U(\mathcal{R})} r\sigma = t$, where $l \to r \in \mathcal{R}$.
2. $t' = l\sigma \xrightarrow{i}_{U(\mathcal{R})} U_1^\rho(s_1, Var(l))\sigma = t$.
3. $t' = U_i^\rho(t_i, Var(l), \dots)\sigma \xrightarrow{i}_{U(\mathcal{R})} U_{i+1}^\rho(s_{i+1}, Var(l), \dots)\sigma = t$.
4. $t' = U_{|\rho|}^\rho(t_{|\rho|}, Var(l), \dots)\sigma \xrightarrow{i}_{U(\mathcal{R})} r\sigma = t$.

The first three cases are easy to prove. In case (4), we have $\nabla(t') = \nabla(l\sigma) = l\sigma_\nabla$. By the inductive hypothesis, $\nabla(t') = l\sigma_\nabla \xrightarrow{i\,*}_{U(\mathcal{R})} t'$ holds true. Moreover, $\nabla(t) = r\sigma_\nabla$. Thus one must show that $l\sigma_\nabla \to_\mathcal{R}^* r\sigma_\nabla \xrightarrow{i\,*}_{U(\mathcal{R})} r\sigma$. The derivation D must contain a subsequence

$$D' : l\sigma_\nabla \xrightarrow{i\,*}_{U(\mathcal{R})} l\sigma \xrightarrow{i}_{U(\mathcal{R})} U_1^\rho(s_1, Var(l))\sigma \xrightarrow{i\,*}_{U(\mathcal{R})} U_1^\rho(t_1, Var(l))\sigma$$
$$\xrightarrow{i}_{U(\mathcal{R})} U_2^\rho(s_2, Var(l), \mathcal{E}Var(t_1))\sigma \xrightarrow{i\,*}_{U(\mathcal{R})} \cdots$$
$$\xrightarrow{i\,*}_{U(\mathcal{R})} U_{|\rho|}^\rho(t_{|\rho|}, Var(l), \dots)\sigma \xrightarrow{i}_{U(\mathcal{R})} r\sigma.$$

Note that $x\sigma_\nabla \xrightarrow{i\,*}_{U(\mathcal{R})} x\sigma$ holds for every variable $x \in Var(l)$. If $length(D') < length(D)$, then the claim follows from the inductive hypothesis. So we have to show it for the case $D' = D$. Consider the derivation $D_1 : \nabla(s_1\sigma) = s_1\sigma_\nabla \xrightarrow{i\,*}_{U(\mathcal{R})} s_1\sigma \xrightarrow{i\,*}_{U(\mathcal{R})} t_1\sigma$. Since $length(D_1) < length(D)$, we infer from the inductive hypothesis that $s_1\sigma_\nabla \to_\mathcal{R}^* \nabla(t_1\sigma) = t_1\sigma_\nabla \xrightarrow{i\,*}_{U(\mathcal{R})} t_1\sigma$. In particular, $x\sigma_\nabla \xrightarrow{i\,*}_{U(\mathcal{R})} x\sigma$ is true for every variable $x \in Var(l) \cup Var(t_1)$. By continuing along these lines, we derive

$$s_j\sigma_\nabla \to_\mathcal{R}^* t_j\sigma_\nabla \xrightarrow{i\,*}_{U(\mathcal{R})} t_j\sigma$$

for all $j \in \{1, \dots, |\rho|\}$. Consequently, $l\sigma_\nabla \to_\mathcal{R} r\sigma_\nabla$. Finally, $r\sigma_\nabla \xrightarrow{i\,*}_{U(\mathcal{R})} r\sigma$ is a consequence of the fact that $x\sigma_\nabla \xrightarrow{i\,*}_{U(\mathcal{R})} x\sigma$ holds for every $x \in Var(l) \cup \bigcup_{j=1}^{|\rho|} Var(t_j)$ in conjunction with $Var(r) \subseteq Var(l) \cup \bigcup_{j=1}^{|\rho|} Var(t_j)$.

Lemma 9. *If $\mathcal{R}$ is a quasi-decreasing deterministic 3-CTRS, then there is no infinite innermost $U(\mathcal{R})$-derivation starting from a term $s \in \mathcal{T}(\mathcal{F}, \mathcal{V})$.*

Proof. Let $\mathcal{R}$ be quasi-decreasing w.r.t. $\succ$. We show by well-founded induction on $\succ$ that every innermost $U(\mathcal{R})$-derivation starting from $s \in \mathcal{T}(\mathcal{F}, \mathcal{V})$ is finite. If $s \to_\mathcal{R}^+ u \in \mathcal{T}(\mathcal{F}, \mathcal{V})$, then $s \succ u$ because $\to_\mathcal{R} \subseteq \succ$ and it follows from the inductive hypothesis that every innermost $U(\mathcal{R})$-derivation starting from $u \in \mathcal{T}(\mathcal{F}, \mathcal{V})$ is finite. Moreover, if t is a proper subterm of s and $t \to_\mathcal{R}^* u \in \mathcal{T}(\mathcal{F}, \mathcal{V})$, then we infer $s \succ t \succeq u$ because $\succ$ has the subterm property and $\to_\mathcal{R} \subseteq \succ$. Hence every innermost $U(\mathcal{R})$-derivation starting from t or u is also finite.

For a proof by contradiction, suppose that there is an infinite innermost $U(\mathcal{R})$-derivation D starting from s. According to the above, D must be of the form

$$D : s \xrightarrow{i\,*}_{U(\mathcal{R})} f(v_1, \dots, v_m) = l\sigma \xrightarrow{i}_{U(\mathcal{R})} U_1^\rho(s_1, Var(l))\sigma \xrightarrow{i}_{U(\mathcal{R})} \cdots$$

where every $v_j \in NF(\to_{U(\mathcal{R})})$, i.e., every v_j is a normal form w.r.t. $\to_{U(\mathcal{R})}$. Since $u_j \xrightarrow{i\ *}_{U(\mathcal{R})} v_j$, we derive from Lemma 8 that $u_j \to_{\mathcal{R}}^* \nabla(v_j) \xrightarrow{i\ *}_{U(\mathcal{R})} v_j$. If $u_j \to_{\mathcal{R}}^+ \nabla(v_j)$, then the derivation

$$s \to_{\mathcal{R}}^+ f(u_1, \ldots, u_{j-1}, \nabla(v_j), u_{j+1}, \ldots u_m) = t \xrightarrow{i\ *}_{U(\mathcal{R})} f(v_1, \ldots, v_m) \xrightarrow{i}_{U(\mathcal{R})} \cdots$$

is infinite which is impossible because $\to_{\mathcal{R}}^+ \subseteq \succ$ and hence there is no infinite innermost $U(\mathcal{R})$-derivation starting from t. Thus $u_j = \nabla(v_j)$ for every $j \in \mathbb{N}$. It is not difficult to check that $s = l\sigma_\nabla$ follows as a consequence. Therefore, D has the form

$$D : s = l\sigma_\nabla \xrightarrow{i\ *}_{U(\mathcal{R})} l\sigma \xrightarrow{i}_{U(\mathcal{R})} U_1^\rho(s_1, Var(l))\sigma \xrightarrow{i}_{U(\mathcal{R})} \cdots$$

The validity of the inequality $l\sigma_\nabla \succ s_1\sigma_\nabla$ is a consequence of the fact that $\mathcal{R}$ is quasi-decreasing. Hence there is no infinite innermost $U(\mathcal{R})$-derivation starting from $s_1\sigma_\nabla$. Since $s_1\sigma_\nabla \xrightarrow{i\ *}_{U(\mathcal{R})} s_1\sigma$, every infinite innermost $U(\mathcal{R})$-derivation starting from $s_1\sigma$ must be finite. The derivation D thus looks like

$$s = l\sigma_\nabla \xrightarrow{i\ *}_{U(\mathcal{R})} l\sigma \xrightarrow{i}_{U(\mathcal{R})} U_1^\rho(s_1, Var(l))\sigma \xrightarrow{i\ *}_{U(\mathcal{R})} U_1^\rho(t_1, Var(l))\sigma \xrightarrow{i}_{U(\mathcal{R})} \cdots$$

Now $s_1\sigma_\nabla \xrightarrow{i\ *}_{U(\mathcal{R})} s_1\sigma \xrightarrow{i\ *}_{U(\mathcal{R})} t_1\sigma$ yields $s_1\sigma_\nabla \to_{\mathcal{R}}^* t_1\sigma_\nabla \xrightarrow{i\ *}_{U(\mathcal{R})} t_1\sigma$ by Lemma 8. It follows $l\sigma_\nabla \succ s_2\sigma_\nabla$ because $\mathcal{R}$ is quasi-decreasing w.r.t. $\succ$ and we may continue with the above reasoning. All in all, D must have the form

$$l\sigma_\nabla \xrightarrow{i\ +}_{U(\mathcal{R})} U_1^\rho(s_1, Var(l))\sigma \xrightarrow{i\ *}_{U(\mathcal{R})} U_{|\rho|}^\rho(t_{|\rho|}, Var(l), \ldots)\sigma \xrightarrow{i}_{U(\mathcal{R})} r\sigma \xrightarrow{i}_{U(\mathcal{R})} \cdots$$

Hence $l\sigma_\nabla \to_{\mathcal{R}} r\sigma_\nabla \xrightarrow{i\ *}_{U(\mathcal{R})} r\sigma$ by Lemma 8. We conclude that there is an infinite innermost $U(\mathcal{R})$-derivation starting from $r\sigma_\nabla$ which is impossible because $s = l\sigma_\nabla \succ r\sigma_\nabla$.

Theorem 10. If $\mathcal{R}$ is a quasi-decreasing deterministic 3-CTRS, then $U(\mathcal{R})$ is innermost terminating.

Proof. We prove by structural induction that there is no infinite innermost $U(\mathcal{R})$-derivation starting from a term $s \in \mathcal{T}(\mathcal{F}', \mathcal{V})$. If (a) s is a variable, then it is in normal form. If (b) s is a constant, then $s \in \mathcal{F}$ and the claim follows from Lemma 9. Suppose (c) $s = U_i^\rho(u_1, \ldots, u_m)$. Every infinite innermost $U(\mathcal{R})$-derivation starting from s must have the form

$$D : s = U_i^\rho(u_1, \ldots, u_m) \xrightarrow{i\ *}_{U(\mathcal{R})} U_i^\rho(v_1, \ldots, v_m) = U_i^\rho(t_i, Var(l), \ldots)\sigma$$
$$\xrightarrow{i}_{U(\mathcal{R})} U_{i+1}^\rho(s_{i+1}, Var(l), \ldots)\sigma \xrightarrow{i}_{U(\mathcal{R})} \cdots$$

where $v_j \in NF(\to_{U(\mathcal{R})})$ for every $1 \le j \le m$. If s_{i+1} is a variable, then $s_{i+1}\sigma \in NF(\to_{U(\mathcal{R})})$. Otherwise $root(s_{i+1}) \in \mathcal{F}$ and by case (d) there is no infinite innermost $U(\mathcal{R})$-derivation starting from $s_{i+1}\sigma$. A repetition of these arguments shows that D has the form

$$D : s = U_i^\rho(u_1, \ldots, u_m) \xrightarrow{i\ *}_{U(\mathcal{R})} U_{|\rho|}^\rho(t_{|\rho|}, Var(l), \ldots)\sigma \xrightarrow{i}_{U(\mathcal{R})} r\sigma \xrightarrow{i}_{U(\mathcal{R})} \cdots$$

Again, if r is a variable, then $r\sigma \in NF(\to_{U(\mathcal{R})})$. Otherwise $root(r) \in \mathcal{F}$ and by case (d) there is no infinite innermost $U(\mathcal{R})$-derivation starting from $r\sigma$.

(d) Suppose $s = f(u_1, \ldots, u_m)$, where $f \in \mathcal{F}$ and $u_j \in \mathcal{T}(\mathcal{F}', \mathcal{V})$. For a proof by contradiction, suppose that there is an infinite innermost $U(\mathcal{R})$-derivation

$$D : s = f(u_1, \ldots, u_m) \xrightarrow{i\ *}_{U(\mathcal{R})} f(v_1, \ldots, v_m) = t \xrightarrow{i}_{U(\mathcal{R})} \cdots$$

where $v_j \in NF(\to_{U(\mathcal{R})})$. If $t \in \mathcal{T}(\mathcal{F}, \mathcal{V})$, then the assertion follows from Lemma 9. Otherwise, t contains U-subterms but all of them are in normal form. We may write $t = C[w_1, \ldots, w_n]$, where $C \in \mathcal{T}(\mathcal{F}, \mathcal{V})$ and every term w_i is a (maximal) U-subterm of t. In order to cope with non-left-linear rules, we have to distinguish between those U-subterms of t which can be created by a term without U-symbols and those which can't. For the sake of simplicity, let us assume that for every $1 \leq j \leq i$ there is a term $w'_j \in \mathcal{T}(\mathcal{F}, \mathcal{V})$ such that $w'_j \xrightarrow{i\ +}_{U(\mathcal{R})} w_j$ but for every $i < j \leq n$ no such term exists. Then there is an infinite innermost $U(\mathcal{R})$-derivation

$$D' : s' = C[w'_1, \ldots, w'_i, w_{i+1}, \ldots, w_n] \xrightarrow{i\ *}_{U(\mathcal{R})} f(v_1, \ldots, v_m) = t \xrightarrow{i}_{U(\mathcal{R})} \cdots$$

In order to get rid of the remaining U-subterms $w_{i+1}, \ldots, w_n$, we mark[1] every w_j, $i < j \leq n$, and choose fresh variables $x_{i+1}, \ldots, x_n$ with the property that $x_j = x_k$ if and only if $w_j = w_k$ for $i < j < k \leq n$. Let Ψ be the transformation which replaces every marked occurrence of w_j in a term with x_j. We claim that the transformed derivation $\Psi(D')$

$$\Psi(s') = C[w'_1, \ldots, w'_i, x_{i+1}, \ldots, x_n] \xrightarrow{i\ *}_{U(\mathcal{R})} \Psi(f(v_1, \ldots, v_m)) = \Psi(t) \xrightarrow{i}_{U(\mathcal{R})} \cdots$$

is an infinite innermost $U(\mathcal{R})$-derivation. Since $\Psi(s') \in \mathcal{T}(\mathcal{F}, \mathcal{V})$, this yields the desired contradiction to Lemma 9. Let $C[l\sigma] \xrightarrow{i}_{U(\mathcal{R})} C[r\sigma]$ be a reduction step in D', where $l \to r \in U(\mathcal{R})$. The reduction step cannot take place in a marked subterm because every marked subterm is in normal form, so $\Psi(C[l\sigma]) = \Psi(C)[\Psi(l\sigma)]$. Moreover, we have $\Psi(l\sigma) = l\sigma_\Psi$, where σ_Ψ is defined by $x\sigma_\Psi = \Psi(x\sigma)$ because no proper subterm of l contains a U-symbol. It is thus sufficient to show $l\sigma_\Psi \xrightarrow{i}_{U(\mathcal{R})} r\sigma_\Psi$ because this yields

$$\Psi(C[l\sigma]) = \Psi(C)[l\sigma_\Psi] \xrightarrow{i}_{U(\mathcal{R})} \Psi(C)[r\sigma_\Psi] = \Psi(C[r\sigma]).$$

We first show $l\sigma_\Psi \to_{U(\mathcal{R})} r\sigma_\Psi$. Since l may be non-left-linear, we have to show that $x\sigma = y\sigma$ implies $x\sigma_\Psi = y\sigma_\Psi$ for every pair x, y of variables from $Var(l)$. So suppose that $x\sigma$ contains a marked U-subterm, say at position p. Then $y\sigma$ contains the same subterm u at position p. Since u hasn't been created in the derivation $\Psi(D')$ – there is no $u' \in \mathcal{T}(\mathcal{F}, \mathcal{V})$ with $u' \xrightarrow{i\ +}_{U(\mathcal{R})} u$ – it is also marked. Therefore, $l\sigma_\Psi \to_{U(\mathcal{R})} r\sigma_\Psi$. Furthermore, by the choice of the fresh variables $x_{i+1}, \ldots, x_n$, $x\sigma_\Psi = y\sigma_\Psi$ also implies $x\sigma = y\sigma$. Consequently, $l\sigma_\Psi \to_{U(\mathcal{R})} r\sigma_\Psi$ is an innermost reduction step (for otherwise $l\sigma \to_{U(\mathcal{R})} r\sigma$ wouldn't be innermost). This concludes the proof.

---

[1] For instance by underlining the root symbol.

5   Application 1: Modularity

From the previous sections, we know that the following implications hold.

$$U(\mathcal{R}) \text{ is terminating } \Rightarrow \mathcal{R} \text{ is quasi-reductive } \Rightarrow \mathcal{R} \text{ is quasi-decreasing}$$
$$\Rightarrow U(\mathcal{R}) \text{ is innermost terminating.}$$

Gramlich [Gra95, Thm. 3.23] showed that a non-overlapping TRS is terminating if and only if it is innermost terminating. Thus, if $U(\mathcal{R})$ is non-overlapping, then the above implications are in fact equivalences. However, non-overlappingness of $U(\mathcal{R})$ is not implied by non-overlappingness of $\mathcal{R}$. For example, the system $\mathcal{R} = \{a \to b \Leftarrow b \to a\}$ is non-overlapping but $U(\mathcal{R}) = \{a \to U(b), U(a) \to b\}$ is not. The situation is different for syntactically deterministic 3-CTRSs which will be considered next.

Definition 11. *A deterministic 3-CTRS $\mathcal{R}$ is called* syntactically deterministic *if, for every $l \to r \Leftarrow s_1 \to t_1, \ldots, s_k \to t_k$ in $\mathcal{R}$, every term t_i is a constructor term[2] or a ground $\mathcal{R}_u$-normal form, where $\mathcal{R}_u = \{l \to r \mid l \to r \Leftarrow c \in \mathcal{R}\}$.*

Syntactically deterministic CTRSs are a natural generalization of normal CTRSs. The *quicksort* system shows that these systems arise quite naturally. As a matter of fact, every syntactically deterministic CTRS is strongly deterministic (see [ALS94] for a definition) but in contrast to the latter property, it is decidable whether a CTRS is syntactically deterministic or not. Strongly deterministic systems are interesting because of the critical pair lemma that holds for them [ALS94, Thm. 4.1].

According to the next lemma, for non-overlapping syntactically deterministic 3-CTRSs all of the above implications are equivalences.

Lemma 12. *The transformed system $U(\mathcal{R})$ of a syntactically deterministic 3-CTRS $\mathcal{R}$ is non-overlapping if $\mathcal{R}$ is non-overlapping.*

Proof. Let $l_1 \to r_1$ and $l_2 \to r_2$ be renamed versions of rewrite rules from $U(\mathcal{R})$ such that they don't have variables in common. If l_1 and l_2 are left-hand sides of rules from $\mathcal{R}$, then they cannot overlap because $\mathcal{R}$ is non-overlapping. If both l_1 and l_2 have a U-symbol at their root, then they cannot overlap either because of the shape of the U-rules (U-symbols only occur at root positions and the root symbols of two different U-rules cannot be the same). Thus let l_1 be a left-hand side of a rule from $\mathcal{R}$ and $l_2 = U_i^p(t_i, Var(l), \ldots)$. For an indirect proof, suppose that l_1 and l_2 do overlap. Obviously, l_1 must overlap with a subterm of t_i. This, however, is impossible because t_i is either a constructor term or a ground $\mathcal{R}_u$-normal form. □

Lemma 12 can be refined to demand only exactly what is required by the proof. For instance, the 3-CTRS $\mathcal{R}$ need not be syntactically deterministic; it is sufficient to demand that no left-hand side l_1 of a rule from $\mathcal{R}$ overlaps a term

---

[2] A *constructor term* is a term without defined symbols.

t_i of another rule $l_2 \to r_2 \Leftarrow s_1 \to t_1, \ldots, s_k \to t_k$ from $\mathcal{R}$. Moreover, non-overlappingness of $\mathcal{R}$ can slightly be weakened in the preceding lemma. For instance, we may allow infeasible critical pairs as in the *quicksort* system by using the "optimized" U-transformation explained earlier.

Now we are in a position to prove a nice modularity result for CTRSs with *extra variables on the right-hand sides* of the rules. The reader is assumed to be familiar with the concepts of the field of modularity. Details and references to the literature can be found e.g. in [Ohl95]. Let $\mathcal{R}$ be a CTRS over the signature $\mathcal{F}$. A function symbol $f \in \mathcal{F}$ is called a *defined symbol* if there is a rewrite rule $l \to r \Leftarrow c \in \mathcal{R}$ such that $f = root(l)$. Function symbols from $\mathcal{F}$ which are not defined symbols are called *constructors*. If $\mathcal{R}_1$ and $\mathcal{R}_2$ are CTRSs over the signatures $\mathcal{F}_1$ and $\mathcal{F}_2$, respectively, then their *combined system* is their union $\mathcal{R} = \mathcal{R}_1 \cup \mathcal{R}_2$ over the signature $\mathcal{F} = \mathcal{F}_1 \cup \mathcal{F}_2$. Its set of defined symbols is $\mathcal{D} = \mathcal{D}_1 \cup \mathcal{D}_2$ and its set of constructors is $\mathcal{C} = \mathcal{F} \setminus \mathcal{D}$, where $\mathcal{D}_i$ $(\mathcal{C}_i)$ denotes the defined symbols (constructors) in $\mathcal{R}_i$.

(1) $\mathcal{R}_1$ and $\mathcal{R}_2$ are *disjoint* if $\mathcal{F}_1 \cap \mathcal{F}_2 = \emptyset$.
(2) $\mathcal{R}_1$ and $\mathcal{R}_2$ are *constructor-sharing* if $\mathcal{F}_1 \cap \mathcal{F}_2 = \mathcal{C}_1 \cap \mathcal{C}_2 \ (\subseteq \mathcal{C})$.
(3) $\mathcal{R}_1$ and $\mathcal{R}_2$ are *composable* if $\mathcal{C}_1 \cap \mathcal{D}_2 = \mathcal{D}_1 \cap \mathcal{C}_2 = \emptyset$ and both systems contain all rewrite rules that define a defined symbol whenever that symbol is shared, that is to say, $\{l \to r \Leftarrow c \in \mathcal{R} \mid root(l) \in \mathcal{D}_1 \cap \mathcal{D}_2\} \subseteq \mathcal{R}_1 \cap \mathcal{R}_2$.

A property P is *modular* for a certain class of CTRSs if, for all CTRSs $(\mathcal{F}_1, \mathcal{R}_1)$ and $(\mathcal{F}_2, \mathcal{R}_2)$ belonging to that class and having property P, their union $(\mathcal{F}_1 \cup \mathcal{F}_2, \mathcal{R}_1 \cup \mathcal{R}_2)$ also belongs to that class and has the property P.

Proposition 13. *Let $\mathcal{R}_1$ and $\mathcal{R}_2$ be quasi-reductive (quasi-decreasing, respectively) deterministic 3-CTRSs. Their combined system $\mathcal{R}_1 \cup \mathcal{R}_2$ is quasi-reductive if*

1. *$U(\mathcal{R}_1)$ and $U(\mathcal{R}_2)$ belong to a class of TRSs for which innermost termination is modular, and*
2. *$U(\mathcal{R}_1 \cup \mathcal{R}_2)$ is non-overlapping.*

Proof. Since $\mathcal{R}_1$ and $\mathcal{R}_2$ are quasi-reductive, they are quasi-decreasing by Lemma 4. Thus the transformed TRSs $U(\mathcal{R}_1)$ and $U(\mathcal{R}_2)$ are innermost terminating by Theorem 10. Their combination $U(\mathcal{R}_1) \cup U(\mathcal{R}_2) = U(\mathcal{R}_1 \cup \mathcal{R}_2)$ is also innermost terminating because innermost termination is modular. Since innermost termination and termination coincide for non-overlapping systems, $U(\mathcal{R}_1 \cup \mathcal{R}_2)$ is terminating. Now the assertion follows from Proposition 6.

Theorem 14. *Quasi-reductivity (quasi-decreasingness, respectively) is modular for non-overlapping syntactically deterministic composable 3-CTRSs.*

Proof. Let $\mathcal{R}_1$ and $\mathcal{R}_2$ be quasi-reductive non-overlapping syntactically deterministic composable 3-CTRSs. It is relatively easy to verify that $U(\mathcal{R}_1)$ and $U(\mathcal{R}_2)$ are composable since $\mathcal{R}_1$ and $\mathcal{R}_2$ are composable (note that the U-symbols

U_i^ρ used in the transformation $U(\rho)$ are marked with the rule ρ). Note that innermost termination is modular for composable TRSs; see [Ohl95]. According to Lemma 12, the TRSs $U(\mathcal{R}_1)$ and $U(\mathcal{R}_2)$ are non-overlapping. The system $U(\mathcal{R}_1 \cup \mathcal{R}_2) = U(\mathcal{R}_1) \cup U(\mathcal{R}_2)$ is non-overlapping as well because the union of two non-overlapping composable TRSs is again non-overlapping. Hence the combined system $\mathcal{R}_1 \cup \mathcal{R}_2$ is quasi-reductive by Proposition 13. Furthermore, $\mathcal{R}_1 \cup \mathcal{R}_2$ is obviously non-overlapping and syntactically deterministic.

As already mentioned, Lemma 12 can be generalized as follows: If functions are defined by distinct cases, then the "optimized" transformation described earlier still yields a non-overlapping transformed system $U(\mathcal{R})$. Clearly, Theorem 14 remains valid for these systems. For example, this generalized version of Theorem 14 can be applied to the function *quorem* which computes the quotient and the remainder of m and n

$$0 - s(y) \to 0$$
$$x - 0 \to x$$
$$s(x) - s(y) \to x - y$$
$$x < 0 \to false$$
$$0 < s(x) \to true$$
$$s(x) < s(y) \to x < y$$
$$quorem(0, s(y)) \to \langle 0, 0 \rangle$$
$$quorem(s(x), s(y)) \to \langle 0, s(x) \rangle \Leftarrow x < y \to true$$
$$quorem(s(x), s(y)) \to \langle s(q), r \rangle \Leftarrow x < y \to false,$$
$$quorem(x - y, s(y)) \to \langle q, r \rangle$$

and the function *filter* which filters all elements out of a list of natural numbers that have remainder r when divided by n

$$0 - s(y) \to 0$$
$$x - 0 \to x$$
$$s(x) - s(y) \to x - y$$
$$0 \le y \to true$$
$$s(x) \le 0 \to false$$
$$s(x) \le s(y) \to x \le y$$
$$eq(0, 0) \to true$$
$$eq(s(x), 0) \to false$$
$$eq(0, s(y)) \to false$$
$$eq(s(x), s(y)) \to eq(x, y)$$
$$mod(0, y) \to 0$$
$$mod(s(x), 0) \to 0$$
$$mod(s(x), s(y)) \to mod(x - y, s(y)) \Leftarrow y \le x \to true$$
$$mod(s(x), s(y)) \to s(x) \qquad\qquad \Leftarrow y \le x \to false$$
$$filter(n, r, nil) \to nil$$
$$filter(n, r, x : xs) \to x : filter(n, r, xs) \Leftarrow mod(x, n) \to r', eq(r, r') \to true$$
$$filter(n, r, x : xs) \to filter(n, r, xs) \quad \Leftarrow mod(x, n) \to r', eq(r, r') \to false$$

Both systems are syntactically deterministic composable 3-CTRSs which can be shown quasi-reductive by Proposition 6 in conjunction with the dependency pair technique. Hence we can conclude from the generalized version of Theorem 14 that their combined system is also quasi-reductive.

6   Application 2: Well-Moded Logic Programs

Next we will show how our results can be used to show termination of well-moded logic programs. We assume that the reader is familiar with logic programming and SLD derivations and will only review the following notions.

If P is a predicate symbol and $t_1, \ldots, t_n$ are terms, then $P(t_1, \ldots, t_n)$ is an *atom*. A *Horn-clause* is a formula of the form $A \leftarrow B_1, \ldots, B_m$ where $m \geq 0$ and A, B_i are atoms. A *logic program* $\mathcal{P}$ is a set of Horn-clauses. A *query* is a formula of the form $\leftarrow B_1, \ldots, B_m$ where $m \geq 1$ and B_i are atoms.

A logic program $\mathcal{P}$ is *moded* if for each occurrence of an atom $A = P(t_1, \ldots, t_n)$ there is a function $m_A : \{1, \ldots, n\} \to \{in, out\}$. If $m_A(i) = in$ $(m_A(i) = out)$ then position i is called an *input position (output position)* of A. A variable x occurs in an input (output) position in A if $x \in Var(t_i)$ for some i with $m_A(i) = in$ $(m_A(i) = out)$.

Here only left-to-right SLD-derivations will be considered. In these derivations it is always the leftmost literal of a query that is selected for the next resolution step. Moreover, we will restrict our attention to LR-well-moded programs.

Definition 15. *1. Let $C = A \leftarrow B_1, \ldots, B_m$ be a clause and $x \in Var(C)$. The head A of C is called a* producer (consumer) *of x, if x occurs in an input (output) position of A. The body atom B_j is called a producer (consumer) of x, if x occurs in an output (input) position of B_j.*

2. The clause $B_0 \leftarrow B_1, \ldots, B_m$ is called LR-well-moded, if every variable x in the clause has a producer B_i $(0 \leq i \leq m)$ and $i < j$ for every consumer B_j $(1 \leq j \leq m)$ of x in the body of the clause. A logic program $\mathcal{P}$ is LR-well-moded if every clause in $\mathcal{P}$ is LR-well-moded.

3. A query $\leftarrow B_1, \ldots, B_m$ is LR-well-moded if every variable x in the query has a producer B_i such that for every consumer B_j of x we have $i < j$.

By this definition, if $\leftarrow B_1, \ldots, B_m$ is LR-well-moded and $B_1 = P(t_1, \ldots, t_n)$, then, for all input positions i of B_1, t_i is a ground term.

We transform every LR-well-moded logic program $\mathcal{P}$ into a deterministic 3-CTRS $R_{\mathcal{P}}$ as in [GW93,ALS94]. For every atom $A = P(t_1, \ldots, t_n)$ with input positions $i_1, \ldots, i_k$ and output positions $i_{k+1}, \ldots, i_n$ there are two new function symbols P_{in} and P_{out} and we define $\rho_{in}(A) = P_{in}(t_{i_1}, \ldots, t_{i_k})$, $\rho_{out}(A) = P_{out}(t_{i_{k+1}}, \ldots, t_{i_n})$, and $\rho(A) = \rho_{in}(A) \to \rho_{out}(A)$. The transformation $\rho(C)$ of a clause $C = A \leftarrow B_1, \ldots, B_m$ is defined to be the rule

$$\rho(A) \Leftarrow \rho(B_1), \ldots, \rho(B_m)$$

and with every logic program $\mathcal{P}$ we associate $R_{\mathcal{P}} = \{\rho(C) \mid C \text{ in } \mathcal{P}\}$.

Note that $R_\mathcal{P}$ is a syntactically deterministic 3-CTRS over the signature $F_\mathcal{P} = F_\mathcal{P}^P \cup F_\mathcal{P}^T$, where $F_\mathcal{P}^P = \{P_{in}, P_{out} \mid P \text{ is a predicate in } \mathcal{P}\}$ and $F_\mathcal{P}^T = \{f \mid f \text{ occurs in a term of an atom in } \mathcal{P}\}$.

As an example, consider the logic program $\mathcal{P}$ which implements the *quicksort* algorithm:

$$qsort([],[]) \leftarrow$$
$$qsort(x:l,s) \leftarrow split(l,x,l_1,l_2), qsort(l_1,s_1), qsort(l_2,s_2), app(s_1,x:s_2,s)$$

$$split([],x,[],[]) \leftarrow$$
$$split(x:l,y,x:l_1,l_2) \leftarrow less(x,y), split(l,y,l_1,l_2)$$
$$split(x:l,y,l_1,x:l_2) \leftarrow geq(x,y), split(l,y,l_1,l_2)$$

with input positions $m_{qsort}(1) = m_{split}(1) = m_{split}(2)$ and output positions $m_{qsort}(2) = m_{split}(3) = m_{split}(4)$. The transformation yields the deterministic 3-CTRS $R_\mathcal{P}$

$$qsort_{in}([]) \rightarrow qsort_{out}([])$$
$$qsort_{in}(x:l) \rightarrow qsort_{out}(s) \Leftarrow split_{in}(l,x) \rightarrow split_{out}(l_1,l_2),$$
$$qsort_{in}(l_1) \rightarrow qsort_{out}(s_1),$$
$$qsort_{in}(l_2) \rightarrow qsort_{out}(s_2),$$
$$app_{in}(s_1,x:s_2) \rightarrow app_{out}(s)$$

$$split_{in}([],x) \rightarrow split_{out}([],[])$$
$$split_{in}(x:l,y) \rightarrow split_{out}(x:l_1,l_2) \Leftarrow less_{in}(x,y) \rightarrow less_{out},$$
$$split_{in}(l,y) \rightarrow split_{out}(l_1,l_2)$$
$$split_{in}(x:l,y) \rightarrow split_{out}(l_1,x:l_2) \Leftarrow geq_{in}(x,y) \rightarrow geq_{out},$$
$$split_{in}(l,y) \rightarrow split_{out}(l_1,l_2)$$

Note that each rule of $R_\mathcal{P}$ has the form $P_{in}^0(u_1^0,\ldots,u_{m_0}^0) \rightarrow P_{out}^0(v_1^0,\ldots,v_{n_0}^0) \Leftarrow P_{in}^1(u_1^1,\ldots,u_{m_1}^1) \rightarrow P_{out}^1(v_1^1,\ldots,v_{n_1}^1),\ldots,P_{in}^k(u_1^k,\ldots,u_{m_k}^k) \rightarrow P_{out}^k(v_1^k,\ldots,v_{n_k}^k)$, where $u_i^j,v_i^j \in \mathcal{T}(F_\mathcal{P}^T,\mathcal{V})$. In particular, every $l \rightarrow r \Leftarrow s_1 \rightarrow t_1,\ldots,s_k \rightarrow t_k$ in $R_\mathcal{P}$ satisfies: (1) The root symbol is the only defined symbol in l and s_i, and (2) r and t_i are constructor terms.

Definition 16. *An LR-well-moded logic program $\mathcal{P}$ is (uniquely) terminating if, for every LR-well-moded query $\leftarrow A$, every left-to-right SLD-derivation is terminating (and every left-to-right SLD-refutation computes the same answer substitution).*

Ganzinger and Waldmann [GW93, Thm. 14] showed that quasi-reductivity of $R_\mathcal{P}$ proves termination of an LR-well-moded logic program $\mathcal{P}$. Avenhaus and Loría-Sáenz [ALS94, Thm. 5.1] proved that unique termination follows from quasi-reductivity and the joinability of all conditional critical pairs.

By means of the following implications

$$U(R_\mathcal{P}) \text{ is terminating} \Rightarrow R_\mathcal{P} \text{ is quasi-reductive} \Rightarrow \mathcal{P} \text{ is terminating}$$

it suffices to show termination of $U(R_{\mathcal{P}})$ in order to prove termination of the *quicksort* program. Termination of $U(R_{\mathcal{P}})$ can automatically be shown with the dependency pair technique; see [AG97a]. Thus the *quicksort* program is terminating. Since every conditional critical pair in $R_{\mathcal{P}}$ is infeasible (hence joinable), the logic program is also uniquely terminating.

Arts and Zantema [AZ95,AZ96] stated an imperative procedure[3] which directly transforms a logic program $\mathcal{P}$ into an *unconditional* TRS. The TRS obtained by this imperative procedure[4] is essentially the same as $U(R_{\mathcal{P}})$. Arts and Zantema showed that single-redex termination of $U(R_{\mathcal{P}})$ suffices to prove termination of $\mathcal{P}$; see [AZ95, Thm. 4.8] and [Art97, Thm. 8.2.9]. We recall the definition:

Definition 17. *A reduction step $s \to t$ is called a* single-redex *reduction step if s contains exactly one redex. If a term does not have exactly one redex, then it is in* single-redex *normal form. A* single-redex *derivation is a reduction sequence consisting solely of single-redex reduction steps. A TRS $\mathcal{R}$ is called* single-redex *terminating if all single-redex derivations are finite.*

Note that innermost termination implies single-redex termination. Due to the following hierarchy (note that $U(R_{\mathcal{P}})$ may be overlapping)

$U(R_{\mathcal{P}})$ is terminating $\Rightarrow R_{\mathcal{P}}$ is quasi-reductive $\Rightarrow R_{\mathcal{P}}$ is quasi-decreasing
$\Rightarrow U(R_{\mathcal{P}})$ is innermost terminating $\Rightarrow U(R_{\mathcal{P}})$ is single-redex terminating

it seems that the method of Arts and Zantema is more powerful than Ganzinger and Waldmann's, in the sense that more logic programs can be proven terminating by the former method. Theorem 19, however, implies that both methods are *equally powerful*. To prove it, we need the following lemma.

Lemma 18. *Suppose $U(R_{\mathcal{P}})$ is single-redex terminating. If every v_j in $u = P_{in}(v_1, \ldots, v_m)$ is a term in $\mathcal{T}(F_{\mathcal{P}}^T, \mathcal{V})$, then every $U(R_{\mathcal{P}})$-derivation starting from u is finite.*

Proof. It is fairly easy to see that every $U(R_{\mathcal{P}})$-derivation starting from u is a single-redex derivation. Thus it is finite.

Theorem 19. *If $U(R_{\mathcal{P}})$ is single-redex terminating, then it is terminating.*

Proof. By structural induction on u, it will be shown that every $U(R_{\mathcal{P}})$-derivation starting from u is finite. If u is a variable, then it is in normal form. If u is a constant, then it is either in normal form or Lemma 18 applies. If u has a U-symbol at its root, then the assertion follows as in the proof of case (c) in Theorem 10. So suppose $u = P_{in}(v_1, \ldots, v_m)$, where at least one of the v_j contains a function symbol $f \notin F_{\mathcal{P}}^T$. By the inductive hypothesis, every $U(R_{\mathcal{P}})$-derivation starting from v_j is finite. For a proof by contradiction suppose there is an infinite $U(R_{\mathcal{P}})$-derivation

$$D : u = u_0 \to u_1 \to u_2 \to \ldots$$

---

[3] There is a flaw in the procedure which has been corrected in [Art97, Def. 8.2.2].
[4] More precisely, by the imperative procedure in [Art97, Def. 8.2.2].

The proof idea is to eliminate all "aliens" in the terms u_j by a function Ψ and to show that the derivation $\Psi(D)$ is still infinite. In u, every maximal proper subterm t with a U-symbol or a function symbol from $F_{\mathcal{P}}^P$ at the root is an alien. Informally, every "descendant" of an alien from u is an alien in u_j. In order to formally define what an alien is, we need the two functions Φ and Ψ defined below.

$$\Phi(t) = \begin{cases} t & \text{if } t \in \mathcal{V}, \\ f(\Phi(t_1), \dots, \Phi(t_n)) & \text{if } t = f(t_1, \dots, t_n),\ f \in F_{\mathcal{P}}^T, \\ z & \text{otherwise} \end{cases}$$

where z is a fresh variable (i.e., it does not occur in t). So if $t = C[t_1, \dots, t_n]$, where $C \in \mathcal{T}(F_{\mathcal{P}}^T, \mathcal{V})$ and either $root(t_j)$ is a U-symbol or $root(t_j) \in F_{\mathcal{P}}^P$, then $\Phi(t) = C[z, \dots, z]$.

$$\Psi(t) = \begin{cases} p(\Phi(t_1), \dots, \Phi(t_n)) & \text{if } t = p(t_1, \dots, t_n),\ p \in F_{\mathcal{P}}^P, \\ U_i^\rho(\Psi(t_1), \Phi(t_2), \dots, \Phi(t_n)) & \text{if } t = U_i^\rho(t_1, \dots, t_n). \end{cases}$$

Note that Ψ is only partially defined. Suppose t has only U-symbols above the leftmost outermost function symbol which is in $F_{\mathcal{P}}^P$. Ψ does not modify this symbol or any of the U-symbols above it. All other function symbols in t that are not in $F_{\mathcal{P}}^T$ are then replaced with the variable z by the function Φ.

Now the aliens in u_j are those subterms of u_j which are replaced with the fresh variable z when Ψ is applied to u_j. We write $u_j \to_a u_{j+1}$ if the contracted redex is a subterm of an alien in u_j and $u_j \to_{na} u_{j+1}$ otherwise. It is not difficult to show that for every alien t in u_j there is an alien s in u such that $s \to^* t$. Since every $U(R_{\mathcal{P}})$-derivation starting from s is finite, the relation $\to_a$ is terminating. Consequently, D must contain infinitely many $\to_{na}$ steps. It is obvious that $u_j \to_a u_{j+1}$ implies $\Psi(u_j) = \Psi(u_{j+1})$. Moreover, if $u_j \to_{na} u_{j+1}$, then $\Psi(u_j) \to \Psi(u_{j+1})$. This fact can be proven as follows. Write $u_j = C[l\sigma] \to_{na} C[r\sigma] = u_{j+1}$, where $l \to r \in U(R_{\mathcal{P}})$. By the form of the rewrite rules in $U(R_{\mathcal{P}})$, we have $\Psi(l\sigma) = l\tau$, where τ is defined by $x\tau = \Phi(x\sigma)$. It is fairly simple to prove that $l\tau \to r\tau = \Psi(r\sigma)$ which yields $\Psi(u_j) = \Psi(C)[\Psi(l\sigma)] \to \Psi(C)[\Psi(r\sigma)] = u_{j+1}$. By putting all the facts together, we conclude that the $U(R_{\mathcal{P}})$-derivation

$$\Psi(D) : \Psi(u) = \Psi(u_0) \to^* \Psi(u_1) \to^* \Psi(u_2) \to^* \dots$$

is infinite. Furthermore, $\Psi(u) = P_{in}(\Phi(v_1), \dots, \Phi(v_m))$ and every $\Phi(v_j)$ is an element of $\mathcal{T}(F_{\mathcal{P}}^T, \mathcal{V})$. This, however, contradicts Lemma 18.

We have seen that the termination proof technique of Ganzinger and Waldmann is as powerful as that of Arts and Zantema. All in all, we suggest that one takes the best of both worlds:

1. The two-stage transformation consisting of the phases (i) translation of a logic program $\mathcal{P}$ into a deterministic 3-CTRS $R_{\mathcal{P}}$ and (ii) translation of $R_{\mathcal{P}}$ into an unconditional TRS $U(R_{\mathcal{P}})$ is much easier to grasp than a direct transformation via an imperative procedure. It is thus preferable.

2. Unique termination of $\mathcal{P}$ can be proven on the level of 3-CTRSs whereas there is no similar method for TRSs. So the two-stage transformation has another advantage over the direct transformation.

3. We have seen that in both approaches to proving termination of an LR-well-moded logic program $\mathcal{P}$ it boils down to proving innermost termination of the unconditional TRS $U(R_\mathcal{P})$. Since the latter can be automated by the dependency pair technique [AG97b], the whole method can be automated; cf. [Art97].

It should be pointed out that the methods don't yield a complete criterion for proving termination of LR-well-moded logic programs; see [GW93].

7   Related Work

As already mentioned, the idea of transforming conditional rewrite systems into unconditional ones dates back to the work of Bergstra and Klop [BK86], where such transformations were used as a heuristic tool to construct counterexamples to confluence of certain classes of CTRSs. Bergstra and Klop did not explore the formal aspects of these transformations. This was done ten years later by Marchiori [Mar96]. He showed that some parts of the theory of CTRSs "can be *automatically* recovered from the theory of TRSs". In [Mar97], the limits of transformational approaches are discussed. Other transformations can be found in [GM88] and [Hin95]. The applicability of Giovanetti and Moiso's [GM88] transformation is rather limited because it is designed to preserve "the equivalence relation induced on terms". Hintermeier [Hin95] provides a two-phase transformation (based on order-sorted rewriting) from the class of decreasing and ground confluent CTRSs to TRSs.

Many methods have been proposed to prove termination of logic programs and we will not attempt to review all of these here. Instead, we refer to the overview article of de Schreye and Decorte [SD94]. More recent approaches to proving termination of logic programs are discussed in Krishna Rao et al. [KRKS98]. We will only briefly comment on other transformational techniques. To the best of our knowledge, the first termination proof technique for well-moded logic programs which uses a transformation of logic programs into TRSs was described by Krishna Rao et al. [KRKS92]. However, Ganzinger and Waldmann's method is not only conceptually easier but it is also able to prove termination of logic programs for which the method in [KRKS92] fails. An approach similar to that of Arts and Zantema was suggested by Aguzzi and Modigliani [AM93]. In contrast to the other techniques, however, their method does not require any prior information about modes of predicates because these are computed during the transformation according to a given query. The transformational approach of Marchiori [Mar94] is rather complex but it can handle logic programs for which the methods described above fail. It is sound and complete for two subclasses of the class of well-moded logic programs, viz. simply well-moded and flatly well-moded programs. Lastly, another translation of logic programs into conditional rewrite systems can be found in van Raamsdonk [Raa97].

Acknowledgment: I thank Michael Hanus for the (email) discussion which led to the development of the transformation U. He also pointed out that the elimination of local definitions via program transformations is well-known in the implementation of functional programming languages; see [Joh85].

References

[AG97a]   T. Arts and J. Giesl. Automatically proving termination where simplification orderings fail. In *Proceedings of the 22nd International Colloquium on Trees in Algebra and Programming*, volume 1214 of *Lecture Notes in Computer Science*, pages 261–272, Berlin, 1997. Springer-Verlag.

[AG97b]   T. Arts and J. Giesl. Proving innermost normalisation automatically. In *Proceedings of the 8th International Conference on Rewriting Techniques and Applications*, volume 1232 of *Lecture Notes in Computer Science*, pages 157–172, Berlin, 1997. Springer-Verlag.

[ALS94]   J. Avenhaus and C. Loría-Sáenz. On conditional rewrite systems with extra variables and deterministic logic programs. In *Proceedings of the 5th International Conference on Logic Programming and Automated Reasoning*, volume 822 of *Lecture Notes in Artificial Intelligence*, pages 215–229, Berlin, 1994. Springer-Verlag.

[AM93]   G. Aguzzi and U. Modigliani. Proving termination of logic programs by transforming them into equivalent term rewriting systems. In *Proceedings of the 13th Conference on the Foundations of Software Technology and Theoretical Computer Science*, volume 761 of *Lecture Notes in Computer Science*, pages 114–124, Berlin, 1993. Springer-Verlag.

[Art97]   T. Arts. *Automatically Proving Termination and Innermost Normalisation of Term Rewriting Systems*. PhD thesis, Utrecht University, 1997.

[AZ95]   T. Arts and H. Zantema. Termination of logic programs via labelled term rewrite systems. In *Proceedings of Computing Science in the Netherlands*, pages 22–34, 1995.

[AZ96]   T. Arts and H. Zantema. Termination of logic programs using semantic unification. In *Proceedings of the 5th International Workshop on Logic Program Synthesis and Transformation*, volume 1048 of *Lecture Notes in Computer Science*, pages 219–233, Berlin, 1996. Springer-Verlag.

[BG89]   H. Bertling and H. Ganzinger. Completion-time optimization of rewrite-time goal solving. In *Proceedings of the 3rd International Conference on Rewriting Techniques and Applications*, volume 355 of *Lecture Notes in Computer Science*, pages 45–58, Berlin, 1989. Springer-Verlag.

[BK86]   J.A. Bergstra and J.W. Klop. Conditional rewrite rules: Confluence and termination. *Journal of Computer and System Sciences*, 32(3):323–362, 1986.

[BN98]   F. Baader and T. Nipkow. *Term Rewriting and All That*. Cambridge University Press, 1998.

[DOS88]   N. Dershowitz, M. Okada, and G. Sivakumar. Canonical conditional rewrite systems. In *Proceedings of the 9th Conference on Automated Deduction*, volume 310 of *Lecture Notes in Computer Science*, pages 538–549, Berlin, 1988. Springer-Verlag.

[Gan91]   H. Ganzinger. Order-sorted completion: The many-sorted way. *Theoretical Computer Science*, 89:3–32, 1991.

[GM88]   E. Giovannetti and C. Moiso. Notes on the elimination of conditions. In *Proceedings of the 1st International Workshop on Conditional and Typed Rewriting Systems*, volume 308 of *Lecture Notes in Computer Science*, pages 91–97, Berlin, 1988. Springer-Verlag.

[Gra95]   B. Gramlich. Abstract relations between restricted termination and confluence properties of rewrite systems. *Fundamenta Informaticae*, 24:3–23, 1995.

[GW93]   H. Ganzinger and U. Waldmann. Termination proofs of well-moded logic programs via conditional rewrite systems. In *Proceedings of the 3rd International Workshop on Conditional Term Rewriting Systems*, volume 656 of *Lecture Notes in Computer Science*, pages 113–127, Berlin, 1993. Springer-Verlag.

[Han94]   M. Hanus. The integration of functions into logic programming: From theory to practice. *The Journal of Logic Programming*, 19&20:583–628, 1994.

[Hin95]   C. Hintermeier. How to transform canonical decreasing CTRSs into equivalent canonical TRSs. In *Proceedings of the 4rd International Workshop on Conditional and Typed Rewriting Systems*, volume 968 of *Lecture Notes in Computer Science*, pages 186–205, Berlin, 1995. Springer-Verlag.

[Joh85]   T. Johnsson. Lambda lifting: Transforming programs to recursive functions. In *Functional Programming Languages and Computer Architecture*, volume 201 of *Lecture Notes in Computer Science*, pages 190–203, Berlin, 1985. Springer-Verlag.

[KRKS92] M.R.K. Krishna Rao, D. Kapur, and R.K. Shyamasundar. A transformational methodology for proving termination of logic programs. In *Proceedings of the 5th Workshop on Computer Science Logic*, volume 626 of *Lecture Notes in Computer Science*, pages 213–226, Berlin, 1992. Springer-Verlag.

[KRKS98] M.R.K. Krishna Rao, D. Kapur, and R.K. Shyamasundar. Transformational methodology for proving termination of logic programs. *The Journal of Logic Programming*, 34(1):1–42, 1998.

[Mar94]   M. Marchiori. Logic programs as term rewriting systems. In *Proceedings of the 4th International Conference on Algebraic and Logic Programming*, volume 850 of *Lecture Notes in Computer Science*, pages 223–241, Berlin, 1994. Springer-Verlag.

[Mar95]   M. Marchiori. Unravelings and ultra-properties. Technical Report 8, Dept. of Pure and Applied Mathematics, University of Padova, Italy, 1995.

[Mar96]   M. Marchiori. Unravelings and ultra-properties. In *Proceedings of the 5th International Conference on Algebraic and Logic Programming*, volume 1139 of *Lecture Notes in Computer Science*, pages 107–121, Berlin, 1996. Springer-Verlag.

[Mar97]   M. Marchiori. On the expressive power of rewriting. In *Proceedings of the 17th International Conference on the Foundations of Software Technology and Theoretical Computer Science*, volume 1346 of *Lecture Notes in Computer Science*, pages 88–102, Berlin, 1997. Springer-Verlag.

[Ohl95]   E. Ohlebusch. Modular properties of composable term rewriting systems. *Journal of Symbolic Computation*, 20:1–41, 1995.

[Raa97]   F. van Raamsdonk. Translating logic programs into conditional rewriting systems. In *Proceedings of the 14th International Conference on Logic Programming*, pages 168–182. MIT Press, 1997.

[SD94]   D. de Schreye and S. Decorte. Termination of logic programs: The never-ending story. *The Journal of Logic Programming*, 19&20:199–260, 1994.

Cancellative Superposition Decides the Theory of Divisible Torsion-Free Abelian Groups

Uwe Waldmann

Max-Planck-Institut für Informatik, Im Stadtwald,
66123 Saarbrücken, Germany, uwe@mpi-sb.mpg.de

Abstract. In divisible torsion-free abelian groups, the efficiency of the cancellative superposition calculus can be greatly increased by combining it with a variable elimination algorithm that transforms every clause into an equivalent clause without unshielded variables. We show that the resulting calculus is not only refutationally complete (even in the presence of arbitrary free function symbols), but that it is also a decision procedure for the theory of divisible torsion-free abelian groups.

1 Introduction

Equational reasoning in the presence of the associativity and commutativity axioms is known to be difficult – theoretically [5, 12], as well as practically [1, 13–17, 21]. Using AC-unification and extended clauses the worst inefficiencies of a naïve approach can be avoided, but still the extended clauses lead to numerous variable overlaps – one of the most prolific types of inferences in resolution or superposition style calculi. Besides, minimal complete set of AC-unifiers may have doubly exponential size. If the theory contains also the identity law

$$x + 0 \approx x \,, \tag{U}$$

then AC-unification can be replaced by ACU-unification, but the minimal complete set is still simply exponential.

A substantial improvement can be observed when we consider structures that satisfy also the cancellation axiom

$$x + y \approx x + z \Rightarrow y \approx z \,, \tag{K}$$

or the inverse axiom

$$x + (-x) \approx 0 \,, \tag{Inv}$$

(which implies (K)), that is, when we switch over from abelian semigroups or monoids to abelian groups (ACUInv) or at least cancellative abelian monoids (ACUK). The cancellative superposition calculus (Ganzinger and Waldmann [10, 18]) is a refined superposition calculus for cancellative abelian monoids which requires neither explicit inferences with the theory clauses nor extended equations or clauses. Strengthened ordering constraints lead to a significant reduction of the number of variable overlaps, compared with traditional AC-calculi. Some variable overlaps remain necessary, however.

In (non-trivial) divisible torsion-free abelian groups, e. g., the rational numbers and rational vector spaces, the abelian group axioms ACUInv are extended by the torsion-freeness axioms

$$kx \approx ky \Rightarrow x \approx y \qquad (T)$$

(for all $k \in \mathbf{N}^{>0}$), the divisibility axioms[1]

$$k \ div\text{-}by_k(x) \approx x \qquad (Div)$$

(for all $k \in \mathbf{N}^{>0}$), and the non-triviality axiom[2]

$$a \not\approx 0. \qquad (Nt)$$

Divisible torsion-free abelian groups (DTAGs) allow quantifier elimination: For every quantified formula over 0, +, and $\approx$ there exists a quantifier-free formula that is equivalent modulo the theory axioms. In particular, every closed formula over this vocabulary is provably true or false: the theory of DTAGs is complete and decidable. Superposition calculi, however, work on formulae that do not contain any existential quantifiers, but that may contain free function symbols – possibly introduced by skolemization, possibly given initially. In the presence of free function symbols, there is of course no way to eliminate all variables from a formula – not even all universally quantified ones – but we can at least give an effective method to eliminate all *unshielded* variables, that is, all variables not occurring below any free function symbol. This elimination algorithm has been integrated into the cancellative superposition calculus in (Waldmann [20]). The resulting calculus is refutationally complete with respect to the DTAG axioms and allows us to dispense with variable overlaps completely.

Starting with Joyner [11], resolution and superposition calculi have been shown to be decision procedures for various classes of formulae (e. g., [3, 6–9]). As the theory of DTAGs is decidable, it is now a natural question to ask whether the combination of cancellative superposition and variable elimination for unshielded universally quantified variables is powerful enough to be usable as a decision procedure for the theory of DTAGs. We show in this paper that this is indeed the case: The combined calculus is refutationally complete in the presence of arbitrary free function symbols; and it is a decision procedure, if all free function symbols are the result of skolemization.

---

[1] In non-skolemized form: $\forall x \ \exists y$: $ky \approx x$ for all $k \in \mathbf{N}^{>0}$.
[2] In non-skolemized form: $\exists y$: $y \not\approx 0$.

2   Preliminaries

We will first give a short overview over the cancellative superposition calculus and its specialization for DTAGs. The reader is referred to (Waldmann [18, 20]) for more technical details.[3]

Throughout this paper we assume that our signature contains a binary function symbol $+$ and a constant 0. If t is a term and $n \in \mathbf{N}$, then nt is an abbreviation for the n-fold sum $t + \cdots + t$; in particular, $0t = 0$ and $1t = t$.

A function symbol different from 0 and $+$ is called free. A term is called atomic, if it is not a variable and its top symbol is different from $+$. We say that a term t occurs at the top of s, if there is a position $o \in \mathrm{pos}(s)$ such that $s|_o = t$ and for every proper prefix o' of o, $s(o')$ equals $+$; the term t occurs in s below a free function symbol, if there is an $o \in \mathrm{pos}(s)$ such that $s|_o = t$ and $s(o')$ is a free function symbol for some proper prefix o' of o.

The equality symbol $\approx$ is the only predicate of our language. Hence a literal is either an equation $t \approx t'$ or a negated equation $t \not\approx t'$. The symbol $\dot{\approx}$ denotes either $\approx$ or $\not\approx$. A clause is a finite multiset of literals, usually written as a disjunction.

A variable x is called shielded in a clause C, if it occurs at least once below a free function symbol in C. Otherwise, x is called unshielded.

We say that an ACU-compatible ordering $\succ$ has the multiset property, if whenever a ground atomic term u is greater than v_i for every i in a finite non-empty index set I, then $u \succ \sum_{i \in I} v_i$.

From now on we will work only with ACU-congruence classes, rather than with terms. So all terms, equations, substitutions, inference rules, etc., are to be taken modulo ACU, i.e., as representatives of their congruence classes. The symbol $\succ$ will always denote an ACU-compatible reduction ordering that has the multiset property and is total on ground ACU-congruence classes.[4]

Let A be a ground literal $nu + \sum_{i \in I} s_i \dot{\approx} mu + \sum_{j \in J} t_j$, where u, s_i, and t_j are atomic terms, $n \geq m \geq 0$, $n \geq 1$, and $u \succ s_i$ and $u \succ t_j$ for all $i \in I$, $j \in J$. Then u is called the maximal atomic term of A.

The ordering $\succ_{\mathrm{L}}$ on literals compares lexicographically first the maximal atomic terms of the literals, then the polarities (negative $\succ$ positive), then the multisets of all non-zero terms occurring at the top of the literals, and finally the multisets consisting of the left and right hand sides of the literals. The ordering $\succ_{\mathrm{C}}$ on clauses is the multiset extension of the literal ordering $\succ_{\mathrm{L}}$. Both $\succ_{\mathrm{L}}$ and $\succ_{\mathrm{C}}$ are noetherian and total on ground literals/clauses.

We denote entailment modulo equality and ACUKT by $\models_{\mathrm{ACUKT}}$. In other words, $\{C_1, \ldots, C_n\} \models_{\mathrm{ACUKT}} C_0$ if and only if $\mathrm{ACUKT} \cup \{C_1, \ldots, C_n\} \models C_0$.

---

[3] The cancellative superposition calculus as described in (Waldmann [18, 20]) works in a many-sorted framework. For the purposes of this paper, it is sufficient to restrict to the one-sorted case.

[4] For ground terms, such an ordering can be obtained for instance from the recursive path ordering with precedence $f_n \succ \ldots \succ f_1 \succ + \succ 0$ and multiset status for $+$ by comparing normal forms w.r.t. $x + 0 \rightarrow x$ and $0 + x \rightarrow x$. If clauses are fully abstracted eagerly (cf. Sect. 5), the compatibility requirement becomes void.

3 Cancellative Superposition

Saturation-based theorem proving methods such as resolution or superposition aim at deducing a contradiction from a set of clauses by recursively inferring new clauses from given ones according to some inference system. A theorem prover computes one of the possible inferences of the current set of clauses and adds its conclusion to the current set, until a contradiction has been derived or a "closed" (or "saturated") set is reached.

To reduce the search space, the inference system is complemented by a redundancy criterion, which specifies inferences and clauses deemed to be unnecessary for deriving a contradiction. An inference that is redundant with respect to the current set N of clauses need not be computed; a clause that is redundant with respect to N may be removed from N.[5] In particular, a clause may be replaced by another equivalent clause, if the new clause renders the old one redundant; such a replacement is called a simplification. We call a (finite or infinite) sequence $N_0 \vdash N_1 \vdash \ldots$ a theorem proving derivation, if every N_{i+1} follows logically from N_i and every clause in $N_{i+1} \setminus N_i$ is redundant with respect to N_i. The derivation is said to be fair if every inference from persisting clauses is redundant with respect to some N_j.[6]

A set N of clauses is called saturated with respect to an inference system and a redundancy criterion, if every inference from clauses in N is redundant with respect to N. The inference system is called refutationally complete if saturated sets are unsatisfiable if and only if they contain the empty clause, or equivalently, if every fair theorem proving derivation starting from an unsatisfiable set of clauses will eventually derive the empty clause [4, 18].

The cancellative superposition calculus (Waldmann [18]) is a refutationally complete variant of the standard superposition calculus (Bachmair and Ganzinger [2]) for sets of clauses that contain the axioms ACUK and (optionally) T. Compared with standard or AC superposition calculi, the ordering restrictions of its inference rules are strengthened: Inferences are not only limited to maximal sides of maximal literals, but also to maximal summands thereof. As shielded variables are non-maximal, this excludes in particular overlaps with such variables. Besides any explicit inferences with the axioms ACUKT are unnecessary.

The inference system $\mathfrak{K}$ of the cancellative superposition calculus[7] consists of the inference rules cancellation, equality resolution, standard superposition, cancellative superposition, abstraction, and cancellative equality factoring. Ground versions of four of these rules are given below.[8]

The following conditions are common to the rules of $\mathfrak{K}$: Every literal involved in an inference must be maximal in the respective premise (except for the last

---

[5] Redundancy criteria need not be (and usually are not) decidable. For an implementation, having a decidable approximation is sufficient.

[6] In particular, every inference whose conclusion is contained in N_j is redundant with respect to N_j.

[7] In [18], this inference system is denoted by $CS\text{-}Inf_{N>0}$.

[8] We leave out the rules standard superposition and abstraction, as the restriction to fully abstracted clauses (in Section 5) will make them superfluous anyway.

but one literal in *cancellative equality factoring* inferences); a positive literal involved in a *superposition* inference must be strictly maximal. In *superposition* inferences, the left premise is smaller than the right premise.

Cancellation
$$\frac{C' \vee mu + s \approx m'u + s'}{C' \vee (m - m')u + s \approx s'}$$
if $m \geq m' \geq 1$ and $u \succ s$, $u \succ s'$.

Equality Resolution
$$\frac{C' \vee 0 \not\approx 0}{C'}$$

Canc. Superposition
$$\frac{D' \vee nu + t \approx t' \qquad C' \vee mu + s \approx s'}{D' \vee C' \vee \psi s + \chi t' \approx \chi t + \psi s'}$$
if $m \geq 1$, $n \geq 1$, $\psi = n/\gcd(m,n)$, $\chi = m/\gcd(m,n)$, and $u \succ s$, $u \succ s'$, $u \succ t$, $u \succ t'$.

Canc. Eq. Factoring
$$\frac{C' \vee nu + t \approx n'u + t' \vee mu + s \approx s'}{C' \vee \psi t + \chi s' \not\approx \chi s + \psi t' \vee nu + t \approx n'u + t'}$$
if $m \geq 1$, $n > n' \geq 0$, $\nu = n - n'$, $\psi = m/\gcd(m,\nu)$, $\chi = \nu/\gcd(m,\nu)$, and $u \succ s$, $u \succ s'$, $u \succ t$, $u \succ t'$.

The system $\mathcal{R}$ is sound with respect to ACUKT. That is, for every inference with premises $C_1, \ldots, C_n$ and conclusion C_0, we have $\{C_1, \ldots, C_n\} \models_{\mathrm{ACUKT}} C_0$.

Lifting the inference rules to non-ground clauses is relatively straightforward as long as we restrict to clauses without unshielded variables. We have to take into account that, in a clause $C = C' \vee A$, the maximal literal A need no longer have the form $mu + s \approx s'$, where u is the unique maximal atomic term. Rather, a non-ground literal such as $f(x) + 2f(y) + b \not\approx c$ may contain several (distinct but ACU-unifiable) maximal atomic terms u_k with multiplicities m_k, where k ranges over some finite non-empty index set K. We obtain thus $A = \sum_{k \in K} m_k u_k + s \approx s'$, where $\sum_{k \in K} m_k$ corresponds to m in the ground literal above. As in the standard superposition calculus, the substitution σ that unifies all u_k (and the corresponding terms v_l from the other premise) is applied to the conclusion. For instance, the *cancellative superposition* rule has now the following form:

Cancellative Superposition
$$\frac{D' \vee A_2 \qquad C' \vee A_1}{(D' \vee C' \vee A_0)\sigma}$$

if the following conditions are satisfied:

- $A_1 = \sum_{k \in K} m_k u_k + s \approx s'$.
- $A_2 = \sum_{l \in L} n_l v_l + t \approx t'$.

- $m = \sum_{k \in K} m_k \geq 1$, $n = \sum_{l \in L} n_l \geq 1$.
- $\psi = n/\gcd(m,n)$, $\chi = m/\gcd(m,n)$.
- u is one of the u_k or v_l ($k \in K, l \in L$).
- σ is a most general ACU-unifier of all u_k and v_l ($k \in K, l \in L$).
- $u \not\leq s$, $u \not\leq s'$, $u \not\leq t$, $u \not\leq t'$.
- $A_0 = \psi s + \chi t' \approx \chi t + \psi s'$.

The lifted versions of the rules *cancellation* and *cancellative equality factoring* are obtained analogously.

In the presence of unshielded variables, it is still possible to devise (more complicated) lifted inference rules that produce only finitely many conclusions for a given tuple of premises. We do not repeat these rules here, as the additional theory axioms DivInvNt make it possible to eliminate unshielded variables completely. The elimination of unshielded variables happens in two stages. First we show that every clause is logically equivalent to a clause without unshielded variables. Then this elimination algorithm has to be integrated into cancellative superposition. Our main tool for the second step is the concept of redundancy.

Let $C_0, C_1, \ldots, C_k$ be clauses and let θ be a substitution such that $C_i\theta$ is ground for all $i \in \{1, \ldots, k\}$. If there are inferences

$$\frac{C_k \ \ldots \ C_1}{C_0}$$

and

$$\frac{C_k\theta \ \ldots \ C_1\theta}{C_0\theta}$$

then the latter is called a ground instance of the former.

Let N be a set of clauses, let $\bar{N}$ be the set of ground instances of clauses in N. An inference is called ACUKT-redundant with respect to N if for each of its ground instances with conclusion $C_0\theta$ and maximal premise $C\theta$ we have $\{D \in \bar{N} \mid D \prec_c C\theta\} \models_{\text{ACUKT}} C_0\theta$. A clause C is called ACUKT-redundant with respect to N, if for every ground instance $C\theta$, $\{D \in \bar{N} \mid D \prec_c C\theta\} \models_{\text{ACUKT}} C\theta$.

Theorem 1. *The inference system $\mathfrak{K}$ is refutationally complete with respect to ACUKT, that is, a $\mathfrak{K}$-saturated set of clauses is unsatisfiable modulo ACUKT if and only if it contains the empty clause (Waldmann [18]).*

4   Variable Elimination: The Logical Side

It is well-known that the theory of DTAGs allows quantifier elimination: For every quantified formula over 0, $+$, and $\approx$ there exists an equivalent quantifier-free formula. In the presence of free function symbols, there is of course no way to eliminate all variables from a clause, but we can at least give an effective method to eliminate all *unshielded* variables.

Let x be a variable. We define a binary relation $\to_x$ over clauses by

CancelVar $C' \lor mx + s \approx m'x + s' \quad \to_x \quad C' \lor (m-m')x + s \approx s'$
if $m \geq m' \geq 1$.

ElimNeg $C' \lor mx + s \not\approx s' \quad \to_x \quad C'$
if $m \geq 1$ and x does not occur in C', s, s'.

ElimPos $C' \lor m_1 x + s_1 \approx s'_1 \lor \ldots \lor m_k x + s_k \approx s'_k \quad \to_x \quad C'$
if $m_i \geq 1$ and x does not occur in C', s_i, s'_i, for $1 \leq i \leq k$.

Coalesce $C' \lor mx + s \not\approx s' \lor nx + t \approx t'$
$\to_x C' \lor mx + s \not\approx s' \lor \psi t + \chi s' \approx \psi t' + \chi s$
if $m \geq 1$, $n \geq 1$, $\psi = m/\gcd(m,n)$, $\chi = n/\gcd(m,n)$, and x does
not occur at the top of s, s', t, t'.

The relation $\to_x$ is noetherian. Let the binary relation $\to_{\mathrm{elim}}$ over clauses be defined in such a way that $C_0 \to_{\mathrm{elim}} C_1$ if and only if C_0 contains an unshielded variable x and C_1 is a normal form of C_0 with respect to $\to_x$. Then $\to_{\mathrm{elim}}$ is again noetherian. For any clause C, let $\mathrm{elim}(C)$ denote some (arbitrary but fixed) normal form of C with respect to the relation $\to_{\mathrm{elim}}$.

Lemma 2. *For every clause C, $\mathrm{elim}(C)$ contains no unshielded variables.*

Lemma 3. *For every clause C, $\{C\} \cup \mathrm{DivInvNt} \models_{\mathrm{ACUKT}} \mathrm{elim}(C)$ and $\{\mathrm{elim}(C)\} \models_{\mathrm{ACUKT}} C$. For every ground $C\theta$, $\{\mathrm{elim}(C)\theta\} \models_{\mathrm{ACUKT}} C\theta$ [18].*

Proof. If $C_0 \to_x C_1$ by *CancelVar*, the equivalence of C_0 and C_1 modulo ACUKT follows from cancellation; for *Coalesce*, from cancellation and torsion-freeness. The soundness of *ElimNeg* follows from the inverse and divisibility axioms, for *ElimPos* it is implied by torsion-freeness and non-triviality. $\square$

Using the technique sketched so far, every clause C_0 can be transformed into a clause $\mathrm{elim}(C_0)$ that does not contain unshielded variables, follows from C_0 and the DTAG axioms, and implies C_0 modulo ACUKT. Obviously, we can perform this transformation for all initially given clauses *before* we start the saturation process. However, $\Re$-inferences from clauses without unshielded variables may produce clauses with unshielded variables. To eliminate these clauses *during* the saturation process, it is not sufficient that they follow logically from *some* other clauses: redundancy requires that they follow from *some sufficiently small* clauses. Unfortunately, under certain circumstances the transformed clause $\mathrm{elim}(C_0)$ may not be small enough. Hence, to integrate the variable elimination algorithm into the cancellative superposition calculus, it has to be supplemented by a case analysis technique.

5   Variable Elimination: The Operational Side

Let ι be an inference. We call the unifying substitution σ that is computed during ι and applied to the conclusion the pivotal substitution of ι. (For ground inferences, the pivotal substitution is the identity mapping.) If A is the last literal of the last premise of ι, we call $A\sigma$ the pivotal literal of ι. Finally, if u_0 is the atomic term that is cancelled out in ι, or in which some subterm is replaced or abstracted out, then we call $u_0\sigma$ the pivotal term of ι. Pivotal terms have two important properties: First, whenever an inference ι from clauses *without* unshielded variables produces a conclusion *with* unshielded variables, then all these unshielded variables occur in the pivotal term of ι. Second, no atomic term in the conclusion of ι can be larger than the pivotal term of ι.

A clause C is called fully abstracted, if no non-variable term occurs below a free function symbol in C. Every clause C can be transformed into an equivalent fully abstracted clause abs(C) by iterated rewriting

$$C[f(\ldots,t,\ldots)] \quad \rightarrow \quad x \not\approx t \vee C[f(\ldots,x,\ldots)],$$

where x is a new variable and t is a non-variable term occurring immediately below the free function symbol f in C. It should be noted that the variable elimination algorithm preserves full abstraction, so that for every clause C, elim(abs(C)) is a logically equivalent clause that is fully abstracted and does not contain unshielded variables.

In the sequel we assume that every clause C in the input of the inference system is replaced by elim(abs(C)) before we start the saturation process. The inference system $\mathfrak{D}^{abs}$ that we will describe now preserves both properties: the set of all fully abstracted clauses without unshielded variables is closed under $\mathfrak{D}^{abs}$. The system $\mathfrak{D}^{abs}$ is given by two meta-inference rules:

Eliminating Inference

$$\frac{C_n \quad \ldots \quad C_1}{\text{elim}(C_0)}$$

if the following condition is satisfied:

- $\dfrac{C_n \quad \ldots \quad C_1}{C_0}$ is a non-*abstraction* and non-*standard superposition* $\mathfrak{K}$-inference.[9]

Instantiating Inference

$$\frac{C_n \quad \ldots \quad C_1}{C_0\tau}$$

if the following conditions are satisfied:

- $\dfrac{C_n \quad \ldots \quad C_1}{C_0}$ is a non-*abstraction* and non-*standard superposition* $\mathfrak{K}$-inference with pivotal literal A and pivotal term u.

---

[9] In the one-sorted case considered in this paper, *standard superposition* inferences from fully abstracted clauses are impossible. In the general many-sorted case, *standard superposition* inferences must not be ignored.

- The multiset difference $\text{elim}(C_0) \setminus C_0$ contains a literal A_1 with the same polarity as A.
- An atomic term u_1 occurs at the top of A_1.
- τ is contained in a minimal complete set of ACU-unifiers of u and u_1.

The redundancy of $\mathfrak{D}^{abs}$-inferences is defined in a slightly complicated way. Essentially, a $\mathfrak{D}^{abs}$-inference is redundant if sufficiently many ground instances of the $\mathfrak{K}$-inference on which it is based are redundant. For our purposes, it is sufficient to know that any inference is redundant with respect to a set N of clauses as soon as its conclusion (or a simplified version thereof) is present in N.

Theorem 4. *If a set of fully abstracted clauses is saturated with respect to $\mathfrak{D}^{abs}$ and none of the clauses contains unshielded variables, then it is also saturated with respect to $\mathfrak{K}$, and it is unsatisfiable modulo $\text{ACUKT} \cup \text{DivInvNt}$ if and only if it contains the empty clause (Waldmann [18, 20]).*

If all clauses are fully abstracted, then the terms that have to be compared during the saturation do not contain the operator $+$. In this situation, the requirement that the ordering $\succ$ has to be ACU-compatible becomes void, and we may use an arbitrary reduction ordering over terms not containing $+$ that is total on ground terms and for which 0 is minimal. As every ordering of this kind can be extended to an ordering that is ACU-compatible and has the multiset property (Waldmann [19]), the completeness proof is still justified.

6 Deciding the Theory of DTAGs

A refutationally complete calculus derives a contradiction (and terminates) whenever the set of input formulae is inconsistent. To show that a refutationally complete calculus is actually a decision procedure, one has to prove that it terminates even on consistent inputs. Following this general scheme, we will now demonstrate that the calculus $\mathfrak{D}^{abs}$ is a decision procedure for the theory of divisible torsion-free abelian groups.

Let us denote by $\mathcal{D}$ the class of all closed first-order formulae with arbitrary quantifiers and logical connectives and containing not more than the function symbols $+$ (binary), 0 (constant), $-$ (unary), $div\text{-}by_k$ (unary) for $k \in \mathbf{N}^{>0}$, and the binary predicate symbol $\approx$. Given a formula $F \in \mathcal{D}$, our task is to decide whether F is equivalent to true or to false with respect to the theory of DTAGs. As this theory is complete, every formula in $\mathcal{D}$ is equivalent either to true or to false, hence F is equivalent to true if and only if it is satisfiable.

We can first of all eliminate the symbols $-$ and $div\text{-}by_k$ from F by recursively replacing any atom $s[-t] \approx s'$ by $\forall x(\neg\, x + t \approx 0 \lor s[x] \approx s')$ and any atom $s[div\text{-}by_k(t)] \approx s'$ by $\forall x(\neg\, kx \approx t \lor s[x] \approx s')$, where x is a new variable. The resulting formula F_1 is then converted into a formula F_2 in prenex normal form. By skolemization, F_2 can be further translated into a formula F_3 without existentially quantified variables, such that F_3 is satisfiable if and only if F is satisfiable. Skolemization replaces the existentially quantified variables of F_2 by terms $f_k(x_1, \ldots, x_i)$, where the x_j are universally quantified variables and f_k is a new free function symbol. The formula F_3 can be transformed into conjunctive normal form, which we represent as a finite set N' of clauses. This set N' is a subset of the class $\mathcal{D}_c$ defined as follows: A clause C is contained in $\mathcal{D}_c$ if and only if there exists a finite sequence of distinct variables $x_1, \ldots, x_n$ such that, for every literal $s \stackrel{.}{\approx} s'$ in C, both s and s' are sums $\sum n_k t_k$, and each t_k is either an atomic term $f(x_1, \ldots, x_i)$ or a variable x_i for some $i \leq n$. The class of all clauses C in $\mathcal{D}_c$ without unshielded variables is denoted by $\mathcal{D}_c^{\text{elim}}$. Obviously, $N' \subseteq \mathcal{D}_c$ can be converted into an equivalent subset N of $\mathcal{D}_c^{\text{elim}}$ using the variable elimination algorithm described above.

We claim that there is a fair strategy for $\mathfrak{D}^{abs}$-superposition that is guaranteed to terminate on every finite subset of $\mathcal{D}_c^{\text{elim}}$. Termination implies that with this strategy $\mathfrak{D}^{abs}$-superposition becomes a decision procedure for the satisfiability of finite subsets of $\mathcal{D}_c^{\text{elim}}$ (and hence of formulae in $\mathcal{D}$) with respect to $\text{ACUKT} \cup \text{DivInvNt}$.

In the rest of this paper, we assume $\succ$ to be a lexicographic path ordering based on a total precedence relation that respects the arity of function symbols (greater arity implying higher precedence). Apart from satisfying this restriction, the precedence can be arbitrary. Without loss of generality, we assume that the function symbols occurring in the input clauses are $f_m \succ \cdots \succ f_1$. We note that $f_j(x_1, \ldots, x_l) \succ f_k(x_1, \ldots, x_i)$ if and only if $f_j \succ f_k$ if and only if $j > k$.

In the one-sorted case, the inference system $\mathfrak{D}^{abs}$ consists of the eliminating and the instantiating variants of the rules *cancellation*, *equality resolution*, *cancellative superposition*, and *cancellative equality factoring*. We will show that for the special class of clauses $\mathcal{D}_c^{\text{elim}}$, instantiating inferences are not needed:

Lemma 5. *Every $\mathfrak{D}^{abs}$-inference from clauses in $\mathcal{D}_c^{\text{elim}}$ is an eliminating inference.*

Proof. Assume that there is an instantiating $\mathfrak{D}^{abs}$-inference

$$\frac{C_n \quad \ldots \quad C_1}{C_0 \tau}$$

with premises in $\mathcal{D}_c^{\text{elim}}$. Then

$$\frac{C_n \quad \ldots \quad C_1}{C_0}$$

is a $\mathfrak{K}$-inference with pivotal literal A, pivotal term u, and pivotal substitution σ. Furthermore, the multiset difference $\text{elim}(C_0) \setminus C_0$ contains a literal A_1 with the same polarity as A, and $u\tau = u_1\tau$ for some atomic term u_1 occurring at the top of A_1. As $\text{elim}(C_0) \neq C_0$, the clause C_0 must contain some unshielded variable x, and since the premises have no unshielded variables, x must occur in the pivotal term u. Now, as the premises C_i are clauses in $\mathcal{D}_c^{\text{elim}}$, there exists a fixed list of variables $x_1, x_2, \ldots$ such that all atomic terms in $C_i\sigma$, and thus in C_0 and $\text{elim}(C_0)$, have the form $f_j(x_1, \ldots, x_l)$ for some j and l. Consequently, any two atomic terms in $C_i\sigma$, C_0, and $\text{elim}(C_0)$ are either equal or not unifiable. By assumption, u and u_1 have the unifier τ, hence $u = u_1$. So x occurs in u_1, and thus in an atomic term in $\mathrm{elim}(C_0)$, and thus in an atomic term in C_0. Hence x is shielded in C_0, which refutes our assumption. $\qquad\qquad\qquad\qquad\qquad\square$

In order to force the termination of $\mathfrak{D}^{abs}$-superposition, certain simplification techniques are necessary. For a clause C, let $\mathrm{sfact}(C)$ be the clause obtained from C by syntactic factoring, that is, by replacing every repeated literal $A \vee \ldots \vee A$ by A. Let $\mathrm{scanc}(C)$ be the clause obtained from C by syntactic cancellation, that is, by replacing every literal $s + t \mathrel{\dot{\approx}} s' + t$ with non-zero t by $s \mathrel{\dot{\approx}} s'$.

Unlike syntactic factoring, syntactic cancellation may introduce unshielded variables (if the term that was cancelled out was the last term shielding some variable). During elimination of these unshielded variables, the *Coalesce* rule may again produce syntactically equal terms on both sides of a literal. Let the binary relation $\rightarrow_{\mathrm{sce}}$ over clauses be defined in such a way that $C_0 \rightarrow_{\mathrm{sce}} C_1$ if and only if $C_1 = \mathrm{elim}(\mathrm{scanc}(C_0))$ and $C_1 \neq C_0$. It is easy to show that $\rightarrow_{\mathrm{sce}}$ terminates. Let us denote the normal form of a clause C with respect to $\rightarrow_{\mathrm{sce}}$ by $\mathrm{scanc}^*(C)$, and let $\mathrm{simp}(C)$ be the clause $\mathrm{sfact}(\mathrm{scanc}^*(C))$.

Lemma 6. *For every $C \in \mathcal{D}_c^{\mathrm{elim}}$, if $\mathrm{simp}(C) \neq C$, then C is redundant with respect to $\{\mathrm{simp}(C)\}$, that is, replacing C by $\mathrm{simp}(C)$ is a simplification.*[10]

Proof. We have to show that, for every ground instance $C\theta$, $\{\mathrm{simp}(C)\theta\} \models_{\mathrm{ACUKT}} C\theta$ and $\mathrm{simp}(C)\theta \prec_c C\theta$. The first part follows directly from Lemma 3. To show that $\mathrm{simp}(C)\theta$ is smaller than $C\theta$, two cases have to be distinguished: If the transformation from C to $\mathrm{simp}(C)$ does not use variable elimination steps, that is, if $\mathrm{simp}(C) = \mathrm{sfact}(\mathrm{scanc}(C))$, then $\mathrm{simp}(C)\theta \prec_c C\theta$ is obvious. Otherwise, $\mathrm{scanc}(C)$ contains some unshielded variable. This can only happen if one of the cancelled terms is $f_j(x_1, \ldots, x_l)$, where f_j is the largest function symbol occurring in C. Then $\mathrm{simp}(C)\theta \prec_c C\theta$, since every atomic term occurring in $\mathrm{scanc}(C)\theta$ and $\mathrm{simp}(C)\theta$ is smaller than $f_j(x_1, \ldots, x_l)\theta$. $\qquad\square$

In descriptions of resolution or paramodulation style inference systems, one assumes conventionally that all clauses are variable disjoint, so that overlapping terms or literals can always be unified in the inference rules. To simplify the termination proof, we will exploit the fact that the particular structure of $\mathcal{D}_c^{\mathrm{elim}}$ allows us to use quite the opposite approach: Consider a $\mathfrak{D}^{abs}$-inference from two clauses C_2 and C_1 in $\mathcal{D}_c^{\mathrm{elim}}$. During this inference, the maximal atomic term of C_2, say $f_k(x_1'', \ldots, x_i'')$, and the maximal atomic term of C_1, say $f_k(x_1', \ldots, x_i')$, are overlapped. By definition of the ordering and of the class $\mathcal{D}_c^{\mathrm{elim}}$, the set of variables of C_1 is exactly $\{x_1', \ldots, x_i'\}$, and all atomic terms in C_1 have the form $f_j(x_1', \ldots, x_l')$ with $j \leq k$ and $l \leq i$ (and analogously for C_2). Therefore, essentially the same inference is also possible, if we assume that all clauses share the *same* variables $x_1, x_2, \ldots$, and all non-variable terms occurring in the *clause set* have the form $f_j(x_1, \ldots, x_l)$ for some j and l. The pivotal substitution can then always be assumed to be the identity mapping, and it is trivial to check

---

[10] The restriction to clauses in $\mathcal{D}_c^{\mathrm{elim}}$ is crucial for the correctness of this lemma.

that the conclusion of any $\mathfrak{D}^{abs}$-inference uses again the variables $x_1, x_2, \ldots$ in the required way.

To saturate a given finite subset of $\mathcal{D}_c^{\text{elim}}$, we proceed in a stratified way: We compute first all inferences involving the maximal function symbol f_m, then continue with the function symbols $f_{m-1}, \ldots, f_1$, and finally compute all *equality resolution* inferences. More formally, our strategy is defined as follows:

Let $N \subseteq \mathcal{D}_c^{\text{elim}}$ be the set of all input clauses.
Let $f_m \succ \cdots \succ f_1$ be the function symbols occurring in N.
Let $N_{m+1}^* = \{ \text{sfact}(C) \mid C \in N \}$.
For $k = m, m-1, \ldots, 1$:
  If N_{k+1}^* is defined, let N_k^0 be the set obtained from N_{k+1}^* by replacing every clause C whose maximal function symbol is f_k by $\text{simp}(C)$.
  For $r = 0, 1, \ldots$:
    If N_k^r is defined and if there are non-redundant *cancellative superposition* or *cancellative equality factoring* $\mathfrak{D}^{abs}$-inferences from clauses in N_k^r with pivotal term $f_k(x_1, \ldots, x_i)$, pick one of them "don't care" non-deterministically, let C be its conclusion, and let $N_k^{r+1} = N_k^r \cup \{\text{sfact}(C)\}$;
    if N_k^r is defined and if there is no such inference, let $N_k^* = N_k^r$.
If N_1^* is defined, let N^* be the union of N_1^* and the set of all conclusions of all non-redundant *equality resolution* $\mathfrak{D}^{abs}$-inferences from clauses in N_1^*.

Example 7. Let $N = \{3\underline{f_2(x,y)} \approx f_1(x), \; 2\underline{f_2(x,y)} + y \not\approx 0 \lor f_2(x,y) \not\approx f_1(x)\}$, where maximal atomic terms of maximal sides of maximal literals are underlined. Then $N_3^* = N$,

$N_2^0 = N_3^*$,

$N_2^1 = N_2^0 \cup \{2f_1(x) + 3y \not\approx 0 \lor \underline{f_2(x,y)} \not\approx f_1(x)\}$
    – by *cancellative superposition* of input clauses 1 and 2,

$N_2^2 = N_2^1 \cup \{f_1(x) \not\approx 3\underline{f_1(x)}\}$
    – by *cancellative superposition* of clause 1 and the newly generated clause (note elimination of y by *ElimNeg*),

$N_2^* = N_2^2$
    – as all inferences from N_2^2 with pivotal term $f_2(x,y)$ have been computed and are thus redundant,

$N_1^0 = N_2^* \setminus \{f_1(x) \not\approx 3\underline{f_1(x)}\} \cup \{0 \not\approx 2\underline{f_1(x)}\}$
    – by simp,

$N_1^* = N_1^0$
    – as there are no inferences from N_1^0 with pivotal term $f_1(x)$,

$N^* = N_1^*$.

As N^* is saturated and does not contain the empty clause, N^* and N are satisfiable.

Our task is now to show that the saturation of every stratum must terminate:

Lemma 8. *Let $k \in \{1, \ldots, m\}$. If N_{k+1}^* is defined, then there exists an $r \in \mathbf{N}$ such that there is no non-redundant cancellative superposition or cancellative equality factoring $\mathfrak{D}^{abs}$-inference from clauses in N_k^r with pivotal term $f_k(x_1, \ldots, x_i)$.*

Proof. Every $\mathfrak{D}^{abs}$-inference is redundant with respect to N_k^r if its conclusion C or an equivalent smaller clause, such as sfact(C), is contained in N_k^r. All inclusions in the sequence $N_k^0 \subseteq N_k^1 \subseteq \cdots \subseteq N_k^r \subseteq \ldots$ must therefore be strict. A clause can participate in an inference with pivotal term $f_k(x_1, \ldots, x_i)$ only if it contains f_k and if it does not contain any f_j with $j > k$, or in other words, if $f_k(x_1, \ldots, x_i)$ is its maximal atomic term. The set of all such clauses in N_k^0 is obviously finite. We will show below that the number of such clauses in $\bigcup_r N_k^r$ is also finite. From these finitely many clauses only finitely many conclusions of inferences can be derived, hence $\bigcup_r N_k^r$ must be finite. As the inclusions in the sequence are strict, the sequence is finite.

It remains to be proved that the number of clauses with maximal atomic term $f_k(x_1, \ldots, x_i)$ in $\bigcup_r N_k^r$ is finite. Let M be the subset of N_k^0 containing all clauses with maximal atomic term $f_k(x_1, \ldots, x_i)$. Let L be the set of all literals of clauses in M, let L_1 be the set of all literals in L in which f_k occurs, and let $L_0 = L \setminus L_1$. Note that there is no literal in L_1 in which f_k occurs on both sides. Let L_0' be the set of all literals A, such that there is a *cancellative superposition* $\mathfrak{K}$-inference

$$\frac{A_2 \quad A_1}{A}$$

with literals A_1 and A_2 from L_1. Let L_0'' be the set of all literals A, such that there is a *cancellative equality factoring* $\mathfrak{K}$-inference

$$\frac{A_2 \vee A_1}{A \vee A_2}$$

with literals A_1 and A_2 from L_1. Note that f_k does not occur in literals from $L_0' \cup L_0''$. Let M^* be the set of all clauses consisting of literals in $L_0 \cup L_0' \cup L_0'' \cup L_1$ (without duplicated literals).

Consider an arbitrary eliminating *cancellative superposition* or *cancellative equality factoring* $\mathfrak{D}^{abs}$-inference

$$\frac{C_n \quad \cdots \quad C_1}{\text{elim}(C_0)}$$

from premises in M^* with pivotal term $f_k(x_1, \ldots, x_i)$ and conclusion $D = \text{elim}(C_0)$. If $f_k(x_1, \ldots, x_i)$ occurs in sfact(D), then it occurs also in C_0. In this case, all variables in C_0 are shielded, thus $\text{elim}(C_0) = C_0$. Since

$$\frac{C_n \quad \cdots \quad C_1}{C_0}$$

is a *cancellative superposition* or *cancellative equality factoring* $\Re$-inference, $\mathrm{sfact}(D) = \mathrm{sfact}(C_0)$ is again contained in M^*. As $M \subseteq M^*$, we can conclude that all clauses in $\bigcup_r N_k^r$ with maximal atomic term $f_k(x_1, \ldots, x_i)$ are contained in M^*. Since M^* is finite, this completes the proof.   □

Corollary 9. N_k^* and N^* are defined for every $k \in \{1, \ldots, m+1\}$.

Theorem 10. $N \vdash N_{m+1}^* \vdash N_m^0 \vdash N_m^1 \vdash \ldots \vdash N_m^* \vdash \ldots \vdash N_1^0 \vdash N_1^1 \vdash \ldots \vdash N_1^* \vdash N^*$ is a finite theorem proving derivation; N and N^* are equivalent modulo $\mathrm{ACUKT} \cup \mathrm{DivInvNt}$.

Lemma 11. Let $1 \le k \le j \le m$. Then all $\mathfrak{D}^{abs}$-inferences with pivotal term $f_j(x_1, \ldots, x_l)$ from clauses in N_k^* are redundant with respect to N_k^*.

Proof. By induction, we may assume that all $\mathfrak{D}^{abs}$-inferences with pivotal term $f_p(x_1, \ldots, x_l)$, $p > k$ from clauses in N_{k+1}^* are redundant with respect to N_{k+1}^*.

The clauses in $N_k^* \setminus N_{k+1}^*$ contain only function symbols f_p with $p \le k$. Therefore, every $\mathfrak{D}^{abs}$-inference from clauses in N_k^* with pivotal term $f_p(x_1, \ldots, x_i)$ and $p > k$ is an inference from clauses in N_{k+1}^*, hence it is redundant with respect to N_{k+1}^*. As all clauses in $N_{k+1}^* \setminus N_k^*$ are redundant with respect to N_{k+1}^*, every inference that is redundant with respect to N_{k+1}^* is also redundant with respect to N_k^*. Therefore it suffices to show that all $\mathfrak{D}^{abs}$-inferences with pivotal term $f_k(x_1, \ldots, x_i)$ from clauses in N_k^* are redundant with respect to N_k^*.

It is easy to check that literals with f_k occurring on both sides cannot occur at all in clauses in $N_k^* \setminus N_k^0$, and that they can occur in a clause C in N_k^0 only if some f_p with $p > k$ occurs in C. Hence there are no *cancellation* inferences with pivotal term $f_k(x_1, \ldots, x_i)$ from clauses in $N_k^* = N_k^0 \cup (N_k^* \setminus N_k^0)$. This means that all inferences from clauses in N_k^* with pivotal term $f_k(x_1, \ldots, x_i)$ are either *cancellative superposition* or *cancellative equality factoring* inferences, hence they are redundant with respect to N_k^* by construction of N_k^*.   □

Theorem 12. N^* is saturated, that is, all inferences from clauses in N^* are redundant with respect to N^*.

Proof. By Lemma 11, all $\mathfrak{D}^{abs}$-inferences with pivotal terms $f_j(x_1, \ldots, x_l)$ from clauses in N_1^* are redundant with respect to N_1^* (and hence with respect to N^*). Furthermore, by construction of N^*, all *equality resolution* inferences from clauses in N_1^* are redundant with respect to N^*. Since *equality resolution* applies only to clauses with maximal literals $0 \not\approx 0$ and since no clause in N_1^* contains repeated literals, no inferences are possible from clauses in $N^* \setminus N_1^*$.   □

As N^* is saturated, it contains the empty clause if and only if it is unsatisfiable modulo $\mathrm{ACUKT} \cup \mathrm{DivInvNt}$. Since N and N^* are equivalent modulo the theory axioms, the main theorem of this paper is proved:

Theorem 13. *The saturation strategy terminates for every finite input set $N \subseteq \mathcal{D}_c^{\mathrm{elim}}$; N is unsatisfiable modulo $\mathrm{ACUKT} \cup \mathrm{DivInvNt}$ if and only if the strategy derives the empty clause from N.*

7   Conclusions

In previous work, we have demonstrated that the cancellative superposition calculus $\mathfrak{K}$ can be augmented by a variable elimination algorithm for DTAGs. The resulting calculus $\mathcal{D}^{abs}$ is refutationally complete with respect to the axioms of divisible torsion-free abelian groups and allows us to dispense with variable overlaps altogether. As variable overlaps are one of the most prolific types of inferences in resolution or superposition style calculi, integration of the variable elimination algorithm leads to a dramatically reduced search space compared with the usual cancellative superposition calculus or, even worse, AC or ACU superposition calculi.

Since 1976 several resolution or superposition calculi have been shown to be decision procedures for certain classes of formulae (e. g., [3, 6–9, 11]). If the calculi in question are known to be refutationally complete, then showing that they are actually decision procedures amounts to proving that they terminate even on consistent inputs. In the present paper we have demonstrated that the calculus $\mathcal{D}^{abs}$ is powerful enough to solve the decision problem for divisible torsion-free abelian groups. Following the general scheme described above, the termination proof is peculiar in two respects: First, we require that the set of clauses is saturated in a stratified way. Termination follows from the two facts that the number of strata is finite and that the number of new clauses derived during the saturation of each stratum is finite. Second, the particular structure of the literals and clauses makes it possible to assume that all clauses share the *same* variables and that the pivotal substitution is always the identity mapping – in some sense, variables are treated as if they were constants.

What remains open at present is the precise computational complexity of our decision procedure. The time bound that can be derived in a straightforward manner from the saturation strategy is non-elementary. Possibly significantly better bounds can be obtained for subclasses of $\mathcal{D}_c^{elim}$, but this is still a matter of further research.

Acknowledgments: I would like to thank Patrick Maier, Jürgen Stuber, and the LPAR'99 referees for helpful comments on this paper.

References

1. Leo Bachmair and Harald Ganzinger. Associative-commutative superposition. In Nachum Dershowitz and Naomi Lindenstrauss, eds., *Conditional and Typed Rewriting Systems, 4th International Workshop, CTRS-94*, Jerusalem, Israel, July 13–15, 1994, LNCS 968, pp. 1–14. Springer-Verlag.

2. Leo Bachmair and Harald Ganzinger. Rewrite-based equational theorem proving with selection and simplification. *Journal of Logic and Computation*, 4(3):217–247, 1994.

3. Leo Bachmair, Harald Ganzinger, and Uwe Waldmann. Superposition with simplification as a decision procedure for the monadic class with equality. In Georg Gottlob, Alexander Leitsch, and Daniele Mundici, eds., *Computational Logic and*

Proof Theory, Third Kurt Gödel Colloquium, Brno, Czech Republic, August 24–27, 1993, LNCS 713, pp. 83–96. Springer-Verlag.

4. Leo Bachmair, Harald Ganzinger, and Uwe Waldmann. Refutational theorem proving for hierarchic first-order theories. *Applicable Algebra in Engineering, Communication and Computing*, 5(3/4):193–212, April 1994.

5. E[dward] Cardoza, R[ichard] Lipton, and A[lbert] R. Meyer. Exponential space complete problems for petri nets and commutative semigroups: Preliminary report. In *Eighth Annual ACM Symposium on Theory of Computing*, Hershey, PA, USA, May 3–5, 1976, pp. 50–54.

6. C[hristian] Fermüller, A[lexander] Leitsch, Tanel Tammet, and Nail Zamov. *Resolution Methods for the Decision Problem*. LNAI 679. Springer-Verlag, Berlin, Heidelberg, New York, 1993.

7. Christian Fermüller and Gernot Salzer. Ordered paramodulation and resolution as decision procedure. In Andrei Voronkov, ed., *Logic Programming and Automated Reasoning, 4th International Conference, LPAR'93*, St. Petersburg, Russia, July 13–20, 1993, LNCS 698, pp. 122–133. Springer-Verlag.

8. Harald Ganzinger and Hans de Nivelle. A superposition decision procedure for the guarded fragment with equality. In *Fourteenth Annual IEEE Symposium on Logic in Computer Science*, Trento, Italy, July 2–5, 1999, pp. 295–303. IEEE Computer Society Press.

9. Harald Ganzinger, Ullrich Hustadt, Christoph Meyer, and Renate Schmidt. A resolution-based decision procedure for extensions of K4. In *Advances in Modal Logic '98*, 1998. To appear.

10. Harald Ganzinger and Uwe Waldmann. Theorem proving in cancellative abelian monoids (extended abstract). In Michael A. McRobbie and John K. Slaney, eds., *Automated Deduction – CADE-13, 13th International Conference on Automated Deduction*, New Brunswick, NJ, USA, July 30–August 3, 1996, LNAI 1104, pp. 388–402. Springer-Verlag.

11. William H. Joyner Jr. Resolution strategies as decision procedures. *Journal of the ACM*, 23(3):398–417, July 1976.

12. Ernst W. Mayr and Albert R. Meyer. The complexity of the word problems for commutative semigroups and polynomial ideals. *Advances in Mathematics*, 46(3):305–329, December 1982.

13. Etienne Paul. A general refutational completeness result for an inference procedure based on associative-commutative unification. *Journal of Symbolic Computation*, 14(6):577–618, December 1992.

14. Gerald E. Peterson and Mark E. Stickel. Complete sets of reductions for some equational theories. *Journal of the ACM*, 28(2):233–264, April 1981.

15. Gordon D. Plotkin. Building-in equational theories. In Bernard Meltzer and Donald Michie, eds., *Machine Intelligence 7*, ch. 4, pp. 73–90. American Elsevier, New York, NY, USA, 1972.

16. Michaël Rusinowitch and Laurent Vigneron. Automated deduction with associative-commutative operators. *Applicable Algebra in Engineering, Communication and Computing*, 6(1):23–56, January 1995.

17. James R. Slagle. Automated theorem-proving for theories with simplifiers, commutativity, and associativity. *Journal of the ACM*, 21(4):622–642, October 1974.

18. Uwe Waldmann. *Cancellative Abelian Monoids in Refutational Theorem Proving*. Dissertation, Universität des Saarlandes, Saarbrücken, Germany, 1997. http://www.mpi-sb.mpg.de/~uwe/paper/PhD.ps.gz.

19. Uwe Waldmann. Extending reduction orderings to ACU-compatible reduction orderings. *Information Processing Letters*, 67(1):43–49, July 16, 1998.
20. Uwe Waldmann. Superposition for divisible torsion-free abelian groups. In Claude Kirchner and Hélène Kirchner, eds., *Automated Deduction – CADE-15, 15th International Conference on Automated Deduction*, Lindau, Germany, July 5–10, 1998, LNAI 1421, pp. 144–159. Springer-Verlag.
21. Ulrich Wertz. First-order theorem proving modulo equations. Technical Report MPI-I-92-216, Max-Planck-Institut für Informatik, Saarbrücken, Germany, April 1992.

Regular Sets of Descendants for Constructor-Based Rewrite Systems

Pierre Réty

LIFO - Université d'Orléans
B.P. 6759, 45067 Orléans cedex 2, France
e-mail : rety@lifo.univ-orleans.fr
http://www.univ-orleans.fr/SCIENCES/LIFO/Members/rety

Keywords : term rewriting, tree automata.

Abstract. Starting from the regular tree language E of ground constructor-instances of any linear term, we build a finite tree automaton that recognizes the set of descendants $R^*(E)$ of E for a constructor-based term rewrite system whose right-hand-sides fulfill the following three restrictions : linearity, no nested function symbols, function arguments are variables or ground terms. Note that left-linearity is not assumed. We next present several applications.

1 Introduction

Tree automata have already been applied to many areas of computer science, and in particular to rewriting techniques [2]. In comparison with more sophisticated refinements, finite tree automata are obviously less powerful, but have plenty of good properties and lead to much simpler algorithms from a practical point of view.

Because of potential applications to automated deduction and program validation, the problem of expressing by a finite tree automaton the transitive closure of a regular set E of ground terms with respect to an equational system, as well as the related problem of expressing the set of descendants of E with respect to a rewrite system, have already been investigated [1, 5, 13, 4, 9][1]. All those papers assume that the right-hand-sides (both sides when dealing with equational systems) of rewrite rules are shallow, up to slight differences. Shallow means that every variable appears at depth at most one.

On the other hand, the possibility of approximating the set of descendants by means of a finite tree automaton, only assuming left-linearity, has been investigated in [7].

Our work is located in between : it adjusts the former papers to constructor-based rewrite systems where right-hand-sides are not necessarily shallow, without making an approximation. Instead, we assume that function calls in right-hand-sides are shallow subterms (Restriction 1). However, to get regular sets of descendants, some additional restrictions are needed (Restrictions 2 and 3) :

---

[1] [9] computes sets of normalizable terms, which amounts to compute sets of descendants by orienting the rewrite rules in the opposite sense.

1. For each rule $l \rightarrow r$ and each function symbol position p in r, $r|_p = f(r_1, \ldots, r_n)$ where for all i, r_i is a variable or a ground term[2].
2. The right-hand-sides are linear and do not contain nested function symbols.
3. E is the set of the ground constructor-instances (also called data-instances) of a given linear term.

Fortunately, there is no need to start from any regular set E for applications. If any among the above restrictions is not satisfied, the set of descendants $R^*(E)$ is not regular in general. If it were, the set of normal forms $R^!(E)$ of E would be regular as well, provided that R is left-linear, because $R^!(E) = R^*(E) \cap IRR(R)$ and the set of irreducible ground terms $IRR(R)$ is regular in this case. The following array shows that $R^!(E)$ is not regular.

Unsatisfied Restriction	Rewrite System	E	$R^!(E)$
Linearity in rhs's	$f(x) \rightarrow c(x, x)$	$\{f(t)\}$	$\{c(t, t)\}$
Function calls in rhs's are shallow subterms	$f(s(x), y) \rightarrow s(f(x, s(y)))$	$f(s^*(0), 0)$	$s^n(f(0, s^n(0)))$
No nested function symbols in rhs's	$f(s(x), y) \rightarrow s(f(x, g(y)))$ $g(x) \rightarrow s(x)$	$f(s^*(0), 0)$	$s^n(f(0, s^n(0)))$
$E = \{t\theta\}$	$f(s(x)) \rightarrow s(f(x))$	$(fs)^*(0)$	$s^n(f^n(0))$

The construction of the automaton is presented in Section 3. It is necessary to nest automata, as defined in Subsection 2.2. Applications to reachability through rewrite steps, unification, program testing, sufficient completeness are outlined in Section 4.

2 Preliminaries

2.1 Term rewriting and finite tree automata

Surveys can be found in [6] about term rewriting, and in [2,8] about tree automata.

Let C be a finite set of *constructors* and F be a finite set of *defined function symbols* (*functions* in a shortened form). For $c \in C \cup F$, $ar(c)$ is the arity of c. *Terms* are denoted by letters t, u. A *data-term* is a *ground* term (i.e. without variables) that contains only constructors. $T(C)$ is the set of data-terms. For a term t, $Var(t)$ is the set of variables appearing in t, $Pos(t)$ is the set of *positions* of t, $\overline{Pos}(t)$ is the set of non-variable positions of t, $PosF(t)$ is the set of function positions of t. t is *linear* if each variable of t appears only once in t. For $p \in Pos(t)$, $t|_p$ is the subterm of t at position p, $t(p)$ is the top symbol of $t|_p$, and $t[t']_p$ denotes the subterm replacement. For positions p, p', $p \geq p'$ means that p is located below p', i.e. $p = p'.v$ for some position v, whereas $p \| p'$ means that p and p' are incomparable, i.e. $\neg(p \geq p') \wedge \neg(p' \geq p)$. The term t contains

---

[2] It can be weakened into a more technical restriction, which allows non-shallow function calls: for each rewrite rule $l \rightarrow r$ and each function symbol position p in r, if $r|_p$ unifies with a left-hand-side l' (after variable renaming to avoid conflicts), then the mgu σ does not instantiate the variables of l', or only into ground subterms of r.

nested functions if there exist $p, p' \in \overline{Pos}(t)$ s.t. $t(p) \in F$, $t(p') \in F$, and $p > p'$. The domain $dom(\theta)$ of a substitution θ is the set of variables x s.t. $x\theta \neq x$.

A *rewrite rule* is an oriented pair of terms, written $l \to r$. We always assume that $Var(r) \subseteq Var(l)$[3]. A *rewrite system* R is a finite set of rewrite rules. *lhs* stands for left-hand-side, *rhs* for right-hand-side. R is *constructor-based* if every lhs l of R is of the form $l = f(t_1, \ldots, t_n)$ where $f \in F$ and $t_1, \ldots, t_n$ do not contain any functions. The rewrite relation $\to_R$ is defined as follows: $t \to_R t'$ if there exist $p \in \overline{Pos}(t)$, a rule $l \to r \in R$, and a substitution θ s.t. $t|_p = l\theta$ and $t' = t[r\theta]_p$. $\to_R^*$ denotes the transitive closure of $\to_R$. t' is a *descendant* of t if $t \to_R^* t'$. t' is a *normal-form* of t if $t \to_R^* t'$ and t' is irreducible. If E is a set of ground terms, $R^*(E)$ denotes the set of descendants of elements of E, and $R^!(E)$ denotes the set of normal-forms. $IRR(R)$ denotes the set of irreducible ground terms. Thus $R^!(E) = R^*(E) \cap IRR(R)$. R is *weakly normalizing* if every term has at least one normal-form.

A (bottom-up) finite tree *automaton* is a quadruple $\mathcal{A} = (C \cup F, Q, Q_f, \Delta)$ where $Q_f \subseteq Q$ and Δ is a set of *transitions* of the form $c(q_1, \ldots, q_n) \to q$ where $c \in C \cup F$ and $q_1, \ldots, q_n, q \in Q$, or of the form $q_1 \to q$. Sets of *states* are denoted by letters Q, S, D, and states by q, s, d. $\to_\Delta$ (also denoted $\to_\mathcal{A}$) is the rewrite relation induced by Δ. A ground term t is *recognized* by $\mathcal{A}$ into q iff $t \to_\Delta^* q$. $L(\mathcal{A})$ is the set of terms recognized by $\mathcal{A}$ into any states of Q_f. The states of Q_f are called *final states*. $\mathcal{A}$ is *deterministic* if whenever $t \to_\Delta^* q$ and $t \to_\Delta^* q'$ we have $q = q'$. A Q-*substitution* σ is a substitution s.t. $\forall x \in dom(\sigma)$, $x\sigma \in Q$.

2.2   Nesting automata

Definition 1. *The automaton $\mathcal{A} = (C \cup F, Q, Q_f, \Delta)$ discriminates the position p into the state q if $L(\mathcal{A}) \neq \emptyset$ and for each $t \in L(\mathcal{A})$, we have $p \in Pos(t)$ and*

- *$t|_p$ is recognized into q (and only into q),*
- *for each $p' \in Pos(t)$ s.t. $p' \neq p$, $t|_{p'}$ is not recognized into q.*

In this case we define the automaton $\mathcal{A}|_p = (C \cup F, Q, \{q\}, \Delta)$.

Remark : $L(\mathcal{A}|_p) = \{t|_p \mid t \in L(\mathcal{A})\}$.

Definition 2. *Let $\mathcal{A} = (C \cup F, Q, Q_f, \Delta)$ be an automaton that discriminates the position p into the state q, and let $\mathcal{A}' = (C \cup F, Q', Q'_f, \Delta')$ s.t. $Q \cap Q' = \emptyset$. We define $\mathcal{A}[\mathcal{A}']_p =$*

$$(C \cup F, Q \cup Q', Q_f, \Delta \backslash \{c(q_1, \ldots, q_n) \to q \mid c \in C \cup F, q_1, \ldots, q_n \in Q\}$$
$$\cup \Delta' \cup \{q'_f \to q \mid q'_f \in Q'_f\})$$

Lemma 1. $L(\mathcal{A}[\mathcal{A}']_p) = \{t[t']_p \mid t \in L(\mathcal{A}), t' \in L(\mathcal{A}')\}$.

Proof. Let $t \in L(\mathcal{A})$ and $t' \in L(\mathcal{A}')$.
There exists $q'_f \in Q'_f$ s.t. $t[t']_p \to_{\Delta'}^* t[q'_f]_p \to_{[q'_f \to q]} t[q]_p$. Since $\mathcal{A}$ discriminates p into q, there exists $q_f \in Q_f$ s.t. $t \to_\Delta^* t[q]_p \to_\Delta^* q_f$ and within $t[q]_p \to_\Delta^* q_f$

---

[3] Left-hand-sides are allowed to be variables.

no transition whose rhs is q is used. Therefore $t[t']_p \rightarrow^*_{A[A']_p} q_f$, i.e. $t[t']_p \in L(A[A']_p)$.

Conversely, let $t \in L(A[A']_p)$. Since the set of final states of $A[A']_p$ is Q_f, necessarily $t \rightarrow^*_{\Delta'} t[q'_{f_1}]_{p'_1} \cdots [q'_{f_n}]_{p'_n} \rightarrow^* t[q]_{p'_1} \cdots [q]_{p'_n} \rightarrow^*_\Delta q_f$ where $q'_{f_1}, \ldots, q'_{f_n} \in Q'_f$ and $q_f \in Q_f$. Since A discriminates p into q, necessarily $n = 1$ and $p'_1 = p$. Therefore $t \rightarrow^*_{\Delta'} t[q'_{f_1}]_p \rightarrow t[q]_p \rightarrow^*_\Delta q_f$, then $t|_p \rightarrow^*_{\Delta'} q'_{f_1}$, i.e. $t|_p \in L(A')$. Since we assume $L(A) \neq \emptyset$, let $u \in L(A)$. Then $u|_p \rightarrow^*_\Delta q$. Thus $t[u|_p]_p \rightarrow^*_\Delta t[q]_p \rightarrow^*_\Delta q_f$, i.e. $t[u|_p]_p \in L(A)$.

As seen in the above proof, the states of Q' concern only the positions located below p. Therefore:

Corollary 1. *If $L(A) \neq \emptyset$ and A discriminates another position p' s.t. $p' \not\geq p$, into the state q', then $A[A']_p$ still discriminates p' into q'.*

3   An automaton that recognizes $R^*(E)$

Definition 3. *We define the automaton A_{data} that recognizes the set of data-terms $T(C)$:*
$A_{data} = (C, Q_{data}, Q_{data_f}, \Delta_{data})$ *where* $Q_{data} = Q_{data_f} = \{q_{data}\}$ *and* $\Delta_{data} = \{c(q_{data}, \ldots, q_{data}) \rightarrow q_{data} \mid c \in C\}$.

Given a linear term t, we define the automaton $A_{t\theta}$ that recognizes the data-instances of t: $A_{t\theta} = (C \cup F, Q_{t\theta}, Q_{t\theta_f}, \Delta_{t\theta})$ where

$$Q_{t\theta} = \{q^p \mid p \in \overline{Pos}(t)\} \cup \{q_{data}\}$$
$$Q_{t\theta_f} = \{q^\epsilon\} \text{ (} q_{data} \text{ if } t \text{ is a variable)}$$
$$\Delta_{t\theta} = \left\{ t(p)(s_1, \ldots, s_n) \rightarrow q^p \mid p \in \overline{Pos}(t), \ s_i = \left| \begin{matrix} q_{data} \text{ if } t|_{p.i} \text{ is a variable} \\ q^{p.i} \text{ otherwise} \end{matrix} \right. \right\}$$
$$\cup \Delta_{data}$$

Note that $A_{t\theta}$ discriminates each position $p \in \overline{Pos}(t)$ into q^p. On the other hand, $A_{t\theta}$ is not deterministic[4] as soon as there is $p \in \overline{Pos}(t)$ s.t. $t|_p$ is a constructor-term. Indeed for any data-instance $t|_p\theta$, $t|_p\theta \rightarrow^*_{[\Delta_{t\theta}]} q^p$ and $t|_p\theta \rightarrow^*_{[\Delta_{t\theta}]} q_{data}$.

Example 1. Let a, s be constructors and f be a function, s.t. a is a constant and s, f are unary symbols. Consider the term $t = f(s(s(y)))$ as well as the automaton $A_{t\theta}$ that recognizes the language $E = f(s(s(s^*(a))))$ of the data-instances of t. $A_{t\theta}$ can be summarized by writing $\overset{q^\epsilon}{f}$ $(\overset{q^1}{s}$ $(\overset{q^{1.1}}{s}$ $(\overset{q_{data}}{s^*(a)})))$, which means that $s^*(a) \rightarrow^*_{[\Delta_{t\theta}]} q_{data}$, $s(s^*(a)) \rightarrow^*_{[\Delta_{t\theta}]} q^{1.1}$, $s(s(s^*(a))) \rightarrow^*_{[\Delta_{t\theta}]} q^1$, $f(s(s(s^*(a)))) \rightarrow^*_{[\Delta_{t\theta}]} q^\epsilon$. Consider now the rewrite system $R = \{f(s(x)) \rightarrow s(f(x))\}$. Obviously $R^*(E) = E \cup s(f(s(s^*(a)))) \cup s(s(s^*(f(s^*(a)))))$.

When rewriting E, some instances of rhs's of rewrite rules are introduced by rewrite steps. So, to build an automaton that can recognize $R^*(E)$, we need to

---

[4] A direct construction of a deterministic automaton is given in [3]. However, it does not distinguish the positions of $\overline{Pos}(t)$.

recognize the instances of rhs's into some states, without making any confusion between the various potential instances of the same rhs. Indeed consider the first two rewrite steps issued from E:

$$f(s(s(s^*(a)))) \to_{[x/s(s^*(a))]} \mathcal{L}' = s(f(s(s(s^*(a))))) \to_{[x/s^*(a)]} s(s(f(s^*(a))))$$

The language that instantiates x along the first step is $s(s^*(a))$ (recognized into $q^{1.1}$), whereas it is $s^*(a)$ (recognized into q_{data}) along the second step. Therefore we encode two versions of the rhs: $\overset{d^\epsilon_{q1.1}}{s} (\overset{d^1_{q1.1}}{f} (\overset{q^{1.1}}{x}))$ and $\overset{d^\epsilon_{q_{data}}}{s} (\overset{d^1_{q_{data}}}{f} (\overset{q_{data}}{x}))$, by adding the states $d^\epsilon_{q1.1}, d^1_{q1.1}, d^\epsilon_{q_{data}}, d^1_{q_{data}}$ and the transitions

$$f(q^{1.1}) \to d^1_{q1.1}, \quad s(d^1_{q1.1}) \to d^\epsilon_{q1.1}, \quad f(q_{data}) \to d^1_{q_{data}}, \quad s(d^1_{q_{data}}) \to d^\epsilon_{q_{data}}$$

Thus the language recognized into $d^\epsilon_{q1.1}$ (resp. $d^\epsilon_{q_{data}}$) is exactly the rhs instantiated by $\overset{q^{1.1}}{s} (\overset{q_{data}}{s^*(a)})$ (resp. $\overset{q_{data}}{s^*(a)}$). In other words $\mathcal{L}' = s(f(s(s(s^*(a))))) \to^* d^\epsilon_{q1.1}$ (resp. $s(f(s(s^*(a)))) \to^* d^\epsilon_{q_{data}}$). More generally we encode a version of the rhs for each state of $Q_{t\theta}$.

Now we can simulate rewrite steps on languages, by adding transitions again. This step is called saturation in the following. For example, consider again the first rewrite step issued from E:

$$\overset{q^\epsilon}{f} (\overset{q^1}{s} (\overset{q^{1.1}}{s} (\overset{q_{data}}{s^*(a)}))) \to_{[x/s(s^*(a))]} \mathcal{L}' = s(f(s(s(s^*(a)))))$$

Since $f(s(x))$ is the rule lhs, and $f(s(q^{1.1})) \to^*_{\mathcal{A}_{t\theta}} q^\epsilon$, we add the transition $d^\epsilon_{q1.1} \to q^\epsilon$. Thus $\mathcal{L}' = s(f(s(s(s^*(a))))) \to^* d^\epsilon_{q1.1} \to q^\epsilon$ which is the final state. So $\mathcal{L}'$ is recognized by the automaton. More generally, whenever $f(s(q)) \to^* q'$ for $q \in Q_{t\theta}$, we add $d^\epsilon_q \to q'$.

In the previous example, the matches used in rewrite steps always instantiate the variable by languages recognized into states of $\mathcal{A}_{t\theta}$, i.e. the instances are (sub)terms of E. This is not the case in the following example.

Example 2. Let E be the data-instances of $t = f(z)$ and $R = \{f(x) \overset{r_1}{\to} g(s(a)), g(y) \overset{r_2}{\to} s(y)\}$. The rewrite steps issued from E are $\overset{q^\epsilon}{f} (\overset{q_{data}}{s^*(a)}) \to_{[r_1]} g(s(a)) \to_{[r_2, y/s(a)]} s(g(a))$. Unfortunately $Q_{t\theta} = \{q^\epsilon, q_{data}\}$ and the language recognized into q^ϵ (resp. q_{data}) is $f(s^*(a))$ (resp. $s^*(a)$). Thus we do not have any states that can exactly recognize the instance of the second rewrite step $\{s(a)\}$. This comes from the fact that $s(a)$ does not come from E, but from the rhs of r_1. Therefore we need to encode $s(a)$ by additional states.

In rhs's, function calls are assumed to be shallow subterms, and nested functions are not allowed. Therefore (see Lemma 5) the matches used in rewrite steps instantiate variables by either subterms of E, or (sub)-arguments of function calls in rhs's (which are data-terms). So, adding to $\mathcal{A}_{t\theta}$ states and transitions to encode all the function call arguments is enough.

Definition 4. *The non-variable arguments of functions in rhs's are encoded by the set of states Q_{arg} and the set of transitions Δ_{arg} as defined below:*

$$Q_{arg} = \{q^{i,p} \mid l_i \to r_i \in R, \ p \in Arg(r_i)\}$$
$$\Delta_{arg} = \{r_i(p)(q^{i,p.1}, \ldots, q^{i,p.n}) \to q^{i,p} \mid q^{i,p} \in Q_{arg}\}$$

where $Arg(r_i)$ are the non-variable argument positions in r_i, i.e.

$$Arg(r_i) = \{p \in \overline{Pos}(r_i) \mid \exists p_{fct} \in PosF(r_i), \ p > p_{fct}\}$$

Actually, for each state of $Q' = Q_{t\theta} \cup Q_{arg}$, we have to encode a version of each rhs. In general, unlike the previous examples, rhs's may contain several variables. This is why we use states of the form d_σ^p where σ is a Q'-substitution, instead of d_q^p where q is a single state of Q', to encode rhs's. Note that function arguments in rhs's are not encoded by new states in the following definition, but by those of Q_{arg}.

Definition 5. *The rhs's of rewrite rules are encoded by the sets of states Q_{arg} and*

$$D = \{d_\sigma^{i,p} \mid l_i \to r_i \in R, \ p \in Pos(r_i) \backslash Arg(r_i),$$
$$\sigma \text{ is a } Q'\text{-substitution s.t. } dom(\sigma) = Var(r_i|_p)\}$$

and the set of transitions

$$\Delta_d = \{r_i(p)(d_{\sigma_1}^{i,p.1}, \ldots, d_{\sigma_n}^{i,p.n}) \to d_{\sigma_1 \cup \ldots \cup \sigma_n}^{i,p} \mid l_i \to r_i \in R,$$
$$p \in Pos(r_i) \backslash Arg(r_i), \ r_i(p) \in C$$
$$\forall j, \ \sigma_j \text{ is any } Q'\text{-substitution s.t. } dom(\sigma_j) = Var(r_i|_{p.j})\}$$
$$\cup \ \{r_i(p)(X_1, \ldots, X_n) \to d_\sigma^{i,p} \mid l_i \to r_i \in R, \ p \in PosF(r_i),$$
$$\sigma \text{ is any } Q'\text{-substitution s.t. } dom(\sigma) = Var(r_i|_p)$$
$$\text{where } \forall j, \ X_j = \begin{vmatrix} x\sigma \mid r_i(p.j) \text{ is any variable } x \\ q^{i,p.j} \in Q_{arg} \text{ otherwise} \end{vmatrix} \}$$
$$\cup \ \{x\sigma \to d_\sigma^{i,\epsilon} \mid l_i \to r_i \in R, \ r_i \text{ is any variable } x,$$
$$\sigma \text{ is any } Q'\text{-substitution s.t. } dom(\sigma) = \{x\}\}$$

Thus, the ground term t is recognized into the state $d_\sigma^{i,\epsilon}$ iff $t = r_i\sigma$.

Let us explain now what happens when adding the transitions that simulate rewrite steps, if some lhs's are not linear.

Example 3. Let E be the data-instances of $t = f(s(x), y)$ and $R = \{f(x,x) \overset{r_1}{\to} x\}$. Thus $E = \overset{q^\epsilon}{f} (\overset{q^1}{s} (\overset{q_{data}}{s^*(a)}), \overset{q_{data}}{s^*(a)})$. Obviously $R^*(E) = E \cup \{s(s^*(a))\}$. If we try to add transitions to simulate rewrite steps as in Example 1, we have to look for the states $q \in Q_{t\theta}$ s.t. $f(q,q) \to_{\Delta_{t\theta}}^* q^\epsilon$. Unfortunately, no state of $Q_{t\theta} = \{q^\epsilon, q^1, q_{data}\}$ works.

Even so, the terms in the non-regular subset of E: $f(\overset{q^1}{s^n(a)}), \overset{q_{data}}{s^{n+1}(a)})$, are reducible. However they instantiate the left x of the lhs by q_1 and the right x by q_{data}, i.e. by two different states. So $s^{n+1}(a) \to_{\Delta_{t\theta}}^* q^1$ and $s^{n+1}(a) \to_{\Delta_{t\theta}}^* q_{data}$. In other words $\mathcal{A}_{t\theta}$ is not deterministic. If it were, the common instances $s^{n+1}(a)$ of the two occurrences of x would be recognized into the same state, so it would work.

In this example $Q_{arg} = \emptyset$. If it is not, we have to start from the automaton $(C \cup F, Q_{t\theta} \cup Q_{arg}, \{q^\epsilon\}, \Delta_{t\theta} \cup \Delta_{arg})$, which is not necessarily deterministic even if $\mathcal{A}_{t\theta}$ is. Therefore this automaton must be determinized before starting.

In all previous examples, t contained only one function. If there are several ones, and in particular, nested ones, we consider each function on its own and work incrementally.

Example 4. Let E be the data-instances of $t = f(g(z))$ and
$$R = \{f(x) \overset{r_1}{\to} x, \ g(x) \overset{r_2}{\to} s(h(x)), \ h(s(x)) \overset{r_3}{\to} x\}$$
Then
$$f(g(s^*(a))) \to_{[r_1]} g(s^*(a)) \to_{[r_2]} s(h(s^*(a))) \to^*_{[r_3]} s(s^*(a))$$
This derivation can be commutated so that the innermost function g is first reduced, as well as the rhs's coming from the reduction of g:
$$f(g(s^*(a))) \to_{[r_2]} f(s(h(s^*(a)))) \to_{[r_3]} f(s(s^*(a))) \to_{[r_1]} s(s^*(a))$$
Thanks to right-linearity, commuting rewrite derivations leaves the final term unchanged. Thus, we can write (roughly) $R^*(E) = R^*_{[r_1]}(f(R^*_{[r_2,r_3]}(g(s^*(a)))))$.

If t is for example $t = f(f(x))$, we must not make any confusion between both occurrences of f in t. This is the goal of the following definitions.

Definition 6. $t \to^+_{[p,rhs's]} t'$ *means that* t' *is obtained by reducing* t *at position* p, *plus possibly at positions coming from the rhs's.*
Formally, there exist some intermediate terms $t_1, \ldots, t_n$ *and some sets of positions* $P(t), P(t_1), \ldots, P(t_n)$ *s.t.*
$$t = t_0 \to_{[p_0,l_0 \to r_0]} t_1 \to_{[p_1,l_1 \to r_1]} \cdots \to_{[p_{n-1},l_{n-1} \to r_{n-1}]} t_n \to_{[p_n,l_n \to r_n]} t'$$
where

- $p_0 = p$ *and* $P(t) = \{p\}$,
- $\forall j, \ p_j \in P(t_j)$,
- $\forall j, \ P(t_{j+1}) = P(t_j) \backslash \{p' \mid p' \geq p_j\} \cup \{p_j.w \mid w \in PosF(r_j)\}$.

Remark : $P(t_j)$ only contains function positions. Since there are no nested functions in rhs's, $p, p' \in P(t_j)$ implies $p \| p'$.

Definition 7. *Given a language* E *and a position* p, *let*
$$R^*_p(E) = E \cup \{t' \mid \exists t \in E, \ t \to^+_{[p,rhs's]} t'\}$$

Example 5. Consider again Example 4. Then
$R^*_1(f(g(s^*(a)))) = f(g(s^*(a))) \cup f(s(h(s^*(a)))) \cup f(s(s^*(a)))$.

Lemma 2. *Let* E *be the set of data-instances of a linear term* t, *and* $\{p_1, \ldots, p_n\}$ *be the function positions of* t *sorted in an innermost way (i.e.* $i < j \Longrightarrow p_j \not\geq p_i$). *Then*
$$R^*(E) = R^*_{p_n}(\ldots(R^*_{p_1}(E))\ldots)$$

Proof. Obviously $R^*_{p_n}(\ldots(R^*_{p_1}(E))\ldots)\subseteq R^*(E)$.

Conversely, since R is right-linear, each rewrite derivation $t\to^* t'$ can be commuted into $t\to_{[p'_1]}\to\cdots\to_{[p'_k]} t'$ s.t. $i<j\implies p'_j\not\geq p'_i$ (see [12, page 74]). Rewrite steps at incomparable positions can also be commuted. Therefore we can get a derivation of the form

$$t=t_1\to^*_{[p_1,rhs's]} t_2\to^*\cdots\to^* t_n\to^*_{[p_n,rhs's]} t_{n+1}=t'$$

where $t_i\to^*_{[p_i,rhs's]} t_{i+1}$ means $t_{i+1}=t_i$ or $t_i\to^+_{[p_i,rhs's]} t_{i+1}$.

From an automaton $\mathcal{A}$, we are now able to define an automaton that recognizes $R^*_p(L(\mathcal{A}))$.

Notation: $\mathcal{A}_{det}$ denotes the automaton obtained by determinizing $\mathcal{A}$.

Definition 8. *Let $\mathcal{A}=(C\cup F,Q,Q_f,\Delta)$ be an automaton that discriminates the position p into the state q, and s.t. $Q\cap Q_{arg}=\emptyset$. We define:*

$$\mathcal{A}'=(C\cup F,Q',Q'_f,\Delta')=(C\cup F,\ Q\cup Q_{arg},\ \{q\},\ \Delta\cup\Delta_{arg})_{det}$$
$$\mathcal{A}''=(C\cup F,Q'',Q''_f,\Delta'')$$
$$=(C\cup F,\ Q'\cup D\cup\{s\},\ \{s\},\ \Delta'\cup\Delta_d\cup\{q'_f\to s\mid q'_f\in Q'_f\})$$

Roughly speaking, $\mathcal{A}''$ is $\mathcal{A}'$ to which the encoding of rhs's has been added. In general $\mathcal{A}''$ is not deterministic although $\mathcal{A}'$ is (for example if two rhs's are identical). Determinizing $\mathcal{A}'$ is useless if every rewrite rule is left-linear. Note that $L(\mathcal{A}')=L(\mathcal{A}|_p)$ and $\mathcal{A}|_p$ discriminates the position ϵ into q. However, due to the determinization, $\mathcal{A}'$ does not necessarily distinguish ϵ. This is why an additional state s has been added into $\mathcal{A}''$. Thus, $L(\mathcal{A}'')=L(\mathcal{A}')=L(\mathcal{A}|_p)$ and $\mathcal{A}''$ discriminates the position ϵ into s. This property is necessary in the saturation process defined below, to ensure that the first rewrite step is performed at position ϵ on the terms recognized by $\mathcal{A}''$, i.e. at position p on the terms recognized by $\mathcal{A}$.

Definition 9. *(saturation)*
Let $\mathcal{B}$ be the automaton obtained from $\mathcal{A}''$ by adding transitions in the following way: whenever there are $l_i\to r_i\in R$, a Q'-substitution σ s.t. $dom(\sigma)=Var(l_i)$ and $l_i\sigma\to^*_{\Delta''} q$ where $q\in\{s\}\cup D$, add the transition $d^{i,\epsilon}_{\sigma|_{Var(r_i)}}\to q$.

q may be in D in order to simulate the rewrite steps issued from the rhs's coming from previous rewrite steps. The saturation process necessarily terminates because it does not add any new states, and the number of transition rules is bounded in a finite automaton.

Lemma 3. $L(\mathcal{B})=R^*_\epsilon(L(\mathcal{A}|_p))$.

Proof. See Subsection 3.1.

Now, the main result is a straightforward consequence of lemmas 3 and 1.

Corollary 2. $L(\mathcal{A}[\mathcal{B}]_p)=R^*_p(L(\mathcal{A}))$.

Remark: From Corollary 1 $\mathcal{A}[\mathcal{B}]_p$ preserves the discrimination of every position $p'\not\geq p$. Thus the construction of $\mathcal{B}$ from $\mathcal{A}$ can be used incrementally to compute $R^*(E)=R^*_{p_n}(\ldots(R^*_{p_1}(E))\ldots)$ as mentioned in Lemma 2.

Lemma 4. *In the worst case, the number of states of the final automaton that recognizes $R^*(E) = R^*_{p_n}(\ldots(R^*_{p_1}(E))\ldots)$ is a tower of exponentials of height n, in the number of positions of t.*

Proof. For simplicity, let us suppose that $card(Q_{arg}) = 0$. Thus

$$\sum_{l_i \to r_i \in R} card(Var(r_i)).card(Q') \leq card(D) \leq \sum_{l_i \to r_i \in R} |r_i|.card(Var(r_i)).card(Q')$$

where $|r_i| = card(Pos(r_i))$. Therefore for a given rewrite system, $card(D)$ is of the same order as $card(Q')$, i.e. $2^{card(Q)}$ because of the determinization. So $card(Q_B) = card(Q'') = card(Q')+card(D)+1$ is of the same order as $card(Q')$, i.e. $2^{card(Q)}$.

The result comes from the fact that building B from A is performed n times incrementally.

3.1 Proof of lemma 3

This proof breaks down into some lemmas.

We first need some properties about the matches used along a rewrite derivation.

Lemma 5. *Let $A = (C \cup F, Q, Q_f, \Delta)$ be an automaton s.t. $Q \cap Q_{arg} = \emptyset$. For all $t \in L(A)$ and $p \in \overline{Pos}(t)$, if $t = t_0 \to^+_{[p,rhs's]} t_n$ then for each step $t_i \to_{[p_i,l_i \to r_i,\theta_i]} t_{i+1}$ within the derivation we have*

$$\forall x \in Var(l_i), x\theta_i \to^*_{\Delta \cup \Delta_{arg}} q \in Q \cup Q_{arg}$$

Proof. By induction on the length of the derivation.

If $n = 1$, $\forall x \in Var(l_0)$, $x\theta_0 = t|_v$ for some $v \in Pos(t)$. Therefore $x\theta_0 \to^*_\Delta q \in Q$.

Induction step. We know that $p_n \in P(t_n)$. Then there exists $j < n$ s.t. $p_n = p_j.w$, $w \in PosF(r_j)$, and $r_j|_w = f(u_1,\ldots,u_k)$. Therefore for each $x \in Var(l_n)$:

- $x\theta_n = u_l|_v$ where u_l is a non-variable function argument. Then, by construction of Δ_{arg}, $x\theta_n \to^*_{\Delta_{arg}} q \in Q_{arg}$.
- Or $x\theta_n = (y\theta_j)|_v$ where $y \in Var(r_j)$. By induction hypothesis, $y\theta_j \to^*_{\Delta \cup \Delta_{arg}} q \in Q \cup Q_{arg}$. Therefore $x\theta_n \to^*_{\Delta \cup \Delta_{arg}} q \in Q \cup Q_{arg}$.

Recall that $L(A|_p) = L(A')$. To prove completeness, i.e. $L(B) \supseteq R^*_\epsilon(L(A'))$, we have to prove a more precise property, to be able to make the induction step.

Lemma 6. *Let $t \in L(A')$ and assume $t \to^+_{[\epsilon,rhs's]} t'$. Let us write $P(t') = \{p_1,\ldots,p_k\}$. Then $\forall p \in P(t')$, $t'|_p \to^*_{\Delta''} q_p \in \{s\} \cup D$ and $t'[q_{p_1}]_{p_1} \ldots [q_{p_k}]_{p_k} \to^*_B s$.*

Proof. By induction on the length of the derivation. Consider the last step $t_n \to_{[v,l \to r,\theta]} t'$. From lemma 5, $x\theta \to^*_{\Delta \cup \Delta_{arg}} q \in Q \cup Q_{arg}$. Thus, after determinizing, there exists one and only one $s_x \in Q'$ s.t. $x\theta \to^*_{\Delta'} s_x$.

Now $v \in P(t_n)$. By induction hypothesis $l\theta = t_n|_v \to_{\Delta''}^* q_n \in \{s\} \cup D$. Let σ be the Q'-substitution defined by $dom(\sigma) = Var(l)$ and $\forall x \in Var(l)$, $x\sigma = s_x$. Then $l\sigma \to_{\Delta''}^* q_n \in \{s\} \cup D$. From the construction of $\mathcal{B}$, $d_{\sigma|_{Var(r)}}^\epsilon \to q_n \in \Delta_{\mathcal{B}}$. Let $p' \in P(t')$.

- If $p' = v.w$ then $t'|_{p'} = (r\theta)|_w \to_{\Delta'}^* (r\sigma)|_w \to_{\Delta''}^* d_\sigma^w \in D$.
- Otherwise $p' \| v$. Then $t'|_{p'} = t_n|_{p'}$ and $p' \in P(t_n)$. By induction hypothesis $t_n|_{p'} \to_{\Delta''}^* q' \in \{s\} \cup D$.

Assume that $p_1, \ldots, p_k$ are sorted s.t. $p_1, \ldots, p_j \geq v$ and $p_{j+1}, \ldots, p_k \| v$. Thus
$$t'[d_\sigma^{w_1}]_{p_1} \cdots [d_\sigma^{w_j}]_{p_j} \to_{\Delta''}^* t'[d_\sigma^\epsilon]_v \to_{\mathcal{B}} t'[q_n]_v = t_n[q_n]_v$$
$$t'[q_{j+1}]_{p_{j+1}} \cdots [q_k]_{p_k} = t_n[q_{j+1}]_{p_{j+1}} \cdots [q_k]_{p_k}$$
Therefore, from the induction hypothesis
$$t'[d_\sigma^{w_1}]_{p_1} \cdots [d_\sigma^{w_j}]_{p_j} [q_{j+1}]_{p_{j+1}} \cdots [q_k]_{p_k} = t_n[q_n]_v[q_{j+1}]_{p_{j+1}} \cdots [q_k]_{p_k} \to_{\mathcal{B}}^* s$$

To prove correctness, i.e. $l(\mathcal{B}) \subseteq R_\epsilon^*(L(\mathcal{A}'))$, we also have to prove a more precise property. We first need an additional definition.

Definition 10. Let Δ_{sat} be the transitions added by the saturation process (so $\Delta_{\mathcal{B}} = \Delta_{sat} \cup \Delta''$). For $t \in L(\mathcal{B})$, let $\|t\| = Min(\{length_{sat}(t \to_{\mathcal{B}}^* s)\})$ where $length_{sat}(t \to_{\mathcal{B}}^* s)$ is the number of steps using a transition of Δ_{sat}. The derivation $t \to_{\mathcal{B}}^* s$ is said minimal if $length_{sat}(t \to_{\mathcal{B}}^* s) = \|t\|$.

The proof of the following lemma shows that $\|t\|$ is the length of the shortest rewrite derivation that can reach t from a term of $L(\mathcal{A}')$.

Lemma 7. If $t \to_{\mathcal{B}}^* s$ is minimal,
then there exists $u \in L(\mathcal{A}')$ s.t. $u \to_{[\epsilon, rhs's]}^* t$, and for each intermediate term $C[q]_p$ in this minimal derivation (thus $t \to_{\mathcal{B}}^* C[q]_p \to_{\mathcal{B}}^* s$) s.t. $t(p)$ is a function and $q \in \{s\} \cup D$, we have $p \in P(t)$.

Proof. By induction on $\|t\|$.

If $\|t\| = 0$, then no minimal derivation $t \to^* q_f \to s$ ($q_f \in Q_f'$) contains any steps in Δ_{sat}, or in $\Delta'' \backslash \Delta'$. Therefore $t \in L(\mathcal{A}')$. If $t \to^* C[s]_p$ then $p = \epsilon$ and $P(t) = \{\epsilon\}$.

Induction step. Consider a minimal derivation
$$t \to_{\Delta''}^* t_1 \to_{[p, d_\sigma^{i,\epsilon} \to q \in \Delta_{sat}]} t_2 \to_{\mathcal{B}}^* s$$
Since $t_2 \to_{\mathcal{B}}^* s$ is minimal, then $\|t_2\| = length_{sat}(t_2 \to_{\mathcal{B}}^* s) < \|t\|$. But t_2 contains some states. By construction of Δ_{sat}, $t_2[l_i\sigma]_p \to_{\Delta''}^* t_2[q]_p = t_2$ and $\forall x \in Var(l_i)$, $x\sigma \in Q'$. From rhs encoding, $\forall x \in Var(r_i)$, $x\theta \to_{\Delta'}^* x\sigma$. Besides, for each $x \in Var(l_i) \backslash Var(r_i)$ we choose a reachable state for $x\sigma$. Thus we can extend θ s.t. $x\theta \to_{\Delta'}^* x\sigma$. Consequently $t_2[l_i\theta]_p \to_{\Delta''}^* t_2 \to_{\Delta_{\mathcal{B}}}^* s$ and it is minimal. Thus $\|t_2[l_i\theta]_p\| < \|t\|$ and it does not contain any states. By induction hypothesis there exists $u \in L(\mathcal{A}')$ s.t. $u \to_{[\epsilon, rhs's]}^* t_2[l_i\theta]_p$ and for each intermediate term $C[q']_{p'}$ in this minimal derivation (thus $t \to_{\mathcal{B}}^* C[q']_{p'} \to_{\mathcal{B}}^* s$) s.t. $t_2[l_i\theta]_p(p)$ is a function and $q' \in \{s\} \cup D$, we have $p' \in P(t_2[l_i\theta]_p)$.

Now $q \in \{s\} \cup D$ because $d_\sigma^{i,\epsilon} \to q \in \Delta_{sat}$ and $t_2[l_i\theta]_p(p) = (l_i\theta)(\epsilon)$ is a function. So $p \in P(t_2[l_i\theta]_p)$. Therefore $u \to^*_{[\epsilon, rhs's]} t_2[r_i\theta]_p = t$, and for each intermediate term $C[q']_{p'}$ in the minimal derivation $t \to^* t_2 \to^*_{\mathcal{B}} s$ s.t. $t(p')$ is a function and $q' \in \{s\} \cup D$:

- if $p' \not\geq p$, then $t(p') = t_2[l_i\theta]_p(p')$, so $p' \in P(t)$.
- Otherwise since $t_2[l_i\theta]_p \to t$ and from the definition of P, we get $p' \in P(t)$.

4   Applications

4.1   Reachability

Reachability between ground terms is obviously decidable since $t_1 \to^* t_2$ is equivalent to $t_2 \in R^*(\{t_1\})$.

4.2   Unification of linear equations

We assume that R is confluent. Thus the equation $t \doteq t'$ admits a solution σ iff $t\sigma$ and $t'\sigma$ rewrite into the same term, i.e. $R^*(L(\mathcal{A}_{t\theta})) \cap R^*(L(\mathcal{A}_{t'\theta})) \neq \emptyset$ provided $Var(t) \cap Var(t') = \emptyset$ and t, t' are linear.

This extends the result of [10, 11] established thanks to TTSG's (Tree Tuple Synchronized Grammars), since left-linearity is not required any more. On the other hand, TTSG's can express unifiers, and they allow to weaken the linearity of the equation to be solved, as we are going to show in some further work.

4.3   Program testing

Let us see term rewrite systems as functional programs. The informal method to test a program usually consists in checking that for finitely many (and well chosen) data, the result is just the expected one. We suggest to do the same starting from an infinite language of data E, by providing an automaton that recognizes the language of expected results, and checking that it is equivalent to the automaton that recognizes $R^{data}(E) = R^*(E) \cap T(C)$.

Example 6. Consider the identity functions Id_2, (resp. Id_3) defined only for even natural integers (resp. integers multiple of three).
$$R = \{ Id_2(s(s(x))) \to s(s(Id_2(x))), \; Id_2(0) \to 0,$$
$$Id_3(s(s(s(x)))) \to s(s(s(Id_3(x)))), \; Id_3(0) \to 0\}$$
Let E be the set of data-instances of $Id_2(Id_3(x))$. An automaton $\mathcal{A}_r$ that recognizes the expected results, i.e. the multiples of 6, can be easily built by the programmer. Then testing the program may consist in checking that $R^{data}(E) = L(\mathcal{A}_r)$.

4.4   Sufficient completeness

R is sufficiently complete if every ground term rewrites into a data-term.

If R is left-linear, a finite automaton that recognizes the set of reducible ground terms can be easily built, since reducible ground terms are the instances of the lhs's, nested in any context. By complementation we get an automaton that recognizes $IRR(R)$. Thus if in addition R is weakly normalizing, sufficient completeness is decidable thanks to the following lemma.

Lemma 8. *Assume that R is weakly normalizing. Then R is sufficiently complete iff $IRR(R) \subseteq T(C)$.*

Proof. $\Rightarrow$ is obvious.

$\Leftarrow$. Each term t admits a normal-form $t{\downarrow} \in T(C)$.

When R is not sufficiently complete, it might be interesting to check that the functions that are supposed to be completely defined, are indeed.

Notation: For each function f, let $E_f = \{f(t_1, \ldots, t_n) \mid t_1, \ldots, t_n \in T(C)\}$. E_f contains the data-instances of $f(x_1, \ldots, x_n)$.

Lemma 9. *[7] Assume that R is weakly normalizing. If $R^!(E_f) \subseteq T(C)$, then f is completely defined.*

Proof. $\forall t_1, \ldots, t_n \in T(C)$, $f(t_1, \ldots, t_n) \to^* f(t_1, \ldots, t_n){\downarrow} \in T(C)$.

5   Conclusion

We think that this work could be used in practice, because the final automaton often includes much fewer states than mentioned in Lemma 4. Indeed, determinization is useless whenever we reduce a function f s.t. every rewrite derivation issued from f uses only left-linear rules, which can be easily checked. Moreover if the encoding of rhs's is performed only when needed, we get a set of states much smaller than D in most cases.

The assumed restrictions about rhs's are not realistic from a programming point of view. We however hope that this work could give rise to approximations dealing with any rhs's, more precise than that of [7].

Another way to weaken the restrictions might consist in using more sophisticated tree languages, at the expense of more complicated algorithms.

Acknowledgments

I would like to thank Sébastien Limet for comments on this work, and Thomas Genet, Florent Jacquemard for helpful discussions.

References

1. H. Comon. Sequentiality, second order monadic logic and tree automata. In *Proc., Tenth Annual IEEE Symposium on Logic in Computer Science*, pages 508–517. IEEE Computer Society Press, 26–29 June 1995.

2. H. Comon, M. Dauchet, R. Gilleron, D. Lugiez, S. Tison, and M. Tommasi. *Tree Automata Techniques and Applications (TATA)*. http://l3ux02.univ-lille3.fr/tata.

3. Hubert Comon and Florent Jacquemard. Ground reducibility is exptime-complete. In *Proc. IEEE Symp. on Logic in Computer Science*, Varsaw, June 1997. IEEE Comp. Soc. Press.

4. J. Coquidé, M. Dauchet, R. Gilleron, and S. Vagvolgyi. Bottom-up Tree Pushdown Automata and Rewrite Systems. In R. V. Book, editor, *Proceedings 4th Conference on Rewriting Techniques and Applications, Como (Italy)*, volume 488 of *LNCS*, pages 287–298. Springer-Verlag, April 1991.

5. M. Dauchet and S. Tison. The theory of ground rewrite systems is decidable. In *Proc., Fifth Annual IEEE Symposium on Logic in Computer Science*, pages 242–248, Philadelphia, Pennsylvania, 1990. IEEE Computer Society Press.

6. N. Dershowitz and J.-P. Jouannaud. Rewrite Systems. In J. Van Leuven, editor, *Handbook of Theoretical Computer Science*, chapter 6, pages 243–320. Elsevier Science Publishers, 1990.

7. T. Genet. Decidable Approximations of Sets of Descendants and Sets of Normal Forms. In *Proceedings of 9th Conference on Rewriting Techniques and Applications, Tsukuba (Japan)*, volume 1379 of *LNCS*, pages 151–165. Springer-Verlag, 1998.

8. R. Gilleron and S. Tison. Regular Tree Languages and Rewrite Systems. *Fundamenta Informaticae*, 24:157–175, 1995.

9. F. Jacquemard. Decidable Approximations of Term Rewrite Systems. In H. Ganzinger, editor, *Proceedings 7th Conference RTA, New Brunswick (USA)*, volume 1103 of *LNCS*, pages 362–376. Springer-Verlag, 1996.

10. S. Limet and P. Réty. E-Unification by Means of Tree Tuple Synchronized Grammars. In *Proceedings of 6th Colloquium on Trees in Algebra and Programming*, volume 1214 of *LNCS*, pages 429–440. Springer-Verlag, 1997.

11. S. Limet and P. Réty. E-Unification by Means of Tree Tuple Synchronized Grammars. *Discrete Mathematics and Theoritical Computer Science* , 1:69–98, 1997. (http://dmtcs.loria.fr/).

12. P. Réty. *Méthodes d'Unification par Surréduction*. Thèse de Doctorat d'Université, Université de Nancy I, March 1988. In french.

13. K. Salomaa. Deterministic Tree Pushdown Automata and Monadic Tree Rewriting Systems. *The Journal of Computer and System Sciences*, 37:367–394, 1988.

Practical Reasoning for Expressive Description Logics

Ian Horrocks[1], Ulrike Sattler[2], and Stephan Tobies[2]

[1] Department of Computer Science, University of Manchester[†]
[2] LuFG Theoretical Computer Science, RWTH Aachen[‡]

Abstract. Description Logics (DLs) are a family of knowledge representation formalisms mainly characterised by constructors to build complex concepts and roles from atomic ones. Expressive role constructors are important in many applications, but can be computationally problematical. We present an algorithm that decides satisfiability of the DL $\mathcal{ALC}$ extended with transitive and inverse roles, role hierarchies, and qualifying number restrictions. Early experiments indicate that this algorithm is well-suited for implementation. Additionally, we show that $\mathcal{ALC}$ extended with just transitive and inverse roles is still in PSPACE. Finally, we investigate the limits of decidability for this family of DLs.

1 Motivation

Description Logics (DLs) are a well-known family of knowledge representation formalisms [DLNS96]. They are based on the notion of concepts (unary predicates, classes) and roles (binary relations), and are mainly characterised by constructors that allow complex concepts and roles to be built from atomic ones. Sound and complete algorithms for the interesting inference problems such as subsumption and satisfiability of concepts are known for a wide variety of DLs [SS91; DLNdN91; Sat96; DL96; CDL99].

To be used in a specific application, the expressivity of the DL must be sufficient to describe relevant properties of objects in the application domain. For example, transitive roles (e.g. "ancestor") and inverse roles (e.g. "successor"/"predecessor") play an important rôle not only in the adequate representation of complex, aggregated objects [HS99], but also for reasoning with conceptual data models [CLN94]. Moreover, reasoning with respect to cyclic definitions is crucial for applying DLs to reasoning with database schemata [CDL98a].

The relevant inference problems for (extensions of) DLs that allow for transitive and inverse roles are known to be decidable [DL96], and appropriate inference algorithms have been described [DM98], but their high degree of nondeterminism appears to prohibit their use in realistic applications. This is mainly due to the fact that these algorithms can handle not just transitive roles but also

---

[†] Part of this work was carried out while being a guest at IRST, Trento.

[‡] This work was supported by the Esprit Project 22469 – DWQ and the DFG, Project No. GR 1324/3-1.

the transitive closure of roles. It has been shown [Sat96] that restricting a DL to transitive roles can lead to a lower complexity, and that transitive roles (even when combined with role hierarchies) allow for algorithms that behave quite well in realistic applications [Hor98]. However, it remained to show that this is still true when inverse roles and qualifying number restrictions are also present.

This paper extends our understanding of these issues in several directions. Firstly, we present an algorithm that decides satisfiability of $\mathcal{ALC}$ [SS91] (which can be seen as a notational variant of the multi modal logic K_m) extended with transitive and inverse roles, role hierarchies, and qualifying number restrictions, i.e., concepts of the form ($\geqslant$ 3 hasChild Female) that allow the description of objects by restricting the number of objects of a given type they are related to via a certain role. The algorithm can also be used for checking satisfiability and subsumption with respect to general concept inclusion axioms (and thus cyclic definitions) because these axioms can be "internalised". The absence of transitive closure leads to a lower degree of non-determinism, and experiments indicate that the algorithm is well-suited for implementation.

Secondly, we show that $\mathcal{ALC}$ extended with both transitive *and* inverse roles is still in PSPACE. The algorithm used to prove this rather surprising result introduces an enhanced *blocking* technique. In general, blocking is used to ensure termination of the algorithm in cases where it would otherwise be stuck in a loop. The enhanced blocking technique allows such cases to be detected earlier and should provide useful efficiency gains in implementations of this and more expressive DLs.

Finally, we investigate the limits of decidability for this family of DLs, showing that relaxing the constraints placed on the kinds of roles allowed in number restrictions leads to the undecidability of all inference problems.

Due to a lack of space we can only present selected proofs. For full details please refer to [HST98; HST99].

2 Preliminaries

In this section, we present the syntax and semantics of the various DLs that are investigated in subsequent sections. This includes the definition of inference problems (concept subsumption and satisfiability, and both of these problems with respect to terminologies) and how they are interrelated.

The logics we will discuss are all based on an extension of the well known DL $\mathcal{ALC}$ [SS91] to include transitively closed primitive roles [Sat96]; we will call this logic S due to its relationship with the proposition (multi) modal logic $S4_{(m)}$ [Sch91].[1] This basic DL is then extended in a variety of ways—see Figure 1 for an overview.

Definition 1. *Let* **C** *be a set of* concept names *and* **R** *a set of* role names *with* transitive role names $R_+ \subseteq R$. *The set of* $\mathcal{SI}$-roles *is* $R \cup \{R^- \mid R \in R\}$. *The*

---

[1] The logic S has previously been called $\mathcal{ALC}_{R+}$, but this becomes too cumbersome when adding letters to represent additional features.

set of $\mathcal{SI}$-concepts is the smallest set such that every concept name is a concept, and, if C and D are concepts and R is an $\mathcal{SI}$-role, then $(C \sqcap D)$, $(C \sqcup D)$, $(\neg C)$, $(\forall R.C)$, and $(\exists R.C)$ are also concepts.

To avoid considering roles such as R^{--}, we define a function Inv on roles such that $\mathsf{Inv}(R) = R^-$ if R is a role name, and $\mathsf{Inv}(R) = S$ if $R = S^-$. We also define a function Trans which returns true iff R is a transitive role. More precisely, $\mathsf{Trans}(R) = \text{true}$ iff $R \in \mathbf{R}_+$ or $\mathsf{Inv}(R) \in \mathbf{R}_+$.

$\mathcal{SHI}$ is obtained from $\mathcal{SI}$ by allowing, additionally, for a set of role inclusion axioms of the form $R \sqsubseteq S$, where R and S are two roles, each of which can be inverse. For a set of role inclusion axioms $\mathcal{R}$,

$$\mathcal{R}^+ := (\mathcal{R} \cup \{\mathsf{Inv}(R) \sqsubseteq \mathsf{Inv}(S) \mid R \sqsubseteq S \in \mathcal{R}\}, \;\sqsubseteq\!\!{}^*)$$

is called a role hierarchy, where $\sqsubseteq\!\!{}^*$ is the transitive-reflexive closure of $\sqsubseteq$ over $\mathcal{R} \cup \{\mathsf{Inv}(R) \sqsubseteq \mathsf{Inv}(S) \mid R \sqsubseteq S \in \mathcal{R}\}$.

$\mathcal{SHIQ}$ is obtained from $\mathcal{SHI}$ by allowing, additionally, for qualifying number restrictions, i.e., for concepts of the form $(\geqslant n\, R\, C)$ and $(\leqslant n\, R\, C)$, where R is a simple (possibly inverse) role and n is a non-negative integer. A role is called simple iff it is neither transitive nor has transitive sub-roles.

$\mathcal{SHIN}$ is the restriction of $\mathcal{SHIQ}$ where qualifying number restrictions may only be of the form $(\geqslant n\, R\, \top)$ and $(\leqslant n\, R\, \top)$. In this case, we omit the symbol $\top$ and write $(\geqslant n\, R)$ and $(\leqslant n\, R)$ instead.

An interpretation $\mathcal{I} = (\Delta^{\mathcal{I}}, \cdot^{\mathcal{I}})$ consists of a set $\Delta^{\mathcal{I}}$, called the domain of $\mathcal{I}$, and a valuation $\cdot^{\mathcal{I}}$ which maps every concept to a subset of $\Delta^{\mathcal{I}}$ and every role to a subset of $\Delta^{\mathcal{I}} \times \Delta^{\mathcal{I}}$ such that, for all concepts C, D, roles R, S, and non-negative integers n, the properties in Figure 1 are satisfied, where $\sharp M$ denotes the cardinality of a set M. An interpretation satisfies a role hierarchy $\mathcal{R}^+$ iff $R^{\mathcal{I}} \subseteq S^{\mathcal{I}}$ for each $R \sqsubseteq\!\!{}^* S \in \mathcal{R}^+$; we denote this fact by $\mathcal{I} \models \mathcal{R}^+$ and say that $\mathcal{I}$ is a model of $\mathcal{R}^+$.

A concept C is called satisfiable with respect to a role hierarchy $\mathcal{R}^+$ iff there is some interpretation $\mathcal{I}$ such that $\mathcal{I} \models \mathcal{R}^+$ and $C^{\mathcal{I}} \neq \emptyset$. Such an interpretation is called a model of C w.r.t. $\mathcal{R}^+$. A concept D subsumes a concept C w.r.t. $\mathcal{R}^+$ (written $C \sqsubseteq_{\mathcal{R}^+} D$) iff $C^{\mathcal{I}} \subseteq D^{\mathcal{I}}$ holds for each model $\mathcal{I}$ of $\mathcal{R}^+$. For an interpretation $\mathcal{I}$, an individual $x \in \Delta^{\mathcal{I}}$ is called an instance of a concept C iff $x \in C^{\mathcal{I}}$.

All DLs considered here are closed under negation, hence subsumption and (un)satisfiability w.r.t. role hierarchies can be reduced to each other: $C \sqsubseteq_{\mathcal{R}^+} D$ iff $C \sqcap \neg D$ is unsatisfiable w.r.t. $\mathcal{R}^+$, and C is unsatisfiable w.r.t. $\mathcal{R}^+$ iff $C \sqsubseteq_{\mathcal{R}^+} A \sqcap \neg A$ for some concept name A.

In [Baa91; Sch91; BBN$^+$93], the internalisation of terminological axioms is introduced, a technique that reduces reasoning with respect to a (possibly cyclic) terminology to satisfiability of concepts. In [Hor98], we saw how role hierarchies can be used for this reduction. In the presence of inverse roles, this reduction must be slightly modified.

Construct Name	Syntax	Semantics	
atomic concept	A	$A^{\mathcal{I}} \subseteq \Delta^{\mathcal{I}}$	
universal concept	$\top$	$\top^{\mathcal{I}} = \Delta^{\mathcal{I}}$	
atomic role	R	$R^{\mathcal{I}} \subseteq \Delta^{\mathcal{I}} \times \Delta^{\mathcal{I}}$	
transitive role	$R \in \mathbf{R}_+$	$R^{\mathcal{I}} = (R^{\mathcal{I}})^+$	
conjunction	$C \sqcap D$	$C^{\mathcal{I}} \cap D^{\mathcal{I}}$	
disjunction	$C \sqcup D$	$C^{\mathcal{I}} \cup D^{\mathcal{I}}$	$\mathcal{S}$
negation	$\neg C$	$\Delta^{\mathcal{I}} \setminus C^{\mathcal{I}}$	
exists restriction	$\exists R.C$	$\{x \mid \exists y.\langle x,y \rangle \in R^{\mathcal{I}} \text{ and } y \in C^{\mathcal{I}}\}$	
value restriction	$\forall R.C$	$\{x \mid \forall y.\langle x,y \rangle \in R^{\mathcal{I}} \text{ implies } y \in C^{\mathcal{I}}\}$	
role hierarchy	$R \sqsubseteq S$	$R^{\mathcal{I}} \subseteq S^{\mathcal{I}}$	$\mathcal{H}$
inverse role	R^-	$\{\langle x,y \rangle \mid \langle y,x \rangle \in R^{\mathcal{I}}\}$	$\mathcal{I}$
number	$\geqslant nR$	$\{x \mid \#\{y.\langle x,y \rangle \in R^{\mathcal{I}}\} \geqslant n\}$	
restrictions	$\leqslant nR$	$\{x \mid \#\{y.\langle x,y \rangle \in R^{\mathcal{I}}\} \leqslant n\}$	$\mathcal{N}$
qualifying number restrictions	$\geqslant nR.C$	$\{x \mid \#\{y.\langle x,y \rangle \in R^{\mathcal{I}} \text{ and } y \in C^{\mathcal{I}}\} \geqslant n\}$	
	$\leqslant nR.C$	$\{x \mid \#\{y.\langle x,y \rangle \in R^{\mathcal{I}} \text{ and } y \in C^{\mathcal{I}}\} \leqslant n\}$	$\mathcal{Q}$

Fig. 1. Syntax and semantics of the $\mathcal{SI}$ family of DLs

Definition 2. *A terminology $\mathcal{T}$ is a finite set of general concept inclusion axioms, $\mathcal{T} = \{C_1 \sqsubseteq D_1, \ldots, C_n \sqsubseteq D_n\}$, where C_i, D_i are arbitrary $\mathcal{SHIQ}$-concepts. An interpretation $\mathcal{I}$ is said to be a model of $\mathcal{T}$ iff $C_i^{\mathcal{I}} \subseteq D_i^{\mathcal{I}}$ holds for all $C_i \sqsubseteq D_i \in \mathcal{T}$. C is satisfiable with respect to $\mathcal{T}$ iff there is a model $\mathcal{I}$ of $\mathcal{T}$ with $C^{\mathcal{I}} \neq \emptyset$. Finally, D subsumes C with respect to $\mathcal{T}$ iff for each model $\mathcal{I}$ of $\mathcal{T}$ we have $C^{\mathcal{I}} \subseteq D^{\mathcal{I}}$.*

The following Lemma shows how general concept inclusion axioms can be *internalised* using a "universal" role U, that is, a transitive super-role of all roles occurring in $\mathcal{T}$ and their respective inverses.

Lemma 1. *Let $\mathcal{T}$ be a terminology, $\mathcal{R}$ a set of role inclusion axioms and C, D $\mathcal{SHIQ}$-concepts and let*

$$C_{\mathcal{T}} := \bigsqcap_{C_i \sqsubseteq D_i \in \mathcal{T}} \neg C_i \sqcup D_i.$$

Let U be a transitive role that does not occur in $\mathcal{T}, C, D$, or $\mathcal{R}$. We set

$$\mathcal{R}_U := \mathcal{R} \cup \{R \sqsubseteq U, \mathsf{Inv}(R) \sqsubseteq U \mid R \text{ occurs in } \mathcal{T}, C, D, \text{ or } \mathcal{R}\}.$$

Then C is satisfiable w.r.t. $\mathcal{T}$ and $\mathcal{R}^+$ iff $C \sqcap C_{\mathcal{T}} \sqcap \forall U.C_{\mathcal{T}}$ is satisfiable w.r.t. $\mathcal{R}_U^+$. Moreover, D subsumes C with respect to $\mathcal{T}$ and $\mathcal{R}^+$ iff $C \sqcap \neg D \sqcap C_{\mathcal{T}} \sqcap \forall U.C_{\mathcal{T}}$ is unsatisfiable w.r.t. $\mathcal{R}_U^+$.

The proof of Lemma 1 is similar to the ones that can be found in [Sch91; Baa91]. Most importantly, it must be shown that, (a) if a $\mathcal{SHIQ}$-concept C is satisfiable with respect to a terminology $\mathcal{T}$ and a role hierarchy $\mathcal{R}^+$, then $C, \mathcal{T}$

have a *connected* model, and (b) if y is reachable from x via a role path (possibly involving inverse roles), then $\langle x, y \rangle \in U^{\mathcal{I}}$. These are easy consequences of the semantics and the definition of U.

Theorem 1. *Satisfiability and subsumption of $\mathcal{SHIQ}$-concepts (resp. $\mathcal{SHI}$-concepts) w.r.t. terminologies and role hierarchies are polynomially reducible to (un)satisfiability of $\mathcal{SHIQ}$-concepts (resp. $\mathcal{SHI}$-concepts) w.r.t. role hierarchies.*

3   Reasoning for $\mathcal{SI}$ Logics

In this section, we present two tableaux algorithms: the first decides satisfiability of $\mathcal{SHIQ}$-concepts, and can be used for all $\mathcal{SHIQ}$ reasoning problems (see Theorem 1); the second decides satisfiability (and hence subsumption) of $\mathcal{SI}$-concepts in PSPACE. Please note that $\mathcal{SHIN}$ (and hence $\mathcal{SHIQ}$) no longer has the finite model property: for example, the following concept, where R is a transitive super-role of F, is satisfiable, but each of its models has an infinite domain.

$$\neg C \sqcap \exists F^-.(C \sqcap {\leqslant} 1F) \sqcap \forall R^-.(\exists F^-.(C \sqcap {\leqslant} 1F))$$

This concept requires the existence of an infinite F^--path, where the first element on the path satisfies $\neg C$ while all other elements satisfy $C \sqcap {\leqslant} 1F$. This path cannot collapse into a cycle: (a) it cannot return to the first element because this element cannot satisfy both C and $\neg C$; (b) it cannot return to any subsequent element on the path because then this node would not satisfy ${\leqslant} 1F$.

The correctness of the algorithms we are presenting can be proved by showing that they create a *tableau* for a concept iff it is satisfiable. For ease of construction, we assume all concepts to be in *negation normal form* (NNF), that is, negation occurs only in front of concept names. Any $\mathcal{SHIQ}$-concept can easily be transformed to an equivalent one in NNF by pushing negations inwards [HNS90]; with $\sim C$ we denote the NNF of $\neg C$. For a concept C in NNF we define $clos(C)$ as the smallest set of concepts that contains C and is closed under subconcepts and $\sim$. Please note that size of $clos(C)$ is linearly bounded by the size of C.

Definition 3. *Let D be a $\mathcal{SHIQ}$-concept in NNF, $\mathcal{R}^+$ a role hierarchy, and $\mathbf{R}_D$ the set of roles occurring in D and $\mathcal{R}^+$ together with their inverses. Then $T = (\mathbf{S}, \mathcal{L}, \mathcal{E})$ is a tableau for D w.r.t. $\mathcal{R}^+$ iff $\mathbf{S}$ is a set of individuals, $\mathcal{L} : \mathbf{S} \to 2^{clos(D)}$ maps each individual to a set of concepts, $\mathcal{E} : \mathbf{R}_D \to 2^{\mathbf{S} \times \mathbf{S}}$ maps each role to a set of pairs of individuals, and there is some individual $s \in \mathbf{S}$ such that $D \in \mathcal{L}(s)$. Furthermore, for all $s, t \in \mathbf{S}$, $C, C_1, C_2 \in clos(D)$, and $R, S \in \mathbf{R}_D$, it holds that:*

1. *if $C \in \mathcal{L}(s)$, then $\neg C \notin \mathcal{L}(s)$,*
2. *if $C_1 \sqcap C_2 \in \mathcal{L}(s)$, then $C_1 \in \mathcal{L}(s)$ and $C_2 \in \mathcal{L}(s)$,*
3. *if $C_1 \sqcup C_2 \in \mathcal{L}(s)$, then $C_1 \in \mathcal{L}(s)$ or $C_2 \in \mathcal{L}(s)$,*
4. *if $\forall S.C \in \mathcal{L}(s)$ and $\langle s, t \rangle \in \mathcal{E}(S)$, then $C \in \mathcal{L}(t)$,*
5. *if $\exists S.C \in \mathcal{L}(s)$, then there is some $t \in \mathbf{S}$ such that $\langle s, t \rangle \in \mathcal{E}(S)$ and $C \in \mathcal{L}(t)$,*

6. *if* $\forall S.C \in \mathcal{L}(s)$ *and* $\langle s,t \rangle \in \mathcal{E}(R)$ *for some* $R \sqsubseteq^* S$ *with* $\mathsf{Trans}(R)$, *then* $\forall R.C \in \mathcal{L}(t)$,

7. $\langle x,y \rangle \in \mathcal{E}(R)$ *iff* $\langle y,x \rangle \in \mathcal{E}(\mathsf{Inv}(R))$,

8. *if* $\langle s,t \rangle \in \mathcal{E}(R)$ *and* $R \sqsubseteq^* S$, *then* $\langle s,t \rangle \in \mathcal{E}(S)$,

9. *if* $(\leqslant n\ S\ C) \in \mathcal{L}(s)$, *then* $\sharp S^T(s,C) \leqslant n$,

10. *if* $(\geqslant n\ S\ C) \in \mathcal{L}(s)$, *then* $\sharp S^T(s,C) \geqslant n$,

11. *if* $(\bowtie n\ S\ C) \in \mathcal{L}(s)$ *and* $\langle s,t \rangle \in \mathcal{E}(S)$ *then* $C \in \mathcal{L}(t)$ *or* $\sim C \in \mathcal{L}(t)$,

where we use $\bowtie$ *as a placeholder for both* $\leqslant$ *and* $\geqslant$ *and we define*

$$S^T(s,C) := \{t \in \mathbf{S} \mid \langle s,t \rangle \in \mathcal{E}(S) \text{ and } C \in \mathcal{L}(t)\}.$$

Tableaux for $\mathcal{SI}$-*concepts are defined analogously and must satisfy Properties 1-7, where, due to the absence of a role hierarchy,* $\sqsubseteq^*$ *is the identity.*

Due to the close relationship between models and tableaux, the following lemma can be easily proved by induction. As a consequence, an algorithm that constructs (if possible) a tableau for an input concept is a decision procedure for satisfiability of concepts.

Lemma 2. *A* $\mathcal{SHIQ}$-*concept (resp.* $\mathcal{SI}$-*concept)* D *is satisfiable w.r.t. a role hierarchy* $\mathcal{R}^+$ *iff* D *has a tableau w.r.t.* $\mathcal{R}^+$.

3.1   Reasoning in $\mathcal{SHIQ}$

In the following, we give an algorithm that, given a $\mathcal{SHIQ}$-concept D, decides the existence of a tableaux for D. We implicitly assume an arbitrary but fixed role hierarchy $\mathcal{R}^+$. The tableaux algorithm works on a finite *completion tree* (a tree some of whose nodes correspond to individuals in the tableau, each node being labelled with a set of $\mathcal{SHIQ}$-concepts), and employs a *blocking* technique [HS99] to guarantee termination: If a path contains two pairs of successive nodes that have pair-wise identical label and whose connecting edges have identical labels, then the path beyond the second pair is no longer expanded, it is said to be blocked. Blocked paths can be "unravelled" to construct an infinite tableau. The identical labels make sure that copies of the first pair and their descendants can be substituted for the second pair of nodes and their respective descendants.

Definition 4. *A* completion tree *for a* $\mathcal{SHIQ}$-*concept* D *is a tree where each node* x *of the tree is labelled with a set* $\mathcal{L}(x) \subseteq clos(D)$ *and each edge* $\langle x,y \rangle$ *is labelled with a set* $\mathcal{L}(\langle x,y \rangle)$ *of (possibly inverse) roles occurring in* $clos(D)$; *explicit inequalities between nodes of the tree are recorded in a binary relation* $\neq$ *that is implicitly assumed to be symmetric.*

Given a completion tree, a node y *is called an* R-successor *of a node* x *iff* y *is a successor of* x *and* $S \in \mathcal{L}(\langle x,y \rangle)$ *for some* S *with* $S \sqsubseteq^* R$. *A node* y *is called an* R-neighbour *of* x *iff* y *is an* R-successor *of* x, *or if* x *is an* $\mathsf{Inv}(R)$-successor *of* y. *Predecessors and ancestors are defined as usual.*

A node is blocked *iff it is directly or indirectly blocked. A node* x *is* directly blocked *iff none of its ancestors are blocked, and it has ancestors* x', y *and* y' *such that*

1. x is a successor of x' and y is a successor of y' and
2. $\mathcal{L}(x) = \mathcal{L}(y)$ and $\mathcal{L}(x') = \mathcal{L}(y')$ and
3. $\mathcal{L}(\langle x', x \rangle) = \mathcal{L}(\langle y', y \rangle)$.

In this case we will say that y blocks *x. Since this blocking technique involves pairs of nodes, it is called* pair-wise blocking.

A node y is indirectly blocked *iff one of its ancestors is blocked, or it is a successor of a node x and $\mathcal{L}(\langle x, y \rangle) = \emptyset$; the latter condition avoids wasted expansions after an application of the $\leq$-rule.*

For a node x, $\mathcal{L}(x)$ *is said to contain a* clash *iff* $\{A, \neg A\} \subseteq \mathcal{L}(x)$ *or if, for some concept C, some role S, and some $n \in \mathbb{N}$:* $(\leq n\ S\ C) \in \mathcal{L}(x)$ *and there are $n + 1$ S-neighbours $y_0, \dots, y_n$ of x such that $C \in \mathcal{L}(y_i)$ and $y_i \neq y_j$ for all $0 \leq i < j \leq n$. A completion tree is called* clash-free *iff none of its nodes contains a clash; it is called* complete *iff none of the expansion rules in Figure 2 is applicable.*

For a $\mathcal{SHIQ}$-concept D*, the algorithm starts with a completion tree consisting of a single node x with $\mathcal{L}(x) = \{D\}$ and $\neq\ =\ \emptyset$. It applies the expansion rules in Figure 2, stopping when a clash occurs, and answers "D is satisfiable" iff the completion rules can be applied in such a way that they yield a complete and clash-free completion tree.*

The soundness and completeness of the tableaux algorithm is an immediate consequence of Lemmas 2 and 3.

Lemma 3. *Let D be an $\mathcal{SHIQ}$-concept.*

1. *The tableaux algorithm terminates when started with D.*
2. *If the expansion rules can be applied to D such that they yield a complete and clash-free completion tree, then D has a tableau.*
3. *If D has a tableau, then the expansion rules can be applied to D such that they yield a complete and clash-free completion tree.*

The proof can be found in the appendix. Here, we will only discuss the intuition behind the expansion rules and their correspondence to the constructors of $\mathcal{SHIQ}$. Roughly speaking,[2] the completion tree is a partial description of a model whose individuals correspond to nodes, and whose interpretation of roles is taken from the edge labels. Since the completion tree is a tree, this would not yield a correct interpretation of transitive roles, and thus the interpretation of transitive roles is built via the transitive closure of the relations induced by the corresponding edge labels.

The $\sqcap$-, $\sqcup$-, $\exists$- and $\forall$-rules are the standard tableaux rules for $\mathcal{ALC}$ or the propositional modal logic K_m. The $\forall_+$-rule is the standard rule for $\mathcal{ALC}_{R+}$ or the propositional modal logic $S4_m$ extended to deal with role-hierarchies as follows. Assume a situation that satisfies the precondition of the $\forall_+$-rule, i.e., $\forall S.C \in$

---

[2] For the following considerations, we employ a simpler view of the correspondence between completion trees and models, and need not bother with the path construction mentioned above.

⊓-rule:	if 1. $C_1 \sqcap C_2 \in \mathcal{L}(x)$, x is not indirectly blocked, and 2. $\{C_1, C_2\} \nsubseteq \mathcal{L}(x)$ then $\mathcal{L}(x) \longrightarrow \mathcal{L}(x) \cup \{C_1, C_2\}$
⊔-rule:	if 1. $C_1 \sqcup C_2 \in \mathcal{L}(x)$, x is not indirectly blocked, and 2. $\{C_1, C_2\} \cap \mathcal{L}(x) = \emptyset$ then $\mathcal{L}(x) \longrightarrow \mathcal{L}(x) \cup \{C\}$ for some $C \in \{C_1, C_2\}$
∃-rule:	if 1. $\exists S.C \in \mathcal{L}(x)$, x is not blocked, and 2. x has no S-neighbour y with $C \in \mathcal{L}(y)$, then create a new node y with $\mathcal{L}(\langle x, y \rangle) = \{S\}$ and $\mathcal{L}(y) = \{C\}$
∀-rule:	if 1. $\forall S.C \in \mathcal{L}(x)$, x is not indirectly blocked, and 2. there is an S-neighbour y of x with $C \notin \mathcal{L}(y)$ then $\mathcal{L}(y) \longrightarrow \mathcal{L}(y) \cup \{C\}$
∀+-rule:	if 1. $\forall S.C \in \mathcal{L}(x)$, x is not indirectly blocked, and 2. there is some R with $\mathsf{Trans}(R)$ and $R \sqsubseteq S$, 3. there is an R-neighbour y of x with $\forall R.C \notin \mathcal{L}(y)$ then $\mathcal{L}(y) \longrightarrow \mathcal{L}(y) \cup \{\forall R.C\}$
choose-rule:	if 1. $(\bowtie n\, S\, C) \in \mathcal{L}(x)$, x is not indirectly blocked, and 2. there is an S-neighbour y of x with $\{C, \sim C\} \cap \mathcal{L}(y) = \emptyset$ then $\mathcal{L}(y) \longrightarrow \mathcal{L}(y) \cup \{E\}$ for some $E \in \{C, \sim C\}$
⩾-rule:	if 1. $(\geq n\, S\, C) \in \mathcal{L}(x)$, x is not blocked, and 2. there are not n S-neighbours $y_1, \ldots, y_n$ of x with $C \in \mathcal{L}(y_i)$ and $y_i \neq y_j$ for $1 \leq i < j \leq n$ then create n new nodes $y_1, \ldots, y_n$ with $\mathcal{L}(\langle x, y_i \rangle) = \{S\}$, $\mathcal{L}(y_i) = \{C\}$, and $y_i \neq y_j$ for $1 \leq i < j \leq n$.
⩽-rule:	if 1. $(\leq n\, S\, C) \in \mathcal{L}(x)$, x is not indirectly blocked, and 2. $\sharp S^{\mathsf{T}}(x, C) > n$ and there are two S-neighbours y, z of x with $C \in \mathcal{L}(y), C \in \mathcal{L}(z)$, y is not an ancestor of x, and not $y \neq z$ then 1. $\mathcal{L}(z) \longrightarrow \mathcal{L}(z) \cup \mathcal{L}(y)$ and 2. if z is an ancestor of x then $\mathcal{L}(\langle z, x \rangle) \longrightarrow \mathcal{L}(\langle z, x \rangle) \cup \mathsf{Inv}(\mathcal{L}(\langle x, y \rangle))$ else $\mathcal{L}(\langle x, z \rangle) \longrightarrow \mathcal{L}(\langle x, z \rangle) \cup \mathcal{L}(\langle x, y \rangle)$ 3. $\mathcal{L}(\langle x, y \rangle) \longrightarrow \emptyset$ 4. Set $u \neq z$ for all u with $u \neq y$

Fig. 2. The complete tableaux expansion rules for $\mathcal{SHIQ}$

$\mathcal{L}(x)$, and there is an R-neighbour y of x with $\mathsf{Trans}(R)$, $R \sqsubseteq S$ and $\forall R.C \notin \mathcal{L}(y)$. If y has an R-successor z, then, due to the transitivity of R, z is also an R-successor of x. Since $R \sqsubseteq S$, it is also an S-successor of x and hence must satisfy C. This is ensured by adding $\forall R.C$ to $\mathcal{L}(z)$

The rules dealing with qualifying number restrictions work similarly to the rules given in [BBH96]. For a concept $(\geq n\, R\, C) \in \mathcal{L}(x)$, the $\geq$-rule generates n R-successors $y_1, \ldots, y_n$ of x with $C \in \mathcal{L}(y_i)$. To prevent the $\leq$-rule from indentifying the new nodes, it also sets $y_i \neq y_j$ for each $1 \leq i < j \leq n$. Conversely, if $(\leq n\, R\, C) \in \mathcal{L}(x)$ and x has more than n R-neighbours that are labelled with C, then the $\leqslant$-rule chooses two of them that are not in $\neq$ and merges them, together with the edges connecting them with x. The definition of a clash takes care of the situation where the $\neq$ relation makes it impossible to merge any two R-neighbours of x, while the *choose*-rule ensures that all R-neighbours of x are labelled with either C or $\sim C$. Without this rule, the unsatisfiability of concepts like $(\geqslant 3\ R\ A) \sqcap (\leqslant 1\ R\ B) \sqcap (\leqslant 1\ R\ \neg B)$ would go undetected. The relation $\neq$ is used to prevent infinite sequences of rule applications for contradicting number restrictions of the form $(\geqslant n\ R\ C)$ and $(\leqslant (m)\ R\ C)$, with $n > m$. Labelling edges with sets of roles allows a single node to be both an R and S-successor of x even if R and S are not comparable with respect to $\sqsubseteq$.

The following theorem is an immediate consequence of Lemma 2 and 3, and Theorem 1.

Theorem 2. *The tableaux algorithm is a decision procedure for the satisfiability and subsumption of $\mathcal{SHIQ}$-concepts with respect to terminologies.*

3.2   A PSpace-algorithm for $\mathcal{SI}$

To obtain a (worst-case) optimal algorithm for $\mathcal{SI}$, the $\mathcal{SHIQ}$ algorithm is modified as follows. (a) Since $\mathcal{SI}$ does not allow for qualifying number restrictions the $\geqslant$-, $\leqslant$-, and *choose*-rule can be omitted. In the absence of the *choose*-rule we may assume all concepts appearing in labels to be in NNF from the (smaller) set of all subconcepts of D denoted by $sub(D)$, and in the absence of role hierarchies, edge labels can be restricted to roles (instead of sets of roles). Due to the absence of number restrictions the logic still has the finite model property, and blocking no longer need involve two pairs of nodes with identical labels, but only two nodes with (originally) identical labels. (b) To obtain a PSPACE algorithm, we employ a refined blocking strategy which further loosens this "identity" condition to a "similarity" condition. This is achieved by using a second label $\mathcal{B}$ for each node. In the following, we will describe and motivate this blocking technique; detailed proofs as well as an extension of this result to $\mathcal{SIN}$ can be found in [HST98].

Establishing a PSPACE-result for $\mathcal{SI}$ is not as straightforward as it might seem at a first glance. One problem is the presence of inverse roles which might lead to constraints propagating upwards in the tree. This is not compatible with the standard trace technique [SS91] that keeps only a single path in memory at the same time, because constraints propagating upwards in the tree may have an influence on paths that have already been visited and have been discarded from memory. There are at least two possibilities to overcome this problem: (1) by guessing which constraints might propagate upwards beforehand; (2) by a *reset-restart* extension of the trace technique described later in this section. Unfortunately, this is not the only problem. To apply either of these two techniques, it is also necessary to establish a polynomial bound on the length of paths in the completion tree. This is easily established for logics such as $\mathcal{ALC}$ that do not allow for transitive roles. For $\mathcal{ALC}$ with transitive roles (i.e., $\mathcal{S}$), this bound is due to the fact that, for a node x to block a node y, it is sufficient that $\mathcal{L}(y) \subseteq \mathcal{L}(x)$. In the presence of inverse roles, we use a more sophisticated blocking technique to establish the polynomial bound.

⊓-rule: if 1. $C_1 \sqcap C_2 \in \mathcal{L}(x)$ and
                2. $\{C_1, C_2\} \not\subseteq \mathcal{L}(x)$
            then $\mathcal{L}(x) \longrightarrow \mathcal{L}(x) \cup \{C_1, C_2\}$
⊔-rule: if 1. $C_1 \sqcup C_2 \in \mathcal{L}(x)$ and
                2. $\{C_1, C_2\} \cap \mathcal{L}(x) = \emptyset$
            then $\mathcal{L}(x) \longrightarrow \mathcal{L}(x) \cup \{C\}$ for some $C \in \{C_1, C_2\}$
∀-rule: if 1. $\forall S.C \in \mathcal{L}(x)$ and
                2. there is an S-successor y of x with $C \notin \mathcal{B}(y)$
            then $\mathcal{L}(y) \longrightarrow \mathcal{L}(y) \cup \{C\}$ and
                    $\mathcal{B}(y) \longrightarrow \mathcal{B}(y) \cup \{C\}$ or
                2'. there is an S-predecessor y of x with $C \notin \mathcal{L}(y)$
            then $\mathcal{L}(y) \longrightarrow \mathcal{L}(y) \cup \{C\}$.
∀+-rule: if 1. $\forall S.C \in \mathcal{L}(x)$ and Trans(S) and
                2. there is an S-succ. y of x with $\forall S.C \notin \mathcal{B}(y)$
            then $\mathcal{L}(y) \longrightarrow \mathcal{L}(y) \cup \{\forall S.C\}$ and
                    $\mathcal{B}(y) \longrightarrow \mathcal{B}(y) \cup \{\forall S.C\}$ or
                2'. there is an S-predecessor y of x with $\forall S.C \notin \mathcal{L}(y)$
            then $\mathcal{L}(y) \longrightarrow \mathcal{L}(y) \cup \{\forall S.C\}$.
∃-rule: if 1. $\exists S.C \in \mathcal{L}(x)$, x is not blocked and no other rule
                is applicable to any of its ancestors, and
                2. x has no S-neighbour y with $C \in \mathcal{L}(y)$
            then create a new node y with $\mathcal{L}(\langle x, y \rangle) = S$ and $\mathcal{L}(y) = \mathcal{B}(y) = \{C\}$

Fig. 3. Tableaux expansion rules for $\mathcal{SI}$

Definition 5. *A completion tree for an $\mathcal{SI}$ concept D is a tree where each node x of the tree is labelled with two sets $\mathcal{B}(x) \subseteq \mathcal{L}(x) \subseteq sub(D)$, and each edge $\langle x, y \rangle$ is labelled with a (possibly inverse) role $\mathcal{L}(\langle x, y \rangle)$ occurring in $sub(D)$.*

R-neighbours, -successors, and -predecessors are defined as in Definition 4 where, in the absence of role hierarchies, ⊑ is the identity on $\mathbf{R}$.

A node x is blocked iff x has a blocked ancestor y, or x has an ancestor y and a predecessor x' with $\mathcal{L}(\langle x', x \rangle) = S$, and

$$\mathcal{B}(x) \subseteq \mathcal{L}(y) \quad and \quad \mathcal{L}(x)/\operatorname{Inv}(S) = \mathcal{L}(y)/\operatorname{Inv}(S),$$

where $\mathcal{L}(x)/\operatorname{Inv}(S) = \{\forall \operatorname{Inv}(S).C \in \mathcal{L}(x)\}$.

For a node x, $\mathcal{L}(x)$ is said to contain a clash iff $\{A, \neg A\} \subseteq \mathcal{L}(x)$. A completion tree to which none of the expansion rules given in Figure 3 is applicable is called complete.

For an $\mathcal{SI}$-concept D, the algorithm starts with a completion tree consisting of a single node x with $\mathcal{B}(x) = \mathcal{L}(x) = \{D\}$. It applies the expansion rules in Figure 3, stopping when a clash occurs, and answers "D is satisfiable" iff the completion rules can be applied in such a way that they yield a complete and clash-free completion tree.

As for $\mathcal{SHIQ}$, correctness of the algorithm can be proved by first showing that a $\mathcal{SI}$-concept is satisfiable iff it has a tableau, and next proving the $\mathcal{SI}$-analogue of Lemma 3, see [HST98].

Theorem 3. *The tableaux algorithm is a decision procedure for satisfiability and subsumption of $\mathcal{SI}$-concepts.*

Since blocking plays a major rôle both in the proof of Theorem 3 and especially in the following complexity considerations, we will discuss it here in more detail. Blocking guarantees the termination of the algorithm. For DLs such as $\mathcal{ALC}$, termination is mainly due to the fact that the expansion rules can only add new concepts that are strictly smaller than the concept that triggered their application.

For $\mathcal{S}$ this is no longer true: the $\forall_+$-rule introduces new concepts that are the same size as the triggering concept. To ensure termination, nodes labelled with a subset of the label of an ancestor are *blocked*. Since rules can be applied "top-down" (successors are only generated if no other rules are applicable, and the labels of inner nodes are never touched again) and subset-blocking is sufficient (i.e., for a node x to be blocked by an ancestor y, it is sufficient that $\mathcal{L}(x) \subseteq \mathcal{L}(y)$), it is possible to give a polynomial bound on the length of paths.

For $\mathcal{SI}$, *dynamic blocking* was introduced in [HS99], i.e., blocks are not established on a once-and-for-all basis, but established and broken dynamically. Moreover, blocks must be established on the basis of label *equality*, since value restrictions can now constrain predecessors as well as successors. Unfortunately, this may lead to completion trees with exponentially long paths because there are exponentially many possibilities to label sets on such a path. Due to the non-deterministic $\sqcup$-rule, these exponentially many sets may actually occur.

This non-determinism is not problematical for $\mathcal{S}$ because disjunctions need not be completely decomposed to yield a subset-blocking situation. For an optimal $\mathcal{SI}$ algorithm, the additional label $\mathcal{B}$ was introduced to enable a sort of subset-blocking which is independent of the $\sqcup$-non-determinism. Intuitively, $\mathcal{B}(x)$ is the restriction of $\mathcal{L}(x)$ to those non-decomposed concepts that x must satisfy, whereas $\mathcal{L}(x)$ contains boolean decompositions of these concepts as well as those that are imposed by value restrictions in descendants. If x is blocked by y, then all concepts in $\mathcal{B}(x)$ are eventually decomposed in $\mathcal{L}(y)$. However, in order to substitute x by y, x's constraints on predecessors must be at least as strong as y's; this is taken care of by the second blocking condition.

Let us consider a path $x_0, x_1, \ldots, x_n$ where all edges are labelled R with $\mathsf{Trans}(R)$, the only kind of path along which the length of the longest concept in the labels might not decrease. If no rules can be applied, then we have, for $1 \leq i < n$,

$$\mathcal{L}(x_{i+1})/\,\mathsf{Inv}(R) \subseteq \mathcal{L}(x_i)/\,\mathsf{Inv}(R) \text{ and}$$
$$\mathcal{B}(x_i) \subseteq \mathcal{B}(x_{i+1}) \cup \{C_i\}$$

(where $\exists R.C_i \in \mathcal{L}(x_i)$ triggered the generation of x_{i+1}). This limits the number of different labels and guarantees blocking after a polynomial number of steps.

Lemma 4. *The paths of a completion tree for a concept D have a length of at most m^4 where $m = |sub(D)|$.*

Finally, a slight modification of the expansion rules given in Figure 3 yields a PSPACE algorithm. This modification is necessary because the original algorithm must keep the whole completion tree in memory—which needs exponential space even though the length of its paths is polynomially bounded. The original algorithm may not forget about branches because restrictions which are pushed *upwards* in the tree might make it necessary to revisit paths which have been considered before. A *reset-restart* mechanism solves this problem as follows:

Whenever the $\forall$- or the $\forall_+$-rule is applied to a node x and its *predecessor* y (Case 2' of these rules), we delete all successors of y from the completion tree (*reset*). While this makes it necessary to *restart* the generation of successors for y, it makes it possible to implement the algorithm in a depth-first manner which facilitates the re-use of space.

This modification does not affect the proof of soundness and completeness for the algorithm, but of course we have to re-prove termination [HST98] as it formerly relied on the fact that we never removed any nodes from the completion tree. Summing up we get:

Theorem 4. *The modified algorithm is a* PSPACE *decision procedure for satisfiability and subsumption of $\mathcal{SI}$-concepts.*

4   The Undecidability of Unrestricted $\mathcal{SHIN}$

Like earlier DLs that combine a hierarchy of (transitive and non-transitive) roles with some form of number restrictions [HS99; HST98], $\mathcal{SHIN}$ only allows *simple* roles in restrictions, i.e. roles that are neither transitive nor have transitive subroles. The justification for this limitation has been partly on the grounds of a doubtful semantics (of transitive functional roles) and partly to simplify decision procedures. In this section, we will show that allowing arbitrary roles in $\mathcal{SHIN}$ number restrictions leads to undecidability. For convenience, we denote $\mathcal{SHIN}$ with arbitrary roles in number restrictions by $\mathcal{SHIN}^+$.

The undecidability proof uses a reduction of the domino problem [Ber66] adapted from [BS96]. This problem asks whether, for a set of domino types, there exists a *tiling* of an $\mathbb{N}^2$ grid such that each point of the grid is covered with exactly one of the domino types, and adjacent dominoes are "compatible" with respect to some predefined criteria.

Definition 6. *A domino system $\mathcal{D} = (D, H, V)$ consists of a non-empty set of domino types $D = \{D_1, \ldots, D_n\}$, and of sets of horizontally and vertically matching pairs $H \subseteq D \times D$ and $V \subseteq D \times D$. The problem is to determine if, for a given $\mathcal{D}$, there exists a tiling of an $\mathbb{N} \times \mathbb{N}$ grid such that each point of the grid is covered with a domino type in D and all horizontally and vertically adjacent pairs of domino types are in H and V respectively, i.e., a mapping $t : \mathbb{N} \times \mathbb{N} \to D$ such that for all $m, n \in \mathbb{N}$, $\langle t(m, n), t(m+1, n) \rangle \in H$ and $\langle t(m, n), t(m, n+1) \rangle \in V$.*

This problem can be reduced to the satisfiability of $\mathcal{SHIN}^+$-concepts, and the undecidability of the domino problem implies undecidability of satisfiability of $\mathcal{SHIN}^+$-concepts.

Ensuring that each point is associated with exactly one domino type and that a point and its neighbours satisfy the compatibility conditions induced by H and

V is simple for most logics (via the introduction of concepts C_{D_i} for domino types D_i, and the use of value restrictions and boolean connectives), and applying such conditions throughout the grid is also simple in a logic such as $\mathcal{SHIN}^+$ which can deal with arbitrary axioms. The crucial difficulty is representing the N × N grid using "horizontal" and "vertical" roles X and Y, and in particular forcing the coincidence of $X \circ Y$- and $Y \circ X$-successors. This can be accomplished in $\mathcal{SHIN}^+$ using an alternating pattern of two horizontal roles X_1 and X_2, and two vertical roles Y_1 and Y_2, with disjoint primitive concepts A, B, C, and D being used to identify points in the grid with different combinations of successors. The coincidence of $X \circ Y$ and $Y \circ X$ successors can then be enforced using number restrictions on transitive super-roles of each of the four possible combinations of X and Y roles. A visualisation of the resulting grid and a suitable role hierarchy is shown in Figure 4, where $S_{ij}^{\oplus}$ are transitive roles.

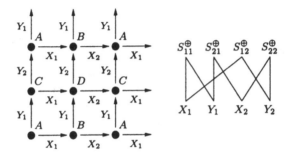

Fig. 4. Visualisation of the grid and role hierarchy.

The alternation of X and Y roles in the grid means that one of the transitive super-roles S_{ij} connects each point (m, n) to the points $(m+1, n)$, $(m, n+1)$ and $(m+1, n+1)$, and to no other points. A number restriction of the form $\leqslant 3S_{ij}$ can thus be used to enforce the necessary coincidence of $X \circ Y$- and $Y \circ X$-successors. A complete specification of the grid is given by the following axioms:

$$A \sqsubseteq \neg B \sqcap \neg C \sqcap \neg D \sqcap \exists X_1.B \sqcap \exists Y_1.C \sqcap \leqslant 3S_{11},$$
$$B \sqsubseteq \neg A \sqcap \neg C \sqcap \neg D \sqcap \exists X_2.A \sqcap \exists Y_1.D \sqcap \leqslant 3S_{21},$$
$$C \sqsubseteq \neg A \sqcap \neg B \sqcap \neg D \sqcap \exists X_1.D \sqcap \exists Y_2.A \sqcap \leqslant 3S_{12},$$
$$D \sqsubseteq \neg A \sqcap \neg B \sqcap \neg C \sqcap \exists X_2.C \sqcap \exists Y_2.B \sqcap \leqslant 3S_{22}.$$

It only remains to add axioms which encode the local compatibility conditions (as described in [BS96]) and to assert that A, B, C, and D are subsumed by the disjunction of all domino types to enforce the placement of a tile on each point of the grid. The concept A is now satisfiable w.r.t. the various axioms (which can be internalised as described in Lemma 1) iff there is a compatible tiling of the grid.

5   Discussion

A new DL system is being implemented based on the $\mathcal{SHIQ}$ algorithm described in Section 3.1. Pending the completion of this project, the existing FaCT system [Hor98] has been modified to deal with inverse roles using the $\mathcal{SHIQ}$ blocking strategy, giving a DL which is equivalent to $\mathcal{SHI}$ extended with functional roles [HS99]; we will refer to this DL as $\mathcal{SHIF}$ and to the modified FaCT system as I-FaCT.

I-FaCT has been used to conduct some initial experiments with a terminology representing (fragments of) database schemata and inter schema assertions from a data warehousing application [CDL+98] (a slightly simplified version of the proposed encoding was used to generate $\mathcal{SHIF}$ terminologies). I-FaCT is able to classify this terminology, which contains 19 concepts and 42 axioms, in less than 0.1s of (266MHz Pentium) CPU time. In contrast, eliminating inverse roles using an embedding technique [CDR98] gives an equisatisfiable FaCT terminology with an additional 84 axioms, but one which FaCT is unable to classify in 12 hours of CPU time.

An extension of the embedding technique can be used to eliminate number restrictions [DL95], but requires a target logic which supports the transitive *closure* of roles, i.e., *converse*-PDL. The even larger number of axioms which this embedding would introduce makes it unlikely that tractable reasoning could be performed on the resulting terminology. Moreover, we are not aware of any algorithm for *converse*-PDL which does not employ a so-called *cut rule* [DM98], the application of which introduces considerable additional non-determinism. It seems inevitable that this would lead to a further degradation in empirical tractability.

As far as complexity is concerned, we have already been successful in extending the PSPACE-result for $\mathcal{SI}$ to $\mathcal{SIN}$ [HST98]. Currently we are working on an extension of this result to $\mathcal{SIQ}$ combining the techniques from this paper with those presented in [Tob99].

References

[Baa91]   F. Baader. Augmenting concept languages by transitive closure of roles: An alternative to terminological cycles. In *Proc. of IJCAI-91*, 1991.

[BBH96]   F. Baader, M. Buchheit, and B. Hollunder. Cardinality restrictions on concepts. *Artificial Intelligence*, 88(1–2):195–213, 1996.

[BBN+93] F. Baader, H.-J. Bürckert, B. Nebel, W. Nutt, and G. Smolka. On the expressivity of feature logics with negation, functional uncertainty, and sort equations. *J. of Logic, Language and Information*, 2:1–18, 1993.

[Ber66]   R. Berger. The undecidability of the dominoe problem. *Mem. Amer. Math. Soc.*, 66, 1966.

[BS96]   F. Baader and U. Sattler. Number restrictions on complex roles in description logics. In *Proc. of KR-96*, pages 328–339, 1996.

[CDL98a] D. Calvanese, G. De Giacomo, and M. Lenzerini. On the decidability of query containment under constraints. In *Proc. of the 17th ACM SIGACT*

SIGMOD SIGART Sym. on Principles of Database Systems (PODS'98), pages 149–158, 1998.

[CDL+98]   D. Calvanese, G. De Giacomo, M. Lenzerini, D. Nardi, and R. Rosati. Source integration in data warehousing. In Proc. of DEXA-98. IEEE Computer Society Press, 1998.

[CDL99]   D. Calvanese, G. De Giacomo, and M. Lenzerini. Reasoning in expressive description logics with fixpoints based on automata on infinite trees. In Proc. of the 16th Int. Joint. Conf. on Artificial Intelligence (IJCAI'99), 1999.

[CDR98]   D. Calvanese, G. De Giacomo, and R. Rosati. A note on encoding inverse roles and functional restrictions in $\mathcal{ALC}$ knowledge bases. In Proc. of DL'98, 1998.

[CLN94]   Diego Calvanese, Maurizio Lenzerini, and Daniele Nardi. A unified framework for class based representation formalisms. Proc. of KR-94, pages 109–120. M. Kaufmann, Los Altos.

[DL95]   G. De Giacomo and M. Lenzerini. What's in an aggregate: Foundations for description logics with tuples and sets. In Proc. of IJCAI-95, 1995.

[DL96]   G. De Giacomo and M. Lenzerini. Tbox and Abox reasoning in expressive description logics. In Proc. of KR-96, pages 316–327. M. Kaufmann, Los Altos, 1996.

[DLNdN91] F. Donini, M. Lenzerini, D. Nardi, and W. Nutt. The complexity of concept languages. In Proc. of KR-91, Boston, MA, USA, 1991.

[DLNS96]   F. M. Donini, M. Lenzerini, D. Nardi, and A. Schaerf. Reasoning in description logics. In G. Brewka, editor, Foundation of Knowledge Representation. CSLI Publication, Cambridge University Press, 1996.

[DM98]   G. De Giacomo and F. Massacci. Combining deduction and model checking into tableaux and algorithms for Converse-PDL. Information and Computation, 1998. To appear.

[HNS90]   B. Hollunder, W. Nutt, and M. Schmidt-Schauss. Subsumption algorithms for concept description languages. In ECAI-90, Pitman Publishing, London, 1990.

[Hor98]   I. Horrocks. Using an expressive description logic: FaCT or fiction? In Proc. of KR-98, pages 636–647, 1998.

[HS99]   I. Horrocks and U. Sattler. A description logic with transitive and inverse roles and role hierarchies. J. of Logic and Computation, 1999. To appear.

[HST98]   I. Horrocks, U. Sattler, and S. Tobies. A PSPACE-algorithm for deciding $\mathcal{ALCI}_{R+}$-satisfiability. Technical Report 98-08, LuFg Theoretical Computer Science, RWTH Aachen, 1998. See http://www-lti.informatik.rwth-aachen.de/Forschung/Papers.html.

[HST99]   I. Horrocks, U. Sattler, and S. Tobies. A description logic with transitive and converse roles, role hierarchies and qualifying number restrictions. LTCS-Report 99-08, LuFg Theoretical Computer Science, RWTH Aachen, Germany, 1999.

[Sat96]   U. Sattler. A concept language extended with different kinds of transitive roles. In 20. Deutsche Jahrestagung für KI, LNAI 1137. Springer-Verlag, 1996.

[Sch91]   K. Schild. A correspondence theory for terminological logics: Preliminary report. In Proc. of IJCAI-91, pages 466–471, Sydney, 1991.

[SS91]   M. Schmidt-Schauß and G. Smolka. Attributive concept descriptions with complements. Artificial Intelligence, 48(1):1–26, 1991.

[Tob99]   S. Tobies. A PSpace algorithm for graded modal logic. In Proc. of CADE-16, LNCS. Springer, 1999.

Appendix

In this appendix we present the proof of Lemma 3, which is repeated here for easier reference.

Lemma. *Let D be an $\mathcal{SHIQ}$-concept.*

1. *(Termination) The tableaux algorithm terminates when started with D.*
2. *(Soundness) If the expansion rules can be applied to D such that they yield a complete and clash-free completion tree, then D has a tableau.*
3. *(Completeness) If D has a tableau, then the expansion rules can be applied to D such that they yield a complete and clash-free completion tree.*

(Termination) Let $m = |clos(D)|$, $k = |\mathbf{R}_D|$, and n_{max} the maximum n that occurs in a concept of the form $(\bowtie n\ S\ C) \in clos(D)$. Termination is a consequence of the following properties of the expansion rules:

- The expansion rules never remove nodes from the tree or concepts from node labels. Edge labels can only be changed by the $\leqslant$-rule which either expands them or sets them to $\emptyset$; in the latter case the node below the $\emptyset$-labelled edge is blocked and this block is never broken.
- Each successor of a node x is the result of the application of the $\exists$-rule or the $\geqslant$-rule to x. For a node x, each concept in $\mathcal{L}(x)$ can trigger the generation of successors at most once.

  For the $\exists$-rule, if a successor y of x was generated for a concept $\exists S.C \in \mathcal{L}(x)$ and later $\mathcal{L}(\langle x, y \rangle)$ is set to $\emptyset$ by the $\leqslant$-rule, then there is some S-neighbour z of x with $C \in \mathcal{L}(z)$.

  For the $\geqslant$-rule, if $y_1, \ldots, y_n$ were generated by the $\geqslant$-rule for $(\geqslant n\ S\ C) \in \mathcal{L}(x)$, then $y_i \neq y_j$ holds for all $1 \leq i < j \leq n$. This implies that there are always n S-neighbours $y'_1, \ldots, y'_n$ of x with $C \in \mathcal{L}(y'_i)$ and $y'_i \neq y'_j$ for all $1 \leq i < j \leq n$, since the $\leqslant$-rule never merges two nodes y'_i, y'_j with $y'_i \neq y'_j$, and, whenever an application of the $\leqslant$-rule sets $\mathcal{L}(\langle x, y'_i \rangle)$ to $\emptyset$, there is some S-neighbour z of x which "inherits" both C and all inequalities from y'_i.

  Since $clos(D)$ contains a total of at most m $\exists R.C$ and $(\geqslant n\ S\ C)$ concepts, the out-degree of the tree is bounded by $m \cdot n_{max}$.
- Nodes are labelled with non-empty subsets of $clos(D)$ and edges with subsets of R_D, so there are at most 2^{2mk} different possible labellings for a pair of nodes and an edge. Therefore, if a path p is of length at least 2^{2mk}, then from the pair-wise blocking condition there must be two nodes x, y on p such that x is directly blocked by y. Furthermore, if a node was generated at distance ℓ from the root node, it always remains at this distance, and thus paths are not curled up or shortened. Since a path on which nodes are blocked cannot become longer, paths are of length at most 2^{2mn}.   □

(Soundness) Let $\mathbf{T}$ be a complete and clash-free completion tree. A path is a sequence of pairs of nodes of $\mathbf{T}$ of the form $p = [\frac{x_0}{x'_0}, \ldots, \frac{x_n}{x'_n}]$. For such a path we define $\mathsf{Tail}(p) := x_n$ and $\mathsf{Tail}'(p) := x'_n$. With $[p|\frac{x_{n+1}}{x'_{n+1}}]$ we denote the path $[\frac{x_0}{x'_0}, \ldots, \frac{x_n}{x'_n}, \frac{x_{n+1}}{x'_{n+1}}]$. The set $\mathsf{Paths}(\mathbf{T})$ is defined inductively as follows:

- For the root node x_0 of **T**, $[\frac{x_0}{x_0}] \in$ Paths(**T**), and
- For a path $p \in$ Paths(**T**) and a node z in **T**:
  - if z is a successor of Tail(p) and z is not blocked, then $[p|\frac{z}{z}] \in$ Paths(**T**), or
  - if, for some node y in **T**, y is a successor of Tail(p) and z blocks y, then $[p|\frac{z}{y}] \in$ Paths(**T**).

Please note that, due to the construction of Paths, for $p \in$ Paths(**T**) with $p = [p'|\frac{x}{x'}]$, we have that x is not blocked, x' is blocked iff $x \neq x'$, and x' is never indirectly blocked. Furthermore, $\mathcal{L}(x) = \mathcal{L}(x')$ holds.

Now we can define a tableau $T = (\mathbf{S}, \mathcal{L}, \mathcal{E})$ with:

$$\mathbf{S} = \text{Paths}(\mathbf{T})$$
$$\mathcal{L}(p) = \mathcal{L}(\text{Tail}(p))$$
$$\mathcal{E}(R) = \{\langle p, q \rangle \in \mathbf{S} \times \mathbf{S} \mid \text{Either } q = [p|\frac{x}{x'}] \text{ and}$$
$$x' \text{ is an } R\text{-successor of Tail}(p)$$
$$\text{or } p = [q|\frac{x}{x'}] \text{ and}$$
$$x' \text{ is an Inv}(R)\text{-successor of Tail}(q)\}.$$

CLAIM: T is a tableau for D with respect to $\mathcal{R}^+$.

We show that T satisfies all the properties from Definition 3.

- $D \in \mathcal{L}([\frac{x_0}{x_0}])$ since $D \in \mathcal{L}(x_0)$.
- **Property 1** holds because **T** is clash-free; **Properties 2,3** hold because Tail(p) is not blocked and **T** is complete.
- **Property 4**: Assume $\forall S.C \in \mathcal{L}(p)$ and $\langle p, q \rangle \in \mathcal{E}(S)$. If $q = [p|\frac{x}{x'}]$, then x' is an S-successor of Tail(p) and thus $C \in \mathcal{L}(x')$ (because the $\forall$-rule is not applicable). Since $\mathcal{L}(q) = \mathcal{L}(x) = \mathcal{L}(x')$, we have $C \in \mathcal{L}(q)$. If $p = [q|\frac{x}{x'}]$, then x' is an Inv(S)-successor of Tail(q) and thus $C \in \mathcal{L}(\text{Tail}(q))$ (because x' is not indirectly blocked and the $\forall$-rule is not applicable), hence $C \in \mathcal{L}(q)$.
- **Property 5**: Assume $\exists S.C \in \mathcal{L}(p)$. Define $x := \text{Tail}(p)$. In **T** there is an S-neighbour y of x with $C \in \mathcal{L}(y)$, because the $\exists$-rule is not applicable. There are two possibilities:
  - y is a successor of x in **T**. If y is not blocked, then $q := [p|\frac{y}{y}] \in \mathbf{S}$ and $\langle p, q \rangle \in \mathcal{E}(S)$ as well as $C \in \mathcal{L}(q)$. If y is blocked by some node z in **T**, then $q := [p|\frac{z}{y}] \in \mathbf{S}$.
  - y is a predecessor of x. Again, there are two possibilities:
    * p is of the form $p = [q|\frac{x}{x'}]$ with Tail(q) = y.
    * p is of the form $p = [q|\frac{x}{x'}]$ with Tail(q) = $u \neq y$. x only has one predecessor in **T**, hence u is not the predecessor of x. This implies $x \neq x'$, x blocks x' in **T**, and u is the predecessor of x' due to the construction of Paths. Together with the definition of the blocking condition, this implies $\mathcal{L}(\langle u, x' \rangle) = \mathcal{L}(\langle y, x \rangle)$ as well as $\mathcal{L}(u) = \mathcal{L}(y)$ due to the pair-wise blocking condition.

In all three cases, $\langle p, q \rangle \in \mathcal{E}(S)$ and $C \in \mathcal{L}(q)$.

- **Property 6:** Assume $\forall S.C \in \mathcal{L}(p)$, $\langle p,q \rangle \in \mathcal{E}(R)$ for some $R \sqsubseteq S$ with $\mathrm{Trans}(R)$. If $q = [p|\frac{x}{x'}]$, then x' is an R-successor of $\mathrm{Tail}(p)$ and thus $\forall R.C \in \mathcal{L}(x')$ (because otherwise the $\forall_+$-rule would be applicable). From $\mathcal{L}(q) = \mathcal{L}(x) = \mathcal{L}(x')$ it follows that $\forall R.C \in \mathcal{L}(q)$. If $p = [q|\frac{x}{x'}]$, then x' is an $\mathrm{Inv}(S)$-successor of $\mathrm{Tail}(q)$ and hence $\mathrm{Tail}(q)$ is an R-neighbour of x'. Because x' is not indirectly blocked, this implies $\forall R.C \in \mathcal{L}(\mathrm{Tail}(q))$ and hence $\forall R.C \in \mathcal{L}(q)$.

- **Property 11:** Assume $(\bowtie\ n\ S\ C) \in \mathcal{L}(p)$, $\langle p,q \rangle \in \mathcal{E}(S)$. If $q = [p|\frac{x}{x'}]$, then x' is an S-successor of $\mathrm{Tail}(p)$ and thus $\{C, \sim C\} \cap \mathcal{L}(x') \neq \emptyset$ (since the *choose*-rule is not applicable). Since $\mathcal{L}(q) = \mathcal{L}(x) = \mathcal{L}(x')$, we have $\{C, \sim C\} \cap \mathcal{L}(q) \neq \emptyset$. If $p = [q|\frac{x}{x'}]$, then x' is an $\mathrm{Inv}(S)$-successor of $\mathrm{Tail}(q)$ and thus $\{C, \sim C\} \cap \mathcal{L}(\mathrm{Tail}(q)) \neq \emptyset$ (since x' is not indirectly blocked and the *choose*-rule is not applicable), hence $\{C, \sim C\} \cap \mathcal{L}(q) \neq \emptyset$.

- Assume **Property 9** is violated. Hence there is some $p \in \mathbf{S}$ with $(\leqslant n\ S\ C) \in \mathcal{L}(p)$ and $\sharp S^T(p, C) > n$. We show that this implies $\sharp S^T(\mathrm{Tail}(p), C) > n$, in contradiction of either the clash-freeness or completeness of $\mathbf{T}$. Define $x := \mathrm{Tail}(p)$ and $P := S^T(p, C)$. Due to the assumption, we have $\sharp P > n$. We distinguish two cases:

  - P contains only paths of the form $q = [p|\frac{y}{y'}]$. We claim that the function Tail' is injective on P. Assume that there are two paths $q_1, q_1 \in P$ with $q_1 \neq q_2$ and $\mathrm{Tail}'(q_1) = \mathrm{Tail}'(q_2) = y'$. Then q_1 is of the form $q_1 = [p|(y_1, y')]$ and q_2 is of the form $q_2 = [p|\frac{y_2}{y'}]$ with $y_1 \neq y_2$. If y' is not blocked in $\mathbf{T}$, then $y_1 = y' = y_2$, contradicting $y_1 \neq y_2$. If y' is blocked in $\mathbf{T}$, then both y_1 and y_2 block y', which implies $y_1 = y_2$, again a contradiction.

    Since Tail' is injective on P, it holds that $\sharp P = \sharp\,\mathrm{Tail}'(P)$. Also for each $y' \in \mathrm{Tail}'(P)$, y' is an S-successor of x and $C \in \mathcal{L}(y')$. This implies $\sharp S^T(x, C) > n$.

  - P contains a path q where p is of the form $p = [q|\frac{x}{x'}]$. Obviously, P may only contain one such path. As in the previous case, Tail' is an injective function on the set $P' := P\backslash\{q\}$, each $y' \in \mathrm{Tail}'(P')$ is an S-successor of x and $C \in \mathcal{L}(y')$ for each $y' \in \mathrm{Tail}'(P')$. To show that indeed $\sharp S^T(x, C) > n$ holds, we have to prove the existence of a further S-neighbour u of x with $C \in \mathcal{L}(u)$ and $u \notin \mathrm{Tail}'(P')$. This will be "supplied" by $z := \mathrm{Tail}(q)$. We distinguish two cases:

    * $x = x'$. Hence x is not blocked. This implies that x is an $\mathrm{Inv}(S)$-successor of z in $\mathbf{T}$. Since $\mathrm{Tail}'(P')$ contains only successors of x, we have that $z \notin \mathrm{Tail}'(P')$ and, by construction, z is an S-neighbour of x with $C \in \mathcal{L}(z)$.

    * $x \neq x'$. This implies that x' is blocked in $\mathbf{T}$ by x and that x' is an $\mathrm{Inv}(S)$-successor of z in $\mathbf{T}$. The definition of pairwise-blocking implies that x is an $\mathrm{Inv}(S)$-successor of some node u in $\mathbf{T}$ with $\mathcal{L}(u) = \mathcal{L}(z)$. Again, since $\mathrm{Tail}'(P')$ contains only successors of x we have that $u \notin \mathrm{Tail}'(P')$ and, by construction, u is an S-neighbour of x and $C \in \mathcal{L}(u)$.

- **Property 10**: Assume $(\geqslant n \; S \; C) \in \mathcal{L}(p)$. Completeness of **T** implies that there exist n individuals $y_1, \ldots, y_n$ in **T** such that each y_i is an S-neighbour of $\mathsf{Tail}(p)$ and $C \in \mathcal{L}(y_i)$. We claim that, for each of these individuals, there is a path q_i such that $\langle p, q_i \rangle \in \mathcal{E}(S)$, $C \in \mathcal{L}(q_i)$, and $q_i \neq q_j$ for all $1 \leq i < j \leq n$. Obviously, this implies $\sharp S^T(p, C) \geqslant n$. For each y_i there are three possibilities:
  - y_i is an S-successor of x and y_i is not blocked in **T**. Then $q_i = [p|\frac{y_i}{y_i}]$ is a path with the desired properties.
  - y_i is an S-successor of x and y_i is blocked in **T** by some node z. Then $q_i = [p|\frac{z}{y_i}]$ is the path with the desired properties. Since the same z may block several of the y_js, it is indeed necessary to include y_i explicitly into the path to make them distinct.
  - x is an $\mathsf{Inv}(S)$-successor of y_i. There may be at most one such y_i. This implies that p is of the form $p = [q|\frac{x}{x'}]$ with $\mathsf{Tail}(q) = y_i$. Again, q has the desired properties and, obviously, q is distinct from all other paths q_j.
- **Property 7** is satisfied due to the symmetric definition of $\mathcal{E}$. **Property 8** is satisfied due to the definition of R-successor that takes into account the role hierarchy $\sqsubseteq^*$.   □

(Completeness) Let $T = (\mathbf{S}, \mathcal{L}, \mathcal{E})$ be a tableau for D w.r.t. $\mathcal{R}^+$. We use this tableau to guide the application of the non-deterministic rules. To do this, we will inductively define a function π, mapping the individuals of the tree **T** to **S** such that, for each x, y in **T**:

$$\left. \begin{array}{l} \mathcal{L}(x) \subseteq \mathcal{L}(\pi(x)) \\ \text{if } y \text{ is an } S\text{-neighbour of } x, \text{ then } \langle \pi(x), \pi(y) \rangle \in \mathcal{E}(S) \\ x \neq y \text{ implies } \pi(x) \neq \pi(y) \end{array} \right\} (*)$$

CLAIM: Let **T** be a completion-tree and π a function that satisfies $(*)$. If a rule is applicable to **T** then the rule is applicable to **T** in a way that yields a completion-tree **T**′ and an extension of π that satisfy $(*)$.

Let **T** be a completion-tree and π be a function that satisfies $(*)$. We have to consider the various rules.

- **The $\sqcap$-rule**: If $C_1 \sqcap C_2 \in \mathcal{L}(x)$, then $C_1 \sqcap C_2 \in \mathcal{L}(\pi(x))$. This implies $C_1, C_2 \in \mathcal{L}(\pi(x))$ due to Property 2 from Definition 3, and hence the rule can be applied without violating $(*)$.
- **The $\sqcup$-rule**: If $C_1 \sqcup C_2 \in \mathcal{L}(x)$, then $C_1 \sqcup C_2 \in \mathcal{L}(\pi(x))$. Since T is a tableau, Property 3 from Definition 3 implies $\{C_1, C_2\} \cap \mathcal{L}(\pi(x)) \neq \emptyset$. Hence the $\sqcup$-rule can add a concept $E \in \{C_1, C_2\}$ to $\mathcal{L}(x)$ such that $\mathcal{L}(x) \subseteq \mathcal{L}(\pi(x))$ holds.
- **The $\exists$-rule**: If $\exists S.C \in \mathcal{L}(x)$, then $\exists S.C \in \mathcal{L}(\pi(x))$ and, since T is a tableau, Property 5 of Definition 3 implies that there is an element $t \in \mathbf{S}$ such that $\langle \pi(x), t \rangle \in \mathcal{E}(S)$ and $C \in \mathcal{L}(t)$. The application of the $\exists$-rule generates a new variable y with $\mathcal{L}(\langle x, y \rangle) = \{S\}$ and $\mathcal{L}(y) = \{C\}$. Hence we set $\pi := \pi[y \mapsto t]$ which yields a function that satisfies $(*)$ for the modified tree.

- **The ∀-rule:** If $\forall S.C \in \mathcal{L}(x)$, then $\forall S.C \in \mathcal{L}(\pi(x))$, and if y is an S-neighbour of x, then also $\langle \pi(x), \pi(y) \rangle \in \mathcal{E}(S)$ due to (∗). Since T is a tableau, Property 4 of Definition 3 implies $C \in \mathcal{L}(\pi(y))$ and hence the ∀-rule can be applied without violating (∗).

- **The ∀$_+$-rule:** If $\forall S.C \in \mathcal{L}(x)$, then $\forall S.C \in \mathcal{L}(\pi(x))$, and if there is some $R \sqsubseteq S$ with $\mathsf{Trans}(R)$ and y is an R-neighbour of x, then also $\langle \pi(x), \pi(y) \rangle \in \mathcal{E}(R)$ due to (∗). Since T is a tableau, Property 6 of Definition 3 implies $\forall R.C \in \mathcal{L}(\pi(y))$ and hence the ∀$_+$-rule can be applied without violating (∗).

- **The *choose*-rule:** If $(\bowtie n\ S\ C) \in \mathcal{L}(x)$, then $(\bowtie n\ S\ C) \in \mathcal{L}(\pi(x))$, and, if there is an S-neighbour y of x, then $\langle \pi(x), \pi(y) \rangle \in \mathcal{E}(S)$ due to (∗). Since T is a tableau, Property 11 of Definition 3 implies $\{C, \sim C\} \cap \mathcal{L}(\pi(y) \neq \emptyset$. Hence the *choose*-rule can add an appropriate concept $E \in \{C, \sim C\}$ to $\mathcal{L}(x)$ such that $\mathcal{L}(y) \subseteq \mathcal{L}(\pi(y))$ holds.

- **The ⩾-rule:** If $(\geq n\ S\ C) \in \mathcal{L}(x)$, then $(\geq n\ S\ C) \in \mathcal{L}(\pi(x))$. Since T is a tableau, Property 10 of Definition 3 implies $\sharp S^T(\pi(x), C) \geq n$. Hence there are individuals $t_1, \ldots, t_n \in \mathbf{S}$ such that $\langle \pi(x), t_i \rangle \in \mathcal{E}(S)$, $C \in \mathcal{L}(t_i)$, and $t_i \neq t_j$ for $1 \leq i < j \leq n$. The ⩾-rule generates n new nodes $y_1, \ldots, y_n$. By setting $\pi := \pi[y_1 \mapsto t_1, \cdots y_n \mapsto t_n]$, one obtains a function π that satisfies (∗) for the modified tree.

- **The ⩽-rule:** If $(\leq n\ S\ C) \in \mathcal{L}(x)$, then $(\leq n\ S\ C) \in \mathcal{L}(\pi(x))$. Since T is a tableau, Property 9 of Definition 3 implies $\sharp S^T(\pi(x), C) \leq n$. If the ⩽-rule is applicable, we have $\sharp S^T(x, C) > n$, which implies that there are at least $n+1$ S-neighbours $y_0, \ldots, y_n$ of x such that $C \in \mathcal{L}(y_i)$. Thus, there must be two nodes $y, z \in \{y_0, \ldots, y_n\}$ such that $\pi(y) = \pi(z)$ (because otherwise $\sharp S^T(\pi(x), C) > n$ would hold). From $\pi(y) = \pi(z)$ we have that $y \neq z$ cannot hold because of (∗), and y, z can be chosen such that y is not an ancestor of z. Hence the ⩽-rule can be applied without violating (∗).

Why does this claim yield the completeness of the tableaux algorithm? For the initial completion-tree consisting of a single node x_0 with $\mathcal{L}(x_0) = \{D\}$ and $\neq = \emptyset$ we can give a function π that satisfies (∗) by setting $\pi(x_0) := s_0$ for some $s_0 \in \mathbf{S}$ with $D \in \mathcal{L}(s_0)$ (such an s_0 exists since T is a tableau for D). Whenever a rule is applicable to **T**, it can be applied in a way that maintains (∗), and, since the algorithm terminates, we have that any sequence of rule applications must terminate. Properties (∗) imply that any tree **T** generated by these rule-applications must be clash-free as there are only two possibilities for a clash, and it is easy to see that neither of these can hold in **T**:

- **T** cannot contain a node x such that $\{C, \neg C\} \in \mathcal{L}(x)$ because $\mathcal{L}(x) \subseteq \mathcal{L}(\pi(x))$ and hence Property 1 of Definition 3 would be violated for $\pi(x)$.
- **T** cannot contain a node x with $(\leq n\ S\ C) \in \mathcal{L}(x)$ and $n+1$ S-neighbours $y_0, \ldots y_n$ of x with $C \in \mathcal{L}(y_i)$ and $y_i \neq y_j$ for $0 \leq i < j \leq n$ because $(\leq n\ S\ C) \in \mathcal{L}(\pi(x))$, and, since $y_i \neq y_j$ implies $\pi(y_i) \neq \pi(y_j)$, $\sharp S^T(\pi(x), C) > n$, in contradiction to Property 9 of Definition 3. $\square$

Complexity of Terminological Reasoning Revisited

Carsten Lutz

RWTH Aachen, LuFG Theoretical Computer Science
Ahornstr. 55, 52074 Aachen

Abstract. TBoxes in their various forms are key components of knowledge representation systems based on description logics (DLs) since they allow for a natural representation of terminological knowledge. Largely due to a classical result given by Nebel [15], complexity analyses for DLs have, until now, mostly failed to take into account the most basic form of TBoxes, so-called *acyclic* TBoxes. In this paper, we concentrate on DLs for which reasoning without TBoxes is PSPACE-complete, and show that there exist logics for which the complexity of reasoning remains in PSPACE if acyclic TBoxes are added and also logics for which the complexity increases. This demonstrates that it is necessary to take acyclic TBoxes into account for complexity analyses.

1 Introduction

A core feature of description logics is their ability to represent and reason about terminological knowledge. Terminological knowledge is stored in so-called TBoxes which mainly come in two flavours. So-called *acyclic* TBoxes are sets of concept definitions that can be thought of as non-recursive macro definitions whereas *general* TBoxes allow to state equivalence of arbitrary, complex concepts. In this paper, we consider the complexity of reasoning with acyclic TBoxes.[1] Surprisingly, although computational complexity of reasoning is a major topic in description logic research, most complexity results available concentrate either on reasoning without TBoxes or on reasoning with general TBoxes (see, e.g., [7], [8], [9], and [10]).

There are two main reasons for this. The first reason is that acyclic TBoxes are a properly subsumed by general TBoxes. However, for many DLs, reasoning with acyclic TBoxes can be expected to be less complex than reasoning with general TBoxes, and, hence, it is interesting to know the exact complexity of reasoning with them. Moreover, there exist description logics for which reasoning with general TBoxes is undecidable but reasoning with acyclic TBoxes is not. In this case, it is obviously desirable to determine the complexity of reasoning with acyclic TBoxes.

---

[1] Hence, when talking of TBoxes, we generally refer to acyclic TBoxes unless otherwise noted.

The second reason can be understood historically. Early DL systems used unfolding to reduce reasoning with acyclic TBoxes to reasoning with concepts. Unfolding a concept C w.r.t. a TBox $\mathcal{T}$ means iteratively replacing concept names in C by their definitions given in $\mathcal{T}$. For example, the result of unfolding the concept *Man ⊓ ∃married-to.Wife* w.r.t. the TBox

$$\{Man \doteq \neg Female, \quad Wife \doteq Female \sqcap Married\}$$

yields *¬Female ⊓ ∃married-to.(Female ⊓ Married)*. In his seminal paper, Nebel showed that, in the worst case, unfolding may result in an exponential blow-up of the concept size [15]. Since the complexity of reasoning with description logics is usually not ExpSpace-hard, this result shows that unfolding is not an adequate means for treating TBoxes. Nebel also showed that in realistic, practical applications, the worst case is almost never encountered. Largely due to these results (and possibly misunderstandings of these results), complexity analyses of reasoning with acyclic TBoxes have long been neglected: First, one could (wrongly) think that reasoning with acyclic TBoxes is necessarily ExpSpace-hard, and that it is sensible to consider only general TBoxes since this—given the misunderstanding—does not seem to make things harder. Second, since the worst case seems not to occur in most practical applications, one could be tempted to think that unfolding is a proper tool for DL systems and that it is not rewarding to search for better alternatives. Last, if one is only interested in decidability of concepts w.r.t. acyclic TBoxes, unfolding is a technique which is easy to use and always applicable.

For many DLs, reasoning without TBoxes is PSpace-complete (see, e.g., [9], [12], [18]). Although the complexity of reasoning with acyclic TBoxes is rarely addressed formally, it is "common knowledge" in the DL community that, if reasoning without TBoxes is in PSpace, then taking into account TBoxes does "usually" not increase complexity. This knowledge has been exploited for efficient practical reasoning with TBoxes [5], but has, to the best of our knowledge, never been used to obtain theoretical complexity results. This is even more surprising since Nebel showed that there exist DLs for which reasoning w.r.t. TBoxes is harder than reasoning with concepts, only (in Nebel's case, complexity moved from P to NP) [15].

In this paper, we focus on logics for which "pure concept satisfiability" (i.e., concept satisfiability w.r.t. the empty TBox) is PSpace-complete and explore the impact of TBoxes on the complexity of the basic DL reasoning tasks satisfiability and subsumption. It turns out that there exist logics for which reasoning remains in PSpace and also DLs for which reasoning gets significantly harder. In the first part of this paper, we focus on $\mathcal{ALC}$, the basic description logic for which pure concept satisfiability is in PSpace [17]. The "common knowledge" mentioned above is used to demonstrate how a pure $\mathcal{ALC}$ concept satisfiability algorithm using the so-called *trace technique* [17] can be modified to take into account TBoxes such that the resulting algorithm can still be executed in polynomial space. Roughly speaking, TBoxes have to be converted to a normal form which allows the tracing algorithm to operate exclusively on concept names (instead of concept expressions). Using the presented modification technique, it is proved that satisfiability of $\mathcal{ALC}$ concepts w.r.t. acyclic TBoxes is still PSPACE-complete.

In the second part of this paper, we show that this technique does not always work: there exist description logics for which pure concept satisfiability is PSPACE-complete but the extension by TBoxes makes reasoning harder. We identify $\mathcal{ALCF}$, i.e., the extension of $\mathcal{ALC}$ with features, feature agreement and feature disagreement, to be such a logic. Pure concept satisfiability is known to be PSPACE-complete for this logic [11]. Using a reduction of a constrained version of the domino problem, it is proved that satisfiability of $\mathcal{ALCF}$ concepts w.r.t. TBoxes is NEXPTIME-hard. Applying the modification technique from the first part to an existing algorithm, it is shown that it is also in NEXPTIME and hence NEXPTIME-complete.

2 Description Logics

In this section, the description logic $\mathcal{ALCF}$ is introduced (see also [11]). All logics considered in this paper are fragments of $\mathcal{ALCF}$.

Definition 1. *Let N_C, N_R, and N_F be disjoint sets of concept, role, and feature names. A composition $f_1 \cdots f_n$ of features is called a* feature chain. *The set of $\mathcal{ALCF}$ concepts is the smallest set such that*

1. *every concept name is a concept (atomic concepts), and*
2. *if C and D are concepts, R is a role or feature, and u_1 and u_2 are feature chains, then the following expressions are also concepts: $\neg C$, $C \sqcap D$, $C \sqcup D$, $\forall R.C$, $\exists R.C$, $u_1 \downarrow u_2$, and $u_1 \uparrow u_2$.*

Let A be a concept name and C be a concept. Then $A \doteq C$ is a concept definition. *Let $\mathcal{T}$ be a finite set of concept definitions. A concept name A* directly uses *a concept name B in $\mathcal{T}$ if there is a concept definition $A \doteq C$ in $\mathcal{T}$ such that B appears in C. Let* uses *be the transitive closure of "directly uses". $\mathcal{T}$ is called* acyclic *if there is no concept name A such that A uses itself in $\mathcal{T}$. If $\mathcal{T}$ is acyclic, and, furthermore, the left-hand sides of all concept definitions in $\mathcal{T}$ are unique, then $\mathcal{T}$ is called a* TBox.

Let $R_1, \ldots, R_n$ be features or roles. We will use $\forall R_1 \ldots R_n.C$ ($\exists R_1 \ldots R_n.C$) as an abbreviation for $\forall R_1.\forall R_2 \ldots \forall R_n.C$ ($\exists R_1.\exists R_2 \ldots \exists R_n.C$). $\mathcal{ALCF}$ concepts which do not contain features are called $\mathcal{ALC}$ concepts. Next, we define the semantics of the language introduced.

Definition 2. *An* interpretation *$\mathcal{I} = (\Delta_\mathcal{I}, \cdot^\mathcal{I})$ is a pair $(\Delta_\mathcal{I}, \cdot^\mathcal{I})$. $\Delta_\mathcal{I}$ is called the* domain *and $\cdot^\mathcal{I}$ the* interpretation function. *The interpretation function maps*

- *each concept name C to a subset $C^\mathcal{I}$ of $\Delta_\mathcal{I}$,*
- *each role name R to a subset $R^\mathcal{I}$ of $\Delta_\mathcal{I} \times \Delta_\mathcal{I}$, and*
- *each feature name f to a partial function $f^\mathcal{I}$ from $\Delta_\mathcal{I}$ to $\Delta_\mathcal{I}$.*

If $u = f_1 \cdots f_k$ is a feature chain, then $u^{\mathcal{I}}$ is defined as the composition $f_1^{\mathcal{I}} \circ \cdots \circ f_k^{\mathcal{I}}$ of the partial functions $f_1^{\mathcal{I}}, \ldots, f_k^{\mathcal{I}}$. Let the symbols C, D, R, u_1, and u_2 be defined as in Definition 1. The interpretation function can inductively be extended to complex concepts as follows:

$$(C \sqcap D)^{\mathcal{I}} := C^{\mathcal{I}} \cap D^{\mathcal{I}}$$

$$(C \sqcup D)^{\mathcal{I}} := C^{\mathcal{I}} \cup D^{\mathcal{I}}$$

$$(\neg C)^{\mathcal{I}} := \Delta_{\mathcal{I}} \setminus C^{\mathcal{I}}$$

$$(\exists R.C)^{\mathcal{I}} := \{a \in \Delta_{\mathcal{I}} \mid \exists b \in \Delta_{\mathcal{I}} : (a, b) \in R^{\mathcal{I}} \wedge b \in C^{\mathcal{I}}\}$$

$$(\forall R.C)^{\mathcal{I}} := \{a \in \Delta_{\mathcal{I}} \mid \forall b : (a, b) \in R^{\mathcal{I}} \to b \in C^{\mathcal{I}}\}$$

$$(u_1 \downarrow u_2)^{\mathcal{I}} := \{a \in \Delta_{\mathcal{I}} \mid \exists b \in \Delta_{\mathcal{I}} : u_1^{\mathcal{I}}(a) = b \wedge u_2^{\mathcal{I}}(a) = b\}$$

$$(u_1 \uparrow u_2)^{\mathcal{I}} := \{a \in \Delta_{\mathcal{I}} \mid \exists b_1, b_2 \in \Delta_{\mathcal{I}} : b_1 \neq b_2 \wedge$$
$$u_1^{\mathcal{I}}(a) = b_1 \wedge u_2^{\mathcal{I}}(a) = b_2\}$$

An interpretation $\mathcal{I}$ is a model of a TBox $\mathcal{T}$ iff it satisfies $A^{\mathcal{I}} = C^{\mathcal{I}}$ for all concept definitions $A \doteq C$ in $\mathcal{T}$. A concept C subsumes a concept D w.r.t. a TBox $\mathcal{T}$ (written $D \preceq_{\mathcal{T}} C$) iff $D^{\mathcal{I}} \subseteq C^{\mathcal{I}}$ for all models $\mathcal{I}$ of $\mathcal{T}$. A concept C is satisfiable w.r.t. a TBox $\mathcal{T}$ iff there exists a model $\mathcal{I}$ of $\mathcal{T}$ such that $C^{\mathcal{I}} \neq \emptyset$.

Subsumption can be reduced to satisfiability since $D \preceq_{\mathcal{T}} C$ iff the concept $D \sqcap \neg C$ is unsatisfiable w.r.t. $\mathcal{T}$. Satisfiability can be reduced to subsumption since C is unsatisfiable w.r.t. $\mathcal{T}$ iff $C \preceq_{\mathcal{T}} \bot$, where $\bot$ is an abbreviation for $A \sqcap \neg A$.

Sometimes, generalized concept definitions called "general concept inclusions" (GCIs) are considered. A GCI has the form $C \sqsubseteq D$, where both C and D are (possibly complex) concepts. An interpretation $\mathcal{I}$ is a model for a GCI $C \sqsubseteq D$ iff $C^{\mathcal{I}} \subseteq D^{\mathcal{I}}$. TBoxes containing GCIs are called *generalized*. In this paper, we will not admit generalized TBoxes unless explicitly mentioned.

2.1 Extending Completion Algorithms

Most satisfiability algorithms for description logics are so-called *completion algorithms*, which check the satisfiability of concepts by trying to explicitly construct a canonical model. Completion algorithms are described by a rule set and a strategy to apply these rules. The rules operate on constraint systems, i.e., partial descriptions of models. Constraints are comprised of objects, concepts and roles. In the following, we will present a completion algorithm for deciding satisfiability of $\mathcal{ALC}$ concepts w.r.t. the empty TBox which was first described in [17]. We will then show how this algorithm can be modified to handle TBoxes. Both the original algorithm and its extension can be executed in polynomial space. The modification scheme presented is also applicable to a variety of other description logics.

The algorithm requires $\mathcal{ALC}$ concepts to be in negation normal form. A concept is in *negation normal form (NNF)* iff negation occurs only in front of atomic concepts. It is easy to see that any $\mathcal{ALC}$ concept can be converted into an equivalent one in NNF in linear time by exhaustively applying the following rewrite rules:

- $\neg(C \sqcap D) \to (\neg C \sqcup \neg D)$, $\quad \neg(C \sqcup D) \to (\neg C \sqcap \neg D)$, $\quad \neg\neg C \to C$
- $\neg(\exists R.C) \to \forall R.\neg C$, $\quad \neg(\forall R.C) \to \exists R.\neg C$

Definition 3. *Let O_A be a set of object names. For $a, b \in O_A$, an $\mathcal{ALC}$ concept C, and $R \in N_R$, the expressions $a : C$ and $(a, b) : R$ are $\mathcal{ALC}$ constraints. A finite set of constraints S is called an $\mathcal{ALC}$ constraint system. Interpretations can be extended to constraint systems by mapping every object name to an element of Δ_I. The unique name assumption is not imposed, i.e. $a^I = b^I$ may hold even if a and b are distinct object names. An interpretation $\mathcal{I}$ satisfies a constraint*

$$a : C \quad \text{iff} \quad a^I \in C^I, \quad \text{and} \quad (a, b) : R \quad \text{iff} \quad (a^I, b^I) \in R^I.$$

An interpretation is a model *of a constraint system S iff it satisfies all constraints in S.*

To decide the satisfiability of an $\mathcal{ALC}$ concept C in NNF (w.r.t. the empty TBox), the algorithm starts with the constraint system $S_0 := \{a : C\}$ and repeatedly applies completion rules. If a constraint system is found which does not contain a contradiction and to which no completion rule is applicable, then this constraint system has a model, which implies the existence of a model for C w.r.t. the empty TBox. If no such constraint system can be found, C is unsatisfiable. One of the completion rules is nondeterministic, i.e., there is more than one possible outcome of a rule application. Hence, the described completion algorithm is a nondeterministic decision procedure, i.e., it returns *satisfiable* iff there is a way to make the nondeterministic decisions such that a positive result is obtained.

Definition 4. *The following* completion rules *replace a given constraint system S nondeterministically by a constraint system S'. S' is called a* descendant *of S. An object $a \in O_A$ is called* fresh *in S if a is not used in S. In the following, C and D denote concepts, R a role, and a and b object names from O_A.*

$R\sqcap$ *The conjunction rule.*
If $a : C \sqcap D \in S$, $\{a : C, \ a : D\} \not\subseteq S$, then $S' := S \cup \{a : C, \ a : D\}$

$R\sqcup$ *The (nondeterministic) disjunction rule.*
If $a : C \sqcup D \in S, \{a : C, a : D\} \cap S = \emptyset$, then $S' := S \cup \{a : C\}$ $\vee$ $S' := S \cup \{a : D\}$

$R\exists C$ *The exists restriction rule.*
If $a : \exists R.C \in S$, and there is no $b \in O_A$ such that $\{(a, b) : R, \ b : C\} \subseteq S$, then $S' := S \cup \{(a, b) : R, \ b : C\}$ where $b \in O_A$ is fresh in S.

$R\forall C$ *The value restriction rule.*
If $a : \forall R.C \in S$ and there is a $b \in O_A$ such that $(a, b) : R \in S \wedge b : C \notin S$, then $S' := S \cup \{b : C\}$

A constraint system S is called contradictory *iff $\{a : C, a : \neg C\} \subseteq S$ for some*

```
define procedure sat(S)
    while a rule r from {R⊓, R⊔} is applicable to S
        S := apply(S, r)
        if S is contradictory then
            return unsatisfiable
    forall a : ∃R.D ∈ S do
        Let b be an object name from O_A.
        if sat({b : D} ∪ {b : E | a : ∀R.E ∈ S}) = unsatisfiable then
            return unsatisfiable
    return satisfiable
```

Fig. 1. The algorithm for deciding satisfiability of $\mathcal{ALC}$ concepts w.r.t. the empty TBox.

$a \in O_A$ and $C \in N_C$. A constraint system to which no completion rules are applicable is called complete.

Let apply be a function which takes a constraint system S and a completion rule r as argument, applies r once to an arbitrary set of constraints in S matching r's premise and returns the resulting constraint system. The algorithm for deciding satisfiability of $\mathcal{ALC}$ concepts is given in Figure 1. It takes a constraint system $\{x : C\}$ as input and returns satisfiable if C is satisfiable w.r.t. the empty TBox and unsatisfiable otherwise. In order to describe the space requirements of the sat algorithm, a formal notion of the size of concepts is introduced.

Definition 5. For a concept C, the size of C (denoted by $\|C\|$) is defined as the number of symbols (operators, concept and role names) it contains. For a TBox $\mathcal{T}$, the size of $\mathcal{T}$ (denoted by $\|\mathcal{T}\|$) is defined as the sum of the sizes of the right-hand sides of all concept definitions in $\mathcal{T}$. The role depth of a concept C is the nesting depth of exists and value restrictions in C.

In [17], it is proved that the described algorithm is correct and can be executed in polynomial space.[2] The latter is a consequence of the following facts:

- The recursion depth of sat is bounded by the role depth.
- In each recursion step, the constraints in the constraint system S involve a single object, only. For each object, there can be at most $\mathcal{O}(\|C\|)$ constraints. The size of each constraint is bounded by $\|C\|$.

As already argued in the introduction, using unfolding to generalize sat to TBoxes is not a good choice since the space requirements of the resulting algorithm would no longer be polynomial. However, there exists a better strategy for dealing with TBoxes, which is described in the following.

In order to allow for a succinct definition of the extended algorithm, we need to introduce a special form of TBoxes.

---

[2] Schmidt-Schauß and Smolka present the algorithm in a different form. In the form presented here, the algorithm first appeared in [4].

Definition 6. *A TBox T is called* simple *iff it satisfies the following requirements:*

- *The right-hand side of each concept definition in T contains exactly one operator.*
- *If the right hand side of a concept definition in T is $\neg A$, then A does not occur on the left hand side of any concept definition in T.*

The following lemma shows that restricting ourselves to simple TBoxes is not a limitation.

Lemma 1. *Any TBox T can be converted into a simple one T' in linear time, such that T' is equivalent to T in the following sense: Any model for T' can be extended to a model for T and vice versa.*

Proof: The conversion can be done in three steps as follows.

1. *eliminate non-atomic negation.* (i) convert the right-hand sides of all concept definitions in T to NNF. (ii) For each definition $A \doteq C$ in T, add a new definition $\overline{A} \doteq nnf(\neg C)$, where $nnf(\neg C)$ denotes the result of converting $\neg C$ to NNF. (iii) For every atomic concept A occurring on the left-hand side of a concept definition in T, replace every occurrence of $\neg A$ in T with $\overline{A}$.
2. *break up concepts.* Exhaustively apply the following rewrite rules. In the following, C denotes a non-atomic concept and D an arbitrary concept.
   - $A \doteq C \sqcap D \;\rightarrow\; A \doteq A' \sqcap D,\ A' \doteq C$ (and analogous for $\sqcup$)
   - $A \doteq D \sqcap C \;\rightarrow\; A \doteq D \sqcap A',\ A' \doteq C$ (and analogous for $\sqcup$)
   - $A \doteq \exists R.C \;\rightarrow\; A \doteq \exists R.A',\ A' \doteq C$ (and analogous for $\forall$)
   In all cases, A' is a concept name not yet used in T. Please note that if a definition $A \doteq \neg C$ is in T, then, due to the first step, C is atomic and does not occur on the left-hand side of a concept definition.
3. *eliminate redundant names.* For each concept definition $A \doteq A'$, where both A and A' are atomic, replace every occurrence of A' in T with A. Remove the definition from T.

The correctness of the above procedure is easily seen. The loosened form of equivalence is necessary since T' contains additional atomic concepts, and, furthermore, some "redundant" atomic concepts from T may not exist in T'. Let T be a TBox and T' be the result of applying the above procedure. The first step can be performed in linear time since NNF conversion needs linear time and the number of concept definitions is at most doubled. Since the number of rewrite rule applications in the second step is bounded by the number of operators in T, this step can also be performed in linear time. This obviously also holds for the third step. □

From the above result, it immediately follows that, for any TBox T, there exists an equivalent simple one T' such that $\|T'\|$ is of order $\mathcal{O}(\|T\|)$. We will now modify the sat algorithm to decide the satisfiability of an atomic concept A w.r.t. a simple TBox T. Using the modified algorithm, it is also possible to decide the satisfiability of non-atomic concepts C w.r.t. TBoxes T: Add a definition $A \doteq C$ to $\mathcal{T}$ (where A is a new concept name in $\mathcal{T}$), convert the resulting TBox to simple form and start the algorithm with $(A, \mathcal{T}')$ where $\mathcal{T}'$ is the newly obtained TBox. The modified algorithm works on constraint systems of a restricted form. In constraints of the form $a : C$, C must be a concept name (which may be the left-hand side of a concept definition in $\mathcal{T}$).

Definition 7. *Let A be an atomic concept and $\mathcal{T}$ be a simple $\mathcal{ALC}$ TBox. Making use of the existing sat algorithm, an algorithm tbsat, which returns satisfiable if A is satisfiable w.r.t. $\mathcal{T}$ and unsatisfiable otherwise, is given as follows.*

1. *Modify the completion rules of sat as follows: In the premise of each completion rule, substitute "$a : C \in S$" by "$a : A \in S$ and $A \doteq C \in \mathcal{T}$". E.g., in the conjunction rule, "$a : C \sqcap D \in S$" is replaced by "$a : A \in S$ and $A \doteq C \sqcap D \in \mathcal{T}$".*
2. *Start the sat algorithm with the initial constraint system $\{x : A\}$, where x is an arbitrary object name. Use the modified rules for the sat run.*

Unlike unfolding, the described algorithm has the advantage that it can be executed in polynomial space.

Proposition 1. *The tbsat algorithm is sound and complete and can be executed in polynomial space.*

Proof: Let $(A, \mathcal{T})$ be an input to tbsat and let C be the result of unfolding A w.r.t. $\mathcal{T}$. Please note that C is in NNF since $\mathcal{T}$ is in simple form. The correctness of tbsat can be proved by showing that a run of tbsat on input $(A, \mathcal{T})$ yields the same result as a run of sat on input C. This, in turn, can be proved by induction over the number of recursion steps. It is important to note that, at every point in the computation where a nondeterministic decision has to be made (deciding which rule to apply or deciding which consequence of the R⊔ rule to use), the available choices are exactly the same for both algorithms.

It is an immediate consequence of the following facts that the tbsat algorithm can be executed in polynomial space.

- The recursion depth of tbsat is bounded by $\|\mathcal{T}\|$. This is the case since (i) runs of tbsat on $(A, \mathcal{T})$ are equivalent to runs of sat on C and (ii) the role depth of C is bounded by $\|\mathcal{T}\|$.[3] The second point can be seen as follows: Assume that the role depth of C exceeds $\|\mathcal{T}\|$. This means that the right hand side of a concept definition $A' \doteq \exists R.D$ or $A' \doteq \forall R.D$ in $\mathcal{T}$ contributes to the role depth more than once. From this, however, it follows that unfolding D w.r.t. $\mathcal{T}$ yields a concept containing A' which is a contradiction to the acyclicity of $\mathcal{T}$.
- In each recursion step, the constraints in the constraint system S involve a single object, only. The number of constraints per object is bounded by the number of definitions in $\mathcal{T}$ and the maximum size of constraints is constant.

□

---

[3] I.e., although unfolding may lead to an exponential blow-up in concept size [15], the role depth is "preserved".

The following theorem is an immediate consequence of the above result.

Theorem 1. *Deciding satisfiability of $\mathcal{ALC}$ concepts w.r.t. acyclic TBoxes is* PSPACE-*complete.*

The use of the presented modification scheme is not limited to $\mathcal{ALC}$. In order to give an intuition of when the proposed modification can be applied to yield a PSPACE algorithm, let us summarize why the modification is successful in the case of $\mathcal{ALC}$. As a prerequisite, a completion algorithms is needed which uses tracing, i.e., which performs depth-first search over role successors. In the case of $\mathcal{ALC}$, the recursion depth of this algorithm is bounded by the role depth of the input concept C. As opposed to the concept size, the role depth is "preserved by unfolding", i.e., if a concept C is unfolded w.r.t. a TBox $\mathcal{T}$, then the role depth of the unfolded concept C' is linear in $||C|| + ||\mathcal{T}||$. This fact is used to argue that the recursion depth of the modified algorithm is linear in the size of its input.

The other important point in the proof of Proposition 1 is that the $\mathcal{ALC}$ tracing algorithm considers constraints for only one object per recursion step and so does the modified algorithm. What is important here is, again, that the number of objects considered in a single recursion step is describable by a function which is "preserved by unfolding" (the constant 1 in the case of $\mathcal{ALC}$).

For a formalization of "preservation by unfolding", the notion of a u-stable function (where "u" stands for unfolding) is introduced. A function f mapping concepts to natural numbers is called *u-stable* w.r.t. a description logic $\mathcal{L}$ iff the following holds: There exists an integer k such that, for all atomic concepts A and all $\mathcal{L}$ TBoxes $\mathcal{T}$, if C is the result of unfolding A w.r.t. $\mathcal{T}$, then $f(C)$ is of order $\mathcal{O}(||\mathcal{T}||^k)$. As was shown in the proof of Proposition 1, the role-depth of concepts is an example for a u-stable function. An example for a function which is not u-stable is the size of concepts (as Nebel proved [15]). A rule of thumb can now be formulated as follows:

> *The described modification can be applied to completion algorithms $\mathcal{A}$ which decide satisfiability for a logic $\mathcal{L}$ w.r.t. the empty TBox. Assume that $\mathcal{A}$ performs depth-first search over role-successors and can be executed in polynomial space. If $\mathcal{A}$ expands the constraints of $\alpha(C)$ objects per recursion step and $\mathcal{A}$'s recursion depth is bounded by $\beta(C)$, where C is the input concept and α and β are functions which are u-stable w.r.t. $\mathcal{L}$, then the modified algorithm can be expected to be executable in polynomial space.*

This rule of thumb can, e.g., be applied to the description logic $\mathcal{ALCNR}$ (see [9]). $\mathcal{ALCNR}$ extends $\mathcal{ALC}$ by (unqualified) number restrictions[4] and role conjunction.

Conjecture. *Deciding the satisfiability of $\mathcal{ALCNR}$ concept w.r.t. TBoxes is a* PSPACE-*complete problem.*

---

[4] We follow Donini et al. and assume unary coding of numbers.

Why is the rule of thumb applicable to $\mathcal{ALCNR}$? Donini et al. [9] give a PSPACE algorithm for deciding satisfiability of $\mathcal{ALCNR}$ concepts w.r.t. empty TBoxes which performs depth-first search over role successors. Its recursion depth is bounded by the role depth of the input concept C. In each recursion step, constraints for at most $ex(C) + 1$ objects are expanded where $ex(C)$ is the number of *distinct* existentially quantified subconcepts of C. It is easy to prove that $ex(\cdot)$ is a u-stable function. Assume that C is the result of unfolding an atomic concept A w.r.t. a TBox $\mathcal{T}$ and that $ex(C) \geq \|\mathcal{T}\|$. It follows that there exists a concept definition $B_0 \doteq \exists R.B_1$ in $\mathcal{T}$ such that B_0 uses an atomic concept B_2 (where possibly $B_1 = B_2$) and that B_2 can be replaced by *different* concepts during unfolding. This, however, is a contradiction to the definition of TBoxes, since the uniqueness of left-hand sides of concept definitions is mandatory.

3 $\mathcal{ALCF}$ and TBoxes: The Lower Bound

Given the modification scheme for satisfiability algorithms described in the previous section, it is a natural question to ask if there are any relevant description logics for which reasoning w.r.t. the empty TBox is in PSPACE but reasoning w.r.t. TBoxes is not. In the following, we will answer this question to the affirmative by showing that the hardness of reasoning with the logic $\mathcal{ALCF}$ [11] moves from PSPACE to NEXPTIME if TBoxes are admitted.

A domino problem is given by a finite set of *tile types*. All tile types are of the same size, each type has a quadratic shape and colored edges. Of each type, an unlimited number of tiles is available. The problem is to arrange these tiles to cover a torus[5] of exponential size without holes or overlapping, such that adjacent tiles have identical colors on their common edge (rotation of the tiles is not allowed). Please note that this is a restricted version of the (undecidable) general domino problem where a tiling of the first quadrant of the plane is asked for.

Definition 8. *Let $\mathcal{D} = (D, H, V)$ be a domino system, where D is a finite set of tile types and $H, V \subseteq D \times D$. Let $U(s,t)$ be the torus $\mathbb{Z}_s \times \mathbb{Z}_t$, where $\mathbb{Z}_n$ denotes the set $\{0, \ldots, n-1\}$. Let $w = w_0, \ldots, w_{n-1}$ be an n-tuple of tiles (with $n \leq s$). We say that $\mathcal{D}$ tiles $U(s,t)$ with initial condition w iff there exists a mapping $\tau : U(s,t) \to D$ such that for all $(x,y) \in U(s,t)$:*

- *if $\tau(x,y) = d$ and $\tau(x \oplus_s 1, y) = d'$ then $(d, d') \in H$*
- *if $\tau(x,y) = d$ and $\tau(x, y \oplus_t 1) = d'$ then $(d, d') \in V$*
- *$\tau(i,0) = w_i$ for $0 \leq i < n$.*

where $\oplus_n$ denotes addition modulo n.

Börger et al. show that it is NEXPTIME-complete to decide if, for a given domino system $\mathcal{D}$ and a given n-tuple w, $\mathcal{D}$ tiles $U(2^n, 2^n)$ with initial condition w [6]. In the following, we will reduce this domino problem to satisfiability of $\mathcal{ALCF}$ concepts w.r.t. TBoxes. We will first give an informal explanation of

---

[5] i.e., a rectangular grid whose edges are "glued" together

$$Tree_0 \doteq \beta^n \gamma \downarrow \alpha^n \sqcap$$
$$\exists \alpha. Tree_1 \sqcap \exists \beta. Tree_1$$
$$\sqcap \alpha \beta^{n-1} \gamma \downarrow \beta \alpha^{n-1}$$
$$Tree_1 \doteq \exists \alpha. Tree_2 \sqcap \exists \beta. Tree_2$$
$$\sqcap \alpha \beta^{n-2} \gamma \downarrow \beta \alpha^{n-2}$$
$$\vdots$$
$$Tree_{n-1} \doteq \exists \alpha. Tree_n \sqcap \exists \beta. Tree_n$$
$$\sqcap \alpha \gamma \downarrow \beta$$
$$Tree_n \doteq Grid_n$$

Fig. 2. The $\mathcal{ALCF}$ reduction TBox $\mathcal{T}[\mathcal{D}, w, n]$: Tree definition. Substitute (α, β, γ) by (f, g, y) or (u, v, x).

how the reduction works and then formally prove its correctness. For the sake of readability, the reduction TBox $\mathcal{T}[\mathcal{D}, w, n]$ is split into two figures. Models of the reduction TBox represent solutions of instances of the domino problem. To be more precise, models of C w.r.t. $\mathcal{T}[\mathcal{D}, w, n]$ (Figure 3) encode a grid of size 2^n which has the form of a torus and is properly tiled by $\mathcal{D}$. The nodes of the grid are represented by domain objects, horizontal edges are represented by the feature x and vertical edges by the feature y. Please note that the grid may "collapse", i.e., the $2^n \times 2^n$ nodes are not necessarily distinct. Nevertheless, models of C w.r.t. $\mathcal{T}[\mathcal{D}, w, n]$ define a tiling of the full $2^n \times 2^n$ torus.

The first task is to enforce two cyclic feature chains of length 2^n, which will be edges of the grid. This is done by defining a binary tree of depth n whose leaf nodes are connected by a cyclic feature chain. The corresponding concept $Tree_0$ can be found in Figure 2. Please note that since two trees are needed, the TBox in the Figure has to be instantiated twice, where (α, β, γ) is substituted by (f, g, y) and (u, v, x), respectively. The first instantiation yields a y chain (of length 2^n) and the second one an x chain.

Consider the concept C in Figure 3, which glues together all the necessary building parts. It refers to the $Tree_0$ concept to build up two trees and it enforces the identification of the "beginning" nodes in the two (cyclic) leaf chains. The next task is to build the remaing grid which is done by the $Grid_i$ concepts in Figure 3. The features $d_1, \ldots, d_n$ are diagonals in the grid (each d_i spans 2^{i-1} "grid cells") and play a central rôle in the grid definition. The use of these diagonals allows the definition of the (exponentially sized) grid by a TBox of polynomial size. First observe that each object on the two cyclic feature chains (row 0 and column 0 of the torus to be defined) is in the extension of $Grid_n$ and hence also of $Grid_0$. Because of this, each object on the chains has d_1, x, and y fillers such that the d_1 filler coincides with the xy and yx filler. Together with the cyclicity of the initial feature chains, this properly defines row 1 and

$$Grid_0 \doteq xy{\downarrow}yx \sqcap xy{\downarrow}d_1 \sqcap Tile$$
$$Grid_1 \doteq Grid_0 \sqcap d_1 d_1{\downarrow}d_2 \sqcap \exists d_1.Grid_0$$

$$\vdots$$

$$Grid_{n-1} \doteq Grid_{n-2} \sqcap d_{n-1} d_{n-1}{\downarrow}d_n \sqcap \exists d_{n-1}.Grid_{n-2}$$
$$Grid_n \doteq Grid_{n-1} \sqcap \exists d_n.Grid_{n-1}$$

$$Tile \doteq \bigsqcup_{d\in\mathcal{D}} D_d \sqcap \prod_{d\in\mathcal{D}} \prod_{d'\in\mathcal{D}\setminus\{d\}} \neg(D_d \sqcap D_{d'})$$
$$\prod_{d\in\mathcal{D}}(D_d \to \exists x.\bigsqcup_{(d,d')\in H} D_{d'})$$
$$\prod_{d\in\mathcal{D}}(D_d \to \exists y.\bigsqcup_{(d,d')\in V} D_{d'})$$

$$Init \doteq \exists u^n.(D_{w_0} \sqcap \exists x.(D_{w_1} \sqcap \ldots \sqcap \exists x.(D_{w_{n-2}} \sqcap \exists x.D_{w_{n-1}})\ldots))$$

$$C \doteq Tree_0(f,g,y) \sqcap Tree_0(u,v,x) \sqcap f^n{\downarrow}u^n \sqcap Init$$

Fig. 3. The $\mathcal{ALCF}$ reduction TBox $\mathcal{T}[\mathcal{D}, w, n]$: Grid definition and tiling.

column 1 of the torus. Since the objects on the initial chains are in the extension of $Grid_1$, the objects on row 1 and column 1, which are d_1 fillers of objects on the initial chains, are in the extension of $Grid_0$. Hence, we can repeat the argument for row/column 1 and conclude the proper definition of row/column 2. Now observe that the objects on row/column 2 are d_2 fillers of the objects on the initial chain. Hence, they are in the extension of both the $Grid_0$ and $Grid_1$ concept and we can repeat the entire argument from above to derive the existence of rows/columns 3 and 4. This "doubling" can be repeated n times because of the existence of the features $d_1,\ldots,d_n$ and yields rows/columns $0,\ldots,2^n$ of the torus. The cyclicity of the initial feature chains ensures that the edges of the grid are properly "glued" to form a torus, i.e., that row/column 2^n coincides with row/column 0. Figure 4 shows a clipping from a grid as enforced by the reduction TBox.

The grid represents the structure to be tiled. The final task is to define the tiling itself. Domino types are represented by atomic concepts D_d. Because of the definition of $Grid_0$, each node in the grid is in the extension of the concept $Tile$. The $Tile$ concept ensures that, horizontally as well as vertically, the tiling condition is satisfied (we use $C \to D$ as an abbreviation for $\neg C \sqcup D$). The $Init$ concept enforces the initial condition w. In the following, a formal proof of the correctness of the reduction is given.

Proposition 2. *Satisfiability and subsumption of $\mathcal{ALCF}$ concepts w.r.t. TBoxes is NExpTime-hard.*

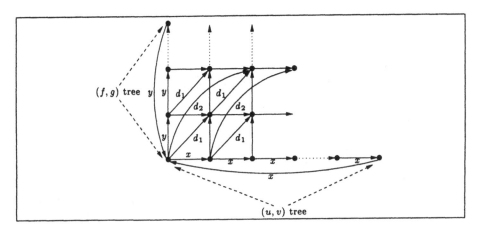

Fig. 4. Clipping of a model of the reduction concept C.

Proof:

($\Rightarrow$) Let $\mathcal{I}$ be a model of C w.r.t. $\mathcal{T}[\mathcal{D}, w, n]$. To prove that $\mathcal{D}$ tiles $U(2^n, 2^n)$ with initial condition w, it needs to be shown that there is a mapping τ as introduced in Definition 8.

As argued above, there exist $2^n \times 2^n$ (not necessarily distinct) objects $a_{i,j}$ in $\Delta_{\mathcal{I}}$ which form a torus w.r.t. the features x and y, i.e., $x^{\mathcal{I}}(a_{i,j}) = a_{(i \oplus_{2^n} 1), j}$ and $y^{\mathcal{I}}(a_{i,j}) = a_{i, (j \oplus_{2^n} 1)}$. All objects in the torus are in the extension of the *Tile* concept. This concept encodes the properties required for τ in Definition 8. Hence, τ can be defined as follows: $\tau := \{(i, j, d) \mid a_{i,j} \in D_d\}$. This function is well-defined since the *Tile* concept ensures that none of the $a_{i,j}$ is in the extension of two concepts D_d and $D_{d'}$, where $d \neq d'$.

($\Leftarrow$) Assume that the domino system $\mathcal{D}$ tiles $U(2^n, 2^n)$ with initial condition w (which is of length n). This means that there exists a mapping τ as defined in Definition 8. In the following, we define a model for C w.r.t. $\mathcal{T}[\mathcal{D}, w, n]$. The model has the form as discussed above: There are two binary trees of depth n whose leaf nodes are connected by a feature chain. These two chains of length 2^n are edges of a grid of size $2^n \times 2^n$. The edges of the grid are "glued" together. Let the interpretation $\mathcal{I}$ be defined as follows:

$$\Delta_{\mathcal{I}} = \{a_{i,j} \mid 0 \leq i,j < 2^n\} \cup \{b_{i,j}, c_{i,j} \mid 0 \leq i < n, 0 \leq j < 2^i\}$$

$$f^{\mathcal{I}}(b_{0,0}) := b_{1,0}, \quad g^{\mathcal{I}}(b_{0,0}) := b_{1,1}, \quad u^{\mathcal{I}}(b_{0,0}) := c_{1,0}, \quad v^{\mathcal{I}}(b_{0,0}) := c_{1,1}$$
$$\forall i, j \text{ where } 0 < i < n-1, \ 0 \leq j < 2^i :$$
$$f^{\mathcal{I}}(b_{i,j}) := b_{(i+1),(2j)}, \quad g^{\mathcal{I}}(b_{i,j}) := b_{(i+1),(2j+1)},$$
$$u^{\mathcal{I}}(c_{i,j}) := c_{(i+1),(2j)}, \quad v^{\mathcal{I}}(c_{i,j}) := c_{(i+1),(2j+1)}$$

$$\forall 0 \leq i < 2^{n-1} :$$
$$f^{\mathcal{I}}(b_{(n-1),i}) := a_{0,(2i)}, \quad g^{\mathcal{I}}(b_{(n-1),i}) := a_{0,(2i+1)},$$
$$u^{\mathcal{I}}(c_{(n-1),i}) := a_{(2i),0}, \quad v^{\mathcal{I}}(c_{(n-1),i}) := a_{(2i+1),0}$$

$$\forall 0 \leq i,j < 2^n : x^{\mathcal{I}}(a_{i,j}) := a_{(i \oplus_{2^n} 1),j}, \quad y^{\mathcal{I}}(a_{i,j}) := a_{i,(j \oplus_{2^n} 1)}$$
$$\forall 0 \leq i,j < 2^n, 1 \leq k \leq n : d_k^{\mathcal{I}}(a_{i,j}) := a_{(i \oplus_{2^n} 2^{k-1}),(j \oplus_{2^n} 2^{k-1})}$$
$$\forall d \in D : D_d^{\mathcal{I}} := \{a_{x,y} \mid \tau(x,y) = d\}$$

It is straightforward to verify that $\mathcal{I}$ is in fact a model for C w.r.t. $\mathcal{T}[\mathcal{D},w,n]$: The $b_{i,j}$ objects form a tree of depth n where edges are labelled with f and g. The n-th level of the tree consists of the objects $a_{0,0},\ldots,a_{0,2^n}$. Similarly, the $c_{i,j}$ objects form a u,v-tree where the n-th level consists of the objects $a_{0,0},\ldots,a_{2^n,0}$ and the root is the object $b_{0,0}$. The $a_{i,j}$ objects make up a grid w.r.t. the features x and y (and diagonals d_i) which satisfies the *Tile* concept since the extension of the D_d concepts is defined through the tiling τ. Hence, it can be concluded that the object $b_{0,0}$ is an instance of C w.r.t. $\mathcal{T}[\mathcal{D},w,n]$.

It is easy to verify that the size of $\mathcal{T}[\mathcal{D},w,n]$ is of order $\mathcal{O}(n^2)$. Hence, the reduction can be performed in polynomial time. □

In contrast to agreements on roles (called "role value maps"), agreements on features are frequently believed to "not harm" w.r.t. decidability and complexity. The presented reduction indicates that this is not always the case. Furthermore, if TBoxes are extended with GCIs, the given reduction can easily be extended to an undecidability proof. Consider the following TBox:

$$D \doteq \top$$
$$\top \sqsubseteq xy{\downarrow}yx$$
$$\top \sqsubseteq Tile$$

where *Tile* is defined as in Figure 3. It induces a (possibly) infinite grid and satisfiability of D implies a complete tiling of the first quadrant.[6] Hence, decidability of $\mathcal{ALCF}$ with GCIs contradicts the undecidability of the general domino problem. For the reduction TBox, only the operators atomic negation, conjunction, disjunction, feature agreement and existential quantification over features is required. The result just obtained is already known in feature logic (see [2, Theorem 6.3], where it was proved by a reduction of the word problem for finitely presented groups).

4 $\mathcal{ALCF}$ and TBoxes: The Upper Bound

In order to prove that the satisfiability of $\mathcal{ALCF}$ concepts w.r.t. TBoxes is a NExpTime-complete problem, it remains to be shown that the satisfiability of $\mathcal{ALCF}$ concepts w.r.t. TBoxes can be decided in nondeterministic exponential time.

---

[6] The induced grid may also have the form of a torus since we don't enforce distinct nodes. In this case, however, a tiling of the torus induces a periodic tiling of the first quadrant.

In [14], a completion algorithm for deciding satisfiability of $\mathcal{ALCF(D)}$ concepts w.r.t. empty TBoxes is given which can be executed in polynomial space. $\mathcal{ALCF(D)}$ is the extension of $\mathcal{ALCF}$ by so-called concrete domains. By removing the completion rules and clash conditions dealing with the concrete domain, we will adapt this algorithm to $\mathcal{ALCF}$. Furthermore, we will show that an extension of the obtained algorithm to TBoxes as described in Section 2.1 can be executed in exponential time. The algorithm operates on constraint systems of the following form.

Definition 9. *Let f be a feature and a and b elements of O_A. Then, the following expressions are $\mathcal{ALCF}$ constraints:*

$$\text{All } \mathcal{ALC} \text{ constraints}, \quad (a,b){:}f, \quad a \neq b$$

A finite set of $\mathcal{ALCF}$ constraints is called an $\mathcal{ALCF}$ constraint system. An interpretation for $\mathcal{ALCF}$ constraint systems is defined identically to interpretations for $\mathcal{ALC}$ constraint systems. An interpretation satisfies a constraint

$$(a,b){:}f \quad \text{iff} \quad (a^{\mathcal{I}}, b^{\mathcal{I}}) \in f^{\mathcal{I}} \text{ and}$$
$$a \neq b \quad \text{iff} \quad a^{\mathcal{I}} \neq b^{\mathcal{I}}.$$

A constraint system S is said to contain a *fork* (for a feature f) if it contains the two constraints $(a,b){:}f$ and $(a,c){:}f$. A fork can be *eliminated* by replacing all occurrences of c in S with b. During rule application, it is assumed that forks are eliminated as soon as they appear (as an integral part of the rule application) with the proviso that newly generated object are replaced by older ones.

Before the algorithm itself is described, we introduce the set of completion rules. In order to provide a succinct description of the rules, two auxiliary functions need to be defined. For an object $a \in O_A$ and a feature chain u, $succ_S(a, u)$ denotes the object b that can be found by following u starting from a in S. If no such object exists, $succ_S(a, u)$ denotes the special object ϵ that cannot be part of any constraint system. Let $a, b \in O_A$ and $u = f_1 \cdots f_k$ be a feature chain. The function *chain* is defined as follows:

$$chain_S(a, b, u) := \{(a, c_1){:}f_1, \ldots, (c_{k-1}, b){:}f_k\}$$
$$\text{where the } c_1, \ldots, c_{k-1} \in O_A \text{ are distinct and fresh in } S.$$

We now give the completion rules for the algorithm.

Definition 10. *The following completion rules replace a given constraint system S nondeterministically by a constraint system S'. In the following, C denotes a concepts, $\hat{R}$ a role, f a feature, u_1 and u_2 feature chains, and a and b object names from O_A.*

R$\sqcap$, R$\sqcup$ As in Definition 4

R$r\exists C$ The role exists restriction rule.
If $a{:}\exists \hat{R}.C \in S$ and there is no $b \in O_A$ such that $\{(a,b){:}\hat{R}, b{:}C\} \subseteq S$
Then $S' := S \cup \{(a,b){:}\hat{R}, b{:}C\}$ where $b \in O_A$ is fresh in S.

Rf∃C The feature exists restriction rule (may create forks).
If $a:\exists f.C \in S$ and there is no $b \in O_A$ such that $\{(a,b):f,\ b:C\} \subseteq S$
Then $S' := S \cup \{(a,b):f,\ b:C\}$ where $b \in O_A$ is fresh in S.

Rr∀C The role value restriction rule.
If $a:\forall \hat{R}.C \in S$ and there is a $b \in O_A$ such that $(a,b):\hat{R} \in S \wedge b:C \notin S$
Then $S' := S \cup \{b:C\}$

Rf∀C The feature value restriction rule.
If $a:\forall f.C \in S$ and there is a $b \in O_A$ such that $(a,b):f \in S \wedge b:C \notin S$
Then $S' := S \cup \{b:C\}$

R↓ The agreement rule (may create forks).
If $a:u_1{\downarrow}u_2 \in S$, there is no $b \in O_A$ such that $succ_S(a,u_1) = succ_S(a,u_2) = b$
Then $S_0 := S \cup chain_S(a,b,u_1)$ where $b \in O_A$ is fresh in S.
$\quad\quad S' := S_0 \cup chain_{S_0}(a,b,u_2)$

R↑ The disagreement rule (may create forks).
If $a:u_1{\uparrow}u_2 \in S$ and there are no $b_1, b_2 \in O_A$ such that
$$succ_S(a,u_1) = b_1, succ_S(a,u_2) = b_2 \text{ and } b_1 \neq b_2 \in S$$
Then $S_0 := S \cup chain_S(a,b_1,u_1)$ and $S' := S_0 \cup chain_{S_0}(a,b_2,u_2) \cup \{b_1 \neq b_2\}$
$\quad\quad$ where $b_1, b_2 \in O_A$ are distinct and fresh in S.

An $\mathcal{ALCF}$ constraint system S is called contradictory *iff* any of the following *clash triggers* apply:

– Primitive clash: $a:C \in S$, $a:\neg C \in S$
– Agreement clash: $a \neq a \in S$

The algorithm expects the input concept C to be in negation normal form. Conversion to NNF can be done in linear time by applying the rules given in Section 2.1 together with the following rules:

– $\neg(u_1{\downarrow}u_2) \to \forall u_1.\bot \sqcup \forall u_2.\bot \sqcup u_1{\uparrow}u_2$
– $\neg(u_1{\uparrow}u_2) \to \forall u_1.\bot \sqcup \forall u_2.\bot \sqcup u_1{\downarrow}u_2$

We are now ready to give the satisfiability algorithm itself.

Definition 11. *The function* sat *decides the satisfiability of $\mathcal{ALCF}$ concepts in NNF w.r.t. the empty TBox. To decide the satisfiability of the concept C,* sat *takes the input $\{x:C\}$.*

define procedure sat(S)
$\quad\quad S' :=$ feature-complete(S)
$\quad\quad$ **if** S' *contains a clash* **then**
$\quad\quad\quad\quad$ **return** *inconsistent*
$\quad\quad$ **forall** $a:\exists \hat{R}.D \in S'$, where $\hat{R}$ is a role, **do**
$\quad\quad\quad\quad$ Let b be an object name from O_A.
$\quad\quad\quad\quad$ **if** sat($\{b:D\} \cup \{b:E \mid a:\forall \hat{R}.E \in S'\}$) = *inconsistent* **then**
$\quad\quad\quad\quad\quad\quad$ **return** *inconsistent*
$\quad\quad$ **return** *consistent*

define procedure feature-complete(S)
      while *a rule* r *from* $\{R\sqcap, R\sqcup, R\exists C, R\forall C, R\downarrow, R\uparrow\}$ *is applicable to* S **do**
          $S := apply(S, r)$
    return S

The correctness of the described algorithm can be easily seen: It corresponds to the algorithm given in [14] for deciding satisfiability of $\mathcal{ALCF}(\mathcal{D})$ concepts with all rules and clash triggers concerning the concrete part left out. Since the original algorithm is correct for $\mathcal{ALCF}(\mathcal{D})$, it is obviously also correct for $\mathcal{ALCF}$. Furthermore, it can easily be verified that, if the original algorithm is started on an $\mathcal{ALCF}$ concept, no concrete domain operators or "concrete objects" are introduced during the algorithm run, and, hence, neither concrete domain related completion rules nor concrete domain related clash rules apply. Thus, they can savely be left away.

Proposition 3. *The* sat *algorithm is sound, complete, and terminates.*

We now investigate the extension of sat to TBoxes as described in Section 2.1. The extended algorithm is called tbsat and takes a pair $(A, \mathcal{T})$ as input, where A is an atomic concept and $\mathcal{T}$ is an $\mathcal{ALCF}$ TBox in simple form. tbsat is also capable of deciding satisfiability of non-atomic concepts w.r.t. TBoxes (see Section 2.1). The correctness of tbsat follows from the correctness of the original algorithm and the fact that a run of tbsat on $(A, \mathcal{T})$ is equivalent to a run of sat on C, where C is the result of unfolding A w.r.t. $\mathcal{T}$ (see Section 2.1). It remains to determine the runtime of the extended algorithm.

Proposition 4. *The algorithm* tbsat *can be executed in exponential time.*

Proof: Let $(A, \mathcal{T})$ be an input to tbsat. Let n denote $\|\mathcal{T}\|$. It needs to be shown that the number of rule applications performed by tbsat is exponential in n. This is a consequence of the next two claims, since each completion rule can be applied at most once per constraint (for the R$\forall$C rule, this holds for the $(a, b) : R$ constraints) and constraints are never removed.

1. Let ρ be the number of objects created during a tbsat run. ρ is exponential in n.
2. For each objects a, there may exist at most exponentially many constraints which refer to a.

In the following, we can savely ignore constraints of the form $a \neq b$ since they do not appear in the premise of any completion rule.

    The validity of claim 1 can be seen as follows: The recursion depth of tbsat is bounded by n since the recursion depth of sat is bounded by the role depth of its input (same argument as in the proof of Proposition 1). In each recursion step, at most n recursive calls are made. Hence, by (implicit) application of the Rr$\exists$C rule, at most $n^n = 2^{n*log(n)} \leq 2^{n^2}$ objects are generated. For each such object, the feature-complete function is called which may generate new objects by application of the Rf∃C, R↓, and R↑ rules. feature-complete generates a structure which has the form of a tree in which some nodes may coincide. Outdegree and depth of this tree-like structure are bounded by n: The outdegree is bounded by the number of distinct features in $\mathcal{T}$ since there may be at most one successor per feature; the depth of the structure is bounded by n since in sat runs, its depth is bounded by the role depth (see again the argument in the proof of Proposition 1). Hence, the total number of objects generated is bounded by $2^{n^2} * 2^{n^2}$ which is obviously exponential in n.

Concerning point 2, fix an object a in a constraint system S considered by tbsat. It is easy to see that there may be at most n constraints of the form $a : C$—one for each concept definition in $\mathcal{T}$. Furthermore, there may be at most n constraints of the form $(a, a') : f$, since there cannot be more than one filler per feature (please note that constraints $(a, a') : R$ are never explicitly created). There may, however, be n constraints $(a', a) : f$ per object a'. Since the number of objects is exponentially bounded (point 1), the number of $(a', a) : f$ constraints is also exponentially bounded.   □

Combining Propositions 2 and 4, we obtain the following result.

Theorem 2. *Deciding the satisfiability of $\mathcal{ALCF}$ concepts w.r.t. acyclic TBoxes is* NExpTime-*complete.*

5 Conclusion

TBoxes are an important component of knowledge representation systems using description logics. However, for most DLs, the exact complexity of reasoning with acyclic TBoxes has never been determinded. This paper concentrates on logics for which satisfiability w.r.t. the empty TBox is in PSpace and investigates how the presence of acyclic TBoxes influences the complexity of reasoning. In the first part of the paper, using the logic $\mathcal{ALC}$, it is demonstrated how completion algorithms for deciding "pure" concept satisfiability can be modified to take into account TBoxes such that the resulting algorithm can still be executed in polynomial space. Using the modified algorithm, it is proved that, for $\mathcal{ALC}$, satisfiability w.r.t. acyclic TBoxes is in PSpace. We claim that the given modification scheme can be applied to a variety of other description logics, too, and give a rule of thumb for when the resulting algorithm can be executed in polynomial space.

In the second part, it is proved that, for the logic $\mathcal{ALCF}$, satisfiability w.r.t. acyclic TBoxes is NExpTime-complete. In contrast, satisfiability of "pure" $\mathcal{ALCF}$ concepts is known to be PSpace-complete and the satisfiability of $\mathcal{ALCF}$ concepts w.r.t. general TBoxes is known to be undecidable. It is suprising that the complexity of reasoning moves up *several* steps in the complexity hierarchy if TBoxes are added. $\mathcal{ALCF}$ is a common description logic appearing as a fragment of several more expressive DLs such as, e.g., the temporal logic $\mathcal{TL\text{-}ALCF}$ [1] or the logic $\mathcal{ALCF(D)}$ for reasoning with concrete domains [14]. Hence, satisfiability w.r.t. acyclic TBoxes is NExpTime-hard for these logics, too.

For the description logic $\mathcal{ALC}(\mathcal{D})$, similar complexity results as for $\mathcal{ALCF}$ can be obtained. The logic $\mathcal{ALC}(\mathcal{D})$ can be parameterized with a so-called concrete domain $\mathcal{D}$, and, hence, the complexity of reasoning with $\mathcal{ALC}(\mathcal{D})$ depends on the complexity of reasoning with the concrete domain $\mathcal{D}$. On the one hand, satisfiability of $\mathcal{ALC}(\mathcal{D})$ concepts w.r.t. the empty TBox is PSPACE-complete provided that reasoning with the concrete domain $\mathcal{D}$ is in PSPACE [14]. On the other hand, there exist concrete domains $\mathcal{D}$ for which reasoning is in NP such that satisfiability of $\mathcal{ALC}(\mathcal{D})$ concepts w.r.t. acyclic TBoxes is NEXPTIME-complete [13].

Acknowledgments I am indebted to Franz Baader who provided most of the ideas underlying Section 2.1. The work in this paper was supported by the "Foundations of Data Warehouse Quality" (DWQ) European ESPRIT IV Long Term Research (LTR) Project 22469.

References

1. A. Artale and E. Franconi. A temporal description logic for reasoning about actions and plans. *Journal of Artificial Intelligence Research (JAIR)*, (9), 1998.
2. F. Baader, H.-J. Bürckert, B. Nebel, W. Nutt, and G. Smolka. On the expressivity of feature logics with negation, functional uncertainty, and sort equations. *Journal of Logic, Language and Information*, 2:1–18, 1993.
3. F. Baader and P. Hanschke. A scheme for integrating concrete domains into concept languages. In *Proceedings of IJCAI-91*, pages 452–457, Sydney, Australia, August 24–30, 1991. Morgan Kaufmann Publ. Inc., San Mateo, CA, 1991.
4. F. Baader and B. Hollunder.set A terminological knowledge representation system with complete inference algorithms. In *Processings of PDK'91*, volume 567 of *LNAI*, pages 67–86, Kaiserslautern, Germany, July 1–3, 1991. Springer-Verlag, Berlin – Heidelberg – New York, 1991.
5. F. Baader, B. Hollunder, B. Nebel, H.-J. Profitlich, and E. Franconi. An empirical analysis of optimization techniques for terminological representation systems – or: Making KRIS get a move on. *Journal of Applied Intelligence*, 4:109–132, 1994.
6. E. Börger, E. Grädel, and Y. Gurevich. *The Classical Decision Problem*. Perspectives in Mathematical Logic. Springer-Verlag, Berlin, 1997.
7. D. Calvanese. Reasoning with inclusion axioms in description logics: Algorithms and complexity. In *Proceedings of ECAI'96, Budapest, Hungary*, pages 303–307, 1996.
8. D. Calvanese, G. De Giacomo, M. Lenzerini, and D. Nardi. Reasoning in expressive description logics. In *Handbook of Automated Reasoning*. Elsevier Science Publishers (North-Holland), Amsterdam, 1999. To appear.
9. F. M. Donini, M. Lenzerini, D. Nardi, and W. Nutt. The complexity of concept languages. *Information and Computation*, 134(1):1–58, 10 Apr. 1997.
10. F. M. Donini, M. Lenzerini, D. Nardi, and A. Schaerf. Reasoning in description logics. In G. Brewka, editor, *Foundation of Knowledge Representation*, pages 191–236. CSLI-Publications, 1996.
11. B. Hollunder and W. Nutt. Subsumption algorithms for concept languages. DFKI Research Report RR-90-04, German Research Center for Artificial Intelligence, Kaiserslautern, 1990.

12. I. Horrocks, U. Sattler, and S. Tobies. Practical reasoning for expressive description logics. In *Proceedings of LPAR'99, LNCS*, Tbilisi, Georgia, 1999. Springer-Verlag, Berlin – Heidelberg – New York, 1999.
13. C. Lutz. On the complexity of terminological reasoning. LTCS-Report 99-04, LuFG Theoretical Computer Science, RWTH Aachen, Germany, 1999.
14. C. Lutz. Reasoning with concrete domains. In *Proceedings of IJCAI-99*, Stockholm, Sweden, July 31 – August 6, 1999. Morgan Kaufmann Publ. Inc., San Mateo, CA, 1999.
15. B. Nebel. Terminological reasoning is inherently intractable. *Artificial Intelligence*, 43:235–249, 1990.
16. B. Nebel. Terminological cycles: Semantics and computational properties. In J. F. Sowa, editor, *Principles of Semantic Networks – Explorations in the Representation of Knowledge*, chapter 11, pages 331–361. Morgan Kaufmann Publ. Inc., San Mateo, CA, 1991.
17. M. Schmidt-Schauß and G. Smolka. Attributive concept descriptions with complements. *Artificial Intelligence*, 48(1):1–26, 1991.
18. S. Tobies. A PSpace algorithm for graded modal logic. In *Proceedings of CADE-16, LNCS*, 1999. Springer-Verlag, Berlin – Heidelberg – New York, 1999.

On the Complexity of Single-Rule Datalog Queries

Georg Gottlob* and Christos Papadimitriou

Computer Science Division,
Dept of Electrical Engineering and Computer Science
University of California, Berkeley
Berkeley, CA 94720

Abstract Datalog is a well-known database query language based on the logic programming paradigm. A general datalog program consists of a number of rules and facts. Programs containing a unique rule and possibly some facts are called *single rule programs (sirups)*. We study both the combined and the program complexity of sirups, ie., the complexity of evaluating sirups over variable and fixed databases, respectively. Moreover, we study the descriptive complexity of sirups, i.e., their expressive power. In all cases it turns out that even very restricted classes of sirups have the same complexity and essentially the same expressive power as general datalog programs. We show that the evaluation of single clause programs is EXPTIME complete (combined complexity), and, if restricted to linear recursive rules, PSPACE complete. Moreover, sirups with one recursive rule and one additional fact capture PTIME on ordered structures, if a certain data representation is assumed and certain predefined relations are provided. Our results are obtained by a uniform product construction which maps a datalog program into a single rule by essentially maintaining its semantics. We also prove that the datalog clause implication problem, i.e., deciding whether a datalog clause implies another one, is EXPTIME complete.

1   Introduction

Datalog is a deductive database query language based on logic programming [3,30,31,7]. Intensive work was dedicated to the study of various complexity aspects of different versions of datalog; for a survey, see [10]. While the complexity of general datalog is well understood, certain complexity issues concerning single rule datalog programs (sirups) were not pinpointed so far. It is the aim of this paper to close this gap.

Sirups are datalog programs consisting of a single rule and a number of *initializations* consisting of ground or nonground facts. A relational database is identified with a finite set of function-free ground atoms.

Following Vardi [32], we distinguish between different kinds of complexity. The *combined complexity* of datalog is the complexity of determining whether for a given

---

* This work was done while this author was on leave from the Institut für Informationssysteme, TU Wien, Austria. Gottlob's work was supported by the Austrian Science Fund Project Z29-INF and by a McKay Lectureship of UC Berkeley. Current email: gottlob@dbai.tuwien.ac.at

datalog program P, database **db**, and fact f, f is derivable from **db** via P (denoted by **db** $\cup P \models f$). The *data complexity* is the complexity of the same problem for a *fixed* program P. If, instead, the database **db** is fixed, then we speak about the *program complexity*.

Results about datalog programs with an arbitrary number of rules are summarized in Table 1, whose last column specifies the expressive power w.r.t. *ordered* structures. The results about general datalog programs are well-known and can be found in [8,32,20,15,16,21,10]. A datalog program P is linear if each rule body of P contains at most one occurrence of an intensional database (IDB) predicate. The results about the data complexity and expressive power of linear programs over ordered structures can be found in [15,16], while the result on the program and combined complexity of linear datalog programs (PSPACE completeness) is proven in the present paper (Theorems 5 and 6).

	Data Complexity	Progr. Complex.	Combined Complex.	Expr. Power
General Programs	PTIME-cmplt	ETIME-cmplt	EXPTIME-cmplt	PTIME
Linear Programs	NLOGSPACE-cmplt	PSPACE-cmplt	PSPACE-cmplt	NLOGSPACE

Table 1: Complexity of Datalog Programs

In this paper we are interested in sirups. It is well-known that even single clause sirups can express PTIME complete problems [29,22]; sirups are thus data-complete for PTIME. Several restricted classes of sirups that are highly parallelizable (i.e., in NC) were studied in e.g. [29,22,4].

It was also shown that several undecidability results for datalog or general logic programming carry over to sirups. Among these are results on the undecidability of datalog boundedness [2,19,26,25] and on the undecidability of the evaluation problem of logic programs in presence of function symbols [1,5,11,24,27,18].

The program and combined complexity, and the expressive power of sirups, however, have remained unexplored until recently.

In this paper we settle this problem by proving that the main complexity results for general logic programs also hold for very simple sirups. We also show that sirups have essentially the same expressive power as general logic programs.

We consider the following classes of sirups:

Absolute Sirups. These are datalog programs made of a single rule and no facts.
Single Ground Fact Sirups (SGF Sirups). This class contains all datalog programs with one rule and at most one ground fact.
General Sirups. This class contains all sirups, i.e., all datalog programs with one rule and some ground or nonground facts.

For each of these classes we can further consider the corresponding subclass linear sirups.

The main results of this paper are summarized in Table 2, whose last column specifies the expressive power of sirups over ordered, completed, and enriched structures, as explained later on.

	Program Complexity	Combined Complexity	Expressive Power
Absolute Sirups	NP-complete	EXPTIME-complete	$\subseteq$ PTIME
Linear Absolute Sirups	NP-complete	PSPACE-complete	$\subseteq$ NLOGSPACE
General Sirups and SGF Sirups	ETIME-complete	EXPTIME-complete	PTIME
Linear and Linear SGF Sirups	PSPACE-complete	PSPACE-complete	NLOGSPACE

Table 2: Complexity of Sirups

Our main complexity results for sirups are obtained by a product construction mapping an arbitrary logic program P to a sirup XP such that P and XP have essentially the same semantics.

Note that naively constructed products of programs fail to deliver a semantically equivalent program. For a simple example of this failure, assume that a database has a binary relation p, and the original datalog program is:

$$r(X) \leftarrow p(a, X).$$
$$r(X) \leftarrow p(b, X).$$

Then, a naively constructed sirup constructed from this program would have both $p(a, X)$ and $p(b, X)$ in its rule's body, and would thus fail to deliver the correct result. In fact, the disjunction implicit in the original program would be transformed into a conjunction.

We show that this problem can be circumvented by adding to the database a set BASIC of auxiliary relations: A relation *and* corresponding to the Boolean conjunction, a relation *equal* for equality, and a relation *select* which "hardwires" a conditional statement. By use of the BASIC relations, disjunctions can be simulated correctly with single rule programs. Note that enriching a database by the corresponding BASIC relations results in a polynomial increase of the database size only.

By use of BASIC we are able to realize rather sophisticated programming constructs within a datalog rule body. In particular, we show how to implement a kind of CASE statement in a rule body which can perform different variable substitutions depending on corresponding conditions.

Our main construction, the product sirup XP for a program P, uses such a CASE statement. In particular, each clause C of P is simulated by a particular case of the CASE statement. To be able to do this, we introduce the concept of a *mould* for a datalog rule. A mould is a generalization of the rule containing no constants and having no double occurrence of variables. For each clause C of P, XP contains as subclause a mould $\hat{C}$ for C. For each substitution ϑ satisfying C, XP "forces" $\hat{C}$ via appropriate instantiations to become equivalent to C, and makes all other (in this case irrelevant) atoms succeed. Thus, XP becomes—for the particular substitution ϑ—equivalent to C. In summary, XP is in essence equivalent to the original program P.

All our complexity and expressiveness results follow rather straightforwardly from this construction and from the corresponding results for general datalog programs (see Table 1).

Note that a different product construction was given by Abiteboul [2] in order to show that the boundedness problem for datalog sirups is undecidable. That construction does preserve program boundedness, but not equivalence. Moreover, it uses additional nonrecursive rules. It is thus not suited for the purposes pursued here. Note also that the above cited undecidability proofs for the evaluation problem of sirups with function symbols cannot be exploited to solve the complexity of datalog. All those proofs rely heavily on the coding-power of functions, but datalog is function-free.

As a corollary to the EXPTIME complexity of evaluating sirups, it follows that checking whether a datalog rule C logically implies a datalog rule D is EXPTIME-complete. (Here datalog rules are conceived as universally closed first order sentences.) Note that the implication problem for datalog rules is relevant in the context of inductive logic programming (cf. [23]). Its precise complexity was settled only for restricted versions.

The paper is organized as follows. In Section 2, we define a number of relevant concepts and complexity classes. In Section 3, we describe the BASIC relations and show how the CASE construct can be implemented. In Section 4, we introduce the concept of a mould and show how moulds can interact with a CASE statement. The product construction is described in Section 5. Our main complexity results are then easily derived in Section 6. In Section 7, we argue that the expressive power of datalog sirups is essentially the same as the expressive power of general datalog programs.

2 Preliminaries and Notation

2.1 Relational Databases and Datalog

A database **db** consists of a finite universe U and a finite set of relations of specified arity over U. An element of a relation is called a *tuple*. In this paper, w.l.o.g., every database universe U is identified with an initial segment $[0, n-1]$ of the natural numbers. Moreover, we always assume that U has at least two elements, and thus the integers 0 and 1 belong to U. When it is clear from the context, we may identify a database **db** with the set of all tuples contained in its relations.

A *datalog term* is either a variable X or a constant c. An *atom* is a formula $p(t_1, \ldots, t_n)$, where p is a predicate symbol of arity n and each t_i is a term. An atom is *ground*, if all t_i are constants.

A *datalog clause* (or *rule*) is an expression of the form $A_0 \leftarrow A_1, \ldots, A_m$, where each A_i is an atom. The parts on the left and on the right of "$\leftarrow$" are the *head* and the *body* of the rule, respectively. A rule r of the form $A_0 \leftarrow$, i.e., whose body is empty, is called a *fact*, and if A_0 is a ground atom, then r is called a *ground fact*.

A datalog clause C is a *subclause* (or *subrule*) of a datalog clause D if the heads of C and D coincide and if every body atom of C also occurs in the body of D. (Note that the order of occurrence is irrelevant.)

A *datalog program* is a finite set of datalog clauses. A rule or a datalog program is ground, if all terms in it are ground. A datalog program is evaluated over relational databases.

The predicate symbols appearing in the head of a datalog program are referred to as the *intensional database predicates (IDB predicates)*, while those occurring only in rule bodies are called *extensional databases (EDB predicates)*. The IDB predicates can be further subdivided into *output predicates* (containing the output of the program) and *auxiliary predicates* (containing intermediate results). This division is, however, not of great importance for the present paper.

For the definition of various classes of sirups, refer to the introduction.

If Ω is a syntactic object, e.g., an atom, a clause, or a program, then we denote by $var(\Omega)$ the set of all variables occurring in Ω. If V is a set of variables and A a set of constants, then a substitution $\vartheta : V \longrightarrow A$ is a mapping from V to A. If Ω is a syntactic object and ϑ a substitution having domain V, then the *substitution instance* $\Omega\vartheta$ is obtained from Ω by (simultaneously and uniformly) substituting $\vartheta(X)$ for X for each variable $X \in V$ occurring in Ω.

The semantics of datalog is as follows. Let P be a datalog program and let **db** be a database over universe U. The program $ground(P,U)$ is defined by $\bigcup_{C \in P} ground(C,U)$, where ground $ground(C,U)$ consists of the set of all substitution instances $C\vartheta$ of clause C, for all substitutions $\vartheta : var(P) \longrightarrow U$. Ground atoms can be identified with propositional atoms. A ground fact f is deducible from a database **db** with universe U via datalog program P, denoted by **db** $\cup P \models f$ iff **db** $\cup ground(P,U) \models f$, i.e., if f is a logical consequence of the set of all database and ground program atoms. Two datalog rules are *equivalent* if for any database they derive the same facts.

Note: We do not require that that the IDB relations be initially empty; rather, the IDB relations of a datalog program may occur in the database with some initial value. This setting, which is also adopted in [4], makes sense in the context of absolute sirups, for otherwise a recursive absolute sirup does not compute anything. However, this assumption is of relevance to absolute sirups only. All results of this paper on all other types of sirups remain valid if we adopt the more standard assumption that IDB relations do not occur in the database and are initially empty (see also the remark in Section 6.1).

It is easy to see that for each database **db**, **db** $\cup P \models f$ iff there exists a *proof tree* for f based on P and **db** over universe U. The vertices of such a tree are IDB ground atoms g, the root being f. For each vertex there exists a clause $C : head \leftarrow body$ in P and a ground substitution ϑ such that $head\vartheta = g$ and all EDB atoms in $body\vartheta$ are in EDB and the IDB atoms in $body\vartheta$ are the children of g in the proof tree.

2.2   Relevant Complexity Classes

The concepts of *data complexity*, *combined complexity*, and *program complexity* were already defined in the introduction.

The complexity classes relevant to this paper are the well-known classes LOGSPACE, PTIME, NP, and PSPACE, as well as the following exponential classes:

$$\text{ETIME} = \bigcup_{d>0} \text{DTIME}(2^{dn}) \qquad \qquad \text{EXPTIME} = \bigcup_{d>0} \text{DTIME}(2^{n^d}).$$

It is well-known that ETIME is not closed under logspace reductions and that every problem complete for ETIME is also complete for EXPTIME. Moreover, EXPTIME is the closure under LOGSPACE many-one reductions of ETIME. ETIME is thus not a robust complexity class. Nevertheless, stating that a problem is ETIME-complete is more informative than stating it is EXPTIME-complete. In fact, if a problem is ETIME-complete, then it is EXPTIME-complete *and* it is in ETIME. Note that ETIME is a proper subclass of EXPTIME and not all EXPTIME-complete problems are in ETIME.

All reductions performed in the present paper are LOGSPACE many-one reductions, and all completeness results are w.r.t. such reductions.

2.3 Descriptive Complexity

Descriptive complexity theory [17,12,21] deals with the expressive power of logical formalisms over finite structures and describes it in terms of complexity classes.

A *database property* π is an isomorphism-invariant Boolean property of databases of a given schema. For example, graph three-colorability is a database property over databases with a single binary relation representing a graph.

Let C be a complexity class. A database property π is C-decidable if the problem of deciding whether a given database satisfies π (written $\pi(\mathbf{db})$) is in C.

A *Boolean datalog query* consists of a datalog program P and a ground fact f. For a database $\mathbf{db}$, the query answer is *yes* if $\mathbf{db} \cup P \models f$, otherwise the answer is *no*.

Let us refer to finite Γ-*structures* when we speak about the set of all finite structures that are restricted by some qualification Γ. For example the *ordered* structures are all those structures equipped with a linear order (successor relation) over the universe. In Section 7 we will define other relevant qualifications of structures.

A class $\mathcal{P}$ of datalog programs *captures* the complexity class C over finite Γ-structures if for all such structures, the evaluation problem for Boolean $\mathcal{P}$-queries is in C, and if every C-decidable database property over finite Γ-structures is expressible by a Boolean $\mathcal{P}$-query.

Well-known results about the expressive power of general and linear datalog programs over ordered structures are given in Table 1 of the introduction.

3   Useful Features of Single-Rule Programs

In this section we discuss different useful features that can be achieved by datalog programs that consist of a single clause, provided the database contains some basic facts. First, in Subsection 3.1, we define for each universe U a set $BASIC(U)$ of basic auxiliary facts. The following subsections describe more and more complex program constructs we are able to build by use of the basic facts. The most important one is the CASE statement explained in Section 3.4.

3.1   Basic Auxiliary Facts

Let $and(X, Y, Result)$ be a relation encoding the logical conjunction:

$$and = \{and(0,0,0), and(0,1,0), and(1,0,0), and(1,1,1)\}.$$

Moreover, for each finite universe U, define the relation instances $equal_U$ and $select_U$ over the respective relation schemas $equal(X, Y, R)$ and $select(Cond, X, Y, Res)$ as follows:

$$equal_U = \{equal(X, X, 1)|X \in U\} \cup \{equal(X, Y, 0)|X, Y \in U \wedge X \neq Y\},$$

thus $equal(X, Y, R)$ "assigns" 1 to the result R if X and Y are bound to the same value and assigns zero to R otherwise.

$$select_U = \{select(0, X, Y, X)|X, Y \in U\} \cup \{select(1, X, Y, Y)|X, Y \in U\},$$

thus $select(Cond, X, Y, Res)$ assigns X to Res if $Cond$ is 0 and Y if $Cond$ is 1.

By $BASIC(U)$ we denote the union of all facts contained in the relations *and*, $equal_U$ and $select_U$; when U is understood, we refer to these facts simply as the BASIC facts. We always assume w.l.o.g. that an original database **db** does not contain any *and, equal* or *select* facts. We can then extend every database **db** over universe U to a database $\mathbf{db}^+$ by adding the facts $BASIC(U)$ to **db**.

We will furthermore consider the following special relations $succ(., .)$, $min(.)$, and $max(.)$: The relation $succ$ is a successor relation for some linear order on U, and min and max are singleton relations that identify the first and the last element w.r.t. this order, respectively. We will denote by $ORDER$ the facts corresponding to these three relations, and by $\mathbf{db}_s$ the extension of any database **db** by such a successor ordering. In particular, $\mathbf{db}_s^+$ is the extension of **db** by both, successor ordering and BASIC facts.

3.2 Vectorized Equality-Checks and Selections

Here we show how to extend the primitive relations *equal* and *select* to arguments that are *vectors* (i.e., lists) of variables instead of single variables. This will not require to add any new facts to the database, but can be entirely done within the body of a rule.

Let $\mathbf{X} = X_1, X_2, \ldots, X_k$ and $\mathbf{Y} = Y_1, Y_2, \ldots, Y_k$ be k-ary lists of terms, $\mathbf{Z} = Z_1, Z_2, \ldots, Z_k$ a k-ary list of variables, and $Cond$ and R single variables. We define the following abbreviations for conjunctions of literals in a rule body:

$$EQUAL(\mathbf{X}, \mathbf{Y}, R) = \left(\bigwedge_{1 \leq i \leq k} equal(X_i, Y_i, R_i)\right) \wedge and(R_1, R_2, R_2') \wedge$$
$$\left(\bigwedge_{2 \leq i \leq k-2} and(R_i', R_{i+1}, R_{i+1}')\right) \wedge and(R_{k-1}', R_k, R),$$

where the variables R_i and R_j' $1 \leq i \leq k, 2 \leq j \leq k - 1$ are fresh variables not used anywhere else.

$$SELECT(Cond, \mathbf{X}, \mathbf{Y}, \mathbf{Z}) = \bigwedge_{1 \leq i \leq k} select(Cond, X_i, Y_i, Z_i).$$

It is easy to see that the $EQUAL$ and $SELECT$ constructs fullfil their intended purposes. We omit a formal proof.

3.3   Negation and Disjunction

From the basic relations *and* and *equal*, we can define negation and disjunction as abbreviations as follows. $NOT(X,Y) \equiv equal(X,Y,0)$, and
$OR(X,Y,Z) \equiv NOT(X,X') \wedge NOT(Y,Y') \wedge and(X',Y',Z') \wedge NOT(Z',Z)$,
where the primed variables are fresh variables not occurring anywhere else.

From the definition of *equal* and by De Morgans laws it follows immediately that over the restricted domain $\{0,1\}$ NOT and OR have their intended meaning when evaluated over any database $\mathbf{db}^+$.

3.4   Simple Case Statements in Rule Bodies

We now show how to simulate – within a clause body – simple CASE statements such as the following:

$$\text{CASE}$$
$$\mathbf{X}^1 = \mathbf{T}^1 \text{ DO } \mathbf{Y} := \mathbf{Z}^1;$$
$$\mathbf{X}^2 = \mathbf{T}^2 \text{ DO } \mathbf{Y} := \mathbf{Z}^2;$$
$$\cdots \qquad \cdots\cdots\cdots$$
$$\mathbf{X}^k = \mathbf{T}^k \text{ DO } \mathbf{Y} := \mathbf{Z}^k;$$
$$\text{ENDCASE}$$

where for $1 \leq i \leq k$, $\mathbf{X}^i$ and $\mathbf{T}^i$ are vectors of variables or constants of length r_i, and $\mathbf{Y}$ is a block of variables of length s, disjoint from any other variable list occurring in the CASE statement, and each $\mathbf{Z}^i$ $(1 \leq i \leq k)$ is a block of s variables, respectively.

The intended meaning of the CASE statement occurring within the body of a clause C is intuitively described as follows. Assume the CASE statement is evaluated over a database $\mathbf{db}^+$ in a context where all variables, except those in $\mathbf{Y}$, have already been unified with some constant values via a substitution ϑ. It then should hold that:

- If ϑ falsifies all conditions $\mathbf{X}^i = \mathbf{T}^i$, then C fails over $\mathbf{db}^+$.
- If exactly one of the conditions $\mathbf{X}^i = \mathbf{T}^i$ is satisfied by ϑ, then there is precisely one "legal" extension $\vartheta' \supset \vartheta$ of ϑ to the variables in $\mathbf{Y}$, and this extension is given by the assignment $\mathbf{Y} := \mathbf{Z}^i$.
- If more than one conditions are satisfied, then the meaning of the CASE statement is undefined (this case will never occur in the programs used below).

The above CASE statement is a syntactic shorthand for the conjunction of the following three conjunctions of atoms:

1. $\bigwedge_{1 \leq i \leq k} EQUAL(\mathbf{X}^i, \mathbf{T}^i, T_i)$ where each T_i, for $1 \leq i \leq k$ is a fresh variable;
2. The conjunction

$$SELECT(T_1, \mathbf{Z}^1, \mathbf{Z}^1, \mathbf{Y}^1) \wedge SELECT(T_2, \mathbf{Y}^1, \mathbf{Z}^2, \mathbf{Y}^2) \wedge \cdots \wedge$$
$$SELECT(T_i, \mathbf{Y}^{i-1}, \mathbf{Z}^i, \mathbf{Y}^i) \wedge \cdots \wedge \cdots \wedge$$
$$SELECT(T_{k-1}, \mathbf{Y}^{k-2}, \mathbf{Z}^{k-1}, \mathbf{Y}^{k-1}) \wedge SELECT(T_k, \mathbf{Y}^{k-1}, \mathbf{Z}^k, \mathbf{Y})$$

where the $\mathbf{Y}^i$ are blocks of fresh variables for $1 \leq i \leq k-1$;

3. $OR(T_1, T_2, T'_2) \wedge OR(T'_2, T_3, T'_3) \wedge \cdots \wedge OR(T'_{k-1}, T_k, 1)$, where the T'_j are fresh variables.

We refer to the *expansion* of a CASE statement $CASE$ as the conjunction of all literals occurring in the above described realization of $CASE$. The *hidden variables* $hiddvar(CASE)$ of CASE are all the variables occurring in the expansion of $CASE$ but not in the presentation of the statement itself.

The correctness of the construction is formally stated by the following lemma.

Lemma 1. *Assume a simple CASE statement $CASE$ as above appears in the body $body(C)$ of some clause C. Let db be a database. Assume ϑ is a substitution mapping each variable in $\mathbf{X}^1, \ldots, \mathbf{X}^k, \mathbf{T}^1, \ldots, \mathbf{T}^k$, and $\mathbf{Z}^1, \ldots, \mathbf{Z}^k$ to some element of the universe U of db.*

(i) *If for each $1 \leq i \leq k$, $\mathbf{X}^i\vartheta \neq \mathbf{T}^i\vartheta$, then $CASE\vartheta$ evaluates to false over $\mathbf{db}^+$ and thus $body(C)\vartheta$ evaluates to false over $\mathbf{db}^+$.*

(ii) *If exactly one condition $\mathbf{X}^i\vartheta = \mathbf{T}^i\vartheta$ is true, then there is exactly one way to extend ϑ to a substitution $\vartheta' \supset \vartheta$ covering $hiddvar(CASE)$ and all variables in $\mathbf{Y}$ such that $CASE\vartheta'$ evaluates to true over $\mathbf{db}^+$. Moreover, this substitution ϑ' is such that $\mathbf{Y}\vartheta' = \mathbf{Z}^i\vartheta$.*

3.5 Extended Case Statements

For the sake of a more comfortable reading of simple CASE statements, we adopt the following syntactic conventions and extensions of the CASE statement.

Conjunctive conditions. Conditions of the form $\mathbf{X}^1\mathbf{X}^2 \cdots \mathbf{X}^r = \mathbf{T}^1\mathbf{T}^2 \cdots \mathbf{T}^r$, where $|\mathbf{X}^i| = |\mathbf{T}^i|$ for $1 \leq i \leq r$, can be written in the more suggestive form $\mathbf{X}^1 = \mathbf{T}^1 \wedge \mathbf{X}^2 = \mathbf{T}^2 \wedge \ldots \wedge \mathbf{X}^r = \mathbf{T}^r$.

Compound Assignments. An assignment of the form $\mathbf{Y}^1\mathbf{Y}^2 \cdots \mathbf{Y}^r := \mathbf{Z}^1\mathbf{Z}^2 \cdots \mathbf{Z}^r$ may be rewritten as a the compound assignment $\mathbf{Y}^1 := \mathbf{Z}^1; \mathbf{Y}^2 := \mathbf{Z}^2; \ldots; \mathbf{Y}^r := \mathbf{Z}^r$.

Inequality tests We may use inequalities in the conditions. For example, we may write a condition $\mathbf{X} \neq \mathbf{T}^i$. This can be simulated as follows by an equality. Introduce a new variable W. Add the construct $EQUAL(\mathbf{X}, \mathbf{T}^i, W)$ to the body of the clause containing the CASE statement, and replace the condition $\mathbf{X} \neq \mathbf{T}^i$ by $W = 0$.

4 Moulds

A datalog rule C is a *mould* if it has no occurrences of constants and no double occurrences of variables. If C and D are rules of the form:

$$C: \quad H \leftarrow B_1, \ldots, B_n$$

$$D: \quad H' \leftarrow B'_1, \dots, B'_n$$

then C *is a mould for* D if C is a mould and there exists a substitution ϑ defined on $var(C)$ such that $H\vartheta = H'$ and for each $1 \leq i \leq n$, $B_i\vartheta = B'_i$.

If C is a mould for D via substitution ϑ, we define two syntactic objects $cond(C, D)$ and $assgt(C, D)$ as follows.

$cond(C, D)$: Let ϑ be the unique substitution that translates C "literalwise" into D as above. Then $cond(C, D)$ is a conjunction containing, for each variable X occurring in the body of C, the equation $X = a$ if $X\vartheta = a$ for some constant a, and, if $X\vartheta$ is not a constant but coincides with the ϑ-image of some other (lexicographically smaller) body-variable of C, the equation $X = Y$ for the lexicographically smallest variable Y in the body of C such that $Y\vartheta = X\vartheta$.

$assgt(C, D)$: $assgt(C, D)$ is a list of assignments containing precisely the following assignments:

- an assignment $X := a$ for each head variable X of C, where $X\vartheta = a$;
- an assignment $X := Y$, for each head variable X of C, where $\vartheta(X)$ is a variable, and where Y is the lexicographically smallest variable in the body of C such that $X\vartheta = Y\vartheta$. (Note: We assume w.l.o.g. that clause D is range-restricted, i.e., each head-variable of D also occurs in the body of D; thus, a variable Y as above always exists in C.)

Example 1. Consider the following two clauses:

$$C: \quad p(X_1, X_2) \leftarrow p(X_3, X_4), q(X_5, X_6), r(X_7, X_8, X_9).$$
$$D: \quad p(a, X) \leftarrow p(X, Y), q(Y, Y), r(X, b, Y).$$

Here, C is a mould for D, and we have:

$$cond(C, D) = X_5 = X_4 \wedge X_6 = X_4 \wedge X_7 = X_3 \wedge X_8 = b \wedge X_9 = X_4 \text{ and}$$
$$assgt(C, D) = X_1 := a; X_2 := X_3.$$

Let us denote by $\sigma_c(C, D)$ the substitution $\{X/t \mid (X = t) \in cond(C, D)\}$ and by $\sigma_a(C, D)$ the substitution $\{X/t \mid (X := t) \in assgt(C, D)\}$.

Lemma 2. *If* $C = Head \leftarrow Body$ *is a mould for* D, *then the clause* $C' \equiv Head\sigma_a(C, D) \leftarrow Body\sigma_c(C, D)$ *is equivalent to* D.

In Section 5 we will show how a datalog program P with several rules $R_1, \dots, R_r$ can be simulated by a program XP containing a single rule R. The basic idea is to design R such that an appropriate subset R'_i of R will act as a mould for R_i. A CASE statement in the body of R will then distinguish between r different cases (corresponding to the r different rules of P). The i-th case will "force" R'_i to become equivalent to R_i by suitable conditions and assignments.

The following technical lemma will be useful to prove the correctness of this approach.

Lemma 3. *Let* C : $head(C) \leftarrow body(C)$ *be a mould for a clause* D : $head(D) \leftarrow body(D)$. *Let* $Case$ *denote a CASE statement whose i-th case is of the form:*

$$choice \wedge cond(C, D) \ \text{DO} \ assgt(C, D),$$

where choice is a conjunction of equations whose variables are disjoint from those in C.

Consider a Datalog rule R *of the form*

$$head(C) \leftarrow body(C) \wedge Case \wedge Rest,$$

where Rest is a conjunction of literals that have no variables in common with C, *such that* $var(choice) \subseteq var(Rest)$. *Let* **db** *be a database over a universe* U, *and let* λ *be a substitution* $\lambda : Var(Rest) \longrightarrow U$. *If*

- *choiceλ evaluates to true, and*
- *the conditions of all other cases of the CASE statement are inconsistent with* λ, *and*
- *Rest$\lambda \subseteq$ **db**$^{+}$,*

then $R\lambda$ *is equivalent to* D *over* **db**$^{+}$, *i.e.*, $ground(R\lambda, U)$ *and* $ground(D, U)$ *compute the same atoms over* **db**$^{+}$.

5   The Product Construction

In this section we present the product construction, which for each datalog program P defines an essentially equivalent single-rule program XP. Before describing this construction, we deal with two standardization features.

5.1   Program Degrees

The *degree* $deg(P)$ of a datalog program P is the maximal number of occurrences of IDB predicates in a rule body of P. P is *linear* if $deg(P) \leq 1$. P is *quadratic* if $deg(P) \leq 2$.

Recall that datalog programs have input, output and auxiliary predicates. Two datalog programs are *equivalent* if they have the same input and output predicates and compute the same result over each database. Equivalent programs may have different auxiliary predicates. Each datalog program can be transformed into an equivalent quadratic program as follows: Break rules with more than two IDB atoms in the body into several rules by using new auxiliary predicates.

Lemma 4. *Each datalog program* P *can be transformed into an equivalent quadratic program* P'. *The transformation is feasible in logspace.*

5.2   Eliminating Multiple IDB Predicates

To transform a program P with several IDB predicates into an essentially equivalent program P^* with a unique IDB predicate, we proceed in two steps:

1. Pad all relations with a dummy constant 0 so that they are all of the same arity.
2. Let $p_1, \ldots, p_h$ be the different names of IDB predicate in P. Replace all instances $p_i(V)$ with $r(V, \mathbf{i})$, where $\mathbf{i}$ is the $\lceil \log(h) \rceil + 1$ long binary encoding of i.

In summary, we obtain P^* from P by replacing each IDB literal $p_i(t_1, \ldots, t_k)$ with a suitable literal $r(t_1, \ldots, t_k, 0^{a-k}, \mathbf{i})$, where a be the maximum arity of any IDB predicate in P.

Note that the vector $\mathbf{0}$ of $\lceil \log h \rceil + 1$ zeroes does not encode any IDB predicate in P, but will be used as a dummy value in our subsequent product construction.

Lemma 5. *For any program P with maximum IDB arity a, for any database* db, *and for any k-tuple* b *of elements of the universe U of* db, *and predicate p_i of P,* $P \cup$ db $\models$ $p_i(\mathbf{b})$ *iff* $P^* \cup$ db $\models r(\mathbf{b}, 0^{a-k}, \mathbf{i})$.

5.3   The Product Program

Let P be a datalog program. Without loss of generality we assume that $deg(P) \leq 2$. Let $p_1, \ldots p_h$ be the IDB predicates occurring in P.

Transform P, as described above, into an equivalent program P^* having a unique IDB predicate r. The r-atoms have thus the form $r(\mathbf{A}, \mathbf{B})$, where $\mathbf{A}$ and $\mathbf{B}$ are term vectors of dimension a and $\lceil \log h \rceil + 1$, respectively.

The *multiplicity* $mult(q)$ of an EDB predicate q occurring in P^* is the maximal number of q-atoms occurring in a rule body of P^*.

We now proceed by describing various conjuncts of atoms which will serve as constituents of the sirup XP.

Generic EDB Atoms of XP. For each EDB predicate q of arity α occuring in P^*, define the set of *generic q atoms* $Gen(q) = \{gen_i(q) | 1 \leq i \leq mult(q)\}$, where $gen_i(q)$ is the atom $q(\mathbf{X}_i^q)$, where $\mathbf{X}_i^q$ is a list of α fresh variables that are mutually distinct and distinct from all other variables occurring in XP.

Let GEN denote the conjunction of all such generic atoms.

Recursive Atoms of XP. We define the conjunction of atoms REC as follows:

- $REC \equiv r(\mathbf{V}, \mathbf{J})$ if $deg(P) < 2$, and
- $REC \equiv r(\mathbf{V}, \mathbf{J}) \wedge r(\mathbf{W}, \mathbf{K})$ if $deg(P) = 2$.

Here $\mathbf{V}, \mathbf{W}$ are a-ary vectors of variables, where a is the maximum IDB arity, and $\mathbf{J}, \mathbf{K}$ are ℓ-ary vectors of variables (with $\ell = \lceil \log h \rceil + 1$), and all variables in $\mathbf{V}, \mathbf{W}, \mathbf{J}, \mathbf{K}$ are mutually distinct and distinct from all previously defined variables.

The Head Atom. Let $HEAD$ be the atom $r(\mathbf{U}, \mathbf{I})$, where $\mathbf{U}$ is an a-ary vector of variables, and $\mathbf{I}$ is an ℓ-ary vector of variables, and all variables in $\mathbf{U}, \mathbf{I}$ are mutually distinct and distinct from all previously defined variables.

Moulds for Rules in P^*. Consider the rule $\Gamma : HEAD{\leftarrow}REC \wedge GEN$. Note that Γ contains as subrule a mould for each rule D of P^* (even several such moulds may be possible). Choose one such mould for each clause D of P^* and denote it by $\hat{D}$.

The Choice Construct. Let s be the number of rules in P^*. The program XP needs to choose (via unification) one rule of P at a time. This is realized by a conjunction of atoms $CHOICE(\mathbf{C})$, where $\mathbf{C} = C_1 C_2 \cdots C_\rho$ is a vector of $\rho = \lceil \log s \rceil$ variables. In particular, if the variable $\mathbf{C}$ in $CHOICE(\mathbf{C})$ are instantiated by a vector $\mathbf{T}$ of Boolean values, then $\mathbf{T}$ identifies (at most) one rule of P^*. $CHOICE(\mathbf{C})$ is realized as follows:

$$CHOICE(\mathbf{C}) \equiv and(C_1, R_1, S_1) \wedge and(C_2, R_2, S_2) \wedge \cdots \wedge and(C_\rho, R_\rho, S_\rho),$$

where the C, R, and S variables are all mutually distinct fresh variables (not occurring in P^*). The role of CHOICE is simply to determine a particular rule, say, rule number i, by binding the vector of variables $C_1 \ldots C_\rho$ to the corresponding binary representation $\mathbf{i}$ of i. (The fact that this is realized via *and* atoms should not confuse the reader; we could have used *select* atoms instead; the R and S variables are just fillers that will not be used outside the CHOICE construct.)

Main rule of XP. The program XP consists of a single rule of the form

$$\boxed{HEAD \leftarrow REC \wedge GEN \wedge CHOICE(\mathbf{C}) \wedge CASE}$$

where $CASE$ denotes the following statement:

```
CASE
C = 1 ∧ cond(D̂₁, D₁)  DO  assgt(D̂₁, D₁);
...                   ... ...
C = i ∧ cond(D̂ᵢ, Dᵢ)  DO  assgt(D̂ᵢ, Dᵢ);    (1 < i < r)
...                   ... ...
C = r ∧ cond(D̂ᵣ, Dᵣ)  DO  assgt(D̂ᵣ, Dᵣ);
ENDCASE
```

where $D_1, \ldots, D_r$ are the clauses of P^*. Intuitively, the role of the i-th line of the CASE statement is to emulate the i-th rule in the program P^*.

This completes the description of XP. Obviously XP can be constructed from P in LOGSPACE.

For a program XP, we denote by $r(\mathbf{0})$ the fact $r(0, 0, \ldots, 0)$.

Theorem 1. *Let db be a database over universe U, whose relations are all nonempty. Let P be a datalog program over db whose IDB predicates are of maximal arity a. Let*

p_j be the j-th IDB predicate symbol in P, and let c be its arity. Let $\mathbf{t}$ be a vector in U^c. We then have:

$$\mathbf{db} \cup P \models p_j(\mathbf{t}) \quad \text{iff} \quad \mathbf{db}^+ \cup \{r(0)\} \cup XP \models r(\mathbf{t}, 0^{a-c}, \mathbf{j}).$$

Proof.   By Lemma 5 it suffices to show that

$$\mathbf{db} \cup P^* \models r(\mathbf{t}, 0^{a-c}, \mathbf{j}) \quad \text{iff} \quad \mathbf{db}^+ \cup \{r(0)\} \cup XP \models r(\mathbf{t}, 0^{a-c}, \mathbf{j}).$$

We use induction on the minimal derivation depth δ of the ground fact $r(\mathbf{t}, 0^{a-c}, \mathbf{j})$ w.r.t. program P^*, i.e., the depth of a minimal derivation tree. For $\delta = 0$, the claim holds because we can infer only $\mathbf{db}$ facts via P^* and only $\mathbf{db}^+$ facts and $r(0)$ via XP in zero steps. None of these facts fit the pattern $r(\mathbf{t}, \mathbf{i})$ where $\mathbf{i} \neq 0$.

Assume the claim holds for derivation depth m. We show it for $\delta = m + 1$.

Define the following EDBs:

$\mathbf{db}_m$ is the database consisting of all facts derivable from $\mathbf{db}$ via P^* having derivation depth $\leq m$

$\overline{\mathbf{db}_m^+}$ is the database consisting of all facts derivable from $\mathbf{db}^+ \cup \{r(0)\}$ via XP having derivation depth $\leq m$.

By the induction hypothesis we have $\overline{\mathbf{db}_m^+} = \mathbf{db}_m^+ \cup \{r(0)\}$.

If. Assume $\mathbf{db} \cup \{r(0)\} \cup XP \models r(\mathbf{t}, 0^{a-c}, \mathbf{j})$, where the ground fact $r(\mathbf{t}, 0^{a-c}, \mathbf{j})$ has derivation depth $\delta = m + 1$. Consider the last derivation step. In this step the body of rule XP succeeds over $\overline{\mathbf{db}_m^+}$. $CHOICE(\mathbf{C})$ in XP must succeed and thus $\mathbf{C}$ is instantiated to a Boolean vector $\mathbf{j}$ corresponding to some integer i. Since also the $CASE$ construct suceeds, this means that $i > 0$ and that the instantiation of $\mathbf{C}$ is consistent with precisely the precondition of the i-th case in the CASE statement. By Lemma 3 it then follows that $r(\mathbf{t}, 0^{a-c}, \mathbf{j})$ can be derived in one step by some rule D of P^* from the database $\overline{\mathbf{db}_m^+}$. Since rule D of P^* cannot use fact $r(0)$ nor the BASIC facts, $r(\mathbf{t}, 0^{a-c}, \mathbf{j})$ can be derived in one step by rule D of P^* from $\mathbf{db}_m$. Hence $\mathbf{db} \cup P^* \models r(\mathbf{t}, 0^{a-c}, \mathbf{j})$.

Only if. Assume that $\mathbf{db} \cup P^* \models r(\mathbf{t}, 0^{a-c}, \mathbf{j})$ and that this fact has derivation depth δ by P^*. Let D be the rule of P^* deriving this fact in one step from $\mathbf{db}_m$ and assume D is the i-th rule of P^*. Let γ be the ground substitution for the variables of D in the last step of the derivation of $r(\mathbf{t}, 0^{a-c}, \mathbf{j})$.

Let $\hat{D} \subseteq XP$ be the mould for D according to the construction of XP as described above, and let ϑ be the substitution translating $\hat{D}$ into D. Let $Rest$ denote all atoms in the body of XP which are neither in $\hat{D}$ nor in $CASE$. Consider the following substitution $\lambda : var(Rest) \longrightarrow U$:

- $\lambda(\mathbf{C}) := \mathbf{i}$; the other variables of $CHOICE$ are defined accordingly.
- Let GEN' denote the atoms of GEN which do not occur in $\hat{D}$. Let σ be any substitution such that $GEN'\sigma \subseteq \mathbf{db}$. Note that such a substitution exists because no EDB relation is empty. For each $X \in var(GEN')$ define $\lambda(X) := \sigma(X)$. (All atoms in GEN' are irrelevant, they are satisfied via arbitrary ground substitutions in order to make the body of XP succeed.)

- For any r-atom R in $Rest$, extend λ to $var(R)$ in such a way that $R\lambda = r(0)$. (Note that there may be up to $deg(P)$ such r-atoms; these are the irrelevant r-atoms of case i; they are mapped into the dummy fact $r(0)$ in order to succeed.)

It is clear that $Rest\lambda \subseteq \mathbf{db}_m^+ \cup \{r(0)\}$, and thus $Rest\lambda \subseteq \overline{\mathbf{db}_m^+}$, The other two conditions of Lemma 3 also apply. By Lemma 3, we thus conclude that $XP\lambda$ is equivalent over $\overline{\mathbf{db}_m^+}$ to D. Hence $XP\lambda\vartheta$, whose body is satisfied in $\overline{\mathbf{db}_m^+}$, fires on that database and allows us to derive $r(\mathbf{t}, 0^{a-c}, \mathbf{j})$ in one step from it. It thus holds that $\mathbf{db} \cup \{r(0)\} \cup XP \models r(\mathbf{t}, 0^{a-c}, \mathbf{i})$. ∎

6 Main Complexity Results

6.1 Combined Complexity of Datalog Sirups

The following theorem determines the combined complexity of absolute sirups.

Theorem 2 (Combined Complexity of Absolute Sirups). *Given an absolute sirup P, a database $\mathbf{db}$, and a ground fact f, determining whether $P \cup \mathbf{db} \models f$ is EXPTIME complete. This remains true even if P is quadratic and $\mathbf{db}$ contains no EDB predicates, and the universe of $\mathbf{db}$ has cardinality 2.*

Proof. It is well-known (implicit in [8,32], see also [10]) that the combined complexity of (general) Datalog is EXPTIME complete. For a simple proof cf. [10], where the EXPTIME result is shown for instances $(\mathbf{db}', P', f')$, where $\mathbf{db}'$ contains no EDB predicates, and the universe of $\mathbf{db}$ is the set $\{0, 1\}$. It is thus sufficient to show that the problem remains EXPTIME hard for absolute sirups. By our product construction we transform each instance $(\mathbf{db}', P', f')$ as above to an equivalent instance $(\mathbf{db}' \cup BASIC \cup r(0), XP, f)$ of the derivation problem for absolute sirups. The equivalence is guaranteed by Theorem 1. Note that XR is quadratic. ∎

As an immediate consequence of Theorem 2, we get:

Corollary 1. *Any class of datalog sirups containing the absolute sirups has EXPTIME-complete combined complexity.*

Theorem 2 can be reinterpreted as a complexity result on the datalog clause implication problem, where datalog clauses are conceived as universally closed formulas.

Corollary 2 (Complexity of the Implication Problem for Datalog Clauses).
Determining whether a datalog rule C logically implies a datalog rule D is EXPTIME complete.

Proof. It is well-known [14] that the problem of deciding whether C implies D is equivalent to the problem of deciding

$$(\{A\vartheta|\ A \text{ is an atom in } body(D)\} \cup C\ ) \models head(D)\vartheta,$$

where ϑ is an arbitrary ground substitution replacing every variable of D with a distinct fresh constant. Thus the datalog clause implication problem is in EXPTIME. Conversely, the problem of checking whether for a database **db**, a sirup P and a ground fact f it holds that $\mathbf{db} \cup P \models f$ is equivalent to deciding whether the datalog clause P logically implies the ground rule D whose head is f and whose body consists of the conjunction of all atoms in **db**. Thus the datalog clause implication problem is EXPTIME hard.   ∎

Remark. Theorem 2 is formulated in the liberal setting, where an IDB relation may have a nonempty initial value in the given database **db**. In fact, in our proof we assume that the IDB relation r initially contains the tuple $r(0)$. In a more restricted setting, where this is forbidden, Theorem 2 does not hold. In such a restricted setting, absolute sirups are equivalent to conjunctive queries which are NP-complete both w.r.t. program and to combined complexity [9]. However, in the restricted setting, an analogous statement to Theorem 2 holds for single ground fact sirups (just add $r(0)$ as ground fact to the program).

6.2   Program Complexity of Datalog Sirups

General datalog programs are known to be program complete in EXPTIME (implicit in [8,32], cf. [10] for a simple proof) and are actually in ETIME and thus complete for ETIME. In fact, the fixed size of the universe ensures that the ground version of a program has only linear exponential size in the original program, and thus the entire evaluation problem can be solved in linear exponential time.

What about the *program complexity* for absolute sirups? The classical definition of program complexity [32] asks for the evaluation of (variable) datalog programs over a *fixed* database. While general datalog programs are program-complete in ETIME, this is not the case for absolute sirups.

Theorem 3 (Program Complexity of Absolute Sirups). *Evaluating absolute sirups over fixed databases is* NP *complete.*

Proof. *Membership.* Note that a *recursive* absolute sirup has no rule for initializing its head relation r and fails if this relation is initially empty. Thus the fixed database **db** must contain some initial value. This means that the arity of r is fixed. It follows that for a fixed database universe the set of all possible ground instances of r is predetermined and of constant size k. It follows that every derivable goal f has a proof tree of depth at most k, and thus of polynomial size. Guessing and verifying such a proof tree for a given goal is clearly in NP.

Hardness. For hardness it suffices to consider nonrecursive absolute sirups. The evaluation problem for such sirups is clearly equivalent to the problem of evaluating conjunctive queries, which is NP complete even in case of a fixed database [9].   ∎

This pathology disappears if we move from absolute sirups to the (syntactically) slightly more general class of single ground fact sirups (SGF Sirups).

Theorem 4 (Program Complexity of SGF and General Sirups).
SGF sirups are program-complete in ETIME. The same holds for all classes of sirups containing the SGF sirups.

Proof. The ETIME upper bound is inherited from the class of general datalog programs for which this bound holds. To see hardness, recall from the proof of Theorem 2 that EXPTIME hardness for absolute sirups P holds even in case the universe is fixed and the database contains only the BASIC facts and $r(0)$. Note that BASIC is fixed for the fixed universe U. The only nonfixed fact in the database is $r(0)$. For obtaining a *fixed* database, it is thus sufficient to eliminate $r(0)$ from the database and add it to the absolute sirup. This yields an SGF sirup. ∎

Note. If we slightly modify the classical definition of program complexity by requiring only a fixed database *universe* instead of a fixed database, then even the evaluation problem for absolute sirups is program complete in ETIME.

6.3   Linear Sirups

The combined complexity of linear sirups is in PSPACE. This is actually true for all linear datalog programs, and not just for linear sirups.

Theorem 5. *Given a linear datalog program P, a database* **db** *and a ground fact f, it can be tested in* PSPACE *whether $P \cup \mathrm{db} \models f$.*

Proof. As said in Section 2.1, derivations of facts by datalog programs can be represented by proof trees. In general, such proof trees are truly branching. For linear programs, however, they correspond to chains (if we do not explicitly represent EDB atoms). Each element of such a chain corresponds to a fact derived (via an appropriate rule and instantiation) from its predecessor, i.e., its child. The top element of the chain is f. Clearly, each chain element fits into polynomial space. We can thus generate the chain elements nondeterministically one by one, bottom to top in PSPACE by reusing space. At each step we generate a new chain element and check whether there exists a rule in P and some ground facts in EDB such that the new chain element is generated from the previous one in one inference step. This requires us to keep only two chain elements in memory at a time. The procedure stops if f is obtained. The procedure is in NPSPACE and thus in PSPACE. ∎

The PSPACE hardness of the evaluation problem for linear general programs can be proven via a particularly simple Turing machine simulation.

Theorem 6. *Given a linear datalog program P, a database* **db** *and a ground fact f, deciding whether $P \cup \mathrm{db} \models f$ is* PSPACE *complete. This remains true if both the universe of* **db** *is fixed to be $\{0, 1\}$ and if* **db** *does not contain any EDB relations.*

Proof. Membership in PSPACE was already shown in Theorem 5. We show hardness. We use a reduction from the following well-known PSPACE-complete problem: Given an integer k as unary string and the description of a deterministic Turing machine T, decide whether T accepts the empty input string in space k, i.e., without ever leaving the first k tape cells. Without loss of generality, we may assume that T accepts iff it halts in a special state α with a completely blank tape and having the cursor in the leftmost position.

Assume the machine has a tape alphabet of a letters and a state set of s states. We encode letters and states by binary strings of length $\lceil \log a \rceil$ and $\lceil \log s \rceil$, respectively. We denote the code of an object o by $\lceil o \rceil$.

A configuration $\mathcal{E}$ of the machine is represented by a datalog atom of the form

$$conf(state, cell_1, cur_1, cell_2, cur_2, \ldots, cell_k, cur_k),$$

where $state$ is a Boolean vector of length s encoding the state of $\mathcal{E}$, the $cell_i$ items are a-ary Boolean vectors encoding the cell-contents of cell i, respectively, and cur_i is 1 if the cursor is at cell i and 0 otherwise.

We now describe a datalog program P simulating the evolution of T when started with a blank worktape (i.e., with empty input). The unique predicate of program P is the IDB predicate $conf$.

P consists of an initialization rule and a number of transition rules. The initialization rule is:

$$conf(\lceil init \rceil, \lceil b \rceil, 1, \lceil b \rceil, 0, \lceil b \rceil, 0 \ldots, \lceil b \rceil, 0),$$

where $init$ denotes the initial state and b the blank symbol.

For each transition τ and each cursor position from which τ is possible, P contains a corresponding rule. For example, the transition *if symbol read is a and state is q, then write b, move right, and enter state q'* is represented by a datalog rule of the following form for $1 \le i \le k-1$:

$$conf(\lceil q' \rceil, \mathbf{X}_1, 0, \ldots, \mathbf{X}_{i-1}, 0, \lceil b \rceil, 0, \mathbf{X}_{i+1}, 1, \mathbf{X}_{i+2}, 0, \ldots, \mathbf{X}_k, 0) \leftarrow$$
$$conf(\lceil q \rceil, \mathbf{X}_1, 0, \ldots, \mathbf{X}_{i-1}, 0, \lceil a \rceil, 1, \mathbf{X}_{i+1}, 0, \mathbf{X}_{i+2}, 0, \ldots, \mathbf{X}_k, 0).$$

It is clear that T halts in the accepting state iff from the datalog program P operating over the empty database, the following fact can be derived:

$$conf(\lceil \alpha \rceil, \lceil b \rceil, 1, \lceil b \rceil, 0, \lceil b \rceil, 0 \ldots, \lceil b \rceil, 0).$$

■

Theorem 7 (Combined Complexity of Absolute Linear Sirups). *Given an absolute linear sirup P, a database* db, *and a ground fact f, determining whether $P \cup$ db $\models f$ is PSPACE complete. This remains true even if* db *has no EDB predicates, and the universe of* db *has cardinality 2.*

Proof.   Membership follows from Theorem 5. To see PSPACE hardness, form the product of general linear programs as in Theorem 6. The resulting absolute sirup is linear. The theorem follows.   ■

The following theorems state some additional complexity results that can be proven in a completely analogous way as the corresponding results for nonlinear sirups. The proofs are thus omitted.

Theorem 8 (Program Complexity of Absolute Linear Sirups). *Absolute linear sirups are program-complete in NP.*

Theorem 9 (Program Complexity of Linear SGF Sirups). *Linear SGF sirups are program-complete in PSPACE. The same holds for all classes of linear sirups containing the linear SGF sirups.*

7 Descriptive Complexity of Sirups

It is well-known that semipositive Datalog, i.e., datalog, where negation may be applied to EDB relations only, captures PTIME on ordered structures. In this section we show that similar results hold even for very restricted versions of sirups. We limit ourselves to the feature of expressing Boolean database properties. Thus, when speaking about *capturing*, we mean the capability of expressing Boolean database properties in a certain class via the evaluation problem for a particular class of sirups.

The main message of this section is that *in essence* even very restricted classes of sirups such as SGF sirups have the same expressive power as full datalog. "In essence" means that we have to move to a slightly different representation of relational data for achieving our goals, and that we have to assume that the database contains the BASIC facts as predefined facts.

Let us start by considering absolute sirups. Clearly, absolute sirups *do not* capture PTIME on ordered structures, even if negation of EDB facts is allowed in the rule body and even on databases where the $BASIC$ relations are available as predefined relations. There are two main reasons for this:

1. The database must contain at least one ground fact for the recursive IDB predicate, otherwise the recursive rule fails. A database is not guaranteed to contain such a fact, and even if so, this fact is not guaranteed to be the right one (e.g. fact $r(0)$, c.f. Section 6).
2. If the absolute sirup contains, say, an atom $q(X)$ in its rule body for some EDB predicate q, then, if the relation q is empty, the rule will fail regardless of the value of other predicates. Similarly, if the rule contains in its body a literal $\neg q(X)$, and if q happens to be the total relation, then the rule will fail.

The first of the above inconveniences does not subsist for SGF sirups, where we can explicitly add the required IDB ground fact. The second problem, however, applies also to SGF sirups. To circumvent it, we switch to another data representation format.

In a *completed* database (finite structure), each non-predefined EDB predicate p has, in addition to its regular arguments an additional Boolean argument that states whether the intended fact is or is not in the database. In a completed database a k-ary relation p over a universe U is represented by the following *completion* $\hat{p}$:

$$\hat{p} = \{\hat{p}(t_1, \dots, t_k, 1) \mid p(t_1, \dots, t_k) \in p\} \cup$$
$$\{\hat{p}(t_1, \dots, t_k, 0) \mid t_1, \dots, t_k \in U \land p(t_1, \dots, t_k) \notin p\}.$$

It is obvious that, over a fixed schema, each database can be translated into its completion in logspace, and vice-versa.

We call a structure *enriched*, if it contains the BASIC predicates as predefined predicates.

Theorem 10 (Expressive Power of SGF Sirups). *Over completed, ordered, and enriched databases, SGF sirups, and, in particular, quadratic SGF sirups capture PTIME, and linear SGF sirups capture NLOGSPACE.*

Proof.   First observe that datalog (without negation of EDB predicates) captures PTIME over ordered completed structures: Negated EDB literals can be replaced by appropriately tagged positive atoms. Thus, for any given schema, any PTIME database property π can be represented by an appropriate program P_π and a ground fact $p_j(t)$ such that for every completed, ordered, and enriched database **db**, **db** $\cup P_\pi \models p_j(t)$ iff $\pi(\mathbf{db})$ holds. Now consider the SGF sirup $P'_\pi = XP_\pi \cup \{r(0)\}$. By Theorem 1 it follows that $\pi(\mathbf{db})$ holds iff **db** $\cup P'_\pi \models r(t, 0^{a-c}, \mathbf{j})$, where a is the maximal arity of IDB predicates in P_π. Note that P'_π is a quadratic SGF sirup.

The result for linear SGF sirups can be obtained in a similar way from the result that linear datalog programs capture NLOGSPACE [16], and from the fact that the product XP of a linear program is itself linear.   ∎

From the above result we can obtain various extremely restricted versions of semipositive datalog that capture PTIME or NLOGSPACE on (regular) ordered structures with equality. In fact, restricted versions of semipositive datalog in which BASIC and the completion relations can be defined by subprograms are good candidates for such expressiveness results. As an example, consider the class SIMPLE defined as follows. The programs in SIMPLE contain a single recursive rule whose body has no occurrence of the negation sign, plus nonrecursive initialization rules whose right-hand side is either empty or contains a negated or unnegated EDB or equality atom. The class LINSIMPLE, in addition, restricts the recursive rule to be linear.

Theorem 11. *Over ordered structures with equality SIMPLE captures PTIME and LINSIMPLE captures NLOGSPACE.*

Proof.   It is sufficient to show that the BASIC facts and an IDB predicate corresponding to $\hat{p}$ for each EDB predicate p can be defined by initialization rules. This is done as follows:

$$and(0,0,0) \leftarrow$$
$$and(0,1,0) \leftarrow$$
$$and(1,0,0) \leftarrow$$
$$and(1,1,1) \leftarrow$$
$$select(0,X,Y,X) \leftarrow$$
$$select(1,X,Y,Y) \leftarrow$$
$$equal(X,X,1) \leftarrow$$
$$equal(X,Y,0) \leftarrow \neg(X=Y)$$
$$\hat{p}(\mathbf{t},1) \leftarrow p(\mathbf{t}) \qquad \text{for each EDB predicate } p$$
$$\hat{p}(\mathbf{t},0) \leftarrow \neg p(\mathbf{t}) \qquad \text{for each EDB predicate } p$$

∎

Acknowledgments

We thank Robert Baumgartner, Hans Tompits, and Andrei Voronkov for useful comments on an earlier version of this paper.

References

1. S. Aanderaa. On the Decision Problem for Formulas in which all Disjunctions are binary. *Proc. of the 2nd Scandinavian Logic Symposium*, pp. 1–18, North Holland Publishing Company, 1971.
2. S. Abiteboul. Boundedness is undecidable for datalog programs with a single recursive rule. *Information Processing Letters*, 32(6):281–289, 1989.
3. S. Abiteboul, R. Hull, and V. Vianu. *Foundations of Databases*. Addison-Wesley, 1995.
4. F. Afrati and C. H. Papadimitriou. The parallel complexity of simple logic programs. *Journal of the Association for Computing Machinery*, 40(4):891–916, 1993.
5. E. Börger *Reduktionstypen in Krom- und Hornformeln*. Ph.D. Dissertation, Münster, Germany, 1971.
6. E. Börger, E. Grädel, and Y. Gurevich. *The Classical Decision Problem*. Springer, Berlin Heidelberg, 1997.
7. S. Ceri, G. Gottlob, and L. Tanca. *Logic Programming and Databases*. Surveys in Computer Science. Springer Verlag, 1990.
8. A. K. Chandra, H. Lewis, and J. Makowsky. Embedded implicational dependencies and their inference problem. In *ACM Symposium on Theory of Computing (STOC)*, pages 342–354, 1981.
9. A. Chandra and P. Merlin. Optimal implementation of conjunctive queries in relational databases. In *Proc. Ninth ACM Symposium on the Theory of Computing*, pages 77–90, 1977.
10. E. Dantsin, T. Eiter, G. Gottlob, and A. Voronkov. Complexity and expressive power of logic programming. In *Proceedings Twelfth Annual IEEE Conference on Computational Complexity*, pages 82–101, Ulm, Germany, June 1997. Full version available from the authors.
11. P. Devienne, P. Lebègue, and J.-C. Routier. Halting problem of one binary Horn clause is undecidable. In P. Enjalbert, A. Finkel, and K. Wagner, editors, *Proceedings Tenth Symposium on Theoretical Aspects of Computing (STACS-93)*, number 665 in LNCS, pages 48–57, Würzburg, February 1993. Springer.
12. H.-D. Ebbinghaus and J. Flum. *Finite Model Theory*. Perspectives in Mathematical Logic. Springer, 1995.
13. M. Gelfond and V. Lifschitz. The stable model semantics for logic programming. In *Proc. 5th International Conference and Symposium on Logic Programming*, pages 1070–1080. The MIT Press, 1988.
14. G. Gottlob. Subsumption and implication. *Information Processing Letters*, 24(2):109–111, 1987.
15. E. Grädel. The Expressive Power of Second-Order Horn Logic. In *Proceedings STACS-91*, LNCS 480, pages 466–477, 1991.
16. E. Grädel. Capturing Complexity Classes with Fragments of Second Order Logic. *Theoretical Computer Science*, 101:35–57, 1992.
17. Y. Gurevich. Logic and the Challenge of Computer Science. In E. Börger, editor, *Trends in Theoretical Computer Science*, chapter 1. Computer Science Press, 1988.
18. P. Hanschke and J. Würtz. Satisfiability of the smallest binary program. *Information Processing Letters*, 45(5):237–241, 1993.

19. G. G. Hillebrand, P. C. Kanellakis, H. G. Mairson, and M. Y. Vardi. Undecidable boundedness problems for datalog programs. *Journal of Logic Programming*, 25(2):163–190, 1995.
20. N. Immerman. Relational queries computable in polynomial time. *Information and Control*, 68:86–104, 1986.
21. N. Immerman. *Descriptive Complexity Theory*. Springer, 1998 (to appear).
22. P. Kanellakis. Logic programming and parallel complexity. In J. Minker, editor, *Foundations of Deductive Databases and Logic Programming*, pp. 547–586. Morgan Kaufmann, 1988.
23. J. U.Kietz, S. Dzeroski. Inductive Logic Programming and Learnability. *SIGART Bulletin* 5(1), pp. 22–32,1994.
24. H. Lewis. Krom Formulas with One Dyadic Predicate Letter. *Journal of Symbolic Logic*, 46(2):341–362, 1976.
25. J. Marcinkowski. The 3 frenchmen method proves undecidability of the uniform boundedness for single recursive rule ternary DATALOG programs. In *ACM Symposium on Theory of Computing (STOC)*, volume 1046 of *Lecture Notes in Computer Science*, pages 427–438. Springer Verlag, 1996.
26. J. Marcinkowski. DATALOG SIRUPs uniform boundedness is undecidable. In *Proc. IEEE Conference on Logic in Computer Science (LICS)*, pages 13–24. IEEE Computer Society Press, 1996.
27. J. Marcinkowski and L. Pacholski. Undecidability of the Horn-clause implication problem. In *Proc. IEEE International Conference of Foundations of Computer Science (FOCS)*, pages 354–362. IEEE Computer Society Press, 1992.
28. L. J. Stockmeyer. The Polynomial-Time Hierarchy. *Theoretical Computer Science*, 3:1–22, 1977.
29. J. D. Ullman and A. van Gelder. Parallel complexity of logical query programs. *Algorithmica*, 3:5–42, 1988.
30. J. Ullman. *Database and Knowledge-Base Systems*, volume I. Computer Science Press, 1988.
31. J. Ullman. *Database and Knowledge-Base Systems*, volume II. Computer Science Press, 1989.
32. M. Vardi. Complexity of Relational Query Languages. In *Proceedings 14th STOC*, pages 137–146, San Francisco, 1982.

Abstracting Properties in Concurrent Constraint Programming

René Moreno

Dipartimento di Informatica, Università di Pisa,
Corso Italia 40, 56125, Pisa, Italy
moreno@di.unipi.it

Abstract. We present a denotational semantics for concurrent constraint programming based on derivations containing sequences of interactions of a process with the environment. Our semantic is then used as collecting semantics for abstracting properties of computations by applying techniques of abstract interpretation.

1 Introduction

The concurrent constraint programming (*ccp*) paradigm [7] combines elegantly logical concepts and concurrency mechanisms. It is based on the notion of computing with systems of partial information and its computational model relays on the concept of *constraint system*, consisting of a set of constraints ordered with respect to logical implication. The *store* is seen as a constraint on the range of values that variables can assume, i.e. it is seen as a set of valuations, and constraints are finite representations of these sets.

All processes interact through a common store, which represents the constraint established until that moment of the computation. Communication is achieved by *telling* (adding) a given constraint to the store, and by *asking* (checking whether the store entails) a given constraint. Synchronization is based on the mechanism of *blocking ask*, i.e. a process waits until the store is strong enough to entail a given constraint. The execution of an ask depends monotonically upon the store, which in turn is monotonically increased by the tell operation. This means that the store evolves monotonically from the initial store *true* (meaning no restriction on the values of variables) and gets more refined while the computation proceeds.

Like for most of concurrent languages, the presence of guarded nondeterminism causes the denotational semantics of *ccp* to be rather complicated, and therefore programs are difficult to analyze and to reason about. We address the problem of defining a compositional semantics for *ccp*, and introduce a semantics expressed in term of derivations. The basic idea in our approach is the *goal independent program denotation*, which we specify by a bottom-up construction as the least fixpoint of a suitable operator.

The idea of defining compositional semantics for *ccp* has been extensively investigated (see [3, 6]). The different semantics presented are defined at different levels of abstraction, according with the specific problem to solve and are more or less concrete. The goal of our work is to define a semantics which should be the most concrete one, with the scope of using it as collecting semantics for an abstract interpretation framework in which we can characterize properties of *ccp* computations by means of suitable abstractions.

We define a *denotational semantics* on domains consisting of sets of derivations, which deals with low-level operational details. Moreover, the typical compositional style of denotational semantics allows us to identify a small set of *primitive semantic operators*, which are the semantic counterparts of the language syntactic operators. This derivations semantics is the most natural choice for a collecting semantics and is essentially a traces semantics containing all the relevant information of *ccp*-computations.

2 Abstract Interpretation

Abstract Interpretation [1, 2] is a theory to reason about the abstraction relation between two different semantics, the concrete and the abstract semantics. The main idea is to relate both semantics by a pair of functions, the abstraction α and the concretization γ, which form a Galois connection.

Definition 1. *Let $(C, \sqsubseteq)$ and $(A, \leq)$ be two posets (the concrete and the abstract domain). A Galois Connection $\langle \alpha, \gamma \rangle : (C, \sqsubseteq) \rightleftharpoons (A, \leq)$ is a pair of maps $\alpha : C \to A$ and $\gamma : A \to C$ such that*

1. *α and γ are monotonic,*
2. *for each $x \in C$, $x \sqsubseteq (\gamma \circ \alpha)(x)$ and*
3. *for each $y \in A$, $(\alpha \circ \gamma)(y) \leq y$.*

Moreover, a Galois insertion (of A in C) $\langle \alpha, \gamma \rangle : (C, \sqsubseteq) \rightleftharpoons (A, \leq)$ is a Galois connection where $\alpha \circ \gamma = Id_A$.

Given a concrete semantics and a Galois insertion between the concrete and the abstract domain, we want to define an abstract semantics. The theory requires the concrete semantics to be the least fixpoint of a semantic function $F : C \to C$. The abstract semantics function $\tilde{F} : A \to A$ is correct if $\forall x \in C.F(x) \sqsubseteq \gamma \left(\tilde{F}(\alpha(x)) \right)$.

F in turn is often defined as composition of "primitive" operators. Let $f : C^n \to C$ be one such an operator and assume $\tilde{f}$ is its abstract counterpart. Then $\tilde{f}$ is locally correct w.r.t. f if $\forall x_1, \cdots, x_n \in C$ we have $f(x_1, \cdots, x_n) \sqsubseteq \gamma \left(\tilde{f}(\alpha(x_1), \cdots, \alpha(x_n)) \right)$. The local correctness of all the primitive operators implies the global correctness. Hence, we can define an abstract semantics by defining locally correct abstract primitive operators. An abstract computation is then related to the concrete computation by replacing the concrete operators by the corresponding abstract operators. According to the theory, for each operator f, there exists an optimal (most precise) locally correct abstract operator $\tilde{f}$ defined as $\tilde{f}(y_1, \cdots, y_n) = \alpha (f (\gamma(y_1), \cdots, \gamma(y_n)))$.

3   Concurrent Constraint Programming

3.1   Cylindric Constraint Systems

A constraint system can be any system of partial information that supports the notion of consistency and entailment. Here we consider an abstract definition of such systems as lattices, following [7]

Definition 2. *A cylindric constraint system is a structure*

$$\mathbf{C} = \langle C, \leq, \sqcup, true, false, Var, \exists, \delta \rangle$$

such that

1. $\langle C, \leq, \sqcup, true, false \rangle$ *is a lattice, where* $\sqcup$ *is the lub operation (representing the logical and), and* $true, false$ *are the least and the greatest elements of* C, *respectively[1]. The elements of* C *are called constraints.*
2. *Var is a denumerable set of variables , and for each* $x \in Var$ *the function* $\exists_x : C \to C$ *is a cylindrification operator [5], i.e. it satisfies the following properties:*

    (a) $\exists_x c \leq c$,
    (b) *if* $c \leq d$ *then* $\exists_x c \leq \exists_x d$,
    (c) $\exists_x (c \sqcup \exists_x d) = \exists_x c \sqcup \exists_x d$,
    (d) $\exists_x \exists_y c = \exists_y \exists_x c$.
3. *For each* $x, y \in Var$, $\delta_{xy} \in C$ *is a diagonal element [5], i.e. it satisfies the following properties:*

    (a) $\delta_{xx} = true$,
    (b) *if* z *is different from* x, y *then* $\delta_{xy} = \exists_z (\delta_{xz} \sqcup \delta_{zy})$,
    (c) *if* x *is different from* y *then* $c \leq \delta_{xy} \sqcup \exists_x (c \sqcup \delta_{xy})$.

The cylindrification operators model a sort of existential quantification and are used for defining a hiding operator in the language. The diagonal elements are useful to model parameter passing. If **C** contains an equality theory, then the elements δ_{xy} can be thought of as the formulas $x = y$.

3.2   The Ccp Language

We present a language containing the basic features of concurrent contraint programming, we define its syntax and its standard computational model, which are parametric with respect to an underlying cylindric constraint system.

Queries, programs and agents (processes) are described by the following grammar

---

[1] The entailment relation $\vdash$, which is commonly used in the literature, is the reverse of $\leq$. Formally: for $c, d \in C$, $c \vdash d$ iff $d \leq c$.

$$QUERY ::= AGENT \text{ } in \text{ } PROG$$
$$PROG ::= \emptyset \mid \{CLAUSE\} \cup PROG$$
$$CLAUSE ::= ATOM :-AGENT$$
$$AGENT ::= \textbf{Stop} \mid ATOM \mid \exists_x AGENT \mid$$
$$\textbf{tell}(c) \rightarrow AGENT \mid \textbf{ask}(c) \rightarrow AGENT \mid$$
$$AGENT + AGENT \mid AGENT \parallel AGENT$$

where c is a constraint and $ATOM$ stands for the usual notion of atomic goal. In the following we denote by *Goals* the set of all agents.

The agent **Stop** represents termination. The **ask** an **tell** operations are the communication primitives and work on a common *store* which ranges over C. If d is the current store, then the execution of $\textbf{tell}(c) \rightarrow A$ adds c to the store, that is, it sets the store to be $c \sqcup d$, and then behaves like A. The $\textbf{ask}(c)$ operation is a *guard* and its execution does not modify the store: it just tests the current store for entailment of the constraint c. We say that $\textbf{ask}(c)$ is *enabled* in d if $c \leq d$. The operations $\textbf{tell}(c)$ and $\textbf{ask}(c)$ fail when c is inconsistent with the store. The operators $\parallel$ and $+$ are the parallel composition and the nondeterministic choice, respectively. We use $\exists_x$ to indicate a *hiding operator* . The intended meaning of $\exists_x A$ is that of an process which behaves like A, but where x is considered *local* or *private* in A. Finally, the agent $p(\textbf{t})$ is a procedure call, where p is the name of the procedure and $\textbf{t}$ is the actual parameters list. The meaning of $p(\textbf{t})$ is given with respect to a set of procedure declarations P (program) of the form $p(\textbf{x}) : -A$, where $\textbf{x}$ is the formal parameters list. An instantiation of $p(\textbf{x}) : -A$ is an object of the form $p(\textbf{t}) : -A'$, where A' is obtained by replacing every formal parameter by its corresponding actual parameter, and by renaming all the other variables to avoid clashes with $\textbf{t}$. Given a Program P we denote by *Inst(P)* the set of all instantiations of the clauses in P.

3.3   The Operational Model

The informal computational model of *ccp* introduced above can be defined in terms of an operational model based on interactions between a process and the environment, first presented in [3], and similar to that presented in [6]. These interactions are constraints labeled by **a** (assume) or **t** (tell). An assume constraint represents an action performed by the environment, while a tell constraint represents an action performed by the process itself. We will use $\mathcal{L}$ to range over $\{\textbf{a}, \textbf{t}\}$. The interactions encode also the hiding of local variables, by means of existential quantifiers, allowing to model compositionally the hiding operator.

A sequence of interactions has the form $c_1^{l_1} \cdots c_n^{l_n}$, where each c_i can be of the form $\exists_x.c$, and is interpreted as a conjunction, where the scope of an existential quantifier is the whole subsequence that follows. Formally

- $EStore(\varepsilon) = true$
- $EStore\left((\exists_x.c)^l.s\right) = \exists x \left(c \sqcup EStore(s)\right)$

For technical convenience we introduce the following notations. Given an object $\mathcal{X}$ (a constraint, an agent or a derivation) we will denote by

- $vars(\mathcal{X})$ the set of variables of $\mathcal{X}$.
- $FV(\mathcal{X})$ the set of free variables of $\mathcal{X}$.
- $BV(\mathcal{X})$ the set of bounded (by the hiding operator) variables of $\mathcal{X}$.
- $BV^l(\mathcal{X})$, $l \in \mathcal{L}$ the set of bounded variables of $\mathcal{X}$ occurring in constraints labeled by l . Note that the local variables introduced by the process are given by BV^t and those introduced by the environment are given by BV^a.
- $FV^l(\mathcal{X})$, $l \in \mathcal{L}$ the set of free variables of $\mathcal{X}$ occurring in constraints labeled by l.

We describe the operational model of ccp in terms of a labelled transition system $T_P = (Conf, \longrightarrow)$ which is specified with respect to a given program P. The configurations in $Conf$ are pairs consisting of a goal or a *termination mode* [3] and a constraint, representing the global store. The termination modes τ are the symbols **ss**, **ff** and **dd**, denoting success, failure and deadlock respectively. The labels of the transition relation are interactions between the process and the environment.

Table 1 describe the rules of T_P. We assume that variables existentially quantified occurring inside a **tell** or **ask** have different names from all the others occurring in the process or introduced during the computation. We assume also a renaming mechanism that takes care of using fresh variables each time a clause is used.

Note that Rule *R14* models the interaction with the environment. The computation of a process is not immediately affected by actions made by the environment, only its future behavior will depend on them. The environment can then produce an arbitrary constraint without changing the state of the process. Therefore, a process can make an arbitrary assumption about the store, where assumptions involving local variables of the process are not allowed, because these variables are hidden from the environment. Formally this means that the free variables of an assumption may not occur in the scope of the bound variables introduced by the process, i.e. $FV(c) \cap BV^t(d) = \emptyset$, where c is the assumption and d represents the current store. The restrictions $BV(c) \cap vars(A) = \emptyset$ and $BV(c) \cap vars(d) = \emptyset$ ensure the absence of variable clashes between the local variables of the environment and the variables of the process.

Definition 3. *A* derivation *of the query* **G** *in* P *consists of a sequence*

$$\langle \mathbf{G}_0, true \rangle \xrightarrow[A_1]{\alpha_1} \langle \mathbf{G}_1, c_1 \rangle \xrightarrow[A_2]{\alpha_2} \cdots \xrightarrow[A_n]{\alpha_n} \langle \mathbf{G}_n, d \rangle \xrightarrow[A_{n+1}]{\alpha_{n+1}} \cdots$$

where $A_1, A_2, \ldots, A_n, \ldots$ *are the selected agents of each transition and* $s = \alpha_1 \alpha_2 \ldots \alpha_n \ldots$ *is a sequence of interactions with the environment (called reactive sequence), such that* $\mathbf{G}_0 = \mathbf{G}$ *and* $\langle \mathbf{G}_{i-1}, c_{i-1} \rangle \xrightarrow{\alpha_i} \langle \mathbf{G}_i, c_i \rangle$, *for* $i \geq 1$ *(by means of the transition system* T_P), *where the selected agent of* $\mathbf{G}_{i-1}$ *is* A_i *and* $c_i = c_{i-1} \sqcup \alpha_i$.

In the following $\langle \mathbf{G}, true \rangle \xrightarrow[A_1]{\alpha_1} \cdots \xrightarrow[A_n]{\alpha_n} \langle \mathbf{G}_n, d \rangle$ $(n \geq 0)$, where $\mathbf{G}_n$ is a goal or a termination mode in $\{\mathbf{ss}, \mathbf{dd}, \mathbf{ff}\}$, denotes a (partial and finite) derivation of

R1	$\langle \mathbf{Stop}, d \rangle \xrightarrow{true^t} \langle \mathbf{ss}, d \rangle$	
R2	$\langle \mathbf{ask}(c), d \rangle \xrightarrow{true^t} \langle \mathbf{ss}, d \rangle$	if $c \leq d$
R3	$\langle \mathbf{ask}(c), d \rangle \xrightarrow{true^t} \langle \mathbf{dd}, d \rangle$	if $c \nleq d$ and $\models c \sqcup d$
R4	$\langle \mathbf{ask}(c), d \rangle \xrightarrow{true^t} \langle \mathbf{ff}, d \rangle$	if $\nvDash c \sqcup d$
R5	$\langle \mathbf{tell}(c), d \rangle \xrightarrow{e^t} \langle \mathbf{ss}, d \sqcup e \rangle$	$\models d \sqcup c,$ $d \sqcup c \equiv_C d \sqcup e,$ $BV(e) \cap vars(d) = \emptyset$
R6	$\langle \mathbf{tell}(c), d \rangle \xrightarrow{true^t} \langle \mathbf{ff}, d \rangle$	if $\nvDash c \sqcup d$
R7	$\dfrac{\langle G, d \rangle \xrightarrow{c^t} \langle \mathbf{ss}, d' \rangle \mid \langle \alpha, d \rangle}{\langle G \to A, d \rangle \xrightarrow{c^t} \langle A, d' \rangle \mid \langle \alpha, d \rangle}$	$\alpha \in \{\mathbf{ff}, \mathbf{dd}\}$
R8	$\dfrac{\langle A\{^y/_x\}, d \rangle \xrightarrow{c^t} \langle B, d \sqcup c \rangle}{\langle \exists_x A, d \rangle \xrightarrow{\exists_y c^t} \langle B, d \sqcup \exists_y c \rangle}$	$y \cap vars(A) = \emptyset,$
R9	$\langle p(t), d \rangle \xrightarrow{true^t} \langle A', d \rangle$	$p(t)- : A' \in Inst(P)$
R10	$\dfrac{\langle A, d \rangle \xrightarrow{c^t} \langle A', d \sqcup c \rangle \mid \langle \mathbf{ss}, d \sqcup c \rangle}{\begin{array}{l}\langle A \parallel B, d \rangle \xrightarrow{c^t} \langle A' \parallel B, d \sqcup c \rangle \mid \langle B, d \sqcup c \rangle \\ \langle B \parallel A, d \rangle \xrightarrow{c^t} \langle B \parallel A', d \sqcup c \rangle \mid \langle B, d \sqcup c \rangle \end{array}}$	$BV(c) \cap vars(B) = \emptyset$
R11	$\dfrac{\langle A, d \rangle \xrightarrow{true^t} \langle \mathbf{ff}, d \rangle}{\begin{array}{l}\langle A \parallel B, d \rangle \xrightarrow{true^t} \langle \mathbf{ff}, d \rangle \\ \langle B \parallel A, d \rangle \xrightarrow{true^t} \langle \mathbf{ff}, d \rangle \end{array}}$	
R12	$\dfrac{\langle A, d \rangle \xrightarrow{c^t} \langle A', d \sqcup c \rangle \mid \langle \mathbf{ss}, d \sqcup c \rangle}{\begin{array}{l}\langle A + B, d \rangle \xrightarrow{c^t} \langle A', d \sqcup c \rangle \mid \langle \mathbf{ss}, d \sqcup c \rangle \\ \langle B + A, d \rangle \xrightarrow{c^t} \langle A', d \sqcup c \rangle \mid \langle \mathbf{ss}, d \sqcup c \rangle \end{array}}$	
R13	$\dfrac{\langle A, d \rangle \xrightarrow{true^t} \langle \mathbf{dd}, d \rangle, \ \langle B, d \rangle \xrightarrow{true^t} \langle \alpha, d \rangle}{\begin{array}{c}\langle A \parallel B, d \rangle \xrightarrow{true^t} \langle \alpha, d \rangle \\ \langle B \parallel A, d \rangle \xrightarrow{true^t} \langle \alpha, d \rangle \\ \langle A + B, d \rangle \xrightarrow{true^t} \langle \mathbf{dd}, d \rangle \\ \langle B + A, d \rangle \xrightarrow{true^t} \langle \mathbf{dd}, d \rangle \end{array}}$	$\alpha \in \{\mathbf{ff}, \mathbf{dd}\}$
R14	$\langle A, d \rangle \mid \langle \mathbf{ss}, d \rangle \xrightarrow{c^\bullet} \langle A, d \sqcup c \rangle \mid \langle \mathbf{ss}, d \sqcup c \rangle$	$\models d \sqcup c,$ $FV(c) \cap BV^t(d) = \emptyset,$ $BV(c) \cap vars(A) = \emptyset,$ $BV(c) \cap vars(d) = \emptyset$

Table 1. The Transition System T_P

the query **G** *in P*, with selected agents $A_1, \ldots, A_n$, reactive sequence $\alpha_1 \alpha_2 \ldots \alpha_n$ and final store d. We also denote by $\langle \mathbf{G}, true \rangle \xrightarrow[A_P]{s} \langle \mathbf{B}, d \rangle$ a finite derivation of the query **G** *in P* , using the reflexive and transitive closure of $\rightarrow$, where **B** is the last goal or a termination mode, s is the sequence of interactions and A_P is the sequence of agents.

Given a derivation d, *first*(d) and *last*(d) (with d finite) are the first and the last goal or termination mode of d . *length*(d) denotes the length of the derivation, *agents*(d) denotes the sequence of selected agents of the derivation, *sequence*(d) denotes the reactive sequence of d and *EStore*(d) stands for *EStore*(*sequence*(d)). We will denote by *Derivs* the set of all derivations. We will use the following notions regarding derivations.

Between finite derivations, we define the following equivalence relation:
$d_1 \approx d_2$ *iff* $first(d_1) = fisrt(d_2), agents(d_1) \equiv agents(d_2)$
and $sequence(d_1) \equiv_C sequence(d_2)^2$

Given a set of derivations *SD* the notation *sequence*(*SD*) stands for the set $\{ sequence(d) \mid d \in SD \}$.

Definition 4. *A derivation d is called* real *if it is entirely composed by tell constraints, i.e. if $sequence(d) = c_1^t \cdots c_n^t$.*

A derivation d is called convergent *if $last(d) \in \{\mathbf{ss}, \mathbf{dd}, \mathbf{ff}\}$.*

Note that in a real derivation each constraint we observe has been really produced by the process and that a convergent derivation represents a computation which has reached a final state.

4   The Collecting Semantics

4.1   Semantics Domains

In this section we present the semantics domains used to define a denotational semantics, based in the notion of derivation presented above.

A set of derivations *SD* is *well-formed* if and only if $d_1 \approx d_2$ implies $d_2 \in SD$. We denote by $(WFD, \subseteq)$ the complete lattice of well-formed sets of derivations, partially ordered by inclusion. A *collection* D is a partial function $Goals \rightharpoonup WFD$ such that, for every $\mathbf{G} \in Goals$, $D(\mathbf{G})$, if defined, is a well-formed set of derivations all starting from **G**.

We denote by $\mathbb{D}$ the domain of all collections ordered by $\sqsubseteq$ where $D_1 \sqsubseteq D_2$ if and only if $\forall \mathbf{G}.D_1(\mathbf{G}) \subseteq D_2(\mathbf{G})$. $(\mathbb{D}, \sqsubseteq)$ is easy shown to be a complete lattice.

For collections D_1 and D_2 we say D_1 is *equivalent modulo variance* to D_2, $D_1 \equiv_{\mathbf{D}} D_2$, if and only if for any **G** there exist a renaming **G'** of **G** such that, if $D_1(\mathbf{G})$ is defined, then $D_2(\mathbf{G'})$ is defined and, for any $d \in D_1(\mathbf{G})$, there exists $d' \in D_2(\mathbf{G'})$, such that $d \approx d'$ and viceversa.

---

[2] Here $\equiv$ denotes the variance relation on terms defined over a given signature.

A *pure collection* is a collection defined only for pure atomic goals[3]. We denote by $\mathbb{PD}$ the sublattice of pure $\mathbb{D}$-collections. An *interpretation* I ($\mathbb{D}$-*Interpretation*) is a pure collection modulo variance. We denote by $\mathbb{I_D}$ the set of interpretations. $(\mathbb{I_D}, \sqsubseteq)$ is a complete lattice with the induced quotient order.

4.2   Denotational Semantics

The equivalence class modulo variance of a collection D is denoted by D itself. Any interpretation I of $\mathbb{I_D}$ is considered also as an arbitrary collection obtained by choosing an arbitrary representative of I . The semantics operators used on interpretations are independent of the choice of the representative. Therefore, we can define any operator on $\mathbb{I_D}$ in terms of its counterpart on $\mathbb{D}$, independently from the choice of the representative. We will denote the corresponding operators on $\mathbb{I_D}$ and $\mathbb{D}$ by the same name.

We define the denotational semantics inductively on the syntax of *ccp* programs presented in Section 3.2. The semantics functions are

$\mathcal{Q} : QUERY \to \mathbb{D}$
$\mathcal{P} : PROG \to (\mathbb{I_D} \to \mathbb{I_D})$
$\mathcal{C} : CLAUSE \to (\mathbb{I_D} \to \mathbb{I_D})$
$\mathcal{A} : AGENT \to (\mathbb{I_D} \to \mathbb{D})$

and are defined in term of the operators $\otimes, \bowtie, \|, \oplus, \rhd, \lhd, \exists$ and $\bullet$ defined in section 4.2. The choice of this semantic operators is induced by the syntactic operations, due to the compositional nature of denotational semantics.

$$\mathcal{Q}[\mathbf{G}\ in\ P] \quad := \mathcal{G}[\mathbf{G}]_{lfp\,\mathcal{P}[P]}$$
$$\mathcal{P}[\{cl\} \cup P]_I \quad := \mathcal{C}[cl]_I \otimes \mathcal{P}[P]_I$$
$$\mathcal{P}[\emptyset] \quad := Id_{\mathbb{I_D}}$$
$$\mathcal{C}[p(\mathbf{x}){\vdash}: \mathbf{B}]_I \quad := tree(p(\mathbf{x}) :- \mathbf{B}) \bowtie \mathcal{A}[\mathbf{B}]_I$$
$$\mathcal{A}[\mathbf{A} \| \mathbf{B}]_I \quad := \mathcal{A}[\mathbf{A}]_I \| \mathcal{A}[\mathbf{B}]_I$$
$$\mathcal{A}[\mathbf{A} + \mathbf{B}]_I \quad := \mathcal{A}[\mathbf{A}]_I \oplus \mathcal{A}[\mathbf{B}]_I$$
$$\mathcal{A}[\mathbf{Stop}]_I \quad := \phi\left[^{\mathsf{StopSet}}/_{\mathsf{Stop}}\right]$$
$$\mathcal{A}[\mathbf{tell}(c) \to \mathbf{A}]_I := c \rhd \mathcal{A}[\mathbf{A}]_I$$
$$\mathcal{A}[\mathbf{ask}(c) \to \mathbf{A}]_I := c \lhd \mathcal{A}[\mathbf{A}]_I$$
$$\mathcal{A}[\exists_x \mathbf{A}]_I \quad := \exists_x^A \mathcal{A}[\mathbf{A}]_I$$
$$\mathcal{A}[\mathbf{p}]_I \quad := \mathbf{p} \bullet I$$

where $lfp\,\mathcal{P}[P]$ means $lfp_{\mathbb{I_D}} \lambda I.\mathcal{P}[P]_I$.

Using standard techniques it can be proved that $\mathcal{P}[P]$ is continuous [6], hence we can define the fixpoint denotation of a program P as the interpretation $\mathcal{F} := lfp\,\mathcal{P}[P]$.

Operations on Derivations   We define now various auxiliary operations on derivations, used later to define the semantic operators on collections.

1. Let $d_1 = \langle \mathbf{G}, c \rangle \xrightarrow[A_P^1]{s_1} \langle \mathbf{B}_1, d_1 \rangle$ and $d_2 = \langle \mathbf{B}_1, d_1 \rangle \xrightarrow[A_P^2]{s_2} \langle \mathbf{B}_2, d_2 \rangle$ be two derivations with $last(d_1) = first(d_2)$ and $vars(d_1) \cap vars(d_2) = vars(first(d_2))$.

---

[3] An atom is called *pure* if it is of the form $p(\mathbf{x})$, where $\mathbf{x}$ is a tuple of distinct variables.

Then $d_1 :: d_2 := \langle G, c\rangle \xrightarrow[A_P^1]{s_1} \langle B_1, d_1\rangle \xrightarrow[A_P^2]{s_2} \langle B_2, d_2\rangle$ denotes the concatenation of d_1 and d_2. This operation is naturally extended to sets of derivations. The operator $\bowtie$ is a special case of the operator $::$ and is defined only for two derivations d_1 and d_2 with $d_1 = \langle \mathbf{p(t)}, c\rangle \xrightarrow[\mathbf{p(t)}]{true^t} \langle B', true\rangle$ and $d_2 = \langle B', true\rangle \xrightarrow[A_P]{s} \langle B, d\rangle$, i.e. $last(d_1) = first(d_2)$. Then $d_1 \bowtie d_2$ is defined as

the collection $\langle \mathbf{p(t)}, true\rangle \xrightarrow[\mathbf{p(t)}]{true^t} \langle B', true\rangle \xrightarrow[A_P]{s} \langle B, d\rangle$

2. Let $d = \langle G, c\rangle \xrightarrow[A_P]{s} \langle B, d\rangle$ be a derivation and ρ be a renaming such that $vars(G\rho) \cap (vars(agents(d)) \cup vars(sequence(d)) = \emptyset$. Then $\partial_\rho(d)$ is defined as the collection $\langle G\rho, c\rho\rangle \xrightarrow[A_P\rho]{s\rho} \langle B\rho, d\rho\rangle$

3. The operator $\triangleright$ acting on a constraint c and a derivation d if defined as follows: Let $G' = \mathbf{tell}(c) \to G$, and $s^a = c_1^a \cdots c_n^a$, then

   - If $\models d_i \sqcup c$ and $d_i \sqcup c \equiv_C d_i \sqcup e$ and $FV(e) \cap BV(d) = \emptyset$ and $BV(e) \cap FV(d) = \emptyset$, then

   $$c \triangleright \langle G, d_0\rangle \xrightarrow[A_P^0]{s_0^a} \langle G, d_i\rangle \xrightarrow[Env]{e^a} \langle G, d_{i+1}\rangle \xrightarrow[A_P^1]{s_1} \langle \tau, d_n\rangle :=$$
   $$\langle G', d_0\rangle \xrightarrow[A_P^0]{s_0^a} \langle G', d_i\rangle \xrightarrow[G']{e^t} \langle G, d_{i+1}\rangle \xrightarrow[A_P^1]{s_1} \langle \tau, d_n\rangle$$

   - If $\not\models d_i \sqcup c$, then

   $$c \triangleright \langle G, d_0\rangle \xrightarrow[A_P^0]{s_0^a} \langle G, d_i\rangle \xrightarrow[A_P^1]{s_1} \langle \tau, d_n\rangle := \langle G', d_0\rangle \xrightarrow[A_P^0]{s_0^a} \langle G', d_i\rangle \xrightarrow[G']{true^t} \langle \mathbf{ff}, d_i\rangle$$

   - $c \triangleright \langle G, d\rangle \xrightarrow[A_P]{s} \langle \bot, d_n\rangle := \langle G', d\rangle \xrightarrow[A_P]{s} \langle \bot, d_n\rangle$

4. The operator $\triangleleft$ acting on a constraint c and a derivation d if defined as follows:. Let $G' = \mathbf{ask}(c) \to G$, and $s^a = c_1^a \cdots c_n^a$, then

   - If $c \leq d_i$, then

   $$c \triangleleft \langle G, d_0\rangle \xrightarrow[A_P^0]{s_0^a} \langle G, d_i\rangle \xrightarrow[Env]{c^a} \langle G, d_{i+1}\rangle \xrightarrow[A_P^1]{s_1} \langle \tau, d_n\rangle :=$$
   $$\langle G', d_0\rangle \xrightarrow[A_P^0]{s_0^a} \langle G', d_i\rangle \xrightarrow[Env]{c^a} \langle G', d_{i+1}\rangle \xrightarrow[G']{true^t} \langle G, d_{i+1}\rangle \xrightarrow[A_P^1]{s_1} \langle \tau, d_n\rangle$$

   - If $\not\models d_i \sqcup c$, then

   $$c \triangleleft \langle G, d_0\rangle \xrightarrow[A_P^0]{s_0^a} \langle G, d_i\rangle \xrightarrow[A_P^1]{s_1} \langle \tau, d_n\rangle := \langle G', d_0\rangle \xrightarrow[A_P^0]{s_0^a} \langle G', d_i\rangle \xrightarrow[G']{true^t} \langle \mathbf{ff}, d_i\rangle$$

   - If $\models d_i \sqcup c$ and $c \not\leq d_i$, then

   $$c \triangleleft \langle G, d_0\rangle \xrightarrow[A_P^0]{s_0^a} \langle G, d_i\rangle \xrightarrow[A_P^1]{s_1} \langle \tau, d_n\rangle := \langle G', d_0\rangle \xrightarrow[A_P^0]{s_0} \langle G', d_i\rangle \xrightarrow[G']{true^t} \langle \mathbf{dd}, d_i\rangle$$

   - $c \triangleleft \langle G, d\rangle \xrightarrow[A_P]{s} \langle \bot, d_n\rangle := \langle G', d\rangle \xrightarrow[A_P]{s} \langle \bot, d_n\rangle$

5. The operator $\|$, first introduced in [4] for sequences of constraints, allows to combine derivations whose sequences are equal at each point, apart from the modes, modeling the interaction of a process with its environment. It amounts to verify that the assumptions made by one process are validated by the other one (i.e. it tells or assumes the same contraint). Formally,

the operator is defined on derivations d_1 and d_2, such that $sequence(d_1) = c_1^{l_1} c_2^{l_2} \cdots c_n^{l_n}$,and $sequence(d_2) = c_1^{l'_1} c_2^{l'_2} \cdots c_n^{l'_n}$.

$$\langle A, d\rangle \xrightarrow[A_P^1]{s_1} \langle \tau_1, e\rangle \, \| \, \langle B, d\rangle \xrightarrow[A_P^2]{s_2} \langle \tau_2, e\rangle = \langle B, d\rangle \xrightarrow[A_P^2]{s_2} \langle \tau_2, e\rangle \, \| \, \langle A, d\rangle \xrightarrow[A_P^1]{s_1} \langle \tau_1, e\rangle$$

$$\langle A, d\rangle \xrightarrow[Env]{c^\bullet} \langle A_1, d_1\rangle \xrightarrow[A_P^1]{s_1} \langle \tau_1, e\rangle \, \| \, \langle B, d\rangle \xrightarrow[G_1]{c'} \langle B_1, d_1\rangle \xrightarrow[A_P^2]{s_2} \langle \tau_2, e\rangle :=$$

$$\langle A \, \| \, B, d\rangle \xrightarrow[G_1]{c'} \langle A \, \| \, B_1, d_1\rangle :: \left(\langle A, d_1\rangle \xrightarrow[A_P^1]{s_1} \langle \tau_1, e\rangle \, \| \, \langle B_1, d_1\rangle \xrightarrow[A_P^2]{s_2} \langle \tau_2, e\rangle \right)$$

Syntactically, we apply the notation $\mathbf{Stop} \, \| \, A = A \, \| \, \mathbf{Stop} = A$. Furthermore we have the rules

- $\langle \tau, e\rangle \, \| \, \langle \mathbf{ss}, e\rangle := \langle \tau, e\rangle$
- $\langle \tau, e\rangle \, \| \, \langle \mathbf{ff}, e\rangle := \langle \mathbf{ff}, e\rangle$
- $\langle \mathbf{dd}, e\rangle \, \| \, \langle \mathbf{dd}, e\rangle := \langle \mathbf{dd}, e\rangle$
- $\langle \perp, e\rangle \, \| \, \langle \perp, e\rangle := \langle \perp, e\rangle$

6. The hiding operator on derivations, defined if $X \cap (FV^{\mathbf{a}}(d_i) \cup FV^{\mathbf{a}}(s_1)) = \emptyset$, is given by

$$\exists_x \left(\langle G, d_0\rangle \xrightarrow[A_P^0]{s_0^\bullet} \langle G, d_i\rangle \xrightarrow[A_i]{c'} \langle G_{i+1}, d_{i+1}\rangle \xrightarrow[A_P^1]{s_1} \langle \tau, d_n\rangle \right) :=$$

$$\langle G, d_0\rangle \xrightarrow[A_P^0]{s_0^\bullet} \langle G, d_i\rangle \xrightarrow[A_i]{\exists_x c^\bullet} \langle G_{i+1}, d_i \sqcup \theta_x c)\rangle \xrightarrow[A_P^1]{s_1} \langle \tau, d_n\rangle$$

Operations on Collections The *void collection* ϕ is the collection $\lambda G.\mathfrak{N}$, (the undefined function), where $\mathfrak{N}$ stands for the undefined element. The identity collection Id_D is the collection of zero-length derivations for each goal, i.e. $\lambda G.\{\langle G, true\rangle\}$, while the pure identity collection Id_{I_D} is the collection $\lambda p(x).\{\langle p(x), true\rangle\}$[4]. Moreover ϕ_G stands for the collection $\phi\left[^{\langle G, true\rangle}/_G\right]$.

We introduce a special set of derivations, the **StopSet**, defined as

$$\mathbf{StopSet} := \left\{ \langle \mathbf{Stop}, true\rangle \xrightarrow[Env]{c_1^\bullet} \langle \mathbf{Stop}, d_1\rangle \cdots \xrightarrow[\mathbf{Stop}]{true^t} \langle \mathbf{ss}, d_n\rangle \mid d_i = d_{i-1} \sqcup c_i \right\}$$

1. The *sum* of a class of collections $\{D_j\}_{j \in J}$ is defined as $\bigotimes \{D_j\}_{j \in J} :=$ $\lambda G. \bigcup_{j \in J} D_j(G)$

2. The *extension* of D_1 by D_2 is given by
$D_1 \bowtie D_2 := \lambda G. \{d_1 \bowtie d_2 \mid d_1 \in D_1(G), d_2 \in D_2(last(d_1))\}$

3. The *tree* operation maps clauses to collections. For a clause $cl := p(x) \leftarrow : B$ we define
$$tree(cl) := \phi \left[\left\{ \langle p(t), true\rangle \xrightarrow[p(t)]{true^t} \langle B', true\rangle \mid p(t): -B' \in Inst(P) \right\} \big/_{p(t)} \right]$$

4. The *parallel composition* of D_1 and D_2 is defined as
$D_1 \| D_2 := \lambda G. \{d_1 \, \| \, d_2 \mid G = G_1 \, \| \, G_2, d_1 \in D_1(G_1), d_2 \in D_2(G_2)\}$

5. Given a constraint c and a collection D, the $\triangleright$ operator is defined by
$c \triangleright D := \lambda G. \{c \triangleright d \mid G = tell(c) \to A, d \in D(A), c \triangleright d \text{ is defined}\}$

---

[4] Note that when we write $\lambda p(x).E$ we denote a partial function which is defined only for inputs of the form $p(x)$ and is otherwise undefined.

6. Given a constraint c and a collection D , the $\triangleleft$ operator is defined by

$$c \triangleleft D = \lambda G. \{c \triangleleft d \mid G = \mathbf{ask}(c) \to \mathbf{A}, d \in D(\mathbf{A}), c \triangleleft d \text{ is defined}\}$$

7. Let $\{^x/_z,^y/_x\}$ denotes the simultaneous substitution of the free occurrences of the variables z by its corresponding variables x , and the variables x by its corresponding variables y . Furthermore we require that $z \cap vars(\mathbf{A}) = \emptyset$, $y \cap vars(d) = \emptyset$. Then the hiding operator on collections is defined by

$$\exists_x^A D = \lambda G. \{\exists_y d \{^x/_z,^y/_z\} \mid G = \exists_x A, d \in D(\mathbf{A})\}$$

8. To define the choice operator on collections, we make the following considerations. Apart from the cases of deadlock and failure, an alternative derivation can be always selected, therefore the successful and unfinished computations are given by set union. In case of failed or deadlocked computations, observe that the successful execution of an action is made visible by a tell constraint, hence, when a tell constraint is present, the alternative can be selected and we have set union again. On the other side, derivations whose actions are only assume actions and end in failure or deadlock, are present in the result collection only if they are present in all collections. Given a set of derivations S , we use the following notations

$$\{S\}^{\mathbf{T}} = \{d \in S \mid \text{there exists } c^l \in sequence(d) \text{ with } l = \mathbf{t} \text{ and } c \ne \mathbf{true}\}$$

$$\{S\}^{\mathbf{A}} = \{d \in S \mid \text{for all } c^l \in sequence(d) \text{ with } c \ne \mathbf{true} \text{ we have } l = \mathbf{a}\}$$

Formally, we define

$$D_1 \oplus D_2 := \lambda G. \{(D_1(\mathbf{A}_1) \cup^{\mathbf{ss}} D_2(\mathbf{A}_2)) \cup (D_1(\mathbf{A}_1) \cup^{\mathbf{ff}} D_2(\mathbf{A}_2)) \cup \\ (D_1(\mathbf{A}_1) \cup^{\mathbf{dd}} D_2(\mathbf{A}_2)) \cup (D_1(\mathbf{A}_1) \cup^{\perp} D_2(\mathbf{A}_2)) \\ \mid G = \mathbf{A}_1 + \mathbf{A}_2\}$$

where

$$S_1 \cup^{\mathbf{ss}} S_2 = \{d \in S_1 \cup S_2 \mid last(d) = \mathbf{ss}\}$$

$$S_1 \cup^{\mathbf{ff}} S_2 = \{d \in S_1 \cup S_2 \mid last(d) = \mathbf{ff}\}^{\mathbf{T}} \\ \cup \{d \in S_1 \cup S_2 \mid last(d) = \mathbf{ff} \text{ and} \\ sequence(d) \in sequence(S_1) \cap sequence(S_2)\}^{\mathbf{A}}$$

$$S_1 \cup^{\mathbf{dd}} S_2 = \{d \in S_1 \cup S_2 \mid last(d) = \mathbf{dd}\}^{\mathbf{T}} \\ \cup \{d \in S_1 \cup S_2 \mid last(d) = \mathbf{dd} \text{ and} \\ sequence(d) \in sequence(S_1) \cap sequence(S_2)\}^{\mathbf{A}} \\ \cup \{d \in S_1 \mid \exists d' \in S_2.sequence(d) = sequence(d') \\ \text{and } last(d) = \mathbf{dd} \text{ and } last(d') = \mathbf{ff}\}^{\mathbf{A}} \\ \cup \{d \in S_2 \mid \exists d' \in S_1.sequence(d) = sequence(d') \\ \text{and } last(d) = \mathbf{dd} \text{ and } last(d') = \mathbf{ff}\}^{\mathbf{A}}$$

$$S_1 \cup^{\perp} S_2 = \{d \in S_1 \cup S_2 \mid last(d) = \perp\}$$

9. Given an atom $p(t)$ and a collection D , the operator $\bullet$ solves the atom using the collection. We define $p(t) \bullet D := \phi \, [^S/_{p(t)}]$, where

$$
\begin{aligned}
\mathbf{S} = \quad & \{\partial_\rho(\mathrm{d}) \mid \text{There exists renaming } \rho \text{ such that} \\
& \qquad A' = \mathbf{p(t)}\rho, \ \mathrm{d} \in D(A'), last(\mathrm{d}) \in \{\mathbf{ss, ff, dd}\}\} \\
\cup \ & \{\partial_\rho(\mathrm{d}') \mid \text{There exists renaming } \rho \text{ such that} \\
& \qquad A' = \mathbf{p(t)}\rho, \ \mathrm{d} \in D(A'), \\
& \qquad \mathrm{d} = \langle \mathbf{A}', true \rangle \xrightarrow[A_P]{s} \langle \mathbf{G}, c \rangle, \mathbf{G} \in Goals \\
& \qquad \mathrm{d}' = \langle \mathbf{A}', true \rangle \xrightarrow[A_P]{s} \langle \bot, c \rangle \}
\end{aligned}
$$

5   The Abstraction Framework

General semantic frameworks taking into account approximation can be defined using Abstract Interpretation [1,2]. We define a semantic framework whose ingredients are a concrete semantics and an observable. Our concrete semantics models *ccp*-computations and is formalized denotationally.

An observable is a Galois insertion between the domain of computations and an abstract domain of computations over the same constraint system, describing the properties to be modelled. The abstract denotational definition and goal-independent denotation are systematically derived from the concrete ones, by replacing the concrete semantic operators by they optimal abstract versions.

We recall that we are interested in extracting some properties from the concrete semantics *without abstracting the constraint system*, hence we can apply the general framework of Abstract Interpretation in order to define abstract semantics which characterize the properties of computations.

5.1   Extracting Properties of Computations

An observable property domain is a set of properties of derivations with an ordering relation which can be viewed as an approximation structure. An observation consists of looking at an computation, and then extracting some property (abstraction). Since we represent computations as collections, an observable is a function from $\mathbb{D}$ to a suitable domain $\mathcal{A}$, which preserves the approximation structure. Such a function must be a Galois insertion.

Let $(\mathcal{A}, \preceq)$ be a complete lattice. A function $\alpha : WFD \to \mathcal{A}$ is a *domain abstraction* if there exists γ such that $\langle \alpha, \gamma \rangle : (WFD, \subseteq) \rightleftharpoons (\mathcal{A}, \preceq)$ is a Galois insertion. Given an abstract domain A we are generally interested in the *abstract behaviour* of the queries, which are elements of a domain of partial functions $A \subseteq [Goals \to \mathcal{A}]$ (ordered by the trivial extension $\leq$ of $\preceq$) and are called A-*collections*.

The insertion $\langle \alpha, \gamma \rangle$ can be lifted to collections by defining[5] $A = \alpha^\star(\mathbb{D})$, where $\alpha^\star(D) := \lambda G.\alpha(D(G))$, and $\forall S \in \mathrm{A}.\gamma^\star(S) := wf_G(\gamma(S(\mathbf{G})))$, where $wf_G(S)$ is the greatest well-formed subset of S, restricted to the derivations starting from $\mathbf{G}$. The pair $\langle \alpha^\star, \gamma^\star \rangle : (\mathbb{D}, \sqsubseteq) \rightleftharpoons (\mathrm{A}, \leq)$ is a Galois insertion. We will often abuse notation and denote $\alpha^\star$ by α. As in the concrete case, a pure

---

[5] Remember that if $D(\mathbf{G})$ is undefined then also $\alpha(D(\mathbf{G}))$ is undefined.

A-collection is any element $\mathcal{X} \in A$ which is defined for pure atomic goals only. We denote by $\mathbb{P}A$ the sub-lattice of pure A-collections.

Definition 5. *Let* $(A, \leq)$ *be a complete lattice of A-collections. A function* $\alpha :$ $A \to \mathbb{D}$ *is an observable if it maps finite elements of* $\mathbb{D}$ *to finite elements[6] of* A *and there exists* γ *such that*

1. $\langle \alpha, \gamma \rangle : (\mathbb{D}, \sqsubseteq) \rightleftharpoons (A, \leq)$ *is a Galois insertion,*
2. $\alpha(\mathbb{P}\mathbb{D}) = \mathbb{P}A$ *and* $\gamma(\mathbb{P}A) \subseteq \mathbb{P}\mathbb{C}$,
3. $\forall D, D' \in \mathbb{P}\mathbb{D}.D \equiv_{\mathbb{D}} D' \Rightarrow (\gamma\alpha)D \equiv_{\mathbb{D}} (\gamma\alpha)D'$.

Note that given a domain abstraction it is easy to obtain an observable by the above mentioned lifting.

We can then define an abstract enhanced variance relation $\equiv_A$ on abstract collections as follows: for any $\mathcal{X}, \mathcal{X}', \mathcal{X} \equiv_A \mathcal{X}' \Leftrightarrow \gamma(\mathcal{X}) \equiv_{\mathbb{D}} \gamma(\mathcal{X}')$. An A-interpretation is a pure A-collection modulo $\equiv_A$. We denote by $(\mathbb{I}_A, \leq)$ the complete lattice of A-interpretations with the induced quotient order.

5.2   From the Observables to the Abstract Semantics

Once we have an observable $\alpha : A \to \mathbb{D}$, we want to derive the abstract semantics. The idea is to define the optimal abstract versions of the various semantic operators. The optimal abstract counterparts of the basic operators defined on $\mathbb{D}$ are given by the following definitions, $\forall \mathcal{X}, \mathcal{X}', \mathcal{X}_i \in A, c \in C, \mathbf{A} \in Agents$

$$\widetilde{\bigotimes_{i \in J}} \mathcal{X}_i := \alpha \left(\bigotimes_{i \in J} \gamma(\mathcal{X}_i) \right) \tag{1}$$

$$\mathcal{X} \widetilde{\bowtie} \mathcal{X}' := \alpha \left(\gamma(\mathcal{X}) \bowtie \gamma(\mathcal{X}') \right) \tag{2}$$

$$\mathcal{X} \widetilde{\parallel} \mathcal{X}' := \alpha \left(\gamma(\mathcal{X}) \parallel \gamma(\mathcal{X}') \right) \tag{3}$$

$$\mathcal{X} \widetilde{\oplus} \mathcal{X}' := \alpha \left(\gamma(\mathcal{X}) \oplus \gamma(\mathcal{X}') \right) \tag{4}$$

$$c \widetilde{\triangleright} \mathcal{X}' := \alpha \left(c \triangleright \gamma(\mathcal{X}) \right) \tag{5}$$

$$c \widetilde{\triangleleft} \mathcal{X} := \alpha \left(c \triangleleft \gamma(\mathcal{X}) \right) \tag{6}$$

$$\widetilde{\exists_x^{\mathbf{A}}} \mathcal{X} := \alpha \left(\exists_x^{\mathbf{A}} \gamma(\mathcal{X}) \right) \tag{7}$$

$$\mathbf{p} \widetilde{\bullet} \mathcal{X} := \alpha \left(\mathbf{p} \bullet \gamma(\mathcal{X}) \right) \tag{8}$$

The Output Observable An interesting property is the notion of output observable, which gives the store resulting of the computation of a goal, together with the termination mode. Using the domain $OObs \subseteq \mathcal{P}(Goals \times \mathbf{TM} \times \mathbb{C})$,

---

[6] Let $A \subseteq [Goals \rightharpoonup A]$. We assume that the elements of A can be represented by means of a syntactic expression built over the free variables which appear in the corresponding derivations in WFD. By finite element of A we mean any element which is finitely representable in the domain A.

where $\mathbf{TM} = \{\mathbf{ss}, \mathbf{ff}, \mathbf{dd}\} \cup Goals$, we can define the abstraction $\langle \xi_o, \xi_o^\gamma \rangle : \mathbb{D} \rightleftharpoons \mathbb{A}_{oo}$, where $\mathbb{A}_{oo} \subseteq [Goals \rightharpoonup OObs]$, by

$$\xi_o(D) := \lambda \mathbf{G}. \{\langle \mathbf{G}, \tau, c \rangle \mid \mathbf{d} \in D(\mathbf{G}), EStore(\mathbf{d}) = c,$$
$$last(\mathbf{d}) = \tau, \mathbf{d} \text{ is real and convergent}\}$$

$$\xi_o^\gamma(\mathcal{X}) := \lambda \mathbf{G}. \{\mathbf{d} \mid first(\mathbf{d}) = \mathbf{G}, EStore(\mathbf{d}) = c,$$
$$last(\mathbf{d}) = \tau, \mathbf{d} \text{ is real and convergent}, \langle \mathbf{G}, \tau, c \rangle \in \mathcal{X}(\mathbf{G})\}$$
$$\cup \quad \{\mathbf{d} \mid first(\mathbf{d}) = \mathbf{G}, last(\mathbf{d}) = \bot\}$$
$$\cup \quad \{\mathbf{d} \mid first(\mathbf{d}) = \mathbf{G}, \mathbf{d} \text{ is not real}\}$$

Using equations 1 to 8 of section 5.2 we have the following definitions of the abstract semantic operators.

1. $\displaystyle \widetilde{\bigotimes_{i \in J}} \mathcal{X}_i := \lambda \mathbf{G}. \bigcup_{j \in J} \mathcal{X}_j(\mathbf{G}).$

2. Before we define the operator $\widetilde{\bowtie}$, we have to define the $\widetilde{tree}$ operation, which maps clauses to A-collections. The clause $cl := p(\mathbf{x}) \!\!- : \mathbf{B}$ can be viewed as the A-collection
$$\widetilde{tree}(cl) := \phi \left[\{\{\langle p(t), \mathbf{B}', true \rangle \mid p(t) :- \mathbf{B}' \in Inst(P)\} /_{p(t)} \right].$$
The operator $\widetilde{\bowtie}$ is then defined as
$$\mathcal{X}_1 \widetilde{\bowtie} \mathcal{X}_2 := \lambda \mathbf{G}. \{ \langle \mathbf{G}, \tau, c \rangle \mid a_1 \in \mathcal{X}_1(\mathbf{G}), a_1 = \langle \mathbf{G}, \mathbf{B}, true \rangle,$$
$$a_2 \in \mathcal{X}_2(\mathbf{B}), a_2 = \langle \mathbf{B}, \tau, c \rangle\}$$

3. The abstract parallel operator is defined as
$$\mathcal{X}_1 \widetilde{\|} \mathcal{X}_2 := \lambda \mathbf{G}. \left\{ \left\langle \mathbf{G}_1 \| \mathbf{G}_2, \tau_1 \widetilde{\|} \tau_2, c \right\rangle \mid \mathbf{G} = \mathbf{G}_1 \| \mathbf{G}_2, \right.$$
$$\left. \langle \mathbf{G}_1, \tau_1, c \rangle \in \mathcal{X}_1(\mathbf{G}_1), \langle \mathbf{G}_2, \tau_2, c \rangle \in \mathcal{X}_2(\mathbf{G}_2)\} \right.$$
where we apply the rules $\tau \widetilde{\|} \mathbf{ss} = \tau, \tau \widetilde{\|} \mathbf{ff} = \mathbf{ff}$ and $\mathbf{dd} \widetilde{\|} \mathbf{dd} = \mathbf{dd}$.

4. $\mathcal{X}_1 \widetilde{\oplus} \mathcal{X}_2 = \lambda \mathbf{G}. \{\mathcal{X}_1(\mathbf{A}_1) \cup \mathcal{X}_2(\mathbf{A}_2) \mid \mathbf{G} = \mathbf{A}_1 + \mathbf{A}_2\}$

5. Given a constraint c and a A-collection $\mathcal{X}$, the $\widetilde{\flat}$ operator is defined by
$$c\widetilde{\flat}\mathcal{X} := \lambda \mathbf{G}. \{c\widetilde{\flat} \langle \mathbf{A}, \tau, c \rangle \mid \mathbf{G} = \mathbf{tell}(c) \rightarrow \mathbf{A}, \langle \mathbf{A}, \tau, c \rangle \in \mathcal{X}(\mathbf{A})\},$$
where
$$c\widetilde{\flat} \langle \mathbf{A}, \tau, d \rangle = \langle \mathbf{tell}(c) \rightarrow \mathbf{A}, \tau, d \sqcup c \rangle \text{ if } \models d \sqcup c$$
$$c\widetilde{\flat} \langle \mathbf{A}, \tau, d \rangle = \langle \mathbf{tell}(c) \rightarrow \mathbf{A}, \mathbf{ff}, d \rangle \quad \text{ if } \not\models d \sqcup c$$

6. Given a constraint c and a A-collection $\mathcal{X}$, the $\widetilde{\triangleleft}$ operator is defined by
$$c\widetilde{\triangleleft}\mathcal{X} := \lambda \mathbf{G}. \{c\widetilde{\triangleleft} \langle \mathbf{A}, \tau, c \rangle \mid \mathbf{G} = \mathbf{ask}(c) \rightarrow \mathbf{A}, \langle \mathbf{A}, \tau, c \rangle \in \mathcal{X}(\mathbf{A})\},$$
where
$$c\widetilde{\triangleleft} \langle \mathbf{A}, \tau, d \rangle = \langle \mathbf{ask}(c) \rightarrow \mathbf{A}, \mathbf{ff}, d \rangle \text{ if } \not\models d \sqcup c$$
$$c\widetilde{\triangleleft} \langle \mathbf{A}, \tau, d \rangle = \langle \mathbf{ask}(c) \rightarrow \mathbf{A}, \mathbf{dd}, d \rangle \text{ if } \models d \sqcup c$$

7. Let $\{^x/_{\mathbf{z}}, ^y/_{\mathbf{x}}\}$ denotes the simultaneous substitution of the free occurrences of the variables $\mathbf{z}$ by its corresponding variables $\mathbf{x}$, and the variables $\mathbf{x}$ by its corresponding variables $\mathbf{y}$. As before we require $\mathbf{z} \cap vars(\mathbf{A}) = \emptyset$, $\mathbf{y} \cap vars(c) = \emptyset$. Then
$$\widetilde{\exists}_{\mathbf{x}}^{\mathbf{A}} \mathcal{X} = \lambda \mathbf{G}. \{\langle \mathbf{G}, \tau, \exists_{\mathbf{x}} c\{^x/_{\mathbf{z}}, ^y/_{\mathbf{x}}\} \rangle \mid \mathbf{G} = \exists_{\mathbf{x}} \mathbf{A}, \langle \mathbf{A}, \tau, c \rangle \in \mathcal{X}(\mathbf{A})\}.$$

8. $p(t)\widetilde{\bullet}\mathcal{X} := \phi [^S/_{p(t)}]$, where
$$S := \{\langle \mathbf{A}\rho, \tau, d\rho \rangle \mid \mathbf{A} = p(t)\rho, \langle \mathbf{A}, \tau, d \rangle \in \mathcal{X}(\mathbf{A}) \text{ for a renaming } \rho\}.$$

6   Conclusions and Future Work

We presented a denotational semantics for Concurrent Constraint Programming based in sequences of interactions of a process with the environment. The semantics is defined using a set of primitive semantic operators, induced by the syntax of programs and is a good basis for building semantic framworks for the analysis of *ccp* programs, using Abstract Interpretation techniques. We indeed show, how to use the semantics for extracting properties of computations, without changing the underlyning constraint system.

The future work will be concentred in defining abstractions of computations from one concrete constraint system to an abstract one. In this case we have to state the conditions that ensure the correctness of all the constraint system operators and to define a correct approximation for the entailment test. The problem is that intuitively a correct approximation of the program meaning generates weaker answers for any possible program behavior. Thus, in order to characterize answers associated with suspended computations, we must guarantee that whenever a concrete computation suspends the corresponding abstract computation suspends too. This can only be obtained by replacing ask constraints with stronger constraints, which is usually not the case in abstract interpretation.

References

1. P. Cousot and R. Cousot. Systematic Design of Program Analysis Frameworks. In *Proc. Sixth ACM Symp. Principles of Programming Languages*, pages 269–282, 1979.
2. P. Cousot and R. Cousot. Abstract Interpretation Frameworks. *Journal of Logic and Computation*, 2(4):511–549, 1992.
3. F. S. de Boer and C. Palamidessi. A Fully Abstract Model of Concurrent Logic Languages. Technical report, Dipartimento di Informatica, Università di Pisa, 1990.
4. R. Gerth, M. Codish, Y. Lichtenstein, and E. Shapiro. Fully abstract denotational semantics for Concurrent Prolog. In *Proc. Third IEEE Symp. on Logic In Computer Science*, pages 320–335. IEEE Computer Society Press, 1988.
5. L. Henkin, J. D. Monk, and A. Tarski. *Cylindric Algebras. Part I and II*. North-Holland, Amsterdam, 1971.
6. R. Moreno. A Semantic Framework for the Analysis of Concurrent Constraint Programming. In M. Falaschi, M. Navarro, and A. Policriti, editors, *Proceedings of the APPIA-GULP-PRODE'97 Joint Conference on Declarative Programming*, 1997.
7. V. A. Saraswat, M. Rinard, and P. Panangaden. Semantic Foundation of Concurrent Constraint Programming. In *Proc. Eighteenth Annual ACM Symp. on Principles of Programming Languages*, pages 333–353. ACM, 1991.

A Fixpoint Semantics for Reasoning about Finite Failure

Roberta Gori

Dipartimento di Informatica, Università di Pisa, Corso Italia 40, 56125 Pisa, Italy
gori@di.unipi.it
Ph.: +39-050-887248   Fax: +39-050-887226

Abstract. Our aim is to define a new fixpoint semantics which correctly models finite failure. In order to achieve this goal a new fixpoint operator is derived from a "suitable" concrete semantics by defining a Galois insertion modeling finite failure. The corresponding abstract fixpoint semantics correctly models finite failure and is and-compositional.

Keywords: *Abstract interpretation, Logic programming, Finite failure.*

1   Which semantics for finite failure

The (ground) finite failure set FF_P (the set of ground atoms which finitely fail in P) [2, 11] does not correctly model finite failure. In fact if we take the observational equivalence relation $\approx_{FF}$ induced on programs by finite failure defined as

Definition 1. *Let P_1 and P_2 be programs, G be a goal and T_1 and T_2 be SLD-trees (defined by a fair selection rule) for G in P_1 and P_2 respectively. Then $P_1 \approx_{FF} P_2$ if, for every goal G, T_1 is finitely failed if and only if T_2 is finitely failed.*

and

$FF_P = \{ \ A \ | \ A$ is a ground atom and $\leftarrow A$ has a fair finitely failed SLD-tree $\}$,

it is easy to see that FF_P is not able to model the behavior of finite failure. Namely, the ground finite failure set cannot distinguish programs which have different sets of goals having a fair finitely failed SLD-tree. Here is a counterexample.

Example 1.

$$P_1 : p(f(X)) :-p(X) \qquad\qquad P_2 : p(f(X)) :-p(X),p(a)$$
$$s(a) \qquad\qquad\qquad\qquad\qquad s(a)$$

P_1 and P_2 have the same finite failure set.

$$FF_{P_1} = FF_{P_2} = \{ \ p(a), p(f(a)), p(f(f(a))), \ldots$$
$$s(f(a)), s(f(f(a))), s(f(f(f(a)))), \ldots \}$$

However the goal $\leftarrow p(X)$ has a fair finitely failed SLD-tree in P_2 while $\leftarrow p(X)$ has only infinite fair SLD-trees in P_1.

In [9], the Non-Ground Finite Failure set, introduced in [12],
$NGFF_P = \{A \mid \leftarrow A$ has a fair finitely failed SLD-tree $\}$,
was proved to be correct w.r.t. finite failure. Moreover $NGFF_P$ was also proved
to be and-compositional (i.e. the failure of conjunctive goals can be derived from
the behavior of atomic goals only). The proof in [9] is rather complex and needs
a construction of ideals of substitutions. However it is important since for the
first time shows that the property of finite failure is indeed AND-compositional.

However, $NGFF_P$ has no fixpoint characterization. This implies that $NGFF_P$
can not be computed by an iterative fixpoint operator. Therefore all the semantics-
based analysis and verification methods which use a "denotational" approach
(inductive verification, bottom-up goal independent abstract interpretation, etc)
can not be applied to finite failure.

Our aim was to find a fixpoint characterization of the set of non ground finite failure. In order to achieve this goal a new fixpoint operator is derived from
a "suitable" concrete semantics by defining a Galois insertion modeling finite
failure. The corresponding abstract fixpoint semantics correctly models finite
failure and is and-compositional. The "suitable" concrete semantics which we
will consider is an extension with infinite computations of the traces semantics
in [4]. In fact, in order to model finite failure we need information on the atoms
which can not be rewritten (either finitely or infinitely) via a fair selection rule.
Moreover, from this concrete semantics other new interesting fixpoint semantics
can be derived by defining a Galois insertion modeling a property "observable"
on the concrete semantics. An example is a fixpoint semantics which captures
infinite derivations. This is why in the following we will define a general framework for defining new semantics as abstractions of our concrete semantics and
then we apply it to derive a correct fixpoint semantics for finite failure.

The paper is organized as follows. In Section 2 we define the general framework. We apply the framework to the finite failure observable in Section 3, deriving a fixpoint semantics which correctly models finite failure. Finally, Section
4 relates this new semantics to other well known semantics. All the proofs of the
results of this paper can be found in [8].

2   The General Framework

The reader is assumed to be familiar with the terminology of and the basic
results in the semantics of logic programs [1, 13] and with the theory of abstract
interpretation as presented in [5, 6]. Moreover, we will denote by x and t a tuple
of distinct variables and a tuple of terms respectively, while B and G will denote
a (possible empty) conjunction of atoms. By $G_0 \xrightarrow[p_1,c_1]{\vartheta_1} \cdots \xrightarrow[p_n,c_n]{\vartheta_n} G_n, (n \geq 0)$,
we denote a finite SLD-derivation of goal G via the parallel selection rule. At
each step we rewrite the atom in position p_i of the goal G_{i-1} using a renamed
apart clause c_i, and computing a substitution ϑ_i. Infinite SLD-derivations will
be indicate by $G_0 \xrightarrow[p_1,c_1]{\vartheta_1} \cdots \xrightarrow[p_n,c_n]{\vartheta_n} G_n \ldots \ldots$

2.1 Semantic Domain

We consider sets of SLD traces via a particular fair selection rule which we call *parallel selection rule* R. Consider a goal $G = A_1, \ldots, A_n$. The rule R, at the first step, selects one of the atoms A_i. Then, at rewriting step $i+1$, if R has selected the atom in position j in G_{i-1}, rewriting it with the clause $A \leftarrow B$ obtaining G_i, then, at step $i+1$, R selects the atom in position $(j + lenght(B))modulo(lenght(G_i))$ in G_i, where $lenght(A_1, \ldots, A_n) = n$.

A set of derivations S for the goal $G = A_1, \ldots, A_n$ is *well-formed* if and only if, for any d in S obtained by selecting as first atom A_i, any prefix of d is also in S and any d' obtained by selecting as first atom A_j and using the same clauses (as long as possible) than the ones in d, is also in S. A *collection* D is a partial function *Goals* $\rightharpoonup$ *WFS* such that, for every G, if D(G) is defined, then it is a well-formed set of derivations in P (via the parallel selection rule) *all starting from the goal G*.

Hence a collection is a function which associates to any goal G a (representation of) a partial *SLD*-tree of G *in* P. A pure collection is a collection defined for pure atomic goals only. $\mathbb{C}$ is the domain of all the collections ordered by $\sqsubseteq$, where $D \sqsubseteq D'$ if and only if $\forall G$, $D(G) \subseteq D'(G)$. The partial order on $\mathbb{C}$ formalizes the evolution of the computation process. $(\mathbb{C}, \sqsubseteq)$ is a complete lattice. $\mathbb{PC}$ denotes the sub-lattice of all pure collections.

The *equivalence modulo enhanced variance* $\equiv_C$ on collections is defined as $D \equiv_C D'$ if and only if, for any G such that D(G) is defined, there exists a variant G' of G such that $D'(G')$ is defined and, for any $d \in D(G)$, there exists $d' \in D'(G')$, such that clauses(d) $\equiv$ clauses(d') and vice versa.

Example 2. Consider the following program:

$$P_1$$
$$c_1 : p(f(X)) : -p(X)$$
$$c_2 : q(f(g(X))) : -q(X)$$
$$c_3 : s(f(g(a)))$$

For every collection D, $D(p(X), q(X), s(X))$ is a representation of a *partial* SLD-tree of the goal $p(X), q(X), s(X)$ in P via the parallel selection rule. Indeed, we can consider the collection D', a partial function which associates to $p(X), q(X), s(X)$ the *well-formed* set of derivations

$$p(X), q(X), s(X) \overset{\{X/f(Y)\}}{\rightarrow}_{1, c_1} p(f(Y)), q(f(Y)), s(f(Y)) \overset{\{Y/g(T)\}}{\rightarrow}_{2, c_2}$$
$$p(f(g(T))), q(f(g(T))), s(f(g(T))) \overset{\{T/a\}}{\rightarrow}_{3, c_3}$$
$$p(f(g(a))), q(f(g(a))) \overset{\epsilon}{\rightarrow}_{1, c_1}$$
$$p(f(g(a))), q(f(g(a))) \overset{\epsilon}{\rightarrow}_{2, c_2}$$
$$p(f(g(a))), q(f(g(a))) \ldots \ldots$$

$$p(X), q(X), s(X) \overset{\{X/f(Y)\}}{\rightarrow}_{1, c_1} p(f(Y)), q(f(Y)), s(f(Y))$$

$$p(X), q(X), s(X) \overset{\{X/f(Y)\}}{\rightarrow}_{1, c_1} p(f(Y)), q(f(Y)), s(f(Y)) \overset{\{Y/g(T)\}}{\rightarrow}_{2, c_2}$$
$$p(f(g(T))), q(f(g(T))), s(f(g(T)))$$

$$p(X), q(X), s(X) \overset{\{X/f(Y)\}}{\rightarrow}_{1,c_1} \quad p(f(Y)), q(f(Y)), s(f(Y)) \overset{\{Y/g(T)\}}{\rightarrow}_{2,c_2}$$
$$p(f(g(T))), q(f(g(T))), s(f(g(T))) \overset{\{T/a\}}{\rightarrow}_{3,c_3}$$
$$p(f(g(a))), q(f(g(a)))$$

$$p(X), q(X), s(X) \overset{\{X/f(Y)\}}{\rightarrow}_{1,c_1} \quad p(f(Y)), q(f(Y)), s(f(Y)) \overset{\{Y/g(T)\}}{\rightarrow}_{2,c_2}$$
$$p(f(g(T))), q(f(g(T))), s(f(g(T))) \overset{\{T/a\}}{\rightarrow}_{3,c_3}$$
$$p(f(g(a))), q(f(g(a))) \overset{\epsilon}{\rightarrow}_{1,c_1}$$
$$p(f(g(a))), q(f(g(a)))$$

$$p(X), q(X), s(X) \overset{\{X/f(Y)\}}{\rightarrow}_{1,c_1} \quad p(f(Y)), q(f(Y)), s(f(Y)) \overset{\{Y/g(T)\}}{\rightarrow}_{2,c_2}$$
$$p(f(g(T))), q(f(g(T))), s(f(g(T))) \overset{\{T/a\}}{\rightarrow}_{3,c_3}$$
$$p(f(g(a))), q(f(g(a))) \overset{\epsilon}{\rightarrow}_{1,c_1}$$
$$p(f(g(a))), q(f(g(a))) \overset{\epsilon}{\rightarrow}_{2,c_2}$$
$$p(f(g(a))), q(f(g(a)))$$

$$\vdots$$
$$\vdots$$

$$p(X), q(X), s(X) \overset{\{X/f(g(Y))\}}{\rightarrow}_{2,c_2} p(f(g(Y))), q(f(g(Y))), s(f(g(Y))) \overset{\{Y/a)\}}{\rightarrow}_{3,c_3}$$
$$p(f(g(a))), q(f(g(a))) \overset{\epsilon}{\rightarrow}_{1,c_1}$$
$$p(f(g(a))), q(f(g(a))) \overset{\epsilon}{\rightarrow}_{2,c_2}$$
$$p(f(g(a))), q(f(g(a))) \overset{\epsilon}{\rightarrow}_{1,c_1}$$
$$p(f(g(a))), q(f(g(a))). \ldots \ldots$$

$$p(X), q(X), s(X) \overset{\{X/f(g(Y))\}}{\rightarrow}_{2,c_2} p(f(g(Y))), q(f(g(Y))), s(f(g(Y)))$$
$$\vdots$$
$$\vdots$$

$$p(X), q(X), s(X) \overset{\{X/f(g(a))\}}{\rightarrow}_{3,c_3} p(f(g(a))), q(f(g(a))) \overset{\epsilon}{\rightarrow}_{1,c_1}$$
$$p(f(g(a))), q(f(g(a))) \overset{\epsilon}{\rightarrow}_{2,c_2}$$
$$p(f(g(a))), q(f(g(a))) \overset{\epsilon}{\rightarrow}_{1,c_1}$$
$$p(f(g(a))), q(f(g(a))) \overset{\epsilon}{\rightarrow}_{2,c_2}$$
$$p(f(g(a))), q(f(g(a))). \ldots \ldots$$
$$p(X), q(X), s(X) \overset{\{X/f(g(a))\}}{\rightarrow}_{3,c_3} p(f(g(a))), q(f(g(a)))$$

$$\vdots$$
$$\vdots$$

Note that $D'(p(X), q(X), s(X))$ is a representation of the *maximal* SLD-tree of $p(X), q(X), s(X)$ in P. While the collection D'' which associates to the goal $p(X), q(X), s(X)$ the *well-formed* set of derivations

$$p(X), q(X), s(X) \stackrel{\{X/f(Y)\}}{\longrightarrow}{}_{1,c_1} \quad p(f(Y)), q(f(Y)), s(f(Y)) \stackrel{\{Y/g(T)\}}{\longrightarrow}{}_{2,c_2}$$
$$p(f(g(T))), q(f(g(T))), s(f(g(T)))$$

$$p(X), q(X), s(X) \stackrel{\{X/f(Y)\}}{\longrightarrow}{}_{1,c_1} \quad p(f(Y)), q(f(Y)), s(f(Y))$$

$$p(X), q(X), s(X) \stackrel{\{X/f(g(Y))\}}{\longrightarrow}{}_{2,c_1} p(f(g(Y))), q(f(g(Y))), s(f(g(Y)))$$

represents a *partial SLD-tree* of $p(X), q(X), s(X)$ in P.

An interpretation I ($\mathbb{C}$-interpretation) is a pure collection modulo enhanced variance. $\mathbb{I}_{\mathbb{C}}$ denotes the set of interpretations and, by abuse of notation, the quotient order on $\mathbb{I}_{\mathbb{C}}$ is denoted by $\sqsubseteq$. ($\mathbb{I}_{\mathbb{C}}, \sqsubseteq$) is a complete lattice. σ denotes also the equivalence class (modulo enhanced variance) of the collection σ. Moreover, any interpretation I of $\mathbb{I}_{\mathbb{C}}$ is implicitly considered also as an arbitrary collection obtained by choosing an arbitrary representative of I. Since all the operators defined on interpretations will be independent from the choice of the representative, we can define any operator on $\mathbb{I}_{\mathbb{C}}$ in terms of its counterpart defined on $\mathbb{C}$. All the definitions are independent from the choice of the syntactic object. To simplify the notation, we denote the corresponding operators on $\mathbb{I}_{\mathbb{C}}$ and $\mathbb{C}$ by the same name.

2.2 Denotational semantics

Queries and programs are described by the following grammar,

$$QUERY ::= GOAL \text{ in } PROG,$$
$$GOAL ::= \emptyset \mid ATOM, GOAL,$$
$$PROG ::= \emptyset \mid \{CLAUSE\} \cup PROG,$$
$$CLAUSE ::= ATOM \leftarrow GOAL.$$

We define the denotational semantics inductively on the syntax. The semantic functions are

$$\mathcal{Q}J\cdot K : QUERY \longrightarrow \mathbb{C},$$
$$\mathcal{G}J\cdot K : GOAL \longrightarrow (\mathbb{I}_{\mathbb{C}} \to \mathbb{C}),$$
$$\mathcal{A}J\cdot K : ATOM \longrightarrow (\mathbb{I}_{\mathbb{C}} \to \mathbb{C}),$$
$$\mathcal{P}J\cdot K : PROG \longrightarrow (\mathbb{I}_{\mathbb{C}} \to \mathbb{I}_{\mathbb{C}})$$
$$\mathcal{C}J\cdot K : CLAUSE \longrightarrow (\mathbb{I}_{\mathbb{C}} \to \mathbb{I}_{\mathbb{C}}).$$

Our semantic functions are described in terms of some semantic operators, whose choice is induced by the syntactic operations, so that the resulting denotational semantics is compositional w.r.t. all the syntactic operations. The semantic operations, formally defined in section 2.4, are $\times$, $\odot$, $\triangleright$, $+$ and *tree* whose informal meaning is the following. The operator $\times$, ($D_1 \times D_2$, $D_1, D_2 \in \mathbb{C}$), computes a new collection which contains all the traces (via a parallel rule) for the goal G_1, G_2, using the information on the traces (via a parallel rule) for the goal G_1 in D_1 and the traces (via a parallel rule) for the goal G_2 in D_2. The operator

$\odot$, $(A \odot D, A \in Atoms, D \in \mathbb{C})$, computes the set of traces for A using the information on the traces for A', $A' \leq A$ ($A' \leq A$ if there exists a substitution ϑ such that $A = A'\vartheta$), in D. The operator $\triangleright$, $(D_1 \triangleright D_2, D_1, D_2 \in \mathbb{C})$, computes a new collection obtained by extending, whenever it is possible, the traces of D_1 with the traces of D_2. The operator $+$, $(D_1 + D_2, D_1, D_2 \in \mathbb{C})$, computes a new collection obtained by considering for every goal G all the traces for G in D_1 and all the traces for G in D_2. Finally, *tree*, $(tree(c), c \in Clauses)$ maps clauses to collections. Indeed every clause $c := p(t) \leftarrow B$ can be viewed as the "one step" interpretation (collection).

The semantic functions are,

$$\mathcal{Q}JG \ in \ PK := \mathcal{G}JGK_{\text{gfp} \, \mathcal{P}JPK}$$
$$\mathcal{G}JA, GK_I := \mathcal{A}JAK_I \times \mathcal{G}JGK_I \qquad\qquad \mathcal{G}J\emptyset K_I := \phi_\emptyset$$
$$\mathcal{A}JAK_I := A \odot I$$
$$\mathcal{P}J\{c\} \cup PK_I := \mathcal{C}JcK_I + \mathcal{P}JPK_I \qquad\qquad \mathcal{P}J\emptyset K_I := Id_I$$
$$\mathcal{C}JH \leftarrow BK_I := tree(H \leftarrow B) \triangleright \mathcal{G}JBK_I.$$

where the *void collection* ϕ is the collection $\lambda G.\, \aleph$, i.e., the undefined function.

Note that the semantics of a set of clauses (a program) is the greatest fixpoint of $\mathcal{P}JPK$.

The *pure identity collection* Id_I is the pure collection of zero-length derivations for each goal, $\lambda p(x).\{p(x)\}^1$. Moreover ϕ_G denotes the collection $\phi[\{G\}/G]$ and $\square$ denotes the empty goal. Let us now give some intuitions on what the gfp $\mathcal{P}J.K$ computes.

Example 3. Consider the program P_1 in Example 2.
gfp $\mathcal{P}JP_1K(p(X)) = \{$

$p(X) \xrightarrow{\{X/f(Y)\}}_{1,c_1} \quad p(f(Y)) \xrightarrow{\epsilon}_{1,c_1} p(f(Y)) \xrightarrow{\epsilon}_{1,c_1} p(f(Y)) \ldots\ldots$

$p(X) \xrightarrow{\{X/f(Y)\}}_{1,c_1} \quad p(f(Y))$

$p(X) \xrightarrow{\{X/f(Y)\}}_{1,c_1} \quad p(f(Y)) \xrightarrow{\epsilon}_{1,c_1} p(f(Y))$
$p(X) \xrightarrow{\{X/f(Y)\}}_{1,c_1} \quad p(f(Y)) \xrightarrow{\epsilon}_{1,c_1} p(f(Y)) \xrightarrow{\epsilon}_{1,c_1} p(f(Y))$

$\qquad\vdots \qquad\qquad\qquad\qquad\qquad\qquad\qquad\qquad\qquad \}$

---

[1] Note that when we write $\lambda p(x).\, E$ we denote a partial function which is defined only for inputs of the form $p(x)$ and is otherwise undefined.

$\text{gfp } \mathcal{P}JP_1K(q(X)) = \{$

$q(X) \overset{\{X/f(g(Y))\}}{\rightarrow}_{1,c_2} \quad q(f(g(Y))) \overset{\epsilon}{\rightarrow}_{1,c_2} q(f(g(Y))) \overset{\epsilon}{\rightarrow}_{1,c_2} q(f(g(Y)))\ldots\ldots$

$q(X) \overset{\{X/f(g(Y))\}}{\rightarrow}_{1,c_2} \quad q(f(g(Y)))$

$q(X) \overset{\{X/f(g(Y))\}}{\rightarrow}_{1,c_2} \quad q(f(g(Y))) \overset{\epsilon}{\rightarrow}_{1,c_2} q(f(g(Y)))$

$q(X) \overset{\{X/f(g(Y))\}}{\rightarrow}_{1,c_2} \quad q(f(g(Y))) \overset{\epsilon}{\rightarrow}_{1,c_2} q(f(g(Y))) \overset{\epsilon}{\rightarrow}_{1,c_2} q(f(g(Y)))$

$\vdots$ $\}$

$\text{gfp } \mathcal{P}JP_1K(s(X)) = \{\ s(X) \overset{\{X/f(g(a))\}}{\rightarrow}_{1,c_3} \square \qquad\qquad\qquad\qquad \}$

Consider now the program

$$P_2$$
$$c_1 : q(a) : -p(X)$$
$$c_2 : p(f(X)) : -p(X)$$

$\text{gfp } \mathcal{P}JP_2K(q(Y)) = \{$

$q(Y) \overset{\{Y/a\}}{\rightarrow}_{1,c_1} p(X) \overset{\{X/f(X_1)\}}{\rightarrow}_{1,c_2} p(f(X_1)) \overset{\{X_2/f(X_3)\}}{\rightarrow}_{1,c_2} p(f(f(X_3)))$

$\qquad\qquad\qquad \overset{\{X_3/f(X_4)\}}{\rightarrow}_{1,c_2} p(f(f(f(X_4))))\ldots\ldots$

$q(Y) \overset{\{Y/a\}}{\rightarrow}_{1,c_1} p(X)$

$q(Y) \overset{\{Y/a\}}{\rightarrow}_{1,c_1} p(X) \overset{\{X/f(X_1)\}}{\rightarrow}_{1,c_2} p(f(X_1))$

$\vdots$ $\}$

$\text{gfp } \mathcal{P}JP_2K(p(X)) = \{$

$p(X) \overset{\{X/f(X_1)\}}{\rightarrow}_{1,c_2} p(f(X_1)) \overset{\{X_1/f(X_2)\}}{\rightarrow}_{1,c_2} p(f(f(X_2))) \overset{\{X_2/f(X_3)\}}{\rightarrow}_{1,c_2}$

$\qquad\qquad p(f(f(f(X_3))))\ldots\ldots$

$p(X) \overset{\{X/f(X_1)\}}{\rightarrow}_{1,c_2} p(f(X_1))$

$\vdots$ $\}$

2.3   Basic operations on derivations

By $d = G_0 \xrightarrow[p_1,c_1]{\theta_1} \cdots \xrightarrow[p_n,c_n]{\theta_n} G_n \rightarrow \ldots$, we denote a possibly infinite SLD-derivation of G via the parallel selection rule, where $first(d) = G_0$, $clauses(d) = c_1, \ldots, c_n$. By $var(d)$ we denote all the variables appearing in the derivation d.

We now define some auxiliary operations on derivations. These operations will be used in section 2.4 in order to define the semantic operators on collections.

- $d_1 :: d_2$ denotes the concatenation of d_1 and d_2.
  Let $d_1 = G \xrightarrow[p_1,c_1]{\vartheta_1} \cdots \xrightarrow[p_n,c_n]{\vartheta_n} G'$ and

  $d_2 = G' \xrightarrow[p_1',c_1']{\vartheta_1'} \cdots \xrightarrow[p_n',c_n']{\vartheta_n'} G_n' \to \ldots$,

  $var(d_1) \cap var(d_2) = var(first(d_2))$ and
  $p_1' = (p_n + lenght(body(c_n)))modulo(lenght(G')))$ then $d_1 :: d_2$ is defined.

- $\partial_\gamma(d)$ is the derivation obtained by applying the substitution γ to $first(d)$
  and building a derivation as long as possible (until a failure in finding *mgus*
  occurs) by selecting the same atoms and by using the same clauses as in d.

  Let $d := G_0' \xrightarrow[p_1',c_1']{\vartheta_1'} \cdots \xrightarrow[p_k',c_k']{\vartheta_k'} G_k' \to \ldots$,

  be a derivation and γ be an idempotent substitution such that $var(G_0'\gamma) \cap var(clauses(d)) = \emptyset$.
  Then $\partial_\gamma(d) := G_0 \xrightarrow[p_1',c_1']{\vartheta_1} \cdots \xrightarrow[p_h',c_h']{\vartheta_h} G_h \to \ldots$, where

  • $G_0 := G_0'\gamma$ and
  • for any i, if $G_{i-1} = (\bar{G}_1, A, \bar{G}_2)$ and A is the p_i' atom in G_{i-1}, $c_i' = H \leftarrow B$ then (if an *mgu* exists) $\vartheta_i := mgu(A, H)$ and $G_i := (\bar{G}_1, B, \bar{G}_2)\vartheta_i$.

- $d_1 \wedge^i d_2$, for $i = 1, 2$, is the derivation obtained by trying to build a derivation
  for the goal $(first(d_1), first(d_2))$ by a parallel selection rule (starting from
  the first atom selected in the derivation d_i) as long as possible using the
  same clauses as in d_1 and d_2.
  $d_1 \wedge^i d_2$ is defined if $var(d_1) \cap var(d_2) \subseteq first(d_1) \cap first(d_2)$.
  For the sake of simplicity we omit the formal definition, which can be found
  in [8].

Note that the operators on derivations are defined so that variable name clashes
in the clauses are avoided. Hence the results of the construction are independent
(modulo variance) from the choice of the mgu.

Lemma 1. *Let d_1, d_2 be derivations and γ be an idempotent substitution. Then
the following properties hold.*

1. *If $d_1 :: d_2$ is defined then $d_1 :: d_2$ is a derivation.*
2. *If $\partial_\gamma(d)$ is defined then $\partial_\gamma(d)$ is a derivation.*
3. *If $d_1 \wedge^i d_2$ is defined then $d_1 \wedge^i d_2$ is a derivation.*

2.4   Basic operators on collections

The *sum* of a class $\{D_j\}_{j \in J}$ is
$\sum\{D_j\}_{j \in J} := \lambda G. \bigcup_{j \in J} D_j(G)$ and $D_1 + D_2$ denotes $\sum\{D_1, D_2\}$.

The *product* of a class $\{D_j\}_{j \in J}$ is
$$\Pi\{D_j\}_{j \in J} := \lambda G. \bigcap_{j \in J} D_j(G).$$

The *instantiation* of D with A is
$$A \odot D := \phi\left[{}^S/_A\right] \text{ where}$$

$S := \{\partial_\gamma(d) \mid S'$ is a renamed apart (from A)

version of $D(A')$, for some $A' \leq A$, $d \in S'$ and there

exists γ such that $A = \text{first}(d)\gamma$ and $\partial_\gamma(d)$ is defined $\}$.

The *and-composition* of D_1 and D_2 is
$$D_1 \times D_2 := (D_1 \times^1 D_2) + (D_1 \times^2 D_2) \text{ where for } i = 1, 2,$$

$D_1 \times^i D_2 := \lambda G.\{d_1 \wedge^i d_2 \mid G = (G_1, G_2)$ and for $i = 1, 2$, $G'_i \equiv G_i$,

d_i is a renamed version of an element

in $D_i(G'_i)$, such that $G_i = \text{first}(d_i)$

and $d_1 \wedge^i d_2$ is defined $\}$.

The *(compatible) extension* of D_1 by D_2 is

$D_1 \triangleright D_2 := \lambda G. D_1(G) \cup \{d_1 :: d_2 \mid d_1 \in D_1(G), G_2 \equiv \text{last}(d_1)$ and d_2 is a

renamed version of an element in

$D_2(G_2)$ such that $d_1 :: d_2$ is defined $\}$.

The *tree* operation maps clauses to collections.

$$\text{tree}(c) := \phi\left[\left.{}^{\{p(x), p(x) \xrightarrow[1, c]{\{x/t\}} B\}}\middle/_{p(x)}\right.\right],$$

where x is a tuple of new distinct variables and $c = p(t) \leftarrow B$.

2.5   Program denotation

The *fixpoint denotation* of the program P is the interpretation $\mathcal{F}\text{JPK} := \text{gfp } \mathcal{P}\text{JPK}$.

Theorem 1. $\mathcal{P}\text{JPK}$ *is continuous and co-continuous on* $(\mathbb{C}, \sqsubseteq)$.

We can define the ordinal powers of $\mathcal{P}\text{JPK}$ so that

$$\mathcal{F}\text{JPK} = \text{glb}(\mathcal{P}\text{JPK} \downarrow i)_{i < \omega} = \Pi_{i < \omega}(\mathcal{P}\text{JPK} \downarrow i).$$

In [8] we have also defined an operational semantics $\mathcal{O}$JPK, in terms of a transition system and a completion on sets of derivations. $\mathcal{O}$JPK correctly models the finite and infinite SLD traces (via a parallel rule) derivable by a program P. Namely, if we define the equivalence on programs P_1 and P_2 as the equivalence of their behaviors,

i.e., $P_1 \approx P_2 \Longleftrightarrow \forall G \in \textit{Goals}$,

$\qquad$ { d | d is a infinite or finite (possibly partial)
$\qquad\qquad$ derivation for **G** in P_1, via a parallel rule} =
$\qquad$ { d | d is a infinite or finite (possibly partial)
$\qquad\qquad$ derivation for **G** in P_2, via a parallel rule },

the following result hold,

- $\mathcal{O}$J.K is *correct* w.r.t. $\approx$, i.e. $\mathcal{O}$JP$_1$K $= \mathcal{O}$JP$_2$K $\Longrightarrow P_1 \approx P_2$.
- and $\mathcal{O}$J.K is *minimal* w.r.t. $\approx$, i.e. $P_1 \approx P_2 \Longrightarrow \mathcal{O}JP_1$K $= \mathcal{O}$JP$_2$K.

An important result is that

Theorem 2. $\mathcal{O}$JPK $= \mathcal{F}$JPK.

which ensures the equivalence of the operational and denotational semantics and states that the denotational semantics is also correct and minimal w.r.t. $\approx$.

2.6   The observable

Once we have defined the concrete fixpoint semantics we can derive abstract fixpoint semantics which model different observable behaviors of the program. An observable behavior is any property which we can be "observed" on the concrete semantics and can be formalized as a Galois insertion.

Example 4. Assume that we are interested in defining a semantics modeling *computer answers* as defined in [7, 3]. We can "observe" this property on our concrete semantics. Then, we can define an abstraction function on collections D, which, for every goal **G**, associates to **G**, the set of substitutions $(\vartheta_1 \cdot \ldots \cdot \vartheta_n)_{|var(G)}$, where the derivation $G \xrightarrow[p_1,c_1]{\vartheta_1} \cdots \xrightarrow[p_n,c_n]{\vartheta_n} G_n \to \square$ belongs to D(G). Indeed, the abstraction function α_{ca} for computed answer applied to the collection gfp $\mathcal{P}$JP$_1$K (Example 3) yields as result the partial function

$$\alpha_{ca}(\text{gfp } \mathcal{P}\text{JP}_1\text{K})(p(X)) = \{ \ \}$$
$$\alpha_{ca}(\text{gfp } \mathcal{P}\text{JP}_1\text{K})(q(X)) = \{ \ \}$$
$$\alpha_{ca}(\text{gfp } \mathcal{P}\text{JP}_1\text{K})(s(X)) = \{ \ X/f(g(a)) \}$$

Once we have formalized the property of interest as a Galois insertion, we define the optimal abstract fixpoint operator.

Here we want to establish sufficient conditions so that the abstract fixpoint semantics that we derive is precise with respect to the concrete one and inherits all the desirable properties from the concrete denotation.

Consider an abstract domain $(\mathcal{D}, \preceq)$, which is a complete lattice. A function $\alpha : WFS \rightarrow \mathcal{D}$ is a *domain abstraction* if there exists γ such that $\langle \alpha, \gamma \rangle :$ $(WFS, \subseteq) \rightleftharpoons (\mathcal{D}, \preceq)$ is a Galois insertion. Given an abstract domain $\mathcal{D}$ we are interested in the *abstract behavior* of queries, which are elements of a domain $A \subseteq [Goals \rightarrow \mathcal{D}]$ (ordered by the trivial extension $\leq$ of $\preceq$) and are called A-collections.

It is easy to see that the insertion $\langle \alpha, \gamma \rangle$ can be *lifted* to collections as following. For all $G \in Goals$, $\forall D \in \mathbb{C}$, $\alpha^*(D) := \lambda G. \alpha(D(G))$, $A := \alpha^*(\mathbb{C})$ and $\forall S \in A$, $\gamma^*(S) := \lambda G.$ wf$_G(\gamma(S(G)))$, where wf$_G(S)$ is the greatest well-formed subset of derivations starting from G only, of any set of derivations S. The pair $\langle \alpha^*, \gamma^* \rangle : (\mathbb{C}, \subseteq) \rightleftharpoons (A, \leq)$ is a Galois insertion. We will often abuse notation and denote simply α^* by α. As in the concrete case, a pure A-collection is any element of $X \in A$ which is defined for pure atomic goals only. We denote by $\mathbb{P}A$ the sub-lattice of pure A-collections.

Definition 2. *Let $(A, \leq)$ be a complete lattice of A-collections. A function $\alpha : \mathbb{C} \rightarrow A$ is an* observable *if there exists γ such that*

1. $\langle \alpha, \gamma \rangle : (\mathbb{C}, \subseteq) \rightleftharpoons (A, \leq)$ *is a Galois insertion,*
2. $\alpha(\mathbb{P}\mathbb{C}) = \mathbb{P}A$ *and* $\gamma(\mathbb{P}A) \subseteq \mathbb{P}\mathbb{C}$,
3. $\forall D, D' \in \mathbb{P}\mathbb{C}$, $D \equiv_\mathbb{C} D' \Longrightarrow (\gamma\alpha)(D) \equiv_\mathbb{C} (\gamma\alpha)(D')$.

Note that given a domain abstraction it is easy to obtain an observable by the above mentioned lifting.

We can define an abstract enhanced variance relation $\equiv_A$ on A-collections as follows. For any A-collections X, X', $X \equiv_A X' \Longleftrightarrow \gamma(X) \equiv_\mathbb{C} \gamma(X')$. An A-*interpretation* is a pure A-collection modulo $\equiv_A$. We denote by $(\mathbb{I}_a, \leq)$ the complete lattice of A-interpretations with the induced quotient order. Condition 3 of Definition 2 states that the observation does not depend on the choice of the variable names and on the choice of the *mgus* used in the derivations. Namely $D \equiv_\mathbb{C} D'$ implies $\alpha(D) \equiv_A \alpha(D')$. Hence for any $\mathbb{C}$-interpretation I, the A-interpretation $\alpha(I)$ is well defined by taking the abstraction of any representative of I as a representative of the intended A-interpretation.

Once we have an observable $\alpha : \mathbb{C} \rightarrow A$, we want to systematically derive the abstract semantics. The idea is to define the optimal abstract versions of the various semantic operators, defined on $\mathbb{C}$. Hence $\forall X, X', X_i \in A$

$$A \,\tilde{\odot}\, X := \alpha(A \odot \gamma(X)),$$

$$X \,\tilde{\times}\, X' := \alpha(\gamma(X) \times \gamma(X')),$$

$$X \,\tilde{\triangleright}\, X' := \alpha(\gamma(X) \triangleright \gamma(X')),$$

$$\widetilde{\sum}\{X_i\}_{i \in I} := \alpha \left(\sum \{\gamma(X_i)\}_{i \in I} \right),$$

$$\widetilde{\prod}\{X_i\}_{i \in I} := \alpha \left(\prod \{\gamma(X_i)\}_{i \in I} \right).$$

Moreover, if the abstract operators also satisfy the following conditions,

$$\alpha(A \odot D) = \alpha(A \odot (\gamma \circ \alpha)D), \tag{2.1}$$

$$\alpha(D \times D') = \alpha((\gamma \circ \alpha)D \times (\gamma \circ \alpha)D'), \tag{2.2}$$

$$\alpha(D \triangleright D') = \alpha(D \triangleright (\gamma \circ \alpha)D'). \tag{2.3}$$

$$\alpha(\textstyle\prod\{D_i\}_{i \in I}) = \alpha(\textstyle\prod(\gamma \circ \alpha)\{D_i\}_{i \in I}) \ \{D_i\}_{i \in I} \text{ descending chain of collections.} \tag{2.4}$$

$$\alpha(\textstyle\prod \gamma(\{X_i\}_{i \in I})) = glb\{X_i\}_{i \in I} \ \{X_i\}_{i \in I} \text{ descending chain of abstract collections.} \tag{2.5}$$

then the abstract denotational semantics is defined by using the abstract optimal operators as follows

Denotational semantics

$$\mathcal{Q}_\alpha JG \ in \ PK := \mathcal{G}_\alpha JGK_{gfp \, \mathcal{P}_\alpha JPK}$$

$$\mathcal{G}_\alpha JA, GK_X := \mathcal{A}_\alpha JAK_X \ \widetilde{\times} \ \mathcal{G}_\alpha JGK_X \qquad \mathcal{G}_\alpha J\emptyset K_X := \alpha(\phi_\emptyset)$$

$$\mathcal{A}_\alpha JAK_X := A \ \widetilde{\odot} \ X$$

$$\mathcal{P}_\alpha J\{c\} \cup PK_X := \mathcal{C}_\alpha JcK_X \ \widetilde{+} \ \mathcal{P}_\alpha JPK_X \qquad \mathcal{P}_\alpha J\emptyset K_X := \alpha(Id_I)$$

$$\mathcal{C}_\alpha JH \leftarrow BK_X := \alpha \circ \mathcal{C}JH \leftarrow BK \circ \gamma(X).$$

$$\mathcal{F}_\alpha JPK := gfp \, \mathcal{P}_\alpha JPK$$

has the following properties,

Theorem 3. *Let $\alpha : \mathbb{C} \to \mathbb{A}$ be observable which satisfies the previous conditions, c be a clause, A be an atom, G be a goal and P be a program. Then*

1. $\alpha(\mathcal{A}JAK_I) = \mathcal{A}_\alpha JAK_{\alpha(I)}$,
2. $\alpha(\mathcal{G}JGK_I) = \mathcal{G}_\alpha JGK_{\alpha(I)}$,
3. $\alpha(\mathcal{C}JcK_I) = \mathcal{C}_\alpha JcK_{\alpha(I)}$,
4. $\alpha(\mathcal{P}JPK_I) = \mathcal{P}_\alpha JPK_{\alpha(I)}$,
5. $\mathcal{P}_\alpha JPK$ *is co-continuous on $\mathbb{A}$ and $\mathcal{F}_\alpha JPK = \mathcal{P}_\alpha JPK \downarrow \omega$,*
6. $\alpha(\mathcal{F}JPK) = \mathcal{F}_\alpha JPK$ *and $\alpha(\mathcal{Q}JG \ in \ PK) = \mathcal{Q}_\alpha JG \ in \ PK$.*

This means that for any observable property on the concrete semantics which can be formalized by a Galois insertion (α), if the optimal abstract operators satisfy properties 2.1-2.5, we are guaranteed that the induced abstract denotational semantic functions are precise w.r.t. the concrete one and that the fixpoint operator $\mathcal{P}_\alpha J.K$ is co-continuous. The precision of the abstract denotational semantic functions implies the correctness of the abstract denotational semantics w.r.t. the observable property α.

3   On finite failure

3.1   The Semantic Domain

By $\vartheta_1 :: \ldots :: \vartheta_n :: \ldots$ we indicate a (possibly infinite) sequence of relevant substitutions for a goal G such that $G\vartheta_i \leq G\vartheta_{i+1}$.

Finite failure is a downward closed property, i.e., if G finitely fails then $G\vartheta$ finitely fails too. Moreover it enjoys a kind of "upward closure". Namely, if the goal G does not finitely fail, then there exists a (possibly infinite) sequence of substitutions $\vartheta_1 :: \ldots :: \vartheta_n :: \ldots$, such that for every G' which finitely fails, there exists a j, such that G' does not unify with $G\vartheta_h$, for $h > j$. Note that the above mentioned sequence of substitutions can be viewed as the one computed by an infinite or successful derivation for the goal G. If we cannot find such a sequence for the goal G, then G finitely fails. Now, suppose we know that a given set C of goals finitely fails. We can infer that an instance $G\vartheta$ of a goal G finitely fails if for all sequences of substitutions $\vartheta_1 :: \ldots \ldots :: \vartheta_n :: \ldots$, there exists a $G' \in C$ such that $\forall i$, G', unifies with $G\vartheta_i$.

The intuition behind the above remarks can be formalized by an operator on *Goals*, where *Goals* is the domain of goals of the program P.

Definition 3. *Let* $C \subseteq Goals$ *and* $G \in Goals$.

$$up_G^{ff}(C) = C \cup \{G\vartheta \mid \text{for all (possibly infinite) sequences}$$
$$\text{of relevant substitutions for the goal } G$$
$$\vartheta_1 :: \ldots \ldots :: \vartheta_n :: \ldots,$$
$$\text{there exists a } \bar{G} \in C \text{ such that}$$
$$\forall i, \bar{G} \text{ unifies with } G\vartheta\vartheta_i \qquad \}.$$

up_G^{ff} is a closure operator, i.e., it is monotonic w.r.t. set inclusion, idempotent and extensive.

Let S be the domain of sets of downward closed instances of a goal G, which are also closed with respect to up_G^{ff}.

3.2   The non ground finite failure observable

By $d' \leq_d d$ we mean that d' is a prefix of d, while d^j denotes the prefix of length j of d.

Let us first introduce some new operators useful in the definition of the abstraction and concretization functions.

Definition 4. *Let* G *be a goal and* A *be an atom.*

$$NUnif_G(A) = \{G\gamma \mid G\gamma \text{ is not unifiable with } A\}$$

Definition 5. *Let* G *be a goal and* $S \in \mathcal{S}$.

$$NUnifseq_G(S) = \{\vartheta_1 :: \ldots :: \vartheta_n :: \ldots \mid \forall \bar{G} \in S \text{ there exists an } i \text{ such that}$$
$$\bar{G} \text{ is not unifiable with } G\vartheta_i\}$$

Consider now the abstract domain $A_{ff} \subseteq [Goals \rightharpoonup S]$. A_{ff} is the domain of all the partial functions ordered by $\sqsubseteq_{ff}$, where $F \sqsubseteq_{ff} F'$ if and only if $\forall G, F(G) \supseteq F'(G)$. $(A_{ff}, \sqsubseteq_{ff})$ is a complete lattice.

Intuitively a goal G has a finite failure if it can not be rewritten successfully or infinitely.

Example 5. Consider the program P_1 of Example 2 and its concrete semantics gfp $\mathcal{P}JP_1K$ as described in Example 3. The instances of the atom $p(X)$ which finitely fail are the ones which can not be rewritten infinitely or successfully. These are the atoms which do not unify with $p(X)\vartheta_i$ starting from a given i, where the ϑ_i's are the ones in the derivation

$$p(X) \stackrel{\{X/f(Y)\}}{\rightarrow}{}_{1,c_1} p(f(Y)) \stackrel{\epsilon}{\rightarrow}{}_{1,c_1} p(f(Y)) \stackrel{\epsilon}{\rightarrow}{}_{1,c_1} p(f(Y)). \ldots \ldots$$

This intuition is formalized by the following observable $\alpha : \mathbb{C} \rightarrow A_{ff}$

$$\alpha(D) := \lambda G. \bigcap_{\substack{d \in D(G) \text{ and} \\ (last(d) = \square \text{ or} \\ last(d) = \infty)}} \bigcup_{d' \leq_d d} NUnif_G\{G \ answer(d')\},$$

$$\gamma(X) := \lambda G. \{ d \mid \vartheta_1 :: \ldots :: \vartheta_n :: \ldots \in NUnifseq_G(X),$$
$$first(d) = G, \forall i, \exists j_i, answer(d^{j_i}) = \vartheta_i \} \cup$$

$$\{d \mid first(d) = G, last(d) \neq \square \text{ and } last(d) \neq \infty \qquad \}$$

where $last(d)$ is equal to the last goal of the derivation d, if d is a finite and ∞, otherwise. $answer(d)$ is the substitution computed by the derivation d, restricted to $var(first(d))$.

Example 6. Consider P_2 and gfp $\mathcal{P}JP_2K$ in Example 3.

$$\alpha(\text{gfp } \mathcal{P}JP_2K)(q(X)) = \{ q(f(X)), q(f(f(X))), \ldots$$
$$q(f(a)), q(f(f(a))), \ldots \quad \}$$
$$\alpha(\text{gfp } \mathcal{P}JP_2K)(p(X)) = \{ p(a), p(f(a)), p(f(f(a))), \ldots \}$$

Lemma 2. $- \langle \alpha, \gamma \rangle : (\mathbb{C}, \sqsubseteq) \rightleftharpoons (A_{ff}, \sqsubseteq_{ff})$ *is a Galois insertion.*

$- \alpha(\mathbb{PC}) = \mathbb{P}A_{ff}$ *and* $\gamma(\mathbb{P}A_{ff}) \subseteq \mathbb{PC}$,

$- \forall D, D' \in \mathbb{PC}, \quad D \equiv_C D' \Longrightarrow (\gamma \cdot \alpha)(D) \equiv_C (\gamma \cdot \alpha)(D').$

Now that we have stated that α is an observable we can define the optimal abstract operations on A_{ff}.

Lemma 3. *Let X be a pure abstract collection.*

$$A \tilde{\odot} X \quad = \phi[^R/_A] \; where$$
$$R := \quad \{A\vartheta \mid <H, \Theta> \; is \; a \; renamed \; apart \; (from \; A)$$
$$version \; of \; < A', X(A') >, \; for \; some \; A' \leq A,$$
$$A'' \in \Theta, \; and \; \vartheta = mgu(A, A'')_{|A}\}.$$

$$X_1 \tilde{\times} X_2 = \quad \lambda G.up_G^{ff}(\{G\vartheta \mid G = (G^1, G^2), \; for \; i = 1 \; or \; i = 2$$
$$G'^i \equiv G^i, G^i\vartheta \; is \; a \; renamed \; apart$$
$$version \; of \; a \; goal \; in \; X^i(G'^i), \; via \; a \; renaming \; \rho_i$$
$$s.t. \; G'^i\rho_i = G^i,$$
$$var(G^i\vartheta) \cap var(G^l) \subseteq var(G^1) \cap var(G^2)$$
$$l = 1 \; or \; l = 2 \; and \; l \neq i\}).$$

$$\widetilde{\prod} X_i = \quad \lambda G. \, up_G^{ff}(\cup(X_i(G))).$$

$$\widetilde{\sum} X_i = \quad \lambda G. \cap(X_i(G)).$$

As we already pointed out, in [9] we proved that NGFF$_P$ was and-compositional, i.e. the behavior of compound goals could be obtained from the behavior of atomic goals only. However the and-composition relation was rather complex. Here we have automatically derived the and-compositionality operator for finite failure yielding a simpler way to derive information on finite failure of conjunctive goals. Moreover the previously defined optimal operator satisfy conditions 2.1-2.5.

Lemma 4. $\tilde{\odot}, \tilde{\times}, \widetilde{\sum}$ and $\widetilde{\prod}$ *satisfy conditions 2.1- 2.5.*

We can now define the abstract denotational semantics and the optimal fixpoint operator, as described in section 2.6. $\mathcal{P}_\alpha JPK_X$.

Lemma 5.

$$\mathcal{P}_\alpha JPK_X = \lambda p(x).\{ p(\tilde{t}) \mid for \; every \; clause \; defining \; the \; procedure \; p,$$
$$p(t) : -B \in P$$
$$p(\tilde{t}) \in up_{p(x)}^{ff}(Nunif_{p(x)}(p(t)) \cup$$
$$\{p(t)\tilde{\vartheta} \mid \tilde{\vartheta} \; is \; a \; relevant \; substitution \; for \; p(t),$$
$$B\tilde{\vartheta} \in up_B^{ff}(\mathcal{C}) \qquad \})$$
$$where \; \mathcal{C} = \{B\sigma \mid B = (B_1, \dots, B_n)\vartheta \; \exists B_i\vartheta\sigma \in X(B_i)\}$$

By lemma 3, $\mathcal{P}_\alpha JPK$ is co-continuous. By defining the ordinal powers $\mathcal{P}_\alpha JPK \downarrow i$ in the usual way, our semantics will be $gfp(\mathcal{P}_\alpha JPK) = glb(\{ \mathcal{P}_\alpha JPK \downarrow i \mid i < \omega\}) = up_{p(x)}^{ff}(\cup_{i<\omega} \mathcal{P}_\alpha JPK \downarrow i)$.

Let us now show how our semantics works on some examples.

Example 7. Assume $\Sigma_P = \{f, a\}$ and program P_2 in Example 3.

$$\mathcal{P}_\alpha JP_2K \downarrow 1(q(X)) = \{ \quad q(f(X)), q(f(f(X))), \ldots$$
$$q(f(a)), q(f(f(a))), \ldots \quad \}$$
$$\mathcal{P}_\alpha JP_2K \downarrow 1(p(X)) = \{ \quad p(a) \quad \}$$

$$\mathcal{P}_\alpha JP_2K \downarrow 2(q(X)) = \{ \quad q(f(X)), q(f(f(X))), \ldots$$
$$q(f(a)), q(f(f(a))), \ldots \quad \}$$
$$\mathcal{P}_\alpha JP_2K \downarrow 2(p(X)) = \{ \quad p(a), p(f(a)) \quad \}$$
$$\vdots$$

$$gfp(\mathcal{P}_\alpha JP_2K)(q(X)) = \{ \, q(f(X)), q(f(f(X))), \ldots$$
$$q(f(a)), q(f(f(a))), \ldots \quad \}$$
$$gfp(\mathcal{P}_\alpha JP_2K)(p(X)) = \{ \, p(a), p(f(a)), p(f(f(a))), \ldots\}$$

Consider now

$$P_3 : q(a) : -p(X)$$
$$p(f(X)) : -p(a)$$

$$\mathcal{P}_\alpha JP_3K \downarrow 1(q(X)) = \{ \quad q(f(X)), q(f(f(X))), \ldots$$
$$q(f(a)), q(f(f(a))), \ldots \quad \},$$
$$\mathcal{P}_\alpha JP_3K \downarrow 1(p(X)) = \{ \quad p(a) \quad \},$$

$$\mathcal{P}_\alpha JP_3K \downarrow 2(q(X)) = \{ \quad q(f(X)), q(f(f(X))), \ldots$$
$$q(f(a)), q(f(f(a))), \ldots \quad \},$$
$$\mathcal{P}_\alpha JP_3K \downarrow 2(p(X)) = \{ \quad p(X), p(f(X)), \ldots$$
$$p(a), p(f(a)), \ldots \quad \},$$
$$\vdots$$

$$gfp(\mathcal{P}_\alpha JP_3K)(q(X)) = \{ \, q(X), q(f(X)), q(f(f(X))), \ldots$$
$$q(a), q(f(a)), q(f(f(a))), \ldots \ldots\}$$
$$gfp(\mathcal{P}_\alpha JP_3K)(p(X)) = \{ \, p(X), p(f(X)), \ldots$$
$$p(a), p(f(a)), \ldots \quad \}.$$

Finally, consider

$$P_4 : p(f(X), f(f(X))) : -p(X, f(X))$$
$$q(f(Y), f(Y)) : -q(Y, Y)$$

$$gfp(\mathcal{P}_\alpha JP_4K)(p(X)) = \{ \, p(f^n(X), f^m(X)), \quad m \neq n + 1,$$
$$p(t_1, t_2), \quad t_1 \text{ or } t_2 \text{ ground terms}\},$$

$$gfp(\mathcal{P}_\alpha JP_4K)(q(X)) = \{ \, q(f^n(X), f^m(X)), \quad m \neq n,$$
$$q(t_1, t_2), \quad t_1 \text{ or } t_2 \text{ ground terms}\}$$

Then next example shows how it is possible to infer if a conjunctive goals has finite failure from the information on finite failure of atomic goals only.

Example 8. Consider the program P_4 of Example 7. The goal $(p(H,V), q(H,V))$ finitely fails in P_4, since $(p(H,V), q(H,V)) \in up^{ff}_{(p(H,V),q(H,V))}(\mathcal{C})$, where
$$\mathcal{C} = \{ \ p(f^n(X), f^m(X)), q(f^n(X), f^m(X)), m \neq n+1,$$
$$p(f^n(X), f^m(X)), q(f^n(X), f^m(X)), m \neq n,$$
$$p(t_1, t_2), q(t_1, t_2) \ \ t_1 \text{ or } t_2 \text{ ground terms}\}$$
This is true, because, for all possible sequences of substitutions $\vartheta_1 :: \ldots \vartheta_n :: \ldots$ for $(p(H,V), q(H,V))$, there exists a $(p(H,V), q(H,V))\sigma \in \mathcal{C}$ which unifies with each $(p(H,V), q(H,V))\vartheta_i$.

4 Relation to other semantics

In this section we want to relate our semantics for finite failure to the direct characterization of the set of ground atoms FF_P.

This characterization for ground finite failure was introduced in [11] by Lassez and Maher.

Definition 6. *Let P be a program. Let T_P be the fixpoint operator on sets of ground atoms defined in [13]. Then F_P^d, the set of atoms of the Herbrand base, which are finitely failed at depth k is defined as follows.*

1. $A \in F_P^1$ *if* $A \notin T_P \downarrow 1$;
2. $A \in F_P^d$ *for* $d > 1$ *if for all clause* $B \leftarrow B_1, \ldots, B_n$ *in P and for all substitutions* ϑ *such that* $A = B\vartheta$ *and* $B_1\vartheta, \ldots, B_n\vartheta$ *are ground, there exists k such that* $1 \leq k \leq n$ *and* $B_k\vartheta \in F_P^{d-1}$.

Definition 7. *The set of finite failure F_P of P is defined as*
$$F_P = \cup_{d \geq 1} F_P^d.$$

It is worth noting that, if we define the set ground as follows,

Definition 8. *Let R be a set of atoms.*
$$\text{ground}(R) = \{ \ p(t) \mid p(t) \in R \text{ and } p(t) \text{ is ground}\}$$

we can establish the following relation between $\mathcal{P}_\alpha JPK \downarrow k$ and F_P^k.

Theorem 4. *For every finite k.*
$$\cup_{p(x)} \text{ground}(\mathcal{P}_\alpha JPK \downarrow k \ (p(x))) = F_P^k.$$

Moreover our fixpoint operator is co-continuous.

Example 9. Consider program P_2 of Example 3.

$$\bigcup_{p(x)} \mathcal{P}_\alpha JP_2K \downarrow 1 \, (p(x)) = \{ \quad q(f(X)), q(f(f(X))), \ldots$$
$$q(f(a)), q(f(f(a))), \ldots$$
$$p(a) \qquad \qquad \}$$

$$\bigcup_{p(x)} \mathcal{P}_\alpha JP_2K \downarrow 2 \, (p(x)) = \{ \quad q(f(X)), q(f(f(X))), \ldots$$
$$q(f(a)), q(f(f(a))), \ldots$$
$$p(a), p(f(a)) \qquad \qquad \}$$

$\vdots$

$$\bigcup_{p(x)} \mathcal{P}_\alpha JP_2K \downarrow \omega \, (p(x)) = \{ \quad q(f(X)), q(f(f(X))), \ldots$$
$$q(f(a)), q(f(f(a))), \ldots$$
$$p(a), p(f(a)), p(f(f(a))), \ldots\}$$

$$\bigcup_{p(x)} \mathcal{P}_\alpha JP_2K \downarrow \omega + 1 \, (p(x)) = \{ \, q(f(X)), q(f(f(X))), \ldots$$
$$q(f(a)), q(f(f(a))), \ldots$$
$$p(a), p(f(a)), p(f(f(a))), \ldots\}$$

Consider now

$$F_P^1 = \bigcup_{p(x)} \text{ground}(\mathcal{P}_\alpha JP_2K \downarrow 1 \, (p(x))) = \{ \, q(f(a)), q(f(f(a))), \ldots$$
$$p(a) \qquad \qquad \}$$

$$F_P^2 = \bigcup_{p(x)} \text{ground}(\mathcal{P}_\alpha JP_2K \downarrow 2 \, (p(x))) = \{ \, q(f(a)), q(f(f(a))), \ldots$$
$$p(a), p(f(a)) \qquad \qquad \}$$

$\vdots$

$$F_P = \bigcup_{p(x)} \text{ground}(\mathcal{P}_\alpha JP_2K \downarrow \omega \, (p(x))) = \{ \, q(f(a)), q(f(f(a))), \ldots$$
$$p(a), p(f(a)), p(f(f(a))), \ldots\}$$

Note that it is not possible to define a co-continuous operator based on the F_P^i's, since $q(a)$ fails according to the information in F_P.

5 Conclusion

Our goal was defining a fixpoint semantics correctly modeling finite failure. Our approach was to start with a concrete fixpoint semantics modeling the finite and infinite SLD traces via a fair selection rule.

From this concrete semantics, which allows us to observe the finite failure property, by using abstract interpretation techniques, we automatically derive a new fixpoint semantics for finite failure. In fact, once we have formalized the "observable" property of finite failure as a Galois insertion, we can define an abstract fixpoint operator as the optimal (and precise) version of the concrete fixpoint operator. This construction yields a fixpoint semantics which correctly models finite failure, using a fixpoint operator which is co-continuous and a new theorem of and-compositionality for finite failure simpler than the one stated in [9]. It is worth noting that the fixpoint operator for finite failure is not finitary. However, for analysis and verification purposes, we are in general not interested in the standard semantics of a program (which is in any case an infinite object), but in its finitely computable approximations. Also in our case, it is possible to derive approximations of our fixpoint operator which will allow us to derive information on finite failure in an effective way and to use it to define effective verification methods [10].

Moreover, we believe that other interesting semantics can be derived from the concrete SLD-traces semantics. We are now currently working on the definition of a new fixpoint semantics modeling infinite derivations, based on a co-continuous operator. Some computable abstractions of this semantics could be useful for the analysis of termination of logic programs.

Finally, we think that our results are a nice example which shows that abstract interpretation is not for static analysis only. It is well known that abstract interpretation can be used to related existing standard semantics. However here we have used the abstract interpretation technique to derive a new semantics which models an observable property for which a satisfactory fixpoint semantics was hard to define in a direct way.

References

1. K. R. Apt. Introduction to Logic Programming. In J. van Leeuwen, editor, *Handbook of Theoretical Computer Science*, volume B: Formal Models and Semantics, pages 495–574. Elsevier and The MIT Press, 1990.
2. K. R. Apt and M. H. van Emden. Contributions to the theory of logic programming. *Journal of the ACM*, 29(3):841–862, 1982.
3. A. Bossi, M. Gabbrielli, G. Levi, and M. Martelli. The s-semantics approach: Theory and applications. *Journal of Logic Programming*, 19–20:149–197, 1994.
4. M. Comini and M. C. Meo. Compositionality properties of *SLD*-derivations. *Theoretical Computer Science*, 211(1-2):275–309, 1999.
5. P. Cousot and R. Cousot. Abstract Interpretation: A Unified Lattice Model for Static Analysis of Programs by Construction or Approximation of Fixpoints. In *Proc. Fourth ACM Symp. Principles of Programming Languages*, pages 238–252, 1977.
6. P. Cousot and R. Cousot. Systematic Design of Program Analysis Frameworks. In *Proc. Sixth ACM Symp. Principles of Programming Languages*, pages 269–282, 1979.
7. M. Falaschi, G. Levi, M. Martelli, and C. Palamidessi. Declarative Modeling of the Operational Behavior of Logic Languages. *Theoretical Computer Science*, 69(3):289–318, 1989.
8. R. Gori. Which semantics for finite failure. http://www.di.unipi.it/~gori/Papers/, 1999.
9. R. Gori and G. Levi. Finite failure is and-compositional. *Journal of Logic and Computation*, 7(6):753–776, 1997.
10. R. Gori and G. Levi. On verification of finite failure. In Gopalan Nadathur, editor, *Proc. Principles and Practice of Declarative Programming 1999*, 1999.

11. J.-L. Lassez and M. J. Maher. Closures and Fairness in the Semantics of Programming Logic. *Theoretical Computer Science*, 29:167–184, 1984.
12. G. Levi, M. Martelli, and C. Palamidessi. Failure and success made symmetric. In S. K. Debray and M. Hermenegildo, editors, *Proc. North American Conf. on Logic Programming'90*, pages 3–22. The MIT Press, 1990.
13. J. W. Lloyd. *Foundations of Logic Programming*. Springer-Verlag, 1987. Second edition.

Extensions to the Estimation Calculus

Jeremy Gow, Alan Bundy, and Ian Green

Institute for Representation and Reasoning,
Division of Informatics, University of Edinburgh,
80 South Bridge, Edinburgh EH1 1HN, Scotland
jeremygo@dai.ed.ac.uk   {A.Bundy,I.Green}@ed.ac.uk

Abstract. Walther's estimation calculus was designed to prove the termination of functional programs, and can also be used to solve the similar problem of proving the well-foundedness of induction rules. However, there are certain features of the goal formulae which are more common to the problem of induction rule well-foundedness than the problem of termination, and which the calculus cannot handle. We present a sound extension of the calculus that is capable of dealing with these features. The extension develops Walther's concept of an argument bounded function in two ways: firstly, so that the function may be bounded *below* by its argument, and secondly, so that a bound may exist between two arguments of a predicate. Our calculus enables automatic proofs of the well-foundedness of a large class of induction rules not captured by the original calculus.

1   Introduction

An induction rule is *well-founded* iff there is a well-founded order such that for each *step case* of the rule the inductive hypotheses are less in that order than the inductive conclusion. A standard technique for showing validity of an induction rule involves showing the rule to be well-founded, and so automatic techniques for establishing well-foundedness are of interest to the inductive theorem proving community.

The problem of proving an induction rule well-founded is similar to that of proving the termination of a recursive functional program. The current state of the art techniques in automated termination analysis of functional programs are based upon Walther's estimation calculus [10]. Likewise, these techniques currently represent the most powerful approach to automatically proving the well-foundedness of induction rules.

Both termination and well-foundedness proofs involve finding a well-founded relation $\prec$ that satisfies formulae of the form

$$\varphi \to s \prec t \tag{1}$$

In a termination proof of a function[1] f, there is a goal (1), known as a *termination formula*, for each recursive call in a defining equation of f of the form

---

[1] We do not consider functions defined by mutual or nested recursion. [5] describes extending existing termination analysis techniques to such functions.

$$\varphi \to f(t) = \cdots f(s) \cdots \qquad (2)$$

In a well-foundedness proof, there is goal (1), known as a *well-foundedness for-mulae*, for each induction hypothesis in a step case of the induction rule of the form

$$\varphi, \ldots, \psi(s), \ldots \vdash \psi(t) \qquad (3)$$

However, there are two common features of the induction step case (3) which appear less often in (2). Firstly, the term t in (3) can contain defined function symbols (i.e. non-constructor symbols), whereas the t in (2) is often a pattern (i.e., a linear constructor term) – some languages (e.g. ML) demand this is the case. Secondly, the terms s and t in (3) may be related by a predicate in the step case conditions φ. Although this can occur in (2), it is not a common style of programming. Hence well-foundedness formulae have features whose analogues appear less frequently in termination formulae:

(i) the appearance of defined function symbols on the right of the inequality, and,
(ii) the two sides of the inequality are related by a predicate that appears in the preconditions.

As the original estimation calculus was designed to prove termination formulae, it does not take account of either of these features, and so fails on well-foundedness formulae when these features are relevant to the solution (several examples are given below).

In this paper we present a sound extension of the estimation calculus which can handle both of these features of well-foundedness formulae. Furthermore, this extended calculus is readily automated in just the same way as Walther's original calculus. Thus the extended calculus enables automatic proofs of the well-foundedness of a strictly larger class of induction rules not captured by Walther's approach. (We discuss below other extensions of the original calculus.) Likewise, it can prove the termination of a larger class of functions, given some formalisms may allow functions with features analogous to (i) and (ii).

The extension is achieved by developing the concept of *argument bounds*. In the original calculus, an argument bounded function is one whose result is bounded above by one of its arguments under the size order. The size order $<_\#$ orders free data types by their value under the size measure $\#$, e.g., natural numbers are ordered by magnitude, and lists by length.

We extend the concept of argument bounds to functions which are bounded below by their arguments, and to predicates in which one argument bounds another. Using these concepts, the calculus is extended in order to deal with features (i) and (ii) described above. For simplicity in this paper, we concentrate on extending Walther's original calculus [10], although our techniques could be combined with some of the other extensions described in §2.3.

The features particular to well-foundedness formulae and our extensions to estimation calculus are illustrated by the following two examples. Firstly, consider (4) below as an example of an induction rule whose well-foundedness formulae have feature (i):

$$\frac{\begin{array}{c} \vdash \psi(0) \\ \vdash \psi(s(0)) \\ x \neq 0 \wedge y \neq 0, \ \psi(x), \ \psi(y) \vdash \psi(plus(x,y)) \end{array}}{\vdash \forall x{:}nat.\ \psi(x)} \tag{4}$$

where *plus* sums two natural numbers. If we attempt to use the size order # to prove this well-founded, we must show that

$$x \neq 0 \wedge y \neq 0 \rightarrow \#(x) < \#(plus(x,y)) \tag{5}$$
$$x \neq 0 \wedge y \neq 0 \rightarrow \#(y) < \#(plus(x,y)) \tag{6}$$

These well-foundedness formulae both display feature (i): defined function symbols appear on the right of the inequality. If we know that *plus* is bounded below by its first argument, relative to #, and that this bound is strict when the second argument is non-zero, i.e.,

$$v \neq 0 \rightarrow \#(u) < \#(plus(u,v)) \tag{7}$$

then we can easily discharge (5). This is the basic approach taken by the estimation calculus: find an argument bound, synthesise lemmas giving conditions on the strictness of this bound (like (7)) and then show that these conditions hold. Formula (6) can be discharged with a similar insight about the second argument of *plus*.

However, this example cannot be solved by the estimation calculus. Because the termination formulae it was designed to solve rarely display feature (i), it only reasons with functions which are bounded *above* by one of their arguments. The crucial part of this proof is to recognise the *lower* argument bound on *plus*. Our extended calculus can solve such well-foundedness conditions by reasoning about lower argument bounds.

Our second example (8) has well-foundedness formulae which illustrate feature (ii) described above. Here *shorter* is a predicate that holds only when its first argument is a shorter list than its second argument.

$$\frac{\vdash \psi(nil) \qquad shorter(x,y), \ \psi(x) \vdash \psi(y)}{\vdash \forall x{:}list(\tau).\ \psi(x)} \tag{8}$$

To establish well-foundedness using the size order, we need to discharge

$$shorter(x,y) \rightarrow \#(x) < \#(y) \tag{9}$$

This well-foundedness formula displays feature (ii): the two sides of the inequality are related by a predicate that appears in the preconditions. If we know that when *shorter* holds, its first argument is bounded above by the second argument, relative to #, and that this bound is *always* strict, then we can discharge (9). Notice we have taken the estimation calculus approach again: find an argument bound, synthesise a lemma giving conditions on the strictness of this bound and show these conditions hold – in this example the conditions are trivially true.

The original estimation calculus cannot solve this example, as the crucial part of the proof is recognising the relevant argument bound holds between the first and second arguments of *shorter*. The calculus can only reason about argument bounded functions, and not argument bounded *predicates* that appear in the conditions on the inequality. This is because these rarely appear in the termination formulae the calculus was designed to prove. Our extended calculus can solve such well-foundedness conditions by reasoning about bounds between arguments of predicates.

Although there exist more powerful techniques which can reason about features (i) and (ii), i.e. [4] and [1], our calculus has advantages over these. The main contribution of this paper is that such reasoning can be 'built in' to Walther's calculus in a way analogous to the original, and which retains its simplicity. The method is simpler and easier to implement than comparable techniques, and although less powerful, is capable of coping with many common examples.

The remainder of this paper is organised as follows: we provide some background on the estimation calculus in §2. The extension for handling the occurrence of defined function symbols in the conclusion of a step case is presented in §3, and the extension for formulae where the two sides of the inequality are related by a predicate that appears in the conditions is described in §4. Refinements and possible developments of our approach are discussed in §5, and in §6 we draw our conclusions.

Conventions We use $i \in [n]$ to denote $1 \leq i \leq n$, and $\vec{s_n}$ to denote $s_1, \ldots, s_n$. Each n-ary constructor c has n associated destructor functions $d_c^1, \ldots, d_c^n$ which return the arguments of c, defined as $d_c^i(c(\vec{t_n})) = t_i$, a everywhere else, where a is an arbitrary nullary constructor of the appropriate type. It is assumed that such a constructor exists for each type.

2 Background

Proving induction rules well-founded, and functional programs terminating (excluding nested and mutually recursive programs), requires us to find a well-founded relation[2] $\prec$ which satisfies a set of formulae of the form

$$\varphi \rightarrow (\vec{s_n}) \prec (\vec{t_n}) \tag{10}$$

There is a well-foundedness formula of this form for each inductive hypothesis, where the s_i are values of the induction variables in the hypothesis, the t_i are the values in the conclusion of this step case and φ are the conditions on this case. In the case of termination proofs, there is a termination formula (10) for each

---

[2] A relation is well-founded if it does not contain any infinite descending chains.

recursive call – the s_i are the arguments of this call, the t_i are the arguments of the head of this defining case and φ are the case conditions.

If a relation $\prec$ is well-founded on β, a measure functions $m : \alpha \to \beta$ can be used to induce a well-founded relation $\prec_m$, defined by

$$\forall x, y{:}\alpha.\ \left(x \prec_m y \leftrightarrow m(x) \prec m(y)\right)$$

The estimation calculus [10] attempts to prove sets of well-foundedness formulae using the well-founded size order $<_\#$. The size measure $\# : \tau \to nat$ counts the number of reflexive[3] type τ constructors in a type τ data-structure, where substructures of other types are ignored. The rest of this section gives a brief summary of the estimation calculus – for more details see [10].

2.1   Argument Bounds and Difference Predicates

Walther defines an argument bounded function as one whose result is smaller under $\leq_\#$ than one of its arguments. In order to avoid confusion later, we refer to these as *upper* argument bounded functions, because the argument is an upper bound on the function. Formally:

Definition 1 (Upper Argument Bounded Function). *A function* $f : \tau_1 \times \cdots \times \tau_n \to \tau$ *is upper p-bounded iff $p \in [n]$ and*

$$\forall t_1{:}\tau_1 \ldots t_n{:}\tau_n.\ f(\vec{t_n}) \leq_\# t_p$$

A function is upper argument bounded *iff it is upper p-bounded for some p.*

For each upper argument bounded position p of a function f, there is a difference predicate which is true only when the upper bound is strict. Formally:

Definition 2 (Difference Predicate). *If f is upper p-bounded, the* difference predicate Δ_f^p *is defined by*

$$\Delta_f^p(\vec{t_n}) = \left(f(\vec{t_n}) <_\# t_p\right)$$

Note that predicates are treated as functions with the range {TRUE, FALSE}. For an n-ary predicate P we write $P(\vec{x_n}) = \text{TRUE}$ as $P(\vec{x_n})$ (see [10] for further details).

2.2   The Estimation Calculus

Walther's calculus is given in Fig. 1, which we have recast as a sequent-style system. The measured data type has k reflexive constructors $\vec{r_k}$, and l irreflexive constructors $\vec{ir_l}$. Each r_i is reflexive on the set of argument positions R_i.

The calculus is used to derive sequents of the form $\langle s \leq_\# t, \Delta \rangle$, and is sound in that $\vdash_E \langle s \leq_\# t, \Delta \rangle$ implies both $s \leq_\# t$ and $\Delta \leftrightarrow s <_\# t$. Well-foundedness

---

[3] A function is reflexive if its range type is one of its domain types.

Assumption

$$\frac{}{\Gamma \vdash_E A} \text{ if } A \in \Gamma$$

Identity

$$\frac{}{\Gamma \vdash_E \langle t \leq_\# t, \text{FALSE} \rangle}$$

Equivalence

$$\frac{}{\Gamma \vdash_E \langle ir_i(\vec{s_n}) \leq_\# ir_j(\vec{t_m}), \text{FALSE} \rangle} \text{ if } i, j \in [l]$$

Strong Estimation

$$\frac{}{\Gamma \vdash_E \langle ir_i(\vec{s_n}) \leq_\# r_j(\vec{t_m}), \text{TRUE} \rangle} \text{ if } i \in [l], j \in [k]$$

Minimum

$$\frac{}{\Gamma \vdash_E \langle ir_i(\vec{s_n}) \leq_\# t \,,\, t = r_1(d^1_{r_1}(t), \ldots, d^{m_1}_{r_1}(t)) \vee \cdots \\ \cdots \vee t = r_k(d^1_{r_k}(t), \ldots, d^{m_k}_{r_k}(t)) \rangle} \text{ if } i \in [l]$$

Upper Bound Estimation

$$\frac{\Gamma \vdash_E \langle s_p \leq_\# t, \Delta \rangle}{\Gamma \vdash_E \langle f(\vec{s_n}) \leq_\# t, \Delta \vee \Delta^p_f(\vec{s_n}) \rangle} \text{ if } f \text{ is upper } p\text{-bounded}$$

Strong Embedding

$$\frac{\Gamma \vdash_E \langle s \leq_\# t_j, \Delta \rangle}{\Gamma \vdash_E \langle s \leq_\# r_i(\vec{t_m}), \text{TRUE} \rangle} \text{ if } i \in [k], j \in R_i$$

Weak Embedding

$$\frac{\Gamma \vdash_E \langle s_{j_1} \leq_\# t_{j_1}, \Delta_1 \rangle, \ldots, \Gamma \vdash_E \langle s_{j_m} \leq_\# t_{j_m}, \Delta_n \rangle}{\Gamma \vdash_E \langle r_i(\vec{s_n}) \leq_\# r_i(\vec{t_n}), \Delta_1 \vee \cdots \vee \Delta_n \rangle} \quad \begin{array}{l} \text{if } i \in [k], \\ R_i = \{\vec{j_m}\} \end{array}$$

Fig. 1. The estimation calculus

conditions of the form (10) are proved by showing $\vdash_E \langle s_i \leq_\# t_i, \Delta \rangle$ for some $i \in [n]$ and then using a theorem prover to establish $\varphi \rightarrow \Delta$.

The calculus rules can be used in reverse to decompose the goal formula $\langle s \leq_\# t, \Delta \rangle$, where the identity of Δ is initially unknown. If we represent this unknown as a meta-variable which can be instantiated by rule applications, then the difference formula Δ can be constructed during the analysis[4].

---

[4] Walther's original approach to using the calculus was to recast it as a production rule system whose rules constructed Δ as they decomposed the inequality. The approaches are trivially equivalent.

Recognising argument bounded functions and synthesising difference predicates is done automatically using the estimation calculus. An upper p-bounded function f is recognised by performing a meta-induction proof that demonstrates that each defining case of f returns a value no larger under $<_\#$ than the pth argument (see [10] for details). If it exists, the corresponding difference predicate is synthesised as a by-product of this analysis.

2.3   Related Techniques

Based on the estimation calculus, Giesl developed a similar calculus that works with arbitrary measure functions based on polynomial norms [3]. As it is not restricted to using the size measure, it is a much more powerful approach. The method still has the drawback that the user must supply the appropriate measure function. To overcome this Giesl adapted the approach to automatically synthesise these measure functions, using techniques from termination analysis of term rewriting systems [4]. This latter technique is quite different from the estimation calculus, and does not use argument bounded functions. A good overview of this research can be found in [6].

The estimation calculus has also been extended to work with certain non-free data types [9], and has been used as the basis for Walther recursive programs [7], a class of functional programs for which termination is decidable.

3   Lower Argument Bounded Functions

In this section we describe our extension for feature (i): the occurrence of defined function symbols on the right of the inequality. If a well-foundedness formula has this feature, then proving it requires us to show $\vdash_E \langle s \leq_\# t, \Delta \rangle$, where t contains defined function. The calculus fails in these situations because it has no rules which can derive theorems of this form.

We can extend the estimation calculus to allow defined functions f to be added to t, providing that they do not decrease the value of this term under the size measure. In other words, the value of $f(\ldots, t, \ldots)$ is bounded below by the value of t. We call these functions *lower* argument bounded functions, and define them as follows:

Definition 3 (Lower Argument Bounded Function). *A function* $f : \tau_1 \times \cdots \times \tau_n \to \tau$ *is lower p-bounded iff $p \in [n]$ and*

$$\forall t_1{:}\tau_1 \cdots t_n{:}\tau_n. \, t_p \leq_\# f(\vec{t_n})$$

A function is lower argument bounded *iff it is lower p-bounded for some p.*

Before we can extend the calculus to use lower argument bounded functions, we need to be able to synthesise a difference predicate that is true iff the lower argument bound is strict. The process is exactly analogous to the upper bound case – the difference predicate Δ_f^p is synthesised while verifying that f is lower

p-bounded – and is described in §3.1. We can now extend the estimation calculus by adding the following inference rule (11) to handle lower argument bounded functions.

Lower Bound Estimation

$$\frac{\Gamma \vdash_E \langle s \leq_\# t_p, \Delta \rangle}{\Gamma \vdash_E \langle s \leq_\# f(\vec{t_n}), \Delta \vee \Delta_f^p(\vec{t_n}) \rangle} \quad \text{if } f \text{ is lower } p\text{-bounded} \quad (11)$$

Because all constructor functions are argument bounded on their reflexive argument positions, the strong embedding rule (see Fig. 1) is now redundant, being subsumed by rule (11). Below we use $\vdash_E$ to denote the estimation calculus extended with our new rule (11).

Theorem 1. *Rule (11) is sound.*

Proof. Assume f is lower p-bounded and $\langle s \leq_\# t_p, \Delta \rangle$. By definition $s \leq_\# t_p$ and $\Delta \leftrightarrow s <_\# t_p$, and $t_p \leq_\# f(\vec{t_n})$ and $\Delta_f^p(\vec{t_n}) \leftrightarrow t_p <_\# f(\vec{t_n})$. Now:

(a) $s \leq_\# f(\vec{t_n})$, by $s \leq_\# t_p$ and $t_p \leq_\# f(\vec{t_n})$.
(b) $\Delta \vee \Delta_f^p(\vec{t_n}) \to s <_\# f(\vec{t_n})$, as $\Delta \to s <_\# f(\vec{t_n})$ and $\Delta_f^p(\vec{t_n}) \to s <_\# f(\vec{t_n})$ by (a).
(c) $s <_\# f(\vec{t_n}) \to \Delta \vee \Delta_f^p(\vec{t_n})$, because $s \leq_\# t_p \leq_\# f(\vec{t_n})$, so $s <_\# f(\vec{t_n}) \to t_p \neq s \vee t_p \neq f(\vec{t_n})$. Hence $s <_\# f(\vec{t_n}) \to s <_\# t_p \vee t_p <_\# f(\vec{t_n})$.

Therefore $\langle s \leq_\# f(\vec{t_n}), \Delta \vee \Delta_f^p(\vec{t_n}) \rangle$ as required.   □

Given the original estimation calculus and the new rule (11) are both sound, our extended calculus $\vdash_E$ is also sound.

As an example of rule (11) in operation, consider the following induction rule, taken from [8]:

$$\frac{\vdash \psi(nil) \qquad \psi(l) \vdash \psi(app(l, cons(x, nil)))}{\vdash \forall l{:}list(\tau).\,\psi(l)} \quad (12)$$

Here *nil* and *cons* are the list constructors and *app* is a defined function that appends two lists, defined as

$$app(nil, l) = l \quad (13)$$
$$app(cons(h, t), l) = cons(h, app(t, l)) \quad (14)$$

We can verify that *app* is lower 1-bounded, with the associated difference predicate Δ_{app}^1 (see §3.1 for details), defined as

$$\Delta_{app}^1(nil, l) = (l = cons(hd(l), tl(l))) \quad (15)$$
$$\Delta_{app}^1(cons(h, t), l) = \Delta_{app}^1(t, l) \quad (16)$$

We can use the size measure to prove (12) well-founded: $\vdash_E \langle l \leq_\# l,\ \text{FALSE} \rangle$ by the identity rule, and then by lower bound estimation

$$\vdash_E \langle l \leq_\# app(l, cons(x, nil)),\ \text{FALSE} \vee \Delta^1_{app}(l, cons(x, nil)) \rangle$$

It is within the power of current automatic inductive theorem provers (e.g., Clam [2]) to show that the difference formulae $\text{FALSE} \vee \Delta^1_{app}(l, cons(x, nil))$ is true, and so the inequality is strict. Hence the induction rule (12) is well-founded. Note this cannot be established using the original calculus, because of the defined function symbols app appearing on the right hand side of the inequality.

In [4] termination/well-foundedness formulae are converted into a set of constraints on a polynomial measure, and a suitable measure is generated. This relieves the user of having to provide suitable measures for the proof. It is also general enough to handle goal formulae with feature (i), and so could be used as an alternative to the estimation calculus extended with our rule (11). However, our approach is considerably simpler and easier to implement. Of course, it can only be used in situations where the size measure is sufficient, but this includes many common induction rules/functions.

3.1   Recognising Lower Argument Bounded Functions

When an n-ary function is defined, we attempt to prove it is lower p-bounded for each $p \in [n]$. We assume it has been shown terminating, and has a set of mutually exclusive and exhaustive defining equations. To verify that f is lower p-bounded for some p we must show

$$\vdash_E \langle t_p \leq_\# f(\vec{t_n}),\ \Delta^p_f(\vec{t_n}) \rangle \tag{17}$$

for some difference predicate Δ^p_f. As in the upper argument bounded case (for details see [10]), we prove this property by a meta-induction over the estimation calculus which corresponds to the recursive structure of f. The difference predicate Δ^p_f is synthesised during this process – each case of the meta-induction adds an equation to its definition.

So for each defining equation of f

$$\varphi \rightarrow f(\vec{t_n}) = b \tag{18}$$

where b contains k recursive calls $f(s_{1,1}, \ldots, s_{1,n}), \ldots, f(s_{k,1}, \ldots, s_{k,n})$, we must verify a case of our meta-induction corresponding to (18)

$$\begin{aligned} \langle s_{1,p} \leq_\# f(s_{1,1}, \ldots, s_{1,n}),\ \Delta^p_f(s_{1,1}, \ldots, s_{1,n}) \rangle, \\ \vdots \qquad\qquad\qquad\qquad \\ \langle s_{k,p} \leq_\# f(s_{k,1}, \ldots, s_{k,n}),\ \Delta^p_f(s_{k,1}, \ldots, s_{k,n}) \rangle \vdash_E \langle t_p \leq_\# b,\ \Delta \rangle \end{aligned} \tag{19}$$

for some Δ. Note there may be no recursive calls in b, and so they will be no inductive hypotheses.

The corresponding difference predicate Δ_f^p is synthesised as a by-product: for each case of our meta-induction (19), we obtain the following defining equation

$$\varphi \rightarrow \Delta_f^p(\overrightarrow{t_n}) = \Delta \tag{20}$$

The above meta-induction is guaranteed valid, because we demand f is terminating and has a set of mutually exclusive and exhaustive defining equations. If we use this scheme to prove (17), then for each case (18) there is a meta-induction case

$$\varphi, h_1, \ldots, h_k \vdash \langle t_p \leq_\# f(\overrightarrow{t_n}), \Delta_f^p(\overrightarrow{t_n}) \rangle$$

where $h_1, \ldots, h_k$ are the inductive hypotheses of (19). By the definitions of f (18) and Δ_f^p (20) it is sufficient to prove (19). Hence the meta-induction proves (17).

Furthermore, as $\vdash_E$ is sound, (17) implies $t_p \leq_\# f(\overrightarrow{t_n})$ and $\Delta_f^p(\overrightarrow{t_n}) \leftrightarrow t_p \leq_\# f(\overrightarrow{t_n})$. So by definition 3, the meta-induction verifies that f is lower p-bounded and has difference predicate Δ_f^p.

The process of recognising lower argument bounded functions is illustrated by the verification app (see §3) is a lower 1-bounded function. For defining equation (13) we use the minimum rule to show

$$\vdash_E \langle nil \leq_\# l, (l = cons(hd(l), tl(l))) \rangle$$

(15) is extracted from this. For the recursive equation (14) we can use the weak embedding rule to show

$$\langle t \leq_\# app(t, l), \Delta_{app}^1(t, l) \rangle \vdash_E \langle cons(h, t) \leq_\# cons(h, app(t, l)), \Delta_{app}^1(t, l) \rangle$$

from which (16) is extracted. Hence app is lower 1-bounded, with the difference predicate defined by (15) and (16).

4   Argument Bounded Predicates

We now describe our extension for feature (ii): the two sides of the inequality are related by a predicate that appears in the preconditions. A well-foundedness formula with this feature requires us to show $\vdash_E \langle s \leq_\# t, \Delta \rangle$, where s is less than t because of the preconditions. This is not possible in the original calculus, which ignores these conditions.

Although the conditions φ may entail $s \leq_\# t$, it may require arbitrarily hard theorem proving to establish this – and we would still be left with the problem of synthesising the appropriate difference predicate. We adopt a restricted but more practical approach in which $\varphi \rightarrow w(\overrightarrow{t_n})$ is tested using a decision procedure[5], such that $s = t_p$ and $t = t_q$, where w is a predicate that is mentioned in φ and whose pth argument is never greater under the size measure than its qth argument. In other words, w ensures t is bounded below by s. We call w an *argument bounded predicate*, defined as follows:

---
[5] For example, that the formula is a tautology.

Definition 4 (Argument Bounded Predicate). *A predicate* $w : \tau_1 \times \cdots \times \tau_n \to bool$ *is* (p, q)-*bounded iff* $1 \leq p, q \leq n$, $p \neq q$ *and*

$$\forall t_1 : \tau_1 \cdots t_n : \tau_n. \, w(\vec{t_n}) \to t_p \leq_\# t_q$$

A predicate is argument bounded *iff it is* (p, q)-*bounded for some* p, q.

As with argument bounded functions, there is a difference predicate $\Delta_w^{(p,q)}$ that is equivalent to this bound being strict, i.e. $w(\vec{t_n}) \to (\Delta_w^{(p,q)}(\vec{t_n}) \leftrightarrow t_p \leq_\# t_q)$, and which is synthesised while verifying w is (p, q)-bounded. This is described in §4.1. We can now extend the estimation calculus by adding an inference rule (21) to handle argument bounded predicates in the conditions.

Condition Bound

$$\frac{}{\Gamma \vdash_E \langle t_p \leq_\# t_q, \Delta_w^{(p,q)}(\vec{t_n}) \rangle} \tag{21}$$

Providing (p, q)-bounded w in φ and $\varphi \to w(\vec{t_n})$ is a tautology.

Theorem 2. *Rule (21) is sound.*

Proof. Assume w is (p, q)-bounded and $\varphi \to w(\vec{t_n})$ is a tautology. As φ is the current condition, $w(\vec{t_n})$ holds. By definition 4, $w(\vec{t_n}) \to t_p \leq_\# t_q$, so $t_p \leq_\# t_q$. Also, $w(\vec{t_n}) \to (\Delta_w^{(p,q)}(\vec{t_n}) \leftrightarrow t_p <_\# t_q)$, so $\Delta_w^{(p,q)}(\vec{t_n}) \leftrightarrow t_p <_\# t_q$. Hence $\langle t_p \leq_\# t_q, \Delta_w^{(p,q)}(\vec{t_n}) \rangle$ as required. □

Extending $\vdash_E$ with (21) preserves soundness; henceforth we shall refer to this system (i.e., $\vdash_E$ with the addition of rule (21)) as $\vdash_E$.

As an example of the use of rule (21), consider the following induction rule:

$$\frac{\vdash \psi(nil) \qquad leqlen(l, m), \psi(l) \vdash \psi(cons(x, m))}{\vdash \forall l : list(\tau). \, \psi(l)} \tag{22}$$

Here *leqlen* is a predicate that holds when its first argument is a list not longer than its second argument, and is defined as

$$leqlen(nil, m) = \text{TRUE} \tag{23}$$

$$leqlen(cons(g, s), nil) = \text{FALSE} \tag{24}$$

$$leqlen(cons(g, s), cons(h, t)) = leqlen(s, t) \tag{25}$$

We can show that *leqlen* is $(1, 2)$-bounded, and has the difference predicate $\Delta_{leqlen}^{(1,2)}$ (see §4.1 for details), defined as

$$\Delta_{leqlen}^{(1,2)}(nil, m) = (m = cons(hd(m), tl(m))) \tag{26}$$

$$\Delta_{leqlen}^{(1,2)}(cons(g, s), nil) = \text{FALSE} \tag{27}$$

$$\Delta_{leqlen}^{(1,2)}(cons(g, s), cons(h, t)) = \Delta_{leqlen}^{(1,2)}(s, t) \tag{28}$$

To establish the well-foundedness of (22) using the size order, we can use the condition bound rule (21) to derive $\vdash_E \langle l \leq_\# m, \Delta_{leqlen}^{(1,2)}(l,m) \rangle$, followed by lower bound estimation, given that $cons$ is lower 2-bounded.

$$\vdash_E \langle l \leq_\# cons(x,m), \Delta_{leqlen}^{(1,2)}(l,m) \vee \Delta_{cons}^2(x,m) \rangle$$

The difference formula is true, as $\Delta_{cons}^2(x,m)$ is defined as TRUE. Hence induction rule (22) is well-founded. Note that this example cannot be solved using the original estimation calculus, as it does not consider the conditions on the well-foundedness formulae.

Brauburger and Giesl use inductive evaluation to exploit the conditions on the inequality in termination formulae [1], and so their method could also be used as an alternative to the condition bound rule (21). However, this requires an inductive theorem prover to solve subgoals that correspond to proving the predicate is strictly argument bounded. Our approach performs this analysis when the predicate is first defined, and so requires less theorem proving support during execution. It is simpler to identify argument bounded predicates when they are defined, and to use the condition bound rule when possible. Of course, there are many situations where rule (21) is not relevant and inductive evaluation is required.

4.1   Recognising Argument Bounded Predicates

When an n-ary predicate is defined, we attempt to prove it is (p,q)-bounded for each $p \neq q$, $1 \leq p, q \leq n$. We assume it has been shown terminating (recall our predicates are functions onto {TRUE, FALSE}) and has a set of mutually exclusive and exhaustive defining equations. To verify that w is (p,q)-bounded for some p and q we must show that

$$\vdash_E \langle t_p \leq_\# t_q, \Delta_w^{(p,q)}(\overrightarrow{t_n}) \rangle \tag{29}$$

when $w(\overrightarrow{t_n})$ holds, for some difference predicate $\Delta_w^{(p,q)}$. We proceed as in the argument bounded function case (see §3.1 and [10]), by a meta-induction over the estimation calculus according to the recursive structure of w. Again each case of the meta-induction adds an equation to the definition of the difference predicate $\Delta_f^{(p,q)}$.

However, because we have the extra assumption $w(\overrightarrow{t_n})$, the details of the meta-induction are somewhat different from the functional case. For each defining equation of w

$$\varphi \to \quad w(\overrightarrow{t_n}) = b \tag{30}$$

we require that b is a quantifier-free formula over the free variables of $w(\overrightarrow{t_n})$. This formula is converted into disjunctive normal form $b' = d_1 \vee \cdots \vee d_m$. Recall that we only want to establish (29) when $w(\overrightarrow{t_n})$ holds, so if $b = $ FALSE we can ignore the case (30) and do not care what value $\Delta_w^{(p,q)}(\vec{t_n})$ takes – a case assigning it FALSE under the condition φ is added.

Otherwise, we must prove a case of the meta-induction corresponding to (30) when $w(\vec{t_n}) = $ TRUE. The latter implies at least one of the disjuncts d_i must hold. If d_i holds and contains the set of positive literals p_i, we can make the following assumptions

1. For each $w(\vec{s_n})$ in p_i we can assume $\langle s_p \leq_\# s_q, \Delta_w^{(p,q)}(\vec{s_n})\rangle$.
2. For each $z(\vec{s_m})$ is in p_i, such that z is a (u,v)-bounded predicate, we can assume $\langle s_p \leq_\# s_q, \Delta_z^{(u,v)}(\vec{s_n})\rangle$.

For each d_i we collect such a set of assumptions $h_1,\ldots,h_a$ and verify the following meta-induction case

$$h_1,\ldots,h_a \vdash_E \langle t_p \leq_\# t_q, \Delta\rangle \tag{31}$$

If this proof is successful we create the following defining equation for $\Delta_w^{(p,q)}$:

$$\varphi \to \quad \Delta_w^{(p,q)}(\vec{t_n}) = \Delta$$

Compare our meta-induction with the induction based upon the recursive structure of w. Ours has the same case structure, with extra cases splits on the disjuncts $d_1 \vee \cdots \vee d_m$, and only uses inductive hypotheses which would also appear in the latter induction. The meta-induction is valid since w is terminating and has a set of mutually exclusive and exhaustive defining equations. So if the meta-induction succeeds, then (29) is established under the assumption $w(\vec{t_n})$.

Given $w(\vec{t_n})$ implies (29), the soundness of $\vdash_E$ yields $w(\vec{t_n}) \to t_p \leq_\# t_q$ and $w(\vec{t_n}) \to (\Delta_w^{(p,q)}(\vec{t_n}) \leftrightarrow t_p \leq_\# t_q)$. So by definition 4, the meta-induction correctly verifies that w is (p,q)-bounded and has difference predicate $\Delta_w^{(p,q)}$.

Our approach to recognising argument bounded predicates is illustrated by the verification of $leqlen$ (see §4) as a $(1,2)$-bounded predicate. Consider defining equation (23) of $leqlen$: we use the minimum rule to show

$$\vdash_E \langle nil \leq_\# m, (m = cons(hd(m), tl(m)))\rangle$$

which gives us (26). The defining equation (24) has FALSE on the right, so this case is ignored, and $\Delta_{leqlen}^{(1,2)}(cons(g,s), nil)$ set to FALSE. For the third defining equation (28) there is a single disjunct containing a single positive literal $leqlen(s,t)$. Hence we use the weak embedding rule to show

$$\langle s \leq_\# t, \Delta_{leqlen}^{(1,2)}(s,t)\rangle$$
$$\vdash_E \langle cons(g,s) \leq_\# cons(h,t), \Delta_{leqlen}^{(1,2)}(cons(g,s), cons(h,t))\rangle$$

from which (28) is extracted. Hence $leqlen$ is $(1,2)$-bounded, with the difference predicate defined by (26), (27) and (28).

5   Further Work

Our extended calculus consists of the lower bound estimation rule and the condition bound rule added to the original estimation calculus, minus the strong embedding rule – which is subsumed by lower bound estimation. There are a number of refinements that could be made to improve its performance. Many of those suggested by Walther for his original calculus [10] would be similarly applicable to our work, e.g., the optimisation of difference algorithms.

The use of lower argument bounded functions and argument bounded predicates could be incorporated into Giesl's calculus for polynomial norm measure functions [3], given that it works on similar principles to the estimation calculus. This would give our benefits for well-foundedness proofs, without the restriction of using only the size measure.

Argument bounded predicates can give us useful information even when their bound arguments are not simply the terms of the inequality we want to derive. For instance, consider the following induction rule:

$$\frac{\vdash \psi(nil) \qquad less(len(l), len(m)), \psi(l) \vdash \psi(m)}{\vdash \forall l{:}list(\tau).\,\psi(l)} \tag{32}$$

Here $less$ is less than on natural numbers, and len returns the length of a list. $less$ is also $(1,2)$-bounded, so we can use the condition bound rule to derive

$$\langle len(l) \leq_\# len(m),\, \Delta_{less}^{(1,2)}(len(l), len(m))\rangle$$

This can be used to prove induction rule (32) well-founded, providing we know the following properties of len:

$$\forall x, y{:}list(\tau).\, len(x) \leq_\# len(y) \rightarrow x \leq_\# y \tag{33}$$
$$\forall x, y{:}list(\tau).\, len(x) <_\# len(y) \rightarrow x <_\# y \tag{34}$$

Such reasoning could be included in the extended calculus, where properties like (33) and (34) are established when the functions are initially defined.

We also intend to implement the extended calculus as part of the *Clam* inductive theorem prover [2], in order to support automatic well-foundedness proofs for induction rules, e.g. the examples given in this paper. This forms part of a project to automatically construct such induction rules when required.

6   Conclusions

We have presented a fully automatic technique for proving that induction rules are well-founded. It is a sound extension of the estimation calculus designed to handle two common features of well-foundedness formulae for induction rules. These features are i) defined function symbols on the right of the inequality and ii) a predicate in the preconditions which relates the two sides of the inequality. The original estimation calculus did not take account of either of these features, as they rarely appear in the termination formulae it was designed to solve. Consequently, our calculus is more powerful.

Although both features could be tackled using alternative techniques our approach is simpler and easier to implement than comparable methods, as well as requiring less theorem proving support during execution than inductive evaluation.

Acknowledgements Thanks to Jürgen Brauburger, Simon Colton, Stephen Cresswell, Ben Curry, Jürgen Giesl, Andrew Ireland, Christoph Walther and three referees for many helpful comments. This research was supported by the EPSRC grant GR/J/80702.

References

1. J. Brauburger and J. Giesl. Termination analysis by inductive evaluation. In C. Kirchner and H. Kirchner, editors, *15th International Conference on Automated Deduction*, pages 254–269. LNAI 1421, Springer-Verlag, 1998.
2. The DReaM Group. *The Clam proof planner, user manual and programmer manual (version 2.8.1)*, April 1999. Available from ftp://dream.dai.ed.ac.uk/pub/oyster-clam/manual.ps.gz.
3. J. Giesl. Automated termination proofs with measure functions. In I. Wachsmuth, C. Rollinger, and W. Brauer, editors, *19th Annual German Conference on Artificial Intelligence*, pages 149–160. LNAI 981, Springer-Verlag, 1995.
4. J. Giesl. Termination analysis for functional programs using term orderings. In *2nd International Static Analysis Symposium*. LNCS 983, Springer-Verlag, 1995.
5. J. Giesl. Termination of nested and mutually recursive algorithms. *Journal of Automated Reasoning*, 19:1–29, 1997.
6. J. Giesl, C. Walther, and J. Brauburger. Termination analysis for functional programs. In W. Bibel and P.H. Schmitt, editors, *Automated Deduction – A Basis for Applications, Vol III: Applications*, volume 10 of *Applied Logic Series*, chapter 6, pages 135–164. Kluwer Academic, 1998.
7. David McAllester and Kostas Arkoudas. Walther recursion. In M.A. McRobbie and J.K. Slaney, editors, *13th International Conference on Automated Deduction*, pages 643–657. LNAI 1104, Springer Verlag, July 1996.
8. L.C. Paulson. *ML for the Working Programmer*. Cambridge University Press, 1991.
9. C. Sengler. Termination of algorithms over non-freely generated datatypes. In M.A. McRobbie and J.K. Slaney, editors, *13th International Conference on Automated Deduction*, pages 121–135. LNAI 1104, Springer Verlag, July 1996.
10. C. Walther. On proving termination of algorithms by machine. *Artificial Intelligence*, 71(1):101–157, 1994.

Beth Definability for the Guarded Fragment

Eva Hoogland[1], Maarten Marx[2], and Martin Otto[3]

[1] Dept. of WINS, Universiteit van Amsterdam, Plantage Muidergracht 24,
1018 TV Amsterdam, The Netherlands, ehooglan@wins.uva.nl
[2] Dept. of Artificial Intelligence, Faculty of Sciences, Vrije Universiteit Amsterdam,
De Boelelaan 1081a, 1081 HV Amsterdam, The Netherlands, marx@wins.uva.nl
[3] Mathematical Foundations of Computer Science, RWTH Aachen, Ahornstr.55,
52074 Aachen, Germany, otto@informatik.rwth-aachen.de

Abstract. The guarded fragment (GF) was introduced in [ABN98] as
a fragment of first order logic which combines a great expressive power
with nice modal behavior. It consists of relational first order formulas
whose quantifiers are relativized by atoms in a certain way. While GF
has been established as a particularly well-behaved fragment of first order
logic in many respects, interpolation fails in restriction to GF, [HM99].
In this paper we consider the Beth property of first order logic and
show that, despite the failure of interpolation, it is retained in restriction
to GF. Being a closure property w.r.t. definability, the Beth property
is of independent interest, both theoretically and for typical potential
applications of GF, e.g., in the context of description logics. The Beth
property for GF is here established on the basis of a limited form of
interpolation, which more closely resembles the interpolation property
that is usually studied in modal logics. From this we obtain that, more
specifically, even every n-variable guarded fragment with up to n-ary
relations has the Beth property.

1 Introduction

The Guarded Fragment It has proven useful to view modal logics not only as
systems in themselves but also as fragments of first order logic. As is well-known,
the basic modal logic K can be seen as a fragment of first order logic via the
translation t which maps a proposition letter p to the atom Px, which com-
mutes with the Boolean connectives, and which maps formulas of the form $\Diamond\varphi$
to $\exists y(Rxy \wedge \varphi^t(y))$ and $\Box\varphi$ to $\forall y(Rxy \rightarrow \varphi^t(y))$. The image of K under this
translation is referred to as the *modal fragment*. This fragment turns out to be-
have excellently. It shares several nice model-theoretic properties with full first
order logic (e.g., interpolation, Beth definability, or the Los-Tarski property),
and has in addition good algorithmic qualities: it is decidable and every satisfiable modal formula has a finite model and a tree model (in other words, the
modal fragment has the finite model property and the tree model property).
Moreover, the decidability of this fragment is robust in the sense that various
extensions remain decidable. For example, adding features like counting quantifiers or fixed points to the modal fragment does not affect decidability.

The usefulness of the modal fragment brought logicians to search for generalizations of this fragment which retain the afore-mentioned nice properties. An obvious candidate for such a generalization is the two variable fragment of first order logic, denoted by L_2. Although this logic is decidable and has the finite model property, it does not have interpolation nor the Beth property. Neither does it have the tree model property, and also its decidability is not as robust as that of the modal fragment [Var98][GO99].

In [ABN98] it is argued that the distinguishing characteristic of the modal fragment is not its restriction to two variables but its restriction on quantifiers, namely to quantifier patterns $\exists y(Rxy \wedge \varphi(y))$ or $\forall y(Rxy \to \varphi(y)))$. This brings Andréka, van Benthem and Németi to investigate to what extent these quantifier restrictions can be loosened while retaining the attractive modal behavior. The outcome is the *guarded fragment* (GF) which allows for quantifications of the form $\exists \bar{y}(R\bar{x}\bar{y} \wedge \varphi(\bar{x}, \bar{y}))$ and $\forall \bar{y}(R\bar{x}\bar{y} \to \varphi(\bar{x}, \bar{y}))$, where $\bar{x}, \bar{y}$ are finite sequences of variables and φ is a guarded formula with free variables among $\bar{x}, \bar{y}$ which *all* must appear in the atomic formula $R\bar{x}\bar{y}$.

In [ABN98] this fragment is shown to have the finite model property, the Los-Tarski property and, most importantly, to be decidable. Grädel [Grä97] improves on this result by classifying the satisfiability problem for GF to be complete for deterministic double exponential time; satisfiability for the finite variable guarded fragments is even in Exptime, in fact Exptime-complete. This is worth comparing with the satisfiability problem for L_2 which is known to be Nexptime-complete [GKV97]. What is more, GF has a certain tree model property. Since the tree model property of the modal fragment can be seen as the main reason behind the robustness of the decidability of that fragment (cf. e.g., [Var98]), this gives hope as to the robustness of GF. And indeed, adding least and greatest fixed points to GF yields a decidable extension [GW99].

However, as shown in [HM99], the interpolation theorem of first order logic fails for GF. In the present paper it will be shown that GF does have an alternative interpolation property, which closely resembles the interpolation property usually studied in modal logics. This result turns out to be strong enough to entail the Beth definability theorem for GF.

The Beth (Definability) Property In a slogan, the Beth definability property states that implicit definability equals explicit definability. Generally, this property may be regarded as an indication that there is a good balance between syntax and semantics of a logic: the semantic phenomenon that the meaning of a basic relation is implicitly determined, guarantees that there is an explicit syntactic expression for that relation. Intuitively, an *implicit definition* of a relation R is a definition of R, in the sense that it fixes the interpretation of R, in which the relation symbol R may occur. For example, consider the conjunction Σ of formulas saying that $<$ is an irreflexive linear order, there exists a first element

and this element has property R, and an element has property R iff its successor
does not have property R. Note that these statements can be formulated in first
order logic (with equality) using the predicates $<$ and R. It is obvious that on
every finite irreflexive linear order the interpretation of the relation R is fixed.
In other words, on finite models, Σ implicitly defines R. On the other hand,
as first observed by [Háj77], there is no first order formula $\theta(x)$ which does not
mention R and which would *explicitly define* R over the finite models of Σ. I.e.,
there is *no* formula $\theta(x)$ using just $<$ such that $\Sigma \models Rx \leftrightarrow \theta(x)$ would be true
over all finite models. Obviously, every relation that is explicitly definable is also
implicitly definable. As the above example showed, the converse is in general not
true. However, in the classical context of not necessarily finite models, implicit
definability and explicit definability in first order logic coincide. This property of
first order logic has first been observed by E.W. Beth (see [Bet53]). Nowadays,
logics for which an analogous statement holds are said to have the *Beth (definability) property*. So the above-mentioned example shows that first order logic
restricted to finite models does not have the Beth property. Another logic which
fails to have this property is L_2 (cf. [Sai90], see also Remark 2). Besides first
order logic, logics with the Beth property include classical (and intuitionistic)
propositional calculus, or the modal logics K, $\mathsf{K4}$ and $\mathsf{S5}$.

Note that for GF, and the modal logics, as long as we consider *finite* sets of
sentences Σ it does not make a difference for the Beth property whether we are
in the classical context of not necessarily finite models, or regard finite models
only. For, as these logics have the finite model property, a finite set of sentences
Σ implicitly defines a relation over finite models if and only if it does so over all
models. The same for explicit definitions.

Description Logics Description logics were designed for the purpose of knowledge
representation. Roughly speaking, a description logic starts from some set of
primitive concepts (which are unary predicates) and roles (binary predicates).
The logic then specifies (or defines) complex concepts out of these primitives
and makes assertions about these specifications, mostly in terms of modally
expressible dependencies between concepts via roles. E.g., the logic can assert
that a certain object, or all objects related to it via a designated role, belongs to
a certain concept. Although they originated from entirely different backgrounds,
there is therefore a close correspondence between description logics and modal
logics. For example the description logic $\mathcal{ALC}$ is nothing but a syntactic variant
of the basic multi-modal logic K_n [Sch91]. Hence the guarded fragment can also
be seen as a general framework for description logics, which may express more
than the ordinary modal dependencies. In particular, it may go beyond the built-
in arity restriction of modal logics, so that one can speak of higher-arity concepts
and roles. The interested reader is referred to [Grä98] for a proposal of GF as a
framework for description logic and for further references. In the description logic
context, the Beth property seems particularly desirable as it guarantees explicit
definability of concepts (and roles): e.g., concept specification in the framework
of GF is closed in the sense that any concept that can implicitly be characterized
can actually be defined explicitly within the logic.

Outline of the Paper Ever since 1956 when W. Craig gave an alternative proof
of the Beth theorem for first order logic via his interpolation theorem, these
two properties are almost always studied simultaneously. This paper forms no
exception. In Section 3 we will prove a certain interpolation property for GF
from which the Beth property for GF will be derived in Section 4. Even better,
both these properties will be shown to hold for each of the n-variable fragments
of GF individually, in the presence of at most n-ary relations.

2   Preliminaries

In this section we will collect all the necessary preliminaries. It also serves to fix
notation and terminology.

Convention 1 By a *language* $\mathcal{L}$ we will henceforth understand a relational first
order language without function- or constant symbols. Besides variables, and
the parentheses), (, we consider as *logical symbols* the connectives $\wedge$, $\neg$, the
existential quantifier $\exists$ and the identity symbol $=$.   ⊣

Notation 1 Models are denoted by calligraphic letters like $\mathcal{M}$, $\mathcal{N}$, and their
respective universes by M, N, etc. The interpretation of an n-ary predicate R
in the model $\mathcal{M}$ (notation: $I^{\mathcal{M}}(R) \subseteq M^n$) is defined as usual. Moreover, we
extend this terminology to sets. That is, for $X \subseteq M$ we write $X \in I^{\mathcal{M}}(R)$ if the
elements of X are R-related, in any order or multiplicity. E.g., if R is ternary and
$\langle n, m, n \rangle \in I^{\mathcal{M}}(R)$, then $\{m, n\} \in I^{\mathcal{M}}(R)$. For a model $\mathcal{M}$, $m_1, \ldots, m_n \in M$ and
a formula φ with free variables among $\{v_1, \ldots, v_n\}$, we write $\mathcal{M} \models \varphi[m_1, \ldots, m_n]$
iff each assignment which maps v_i to m_i satisfies φ in $\mathcal{M}$. If Σ is a formula (or a
set of formulas) and ψ a formula, then $\Sigma \models \psi$ denotes the *consequence* relation.
That is, $\Sigma \models \psi$ iff any assignment into a model $\mathcal{M}$ which satisfies (all formulas
in) Σ also satisfies ψ. In particular, $\varphi \models \psi$ is the same as to say that $\varphi \rightarrow \psi$ is
valid, i.e., $\models \varphi \rightarrow \psi$. For any formula φ, by $free(\varphi)$ we denote the set of free
variables occurring in φ. By $\mathcal{L}_\varphi$ (read: *the language of* φ) we denote the set of
relation symbols occurring in φ.   ⊣

2.1   Defining the Guarded Fragment: Syntax

Definition 1 (Guarded formula). Let $\mathcal{L}$ be a language. The *atomic $\mathcal{L}$-formulas*
(or, *$\mathcal{L}$-atoms*) are of the usual form:

1. $v_1 = v_2$, for variables v_1, v_2.
2. $P v_1 \cdots v_n$, for n-ary $P \in \mathcal{L}$ and variables $v_1, \ldots, v_n$, not necessarily distinct.

The *guarded $\mathcal{L}$-formulas* are defined by induction as follows.

1. Any atomic $\mathcal{L}$-formula is a guarded $\mathcal{L}$-formula.
2. If φ, ψ are guarded $\mathcal{L}$-formulas, then $\varphi \wedge \psi$ and $\neg\varphi$ are guarded $\mathcal{L}$-formulas.

3. Let $\bar{v}$ be a finite, non-empty sequence of variables, ψ a guarded $\mathcal{L}$-formula, and G an $\mathcal{L}$-atom such that $free(\psi) \subseteq free(G)$. Then $\exists\bar{v}(G \wedge \psi)$ is a guarded $\mathcal{L}$-formula. In this case, the atom G is called the *guard* of the quantifier. ⊣

Note that as a dual of guarded existential quantification we also get guarded universal quantification, of the form $\forall\bar{v}(G \rightarrow \psi)$.

A typical example of a guarded formula is the one expressing symmetry of a relation: $\forall v_1 v_2 (Rv_1 v_2 \rightarrow Rv_2 v_1)$. On the other hand, the formula $\forall v_1 v_2 v_3 ((Rv_1 v_2 \wedge Rv_2 v_3) \rightarrow Rv_1 v_3)$, which expresses the transitivity of the relation R, is not guarded, as $Rv_1 v_2 \wedge Rv_2 v_3$ is not a guard.

Remark 1. For readers familiar with [ABN98] we note that contrary to that paper, Definition 1 allows for identity atoms as guards. Since this issue does not affect decidability nor interpolation, we decided to concentrate on this slightly more general fragment. This also places us in line with [Grä97]. ⊣

Guarded formulas are obviously first order formulas. The fragment of first order logic consisting of guarded formulas is called the *guarded fragment* (GF). We understand by $GF_n, n \in \omega$, the fragment of GF that consists of formulas whose variables (free or bound) are among $v_1, \ldots, v_n$. The collection of formulas in GF_n which are built up from at most k-ary relation symbols is denoted by GF_n^k.

2.2 Semantic Characterization of the Guarded Fragment

Similar to modal logics, the guarded fragment can be semantically analyzed via a suitable notion of bisimulation. This has been done in [ABN98]. Here we will recapitulate as much of these results as needed for the purposes of the present paper.

Definition 2 (live set). Let Z be a finite subset of a model $\mathcal{M}$. The set Z is called *live* in $\mathcal{M}$ if Z is either a singleton, or there exists a relation R and a set X such that $Z \subseteq X \in I^{\mathcal{M}}(R)$. In this case we will say that Z is R-*live* (in $\mathcal{M}$). For any language $\mathcal{L}$ we use the notation $Z \subseteq_{\mathcal{L}}^l \mathcal{M}$ to denote that Z is $\mathcal{L}$-live in $\mathcal{M}$. That is, Z is R-live in $\mathcal{M}$ for some $R \in \mathcal{L}$. We will omit the subscript $\mathcal{L}$ if it does not cause confusion. ⊣

Note that by definition subsets of live sets are again live.

Below, by a finite *partial $\mathcal{L}$-isomorphism* we mean a finite one-to-one partial map between two models which preserves the relations in $\mathcal{L}$ both ways. By the *image* of a map $f : X \longrightarrow Y$ we understand the set $\{f(x) : x \in X\}$, and we refer to X as its *domain*.

Definition 3 (Guarded bisimulation). A *guarded $\mathcal{L}$-bisimulation* between two models $\mathcal{M}$ and $\mathcal{N}$ is a non-empty set F of finite partial $\mathcal{L}$-isomorphisms between $\mathcal{M}$ and $\mathcal{N}$ such that for any $f : X \longrightarrow Y \in F$ the following hold:

1. For any $Z \subseteq_{\mathcal{L}}^{l} \mathcal{M}$ there is a $g \in F$ with domain Z such that g and f agree on the intersection of their domains. (The *zig*-condition)
2. For any $W \subseteq_{\mathcal{L}}^{l} \mathcal{N}$ there is a $g \in F$ with image W such that g^{-1} and f^{-1} agree on the intersection of their domains. (The *zag*-condition)   ⊣

Guarded bisimulations are defined in such a way as to preserve guarded formulas. That is, for a guarded $\mathcal{L}$-formula φ with free variables among $\{v_1, \ldots, v_k\}$, a guarded $\mathcal{L}$-bisimulation F between models $\mathcal{M}, \mathcal{N}$, an $f \in F$, and $m_1, \ldots, m_k \in dom(f)$ it is the case that $\mathcal{M} \models \varphi[m_1, \ldots, m_k] \Leftrightarrow \mathcal{N} \models \varphi[f(m_1), \ldots, f(m_k)]$. This can be shown by a straightforward induction on the complexity of φ. The zig- and zag-conditions precisely take care of the induction step for existential quantification. Indeed, preservation under guarded bisimulations is the characteristic feature of GF, in the sense of the following Characterization Theorem from [ABN98]: up to logical equivalence, GF precisely consists of those first order formulas that are preserved under guarded bisimulations.

Note that in the definition of a guarded bisimulation that can be found in [ABN98], the above role of live sets is taken over by what ABN call *guarded* sets. These are subsets Z of a model $\mathcal{M}$ such that $Z \in I^{\mathcal{M}}(R)$, for some relation R. Mutatis mutandis, all arguments in [ABN98] and in particular the characterization theorem also apply to guarded formulas and guarded bisimulations as defined in this paper. Note e.g., that a guarded formula of the form $\exists v(v = v \land \neg Pv)$ which is not guarded in the ABN-sense, is preserved under guarded bisimulations in our sense by virtue of the fact that singletons are live.

For further use we exhibit, for any relation R, a formula $\lambda_R(v_1, \ldots, v_l)$ which defines the set of R-live l-tuples. More precisely, for models $\mathcal{M}$ and $m_1, \ldots, m_l \in M$: $\mathcal{M} \models \lambda_R(v_1, \ldots, v_l)[m_1, \ldots, m_l]$ iff the set $\{m_1, \ldots, m_l\}$ is R-live in $\mathcal{M}$.

Let s be the arity of R. Let e range over all complete equality types in variables $v_1, \ldots, v_l$. We regard e both as a quantifier-free formula $e(v_1, \ldots, v_l)$ in the empty vocabulary and as an equivalence relation on the set $\{1, \ldots, l\}$ according to $(j, i) \in e$ iff $e \models v_j = v_i$. Let $\rho : \{1, \ldots, s\} \rightarrow \{1, \ldots, l+s\}$ be a mapping that is onto $\{1, \ldots, l\}/e$, i.e., for every $j \in \{1, \ldots, l\}$ there is some $i \in \{1, \ldots, s\}$ such that $\rho(i)$ is in the same e equivalence class with j. Put, for any such pair of e and ρ,

$$\gamma_{e,\rho} = e(v_1, \ldots, v_l) \land \exists \bar{v}\left(Rv_{\rho(1)} \ldots v_{\rho(s)} \land \text{true}\right), \tag{1}$$

where $\bar{v}$ consist of those $v_{\rho(i)}$ for which $\rho(i) > l$ (if there are such; else no quantification is necessary and $\gamma_{e,\rho}$ is actually atomic). The desired formula $\lambda_R(v_1, \ldots, v_l)$ is obtained as the disjunction over all $\gamma_{e,\rho}$ for matching pairs (e, ρ).

For any *finite* language $\mathcal{L}$ we further obtain a formula $\lambda_{\mathcal{L}}(v_1, \ldots, v_l)$ defining the set of $\mathcal{L}$-live l-tuples by putting

$$\lambda_{\mathcal{L}}(v_1, \ldots, v_l) = \left(\bigwedge_{1 \leq i,j \leq l} v_i = v_j\right) \lor \bigvee_{R \in \mathcal{L}} \lambda_R(v_1, \ldots, v_l), \tag{2}$$

where the first disjunct reflects the fact that all singleton sets are regarded as live (namely, as guarded by equality).

We finally note that $\gamma_{e,\rho}$ is equivalent to a formula in $\mathrm{GF}_{\max(l,s)}$. We conclude that for every finite language $\mathcal{L}$ which contains at most k-ary relations and for any $l \leq k$ we may assume $\lambda_{\mathcal{L}}(v_1,\ldots,v_l) \in \mathrm{GF}_k^k$.

3   Interpolation for the Guarded Fragment

As shown in [HM99], GF does not have the interpolation property.

Theorem 1 (Failure of interpolation in GF, [HM99]). *There exist sentences φ, $\psi \in \mathrm{GF}_3^3$ such that $\models \varphi \rightarrow \psi$, without a guarded interpolant (in any number of variables). That is, there does not exist a guarded formula ϑ built up from relation symbols which occur both in φ and ψ such that $\models \varphi \rightarrow \vartheta$ and $\models \vartheta \rightarrow \psi$.*

To see why this property fails for GF, it is useful to compare it to the interpolation property studied in modal logic. In modal logic, the interpolant is usually confined to proposition letters in the common language but may contain non-shared modalities. Strengthening the requirement on the common language to also include common modalities results in a much stronger interpolation property. [Ben99] shows this property for the basic multi-modal K. [Mar99] generalizes this result to Sahlqvist axiomatizable multi-modal logics whose axioms correspond to universal Horn frame conditions which do not specify any interaction between the different accessibility relations (e.g., bi-modal S5). When we have interaction, the stronger interpolation property is easily lost as the following example from [Ben99] shows. Consider the multi-modal logic defined by the axiom $\Diamond_1 p \rightarrow \Diamond_2 p$. This logic does not have the stronger interpolation property. For, in this logic $\Diamond_1 True \rightarrow \Diamond_2 True$ is a theorem whereas the only formulas in the common language (in the strong sense) are $True$ and $False$, which are obviously not interpolants. However, this logic does have the usual interpolation property (cf. [MV97, Corollary B.4.1]).

Thinking of guarded formulas as translations of modal formulas, we see that Theorem 1 formulates exactly this stronger version of interpolation, where 'common language' means the set of common relation symbols, which includes both the relations which are translated proposition letters and the relations that are obtained in translating the modalities. This suggests to consider an alternative interpolation property for GF that more closely resembles the one that is usually studied in modal logic. For this we will distinguish occurrences of relation symbols as guards from other occurrences.

Notation 2 For any guarded formula φ we understand by $\mathcal{L}_{G(\varphi)}$ the set of relations that occur in φ as the guard of some quantifier.   ⊣

Note that the relations in $\mathcal{L}_{G(\varphi)}$ may at the same time occur in φ at non-guard positions. For example, in $\varphi = \exists x(Px \wedge \forall y(Sxy \rightarrow Py))$, the relation P occurs both as a guard and as a non-guard.

Definition 4 (Guarded $\mathcal{L}_1/\mathcal{L}_2$-bisimulation). Let $\mathcal{L}_1 \subseteq \mathcal{L}_2$ be languages. A *guarded $\mathcal{L}_1/\mathcal{L}_2$-bisimulation* between models $\mathcal{M}$ and $\mathcal{N}$ is defined as a non-empty set of finite partial $\mathcal{L}_2$-isomorphisms between $\mathcal{M}, \mathcal{N}$ with zig- and zag- condition stipulated for $\mathcal{L}_1$-live sets only.   ⊣

This type of bisimulation supports a characterization theorem for that fragment of GF in which only $\mathcal{L}_1$-predicates may be used as guards, but all predicates in $\mathcal{L}_1$ and $\mathcal{L}_2$ may occur at non-guard positions. Analogously to the characterization theorem for GF, the following characterization can be shown, using [HM99, Proposition 3.11].

Proposition 1. *Let $\mathcal{L}_1 \subseteq \mathcal{L}_2$ be languages which contain at most k-ary relation symbols. A first order sentence φ is preserved under guarded $\mathcal{L}_1/\mathcal{L}_2$-bisimulations iff φ is logically equivalent to an $\mathcal{L}_2$-sentence $\psi \in \mathrm{GF}_k^k$ with $\mathcal{L}_{G(\psi)} \subseteq \mathcal{L}_1$.*

Notation 3 For models $\mathcal{M}, \mathcal{N}$, and $m_1, \ldots, m_k \in M$, $n_1, \ldots, n_k \in N$, we write $\mathcal{M}, m_1 \cdots m_k \equiv_{\mathcal{L}}^{\mathrm{GF}_k} \mathcal{N}, n_1 \cdots n_k$, if $\mathcal{M} \models \theta[m_1, \ldots, m_k]$ iff $\mathcal{N} \models \theta[n_1, \ldots, n_k]$, for all $\mathcal{L}$-formulas $\theta \in \mathrm{GF}_k$.   ⊣

Recall that for any formula ϑ, by $\mathcal{L}_\vartheta$ we denote the language consisting of all the relation symbols occurring in ϑ. The theorem below states that GF_k^k (and hence GF) has interpolation provided an interpolant for $\varphi \to \psi$ is allowed to contain relations in $\mathcal{L}_{G(\varphi)}$ and $\mathcal{L}_{G(\psi)}$ which are not necessarily in the common language. Modally speaking, an interpolant may use non-shared modalities.

Theorem 2 (GF_k^k has interpolation w.r.t. non-guard occurrences). *Let $k \in \omega$. For any $\varphi, \psi \in \mathrm{GF}_k^k$ such that $\models \varphi \to \psi$, there exists a $\vartheta \in \mathrm{GF}_k^k$ such that*

1. *$\mathcal{L}_\vartheta \subseteq (\mathcal{L}_\varphi \cap \mathcal{L}_\psi) \cup \mathcal{L}_{G(\varphi)} \cup \mathcal{L}_{G(\psi)}$, and*
2. *$\models \varphi \to \vartheta$ and $\models \vartheta \to \psi$.*

Proof of Theorem 2: We will show 'amalgamation via bisimulation' in the same spirit as e.g., the proof of interpolation for the basic modal logic K in [ABN98, Theorem 2.5]. Its main construction is a deviation of a fairly standard amalgamation method as can be found e.g., in [Mar95] and [Ném85].

For the course of this proof, let $k \in \omega$ be fixed but arbitrary. Consider $\varphi, \psi \in \mathrm{GF}_k^k$ such that $\models \varphi \to \psi$. For brevity, write $\mathcal{L}$ for $(\mathcal{L}_\varphi \cap \mathcal{L}_\psi) \cup \mathcal{L}_{G(\varphi)} \cup \mathcal{L}_{G(\psi)}$. Let $\Theta \overset{\mathrm{def}}{=} \{\vartheta \in \mathrm{GF}_k : \mathcal{L}_\vartheta \subseteq \mathcal{L} \ \& \models \varphi \to \vartheta\}$. Our aim is to show that

Claim 1 $\Theta \models \psi$.

Note that in the formulation of this claim free variables play the role of individual constants. By compactness, it then follows that ψ is implied by some finite conjunction ϑ of formulas in Θ. Note that ϑ is again an $\mathcal{L}$-formula in GF_k^k. Hence ϑ is an interpolant for φ, ψ, and we are done.

To prove Claim 1, consider an arbitrary $\mathcal{L}_\psi \cup \mathcal{L}$-model $\mathcal{N}$, and $b_1, \ldots, b_k \in N$ such that $\mathcal{N} \models \vartheta[b_1, \ldots, b_k]$, for every $\vartheta \in \Theta$. Our task is to show that $\mathcal{N} \models \psi[b_1, \ldots, b_k]$.

We first note that there exists some $\mathcal{L}_\varphi \cup \mathcal{L}$-model $\mathcal{M}$ and $a_1, \ldots, a_k \in M$ such that $\mathcal{M} \models \varphi[a_1, \ldots, a_k]$ and $\mathcal{M}, a_1 \cdots a_k \equiv_{\mathcal{L}}^{\mathrm{GF}_k} \mathcal{N}, b_1 \cdots b_k$. For, reasoning to contraposition, assume such $\mathcal{M}, a_1, \ldots, a_k$ do not exist. In that case, $\Phi \stackrel{\mathrm{def}}{=} \{\vartheta \in \mathrm{GF}_k : \mathcal{L}_\vartheta \subseteq \mathcal{L} \ \& \ \mathcal{N} \models \vartheta[b_1, \ldots, b_k]\} \models \neg\varphi$. By compactness it follows that $\models \varphi \rightarrow \neg \bigwedge \Phi_0$, for some finite conjunction of formulas in Φ. Therefore $\neg \bigwedge \Phi_0 \in \Theta$, whence $\mathcal{N} \models \neg \bigwedge \Phi_0[b_1, \ldots, b_k]$. Quod non.

By passing to ω-saturated elementary extensions of $\mathcal{M}$ and $\mathcal{N}$, we may w.l.o.g. assume that $\mathcal{M}, \mathcal{N}$ are ω-saturated. As shown in the proof of the Characterization Theorem for GF in [ABN98, Theorem 4.2.2], the relation of guarded $\mathcal{L}$-equivalence between ω-saturated structures induces a guarded $\mathcal{L}$-bisimulation. The same is true for the relation of $\equiv_{\mathcal{L}}^{\mathrm{GF}_k}$ if $\mathcal{L}$ contains at most k-ary relations. Hence our assumption in particular implies the existence of a guarded $\mathcal{L}$-bisimulation between $\mathcal{M}, \mathcal{N}$ which links $\langle a_1, \ldots, a_k \rangle$ and $\langle b_1, \ldots, b_k \rangle$.

The aim of the rest of this proof is to amalgamate the models $\mathcal{M}$ and $\mathcal{N}$ in such a way that we can define guarded $\mathcal{L}_{G(\varphi)}/\mathcal{L}_\varphi$- (resp. $\mathcal{L}_{G(\psi)}/\mathcal{L}_\psi$-) bisimulations between the amalgamated model and $\mathcal{M}$ (resp. $\mathcal{N}$) which, when composed, will map $\langle a_1, \ldots, a_k \rangle$ to $\langle b_1, \ldots, b_k \rangle$. Chasing the resulting diagram and using the fact that $\varphi \models \psi$ will yield the desired conclusion that $\mathcal{N} \models \psi[b_1, \ldots, b_k]$. This will be made precise in the sequel.

We define a model over the set MN consisting of pairs $\langle m, n \rangle \in M \times N$ whose components cannot be distinguished by $\mathcal{L}$-formulas in GF_k. The interpretation of the predicates is read off coordinatewise. More precisely,

- $MN \stackrel{\mathrm{def}}{=} \{\langle m, n \rangle \in M \times N : \mathcal{M}, m \equiv_{\mathcal{L}}^{\mathrm{GF}_k} \mathcal{N}, n\}$.
- For l-ary $R \in \mathcal{L}_\varphi$, set $\langle \langle m_1, n_1 \rangle, \ldots, \langle m_l, n_l \rangle \rangle \in I^{MN}(R)$ iff
  - $\mathcal{M}, m_1 \cdots m_l \equiv_{\mathcal{L}}^{\mathrm{GF}_k} \mathcal{N}, n_1 \cdots n_l$,
    (i.e., the m_i and n_i are not only pairwise equivalent but jointly so), and
  - $\langle m_1, \ldots, m_l \rangle \in I^{\mathcal{M}}(R)$.
- The interpretation of relations in $\mathcal{L}_\psi$ is defined similarly.

Note that the interpretation of relations in the common language is well-defined thanks to the requirement on live subsets of MN to be jointly $\mathcal{L}$-equivalent. The upshot of amalgamating our models into a product is that we can take projection functions as building blocks for the desired bisimulations. This is the purport of the following lemma, where π_i, $i = 1, 2$, denotes the projection function to the i-th coordinate. Define $F_{\pi_1} \stackrel{\mathrm{def}}{=} \{\pi_1 : X \longrightarrow Y : X \subseteq_{\mathcal{L}_{G(\varphi)}}^l MN$ or $X = \{\langle a_1, b_1 \rangle, \ldots, \langle a_k, b_k \rangle\}\}$, where the elements $a_1, \ldots, a_k \in M, b_1, \ldots, b_k \in N$ are the ones picked at the very beginning of this proof.

Lemma 1 (Amalgamation lemma). *The set F_{π_1} is a guarded $\mathcal{L}_{G(\varphi)}/\mathcal{L}_\varphi$-bisimulation between $\mathcal{MN}$ and $\mathcal{M}$. The analogously defined set F_{π_2} is a guarded $\mathcal{L}_{G(\psi)}/\mathcal{L}_\psi$-bisimulation between $\mathcal{MN}$ and $\mathcal{N}$.*

Before proving the lemma, let us first demonstrate its use and finish the proof of Claim 1. Recall that the model $\mathcal{M}$ and the sequence $a_1, \ldots, a_k \in M$ were chosen in such a way that $\mathcal{M} \models \varphi[a_1, \ldots, a_k]$. We took care to include $\pi_1 :$ $\{\langle a_1, b_1 \rangle, \ldots, \langle a_k, b_k \rangle\} \longrightarrow \{a_1, \ldots, a_k\}$ in F_{π_1}. Since φ is invariant under guarded $\mathcal{L}_{G(\varphi)}/\mathcal{L}_\varphi$-bisimulations, it follows from the amalgamation lemma that $\mathcal{MN} \models$ $\varphi[\langle a_1, b_k \rangle, \ldots, \langle a_k, b_k \rangle]$. By assumption then $\mathcal{MN} \models \psi[\langle a_1, b_1 \rangle, \ldots, \langle a_k, b_k \rangle]$. Since we included $\pi_2 : \{\langle a_1, b_1 \rangle, \ldots, \langle a_k, b_k \rangle\} \longrightarrow \{b_1, \ldots, b_k\}$ in F_{π_2}, the second part of the amalgamation lemma allows us to conclude that $\mathcal{N} \models \psi[b_1, \ldots, b_k]$.
Q.E.D. Claim 1.

Now we turn to the proof of the amalgamation lemma.

Proof of Lemma 1: We will prove the first part of the lemma concerning F_{π_1}. The second statement about F_{π_2} can be shown similarly.

F_{π_1} is obviously non-empty. Let $\pi_1 : X \longrightarrow Y \in F_{\pi_1}$. Then $X = \{x_1, \ldots, x_l\}$, for some $l \leq k$, and $\mathcal{M}, \pi_1(x_1) \cdots \pi_1(x_l) \equiv_{\mathcal{L}}^{\mathrm{GF}_k} \mathcal{N}, \pi_2(x_1) \cdots \pi_2(x_l)$. By construction this implies that for any n-ary $R \in \mathcal{L}_\varphi$, and any $\langle x_{i_1}, \ldots, x_{i_n} \rangle \in X^n$ it is the case that $\langle x_{i_1}, \ldots, x_{i_n} \rangle \in I^{\mathcal{MN}}(R)$ iff $\langle \pi_1(x_{i_1}), \ldots, \pi_1(x_{i_n}) \rangle \in I^{\mathcal{M}}(R)$. In other words, π_1 is a partial $\mathcal{L}_\varphi$-isomorphism.

For the zag-condition, consider $\pi_1 : X \longrightarrow Y \in F_{\pi_1}$, and $W \subseteq_R^l \mathcal{M}$, for some $R \in \mathcal{L}_{G(\varphi)}$. As above, $X = \{x_1, \ldots, x_l\}$, for some $l \leq k$, and $\mathcal{M}, \pi_1(x_1) \cdots \pi_1(x_l) \equiv_{\mathcal{L}}^{\mathrm{GF}_k} \mathcal{N}, \pi_2(x_1) \cdots \pi_2(x_l)$. Recall that the relation $\equiv_{\mathcal{L}}^{\mathrm{GF}_k}$ forms a guarded $\mathcal{L}$-bisimulation between $\mathcal{M}$ and $\mathcal{N}$. We saw that the partial map f from $\mathcal{M}$ to $\mathcal{N}$ which maps $\pi_1(x)$ to $\pi_2(x)$, for $x \in X$, is an element of this bisimulation. By the zig-condition, there exists a partial $\mathcal{L}$-isomorphism g in this bisimulation with domain W which agrees with f on the intersection of their domains. Let $W^* = \{\langle w, g(w) \rangle : w \in W\} \subseteq_R^l \mathcal{MN}$. Then W^* is the desired pre-image for W. As the zig-condition is trivially fulfilled, this completes the proof.
Q.E.D. Lemma 1.
Q.E.D. Theorem 2.

Corollary 1. GF *has interpolation w.r.t. non-guard occurrences.*

4   The Beth Theorem for the Guarded Fragment

In general, an important reason to investigate the interpolation property is that it can be seen as an intermediate stage in proving the Beth definability theorem. It will be shown that the limited form of interpolation expressed in Theorem 2 still serves this purpose for GF.

Let $\mathcal{L}_0$ be a language and R and R' distinct relation symbols of the same arity that are not in $\mathcal{L}_0$. Let $\mathcal{L} = \mathcal{L}_0 \cup \{R\}$. Let Σ be a set of guarded sentences in the language $\mathcal{L}$, and let Σ' denote the result of renaming R to R' in Σ.

Theorem 3 (Beth Theorem for GF$_k^k$). *Let $\mathcal{L}_0$, $\mathcal{L}$, R, R', Σ and Σ' be as above. Let $k \in \omega$ be such that $\Sigma \cup \{R\bar{v}\} \subseteq$ GF$_k^k$. If Σ implicitly defines R, i.e., if $\Sigma, \Sigma' \models \forall \bar{v}(R\bar{v} \leftrightarrow R'\bar{v})$, then there exists some $\varphi(\bar{v}) \in$ GF$_k^k$ in the language $\mathcal{L}_0$ such that $\Sigma \models \forall \bar{v}(R\bar{v} \leftrightarrow \varphi(\bar{v}))$. This formula φ is called an explicit definition for R relative to Σ.*

Proof of Theorem 3: Let all data be as in the theorem, and assume that

$$\Sigma, \Sigma' \models \forall \bar{v}(R\bar{v} \leftrightarrow R'\bar{v}). \tag{3}$$

We first show that (3) implies that any R-live set in a model for Σ is $\mathcal{L}_0$-live.

Claim 2 *Let $\mathcal{M}$ be a model of Σ, and let $Y \subseteq_R^l \mathcal{M}$. Then $Y \subseteq_{\mathcal{L}_0}^l \mathcal{M}$.*

Proof of Claim 2: Let $\mathcal{M}$ be a model of Σ, and let $Y_0 \subseteq_R^l \mathcal{M}$. Reasoning to contraposition, suppose $Y_0 \nsubseteq_{\mathcal{L}_0}^l \mathcal{M}$. We will derive a contradiction from this.

Let $\underline{2}$ denote the two-element universal $\mathcal{L}$-model with domain $\{0,1\}$. That is, $\bar{s} \in I^{\underline{2}}(P)$, for every l-ary $P \in \mathcal{L}$ and every $\bar{s} \in \{0,1\}^l$. Let $\mathcal{M} \times \underline{2}$ denote the usual product model. Writing π_1 for the projection on the first coordinate, this definition entails that $\bar{s} \in I^{\mathcal{M} \times \underline{2}}(P)$ iff $\langle \pi_1(s_1), \ldots, \pi_1(s_l) \rangle \in I^{\mathcal{M}}(P)$, for all $\bar{s} \in (M \times \{0,1\})^l$ and l-ary $P \in \mathcal{L}$. As the reader can easily verify, this in its turn implies that $F_1 \overset{\text{def}}{=} \{\pi_1 : X \longrightarrow Y : X \subseteq_{\mathcal{L}}^l \mathcal{M} \times \underline{2}\}$ is a guarded $\mathcal{L}$-bisimulation between $\mathcal{M} \times \underline{2}$ and $\mathcal{M}$. Since $\mathcal{M} \models \Sigma$, we conclude that $\mathcal{M} \times \underline{2} \models \Sigma$.

Our aim is to modify the interpretation of R on $\mathcal{M} \times \underline{2}$ in such a way that the resulting structure is again a model for Σ, contradicting the fact that Σ implicitly defines R. For this, we consider $X_0 \overset{\text{def}}{=} Y_0 \times \{0\}$. Let $(\mathcal{M} \times \underline{2})'$ be the model which differs from $\mathcal{M} \times \underline{2}$ only in that $X_0 \notin I^{(\mathcal{M} \times \underline{2})'}(R)$. We claim that $F_1' \overset{\text{def}}{=} \{\pi_1 : X \longrightarrow Y : X \subseteq_{\mathcal{L}}^l (\mathcal{M} \times \underline{2})'\}$ is a guarded $\mathcal{L}$-bisimulation between $(\mathcal{M} \times \underline{2})'$ and $\mathcal{M}$.

F_1' is certainly not empty. Consider some $\pi_1 : X \longrightarrow Y$ in F_1'. If $X_0 \not\subseteq X$, then $\mathcal{L}$-relations are obviously preserved by π_1 in both ways. But we changed the interpretation of R such that X_0 is not R-live in $(\mathcal{M} \times \underline{2})'$. As Y_0 is not $\mathcal{L}_0$-live, it follows that X_0 is not $\mathcal{L}_0$-live in $(\mathcal{M} \times \underline{2})'$ either, and hence no superset of X_0 is the domain of some $\pi_1 \in F_1'$.

The zig-condition needs no comment. For the zag-condition, consider some $\pi_1 : X \longrightarrow Y$ in F_1', and $W \subseteq_{\mathcal{L}}^l \mathcal{M}$. If $W \subseteq Y$, the condition is trivially fulfilled. If not, then $\pi_1^{-1}[Y \cap W]$ can be extended in at least two ways to a set Z for which $\pi_1[Z] = W$. For $W \neq Y_0$, either one of these two extensions constitutes the domain of a projection in F_1' fulfilling the zag condition for π_1, W. For $W = Y_0$ any extension other than X_0 can be taken as such.

This shows that $(\mathcal{M} \times \underline{2})' \models \Sigma$. Summarizing, we see that $\mathcal{M} \times \underline{2} \models \Sigma$, $(\mathcal{M} \times \underline{2})' \models \Sigma$ but $I^{\mathcal{M} \times \underline{2}}(R) \neq I^{(\mathcal{M} \times \underline{2})'}(R)$. This contradicts the fact that Σ implicitly defines

R. We conclude that Y_0 is indeed $\mathcal{L}_0$-live, as was to be shown.
Q.E.D. *Claim 2.*

By compactness we may assume Σ to be a single sentence, and $\mathcal{L}_0$ finite. Assume R is l-ary, and let $\lambda_0(v_1, \ldots, v_l)$ be the canonical $\mathcal{L}_0$-formula in GF_k^k saying that the set $\{v_1, \ldots, v_l\}$ is $\mathcal{L}_0$-live (cf. page 278). For brevity, we write λ_0. For all $\mathcal{L}$-models $\mathcal{M}$ we define $R_0 \stackrel{\text{def}}{=} \{\bar{m} \in M^l : \mathcal{M} \models R \wedge \lambda_0[\bar{m}]\}$. Hence for every $\mathcal{L}_0$-model $\mathcal{M}$, $\bar{m} \in M^l$, and every interpretation of R in $\mathcal{M}$: $(\mathcal{M}, R) \models R \wedge \lambda_0[\bar{m}]$ iff $(\mathcal{M}, R_0) \models R[\bar{m}]$. Note that by Claim 2, $I^{\mathcal{M}}(R) = R_0$, for models $\mathcal{M}$ of Σ. Let Σ_0 be the result of replacing in Σ any occurrence of R by the conjunction $R \wedge \lambda_0$. It is now straightforward to check the following:

(i) Σ_0 is preserved under guarded $\mathcal{L}_0/\mathcal{L}$-bisimulations. Hence, by Proposition 1, Σ_0 is equivalent to an $\mathcal{L}$-formula Γ in GF_k^k with $\mathcal{L}_{G(\Gamma)} \subseteq \mathcal{L}_0$.
(ii) $\Sigma \models \Sigma_0$, by Claim 2.
(iii) For every $\mathcal{L}_0$-model $\mathcal{M}$, and every interpretation of R in $\mathcal{M}$: if $(\mathcal{M}, R) \models \Sigma_0$, then $(\mathcal{M}, R_0) \models \Sigma$.

Let Σ_0' be the result of replacing R by R' in Σ_0. It follows from (3) and (iii) that

$$\Sigma_0 \wedge R \wedge \lambda_0 \models \Sigma_0' \rightarrow R'. \tag{4}$$

For, consider an $\mathcal{L}_0 \cup \{R, R'\}$-model $(\mathcal{M}, R, R')$ and some $\bar{m} \in M^l$ such that $(\mathcal{M}, R, R') \models (\Sigma_0 \wedge R \wedge \lambda_0 \wedge \Sigma_0')[\bar{m}]$. We have to show that $(\mathcal{M}, R, R') \models R'[\bar{m}]$. It follows from (iii) that $(\mathcal{M}, R_0, R_0') \models (\Sigma \wedge R \wedge \Sigma')[\bar{m}]$. By (3), then $(\mathcal{M}, R_0, R_0') \models R'[\bar{m}]$. Hence, certainly, $(\mathcal{M}, R, R') \models R'[\bar{m}]$.

Replace Σ_0 and Σ_0' in (4) by $\mathcal{L}_0$-guarded formulae Γ and Γ' according to (i). We then apply Theorem 2 to obtain, as an interpolant for (4), a formula ϑ in GF_k^k such that $\mathcal{L}_\vartheta \subseteq \mathcal{L}_0$ and $(\Sigma_0 \wedge R \wedge \lambda_0) \models \vartheta$ and $\vartheta \models \Sigma_0' \rightarrow R'$. Applying (ii) and Claim 2, we find that $\Sigma \wedge R \models \vartheta$. Renaming R' back into R in the second implication and one more appeal to (ii) gives us that $\vartheta \models \Sigma \rightarrow R$. Hence $\Sigma \models R \leftrightarrow \vartheta$ and ϑ provides the desired explicit definition of R relative to Σ. Q.E.D. *Theorem 3.*

Corollary 2. GF *has the Beth definability theorem.*

Remark 2. Theorem 3 shows that the guarded finite variable fragments behave much nicer w.r.t. definability than the full finite variable fragments of first order logic (FO). For not only does the Beth theorem fail for any n-variable fragment of FO, $n \geq 2$, it fails drastically. In fact, even FO_2^2 (using the terminology FO_n^k for fragments of FO similar to our use of GF_n^k for guarded fragments) does not have the Beth property. For more information, the reader is referred to [Sai90] or [Hod93]. ⊣

References

[ABN98] H. Andréka, J. van Benthem, and I. Németi. Modal logics and bounded fragments of predicate logic. *Journal of Philosophical Logic*, 27(3):217–274, 1998.

[Ben99] J. van Benthem. Modal foundations for predicate logic. In E. Orlowska, editor, *Memorial Volume for Elena Rasiowa*, Studies in fuziness and soft computing, pages 39–55. Physica-Verlag, Heidelberg, New York, 1999.

[Bet53] E. W. Beth. On Padoa's method in the theory of definition. *Nederl. Akad. Wetensch. Proc. Ser. A*. **56** = *Indagationes Math.*, 15:330–339, 1953.

[GKV97] E. Grädel, P. Kolaitis, and M. Vardi. On the decision problem for two–variable first order logics. *Bulletin of Symbolic Logic*, 3:53–69, 1997.

[GO99] E. Grädel and M. Otto. On logics with two variables. *Theoretical Computer Science*, 1999. to appear.

[Grä97] E. Grädel. On the restraining power of guards. Technical report, RWTH Aachen, Lehrgebiet Mathematische Grundlagen der Informatik, 1997. To appear in the Journal of Symbolic Logic.

[Grä98] E. Grädel. Guarded fragments of first-order logic: a perspective for new description logics? In *Proc. of 1998 Int. Workshop on Description Logics DL '98, Trento*, CEUR Electronic Workshop Proceedings, 1998. Extended abstract, available at http://sunsite.informatik.rwth-aachen.de/ Publications/ CEUR-WS/Vol-11.

[GW99] E. Grädel and I Walukiewicz. Guarded fixed point logic. In *Proc. 14th Symp. on Logic in Computer Science, LICS'99*, pages 45–54, 1999.

[Háj77] P. Hájek. Generalized quantifiers and finite sets. Ser. Konfer. No 1 14, Prace Nauk. Inst. Mat. Politech. Wroclaw, 1977.

[HM99] E. Hoogland and M. Marx. Interpolation in guarded fragments. Technical report, Institute for Logic, Language and Computation, University of Amsterdam, 1999.

[Hod93] I. Hodkinson. Finite variable logics. *Bull. Europ. Assoc. Theor. Comp. Sci.*, 51:111–140, 1993. Addendum in vol. 52. Also available at http://www.doc.ic.ac.uk/~imh/papers/yuri.html.

[Mar95] Maarten Marx. *Algebraic Relativization and Arrow Logic*. PhD thesis, Institute for Logic, Language and Computation, University of Amsterdam, 1995.

[Mar99] M. Marx. Interpolation in (fibered) modal logic. In A. Haeberer, editor, *Proc. of AMAST 1998, Amazonia–Manaus, Brazil, 4–8 January 1999*, 1999.

[MV97] M. Marx and Y. Venema. *Multi-dimensional Modal Logic*. Applied Logic Series. Kluwer Academic Publishers, 1997.

[Ném85] I. Németi. Cylindric relativised set algebras have strong amalgamation. *Journal of Symbolic Logic*, 50(3):689–700, 1985.

[Sai90] I. Sain. Beth's and Craig's properties via epimorphisms and amalgamation in algebraic logic. In C. Bergman, R. Maddux, and D. Pigozzi, editors, *Algebraic logic and universal algebra in computer science*, volume 24 of *Lecture Notes in Computer Science*, pages 209–226. Springer Verlag, Berlin, Heidelberg, New York, 1990.

[Sch91] K. Schild. A correspondence theory for terminological logics. In *Proceedings of the 12th IJCAI*, pages 466–471, 1991.

[Var98] M. Vardi. Why is modal logic so robustly decidable? In *Descriptive Complexity and Finite Models: Proceedings of a DIMACS Workshop*, volume 31 of *Series in Discrete Mathematics and Theoretical Computer Science*, pages 149–184. American Mathematical Society, 1998.

Simplification of Horn Clauses That Are Clausal Forms of Guarded Formulas

Michael Dierkes

Laboratoire LEIBNIZ - IMAG
46, av. Félix Viallet; 38 031 Grenoble Cedex; France
e-mail: Michael.Dierkes@imag.fr

Abstract. The guarded fragment of first order logic, defined in [1], has attracted much attention recently due to the fact that it is decidable and several interesting modal logics can be translated into it. Guarded clauses, defined by de Nivelle in [7], are a generalization of guarded formulas in clausal form. In [7], it is shown that the class of guarded clause sets is decidable by saturation under ordered resolution.

In this work, we deal with guarded clauses that are Horn clauses. We introduce the notion of *primitive* guarded Horn clause: A guarded Horn clause is primitive iff it is either ground and its body is empty, or it contains exactly one body literal which is flat and linear, and its head literal contains a non-ground functional term. Then, we show that every satisfiable and finite set of guarded Horn clauses S can be transformed into a finite set of primitive guarded Horn clauses S' such that the least Herbrand models of S and S' coincide on predicate symbols that occur in S.

This transformation is done in the following way: first, de Nivelle's saturation procedure is applied on the given set S, and certain clauses are extracted form the resulting set. Then, a resolution based technique that introduces new predicate symbols is used in order to obtain the set S'. Our motivation for the presented method is automated model building.

1 Introduction

The *guarded fragment*, first described in [1], is a fragment of first order logic with very interesting properties: it is decidable, each of its satisfiable formulas allows a finite model, and many modal logics can be translated into it. Transformation of guarded formulas into clausal form has inspired the class of *guarded clauses*. Decidability of sets of guarded clauses by saturation under ordered resolution has been shown in [8].

Guarded clauses form a class of clauses with very strong syntactic restrictions on variable occurrences: every literal L of a guarded clause must contain the same variables (unless it is flat), and it must be *covering*, which means that every non-ground functional subterm of L must contain all the variables of L. But their name comes actually from the condition that a guarded clause must contain a literal in which all the variables of the clause occur at depth 0 (thus as arguments of the literal), and which contains no deeper variable occurrences. This literal is called the *guard* of the clause.

In this work, we consider guarded clauses that are Horn. A guarded Horn clause is called *primitive* if it either contains only a positive ground literal, or has the form $P(x_1, \ldots, x_n) \to Q(t_1, \ldots, t_n)$ where the x_i are pairwise different variables, and at least one t_i is functional and non-ground. We will show that for every satisfiable and finite set of guarded Horn clauses S, there is a finite set of primitive guarded Horn clauses S' such that in the least Herbrand model of S', the predicate symbols occuring in S are interpreted in the same way as in the least Herbrand model of S. Such a set S' can be found by a transformation of S. This transformation is done in several steps: first, the given set S is saturated using de Nivelle's decision procedure. Then, certain clauses are extracted from the resulting set, which are transformed into primitive guarded Horn clauses. To do this, a resolution-based technique which introduces new predicate symbols is used.

Our motivation for the transformation of guarded Horn clauses is automated model building (see [11, 10, 2, 5, 9, 4]). This subfield of automated deduction deals with the problem of finding (the description of) a model for a given satisfiable logical formula. This model must be expressed in a formalism that allows operations like the evaluation of arbitrary clauses or even arbitrary formulas. The usefulness of a model (counter-example) is evident: it does not only show that a formula is satisfiable (not valid), but also provides interesting semantic information on the formula. For example, it can serve to refine resolution in theorem provers, or it can help a human user to understand why a theorem cannot be proved (in this case, the model/counter-example must be expressed in a formalism that is "understandable" for human users).

By now, no method exists that allows to build models for satisfiable sets of guarded clauses automatically. Such a method should also be useful to build models for formulas of modal logics that can be translated into the guarded fragment, thus providing the same advantages to those logics as model building for first order logic has. Since primitive guarded Horn clauses have a relatively simple structure (they remind in some way of tree automaton rules), they seem to be an appropriate formalism to represent Herbrand models for guarded formulas. Models expressed in this way are likely to be understandable for human users. On the other hand, evaluation of arbitrary clauses in interpretations represented by primitive guarded Horn clauses is still an open problem.

This article is structured as follows: we first review some notions to settle our notation, and we recall the decision procedure by de Nivelle. In Section 3, we discuss the transformation of guarded Horn clauses, and conclude with some final remarks in Section 4.

2   Preliminaries

We assume the reader to be familiar with the standard logic notions as term, formula, clause, Herbrand interpretation, etc.

For a literal L, we denote by $\text{args}(L)$ the n-tuple of arguments of L.

Clauses that contain at most one positive literal are called *Horn clauses*. We often write a Horn clause $C = \{\neg B_1, \ldots, \neg B_n, H\}$ in the form $B_1, \ldots, B_n \to H$. In this case, we consider a clause as a list, i.e. we assume an order on its literals. We call the literal H the *head* of the Horn clause C, and the set of literals $\{\neg B_1, \ldots, \neg B_n\}$ the *body* of C. We write $\text{head}(C)$ resp. $\text{body}(C)$ to denote the head resp. the body of the Horn clause C. Clauses that contain only negative (positive) literals are called *negative (positive)*.

We say that a term t *occurs* in a literal L (or inversely that L *contains* t) iff there is a term $s \in \text{args}(L)$ such that t is a subterm of s. A term t occurs in a clause C iff t occurs in a literal $L \in C$.

The binary resolution rule between two clauses is defined as usual. We call the clause in which the negative literal that is resolved upon occurs the *negative premise*, and the clause in which the positive literal occurs the *positive premise*.

We denote by $\overline{\text{var}}(e)$ the n-tuple of pairwise different variables that occur in the expression e, in the order of their first occurence (w.r.t any fixed traversal of the tree that corresponds to e).

Throughout this article, if not stated otherwise, we will mean *finite set of clauses* if we write *set of clauses*. Furthermore, we will always assume that for two different clauses, there is no variable that occurs in both of them.

Let S be a set of clauses over the signature $(\mathcal{F}, \mathcal{P})$. Then, the *Herbrand base* of S, denoted by HB_S, is the set of all ground atoms over $(\mathcal{F}, \mathcal{P})$.

We will identify a Herbrand interpretation I for a clause set S with a subset of HB_S (a ground atom is true in I iff it is contained in I). $\mathcal{M}_S$ denotes the $\subseteq$-*least Herbrand model* of the set of Horn clauses S.

Let S be a set of non-negative Horn clauses. The immediate consequence operator of S, denoted T_S, is defined in the following way: for a set of ground atoms $\mathcal{G}$,

$$T_S(\mathcal{G}) = \{A \mid \exists C = (B_1, \ldots, B_n \to H) \in S, \exists \text{ ground substitution } \sigma \\ \text{with } \text{var}(C) = \text{dom}(\sigma) : A = H\sigma \text{ and } B_i\sigma \in \mathcal{G}\}.$$

$\mathcal{M}_S$ is the $\subseteq$-least fixpoint of T_S, and it can be obtained in ω iterations of T_S starting with the empty set $\emptyset$. Instead of $T_S^n(\emptyset)$, we will simply write T_S^n.

Definition 1. *Let S be a set of non-negative Horn clauses and A be a ground atom such that $A \in T_S^\omega$. If for a clause $C = B_1, \ldots, B_n \to H \in S$, there is a ground substitution σ with $\text{dom}(\sigma) = \text{var}(C)$ such that $B_i\sigma \in T_S^\omega$ for $1 \le i \le n$ and $A = H\sigma$, we say that A is generated by C.*

If for a clause C a literal $A \in T_{S \cup \{C\}}^\omega$ exists such that A is generated by C, we say that C is active in S (note that C is not necessarily contained in S).

If S is clear from the context, we omit it. If S is a set of Horn clauses from a decidable class, we can decide for each clause $C \in S$ if C is active: this is the case iff the empty clause can be derived from $S \cup \{\text{body}(C)\}$.

Definition 2. *For a term t*, vardepth(t) *is defined in the following way: If t is ground, then* vardepth(t) = -1. *Else, if t is a variable, then* vardepth(t) = 0, *else* $t = f(t_1, \ldots, t_n)$, *and* vardepth(t) = $1 + \max($vardepth(t_1), $\ldots$, vardepth(t_n))*.*

The vardepth of an atom is defined to be the maximal vardepth of its arguments, and the vardepth of a literal is the vardepth of its atom. The vardepth of a clause is the maximal vardepth of its literals.

Based on vardepth, we define the following simple ordering $\succeq_{vd}$ on literals:

Definition 3. *Let L_1 and L_2 be literals. Then $L_1 \succeq_{vd} L_2$ iff* vardepth(L_1) $\geq$ vardepth(L_2)*.*

A literal L is *flat* if all of its arguments are variables. It is *weakly flat* if all of its arguments are either variables or ground terms. A literal L is *weakly covering* if every non-ground functional subterm of L contains all the variables in var(L).

The proofs for the following theorems can be found in [7]:

Theorem 1. *Let L_1 and L_2 be two unifiable weakly covering literals with mgu σ, and $K = L_1\sigma$. Then K is weakly covering, and* vardepth(K) $\leq \max($vardepth(L_1), vardepth(L_2))*.*

Theorem 2. *Let L_1 and L_2 be two weakly covering literals with* var(L_1) $\subseteq$ var(L_2), *and* vardepth(L_1) $\leq$ vardepth(L_2), *and θ a substitution such that $L_2\theta$ is weakly covering. Then $L_1\theta$ is weakly covering, and* vardepth($L_1\sigma$) $\leq$ vardepth($L_2\sigma$)*.*

Now we will show the following lemma:

Lemma 1. *Let L_1 and L_2 be two variable disjoint, unifiable weakly covering literals with* vardepth(L_1) $\leq$ vardepth(L_2)*. Then there exists an mgu σ such that* var(L_1) $\subseteq$ dom(σ) *and for all $x \mapsto t \in \sigma$,*

 - *if $x \in$ var(L_1), then* var(t) $\subseteq$ var(L_2)*, and*
 - *if $x \in$ var(L_2), then t is ground or $t \in$ var(L_2)*.*

Proof. Let θ be an mgu of L_1 and L_2. Clearly, θ can map variables from L_2 only to other variables or to ground terms; otherwise, $L_2\theta$ would have a greater vardepth than L_2, which would contradict Theorem 1. If $\theta = \{x \mapsto y\} \cup \theta'$ with $x \in$ var(L_2) and $y \in$ var(L_1), the substitution $(\theta\{y \mapsto x\}) \cup \{y \mapsto x\}$ is also an mgu of L_1 and L_2. In this way, we can "reverse" all the pairs in θ that map a variable in var(L_2) to a variable in var(L_1). Let σ be the result of this reversing of all such pairs.

Now suppose there is a variable x such that $x \in$ var(L_1) and $x \notin$ dom(σ). Then a functional term t exists such that $t = y\sigma$ with $y \in$ var(L_2) and $x \in$ var(t). But this is not possible.

Finally, since all variables in var(L_1) occur on the left hand side of the pairs in σ, none of them can occur on a right hand side. $\qquad\square$

Remark: It is easy to see that we can find the mgu as in the above lemma simply by applying the standard, rule based unification algorithm with L_1 as first and L_2 as second argument. We will denote the mgu of L_1 and L_2 computed in this way by $\overline{\text{mgu}}(L_1, L_2)$.

Definition 4. *A clause C is* guarded *iff*

1. *every literal $L \in C$ is weakly covering,*
2. *if C is not ground, then there is a negative literal $G \in C$ (the guard) such that $vardepth(G) = 0$ and $var(G) = var(C)$, and*
3. *if for a literal $L \in C$, $vardepth(L) > 1$, then $var(L) = var(C)$.*

The proof for the following lemma can be found in [7]:

Lemma 2. *If C is a non-ground resolvent of clauses C_1 and C_2, then C contains no ground terms that are not in C_1 or C_2. If C is a resolvent of a ground clause C_1 and a non-ground clause C_2, then $depth(C) \leq \max(depth(C_1), depth(C_2))$.*

Definition 5. *A guarded Horn clause is called* primitive *if it is ground and its body is empty, or it has the form $P(x_1, \ldots, x_n) \to Q(t_1, \ldots, t_m)$ where $x_i \neq x_j$ if $i \neq j$ and $1 \leq i, j \leq n$, and $vardepth(Q(t_1, \ldots, t_m)) > 0$.*

In [8], it is shown that finite sets of guarded clauses can always be finitely saturated under ordered resolution and factorization using the following ordering $\sqsubset$ on literals of guarded clauses:

For two literals L_1 and L_2, $L_1 \sqsubset L_2$ iff

1. vardepth$(L_1) <$ vardepth(L_2), or
2. var$(L_1) \subset$ var(L_2).

The ordered resolution rule is defined in the standard way. In order to preserve refutational completeness, the binary factorization rule, defined as usual, is also needed. If a set of guarded clauses S is not satisfiable, the empty clause is contained in the saturated set obtained from S. Therefore we get a decision procedure for sets of guarded clauses.

3   Transformation of Guarded Horn Clauses into Primitive Guarded Horn Clauses

In this section, we will show that for every satisfiable set of guarded Horn clauses S, a set S' of primitive guarded Horn clauses exists such that $\mathcal{M}_S = \mathcal{M}_{S'} \cap HB_S$ (the intersection is necessary because we introduce new predicate symbols).

3.1   Saturation and Extraction

As a first step, we will show that in a satisfiable and saturated set of guarded Horn clauses, already those clauses in which the vardepth of the head is *strictly greater* than the vardepth of any body literal generate the least Herbrand model.

Theorem 3. *Let S be a satisfiable set of guarded Horn clauses, and $\bar{S}$ be the closure of S under $\sqsubset$-ordered resolution and factorization. Let*

$$S' = \{B_1, \ldots, B_n \to H \in \bar{S} \mid H \succ_{vd} B_i \text{ for } 1 \leq i \leq n \text{ and}$$
$$B_1, \ldots, B_n \to H \text{ is active in } \bar{S}\}.$$

Then, $\mathcal{M}_S = \mathcal{M}_{S'}$.

Proof. We clearly have that $\mathcal{M}_\mathcal{S} = \mathcal{M}_{\bar{\mathcal{S}}}$, because all the clauses in $\bar{\mathcal{S}}$ are logical consequences of the clauses in $\mathcal{S}$.

$\mathcal{M}_{\mathcal{S}'} \subseteq \mathcal{M}_\mathcal{S}$: Since $\mathcal{S}' \subseteq \bar{\mathcal{S}}$, we have that $\mathcal{M}_{\mathcal{S}'} \subseteq \mathcal{M}_{\bar{\mathcal{S}}} = \mathcal{M}_\mathcal{S}$.

$\mathcal{M}_\mathcal{S} \subseteq \mathcal{M}_{\mathcal{S}'}$: Let A be a ground atom that is true in $\mathcal{M}_\mathcal{S} = \mathcal{M}_{\bar{\mathcal{S}}}$.

Let $\mathcal{S}'' = \{B_1, \ldots, B_n \to H \in \bar{\mathcal{S}} \mid H \not\sqsubset B_i \text{ for } 1 \leq i \leq n\}$. Then, the empty clause can be deduced from $\{\neg A\} \cup \bar{\mathcal{S}}$ by $\sqsubset$-ordered resolution. In this refutation process, all newly deduced clauses are negative ground clauses: $\bar{\mathcal{S}}$ is already closed under resolution, and if we resolve a negative ground clause with a guarded Horn clause, we obtain again a negative ground clause. The reason for this is that the head of the Horn clause must be $\sqsubset$-maximal according to the ordering restriction, and therefore contain all variables of C.

So for the refutation of $\{\neg A\} \cup \bar{\mathcal{S}}$ we only use clauses in which the head is $\sqsubset$-maximal. But those clauses are contained in $\mathcal{S}''$. Therefore, $A \in \mathcal{M}_{\mathcal{S}''}$.

The set $\mathcal{S}''$ is closed under $\sqsubset$-ordered resolution: Let $A_1, \ldots, A_n \to K$ and $B_1, \ldots, B_m \to H$ be two clauses in $\mathcal{S}''$. W.l.o.g. we assume that we can $\sqsubset$-resolve on A_1 and H. Let $\theta = \mathrm{mgu}(A_1, H)$. Then we obtain the clause $C = B_1\theta, \ldots, B_m\theta, A_2\theta, \ldots, A_n\theta \to K\theta$.

The clause C is contained in $\bar{\mathcal{S}}$ because $\mathcal{S}'' \subseteq \bar{\mathcal{S}}$, and $\bar{\mathcal{S}}$ is closed under $\sqsubset$-resolution. Because according to Theorem 2, for $1 \leq j \leq n$, $K\theta \not\sqsubset A_j\theta$, and for $1 \leq i \leq m$, $H\theta = A_1\theta \not\sqsubset B_i\theta$, we have that $K\theta$ is $\sqsubset$-maximal in C, and therefore $C \in \mathcal{S}''$.

Now, we will show that $\mathcal{M}_{\mathcal{S}''} = T^\omega_{\mathcal{S}''} \subseteq T^\omega_{\mathcal{S}'} = \mathcal{M}_{\mathcal{S}'}$. There is a natural number n such that $A \in T^n_{\mathcal{S}''}$. We will show by induction on n that $A \in T^\omega_{\mathcal{S}'}$.

- $n = 1$: A is a ground atom that is contained in $\mathcal{S}''$, and because $\mathcal{S}'' \subseteq \bar{\mathcal{S}}$, A is trivially active in $\bar{\mathcal{S}}$. It follows from the definition of $\mathcal{S}'$ that $A \in \mathcal{S}'$. So, $A \in T^1_{\mathcal{S}'} \subseteq T^\omega_{\mathcal{S}'}$.
- $n > 1$: let A be generated by a clause $C \in \mathcal{S}''$. Let $C = A_1, \ldots, A_k \to H$. Then, there is a ground substitution θ such that $A = H\theta$, and $A_i\theta \in T^{n-1}_{\mathcal{S}''}$. W.l.o.g. we assume that there is a natural number l such that $\mathrm{vardepth}(A_i) = \mathrm{vardepth}(H)$ for $1 \leq i \leq l$, and $\mathrm{vardepth}(A_i) < \mathrm{vardepth}(H)$ for $l < i \leq k$. According to the induction hypothesis, we have that $A_i\theta \in T^\omega_{\mathcal{S}'}$. Let m_i be the smallest number such that $A_i\theta \in T^{m_i}_{\mathcal{S}'}$, and let $A_i\theta$ be generated by the clause $C_i = B_{i,1}, \ldots, B_{i,k_i} \to H_i$. Since $C_i \in \mathcal{S}'$, we have that $\mathrm{vardepth}(H_i) > \mathrm{vardepth}(B_{i,j})$ for $1 \leq j \leq k_i$ and $1 \leq i \leq k$. Let $m = \max\{m_i\}^l_{i=1}$. Then, for $1 \leq i \leq k$, there is a ground substitution σ_i such that $A_i\theta = H_i\sigma_i$, and $B_{i,j}\sigma_i \in T^{m_i-1}_{\mathcal{S}'}$ for $1 \leq j \leq k_i$. Let $\tau = \theta \cup \sigma_1 \cup \ldots \cup \sigma_k$. Then, τ unifies A_i with H_i for $1 \leq i \leq k$.

  Because for $1 \leq i \leq l$, the A_i are $\sqsubset$-maximal in C, and A_i can be unified with H_i, we can successively apply $\sqsubset$-ordered resolution between C and C_i on A_i and H_i. Let ϕ be the most general substitution such that $A_i\phi = H_i\phi$ for $1 \leq i \leq l$. Then, ϕ is more general than τ. Since the set of clauses $\mathcal{S}''$ is saturated under $\sqsubset$-ordered resolution, it must contain the clause $C' = B_{1,1}\phi, \ldots, B_{1,k_1}\phi, \ldots, B_{l,1}\phi, \ldots, B_{l,k_l}\phi, A_{l+1}\phi, \ldots, A_k\phi \to H\phi$.

  Let $\mathcal{A} = \{B_{i,j} \mid 1 \leq i \leq l, 1 \leq j \leq k_i\} \cup \{A_i \mid l < i \leq k\}$.

  First, let us assume that ϕ is not ground. Then, for $1 \leq i \leq l$, we have that $\mathrm{vardepth}(H\phi) = \mathrm{vardepth}(A_i\phi) = \mathrm{vardepth}(H_i\phi) > \mathrm{vardepth}(B_{i,j}\phi)$ where

$1 \leq j \leq k_i$ (Theorem 2). Therefore, the vardepth of $H\phi$ is strictly maximal in C'.

Finally, for each atom $D \in \mathcal{A}$, we have that $D\tau \in T_{\mathcal{S}'}^m$. Since ϕ is more general than τ, the atom $H\tau = H\theta = A$ is generated by C'. Therefore C' is active in $\bar{S}$ and contained in $\mathcal{S}'$, and $A \in T_{\mathcal{S}'}^{m+1} \subseteq T_{\mathcal{S}'}^{\omega}$.

If ϕ is a ground substitution, then $\phi = \tau$. Consider the negative clause $C'' = \neg B_{1,1}\tau, \ldots, \neg B_{1,k_1}\tau, \ldots, \neg B_{l,1}\tau, \ldots, \neg B_{l,k_l}\tau, \neg A_{l+1}\tau, \ldots, \neg A_k\tau$. This clause is false in $T_{\mathcal{S}''}^{\omega}$, because $D\tau \in T_{\mathcal{S}'}^{\omega} \subseteq T_{\mathcal{S}''}^{\omega}$, for each $D \in \mathcal{A}$. Therefore, it is possible to deduce the empty clause from $\{C''\} \cup \mathcal{S}''$ using $\sqsubset$-ordered resolution. But then, it is also possible to deduce the clause $\{H\tau\}$ from $\mathcal{S}''$, because we obtain C' from C'' by adding the literal $H\tau$. This literal is ground, so it is not greater than any literal in C'', and we can apply the same resolution steps on C' as on C''.

Because $\mathcal{S}''$ is closed under $\sqsubset$-ordered resolution, it must contain $H\tau = A$. A is trivially active in $\bar{S}$. By definition of $\mathcal{S}'$, $A \in \mathcal{S}'$. Finally, we have that $A \in T_{\mathcal{S}'}^1 \subseteq T_{\mathcal{S}'}^{\omega}$.   □

3.2   Flattening of the Body Literals

The second step is the transformation of a set of guarded Horn clauses in which the head is strictly $\succeq_{vd}$-maximal into a set of guarded Horn clauses where all body literals are weakly flat.

We use a transformation similar to the unfolding operation known from logic program transformation: the principle is to replace a clause C by all possible resolvents with other clauses on a certain literal $L \in C$. The goal of this transformation is to decrease the vardepth of the body literals of the present clauses. If we use standard resolution, this is not possible, since variables in L might be instantiated with functional terms. In the case of guarded clauses, the variables in L must occur in all other literals of C, so the vardepth of the literals in C different from L would increase. In order to avoid this, we have to perform a certain decomposition operation on clauses.

This decomposition operation is based on the following observation: let $C = B_1, \ldots, B_n \rightarrow H$ be a guarded Horn clause, and L be a literal that is unifiable with H and such that vardepth(L) < vardepth(H), and $\sigma = \overline{\mathrm{mgu}}(L, H)$. Let $\theta = \{x \mapsto t \in \sigma \mid x \in \mathrm{var}(L)\}$. Then we can decompose C into two guarded Horn clauses $C_1 = B_1\sigma, \ldots, B_n\sigma \rightarrow Q(t_1, \ldots, t_m)$ and $C_2 = Q(x_1, \ldots, x_m) \rightarrow L$, where $\{x_i \mapsto t_i \mid 1 \leq i \leq m\} = \theta$ and Q is a fresh predicate symbol of arity m. Then, C is the resolvent of C_1 and C_2 on the literals containing Q.

So, if L is a negative literal in a guarded Horn clause C' that we resolve upon, we can construct two guarded Horn clauses that are *logically equivalent* to the standard resolvent of C and C', without instantiating the variables of C'.

Example 1. Let $C = R(x, y) \rightarrow P(g(f(x, y), h(y, x)), h(f(x, y), h(y, x)))$ and $C' = U(x, y), P(g(x, y), h(x, y)) \rightarrow S(f(x, y))$. Decreasing the vardepth of the body of C' by resolution with C does not work, because we would get the resolvent $U(f(x, y), h(y, x)), R(x, y) \rightarrow S(f(f(x, y), h(y, x)))$. Using decomposition, we get $U(x, y), Q(x, y) \rightarrow S(f(x, y))$ and $R(x, y) \rightarrow Q(f(x, y), h(y, x))$.

We integrate this decomposition into the resolution rule in order to avoid instantiations of the variables of the negative premise with non-ground, functional terms. We call this modified version of resolution *decomposing resolution*, and for short *d-resolution*.

Definition 6. *Let* $\{\neg A_1\} \cup R_1$ *and* $\{A_2\} \cup R_2$ *be two clauses such that* A_1 *and* A_2 *are unifiable, and* $\sigma = \overline{mgu}(A_1, A_2)$. *Then, the* d-resolution *rule is defined as follows:*

- *if* $vardepth(A_1) \geq vardepth(A_2)$ *or* σ *is a ground substitution,*

$$\frac{\{\neg A_1\} \cup R_1 \quad \{A_2\} \cup R_2}{R_1\sigma \cup R_2\sigma}$$

- *else (i.e.* $vardepth(A_1) < vardepth(A_2)$ *and* σ *is not ground)*

$$\frac{\{\neg A_1\} \cup R_1 \quad \{A_2\} \cup R_2}{\{\neg Q(x_1,\ldots,x_n)\} \cup R_1\theta \quad \{Q(t_1,\ldots,t_n)\} \cup R_2\theta}$$

where
- $\theta = \{x \mapsto t \in \sigma \mid t$ *is ground or* $x \in var(A_2)\}$,
- $(x_1,\ldots,x_n) = \overline{var}(A_1\theta)$,
- $(t_1,\ldots,t_n) = (x_1,\ldots,x_n)\sigma$,
- Q *is a fresh predicate symbol.*

We call $R_1\sigma \cup R_2\sigma$ *resp.* $\{\neg Q(x_1,\ldots,x_n)\}\cup R_1\theta$ *a* d-resolvent *of* $\{\neg A_1\}\cup R_1$ *and* $\{A_2\}\cup R_2$, *and we call* $\{Q(t_1,\ldots,t_n)\}\cup R_2\theta$ *(if it exists) a* d-component *of* $\{A_2\} \cup R_2$. *In this case, we call* Q *a decomposition predicate.*

More generally, we will say that a clause D *is a d-component of a clause* C *if there is a clause* C' *such that* D *can be obtained as d-component from d-resolution of* C *as positive premise with* C' *(with appropriate choice of the decomposition predicate).*

Note that if C is a Horn clause, a d-component D of C is also a Horn clause, and $\text{body}(D)$ is an instance of $\text{body}(C)$.

It is not always necessary to introduce a new decomposition predicate: if we d-resolve a clause C as positive premise with a clause C_1 and then with a clause C_2 as negative premises, and the literals $L_1 \in C_1$ and $L_2 \in C_2$ that are resolved upon are identical (modulo renaming), two d-components of C whose heads have the same argument tuple are introduced. In this case it is enough to introduce one d-component, and use the same decomposition predicate in both of the d-resolvents. This fact is used in the procedure in Fig.1, which implements d-resolution.

A d-resolvent is related to the standard resolvent in the following way:

Proposition 1. *Let* $C_1 = \{\neg A_1\} \cup R_1$ *and* $C_2 = \{A_2\} \cup R_2$ *be two guarded Horn clauses, and let* $vardepth(A_1) > 0$. *Then, the d-resolvent of* C_1 *and* C_2 *on* $\neg A_1$ *and* A_2 *is either the standard resolvent, or a guarded Horn clauses* C_1' *such that the standard resolvent is obtained by resolution of* C_1' *with the corresponding d-component* C_2' *on the literals containing the decomposition predicate. The d-component is also a guarded Horn clause.*

procedure *d-resolve* $((B_1,\ldots,B_n \to H),i,(A_1,\ldots,A_m \to K),S)$
begin
$\quad \sigma = \overline{\mathrm{mgu}}(B_i,K);\ R = \emptyset$
$\quad$ **if** $\mathrm{vardepth}(B_i) \geq \mathrm{vardepth}(K)$ **or** σ is ground **then**
$\quad\quad C = (B_1,\ldots,B_{i-1},A_1,\ldots,A_m,B_{i+1},\ldots,B_n \to H)\sigma$
$\quad$ **else**
$\quad\quad \theta = \{x \mapsto t \in \sigma \mid t$ is ground or $x \in \mathrm{var}(K)\}$
$\quad\quad (x_1,\ldots,x_k) = \overline{\mathrm{var}}(B_i\theta)$
$\quad\quad (t_1,\ldots,t_k) = (x_1,\ldots,x_k)\sigma$
$\quad\quad$ **if** $\exists A'_1,\ldots,A'_m \to Q(s_1,\ldots,s_k) \in S$ such that $(t_1,..,t_k) = (s_1,..,s_k)$ **then**
$\quad\quad\quad P = Q$
$\quad\quad$ **else**
$\quad\quad\quad$ let P be a fresh predicate symbol
$\quad\quad\quad R = \{A_1\theta,\ldots,A_m\theta \to P(t_1,\ldots,t_k)\}$
$\quad\quad$ **end if**
$\quad\quad C = B_1\theta,\ldots,B_{i-1}\theta,P(x_1,\ldots,x_k),B_{i+1}\theta,\ldots,B_n\theta \to H\theta$
$\quad$ **end if**
$\quad$ **result** $= (C,R)$
end procedure

Fig. 1. The *d-resolve* procedure

Proof. It is obvious that the deduced clauses are Horn if the premises are Horn. If $\mathrm{vardepth}(A_1) \geq \mathrm{vardepth}(A_2)$, we get the standard resolvent, which is always guarded (see [7]).

Now consider the case that $\mathrm{vardepth}(A_1) < \mathrm{vardepth}(A_2)$. Then we get the d-resolvent $\{\neg Q(x_1,\ldots,x_n)\} \cup R_1\theta$ and the d-component $\{Q(t_1,\ldots,t_n)\} \cup R_2\theta$ as defined in Definition 6. For every t_i in $Q(t_1,\ldots,t_n)$, there is a subterm s_i of A_2 such that $t_i = s_i\theta$. Because $\mathrm{vardepth}(A_1) < \mathrm{vardepth}(A_2)$, there must be at least one s_j that is a non-ground functional term. Since A_2 is covering, s_j must contain all the variables of A_2, and $Q(s_1,\ldots,s_n)$ is also covering. Because for all $x \in \mathrm{var}(A_2)$, $x\theta$ is a ground term or another variable in $\mathrm{var}(A_2)$, $Q(s_1,\ldots,s_n)\theta = Q(t_1,\ldots,t_n)$ is covering. Finally, because $\mathrm{var}(Q(s_1,\ldots,s_n)) = \mathrm{var}(A_2) = \mathrm{var}(R_2)$, we have that $\mathrm{var}(Q(t_1,\ldots,t_n)) = \mathrm{var}(R_2\theta)$. If R_2 contains a guard G, then $G\theta$ is a guard of $R_2\theta$. So, the d-component is a guarded clause.

Concerning the d-resolvent, we have that $V = \{x_1,\ldots,x_n\} \subseteq \mathrm{var}(A_1) = \mathrm{var}(R_1)$. Since $x\theta = x$ for all the variables in V, and $y\theta$ is ground for $y \in \mathrm{var}(R_1) \setminus V$, we have that $V = \mathrm{var}(R_1\theta)$. So, the d-resolvent is a guarded clause, and $\neg Q(x_1,\ldots,x_n)$ is a guard.

Resolution of $\{\neg Q(x_1,\ldots,x_n)\} \cup R_1\theta$ with $\{Q(t_1,\ldots,t_n)\} \cup R_2\theta$ gives $R_1\theta\tau \cup R_2\theta\tau = R_1\sigma \cup R_2\sigma$ with $\tau = \{x_i \mapsto t_i \mid 1 \leq i \leq n\}$ and $\sigma = \mathrm{mgu}(A_1,A_2)$. $\qquad\square$

The following lemma states that a d-resolvent is always smaller than the positive premise:

Lemma 3. *Let C_1 and C_2 be two guarded Horn clauses in which the head is strictly $\succeq_{vd}$-maximal, and such that we can resolve C_1 and C_2 on the head of C_2 and on a negative literal $L \in C_1$ for which $\mathrm{vardepth}(L) > 0$.*

Then, the d-resolvent D of C_1 and C_2 is strictly $\succeq_{vd}^{mul}$-smaller than C_1, where $\succeq_{vd}^{mul}$ is the multiset extension of $\succeq_{vd}$.

Proof. Let $C_2 = B_1, \ldots, B_n \rightarrow H$, and $\sigma = \overline{mgu}(L, H)$. First, suppose that vardepth$(H) >$ vardepth(L). To obtain D from C_1, some variables in C_1 are instantiated with ground terms, and L is replaced by a literal L' with vardepth 0. Since $L \succ_{vd} L'$, we have that $C_1 \succeq_{vd}^{mul} D$.

If vardepth$(H) \leq$ vardepth(L), then in order to obtain D from C_1, some variables in C_1 are instaciated with other variables or ground terms, and L is replaced by $(B_1, \ldots, B_n)\sigma$. Since vardepth$(L) \geq$ vardepth$(L\sigma) =$ vardepth$(H\sigma) >$ vardepth$(B_i\sigma)$ and thus $L \succ_{vd} B_i\sigma$ for $1 \leq i \leq n$, we have that $C_1 \succeq_{vd}^{mul} D$. □

An important property of d-resolution is that there are only finitely many different ways to decompose a clause, if the set of ground terms that may occur is finite.

Lemma 4. *Let T be a finite set of ground terms, and S be a (possibly infinite) set of guarded Horn clauses such that for every non-ground clause $C' \in S$, every ground term that occurs in C' is contained in T.*

Let C be a guarded Horn clause, and S be the set of all d-components of C that can be deduced by d-resolution between C (as positive premise) and clauses in S.

Then, the set $\{ args(head(D)) \mid D \in S \}$ is finite modulo renaming.

Proof. Let $H = head(C)$. Then, there are only finitely many non-ground weakly covering literals L (modulo renaming) such that vardepth$(L) <$ vardepth(H), the ground subterms of L are contained in T, and L is unifiable with H.   □

Now we will define a transformation algorithm. The idea is to associate to every clause $C \in S$ the set of d-components of C that are generated during the transformation process. Such a set is always finite by Lemma 4, if we introduce a new decomposition predicate only if there is not already an equivalent one. So, our algorithm operates on a set $\mathcal{C}$ of pairs of the form *(clause C, set of d-components of C)*.

If a clause C with $(C, S) \in \mathcal{C}$ contains a body literal B that is not weakly flat, we unfold C on B. This means that we replace C by all d-resolvents we can obtain by d-resolving C on B with a clause C' s.th. $(C', S') \in \mathcal{C}$, which may have the side effect of adding a new d-component of C' to S'.

Then, we perform the same unfolding operation for every d-component $D \in S$ on the literal $B' \in D$ that corresponds to B.

If C is self-resolvent on B, this leads to the addition of new d-components to S itself. Therefore, this possibility has to be considered first.

Clearly, a newly generated clause that is not active can be deleted. If a clause is ground and active, its body can be deleted, because all the body literals are false in the least Herbrand model.

The procedure *flatten* that implements the flattening algorithm is shown in Fig.2. We use the following notation: for a literal L, $pr(L)$ denotes the predicate

procedure *flatten* (S)
begin
  $C = \{(C, \emptyset) \mid C \in S\}$
  while $\exists (C, S) \in C$: body(C) contains a non-weakly-flat literal **do**
    choose $(C = B_1, \ldots, B_n \to H, S) \in C$ and $1 \le i \le n$ s.th. vardepth$(B_i) > 0$
    and vardepth$(H) \ge$ vardepth$(Lit^-_{pr(H)}(Cl(C)))$
    L = list containing all elements of C with (C, S) at head position; $C' = \emptyset$
    for $j = 1$ **to** length(L) **do**
      let $L[j] = (C', S')$
      if *resolve*(C, i, C') exists and is active in $Cl(C)$ **then**
        $(\bar{C}, X) = $ *d-resolve*(C, i, C', S')
        if $\bar{C}$ is ground **then** $\bar{C} = $ head$(\bar{C})$ **end if**
        $S' = S' \cup X$; $A = S$; $R = \emptyset$
        while $A \ne \emptyset$ **do**
          choose $C'' \in A$; $A = A \setminus \{C''\}$
          if *resolve*(C'', i, C') exists and is active in $Cl(C)$ **then**
            $(D, X) = $ *d-resolve*(C'', i, C', S')
            if D is ground **then** $D = $ head(D) **end if**
            $S' = S' \cup X$; $R = R \cup \{D\}$
            if $j = 1$ **then** $A = A \cup \{D\}$ **end if**; **end if**; **end while**
      $C' = C' \cup (\bar{C}, R)$; **end if**; **end for**
    $C = (C \setminus \{(C, S)\}) \cup C'$; **end while**
  result = $Cl(C)$
end procedure

Fig. 2. The *flatten* procedure

symbol in L. If S is a set of clauses and P a predicate symbol, then $Lit^-_P(S)$ denotes the set of all negative literals L with $pr(L) = P$ that occur in S. For a set C of pairs *(clause, clause set)*, $Cl(C) = \bigcup_{(c,s) \in C} \{C\} \cup S$. We denote by *resolve*$(C_1, i, C_2)$, where C_1 and C_2 are Horn clauses, the (standard) resolvent of C_1 and C_2 on the i-th body literal of C_1 and the head of C_2.

Proposition 2. *The procedure* flatten *terminates on every set S of guarded Horn clauses in which the head is strictly $\succeq_{vd}$-maximal, and furnishes as result a set S' of guarded Horn clauses such that for every $C \in S'$,*

- *body$(C) = \emptyset$ and head(C) is ground, or*
- *vardepth$(body(C)) = 0$ and vardepth$(head(C)) > 0$,*

and such that $M_S = M_{S'} \cap HB_S$.

Proof. First, we show termination. Let $>$ be the ordering on pairs *(clause, clause set)* defined as follows: $(C_1, S_1) > (C_2, S_2)$ iff $C_1 \succeq_{vd}^{mul} C_2$. Let $\gg$ be the multiset extension of $>$. Clearly, $>$ is well-founded, and $\gg$ is also well-founded.

Every iteration of the outer while loop replaces a pair $(C, S) \in C$ by a set of pairs $\{(C_i, S_i) \mid 1 \le i \le m\}$ such that all the C_i are d-resolvents of C as negative and a clause C' with $(C', S') \in C$ as positive premise. Since d-resolvents are always strictly smaller than the negative premise, the set of pairs C gets strictly smaller under $\gg$.

Termination of the inner while loop is obvious if $j \neq 1$. If $j = 1$, this means that the chosen clause C and its d-components in S are d-resolved with C itself. Then, if a new d-component D of C is generated, D must also be d-resolved with C, which might lead to the generation of another D-component. But termination is assured by the fact that for every pair (C, S), the set S containing d-components of C is finite. The reason for this is that no new ground terms can be introduced into non-groud clauses (Lemma 2), and we avoid the introduction of different d-components whose head literals have the same argument tuples, so the finiteness of S follows from Lemma 4 and the fact that is not possible to add infinitely many ground clauses (Lemma 2).

In a pair (C, S), all the clauses in S are always d-components of C: this is clearly the case for such clauses that are added to S by the d-resolution procedure. On the other hand, let C be obtained by d-resolution of a clause C' as negative premise on a literal $L \in C'$ with a clause C''. Then, every clause $D \in S$ is obtained by d-resolution of a d-component D' of C' with C'' on a literal $L' \in D'$ which is an instance of L, where body literals of active ground clauses are deleted. Clearly, such clauses are d-components of C.

Therefore, if $C = B_1, \ldots, B_n \to H$, every $\bar{C} \in S$ is either a ground clause with one positive literal H', or it has the form $C' = B_1\sigma, \ldots, B_n\sigma \to H'$, where σ is a substitution such that for all $x \in \mathrm{var}(C)$, $x\sigma$ is ground or a variable from $\mathrm{var}(C)$. So, if there are only weakly flat literals in C, this is also the case for the clauses in S.

It is not necessary to apply d-resolution on literals containing decomposition predicates, because negative literals with decomposition predicates can never contain non-ground functional terms: Suppose a variable of a negative literal with a decomposition predicate in a clause C would be instantiated with a non-ground functional term. This is only possible if C is used as positive premise for d-resolution. But then, the negative literal L we resolve upon has greater vardepth than the head of C. But this is not possible, because if we introduce a decomposition predicate in a d-component generated by a clause C', the head H of C' must have greater vardepth than all negative literals containing the same predicate symbol as H.

Let $\mathcal{A} = \{(C, S) \in \mathcal{C} \mid \mathrm{body}(C)$ contains a non-weakly-flat literal$\}$. If $\mathcal{A}$ is not empty, there is always a pair $(C, S) \in \mathcal{A}$ such that the head of C has greater vardepth than all negative literals with the same predicate symbol in $Cl(C)$. For example, chose (C, S) such that $\mathrm{vardepth}(C) \geq \mathrm{vardepth}(C')$ for all C' with $(C', S') \in \mathcal{A}$. Therefore, there is always a pair in $\mathcal{A}$ that can be chosen, and when the procedure stops, all negative literals in the resulting set S' are weakly flat.

By definition, a d-component has always a head with vardepth greater than 0, and a d-resolvent is either ground, or it has the same vardepth as the positive premise. Since we start with a set S in which all clauses have a head with vardepth greater than 0 (except the ground clauses), $\mathrm{vardepth}(\mathrm{head}(C)) > 0$ for every clause C in the resulting set S' that is not ground. Ground clauses that are not active are deleted, and in active ground clauses, all body literals can be deleted, since we know that they are false. Therefore, every ground clause in S' contains exactly one positive literal.

Finally, the interpretation of a predicate symbol that occurs in S is invariant in the least Herbrand model of $Cl(C)$, because in every iteration of the while-loop, a clause is replaced by all possible d-resolvents and d-components on a certain literal.

Because d-resolution is only applied if the corresponding standard resolvent is active, all the clauses in S' are active.   □

3.3   Condensation of the Body Literals

The next step is the transformation of a set of non-negative Horn clauses with weakly flat body that has been obtained from the flatten procedure into a set of guarded Horn clauses with at most one body literal. Here again, we use d-resolution.

The idea is to replace the body of a clause $B_1, \ldots, B_n \to H$ by a literal $\neg Q(x_1, \ldots, x_m)$ where $\{x_1, \ldots, x_m\} = \mathrm{var}(\{B_1, \ldots, B_n\})$ and Q is a fresh predicate symbol. We call Q a *condensation predicate*.

Then, we unfold the clause $C = B_1, \ldots, B_n \to Q(x_1, \ldots, x_m)$ in the following way: Let B_i be a guard of C. Then we deduce all standard resolvents of C on B_i with all other clauses in the set. In this way, all the variables of C are instantiated. Then we flatten the obtained set of clauses in basically the same way as in the flatten procedure, which means that we replace a clause with non-weakly-flat body literals by all possible d-resolvents and add new d-components if necessary. We do this until only clauses with weakly flat bodies are left.

Example 2. Consider the set $\{T(a, b)\} \cup S$, where

$$S = \{P(x, y), R(x, y) \to S(f(x, y), g(x, y)), \tag{1}$$
$$T(x, y) \to P(f(x, y), h(x, y)), \tag{2}$$
$$T(x, y) \to R(f(x, g(x, y)), h(x, g(x, y))), \tag{3}$$
$$T(x, y) \to T(x, g(x, y))\} \tag{4}$$

First, we replace (1) by the clause

$$Q_1(x, y) \to S(f(x, y), g(x, y)), \tag{5}$$

where Q_1 is a new predicate symbol. Then we unfold the clause $P(x, y), R(x, y) \to Q_1(x, y)$ on $P(x, y)$, which gives $T(x, y), R(f(x, y), h(x, y)) \to Q_1(f(x, y), h(x, y))$ by resolution with (2). By d-resolution with (3), this clause is "flattened" to

$$T(x, y), R'(x, y) \to Q_1(f(x, y), h(x, y)), \tag{6}$$

and the d-component $T(x, y) \to R'(x, g(x, y))$ of (3) is added. Then, (6) is replaced by

$$Q_2(x, y) \to Q_1(f(x, y), h(x, y)), \tag{7}$$

and in the same way as above, the clause

$$T(x,y) \rightarrow Q_2(x, g(x,y)) \tag{8}$$

is generated.

It is possible that variables in negative literals containing decomposition predicates are instantiated with non-ground functional terms. Therefore, d-resolution has to be applied on literals containing decomposition predicates. This may lead to the deduction of a d-component of a d-component of a clause. But this does not cause any problem, because it is easy to see that if D is a d-component of C, and E is a d-component of D, then E is a d-component of C.

Since we have only finitely many predicate symbols, and only finitely many decomposition predicates can be introduced, we need to introduce only finitely many condensation predicates.

We start with the set of pairs obtained from the flatten procedure. For a pair (C,S), it is enough to compute a condensation predicate for the body of C, since the bodies of the clauses in S are instances of the body of C.

The condensation procedure is shown in Fig.3. We denote by $resolve(C, i, S)$ where C is a Horn clause and S a set of Horn clauses, the set of all possible resolvents of C on its i-th body literal with the clauses in S.

Lemma 5. *The procedure* condense *terminates for every set $\mathcal{C}$ of pairs (C,S) where C is a guarded Horn clause and S a set of d-components of C, and such that*

- *(i) $body(C) = \emptyset$ and $head(C)$ is ground, or*
- *(ii) $vardepth(body(C)) = 0$ and $vardepth(head(C)) > 0$,*

and the result is a set S' of guarded Horn clauses such that for each $C \in S'$, either (i) is fulfilled, or (ii) and additionally $|body(C)| = 1$ are fulfilled, and such that $\mathcal{M}_S = \mathcal{M}_{S'} \cap HB_S$, where $S = Cl(\mathcal{C})$.
If all the clauses in S are active, all the clauses in S' are active.

Proof. The set of predicate symbols that may occur in the body of the clauses is finite, because we start with a finite set of clauses, and every clause can only generate a finite number of decomposition predicates. For a finite set of predicate symbols $\mathcal{P}$ and a finite set of ground terms T, there can only be finitely many negative guarded clauses (modulo renaming) that contain literals of the form $P(t_1, \ldots, t_n)$ where $P \in \mathcal{P}$ and for $1 \leq i \leq n$, t_i is either a variable or $t_i \in T$. Since condensation predicates do not appear in negative literals in $\mathcal{C}$, and no new ground terms can occur in non-ground clauses (Lemma 2), only finitely many condensation predicates need to be introduced. Therefore, the set $\mathcal{D}$ is always finite, and the procedure terminates.

Because a clause C is always replaced by all the possible resolvents resp. d-resolvents and d-components that can be obtained from (d-)resolution with other clauses, the interpretation of predicate symbols occuring in $Cl(\mathcal{C})$ is invariant in the least Herbrand model of $Cl(\mathcal{C} \cup \mathcal{A})$.

procedure *condense* ($\mathcal{C}$)
begin
  $\mathcal{D} = \emptyset;\ \mathcal{A} = \emptyset;\ S' = \emptyset$
  while $\mathcal{C} \neq \emptyset$ **do**
    choose a pair $p = (B_1, \ldots, B_n \to H, S) \in \mathcal{C}$
    $\mathcal{C} = \mathcal{C} \setminus \{p\};\ \mathcal{A} = \mathcal{A} \cup \{p\}$
    if $n > 1$ and there is no clause $B'_1, \ldots, B'_n \to H' \in \mathcal{D}$ s.th. $\{B_1, \ldots, B_n\} = \{B'_1 \sigma, \ldots, B'_n \sigma\}$ for a renaming σ
      let $(x_1, \ldots, x_n) = \overline{\mathrm{var}}(H)$
      let Q be a fresh predicate symbol
      $\mathcal{D} = \mathcal{D} \cup \{B_1, \ldots, B_n \to Q(x_1, \ldots, x_n)\}$
      let B_i be a guard of $B_1, \ldots, B_n \to Q(x_1, \ldots, x_n)$
      $\mathcal{R} = resolve(B_1, \ldots, B_n \to Q(x_1, \ldots, x_n), i, Cl(\mathcal{C} \cup \mathcal{A}));\ \mathcal{R}' = \emptyset$
      for all $C' \in \mathcal{R}$ **do**
        if C' is active in $Cl(\mathcal{C} \cup \mathcal{A})$ **then**
          if C' is ground **then** $\mathcal{A} = \mathcal{A} \cup \{(\mathrm{head}(C'), \emptyset)\}$
          else $\mathcal{R}' = \mathcal{R}' \cup \{C'\}$ **end if; end if; end for all**
      while $\exists C \in \mathcal{R}'$: body($C$) contains a non-weakly-flat literal
        choose $C = B_1, \ldots, B_n \to H \in \mathcal{R}'$ and $1 \leq i \leq n$ s.th.vardepth(B_i) > 0
        $\mathcal{R}' = \mathcal{R}' \setminus \{C\}$
        for all $(C', S') \in \mathcal{C} \cup \mathcal{A}$ s.th.for a $C'' \in \{C'\} \cup S'$, $resolve(C, i, C'')$
        exists and is active in $Cl(\mathcal{C} \cup \mathcal{A})$ **do**
          $(D, X) = d\text{-}resolve(C, i, C'', S')$
          if D is ground **then** $D = \mathrm{head}(D)$ **end if**
          $S' = S' \cup X;\ \mathcal{R}' = \mathcal{R}' \cup \{D\};$ **end for all; end while**
      $\mathcal{C} = \mathcal{C} \cup \{(C, \emptyset) \mid C \in R'\};$ **end if; end while**
  for all $(B_1, \ldots, B_n \to H, S) \in \mathcal{A}$
    let $B'_1, \ldots, B'_n \to H' \in \mathcal{D}$ be such that $\{B_1, \ldots, B_n\} = \{B'_1 \sigma, \ldots, B'_n \sigma\}$ for
    a renaming σ
    $S' = S' \cup \{H' \sigma \to H\}$
    for all $(A_1, \ldots, A_n \to K) \in S$
      let τ such that $\{A_1, \ldots, A_n\} = \{B'_1 \tau, \ldots, B'_n \tau\}$
      $S' = S' \cup \{H' \tau \to K\};$ **end for all; end for all**
end procedure

Fig. 3. The *condense* procedure

It is obvious that the clauses in the resulting set have either form (i), or form (ii) and contain one single body literal.

Because d-resolution is only applied if the corresponding standard resolvent is active, all the clauses in S' are active. □

3.4 Transformation into Primitive Guarded Horn Clauses

In the set we obtain from the condense procedure, the body literals of the non-ground clauses are weakly flat. But this means that they may contain ground terms and multiple occurrences of the same variable. A last transformation step is necessary in order to obtain primitive guarded Horn clauses.

Here again, the idea is to replace the body literal L by a literal L' whose arguments are exactly the variables in $var(L)$, and then to unfold $L \vee \neg L'$ on L.

Example 3. Consider the set $\{T(a)\} \cup S$, where

$$S = \{P(x, y, x, a) \to R(f(x, y), x), \tag{1}$$
$$S(x, y, z) \to P(g(x, y, z), h(x, y, z), g(y, x, z), z), \tag{2}$$
$$T(x) \to S(f(x, x), f(x, x), a)\} \tag{3}$$

First, we replace (1) by the clause

$$Q_1(x, y) \to R(f(x, y), x), \tag{4}$$

introducing the new predicate symbol Q_1. In the next step, we unfold the clause $P(x, y, x, a) \to Q_1(x, y)$, which gives $S(x, x, a) \to Q_1(g(x, x, a), h(x, x, a))$ by resolution with (2). This clause is not primitive yet, so we replace it by

$$Q_2(x) \to Q_1(g(x, x, a), h(x, x, a)), \tag{5}$$

and we unfold the clause $S(x, x, a) \to Q_2(x)$, which gives

$$T(x) \to Q_2(f(x, x)) \tag{6}$$

by resolving with (3).

The procedure *primitive* in Fig.4 implements this transformation.

Lemma 6. *The procedure* primitive *terminates for every set S of non-negative Horn clauses such that for each $C \in S$, eihter*

- *$body(C) = \emptyset$ and $head(C)$ is ground, or*
- *$body(C) = \{B\}$ for a weakly flat literal B and $vardepth(head(C)) > 0$,*

and furnishes as result a set of primitive guarded Horn clauses S' such that $M_S = M_{S'} \cap HB_S$.
If all the clauses in S are active, all the clauses in S' are active.

Proof. For a finite set of predicate symbols $\mathcal{P}$ and a finite set of ground terms T, there can only be finitely many negative non-ground literals (modulo renaming) of the form $P(t_1, \ldots, t_n)$ where $P \in \mathcal{P}$ and for $1 \leq i \leq n$, t_i is either a variable or $t_i \in T$. Since newly introduced predicate symbols do not appear in negative literals in S, and no new ground terms can occur in non-ground clauses (Lemma 2), only finitely many new predicate symbols need to be introduced. Therefore, the set $\mathcal{D}$ is finite, and the procedure terminates.

Because in each iteration, a clause C is replaced by two clauses C_1 and C_2 in such a way that C is the resolvent of C_1 and C_2 on literals with a predicate symbol that only occurs in C_1 and C_2, and C_2 is then replaced by all its possible resolvents on a certain literal $L \in C_2$, the interpretation of predicate symbols occuring in S is invariant in the least Herbrand model of $S \cup S'$.

It is obvious that the clauses in the resulting set are primitive. Because newly generated clauses are not kept if they are not active, all the clauses in the resulting set S' are active.   □

```
procedure primitive (S)
begin
  D = ∅; S' = ∅
  while S ≠ ∅
    choose C ∈ S
    S = S \ {C}; S' = S' ∪ {C}
    if C is not primitive then
      let C = B → H
      if there is no B' → H' ∈ D s.th. B = B'σ for a renaming σ then
        let (x₁,...,xₙ) = var̄(B)
        let Q be a fresh predicate symbol
        D = D ∪ {B → Q(x₁,...,xₙ)}
        R = resolve(B → Q(x₁,...,xₙ),1,S ∪ S')
        for all C' ∈ R
          if C' is active in S ∪ S' then
            if C' is ground then C' = head(C') end if
            S = S ∪ {C'}; end if; end for all; end if
    end if; end while
  for all C = B → H ∈ S' s.th. C is not primitive
    let B' → H' ∈ D s.th. B = B'σ for a renaming σ
    S' = (S' \ {C}) ∪ {H'σ → H}; end for all
end procedure
```

Fig. 4. The *primitive* procedure

4   Conclusion and Future Work

We have presented a method that transforms a satisfiable and finite set S of guarded Horn clauses (where guarded clauses are defined as in [7]) into a finite set S' of so-called *primitive* guarded Horn clauses such that the minimal Herbrand models of S and S' coincide on predicate symbols that occur in S. A primitive guarded Horn clause has either an empty body and a ground head, or contains only one body literal, which is flat and linear, and a head literal that has at least one non-ground functional term as argument.

The motivation for our work is automated model building. Primitive guarded Horn clauses have a relatively simple structure, and seem to be suitable to represent Herbrand models for sets of guarded clauses (the model represented by a set of primitive guarded Horn clauses is its least Herbrand model). Whereas it is possible to evaluate flat clauses (i.e. clauses that do not contain functional terms) in models represented in this way (see [3]), the evaluation of arbitrary clauses is still an open problem. At least, primitive guarded Horn clauses may represent models (i.e. counter-examples) in a way that is "understandable" for a human user. Finite models for sets of primitive guarded Horn clauses can be found by a method presented in [3] (the termination of this method has still to be shown).

Future work will also include the attempt to extend our method to non-Horn guarded clauses. For a given set of guarded clauses S, this could be done by computing a set of guarded Horn clauses S' such that $\mathcal{M}_{S'}$ is a model of S. Another interesting candidate for a generalization of our method are *weakly guarded* Horn clauses (see [7]). Recently, it has been shown that the guarded fragment with equality can be decided using superposition (see [6]), which might also open a possibility to extend our method. Furthermore, we will study the application of our method to modal logics, as for example the automatic construction of Kripke models.

We have implemented the presented transformation procedure in the Objective Caml language. The source code is available from the author.

References

1. Hajnal Andréka, Johan van Benthem, and István Nemeti. Modal languages and bounded fragments of predicate logic. Research Report ML-96-03, ILLC, 1996.
2. Ch. Bourely, R. Caferra, and N. Peltier. A method for building models automatically. Experiments with an extension of Otter. In *Proceedings of CADE-12*, pages 72–86. Springer, 1994. LNAI 814.
3. Michael Dierkes. Model building for guarded horn clauses. Research report, LEIBNIZ-IMAG Laboratory, 1999. Available via http://www-leibniz.imag.fr/ATINF/Michael.Dierkes/articles/mbghc.ps.gz.
4. C.G. Fermüller and A. Leitsch. Decision procedures and model building in equational clause logic. *Journal of the IGPL*, 6(1):17–41, 1998.
5. Christian Fermüller and A. Leitsch. Hyperresolution and automated model building. *Journal of Logic and Computation*, 6(2):173–203, 1996.
6. H. Ganzinger and H. de Nivelle. A superposition decision procedure for the guarded fragment with equality. In *Proc. 14th IEEE Symposium on Logic in Computer Science*. IEEE Computer Society Press, 1999.
7. Hans de Nivelle. Resolution decides the guarded fragment. Research Report CT-1998-01, ILLC, 1998.
8. Hans de Nivelle. A resolution decision procedure for the guarded fragment. In *Automated Deduction - CADE -15*, volume 1421 of *LNCS*, 1998.
9. Nicolas Peltier. *Nouvelles Techniques pour la Construction de Modèles finis ou infinis en Déduction Automatique*. PhD thesis, Institut National Polytechnique de Grenoble, 1997.
10. J. Slaney. Finder (finite domain enumerator): Notes and guides. Technical report, Australian National University Automated Reasoning Project, Canberra, 1992.
11. Tanel Tammet. Using resolution for deciding solvable classes and building finite models. In *Baltic Computer Science*, pages 33–64. Springer, LNCS 502, 1991.

Resource Management in
Linear Logic Proof Search Revisited

Pablo López and Ernesto Pimentel

Departamento de Lenguajes y Ciencias de la Computación
Universidad de Málaga
Campus de Teatinos. 29071 Málaga, Spain
Phone: +34 952 13 33 17   Fax: +34 952 13 13 97
{lopez,ernesto}@lcc.uma.es

Abstract. Linear logic provides a logical framework to express fundamental computational concepts in a declarative style. As a consequence,
it has been used as a sound foundation for the design of expressive programming and specification languages. Unfortunately, linearity is as convenient for specifying as difficult to implement. In particular, the successful implementation of linear logic languages and provers involving
context splitting strongly depends on the efficiency of the method computing a suitable split. A number of solutions have been proposed, referred to as *lazy splitting* or *resource management* systems. In this paper,
we present a new resource management system for the Lolli linear logic
language. We show that the choice of the structure employed to represent the contexts has a strong influence on the overall performance of
the resource management system. We also estimate the performance of
previous proposals, and compare them to our new system.
Keywords: Linear Logic, Logic Programming, Lolli, Implementation,
Lazy Splitting

1 Introduction

Linear logic, introduced by Girard in [3], is a refinement of intuitionistic and
classical logics. It provides a finer control on the use of formulae which can be
interpreted as *resources*. As a result, linear logic extends the expressive power
of both intuitionistic and classical logics, in the sense that it allows a simpler
and more concise representation of situations difficult to express within these.
Therefore, linear logic constitutes a sound foundation for the design of expressive
specification and programming languages integrating features such as object orientation and concurrency in a declarative style. On the other hand, the *practical*
support of such features within intuitionistic or classical logic languages usually
requires the use of extra-logical characteristics.

Unfortunately, and because of its high degree of non-determinism, linearity
is as convenient for specifying as difficult to implement. Traditional language
implementation techniques are useless to undertake the *efficient* implementation
of linear logic languages. The linear nature of formulae – the key feature on

which the expressiveness of linear logic holds – implies that they must be used *exactly once* in a proof, arising major problems concerning their management. Some of the linear logic languages proposed, such as LO [1] and ACL [6], are based on rather restricted fragments of linear logic. Although these restrictions considerably simplify their implementations, they also imply a severe expressiveness loss. Other languages, such as Lolli [5], Lygon [13], and Forum [10, 11], are based on larger, more expressive, and harder to implement fragments of linear logic. When implementing these richer languages we are faced with the problem of splitting the contexts between the subproofs introduced by a bottom-up application of the multiplicative rules $\otimes R$, $\invamp L$, and $\multimap L$. A number of solutions have been proposed for the context splitting problem, commonly referred to as *lazy splitting* or *resource management* systems.

This paper presents a new resource management system for the Lolli language, although it can be applied to any linear logic language or prover involving splitting. The main contributions of this paper are: 1) we show that the choice of the structure employed to represent the contexts has a strong influence on the efficiency of the resource management system, 2) we propose a new proof system based on an efficient structure called *frame*, and 3) we estimate and compare the performance of several resource management systems.

The rest of the paper is organized as follows. In section 2 we briefly introduce the Lolli language and its proof system. We then revise the fundamental ideas of and contributions to the resource management strategies. In section 5 we revise two well-known resource management systems for the Lolli language and estimate their performance. We also present and compare our new resource management system with them. Finally, conclusions and further work are outlined.

2   The Lolli Programming Language

Lolli is a linear logic programming language proposed by Hodas and Miller [5, 4]. It can be seen as a linear refinement of λProlog. Lolli is defined as the *uniform* fragment of intuitionistic linear logic freely generated from $\top$, $\&$, $\multimap$, $\Rightarrow$, and $\forall$. In addition, the connectives 1, $\oplus$, $\otimes$, $!$, and $\exists$ can also be added to goal formulae without compromising uniformity; thus the formal syntax of Lolli program and goal formulae are

$$D ::= A \mid D_1 \& D_2 \mid G \multimap D \mid G \Rightarrow D \mid \forall x.D$$

$$G ::= A \mid \top \mid 1 \mid G_1 \& G_2 \mid G_1 \oplus G_2 \mid G_1 \otimes G_2 \mid D \multimap G \mid D \Rightarrow G \mid \forall x.D \mid \exists x.G \mid !G$$

where A denotes an atom. The proof system of Lolli can be described in terms of sequents of the form

$$\Psi; \Delta \longrightarrow G \quad \text{and} \quad \Psi; \Delta \stackrel{D}{\longrightarrow} G$$

where Ψ is a set of program formulae denoting the *intuitionistic* portion of the logic program, Δ is a multiset of program formulae denoting the *linear* portion

$$\frac{}{\Psi;\Delta \longrightarrow \top}\mathcal{L}\,\text{T-R} \qquad \frac{}{\Psi;\emptyset \longrightarrow 1}\mathcal{L}\,\text{1-R}$$

$$\frac{\Psi;\Delta \longrightarrow G_1 \quad \Psi;\Delta \longrightarrow G_2}{\Psi;\Delta \longrightarrow G_1 \,\&\, G_2}\mathcal{L}\,\&\,\text{-R}$$

$$\frac{\Psi;\emptyset \longrightarrow G}{\Psi;\emptyset \longrightarrow \,!G}\mathcal{L}\,!\text{-R} \qquad \frac{\Psi;\Delta \longrightarrow G_i}{\Psi;\Delta \longrightarrow G_1 \oplus G_2}\mathcal{L}\oplus\text{-R }(i=1,2)$$

$$\frac{\Psi;\Delta \uplus \{D\} \longrightarrow G}{\Psi;\Delta \longrightarrow D \multimap G}\mathcal{L}\multimap\text{-R} \qquad \frac{\Psi \cup \{D\};\Delta \longrightarrow G}{\Psi;\Delta \longrightarrow D \Rightarrow G}\mathcal{L}\Rightarrow\text{-R}$$

$$\frac{\Psi;\Delta_1 \longrightarrow G_1 \quad \Psi;\Delta_2 \longrightarrow G_2}{\Psi;\Delta_1 \uplus \Delta_2 \longrightarrow G_1 \otimes G_2}\mathcal{L}\otimes\text{-R}$$

$$\frac{\Psi;\Delta \longrightarrow G[t/x]}{\Psi;\Delta \longrightarrow \exists x.G}\mathcal{L}\exists\text{-R} \qquad \frac{\Psi;\Delta \longrightarrow G[y/x]}{\Psi;\Delta \longrightarrow \forall x.G}\mathcal{L}\forall\text{-R}$$

$$\frac{\Psi \cup \{D\};\Delta \xrightarrow{D} A}{\Psi \cup \{D\};\Delta \longrightarrow A}\mathcal{L}\,\text{decide }\Psi \qquad \frac{\Psi;\Delta \xrightarrow{D} A}{\Psi;\Delta \uplus \{D\} \longrightarrow A}\mathcal{L}\,\text{decide }\Delta$$

$$\frac{}{\Psi;\emptyset \xrightarrow{A} A}\mathcal{L}\,\text{initial}$$

$$\frac{\Psi;\Delta \xrightarrow{D[t/x]} A}{\Psi;\Delta \xrightarrow{\forall x.D} A}\mathcal{L}\forall\text{-L} \qquad \frac{\Psi;\Delta \xrightarrow{D_i} A}{\Psi;\Delta \xrightarrow{D_1\,\&\,D_2} A}\mathcal{L}\,\&\,\text{-L }(i=1,2)$$

$$\frac{\Psi;\Delta \xrightarrow{D} A \quad \Psi;\emptyset \longrightarrow G}{\Psi;\Delta \xrightarrow{G \Rightarrow D} A}\mathcal{L}\Rightarrow\text{-L}$$

$$\frac{\Psi;\Delta_1 \xrightarrow{D} A \quad \Psi;\Delta_2 \longrightarrow G}{\Psi;\Delta_1 \uplus \Delta_2 \xrightarrow{G \multimap D} A}\mathcal{L}\multimap\text{-L}$$

Fig. 1. Lolli proof system $\mathcal{L}$

of the logic program, D is a program formula, and G is a goal formula. Figure 1 shows the Lolli proof system $\mathcal{L}$.

3   Lazy Splitting: Assigning Formulae to Proofs

The successful implementation of linear logic languages and theorem provers involving splitting strongly depends on the efficiency of the method used to compute a suitable context split. As an instance of this, consider the $\mathcal{L}\otimes$-R rule

$$\frac{\Psi;\Delta_1 \longrightarrow G_1 \quad \Psi;\Delta_2 \longrightarrow G_2}{\Psi;\underbrace{\Delta_1 \uplus \Delta_2}_{\Delta} \longrightarrow G_1 \otimes G_2}\mathcal{L}\otimes\text{-R}.$$

When applying this rule bottom-up the context Δ must be split into Δ_1 and Δ_2. The problem above is that we do not know in advance how this split should be done. As the number of possible splits is exponential with respect to the cardinality of Δ, it is clear that a trivial implementation which simply backtracks through all these splits is terribly inefficient. This suggests that a better implementation technique must be developed instead, making it possible the practical application of the expressive power of linear logic. A commonly adopted solution is to split the contexts lazily [5, 4, 13, 2, 8]. In this section we briefly revise the fundamental ideas of and contributions to the lazy splitting strategy.

3.1 The Essence of Lazy Splitting

The key leading to lazy splitting is that, in general, linear logic proofs are *satiable*; i.e., they consume the resources they need but no more. In order to take advantage of this *satiability*, we let proofs receive an excess of formulae and return this excess instead of failing. In other words, we do not split contexts but pass the whole of them to the proofs as *input*, which first consume the formulae they need and then return the unused ones as *output*. That is, as we cannot guess the required split *a priori*, we let the very proofs determine it *a posteriori*, assigning formulae to proofs on demand. The strategy outlined is known as the *input-output model of resource consumption* and was first proposed by Hodas and Miller for the Lolli language [5].

3.2 Input and Output Formulae

According to the previous informal description, lazy splitting requires a sort of lazy sequent calculus such that lazy proofs receive an excess of formulae as input and return it as output. Therefore, lazy sequents must include both input and output portions as follows.

$$\underbrace{\Psi; \Delta \longrightarrow G}_{input} / \underbrace{\Delta'}_{output} \qquad\qquad \underbrace{\Psi; \Delta \overset{D}{\longrightarrow} G}_{input} / \underbrace{\Delta'}_{output}$$

The intended meaning is that the input context Δ could contain an excess of formulae while the output context Δ' returns this excess. Note that lazy splitting is concerned with the linear input Δ only. The intuitionistic input Ψ and the goal formula G are never split, and hence no output is required for them.

Lazy sequent rules must assure a correct flow of input and output. Obviously, input flows from the root to the leaves of the proof tree as rules are applied, while output flows from the leaves to the root along a finished proof branch. Lazy axiom rules appearing at the leaves of the proof tree transfer unused input to output. Lazy unary rules are trivial as they simply propagate input and output on the suitable direction. Lazy splitting rules do "the real work". For example, consider the lazy $\mathcal{L} \otimes$-R rule.

$$\frac{\Psi; \Delta \longrightarrow G_1 / \Delta' \qquad \Psi; \Delta' \longrightarrow G_2 / \Delta''}{\Psi; \Delta \longrightarrow G_1 \otimes G_2 / \Delta''}$$

First, the left subproof receives Δ, consumes the portion it requires and returns the unused one – Δ' – as output. Then, the right subproof receives Δ', consumes the portion it needs and returns the unused portion as output – Δ'' – to be further returned as the overall output of the whole proof. Of course, the lazy sequent at the root of a lazy proof cannot return any formula; i.e., its output context must be empty.

3.3   Returnable and Non-returnable Input

It is quite clear that a lazy proof can return an unused formula as output if and only if the aforementioned formula was previously passed to it as input. That is, a proof cannot return what it has not previously borrowed. Although this fact seems fairly trivial, it must be explicitly controlled by the lazy rules. For example, the naive lazy rule

$$\frac{\Psi; \{D\} \uplus \Delta \longrightarrow G \ / \ \Delta'}{\Psi; \Delta \longrightarrow D \multimap G \ / \ \Delta'}$$

is unsound, as the consumption of D is not enforced; i.e., D can be returned as output in Δ'. In order to avoid returning formulae out of scope, we can reformulate the rule above as follows:

$$\frac{\Psi; \{D\} \uplus \Delta \uplus \Delta' \longrightarrow G \ / \ \Delta'}{\Psi; \Delta \uplus \Delta' \longrightarrow D \multimap G \ / \ \Delta'}$$

Alternatively, we can distinguish two types of linear inputs: the *non-returnable input*, containing formulae which must be consumed; and the *returnable input*, containing formulae which could be consumed. Lazy sequents can then be extended as follows

$$\underbrace{\Psi; \Delta; \Pi \longrightarrow G}_{input} \ / \ \underbrace{\Pi'}_{output} \qquad\qquad \underbrace{\Psi; \Delta; \Pi \xrightarrow{D} G}_{input} \ / \ \underbrace{\Pi'}_{output}$$

where Δ stands for the *non-returnable* input and Π for the *returnable* input. The intended meaning is that the input context Δ must be fully consumed as it is non-returnable, while the input context Π could contain an excess of formulae which is returned by the output context Π'. Now, we can reformulate the rule for $\multimap$ using this extended lazy sequents yielding

$$\frac{\Psi; \{D\} \uplus \Delta; \Pi \longrightarrow G \ / \ \Pi'}{\Psi; \Delta; \Pi \longrightarrow D \multimap G \ / \ \Pi'}$$

where the formula D is added to the non-returnable portion of the linear program, enforcing its consumption within the proof of the goal G. The distinction between *returnable* and *non-returnable* formulae was first exploited by the lazy splitting system proposed by Winikoff and Harland [13] for the Lygon language, and later reintroduced – for different reasons – by Cervesato et al. [2] for the Lolli language.

4   Optimizing the Additive Connectives & and ⊤

The introduction of input and output formulae and the distinction between returnable and non-returnable input remove much – but not all – of the non-determinism from the resource distribution in linear logic proof search. There are, however, important optimizations proposed by Hodas [4] and Cervesato et al. [2] related to the treatment of the additive conjunction & and to the additive truth ⊤, which lead to a fully deterministic and much more efficient solution of the splitting problem. In this section, we briefly revise the aforementioned optimizations.

4.1 Learning from Experience: Looking-Ahead Needs

The $\mathcal{L}$ & -R rule in Fig.1 constitutes a special case not discussed so far: both subproofs must consume exactly the same linear formulae. The non-returnable input causes no problem, as in any case it must be fully consumed by both subproofs. On the other hand, each subproof consumes a portion of the returnable input and returns the remaining portion as output. To ensure that both subproofs consume exactly the same portion of the returnable input, their output contexts must be equal, thus we obtain the following lazy rule.

$$\frac{\Psi; \Delta; \Pi \longrightarrow G_1 \ / \ \Pi' \qquad \Psi; \Delta; \Pi \longrightarrow G_2 \ / \ \Pi'}{\Psi; \Delta; \Pi \longrightarrow G_1 \ \& \ G_2 \ / \ \Pi'}$$

As pointed out in [2] this rule can be optimized. In a sequential implementation, the left subproof determines the portion of the returnable input consumed; that is, $\Pi \backslash \Pi'$, where $\backslash$ denotes multiset difference. We can take advantage of this and pass the consumed portion as non-returnable input to the right subproof, enforcing its consumption. The optimized lazy rule is then

$$\frac{\Psi; \Delta; \Pi \longrightarrow G_1 \ / \ \Pi' \qquad \Psi; \Delta \uplus (\Pi \backslash \Pi'); \emptyset \longrightarrow G_2 \ / \ \emptyset}{\Psi; \Delta; \Pi \longrightarrow G_1 \ \& \ G_2 \ / \ \Pi'}$$

where the returnable input and the output of the right subproof remain empty.

4.2 Lazy Consumption: ⊤ Is Insatiable

The contents of the output are determined at the leaves of the proof tree by transferring the returnable input to the output. For example, the lazy *initial* rule transfers all the formulae from the returnable input to the output.

$$\overline{\Psi; \emptyset; \Pi \xrightarrow{\ A\ } A \ / \ \Pi}$$

On the other hand, the ⊤R rule consumes all of the non-returnable input as well as an unknown portion of the returnable input.

$$\overline{\Psi; \Delta; \Pi \uplus \Pi' \longrightarrow \top \ / \ \Pi'}$$

Determining Π', however, is not trivial. Recall the key idea leading to lazy splitting: linear logic proofs are satiable; that is, they consume what they need but no more. But ⊤ wants it all. In a sense, while the other connectives are satiable, ⊤ is not. The rule above shows that the returnable input must be split into two portions: one consumed by ⊤ and the other one returned as output. Thus, we are apparently faced with a context splitting problem again. Nevertheless, this splitting requires a quite different technique to be accomplished lazily. Hodas provided a first solution to this problem in [4], which was further refined by Cervesato et al. in [2].

The main idea is delaying the consumption of ⊤ by attaching a boolean *discard* indicator – referred to as *slack* indicator in [2] – to the output. This indicator denotes whether the associated output has been returned by a ⊤ or not. The lazy sequents have then the form

$$\Psi; \Delta; \Pi \longrightarrow G \mid \Pi'; d \qquad\qquad \Psi; \Delta; \Pi \stackrel{D}{\longrightarrow} G \mid \Pi'; d$$

where d is the aforementioned discard indicator. Now, the lazy ⊤ rule does not consume any portion of the returnable input but transfers it to the output and sets the discard indicator to 1 as follows.

$$\overline{\Psi; \Delta; \Pi \longrightarrow \top \mid \Pi; 1}$$

By returning all of the returnable input, the real consumption of ⊤ is delayed and all of the returnable input is made available to be consumed elsewhere. In a sense, this is not exactly lazy splitting but *lazy consumption*. On the other hand, the consumption of the output returned by a ⊤ is no longer mandatory, as in any case it could have been consumed by that ⊤. Thus, if a portion of the returned output is not consumed elsewhere, it is assigned to any ⊤ it has visited – if any – and silently discarded. Thus the final consumption of ⊤ is lazily determined when the unused output is discarded. Of course, the other lazy axiom rules set the indicator to 0, as their output must be consumed elsewhere. Lazy unary rules are trivial, as they simply propagate both the contexts and the discard indicator. The lazy binary rules are split into two rules, depending on the value of the discard indicator returned by the left subproof. Further details of this solution can be consulted in [4, 2].

5   A Comparison of Three Resource Management Methods

In this section, we introduce a new resource management system $\mathcal{LL}$ and compare it to previous proposals. In essence, the basic principle of these systems is the same. The main difference comes from the structure employed to represent the contexts. We show that this has a strong influence on the performance of the proof system. It is worth noting that we are concerned with the cost incurred by the management of resources; and hence, we do not take into account the cost of unification or clause selection.

5.1   The $\mathcal{IO}$ Proof System: The List Approach

The $\mathcal{IO}$ proof system for Lolli was proposed by Hodas and Miller in [5]. It is the first system ever devised to solve the context splitting problem; some optimizations were later proposed in [2], whereas the $\top$ optimization was first proposed by Hodas in [4]. The formal definitions and the proof system in this section are taken from [4].

The $\mathcal{IO}$ system uses lists to represent a sort of contexts named $\mathcal{IO}$-contexts, defined as follows.

Definition 1 ($\mathcal{IO}$-context). *An $\mathcal{IO}$-context is a list of formulae, each of which is either a program formula, a program formula marked with a* !, *or a constant named* del. *The list is built with the usual constructors* :: *and* nil.

The lazy sequents, named $\mathcal{IO}$-sequents, have the form $I\{G\}O$ where I and O are $\mathcal{IO}$-contexts and G is a goal formula. The intended reading is that the goal G is solved from the input I and returns the output O. The input I contains the logic program encoded as follows: a program formula stands for a linear clause, a program formula marked with ! for an intuitionistic clause, and a constant *del* for a deleted (i.e., used) clause. The output O contains individual constraints for each program formula in I; that is, the *i-th* element of O imposes a consumption constraint on the *i-th* element of I. These constraints are encoded as follows: if the *i-th* element of O is a program formula – either marked or not with a ! – then the *i-th* element of I must be returned as output. Note that if the *i-th* element of O is a non-!'ed formula, this implies that the *i-th* element of I is a linear clause which cannot be used to construct the proof. The $\mathcal{IO}$ proof system is the only one of the proof systems considered in this paper imposing such a bizarre behavior: an $\mathcal{IO}$ lazy proof receives linear formulae it cannot use. On the other hand, a constant *del* in the *i-th* position of O indicates that the *i-th* element of I is a linear clause which must be consumed. The $\mathcal{IO}$ system works by checking that the logic program I satisfies the constraints O at certain nodes of the proof tree. In order to do that, two relations between $\mathcal{IO}$-contexts must be defined:

Definition 2 (pick(I,O,R)). *The ternary relation* pick(I,O,R) *holds if R occurs in the $\mathcal{IO}$-context I, and O results from replacing that occurrence of R in I with the constant* del. *The relation also holds if* !R *occurs in I, and I and O are equal.*

Definition 3 (subcontext(O,I)). *An $\mathcal{IO}$-context O is a* subcontext *of an $\mathcal{IO}$-context I, denoted by the predicate* subcontext(O,I), *if O arises from replacing zero or more non-!'ed elements from I with* del.

Figure 2 shows the $\mathcal{IO}$ proof system for propositional Lolli. In order to estimate the performance of an implementation of the $\mathcal{IO}$ proof system we need to determine the form of the $\mathcal{IO}$-contexts. It should be clear that the input is always a list of the form $I_1 :: \cdots :: I_m :: nil$, where I_i is a program formula – either !'ed or not – or the constant *del*. To determine the form of the output, consider the $\mathcal{IO} \otimes$ rule. The left subproof introduces a new variable M. On the other hand, each occurrence of an implication in a goal will add a new constraint to the output so, in general, the output $\mathcal{IO}$-contexts have the form

$$\frac{}{I\{1\}I}\mathcal{IO}1 \qquad \frac{subcontext(O,I)}{I\{\top\}O}\mathcal{IO}\top \qquad \frac{I\{G\}I}{I\{!G\}I}\mathcal{IO}\,!$$

$$\frac{I\{G_1\}M \quad M\{G_2\}O}{I\{G_1 \otimes G_2\}O}\mathcal{IO}\otimes \qquad \frac{I\{G_1\}O \quad I\{G_2\}O}{I\{G_1 \,\&\, G_2\}O}\mathcal{IO}\,\&$$

$$\frac{R :: I\{G\}del :: O}{I\{R \multimap G\}O}\mathcal{IO}\multimap \qquad \frac{!R :: I\{G\}!\,R :: O}{I\{R \Rightarrow G\}O}\mathcal{IO}\Rightarrow$$

$$\frac{pick(I,O,A)}{I\{A\}O}\mathcal{IO}\,pickA \qquad \frac{pick(I,M,G \multimap A) \quad M\{G\}O}{I\{A\}O}\mathcal{IO}\,pick{-}\circ$$

$$\frac{pick(I,O,G \Rightarrow A) \quad O\{G\}O}{I\{A\}O}\mathcal{IO}\,pick \Rightarrow$$

Fig. 2. Propositional Lolli proof system $\mathcal{IO}$

$O_1 :: \cdots :: O_n :: M$, where O_i is a !'ed program formula or the constant *del*, and M is a variable; that is, the output has a known prefix $O_1 :: \cdots :: O_n$ and an unknown suffix M. Finally, consider the $\mathcal{IO}\,!$ rule. To apply this rule, the input and the output must be equal; that is, $I_1 :: \cdots :: I_m :: nil = O_1 :: \cdots :: O_n :: M$, where $m \geq n$. This requires to compare the first n elements of both lists and to transfer $m - n$ elements from the input to the output. Note that this is the only way to insert a non-!'ed formula into the output.

Now that we have determined the form of the $\mathcal{IO}$-contexts, it is an easy matter to estimate the cost of the $\mathcal{IO}$ rules. It is clear that the cost of the $\mathcal{IO}\,!$ rule is $O(n)$, i.e., it is proportional to the number of elements of the instantied prefix of O. The same reasoning can be applied to other rules enforcing equality of I and O; namely $\mathcal{IO}1$, $\mathcal{IO}\,pickA$, and $\mathcal{IO}\,pick \Rightarrow$. On the other hand, $\mathcal{IO}\top$ has cost $O(n)$ as well, due to the *subcontext* relation. The rest of the rules are $O(1)$, since they do not involve traversing any structure.

The *pick* problem. Recall that it is possible for an $\mathcal{IO}$ proof to receive formulae as input which cannot be used. This singularity is responsible of a severe flaw in the efficiency of the $\mathcal{IO}$ system, which we call the *pick problem*. Consider, for instance, the proof

$$\frac{\dfrac{I\{a\}M \quad M\{b\}I}{I\{(a \otimes b)\}I}}{I\{!(a \otimes b)\}I}$$

In the proof above, the application of the $\mathcal{IO}\,!$ rule enforces the equality of the input and output $\mathcal{IO}$-contexts. This could transfer non-!'ed formulae from the input to the output, imposing the constraint that these formulae cannot be used to build the proof. On the other hand, the application of $\mathcal{IO}\otimes$ replaces the output context I by a new variable M, eliminating all of the constraints on the subproof of the goal a. Thus, the system attempts to build a proof for a using all of the formulae in the input I, including those we know cannot be used. This constraint is restored for the proof of the goal b and checked at the leaves of the proof subtree. The same problem arises from the rule $\mathcal{IO}pick{-}\!\circ$, where a formula $G \multimap A$ is picked without taking into account the current constraints.

5.2   The $\mathcal{LL}$ Proof System: The Frame Approach

In subsection 3.3 an important principle of the lazy splitting strategy was stated: a lazy proof cannot return a formula that has not borrowed previously. That is, a lazy proof system must preserve the scope of formulae. This was solved for individual formulae introduced by implications by distinguishing two classes of contexts: the non-returnable input context and the returnable one. The splitting rules also introduce a scope problem not discussed so far. Consider the lazy $\otimes$ rule (we drop here the discard indicator)

$$\frac{\Psi; \emptyset; (\Delta \uplus \Pi) \longrightarrow G_1 \; / \; (\Delta' \uplus \Pi') \quad \Psi; \Delta'; \Pi' \longrightarrow G_2 \; / \; \Pi''}{\Psi; \Delta; \Pi \longrightarrow G_1 \otimes G_2 \; / \; \Pi''} .$$

In the rule above, the proof of $G_1 \otimes G_2$ cannot return any formula from Δ; i.e., the scope of Δ must be preserved. On the one hand, Δ must be temporarily combined with Π to be lazily split. On the other hand, the residue Δ' must be restored in the original scope of Δ to ensure that Δ is fully consumed. According to the proof above, the returnable input context $(\Delta \uplus \Pi)$ and the output context $(\Delta' \uplus \Pi')$ should be arranged to preserve the scope of the formulae. In this section we propose a new structure for these contexts which we call a *frame*. We show that frames are an appropriate choice for these contexts, as they encode scope of formulae both effectively and efficiently. A new frame-based lazy proof system $\mathcal{LL}$ for Lolli is presented and proved to be logically equivalent to the original proof system $\mathcal{L}$. Finally, the cost of the $\mathcal{LL}$ lazy rules is estimated.

The $\mathcal{LL}$ proof system uses frames to represent returnable input contexts and output contexts. Frames are formally defined as follows:

Definition 4 (Frame). *A frame is a list of multisets. The empty frame is denoted by the constant* nil, *while* $\Delta :: \Pi$ *denotes the frame obtained by concatenating the multiset* Δ *and the frame* Π.

In order to formulate a frame-based lazy proof system, we need to define the following relations on frames:

Definition 5 (Frame Equality). *The equality on frames is recursively defined upon the equality of multisets as follows:*

1. nil $=$ nil
2. $\Delta_1 :: \Pi_1 = \Delta_2 :: \Pi_2 \Leftrightarrow (\Delta_1 = \Delta_2) \wedge (\Pi_1 = \Pi_2)$

Definition 6 (Inclusion Relation, $\sqsubseteq$). *The inclusion relation on frames is recursively defined upon the inclusion relation on multisets as follows:*

1. nil $\sqsubseteq$ nil
2. $\Delta_1 :: \Pi_1 \sqsubseteq \Delta_2 :: \Pi_2 \Leftrightarrow (\Delta_1 \subseteq \Delta_2) \wedge (\Pi_1 \sqsubseteq \Pi_2)$

Definition 7 (Frame Insert Operator, ◁). *Given a frame Π and a formula F, $\Pi \lhd F$ denotes a frame obtained by inserting one occurrence of F into a multiset of the frame Π.*

Definition 8 (Frame Union, ⊔). *Given two frames, their union frame is defined upon the multiset union ⊎ as follows:*

1. $\text{nil} \sqcup \text{nil} =_{def} \text{nil}$
2. $\Delta_1 :: \Pi_1 \sqcup \Delta_2 :: \Pi_2 =_{def} (\Delta_1 \uplus \Delta_2) :: (\Pi_1 \sqcup \Pi_2)$

Definition 9 (Frame Multiset Difference, −). *Given two frames, their multiset difference is the multiset defined as follows:*

1. $\text{nil} - \text{nil} =_{def} \emptyset$
2. $\Delta_1 :: \Pi_1 - \Delta_2 :: \Pi_2 =_{def} (\Delta_1 \backslash \Delta_2) \uplus (\Pi_1 - \Pi_2)$

where \ denotes the multiset difference.

Figure 3 shows the $\mathcal{LL}$ proof system. The sequents of this system have the form

$$\Psi; \Delta; \Pi \longrightarrow G \;/\; \Pi'; d \quad \text{and} \quad \Psi; \Delta; \Pi \xrightarrow{D} G \;/\; \Pi'; d$$

where Π and Π' are frames, and the rest of the components are defined as in section 4. Most of the lazy rules are obtained by a straightforward application of the ideas presented in sections 3 and 4. The main novelty is in the $\mathcal{LL} \otimes_d$ -R and $\mathcal{LL} \multimap_d$ -L rules, where the frames are effectively used to preserve the scope of the formulae.

Soundness and Completeness The $\mathcal{LL}$ lazy proof system in Fig. 3 is logically equivalent to the $\mathcal{L}$ proof system in Fig. 1. The correctness and completeness theorems are stated below. Formal proofs for a frame-based resource management system for Forum [10, 11] – an asynchronous multiple-conclusion presentation of higher order linear logic – are available [9]. The inclusion proposition states an important property of $\mathcal{LL}$; namely, scope of formulae is preserved.

Proposition 1 (Inclusion). *The output is a subframe of the returnable input:*

1. *If $\Psi; \Delta; \Pi \longrightarrow G \;/\; \Pi'; d$ then $\Pi' \sqsubseteq \Pi$*
2. *If $\Psi; \Delta; \Pi \xrightarrow{D} G \;/\; \Pi'; d$ then $\Pi' \sqsubseteq \Pi$*

In the following results, we refer to either $\mathcal{LL}$ or $\mathcal{L}$ proof systems depending on the aspect of the involved sequent.

Theorem 1 (Soundness). *$\mathcal{LL}$ is sound with respect to $\mathcal{L}$; that is, for all Δ':*

1. *If $\Psi; \Delta; \Pi \longrightarrow G \;/\; \Pi'; 0$ then $\Psi; \Delta \uplus (\Pi - \Pi') \longrightarrow G$*
2. *If $\Psi; \Delta; \Pi \xrightarrow{D} G \;/\; \Pi'; 0$ then $\Psi; \Delta \uplus (\Pi - \Pi') \xrightarrow{D} G$*
3. *If $\Psi; \Delta; \Pi \longrightarrow G \;/\; \Pi'; 1$ then $\Psi; \Delta \uplus (\Pi - \Pi') \uplus \Delta' \longrightarrow G$*

$$\frac{}{\Psi;\Delta;\Pi \longrightarrow \top\ /\ \Pi;1}\,\mathcal{LL}\,\text{T-R} \qquad \frac{}{\Psi;\emptyset;\Pi \longrightarrow 1\ /\ \Pi;0}\,\mathcal{LL}\,1\text{-R}$$

$$\frac{\Psi;\Delta;\Pi \longrightarrow G_1\ /\ \Pi';0 \quad \Psi;\Delta \uplus (\Pi-\Pi');\text{nil} \longrightarrow G_2\ /\ \text{nil};d}{\Psi;\Delta;\Pi \longrightarrow G_1\,\&\,G_2\ /\ \Pi';0}\,\mathcal{LL}\,\&_0\text{-R}$$

$$\frac{\Psi;\Delta;\Pi \longrightarrow G_1\ /\ \Pi';1 \quad \Psi;\Delta \uplus (\Pi-\Pi');\Pi' \longrightarrow G_2\ /\ \Pi'';d}{\Psi;\Delta;\Pi \longrightarrow G_1\,\&\,G_2\ /\ \Pi'';d}\,\mathcal{LL}\,\&_1\text{-R}$$

$$\frac{\Psi;\emptyset;\text{nil} \longrightarrow G\ /\ \text{nil};d}{\Psi;\emptyset;\Pi \longrightarrow\ !G\ /\ \Pi;0}\,\mathcal{LL}\,!\text{-R} \qquad \frac{\Psi;\Delta;\Pi \longrightarrow G_i\ /\ \Pi';d}{\Psi;\Delta;\Pi \longrightarrow G_1 \oplus G_2\ /\ \Pi';d}\,\mathcal{LL}\,\oplus\text{-R}\ (i=1,2)$$

$$\frac{\Psi;\Delta \uplus \{D\};\Pi \longrightarrow G\ /\ \Pi';d}{\Psi;\Delta;\Pi \longrightarrow D \multimap G\ /\ \Pi';d}\,\mathcal{LL}\,\multimap\text{-R} \qquad \frac{\Psi \cup \{D\};\Delta;\Pi \longrightarrow G\ /\ \Pi';d}{\Psi;\Delta;\Pi \longrightarrow D \Rightarrow G\ /\ \Pi';d}\,\mathcal{LL}\,\Rightarrow\text{-R}$$

$$\frac{\Psi;\emptyset;\Delta::\Pi \longrightarrow G_1\ /\ \Delta'::\Pi';0 \quad \Psi;\Delta';\Pi' \longrightarrow G_2\ /\ \Pi'';d}{\Psi;\Delta;\Pi \longrightarrow G_1 \otimes G_2\ /\ \Pi'';d}\,\mathcal{LL}\,\otimes_0\text{-R}$$

$$\frac{\Psi;\emptyset;\Delta::\Pi \longrightarrow G_1\ /\ \Delta'::\Pi';1 \quad \Psi;\emptyset;\Delta'::\Pi' \longrightarrow G_2\ /\ \Delta''::\Pi'';d}{\Psi;\Delta;\Pi \longrightarrow G_1 \otimes G_2\ /\ \Pi'';1}\,\mathcal{LL}\,\otimes_1\text{-R}$$

$$\frac{\Psi;\Delta;\Pi \longrightarrow G[t/x]\ /\ \Pi';d}{\Psi;\Delta;\Pi \longrightarrow \exists x.G\ /\ \Pi';d}\,\mathcal{LL}\,\exists\text{-R} \qquad \frac{\Psi;\Delta;\Pi \longrightarrow G[y/x]\ /\ \Pi';d}{\Psi;\Delta;\Pi \longrightarrow \forall x.G\ /\ \Pi';d}\,\mathcal{LL}\,\forall\text{-R}$$

$$\frac{\Psi \cup \{D\};\Delta;\Pi \xrightarrow{D} A\ /\ \Pi';d}{\Psi \cup \{D\};\Delta;\Pi \longrightarrow A\ /\ \Pi';d}\,\mathcal{LL}\,\text{decide }\Psi \qquad \frac{\Psi;\Delta;\Pi \xrightarrow{D} A\ /\ \Pi';d}{\Psi;\Delta \uplus \{D\};\Pi \longrightarrow A\ /\ \Pi';d}\,\mathcal{LL}\,\text{decide }\Delta$$

$$\frac{\Psi;\Delta;\Pi \xrightarrow{D} A\ /\ \Pi';d}{\Psi;\Delta;\Pi \triangleleft D \longrightarrow A\ /\ \Pi';d}\,\mathcal{LL}\,\text{decide }\Pi$$

$$\frac{}{\Psi;\emptyset;\Pi \xrightarrow{A} A\ /\ \Pi;0}\,\mathcal{LL}\,\text{initial}$$

$$\frac{\Psi;\Delta;\Pi \xrightarrow{D[t/x]} A\ /\ \Pi';d}{\Psi;\Delta;\Pi \xrightarrow{\forall x.D} A\ /\ \Pi';d}\,\mathcal{LL}\,\forall\text{-L} \qquad \frac{\Psi;\Delta;\Pi \xrightarrow{D_i} A\ /\ \Pi';d}{\Psi;\Delta;\Pi \xrightarrow{D_1 \& D_2} A\ /\ \Pi';d}\,\mathcal{LL}\,\&\text{-L}\,(i=1,2)$$

$$\frac{\Psi;\Delta;\Pi \xrightarrow{D} A\ /\ \Pi';d_1 \quad \Psi;\emptyset;\text{nil} \longrightarrow G\ /\ \text{nil};d_2}{\Psi;\Delta;\Pi \xrightarrow{G \Rightarrow D} A\ /\ \Pi';d_1}\,\mathcal{LL}\,\Rightarrow\text{-L}$$

$$\frac{\Psi;\emptyset;\Delta::\Pi \xrightarrow{D} A\ /\ \Delta'::\Pi';0 \quad \Psi;\Delta';\Pi' \longrightarrow G\ /\ \Pi'';d}{\Psi;\Delta;\Pi \xrightarrow{G \multimap D} A\ /\ \Pi'';d}\,\mathcal{LL}\,\multimap_0\text{-L}$$

$$\frac{\Psi;\emptyset;\Delta::\Pi \xrightarrow{D} A\ /\ \Delta'::\Pi';1 \quad \Psi;\emptyset;\Delta'::\Pi' \longrightarrow G\ /\ \Delta''::\Pi'';d}{\Psi;\Delta;\Pi \xrightarrow{G \multimap D} A\ /\ \Pi'';1}\,\mathcal{LL}\,\multimap_1\text{-L}$$

Fig. 3. Lolli proof system $\mathcal{LL}$

4. If $\Psi; \Delta; \Pi \xrightarrow{D} G \mid \Pi'; 1$ then $\Psi; \Delta \uplus (\Pi - \Pi') \uplus \Delta' \xrightarrow{D} G$

This result establishes a mapping between $\mathcal{LC}$ and $\mathcal{L}$ proofs. Basically, a $\mathcal{LC}$ proof is mapped into a $\mathcal{L}$ proof receiving the portion of the returnable input which is actually consumed $\Pi - \Pi'$. In addition, if the $\mathcal{LC}$ proof sets the discard to 1, then the $\mathcal{L}$ proof can be obtained even if arbitrary resources Δ' were considered.

Theorem 2 (Completeness). $\mathcal{LC}$ *is complete with respect to* $\mathcal{L}$*; that is, for all* Π *and* $d = 0 \vee d = 1$:

1. *If* $\Psi; \Delta \longrightarrow G$ *then* $\Psi; \Delta; \Pi \longrightarrow G \mid \Pi; d$
2. *If* $\Psi; \Delta \xrightarrow{D} G$ *then* $\Psi; \Delta; \Pi \xrightarrow{D} G \mid \Pi; d$

The completeness theorem states that every $\mathcal{L}$ proof is mapped into a $\mathcal{LC}$ proof where all of the additional returnable input Π is simply returned.

Estimating the cost of the $\mathcal{LC}$ rules. In order to estimate the cost of a direct implementation of the $\mathcal{LC}$ rules there is an important detail it is worth noting. The output context does not encode any consumption constraint as in the Hodas-Miller method; but it is conceived as a means of transferring unused returnable input from a given subproof to another one. This means that the output remains unknown while a branch of the proof is being constructed. In fact, the lazy sequent rules of $\mathcal{LC}$ can be classified into three groups with respect to the way they cope with output contexts; namely, the transferring rules, the propagating rules and the splitting rules. The transferring rules $\mathcal{LC}$ T-R, $\mathcal{LC}$ 1-R, $\mathcal{LC}$!-R, and $\mathcal{LC}$ initial transfer returnable input to the output. Note that this transfer can be efficiently done in $O(1)$; which is the cost of these rules. The propagating rules simply propagate the output from the premises to the conclusion; that is, the cost of $\mathcal{LC} \oplus$-R, $\mathcal{LC} \multimap$-R, $\mathcal{LC} \Rightarrow$-R, $\mathcal{LC} \exists$-R, $\mathcal{LC} \forall$-R, $\mathcal{LC} \forall$-L, $\mathcal{LC}$ & -L, $\mathcal{LC} \Rightarrow$-L, and the decide rules is $O(1)$ as well. The splitting rules $\mathcal{LC} \otimes_d$-R and $\mathcal{LC} \multimap_d$-L take advantage of the frame structure, and are the main contribution of the $\mathcal{LC}$ proof system. Notice that these rules manipulate the frame as a stack: the left premise pushes the non-returnable input Δ onto the frame, while the right subproof pops Δ' from the frame. Both operations are clearly $O(1)$, and hence, the overall cost of the splitting rules is $O(1)$. This way, the frame structure allows encoding and restoring the scope of the formulae at a minimal cost.

Again, the $\mathcal{LC}$ &$_d$-R rule constitutes a special case. While at first sight it seems to be a propagating rule, it does incur in a higher cost due to the optimization presented in section 4. Note that the left premise of this rule receives $\Delta \uplus (\Pi - \Pi')$ as non-returnable input. The multiset union can be implemented at cost $O(1)$ since we do not need to collapse its elements; but the frame difference requires traversing the frames. Therefore, the cost of this rule is $O(n)$; i.e., it is proportional to the size of the frames involved. This cost seems to be unavoidable: the non-optimized $\& - R$ rule is $O(n)$ as well, since it compares the output contexts of both premises. On the other hand, the optimized rule removes a source of non-determinism, as it enforces the consumption of the formulae. As the rest of the $\mathcal{LC}$ rules are $O(1)$, we consider our $\mathcal{LC}$ system to be optimal.

5.3   The $\mathcal{RM}3$ Proof System: The Labelled Set Approach

The $\mathcal{RM}3$ for Lolli was proposed by Cervesato et al. in [2]. This system introduced an elegant notation for the sequents and the rules. In particular, it explicitly distinguishes non-returnable and returnable input contexts. The system
also replaces the left rules by a resolution calculus which translates a program
formula into a goal one.

The $\mathcal{RM}3$ system represents contexts as labelled sets. A labelled set is formally defined as follows:

Definition 10 (Labelled Set). *A labelled set is a set such that each element
has a unique label attached to it.*

The $\mathcal{RM}3$ system can be described in terms of sequents of the form

$$\Psi; \Delta; \Pi \longrightarrow G \mid \Pi'; d$$

where Ψ, Δ, Π, and Π' are labelled sets of formulae. The intended reading
is the usual one. It is worth noting that the use of labels in $\mathcal{RM}3$ is not an
implementation detail. On the contrary, these labels are required to ensure the
soundness and completeness of the system.

Apart from the resolution calculus, the only difference between $\mathcal{RM}3$ and
$\mathcal{LL}$ is the splitting $\otimes - R$ rule. The rest of the right rules of $\mathcal{LL}$ system are
isomorphic to the rules of $\mathcal{RM}3$[1]. Hence, the cost of these $\mathcal{RM}3$ rules is equal
to the cost of the corresponding $\mathcal{LL}$ rules: $O(n)$ for $\& - R$ and $O(1)$ for the rest.

The $\otimes_d - R$ rules of the $\mathcal{RM}3$ system are as follows:

$$\frac{\Psi; \emptyset; \Delta \uplus \Pi \longrightarrow G_1 \mid \Pi'; 0 \quad \Psi; \Delta \cap \Pi'; \Pi \cap \Pi' \longrightarrow G_2 \mid \Pi''; d}{\Psi; \Delta; \Pi \longrightarrow G_1 \otimes G_2 \mid \Pi'; d}$$

$$\frac{\Psi; \emptyset; \Delta \uplus \Pi \longrightarrow G_1 \mid \Pi'; 1 \quad \Psi; \emptyset; \Pi' \longrightarrow G_2 \mid \Pi''; d}{\Psi; \Delta; \Pi \longrightarrow G_1 \otimes G_2 \mid \Pi \cap \Pi'; 1}$$

Note that a labelled set does not provide structure to encode the scope of the
formulae it contains. Therefore, to restore the formulae on the appropriate scope,
an intersection operation is required. This involves traversing the labelled sets
being intersected; and hence, the rules above are $O(n)$; i.e., their cost is proportional to the cardinal of the labelled sets involved. The same cost arises for the
absent $-\circ - L$ rule, since each occurrence of this connective is translated to a
$\otimes - R$ by the resolution calculus.

The cost incurred by these two connectives is crucial for the overall performance of a practical implementation of Lolli, since these connectives are widely
employed. In particular, $\otimes$ usually occurs deeply nested. This is evidenced by
the concrete syntax of Lolli, which employs :- for $-\circ$ and , (comma) for $\otimes$.

---

[1] However, we first discovered and applied the frame approach to the Lygon lazy
   splitting system [13], and then to the $\mathcal{RM}3$ system

6   Conclusions and Further Work

It is well-known that lazy splitting strongly improves the performance of the implementation of any linear logic language or theorem prover involving context splitting. In this paper, we have shown that the structure employed to represent contexts is crucial for the efficiency of lazy splitting as well. In particular, we have introduced a new data structure we call $frame$ to represent contexts, which encodes the scope of the formulae both effectively and efficiently. We have also shown that, except for the $\& - R$ rule, it is possible to reduce the cost of all of the rules to $O(1)$, excluding the cost of unification and clause selection incurred by the typical implementation of the *decide* rules. To the best of our knowledge, $\mathcal{LC}$ is the only resource management system featuring this performance. According to the results obtained, we think the $\mathcal{LC}$ resource management is optimal. We have applied our frame approach to Forum [11] and implemented UMA Forum (available from http:\\www.lcc.uma.es\~lopez\umaforum), a prototype interpreter of a subset of first order Forum. This implementation employs a single data structure to store the logic program (i.e., the Ψ, Δ, and Π contexts) in such a way that the order of the clauses is preserved. Whereas this is irrelevant from the point of view of automated theorem proving, it endows a logic programming language with a predictable behavior. Given the capability of linear logic to express concurrency, we intend to develop a parallel version of our resource management system.

7   Acknowledgments

The authors are very grateful to Iliano Cervesato, Narciso Martí-Oliet, Dale Miller, Christian Urban, and the anonymous referees for their helpful comments on this work. Pablo López is supported by the Spanish Ministry of Education and Culture through a Ph.D. Research Scholarship. This work has been partially supported by the CICYT project TIC98-0445-C03-03.

References

1. J.M. Andreoli and R. Pareschi. Linear Objects: Logical Processes with Built-in Inheritance. *New Generation Computing*, 9(3-4):445–473, 1991.
2. I. Cervesato, J. Hodas, and F. Pfenning. Efficient Resource Management for Linear Logic Proof Search. *Proceedings of the 1996 International Workshop on Extensions of Logic Programming*, 1996.
3. J.-Y. Girard. Linear Logic. *Theoretical Computer Science*, 50, pp. 1–102. 1987.
4. J.S. Hodas. *Logic Programming in Intuitionistic Linear Logic: Theory, Design and Implementation*. PhD Thesis. University of Pennsylvania, Department of Computer and Information Science, 1994.
5. J.S. Hodas and D. Miller. Logic Programming in a Fragment of Intuitionistic Linear Logic. *Information and Computation*, 110(2), pp. 327–365, 1994.
6. N. Kobayashi and A. Yonezawa. ACL – a Concurrent Linear Logic Programming Paradigm. In *International Logic Programming Symposium*, pp. 279–294, 1993.

7. P. López . *Implementación de un Lenguaje de Programación basado en Lógica Lineal.* Master's Thesis supervised by E. Pimentel. Computer Science Department. University of Málaga. 1996.
8. P. López and E. Pimentel. A Lazy Splitting System for Forum. In M. Falaschi, M. Navarro, and A. Policriti, editors, *Proceedings of the Joint Conference on Declarative Programming – APPIA-GULP-PRODE'97*, pp. 247–258, Grado, Italy, 1997.
9. P. López and E. Pimentel. Resource Managament for Linear Logic Proof Search. Manuscript, 1999.
10. D. Miller. A Multiple-Conclusion Meta-Logic. S. Abramsky, editor, *Proceedings of the 1994 Symposium on Logic in Computer Science*, pp. 272–281, 1994.
11. D. Miller. Forum: A Multiple-Conclusion Specification Logic. *Theoretical Computer Science*, 165(1), pp.201–232, 1996.
12. C. Urban. *Forum and its Implementation.* MPhil Thesis. Department of Computer Science, University of St. Andrews, 1996.
13. M. Winikoff and J. Harland. Implementing the Linear Logic Programming Language Lygon. In J. Lloyd, editor, *Proceedings of the 1995 International Logic Programming Symposium*, pp. 66–80, 1995.

Focusing and Proof-Nets in Linear and Non-commutative Logic

Jean-Marc Andreoli[1] and Roberto Maieli[2]*

[1] Xerox Research Centre Europe, 38240 Meylan, France
Jean-Marc.Andreoli@xrce.xerox.com,
Web: http://www.xrce.xerox.com/people/andreoli
[2] Logica - Università "Roma 3", 00154 Roma, Italy
maieli@phil.uniroma3.it

Abstract. Linear Logic [4] has raised a lot of interest in computer research, especially because of its resource sensitive nature. One line of
research studies proof construction procedures and their interpretation
as computational models, in the "Logic Programming" tradition. An
efficient proof search procedure, based on a proof normalization result
called "Focusing", has been described in [2]. Focusing is described in
terms of the sequent system of commutative Linear Logic, which it refines in two steps. It is shown here that Focusing can also be interpreted
in the proof-net formalism, where it appears, at least in the multiplicative fragment, to be a simple refinement of the "Splitting lemma" for
proof-nets. This change of perspective allows to generalize the Focusing
result to (the multiplicative fragment of) any logic where the "Splitting
lemma" holds. This is, in particular, the case of the Non-Commutative
logic of [1], and all the computational exploitation of Focusing which
has been performed in the commutative case can thus be revised and
adapted to the non commutative case.

1 Introduction

Linear Logic [4] has raised a lot of interest in computer research, especially because of its resource sensitive nature. One line of research, supported by systems
such as LO [3], Lambda-Prolog [8], Forum [9] or Lolli [7], studies proof construction procedures and their interpretation as computational models, in the "Logic
Programming" tradition. An efficient proof-search procedure for Linear Logic,
based on a proof normalization result called "Focusing", has been described
in [2]. Focusing is described there in terms of the sequent system of (commutative) Linear Logic, which it refines in two steps ("Dyadic", resp. "Triadic"
system). Basically, each refinement eliminates redundancies in proof-search due

---

* This work was performed while the second author was visiting XRCE; this visit was
supported by the European TMR (*Training and Mobility for Researchers*) Network
"Linear Logic in Computer Science" (esp. the Rome and Marseille sites, XRCE being
attached to the latter).

to irrelevant sequentializations of inference figures in the sequent-based representation of proofs. The expressive power of Focusing is captured in a crisp way in a fully representative fragment of Linear Logic, called "LinLog", introduced in [2] together with a normalization procedure from Linear Logic to LinLog. This procedure allows to represent in LinLog all the fragments considered in the various systems mentioned above.

It is shown here that Focusing can also be interpreted in the proof-net formalism, where it appears, at least in the multiplicative fragment, to be a simple refinement of the "Splitting lemma" for proof-nets. The Splitting lemma is at the core of the Sequentialization procedures for proof-nets, and Focusing thus appears as a sequentialization strategy. This change of perspective allows to generalize the Focusing result to (the multiplicative fragment of) any logic where the "Splitting lemma" holds. This is, in particular, the case of the Non-Commutative logic of [1], and all the computational exploitation of Focusing which has been performed in the commutative case can thus be revised and adapted to the non commutative case. The expected outcome of such a program is a finer model of computational resources and agent-based coordination of these resources.

But beyond the technical results, the aim of this paper is to show that Focusing is not limited to a technique adapted to the specific problem of computational proof search, although that was its original motivation (in the line of uniform proofs for Intuitionistic Logic [10]). Focusing is an intrinsic property of resource-conscious logics which admit an involutive duality. It captures in a single framework the quite straightforward and well-known property of "invertibility" of some connectives (called "asynchronous" or negative) together with the not-so-well-known dual of this property which applies to the dual connectives (called "synchronous" or positive), through so-called "critical focusing sections". Focusing, just as Cut-elimination, is a purely logical property, and it is not surprising that it appears under different forms in different contexts, for instance in sequent systems (through search procedures), or in proof-nets (through sequentialization), or even in the more ambitious program of reformulation of Logic known as "Ludics" [5, 6].

Section 2 recalls prior art and notations exploited in this paper. Section 3 describes the main result of this paper, i.e. a reformulation of Focusing in terms of proof-nets and its application to Non-commutative logic.

2   Notations and Prior Art

2.1   Notations

We consider here the multiplicative fragment of Linear Logic (resp. Non-commutative Logic). The connectives are split into two categories:

- Asynchronous: $\mathreferenceq$ (par), and, in the Non-Commutative case, ∇ (sequential)
- Synchronous: $\otimes$ (times), and, in the Non-Commutative case, $\odot$ (next)

Formulae are built from a given class of atomic formulae using the above connective. A non atomic formula is said to be asynchronous (resp. synchronous) if its top-most connective is asynchronous (resp. synchronous). We assume an involutive duality operation on atomic formulae, generalized to all the formulae using the traditional De Morgan laws:

$$(A \mathbin{⅋} B)^\perp = B^\perp \otimes A^\perp \quad (A \otimes B)^\perp = B^\perp \mathbin{⅋} A^\perp$$
$$(A \nabla B)^\perp = B^\perp \odot A^\perp \quad (A \odot B)^\perp = B^\perp \nabla A^\perp$$

Furthermore, we assume that the class of atomic formulae is split into two dual, disjoint subclasses, called the positive (resp. negative) atoms.

2.2 Sequent Proofs and Focusing

- Identity rules

$$[I] \; \frac{}{\vdash F, F^\perp} \qquad [C] \; \frac{\vdash \Gamma, F \quad \vdash \Delta, F^\perp}{\vdash \Gamma, \Delta}$$

- Logical rules

$$[⅋] \; \frac{\vdash \Gamma, F, G}{\vdash \Gamma, F \mathbin{⅋} G} \qquad [\otimes] \; \frac{\vdash \Gamma, F \quad \vdash \Delta, G}{\vdash \Gamma, \Delta, F \otimes G}$$

Fig. 1. The standard sequent system of Multiplicative Linear Logic

In the fragment of Linear Logic we consider, the standard sequent system is limited to the one shown in Figure 1. Sequents are simple multisets of formulae. Proofs are obtained by assembling in a connected way instances of the inference figures; the assembling is possible when the conclusion of an instance of inference figure is the premiss of another. The resulting structure is a tree labeled with sequents.

Proof search in this system comes up against two snags, identified in [2]: (i) two proofs can be equivalent up to some irrelevant permutation of inference figures; (ii) two proofs can also be equivalent up to the presence of some "dummy" sub-proofs in which the premisses are all identical and identical to the conclusion (such dummy sub-proofs can simply be discarded). A proof search procedure should not make costly non deterministic choices to distinguish between such pairs of equivalent proofs.

The technique proposed in [2] to deal with these problems relies on a refinement of the sequent system. This refinement satisfies the following main properties:

- Each inference figure in the refined system is a combination of inference figures of the initial one. Hence, each proof in the refined system corresponds straightforwardly to a proof in the initial one. This mapping is called "transduction".

- Each proof in the initial system is equivalent (modulo permutations of inference figures and deletion of dummy sub-proofs, of the kind mentioned above) to a proof obtained by transduction of a proof in the refined system.

In other words, proofs in the refined system fully represent proofs in the initial system, except that the refined system does not distinguish between many equivalent proofs of the initial system, which differ only by irrelevant syntactical differences. Hence, proof search in the refined system yields basically the same proofs and proof constructions as in the initial system, but saves a lot of resources otherwise needed to manage irrelevant non-determinism in the proof search process.

- Logical rules

$$[\mathcal{B}] \frac{\vdash \Gamma \Uparrow L, F, G}{\vdash \Gamma \Uparrow L, F \mathbin{\mathcal{B}} G} \qquad [\otimes] \frac{\vdash \Gamma \Downarrow F \quad \vdash \Delta \Downarrow G}{\vdash \Gamma, \Delta \Downarrow F \otimes G}$$

- Reaction $\Uparrow$: if F is not asynchronous

$$[R\Uparrow] \frac{\vdash \Gamma, F \Uparrow L}{\vdash \Gamma \Uparrow L, F}$$

- Reaction $\Downarrow$: if F is neither synchronous nor a positive atom

$$[R\Downarrow] \frac{\vdash \Gamma \Uparrow F}{\vdash \Gamma \Downarrow F}$$

- Identity: if F is a positive atom

$$[\mathrm{I}] \frac{}{\vdash F^{\perp} \Downarrow F}$$

- Decision: if F is synchronous or a positive atom

$$[D] \frac{\vdash \Gamma \Downarrow F}{\vdash \Gamma, F \Uparrow}$$

Fig. 2. The Focusing sequent system for Multiplicative Linear Logic

---

In the fragment of logic we consider, the refined system described in [2] can be reduced to the one shown in Figure 2. It is called below the "Focusing" system. Focusing sequents are of two types:

1. $\Gamma \Uparrow L$ where Γ is a multiset of non-asynchronous formulae and L an ordered list of formulae;
2. $\Gamma \Downarrow F$ where Γ is a multiset of non-asynchronous formulae and F is a single formula (called the "focus").

The transduction of a Focusing inference figure simply "forgets" the structure of the Focusing sequents (i.e. $\Gamma \Uparrow L$ becomes Γ, L where the order in L is forgotten and $\Gamma \Downarrow F$ becomes Γ, F). In the case of the logical and identity inference figures, transduction yields the corresponding inference figure in the initial system. The transduction of the other Focusing inference figures (Reactions and Decision) yields "dummy" inferences in which the premiss is identical to the conclusion (eliminated in the transduction of a proof).

For a discussion of the Focusing system and its computational interpretations in terms of proof search, consult [2]. Notice a slight difference in conventions w.r.t. [2]: here, the Identity rule can only be triggered by a positive atom in the focus (in $\Downarrow$ sequents). In [2], negative atoms had this triggering role, but clearly, polarities are purely conventional, so this difference is only superficial. The Focusing system is justified by the following theorem (stated and proved in [2]):

Theorem 1 (Andreoli 1992). *Let Γ be a multiset of non-asynchronous formulae and L an ordered list of formulae.*

$$\vdash \Gamma, L \text{ if and only if } \vdash \Gamma \Uparrow L$$

More precisely, any proof of Γ, L in the standard sequent system can be mapped, by permutation of inferences and deletion of dummy sub-proofs, into (the transduction of) a proof of $\Gamma \Uparrow L$ in the Focusing system.

There is no straightforward way to map the demonstration of Theorem 1 to the Non-Commutative case. The shape of the focusing sequents in this case is not obvious, and especially it is not clear how to combine the structuring of sequents brought by Focusing with that induced by non-commutativity. Hence the need to consider proof-nets, where the mapping between commutative and non-commutative proofs is more straightforward.

2.3   Proof-Nets and Splitting

Proof-nets have been designed in an attempt to abstract away the inessential sequentializations inherent in the syntax of sequent systems. Proof-nets are defined in two steps. First, proof structures are defined as simple constructions made of nodes and links. Each node is labeled by a single formula. Links are instances of the following prototypes:

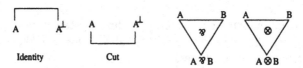

In assembling nodes and links in a proof structure, the following purely syntactical conditions must be respected: (*i*) each node is attached to exactly one conclusion of a link and at most one premiss; (*ii*) no two different nodes can be attached to the same premiss or conclusion of a link; (*iii*) the overall structure is connected. The conclusions of a proof structure are the nodes which are not attached to the premiss of any link.

Proof-nets are proof structures which satisfy a certain correctness criterion. Several equivalent criterions have been proposed in the literature. We use here the criterion based on switching positions and paths: each node in a proof-structure is labeled by a formula, but is also decorated by two "gates" (written ↑ and ↓); a switching position for a link is an undirected graph between the gates of its premiss and conclusion nodes, of one of the following types (dashed lines):

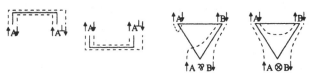

Right switches (Left switches are symmetric)

The "no short-path" criterion [4] states:

> A proof-net is a proof-structure such that for any choice of a switching position for each of its links, the undirected graph induced between its gates, completed by edges $A \uparrow, A \downarrow$ for each conclusion A, contains a single circuit which goes through all the gates of the proof structure.

Furthermore, we make two technical assumptions, justified by our proof search orientation, and which cost no generality:

- The identity link is restricted to atomic formulae only: any identity link with non atomic formulae can be reduced in a straightforward way to atomic identities.
- The cut link is not used: we make use here of the well known cut-elimination result on proof-nets, proved in [4].

Any sequent proof β can straightforwardly be mapped into a proof structure β^* such that the multiset of conclusions of β^* is exactly the conclusion sequent of β. The equivalence between sequent proofs and proof-nets is precisely given by the following theorem (stated and proved in [4]):

Theorem 2 (Girard 1987). *Equivalence between proof-nets and sequent proofs.*

- *Let β be a sequent proof. Then β^* is a proof-net.*
- *Let π be a proof-net. Then there exists a sequent proof β such that $\beta^* = \pi$.*

The first statement of the theorem is straightforward. The second one relies essentially on the following "Splitting lemma", which we detail here since it is essential to our purpose.

Definition 1. *Let π be a proof-net and F be one of its synchronous conclusions. F is splitting for π, and we write $F \in \text{split}(\pi)$ if and only if π consists of two proof nets π_A, π_B plus a synchronous link the premisses of which are conclusions of, resp., π_A and π_B, and the conclusion of which is labeled with F.*

The Splitting lemma (stated and proved in [4]) expresses that, under some conditions, a proof-net can always be split in the sense of the above definition.

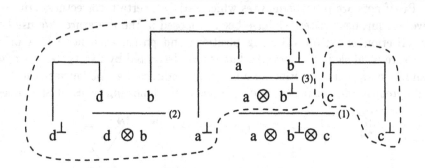

Fig. 3. A sample proof-net and a possible split

Theorem 3. *Let π be a proof-net that contains no asynchronous conclusion and at least one synchronous conclusion. Then* $\mathrm{split}(\pi) \neq \emptyset$

An example of split proof-net is given in Figure 3. The split formula in this case is $a \otimes b^{\perp} \otimes c$. It is easy to check that the two sub-proof-structures obtained by splitting the net at this conclusion are indeed proof-nets. Notice that there is another splitting conclusion, namely $d \otimes b$.

2.4   The Non-commutative Case

Non-Commutative logic, introduced in [1], is a refinement of the commutative case in terms of proof-nets. Two new link types are added (notice here that the premisses are directed), with associated switching positions:

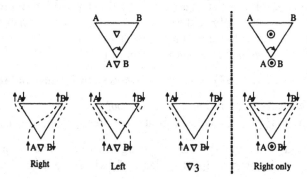

The criterion for proof-net correctness is extended to the non commutative versions of the connectives. A straightforward mapping between non-commutative proof structures and commutative ones is defined by: given a non commutative proof structure π, we build the corresponding commutative proof structure π° by replacing in π the occurrences of non-commutative connectives and links by their corresponding commutative version (i.e. $\nabla \mapsto \mathfrak{N}$ and $\odot \mapsto \otimes$). We then have the following theorem (stated and proved in [1]):

Theorem 4 (Abrusci-Ruet 1998). *Let* π *be a non-commutative proof struc-ture.* π *is a (non-commutative) proof-net if and only if*

- $\pi°$ *is a (commutative) proof-net;*
- *For every* $\nabla 3$*-free switching for* π*, the inner parts of* ∇*-links in the induced cycle contain no conclusions and do not overlap.*

This central theorem allows us to map proof net properties, in particular, as we will see below, Focusing, from the commutative case to the non-commutative one. For a precise definition of "inner parts" of ∇-links and their "overlapping", please refer to [1].

3   Focusing with Proof-Nets

Informally, the main point of this section is to express focusing as a refinement of Theorem 3. This theorem states that whenever a proof-net contains no asynchronous conclusion and at least one synchronous conclusion, there exists a splitting synchronous conclusion. The main refinement we introduce is that the splitting conclusion can be chosen in such a way that each of its premises, if it is synchronous, is itself a splitting conclusion for the sub-proof-net obtained by splitting. Focusing thus appears as a "hereditary" version of Splitting.

3.1   Focusing Conclusions

In Linear Logic, the sequentialization of a proof-net proceeds by induction on the size of the proof-net. At each induction steps, there are three cases to consider:

- If the proof-net contains an asynchronous conclusion, then
  1. remove the corresponding link;
  2. recursively apply sequentialization to the remaining proof-net;
  3. complete the sequent proof obtained with the corresponding asynchronous inference figure.
- If the proof-net contains no asynchronous conclusion but at least one synchronous conclusion, then
  1. use Theorem 3 to choose a splitting synchronous conclusion, and split the proof-net at this formula into two sub-proof-nets;
  2. recursively apply sequentialization to each of these sub-proof-nets;
  3. combine the resulting sequent proofs with the corresponding synchronous inference figure.
- If the proof-net contains neither synchronous nor asynchronous conclusions, i.e. it must be an instance of the identity link, and its sequentialization is reduced to the identity axiom [**I**].

This procedure yields a sequent proof the conclusion of which is the sequent made of the multiset of conclusions of the initial proof-net. However, the resulting proof may not be a focusing proof. For example, the sequentialization of the proof-net of Figure 3, where the conclusions are numbered according to the order in which they are chosen for splitting, yields the following sequent proof:

$$
[\otimes_1] \cfrac{[\otimes_2]\cfrac{[I]\cfrac{}{\vdash d^\perp, d} \quad [\otimes_3]\cfrac{[I]\cfrac{}{\vdash b^\perp, b} \quad [I]\cfrac{}{\vdash a, a^\perp}}{\vdash b, a^\perp, a \otimes b^\perp}}{\vdash d^\perp, d \otimes b, a^\perp, a \otimes b^\perp} \quad [I]\cfrac{}{\vdash c, c^\perp}}{\vdash d^\perp, d \otimes b, a^\perp, a \otimes b^\perp \otimes c, c^\perp}
$$

This proof is not focusing (i.e. it cannot be obtained as the transduction of a proof in the Focusing system). Indeed, the inference figure $[\otimes_1]$ decomposes the synchronous formula $a \otimes b^\perp \otimes c$, but its synchronous sub-formula $a \otimes b^\perp$ is not principal in the next inference figure $[\otimes_2]$, violating the "synchronous critical section" property of focusing proofs. To obtain a focused version of the above proof (assuming a, b, c, d are positive atomic), it is here sufficient to permute the inference figures $[\otimes_2]$ and $[\otimes_3]$. Indeed, the proof thus obtained is the transduction of the following proof in the Focusing system:

$$
[R\Uparrow^*, D]\cfrac{[\otimes_1]\cfrac{[\otimes_3]\cfrac{[I]\cfrac{}{\vdash a^\perp \Downarrow a}}{} \quad [R\Downarrow, D]\cfrac{[\otimes_2]\cfrac{[I]\cfrac{}{\vdash d^\perp \Downarrow d} \quad [I]\cfrac{}{\vdash b^\perp \Downarrow b}}{\vdash d^\perp, b^\perp \Downarrow d \otimes b}}{\vdash d^\perp, d \otimes b \Downarrow b^\perp}}{\vdash d^\perp, d \otimes b, a^\perp \Downarrow a \otimes b^\perp} \quad [I]\cfrac{}{\vdash c^\perp \Downarrow c}}{\vdash d^\perp, d \otimes b, a^\perp, c^\perp \Downarrow a \otimes b^\perp \otimes c}}{\vdash\Uparrow d^\perp, d \otimes b, a^\perp, a \otimes b^\perp \otimes c, c^\perp}
$$

This focused proof could also have been obtained by sequentialization of the initial proof-net, using a different ordering in the choice of splitting conclusions, namely (1-3-2):

$$
a \otimes b^\perp \otimes c \ , \quad a \otimes b^\perp \ , \quad d \otimes b
$$

instead of (1-2-3):

$$
a \otimes b^\perp \otimes c \ , \quad d \otimes b \ , \quad a \otimes b^\perp
$$

Thus, Focusing basically appears as a strategy in the choice of the splitting formula allowed by Theorem 3 in the Sequentialization procedure. More precisely, Focusing expresses that in the conditions of Theorem 3, not only the set of splitting conclusions is not empty, but its subset, consisting of the "focusing" conclusions, defined below, is also non-empty. Sequentialization will yield a focusing proof if, at each choice of a splitting conclusion in the procedure, a focusing conclusion is selected. The set of focusing conclusions of a net is inductively defined as follows:

Definition 2. *Let π be a proof-net and F be one of its conclusions. F is focusing for π, and we write $F \in$ foc(π) if and only if one of the following two conditions holds:*

1. *F is a positive atom and π is reduced to an axiom link.*
2. *$F \in$ split(π) and π is split at F (with subformulae A and B) into two sub-proof-nets π_A, π_B and*

  – A is asynchronous or a negative atom or $A \in \texttt{foc}(\pi_A)$
  – B is asynchronous or a negative atom or $B \in \texttt{foc}(\pi_B)$

From this definition, it is clear that for a proof-net (not reduced to an axiom link), the set of focusing formulae is a subset of the set of splitting formulae.

$$\texttt{foc}(\pi) \subseteq \texttt{split}(\pi)$$

Notice however that, unlike splitting, our definition of focusing also applies to proof-nets reduced to the axiom link. This is essential and allows to capture the particular role of polarities in Focusing, which is fully exploited in LinLog, the normalization procedure for Linear Logic [2].

3.2   The Focusing Theorem

The following theorem is shown in Appendix A.2.

Theorem 5. *Let π be a proof-net containing no asynchronous conclusion. Then $\texttt{foc}(\pi) \neq \emptyset$.*

Thus, Focusing appears as a refinement of Splitting. It expresses a form of "hereditary" Splitting, and, in addition, allows a form of control of the hereditary splitting sequences by the polarities of the atoms found at the end of each sequence (if any). We can now make more precise the view of Focusing as a Splitting strategy in the Sequentialization procedure, illustrated above. For technical reasons, we assume that any proof-net is equipped with a total ordering of its conclusions, which can be straightforwardly expanded to all its nodes in such a way that (*i*) the lowest of two subformulae of the same conclusion is the "left-most, outermost" in the tree representation of that conclusion[1], and (*ii*) the subformulae of different conclusions are in the same order as these conclusions. The ordering of the conclusions can be completely arbitrary; its extension to all the nodes of the proof-net is uniquely defined and induces an ordering of the conclusions for all the sub-proof-nets of the initial one. The ordering is only used here to capture arbitrary choices in the Sequentialization procedure (it has nothing to do with the ordering induced by non-commutativity). Let's enforce that,

  – at each choice of an asynchronous conclusion for decomposition in the Sequentialization procedure, the highest (w.r.t. node ordering) asynchronous conclusion is selected;
  – at each choice of a synchronous conclusion for decomposition in the Sequentialization procedure (when no asynchronous conclusion exist), the highest (w.r.t. node ordering) *focusing* conclusion is selected.

Then, the following property can easily be shown by induction on the size of the proof-net:

---

[1] By convention, a formula is "outer" than its own sub-formulae, and in a formula $F \, c \, G$ — where c is any connective — the subformulae of F are "on the left" of those of G.

330 Jean-Marc Andreoli and Roberto Maieli

> Let π be a proof-net and L be the (ordered) list of its conclusions. Then the sequentialization of π is (a transduction of) a Focusing proof of $\vdash\Uparrow L$.

The induction works on this property together with the following one:

> Let π be a proof-net with no asynchronous conclusion and at least one synchronous one (hence at least one focusing conclusion). Then the sequentialization of π is (a transduction of) a Focusing proof of a sequent of the form $\vdash \Gamma \Downarrow F$ where F is the highest *focusing* conclusion of π.

A careful analysis of the proof of Theorem 5 shows that it relies on two basic features: (*i*) the Splitting lemma and (*ii*) the partition of compound formulae between asynchronous and synchronous formulae, completed by the partition of atomic formulae between positive and negative atoms. The Splitting lemma itself has been reformulated in terms of the asynchronous/synchronous duality in Theorem 3. In fact, the proof of Theorem 5 also makes use of an implicit property (a "Merging" property, the proof of which is quite straightforward):

> Let π_A, π_B be two proof-nets. Then the proof structure obtained by assembling π_A, π_B plus a synchronous link the premisses of which are conclusions of, resp., π_A and π_B, is a proof net.

Consequently, Focusing applies to any logic where

- the synchronous/asynchronous duality holds, and
- the (reformulated version of the) Splitting lemma (and Merging property) hold.

This is the case, for instance, of Multiplicative Non-commutative Logic, as shown in Appendix A.3 (for the Splitting lemma) and Appendix A.4 (for Merging) using only Theorem 4. Therefore, Theorem 5 also holds in this Non-commutative Logic. On the other hand, Theorem 5 does not apply to other logics where the Splitting lemma and the asynchronous/synchronous duality do not hold, such as Pomset logic [11] (the connective $<$ is neither synchronous nor asynchronous).

The link between commutative and non-commutative proof-nets, captured by Theorem 4, and the exact analogy of the Focusing property in the commutative and non commutative cases, show that

Theorem 6. *Let π be a non-commutative proof-net.*

$$\mathrm{foc}(\pi^\circ) \;=\; (\mathrm{foc}(\pi))^\circ$$

In particular, this means that, in terms of proof search, the synchronous/asynchronous duality does not distinguish between the commutative and non-commutative cases.

4 Conclusion and Future Work

We have shown here that Focusing can be expressed in terms of proof-nets, when restricted to the multiplicative fragment of Linear Logic. The only property which is used in the demonstration of this result is the "Splitting lemma", reformulated in terms of the "asynchronous/synchronous" duality of the connectives. Consequently, the result can be generalized to any logic where this property holds, and in particular Non-commutative Logic.

But the sequent system version of Focusing, presented in [2] has the interesting property that it applies to whole Linear Logic, not just its multiplicative fragment. Indeed, the deep symmetry captured by the synchronous/asynchronous duality extends straightforwardly to additive connectives, and even, to some extent, to the exponentials, although, in the latter case, the asynchronous behavior of ? and the synchronous behavior of ! appear only in the "dyadic" sequent system, with some adjustments with respect to the other connectives.

As future work, we intend to re-formulate the Focusing result, obtained here in terms of multiplicative Non-commutative proof-nets, in the sequent system of the whole Non-commutative logic, and thus achieve the same kind of efficiency in proof search as in the commutative case. This can be done in three steps:

- First, we have to state the Focusing result in the multiplicative fragment of the Non-commutative sequent system. The only difficulty here is to choose the most appropriate representation for Non-commutative sequents (either with order-varieties or through explicit rules of "See-saw" and "Entropy" – see [12], which shows the equivalence of the two approaches).
- Then, we have to introduce the additive connectives. Their behavior is *a priori* orthogonal to non-commutativity, since removal of the Exchange rule does not affect their commutativity, but we must check that Focusing extends as straightforwardly to the additives as in the commutative case.
- Finally, introducing the exponentials should not cause any major problem: a similar approach to that taken in the commutative case should work, where unbounded formulae are placed in an "extra-territorial area"[2] and can at any time be materialized at any location (in [2], this area is represented in Focusing sequents by an additional field separated by ":").

However, we expect to go beyond this result, and, by analysing thoroughly the invertibility and permutability of inference figures in the Non-commutative case, to achieve a form of proof search optimization which goes beyond the synchronous/asynchronous duality and exploits the specific features of Non-commutativity (Theorem 6 shows that this duality does not distinguish between the commutative and non-commutative cases). In particular, the See-saw and Entropy rules present interesting invertibility properties which are essential to help deciding when to allow them in a Focusing system, preserving the completeness of Focusing while minimizing the intrinsic non-determinism they carry

---

[2] This expression was originally coined by Jean-Yves Girard, at the Frascati workshop [6]

(reminiscent of the treatment of Weakening and Contraction with Decision rules in the commutative case).

Ultimately, we seek to obtain for Non-commutative Logic a "normal form" analogous to LinLog for Linear Logic, which captures in a restricted, "logic-programming"-like syntax the whole power of Focusing.

Acknowledgement

We would like to thank Michele Abrusci, Paul Ruet and Jean-Yves Girard for fruitful discussions on the topic of this paper, and all the participants at the workshop on Non-commutative Logic, held in Frascati (Italy) in April 1999. This workshop was supported by the TMR network "Linear".

References

1. M. Abrusci and P. Ruet. Non commutative logic I: the multiplicative fragment, 1998. to appear in the *Annals of Pure and Applied Logic*.
2. J-M. Andreoli. Logic programming with focusing proofs in linear logic. *Journal of Logic and Computation*, 2(3), 1992.
3. J-M. Andreoli and R. Pareschi. LO and behold! concurrent structured processes. In *Proc. of OOPSLA/ECOOP'90*, Ottawa, Canada, 1990.
4. J-Y. Girard. Linear logic. *Theoretical Computer Science*, 50:1–102, 1987.
5. J-Y. Girard. On the meaning of logical rules I: syntax vs. semantics II: multiplicatives and additives, 1998. Preprint.
6. J-Y. Girard. Informal communication, 1999. presented at the TMR "Linear" workshop on Non-commutative Logic, Frascati, April 1999.
7. J.S. Hodas and D. Miller. Logic programming in a fragment of intuitionistic linear logic. *Journal of Information and Computation*, 110(2):327–365, 1994.
8. D. Miller. Lexical scoping as universal quantification. In *Proc. of the 6th International Conference on Logic Programming*, Lisboa, Portugal, 1989.
9. D. Miller. Forum: A multiple-conclusion specification logic. *Theoretical Computer Science*, 165(1):201–232, 1996.
10. D. Miller, G. Nadathur, F. Pfenning, and A. Scedrov. Uniform proofs as a foundation for logic programming. *Annals of Pure and Applied Logic*, 51:125–157, 1991.
11. C. Retoré. Pomset logic: A non-commutative extension of classical linear logic. In *Proc. of TLCA'97*, pages 300–318, Nancy, France, 1997.
12. P. Ruet. Non commutative logic II: Sequent calculus and phase semantics, 1998. Preprint.

A   Demonstrations

A.1   A Focusing Lemma

We first prove the following lemma.

Lemma 1. *Let π be a proof-net with no asynchronous conclusion, and $S = A \otimes B$ be a splitting formula of π. Let π_A, π_B be the two proof nets obtained by splitting π at S. If A is not a negative atom, then*

$$\mathtt{foc}(\pi_A) \setminus \{A\} \ \subseteq \ \mathtt{foc}(\pi)$$

(and similarly for the B side)

<u>Demonstration</u>: We proceed by induction on the size of π. Let $F \in \mathtt{foc}(\pi_A) \setminus \{A\}$. Since F is focusing in π_A, there are two cases to consider:

F is a positive atom , and π_A is reduced to an axiom link, with conclusions F and $F^\perp$, one of which being A. But:
 - By hypothesis, A is not a negative atom, hence $A \neq F^\perp$.
 - By hypothesis, $F \in \mathtt{foc}(\pi_A) \setminus \{A\}$, hence $A \neq F$
 Contradiction.

F is a splitting synchronous formula of π_A , of the form $C \otimes D$ and π_A is split at F into two sub-proof-nets π_C, π_D such that
 [P.1]: C is asynchronous or a negative atom or $C \in \mathtt{foc}(\pi_C)$
 [P.2]: D is asynchronous or a negative atom or $D \in \mathtt{foc}(\pi_D)$

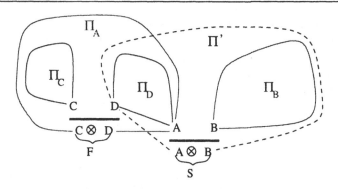

Fig. 4. Different ways of assembling the sub-proof-nets

Since A is a conclusion of π_A different from F and π_A is split at F into π_C, π_D, then A must be in the conclusions of π_C or of π_D. We assume, without loss of generality, that A is a conclusion of π_D (other than D, obviously). Let π' be the proof structure consisting of π_D, π_B and the splitting link of π at S (see Figure 4). It is not difficult to see that

[$\mathcal{P}3$]: π' is a proof-net split at S into π_D and π_B;

[$\mathcal{P}4$]: π is split at F into π_C and π'.

Since π' is smaller (in size) than π, we conclude, by the induction hypothesis applied to [$\mathcal{P}3$], that

$$\mathsf{foc}(\pi_D) \setminus \{A\} \subseteq \mathsf{foc}(\pi')$$

From this, and [$\mathcal{P}2$] and $D \neq A$, we infer that

[$\mathcal{P}5$]: D is asynchronous or a negative atom or $D \in \mathsf{foc}(\pi')$

From [$\mathcal{P}1$] and [$\mathcal{P}5$] and [$\mathcal{P}4$], by application of Definition 2, we obtain that $F \in \mathsf{foc}(\pi)$.

$\square$

A.2   The Focusing Theorem

We make use of the previous lemma to show Theorem 5:

Let π be a proof-net containing no asynchronous conclusion. Then $\mathsf{foc}(\pi) \neq \emptyset$.

Demonstration: We proceed by contradiction. Let's assume that there exists a proof-net π containing no asynchronous conclusion and such that $\mathsf{foc}(\pi) = \emptyset$. We choose π to be of minimal size. We consider two cases:

Either π has no synchronous conclusion , and, since it contains no asynchronous conclusion either, it must be reduced to the axiom link. But then, one of the two conclusions is a positive atom F, which, by Definition 2, is focusing for π. Contradiction.

Or π does contain at least one synchronous conclusion , and, since it contains no asynchronous conclusion, by application of the Splitting lemma, we know that there exists a synchronous conclusion F of π, of the form $A \otimes B$, which splits π into two sub-proof-nets π_A and π_B.

Suppose that

[$\mathcal{P}1$]: A is neither asynchronous nor a negative atom.

– By construction, the conclusions of π_A other than A are conclusions of π (hence not asynchronous). Since A itself is not asynchronous by [$\mathcal{P}1$], we infer that none of the conclusions of π_A are asynchronous. Since π_A is strictly smaller than π, which is a proof-net of minimal size without asynchronous nor focusing conclusions, we conclude that

[$\mathcal{P}2$]: $\mathsf{foc}(\pi_A) \neq \emptyset$

– A is not a negative atom by [$\mathcal{P}1$], hence, by application of Lemma 1, we have

[$\mathcal{P}3$]: $\mathsf{foc}(\pi_A) \setminus \{A\} \subseteq \mathsf{foc}(\pi)$

Since $\mathsf{foc}(\pi) = \emptyset$, we conclude from [$\mathcal{P}3$] that $\mathsf{foc}(\pi_A) \subseteq \{A\}$, and, from [$\mathcal{P}2$], we conclude that $\mathsf{foc}(\pi_A) = \{A\}$. Hence $A \in \mathsf{foc}(\pi_A)$.

Thus, by discharging hypothesis [$\mathcal{P}1$], we conclude

[$\mathcal{P}4$]: A is asynchronous or a negative atom or $A \in \mathsf{foc}(\pi_A)$

By symmetry, we can equally prove that

[$\mathcal{P}5$]: B is asynchronous or a negative atom or $B \in \text{foc}(\pi_B)$

But, from [$\mathcal{P}4$] and [$\mathcal{P}5$], by application of Definition 2, we have that $F \in \text{foc}(\pi)$. Contradiction.

$\square$

A.3   The Splitting Lemma in Non-commutative Logic

We have to show that the Splitting lemma applies to Non-commutative Logic.

Let π be a non-commutative proof-net with no asynchronous conclusion and at least one synchronous one. Then there exists a synchronous conclusion F such that π consists of two proof nets π_A, π_B plus a synchronous link the premisses of which are conclusions of, resp., π_A and π_B, and the conclusion of which is labeled with F.

Demonstration: Let π be a non-commutative proof-net with no asynchronous conclusion and at least one synchronous one. Obviously, π° is a commutative proof-net with no asynchronous conclusion and at least one synchronous one, so is amenable to the commutative splitting lemma (Theorem 3). Hence, π° consists of two proof nets π'_A, π'_B plus a synchronous link the premisses of which are conclusions of, resp., π'_A and π'_B, and the conclusion of which is labeled with F°. By construction of π°, we have that π'_A (resp. π'_B) is of the form π°_A (resp. π°_B), and π consists of π_A, π_B plus a synchronous link the premisses of which are conclusions of, resp., π_A and π_B, and the conclusion of which is labeled with F. Therefore, all we have to check is that π_A and π_B are non-commutative proof-nets (not just proof-structures). In fact, we have that π°_A and π°_B are commutative proof-nets, so, all we have to check is the condition on inner-parts of Theorem 4. Let s_A (resp. s_B) be a $\nabla 3$-free switching for π_A (resp. π_B). We can build a $\nabla 3$-free switching s for π by assembling s_A, s_B and by choosing the Right switching for F (i.e. $R\otimes$ or $R\odot$ depending on the top-most connective in F):

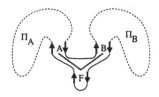

Let l be a ∇-link of π_A, and let's assume its inner-part in $s_A(\pi_A)$ contains a conclusion C of π_A. There are two cases to consider:

- If C is different from A, then it is a conclusion of π; hence the inner part of l in $s(\pi)$ also contains a conclusion of π. Contradiction (by Theorem 4, since π is a proof-net).
- If $C = A$, then the inner part of l in $s_A(\pi_A)$ goes

$$\cdots, A^\downarrow, A^\uparrow, \cdots$$

In $s(\pi)$, the inner part of l becomes

$$\cdots, A^{\downarrow}, B^{\uparrow}, \cdots, B^{\downarrow}, F^{\downarrow}, F^{\uparrow}, A^{\uparrow}, \cdots$$

which contains the conclusion F of π. Contradiction (by Theorem 4, since π is a proof-net).

Hence, the inner-part of a ∇-link of π_A in $s_A(\pi_A)$ is the same as that in $s(\pi)$ and does not visit any conclusion of π_A. Since inner-parts of ∇-links do not overlap in $s(\pi)$ (by Theorem 4), neither do they in $s_A(\pi_A)$. □

A.4   The Merging Property

We have to show the following property in Non-commutative Logic (in commutative logic, it is a straightforward consequence of the "no-short-trip" condition over proof-nets).

Let π_A, π_B be two non-commutative proof-nets. Then the proof structure obtained by assembling π_A, π_B plus a synchronous link the premisses of which are conclusions of, resp., π_A and π_B, is a non-commutative proof net.

Demonstration: Let π_A, π_B be two non-commutative proof-nets and let π be the proof structure obtained by assembling π_A, π_B plus a synchronous link the premisses of which are conclusions A, B of, resp., π_A and π_B. By Theorem 4, we know that π_A° and π_B° are commutative proof-nets, and hence, so is π° (by commutative Merging). Therefore, all we have to prove is that π satisfies the criterion of Theorem 4 on inner-parts. Let s be a $\nabla 3$-free switching of π and l be a ∇-link of π. We can assume without loss of generality that l is in π_A. Let s_A be the switching s restricted to π_A. By Theorem 4, we have that the inner-part of l in $s_A(\pi_A)$ contains no conclusion of π_A, and hence does not visit A. Hence the inner-part of l in $s(\pi)$ is the same as that in $s_A(\pi_A)$. Therefore the inner-part of a ∇-link of π in $s(\pi)$ is exactly its inner-part in the sub-proof-net (π_A or π_B) where it occurs. Consequently, since the condition of Theorem 4 holds in these sub-proof-nets, it also holds in π (the non-overlapping condition is obvious if the two links belong to the two different sub-proof-nets). Hence π is a proof-net.   □

CHAT Is Θ(SLG-WAM)⋆

Bart Demoen[1] and Konstantinos Sagonas[2]

[1] Department of Computer Science, Katholieke Universiteit Leuven, Belgium
bmd@cs.kuleuven.ac.be
[2] Computing Science Department, Uppsala Universitet, Sweden
kostis@csd.uu.se

Abstract. CHAT offers an alternative to SLG-WAM for implementing the suspension and resumption of consumers that tabling needs: unlike SLG-WAM, it does not use freeze registers nor a complicated trail to preserve their execution environments. CHAT also limits the amount of copying of CAT, which was previously put forward as another alternative to SLG-WAM. Although experimental results show that in practice CHAT is competitive with — if not better than — SLG-WAM, there remains the annoying fact that on contrived programs the original CHAT can be made arbitrarily worse than SLG-WAM, i.e. the original CHAT has an intrinsically higher complexity. In this paper we show how to overcome this problem, in particular, we deal with the two sources of higher complexity of CHAT: the repeated traversal of the choice point stack, and the lack of sufficient sharing of the trail. This is achieved without fundamentally changing the underlying principle of CHAT by a technique that manipulates a Prolog choice point so that it assumes temporarily a different functionality and in a way that is transparent to the underlying WAM. There is more potential use of this technique besides lowering the worst case complexity of CHAT: it leads to considering scheduling strategies that were not feasible before either in CHAT or in SLG-WAM. We also discuss extensively issues related to the implementation of the trail in a tabled logic programming system.

1 Introduction

Tabling has by now been recognized as an important feature of logic programming systems. Indeed, a number of applications that were either beyond the reach or very difficult to tackle with conventional Prolog systems are now possible using tabled evaluation. Such application areas include, but are not limited to, verification using model checking [9], program analysis [2], and logic-based databases [12]. Despite this increase in applicability of tabled implementations, for quite a long time, there seemed to be only one possible way of implementing the suspension/resumption mechanism that tabling requires in a logic programming system that was based on WAM. This mechanism is described in [11] as part of the SLG-WAM (the engine of the XSB system [12]) which also defines

---

⋆ A tight correspondence between alternatives for suspension/resumption in the WAM.

and gives alternative implementations for the other components of a tabled logic programming system, i.e. the tables themselves, the scheduling strategy, the extension of the WAM instruction set and the mechanism for detecting completion. It is clear that the issues involved in the tables themselves are rather loosely coupled to the basic engine; i.e. whether one uses tries or not as data structures for tabling, does not affect the underlying WAM. So are issues related to the choice of the scheduling strategy [6], or whether completion detection is based on exact or approximate dependencies. On the other hand, the implementation of suspension/resumption as in SLG-WAM does affect the WAM, because of its introduction of a set of freeze registers and a forward trail. This compromises to a certain extent the efficiency of the underlying abstract machine, even for plain Prolog execution, but more importantly it does not allow for an easy adoption of the mechanism in an existing system. Finally, it is clear that even though the choice of a scheduling strategy can be orthogonal to the underlying LP engine, some strategies are disadvantaged or even impossible when a particular implementation for suspension/resumption is fixed. So it is important to study suspension/resumption implementation models and their properties. [11] describes one implementation of suspension/resumption but no alternative is hinted at, because it was assumed at that time that "reasonable" (i.e. sufficiently efficient) alternatives did not exist.

A first alternative implementation for suspension/resumption in tabling was offered by CAT [3] which stands for the Copying Approach to Tabling. The guiding principle of the design was that the underlying WAM should not be affected by the introduction of tabling and CAT achieved exactly that: starting from a WAM implementation, CAT implements suspension/resumption of consumers without affecting any part of the WAM. In particular, CAT employs the usual WAM trail and no freeze registers. The price to pay for this orthogonality is copying the state of consumers. Although copying has quite horrible worst cases, in practice CAT works quite well. But the high memory consumption of CAT (under certain scheduling strategies) was worrying and in [4] we have tried to remedy this by copying only data that could be reachable in forward execution; i.e. not saving any data that will be garbage on resumption of a consumer. Although this lowers the space requirements of CAT, the worst case complexity of CAT remains unaffected. Thus, still not satisfied, we proposed in [5] another alternative, CHAT, which combines certain features of CAT with SLG-WAM, hence the H in its name which stands for Hybrid. In particular, heap and local stack are frozen without the need for freeze registers and the trail is partially and incrementally copied so that the WAM trail can be retained. CHAT considerably improves on CAT space wise and offers the same added flexibility of scheduling strategies as CAT. Still, in principle, the original CHAT has two sources of added complexity which can result in arbitrarily worse behavior of CHAT than SLG-WAM (see Section 3.3)[1]. Annoyed by this theoretical problem, in this paper, we give a detailed account on how to guarantee that CHAT will not perform arbitrarily worse than SLG-WAM. This is the main contribution of the paper:

---

[1] The SLG-WAM can also be arbitrarily worse space-wise than CHAT; see Section 8.

we show how without fundamentally changing the underlying principle of CHAT (i.e. still without changing the underlying WAM for Prolog execution), CHAT can be implemented in such a way that it performs no worse complexity-wise (in both time and space) than SLG-WAM. We also note, however, that in practice CHAT performs better than SLG-WAM.

CHAT as in [5] is our starting point. We will improve on its incremental copying of trail segments, so that the same sharing of trail between consumers is possible as in SLG-WAM, and on the installation of the equivalent of freeze registers in choice points which in CHAT leads to repeated traversal of the choice point stack. The improvement is based on a technique that modifies choice points dynamically and in a transparent way for the underlying abstract machine: on backtracking to the modified Prolog choice point, it performs the incremental copying task that was formerly reserved for generators and then continues with its original alternative. The technique of modifying choice points opens possibilities for new scheduling strategies in the context of tabling. We also believe that it is of interest outside the relatively small area of tabled LP implementations.

In Section 2 we introduce notation used later in the paper. Section 3 briefly describes CHAT, certain aspects of the SLG-WAM, and gives examples that show the two sources of added complexity in plain CHAT. Section 4 shows how repeated traversal of the choice point stack at CHAT save time can be avoided. Section 5 shows how the same sharing of trail as in SLG-WAM is obtained and Section 6 shows how it is exploited by CHAT. Section 7 discusses details of the implementation of the trail in tabled logic programming systems. Section 8 makes an exhaustive comparison of the space complexity of CHAT and SLG-WAM.

2 Notation and Terminology

We assume familiarity with the WAM [14], SLG-WAM [11], and to some extent with CHAT [5] due to space limitations [2]. However, some aspects of the SLG-WAM and CHAT which are crucial for this paper are presented in Sections 3.1 and 3.2. We assume a four stack WAM, i.e. an implementation with separate stacks for the choice points and the environments as in SICStus Prolog or in XSB; however, this is by no means essential for this paper or for CHAT (see [5]). We will also assume stacks to start from low addresses and to grow downwards; i.e. higher in the stack means older, lower in the stack (or more recent) means younger and a larger address value.

We will use the following notation for WAM registers: **H** for top of heap pointer; **TR** for top of trail pointer; **EB** for top of local stack pointer; **B** for most recent choice point. Three different types of choice points are used: Generator, Consumer or Prolog choice points and are identified by G, C or P respectively. The (relevant for this paper) fields of a choice point are ALT, prevB, H, EB and TR: the next alternative, the previous choice point, the top of heap, local and trail stack respectively upon the creation of the choice point. For a choice point identified by e.g. P, these fields are denoted as P[ALT], P[prevB], P[H], etc.

[2] All relevant papers are accessible at http://www.csd.uu.se/~kostis/Papers/.

In a tabled system, some predicates are designated as *tabled* by means of a declaration; all other predicates are *non-tabled* and are evaluated as in Prolog. The first occurrence of a tabled subgoal is termed a *generator* and uses resolution against the program clauses to derive answers for the subgoal. These answers are recorded in the table (for this subgoal). All other occurrences of identical (e.g. up to variance) subgoals are called *consumers* as they do not use the program clauses for deriving answers but they consume answers from this table.

Implementation of tabling for non-deterministic languages is complicated by the fact that execution environments of consumers need to be retained until they have consumed all answers that the table associated with the generator will ever contain. To partly simplify and optimize tabled execution, implementations of tabling try to determine *completion* of (generator) subgoals: i.e. when the evaluation has produced all their answers. This involves examining dependencies between subgoals and usually interacts with consumption of answers by consumers. The SLG-WAM has a particular stack-based way of determining completion which is based on maintaining *scheduling components*; that is, sets of subgoals which are possibly inter-dependent. A scheduling component is uniquely determined by its *leader*: a (generator) subgoal G_L with the property that subgoals younger than G_L may depend on G_L, but G_L depends on no subgoal older than itself. Obviously, leaders are not known beforehand and they might change in the course of a tabled evaluation. How leaders are maintained is an orthogonal issue beyond the scope of this paper; see [11] for more details. However, we note that besides determining completion, a leader of a scheduling component is usually[3] responsible for scheduling consumers of all subgoals that it leads to consume their answers.

3   SLG-WAM, CHAT and their Complexity Difference

3.1   Suspension/resumption in SLG-WAM: A brief description

Tabling can be implemented by modifying the WAM to preserve execution environments of consumers that suspend by *freezing* the WAM stacks, i.e. by not allowing backtracking to reclaim space in the stacks as is done in the WAM. The SLG-WAM employs a register-based freezing of the WAM stacks, i.e. the SLG-WAM adds an extra set of *freeze registers* to the WAM, one for each stack, and allocation of new information occurs below the frozen part of the stack. Suspension of a consumer is performed in the SLG-WAM by creating a consumer choice point, setting the freeze registers to point to the current top of the stacks, and upon exhausting all answers from the table fall back to the previous choice point by failing as in the WAM (i.e. undoing the variable bindings and restoring the WAM registers) but without reclaiming any space. Frozen space is reclaimed *only* upon determining completion of a scheduling component.

---

[3] "usually" because this depends on the scheduling strategy; however, it holds for all scheduling strategies of the XSB system.

Note that this method of freezing the stacks is a constant time operation. It does impose an overhead — even on plain Prolog execution — because allocation of new information on the stacks requires a comparison of the WAM register and the corresponding freeze register of the stack; but this overhead does not change the complexity of the abstract machine.

To resume a suspended computation of a consumer, the SLG-WAM needs to have a mechanism to reconstitute its execution environment. Besides resetting the WAM registers (e.g. setting $\mathbf{B}$ to point to the consumer choice point), the variable bindings at the time of suspension have to be restored. This can be done using what is known as a *forward trail* [11, 15]. An entry in the forward trail consists of a reference cell, a value cell, and a back-pointer to the previous trail entry (see Fig. 1) as opposed to the regular WAM trail which consists of only the reference cell. Note that the trail back-pointer in the SLG-WAM reflects the fact that the trail stack is used to represent the tree of trails belonging to different computations. By following the back-pointer, parts of the trail that

BackPtr	Pointer to previous trail entry
Value	Value to which the variable was bound
VarAddr	Reference to (address of) the trailed variable

Fig. 1. Format of an SLG-WAM (Forward) Trail Entry.

are not part of the same computation are skipped (see below). Given this trail, restoring the execution environment EE of a consumer from a current execution environment EE_c, is a matter of untrailing from EE_c to a common ancestor of EE_c and EE, and then using values in the forward trail to reconstitute the environment of EE. The exact algorithm of this operation is presented in [11].

Again, it is important to note the following: The forward trail adds a (time and space) overhead to both tabled and plain Prolog execution; however, this overhead is just a constant factor. On the other hand, the SLG-WAM makes good use of the cost of its extended trail: in particular, the back-pointers are used to minimize the cost of switching execution environments. Untrailing does not need to happen up to a generator choice point; instead it is sufficient to untrail to *any* common ancestor of EE_c and EE. In the XSB implementation of the SLG-WAM, this common ancestor is usually related to the nearest choice point; Section 7 elaborates more on this issue. The figure on the right gives a rough idea of the situation for the case of switching execution environments from C_1 to C_3; the common ancestor is P_1.

We finish this section by mentioning the design philosophy of the SLG-WAM: The efficiency of tabled execution is the prime goal. As a consequence, the basic operations of a tabled abstract machine were designed to have constant time (suspension through freezing) or lowest possible cost (resumption by exploiting sharing of trail). The small overhead added to some WAM operations is considered a reasonable price for making tabled execution efficient.

3.2   Suspension/resumption in CHAT: A brief description

CHAT's design philosophy is different: Introduction of tabling into a WAM-based system should leave the underlying WAM *unchanged* for (strictly) non-tabled execution. Naturally, CHAT tries to make the suspension/resumption support for tabling as efficient as possible, but *never* by violating the above requirement.

We describe the actions of CHAT through an example. Consider the following state of a WAM-based abstract machine for tabled evaluation: A generator G has already been encountered and a *generator choice point* has been created for it immediately below a (Prolog) choice point P. Then execution continued with some other non-tabled code and let us, without loss of generality, assume that two Prolog choice points P_1 and P_2 were created and then a consumer C was encountered, G is its generator and G is not completed at this point. Thus, a *consumer choice point* is created for C; see Fig. 2(a). The heap and the trail are shown segmented according to the H and TR values saved in choice points; the same segmentation is not shown for the local stack as it is a spaghetti stack; however the EB values of choice points are also shown by pointers.

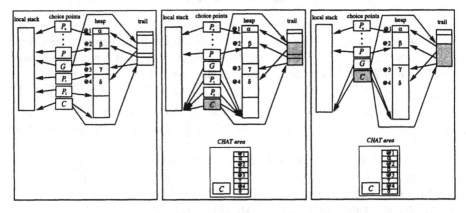

(a) Upon creation of a   (b) After freezing: CPs   (c) Upon reinstalling
consumer choice point.   adapted & CHAT copy.   the CHAT area of C.

Fig. 2. Stacks & CHAT area while executing under the original CHAT implementation.

CHAT preserves the execution environment of consumers partly by freezing and partly by copying. More specifically, CHAT freezes the heap and the local stack by modifying the H and EB fields of all choice points that lie between a consumer C and the nearest generator G, to C[H] and C[EB] respectively. Note that freezing in CHAT does not happen as in the SLG-WAM. We refer to CHAT's way of freezing stacks as *CHAT freeze*. To preserve information from the remaining stacks, CHAT uses copying: from the choice point stack only the consumer choice point is saved; from the trail the entries that lie between the consumer and the generator together with the values that these entries point to are saved. This copied information is saved in what is termed a *CHAT area*. Fig. 2(b) shows such an area and the resulting state of the stacks after modifying the fields of choice points; shaded parts show the information copied by CHAT.

A rigorous argument why this freezing-copying scheme is correct can be found in [5]. For the purposes of this paper, we do not need to fully explain what happens in case that G is not a leader of a scheduling component and execution backtracks over G. Full details can be found in [5], but essentially the same freezing mechanism is applied (now between G and the immediately older generator) and an incremental copy of the trail is saved in a new CHAT area. It is important however to note that this new CHAT area is copied *once* and this incremental copy is shared by *all* consumers that have their state saved up to G.

On the other hand, if upon failing back to G, G is a scheduling generator (e.g. a leader of a scheduling component), G needs to schedule all its consumers to consume answers from the table after it finishes all its program clause resolution. This implies resuming these consumers by restoring their execution environments. In CHAT resumption is also done through copying: the consumer choice point is installed immediately below the choice point of the scheduling generator, and the saved part of the trail is copied from the CHAT area back to the trail stack. Fig. 2(c) gives a rough idea of a consumer's reinstallation; shaded parts of the stacks show the copied information.

3.3   The complexity issue

The source of increase in complexity of CHAT w.r.t. SLG-WAM is two-fold:

1. for each new consumer, C, CHAT traverses the choice point stack from the consumer up to the nearest generator G; if between C and G there are n Prolog choice points $P_1 \ldots P_n$, these can be visited arbitrarily often;
2. assume a generator G and a Prolog choice point P immediately younger, then if the computation starting at P creates consumers $C_1 \ldots C_m$, then in SLG-WAM $C_1 \ldots C_m$ share the part of the trail between P and G, but in CHAT, each consumer's CHAT area contains a separate copy of that trail part. Again, the space and time difference can be arbitrary.

The example program from [5] (Fig. 3) shows both of these problems (the subscripts g and c denote occurrences of a generator or a consumer tabled subgoal). If the compiler recognizes that predicate make_choices/2 (which is supposed to create choice points) is indeed deterministic, a more complicated predicate can be used. The reason for giving the second argument to make_consumers, is to ensure that on every creation of a consumer, H has a different value and an update of the H field of choice points between the new consumer and the generator is needed — otherwise, an obvious optimization of CHAT would be applicable. Against this program, in a query like:

```
?- Choices = 100, Consumers = 200, main(Choices,Consumers).
```

CHAT uses $(Choices * Consumers)$ times more space and time than SLG-WAM.

```
main(Choices,Consumers) :-
    p_g(_), make_choices(Choices,_), make_consumers(Consumers,[]).
make_choices(N,trail) :- N > 0, M is N - 1, make_choices(M,_).
make_choices(0,_).
make_consumers(N,Acc) :-
    N > 0, M is N - 1, p_c(_), make_consumers(M,[a|Acc]).
:- table p/1.
p(1).
```

Fig. 3. A tabled program with different complexity under SLG-WAM and plain CHAT.

We will address these two sources of added complexity separately and we start by dealing with the repeated traversal of the choice point stack as it introduces a technique that is also the basis for the more complicated trail sharing solution.

4 Avoiding Repeated Traversal of Choice Points

First note that visiting each choice point *once* does not affect the complexity. Indeed, this adds only a fixed cost to a choice point that was created already. Next, note that we must cater for the Prolog cut (!/0) which can cut away non-tabled choice points. As a design principle of CHAT is that no changes to the underlying WAM or its instructions should happen for plain Prolog execution, changing the implementation of cut itself is not an option (in many systems, cut is a constant time operation and does not traverse the choice point stack). Thus, we cannot put information in choice points that can disappear. Note however, that generators are used to produce all answers for consumers, so generator choice points are (and must be) immune to cuts. From this, it follows that a generator choice point is a safe place for storing information. Remember that CHAT adapts the H and EB fields of choice points. We will also make use of the ALT field of choice points, which indicates the next alternative. We will assume that one extra field in generator choice points is available: we call this field SALT and we use it for saving the value of an ALT field. However, Prolog choice points remain unchanged. We propose the code below to be executed upon CHAT-freezing a consumer C whose (nearest) generator is G. We also note that CHAT (as SLG-WAM) has constant time access to the choice point of G upon suspension of a consumer; e.g. via the completion stack. In words: for every choice point P between C and G, save its alternative in its EB-field, change its alternative to a chat_choice instruction, set its H-field to point to the generator choice point. Only the generator gets the values of **EB** and **H** which point at the current top of the local stack and the heap. The generator gets as alternative the new instruction chat_generator, which is a version of chat_choice for a generator. We will describe both new instructions later.

Fig. 4 parallels Fig. 2(a) & 2(b) and shows the state of the stacks immediately before and after the above code is executed (the trail remains unaffected and so is not shown). Choice points are now shown in more detail; in particular, their EB, H and (S)ALT fields are shown explicitly (some possible values appear in

```
P := C[prevB];
while (P != G && P[ALT] != chat_choice)
   { P[EB]  := P[ALT];          /* save ALT in the EB field */
     P[ALT] := chat_choice;     /* set ALT to chat_choice */
     P[H]   := G;               /* link P to the generator */
     P := P[prevB];             /* continue with previous choice point */
   }
G[H]  := H;                     /* the H register also equals C[H] */
G[EB] := EB;                    /* the EB register also equals C[EB] */
if (G[ALT] != chat_generator)
   { G[SALT] := G[ALT];         /* save generator's ALT field */
     G[ALT]  := chat_generator; /* install a new alternative */
   }
```

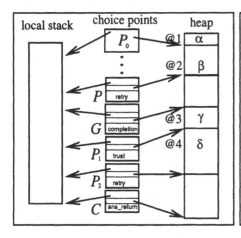
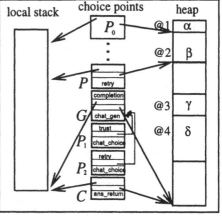

(a) Right upon consumer CP creation   (b) After extended CHAT-freeze

Fig. 4. Stacks while executing under an extended CHAT implementation.

their alternative fields) as it is important to see what takes place. As in Fig. 2, let us assume that there are two Prolog choice points P_1 and P_2 between a generator G and a consumer choice point C. P and all choice points above G are not affected by the execution of the code. The stacks' state shown in Fig. 4(b) is the result of executing the code: the completion instruction is saved in the SALT field of the generator and changed into chat_generator; retry and trust are saved in P_2[EB] and P_1[EB] respectively and the corresponding ALT fields are changed into chat_choice. The values of **EB** and **H** (or alternatively the values of C[EB] and C[H]) are installed in the corresponding fields of G and the Prolog choice points P_1 and P_2 are linked directly to G through their H field.

Note that the above code also handles the case where more that one consumer is present and which lead in the original CHAT to repeated traversal of the whole chain of choice points between the consumer and the generator. Indeed, the test for chat_choice in the condition of the while loop ensures that when a new consumer is frozen, a chain of choice points that was traversed before, is not traversed again; thus, for each backtrack operation to a particular choice point, CHAT visits it at most once more than SLG-WAM. It also shows that setting the H and EB fields of G, updates conceptually the EB and H fields of a set of choice points in a constant time operation.

The above modification of CHAT is enough to get rid of the added complexity of changing the EB and H fields in the choice point stack as performed in the original CHAT. To complete this discussion, we consider the remaining four issues: the implementation of chat_choice and chat_generator, backtracking over a generator, and the actions to be taken in case of a change of leaders:

1. Consider a choice point P which has a chat_choice instruction and consider backtracking to this choice point. For convenience, name α the value of the ALT field that was replaced by chat_choice. α points to a retry or trust instruction (or one of their variants or another form of disjunction). chat_choice first installs the EB and H fields from the generator. Thereby P looses the link to the generator, but this link is indeed no longer needed. After that, chat_choice transfers control to α. The code for chat_choice is given below:

```
alt := P[EB];    /* alt points to α now */
G := P[H];       /* G points to the generator */
P[EB] := G[EB];  /* install top of protected local stack */
P[H]  := G[H];   /* install top of protected heap */
goto alt;        /* transfer control to α */
```

2. chat_generator is a version of chat_choice for generators: its implementation is similar to that shown above taking into account differences in the fields of choice points that are involved. Since in this case $P = G$, it might seem that there was no need to change the ALT field of the generator and in fact, as far as the management of H and EB fields is concerned, this is true. However, all choice points need to have (a variant of) a chat_choice instruction as we will also use this instruction for the purposes of sharing trail (cf. Section 5).

3. On backtracking over G, one case is that G is a leader: then nothing special needs to be done (except releasing frozen space and the CHAT areas), and another that G is not a leader. In the latter, we consider G shortly as a new consumer (for which no CHAT area is needed) and execute the chat_choice code on the part of the choice point stack between G and its nearest generator.

4. A *coup*, i.e. a change of leaders, happens always by the creation of a consumer C which turns one (or more than one) leader G into a non-leader while some other older generator say G_L becomes the leader of the scheduling component that G belongs to. Since G_L is necessarily older than G, the generator nearest to C is always younger or equal to G, so backtracking over a generator as described above deals with this case already. In other words, a *coup* requires no special action in the context of the extended CHAT model.

5 Sharing More Trail

Let us initially assume that each generator G has an associated flat set $S(G)$ of consumers C which have G as nearest generator; $S(G)$ will later get more structure. All consumers in $S(G)$ have copied (in CHAT areas) part of the trail and for each C one can find up to which trail value C has the trail saved. On backtracking to a choice point P with alternative chat_choice, CHAT has the chance to share the segment of the trail between the current top of trail **TR** and P[TR]: for the sake of explanation, let Q be the choice point that is immediately younger than P as in the picture below. Suppose Q once had a chat_choice instruction. This means that all consumers in $S(G)$ that needed it (in the picture C_1, C_2, and C_3) have copied the trail below Q[TR] (shown as the three regions below Q[TR]). Backtracking to P means that execution is about to forget the trail between Q[TR] and P[TR], so this is the moment to save it. CHAT saves it *once* and lets all the affected consumers share it using the same mechanism that is used for incremental copying of the trail on backtracking over a non-leader generator (see [5]). If Q never had a chat_choice instruction, it might appear that the situation is more difficult, but it is sufficient to note is that if Q never had a chat_choice instruction, there never was a consumer below Q. In that case, P must have lost any chat_choice instruction before backtracking from Q to P happened. This means that up to P, the trail was already saved for all relevant consumers.

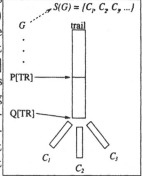

Before presenting code that achieves this sharing, we put some more structure in the set $S(G)$. Suppose execution backtracks to a choice point P with a chat_choice instruction. For each consumer C, we denote by $chat\_tr(C)$ the trail pointer up to which C has the trail in its CHAT area. Then, for every $chat\_tr(C)$ there is (or was) a choice point B such that either:

1. B is still on the stack and $chat\_tr(C) =$ B[TR] or
2. B has been removed (by trust or by cut) and the trail between $chat\_tr(C)$ and P[TR] is still intact

In the first case, B is older than P or $P = B$ and in both cases, no increment of trail must be copied for C. In the second case, if B is older than P, no increment must be copied for C. Otherwise, B is younger than P and the part of the trail between $chat\_tr(C)$ and P[TR] needs to be incrementally added to the CHAT area of C. Note also that the $chat\_tr(C)$ value for a particular C never increases in time, i.e. by copying more of the trail, $chat\_tr(C)$ moves higher in the stack and its value decreases.

The set: $T = \{tr | tr = chat_tr(C) \wedge tr > $ P[TR]$\}$ can be used to partition the set of consumers $S(G)$ into sets $CT(tr_i)$ according to the trail value tr_i up to which these consumers have the trail saved in their CHAT area. More formally, $CT(tr_i) = \{C | C \in S(G) \wedge tr_i \in T \wedge chat\_tr(C) = tr_i\}$ for $i = 1, \ldots, n$ for some n and such that $tr_i > tr_{i+1}$.

For a new consumer C with the same nearest generator G, if $n \neq 0$ $(S(G) \neq \emptyset)$ then $chat\_tr(C) \geq tr_1$: equality is possible if no trailing occurred in the execution from the nearest choice point (whether generator or not) and C. This property is important: it ensures that new consumers can be added to $S(G)$ in constant time and that the set $S(G)$ can be managed with no added complexity.

Trail sharing implementation With the definitions of $CT(tr_i)$ as above, tr_{n+1} defined as P[TR], and $CT(tr_{n+1}) = \emptyset$, the code to achieve trail sharing is:

```
CT := CT(tr₁);
for (i = 1; i ≤ n; i++)
  { construct (in a new CHAT area) the value trail between trᵢ and trᵢ₊₁;
    link this new CHAT area to the CHAT area of each consumer in T;
    CT := CT ∪ CT(trᵢ₊₁);
    S(G) := S(G) \ CT(trᵢ);
  }
S(G) := S(G) ∪ CT; /* all consumers in CT have same chat_tr(C) = P[TR]*/
```

This code is executed at the end of the chat_choice (and chat_generator) instruction, e.g. just before its goto alt statement (see Section 4). n is the number of sets $CT(tr_i)$ in the partition of $S(G)$. In an actual implementation, one would implement and maintain the sets $CT(tr_i)$ as an ordered linked list. There would be no need for having n explicitly, so the use of n does not add extra complexity. The step that links the saved trail to the consumers in T has in CHAT a cost equivalent to the cost of the back-pointers in the forward trail of SLG-WAM.

The tree structure of CHAT areas To further understand how the implementation of trail sharing has the desired complexity, we make explicit the tree structure of CHAT areas and how the trail is shared. When a consumer is frozen, its initial CHAT area is created; it contains just the consumer choice point and a link to a linked list of CHAT trail chunks. One such chunk consists of:

1. the value of the trail pointer up to which this chunk contains a reconstruction of the value trail
2. the reconstructed value trail
3. a link to the next chunk in the chain

So, initially, the chain contains one cell, in which the trail pointer equals C[TR] (if C is the consumer choice point) and an empty value trail: indeed, nothing below C[TR] has been copied (and will never be). This initialization has been chosen for reasons of simplicity, not by necessity. When an incremental part is added to a chain, it is added at the end. Two descendants of one node in the tree necessarily have the same trail pointer value. The set $S(G)$ is actually a forest of such CHAT area trees: there is a tree for each $chat\_tr(C)$ with $C \in S(G)$; see Fig. 5. One can see three consumers with their choice points C_1, C_2, C_3. In the trail chunks, we have indicated the TR value (the numbers 3, 4, 5 and 8) and the reconstructed trail segments: either by [] (for indicating an empty segment) or a number of dots equal to the number of trail entries. This number equals the difference between the TR value of the (any) descendant and the TR value of the chunk itself. In Fig. 5, C_1 and C_2 share the part of the trail between 3 and 5. If backtracking now happens to a choice point with a chat_choice and with a TR value smaller than 3, say 1, then all three consumers will share the segment between 1 and 3.

We can now refine the structure of $S(G)$: it is the list of roots in the forest of CHAT areas. This list is sorted in decreasing order of the values of their TR field. This ordering ensures that adding a new consumer to $S(G)$ is a constant time operation, since the new consumer has a TR root field that is larger than any element of $S(G)$. Also, the set operations in the code above become $O(1)$.

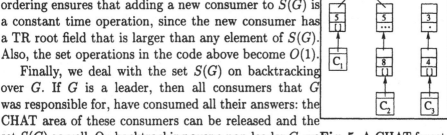

Finally, we deal with the set $S(G)$ on backtracking over G. If G is a leader, then all consumers that G was responsible for, have consumed all their answers: the CHAT area of these consumers can be released and the set $S(G)$ as well. On backtracking over a non-leader G, we merge $S(G)$ with $S(G')$ where G' is the generator immediately younger than G: indeed, $S(G')$ need not be empty !

Fig. 5. A CHAT forest.

The case of consumer below consumer Finally, we explain the only situation that is not described yet: suppose a consumer has been reinstalled and consumed an answer; execution continues and suppose a new consumer is encountered like in the execution of following query ?- p_g(Z). and program:

```
:- table p/1.
p(Z) :- p_c1(X), p_c2(Y), Z is X + Y, Z < 3.
p(1).
```

Here, the second consumer has the same (nearest) generator as the first, but this is immaterial. As far as protecting the execution environment of p_{c_2}(Y) through extended CHAT freeze is concerned, C_1 can be temporarily treated as a Prolog choice point and the same code as in Section 4 can be used. Furthermore, the second consumer should share the part of the trail that the first consumer has in its CHAT area, i.e. the trail between C_1[TR] and G[TR]. This sharing is most naturally established on backtracking over the first consumer, i.e. on backtracking to the generator (note that there is never a choice point between a reinstalled consumer and its scheduling generator; cf. Fig. 2(c)). This is achieved by adapting the code for the answer_return instruction (the instruction through which consumers resolve against answers) so that after consumption of the last answer, the CHAT trail of the consumer is linked to all CHAT areas needing it.

6 Using the Trail Sharing on Reinstalling Consumers

We have shown how CHAT can share trail chunks between suspended consumers in the same way as in SLG-WAM. This is nice, but not enough: CHAT needs to also be able to exploit this trail sharing when restoring environments. Indeed, SLG-WAM will undo and reinstall the minimal set of bindings needed for moving from one node (the source) in the search tree to another (the target). However, note the following: Moving between two non-consumers is the normal Prolog backtracking and sharing between such execution nodes never exists. Similarly, moving from a consumer to a non-consumer is either usual backtracking after the consumer's creation, or backtracking on completion of a scheduling generator and thus does not involve sharing of trail either. Thus, sharing is possible *only* when the target node is a consumer; still the source node can be a consumer or not. We will show that in both cases, the same use of trail sharing as in SLG-WAM can be achieved by CHAT without added complexity.

6.1 Context switching from one consumer to another

This is the situation in which a generator G schedules one consumer after another. To achieve trail sharing in CHAT, generators should be aware of the fact that they have previously scheduled some consumer. The mechanism for this is easy: on scheduling for the first time a consumer, CHAT can simply replace the completion instruction by a new instruction, say next_completion, which takes into account that scheduling has happened before. I.e. backtracking to this G possibly means that a context switch between consumers is about to take place. An alternative is to let a consumer, upon finishing consumption of the current set of available answers, set a flag that the completion instruction tests. Furthermore, each generator should know which consumer it has previously scheduled: again a global variable (set by the consumer) can be used, or the scheduling generator can keep it in one of its slots, or we can simply rely on the fact that in CHAT the consumer choice point is immediately below the generator and find out its identity from there. Let a_1 denote the first trail area of the consumer which was already scheduled, and a_2 likewise for the next consumer to be scheduled. Then CHAT can use the shared trail — which takes the form of a tree, accessible from its leaves — in a way similar to how SLG-WAM finds the common part of the trail between two consumers. Detailed code to achieve this is given in Fig. 6.

In this code, we have assumed that we can go up in the tree of CHAT trail areas with a function up(*area*) and that a function TR(*area*) gives the trail pointer in that area. The test younger() reflects the order in which CHAT trail chunks are allocated; the implementation has to cater for it either using its own memory allocator, or alternatively through timestamps. The code assumes there is a common ancestor and minor modifications cater for the case in which there isn't. The correctness of this code derives partly from the observation that two consumers never share their lowest trail segment.

```
tr₁ := TR(a₁); tr₂ := TR(a₂);
start := a₂;
while (tr₁ != tr₂)
  { if (younger(tr₁,tr₂))
      { a₁ := up(a₁);
        untrail from tr₁ to TR(a₁);
        tr₁ := TR(a₁);
      }
    else
      { a₂ := up(a₂);
        tr₂ := TR(a₂);
      }
  }
while (start != a₂)
  { reinstall_bindings_from(start);
    start := up(start);
  }
```

Fig. 6. CHAT code to context-switch.

In this way, the shared part of the
trail is not de-installed and re-installed
as in the original CHAT. Given the correspondence between the tree structure
of the trail in CHAT and in SLG-WAM (cf. also Section 7), and by comparing
this code to that given for the restore_bindings procedure in [11], it should be
clear that the same use of sharing of trail parts is achieved as in SLG-WAM.

6.2   Context switching from a non-consumer to a consumer

This action happens on backtracking for the first time to a generator that has no
more clauses to execute, so execution goes to the completion instruction which
will schedule some consumer that waits for answers. The execution of the query
?- p_g(X). against the following piece of code shows such a situation.

```
:- table p/1.                              q(1).
p(X) :- comp, q(T), r(T,X).                q(2).
r(1,X) :- pc(Y), X is Y + 1, X =< 200.
r(2,100).
```

Suppose that the goal comp stands for a computation that left something on
the trail but has no more choice points. The goal p_c(Y) suspends. Then the goal
q(T) backtracks to the second and last alternative and the generator gets its first
answer (X = 100). Then backtracking occurs to the generator's chat_generator
instruction, which will cause the addition of the trail part of comp to be added
to the CHAT area of p_c(Y). Then, on failing back to the generator choice point,
a consumer is scheduled: in this case, there is only one consumer and one could
argue that it is clear that its installation does not need to undo and then reinstall
the bindings represented by the trail of comp. In general however, there can be
several consumers. If any of these just got an increment of trail (because the
generator had a chat_generator) and is now scheduled, sharing is easy to get,
on condition that the generator remembers which consumers' CHAT trails were
just added to. It is fairly obvious how to do this and one gets again the same
use of sharing as in SLG-WAM.

In general, it is of course possible that on backtracking to a generator, it has
the completion instruction instead of a chat_generator. This means that no consumer will get the youngest trail increment, simply because the last alternative
of the generator did not have any consumers. That means also that sharing is
impossible both in CHAT and SLG-WAM.

Finally, note that giving up on using the sharing of trail when switching
from a non-consumer to a consumer, does not increase the complexity of overall
execution, as this happens for each generator only once and the extra cost is
proportional to a trail chunk that was constructed before. This applies equally
to both SLG-WAM and CHAT.

7   More about the Trail

In [5] we have already argued how the trail is different from the local stack and
the heap: For the local stack and the heap, it is enough (for correctness) to

maintain a safe approximation of their tops (any over estimation is safe). On the other hand, a WAM-based implementation must keep track *exactly* of which trail entries are between each two choice points. This is the deeper reason why the SLG-WAM uses back-pointers in its trail: the trail has a tree structure which mimics the tree structure of the choice points, but because choice points tend to disappear (by e.g. cut or trust) the trail has to maintain its tree structure independently. CHAT also uses back-pointers to link incremental CHAT trail areas: when each such trail area contains only one reference-value pair, the CHAT trail looks exactly like the backward-linked SLG-WAM trail.

SLG-WAM trail without back-pointers This similarity between the incremental CHAT trail areas and the SLG-WAM trail raises the question whether it is also possible to implement a trail in SLG-WAM *without* all the back-pointers. This is indeed possible: Let trail chunk mean a part of the trail that was created between the execution of two try instructions. Let the first try instruction save TR on the trail stack [4]. Subsequent trailing will consist in pushing only a reference-value pair. On the execution of the next try instruction, push the length of the trail chunk. It is easy to see that this organization still permits finding common ancestors.

Also worth noting is that the SLG-WAM is pessimistic in that the reference-value pair is always constructed, while CHAT postpones construction of a value trail chunk until the trail on the stack is about to be overwritten. It follows that trail chunks in CHAT tend to be larger and less back-pointers will be needed, because choice points can disappear before the trail chunk is constructed.

The concept of "nearest common ancestor" We take this opportunity to dwell on the SLG-WAM mechanism for finding the "nearest common ancestor". Even though intuitively, the nearest common ancestor is a choice point, one has to take into account that choice points (between a consumer and its generator) can die earlier than the consumer because of cut or the trust instruction. This means that the nearest common choice point is time-dependent. However, for the context switch from one consumer to another, one does not need the common choice point, but rather the point up to which in the trail one needs to untrail and from which to start reinstalling bindings. Moreover, the trail reflects the tree of choice points as well, and is (barring tidy trail at cut) time-independent. This leads to the SLG-WAM mechanism for finding the nearest common ancestor, based on the trail and on the back-pointers in the trail entries.

By using the choice points, a worse nearest common ancestor could be found in general: sub-optimal untrailing and reinstallation of bindings can result. Moreover, even if choice points do not disappear, finding the common ancestor in SLG-WAM by following the (frozen) choice points can be arbitrarily worse than by following the backward-linked trail entries and can affect the overall complexity. [5]. To show this, it is enough to construct an example in which there are

---

[4] Note that the top of the trail is (in SLG-WAM) in general not equal to TR

[5] The reverse is not true because untrailing and reinstalling the bindings is obviously linear in the size of the traversed trail.

two execution paths leading from a generator to two consumers. Each path has one trail operation and a number N of choicepoints. It will follow that finding the common ancestor choice point of the consumers is $O(N)$ and while finding the common ancestor trail point is $O(1)$.

8 Space Complexity of CHAT Compared to SLG-WAM

So far, we have argued that CHAT is Θ(SLG-WAM) time-wise. We now compare the space complexity of CHAT and SLG-WAM. In principle, we should consider each of the four stacks separately because each of them can exhibit different behavior. However, note that space requirements of local stack and heap are identical for CHAT and SLG-WAM. They are both based on making these stacks non-recoverable on backtracking and this happens exactly at the same moment in execution for both CHAT and SLG-WAM. Space is retained in both systems until completion of the scheduling component. The fact that the freezing mechanisms of the two tabling implementation alternatives are different plays no role.

The following analysis assumes that SLG-WAM does not compact the stacks and that CHAT does not take advantage from performing selective completion. The reason is that with selective (i.e. non-stack based) completion it is easy for CHAT to release CHAT trail areas in constant time, while SLG-WAM can achieve the same space reclamation only by means of trail stack compaction which has a higher cost. We also do not consider the effects of tidying the trail on cut for reasons of simplicity.

Space Bounds for the Trail Stack As mentioned in Section 3.1, each trail entry of the SLG-WAM requires three cells. In CHAT a trail entry requires one cell while in the (WAM) stack and two cells when in a CHAT area. In the CHAT area, one additional cell *per chunk* is needed to "connect" a saved trail area to its next increment. The latter implies that the worst case for the CHAT trail area occurs when each trail chunk consists of exactly one trail entry: the CHAT trail area corresponds exactly to a forward trail entry in SLG-WAM. Since in CHAT a trail entry can at the same time also be in the active computation, the following equality holds in this worst case:

$$trailsize(\text{CHAT}) = \frac{4}{3}\ trailsize(\text{SLG-WAM})$$

The best case for CHAT occurs when there are no tabled subgoals, because then CHAT uses only one third the space, i.e.

$$trailsize(\text{CHAT}) = \frac{1}{3}\ trailsize(\text{SLG-WAM})$$

In summary, we have that:

$$\frac{1}{3} \leq \frac{trailsize(\text{CHAT})}{trailsize(\text{SLG-WAM})} \leq \frac{4}{3}$$

Space Bound for the Choice Point Stack Concerning choice point space, CHAT can perform worse than SLG-WAM only because at some points of execution a consumer choice point can be both at the stack and in the CHAT area. The only point at which this happens is when a consumer is resumed and as long as it remains resumed: indeed, as long as it is suspended, the consumer resides only in the CHAT area. Since Prolog choice points between the generator and the consumer tend to favor CHAT (see example below) the worst case cannot involve such Prolog choice points. Since each generator G can have at most one resumed consumer C at a time and since each resumed consumer C can only exist if there is a corresponding generator G, the worst case consists in a succession of (G_i, C_i) pairs where each G_i has scheduled C_i. It follows that the following inequality holds as a worst case for CHAT:

$$\frac{choicepointsize(\text{CHAT})}{choicepointsize(\text{SLG-WAM})} \leq \frac{3}{2}$$

This flatters slightly SLG-WAM, as generator choice points tend to be larger than consumer choice points.

On the other hand, CHAT wins from SLG-WAM arbitrarily when non-tabled choice points between the generator and consumer are popped on reinstalling the consumer. This can be seen in the program of Fig. 7: lots of Prolog choice points get trapped under a consumer; in CHAT, they can be reclaimed, while in SLG-WAM they are frozen and retained till completion. When called with

```
query(Choices,Consumers) :- p_g(_), create(Choices,Consumers), fail.
create(Choices,Consumers) :- Consumers > 0,
    ( make_choicepoints(Choices), p_c(Y), Y = 2
    ; C is Consumers - 1, create(Choices,C) ).
make_choicepoints(C) :- C > 0, C1 is C - 1, make_choicepoints(C1).
make_choicepoints(0).
:- table p/1.
p(1).
```

Fig. 7. Tabled program where CHAT has better space complexity than SLG-WAM.

e.g. ?- query(29,97). the maximal choice point usage of SLG-WAM is one generator, $29 * 97$ Prolog choice points plus 97 consumer choice points; while CHAT's maximal choice point usage is the generator, one consumer, 29 Prolog choice points and 97 consumer choice points in the CHAT areas.

9   Related Work

At least in the area of logic programming, "theoretical" implementation papers are not very common. Even at the level of the abstract machine specification, establishing correspondences between different implementation models and relating their properties is quite hard. As a result, the best that theoreticians have thus far achieved is either re-construct a particular abstract machine [8], or verify that the machine [1] or its compiler [10] execute according to the intended semantics of the language. On the other side, implementors are usually content with fully describing their abstract machines, arguing why a particular operation is performed faster in their model (usually at the expense of other operations), and/or comparing their implementation's performance against other systems on a "standard" set of benchmarks (see e.g. [13] and the references therein). To our knowledge, there is no result that a given abstract machine is optimal (i.e. uniformly better that the others): faithful comparisons between abstract machine designs most often show trade-offs. Moreover, worst-case performance of abstract machines is often not mentioned, sometimes not even known by the authors to exist, or all too easily dismissed as unlikely to occur in practice. While this might be true for average uses of an abstract machine, we believe it is important to know in advance how well the design scales and how the abstract machine's performance evolves under extreme circumstances.

There are of course notable exceptions that do prove complexity properties of abstract machines or of execution models. One nice such example is [7] which classifies various Or-parallel execution models based on primitive operations that need to be performed in this context (variable access, task creation and switching) and shows a very strong, negative result: no implementation model (with finite number of processors) can perform all three operations in constant time. While the complexity result in [7] is about a class of execution models, our result is more restricted, as it compares the characteristics of two specific abstract machines. This might account for our result being a positive one: namely that for the control of tabling, the same low cost of suspension/resumption can be obtained with environment sharing (as in SLG-WAM) or with a hybrid approach based on partial copying and partial sharing (as in CHAT). Consequently, the decision on which model to adopt can safely be based on other criteria, like e.g. performance overhead when tabling is not used or simplicity of implementation.

10   Concluding Remarks

We have shown how some adaptations of CHAT lead to an abstract machine for tabled evaluation that does not modify the WAM for non-tabled execution and still guarantees the same time and space complexity of tabled execution as SLG-WAM. Achieving this combination of strengths is by no means straightforward; in fact, for many years, implementors believed this combination was impossible to obtain and the incorporation of tabling into a Prolog system has often been ruled out as too expensive. On the other hand, we have reasons to believe that the complexity result for the modified CHAT described in this paper might be more of theoretical than practical interest because it seems that usually the impact of repeated traversal and sub-optimal trail sharing is very low. Indeed, in practice original CHAT has better performance than SLG-WAM (even on programs dominated by tabled execution), and the worst cases for CHAT have not been observed in real applications. However, as noted, we think that it is essential to know that the original CHAT design is not "just a hacked WAM-based model for implementing tabling that happens to *usually* work well" but that once faced with real programs that suffer from CHAT's worst-case complexity, there exists a "cure" in the form of a relatively simple addition.

Another important idea of independent and more practical interest in this paper is that of manipulating some Prolog choice points — in a way that is transparent to the underlying WAM — to (temporarily) assume a new functionality, which in this case partly overlaps with the functionality that the SLG-WAM reserved for generators. This technique leads naturally to new scheduling strategies of the "premature scheduling" kind, i.e. where scheduling is not only possible by (real) generators, but also by intermediate Prolog choice points that function like scheduling generators for some time. One of the added values of doing so, is that these scheduling strategies have even less context switching overhead (between execution environments of consumers) than strategies currently known. This is because scheduling decisions would then take place lower, or in any case more locally, in the execution tree. Another advantage is that scheduling of some consumers can naturally occur even before the associated generators finish program clause resolution. The performance benefits of doing so are yet to be explored.

Acknowledgements

The second author was supported by a K.U. Leuven junior scientist fellowship.

References

1. E. Börger and D. Rosenzweig. The WAM — Definition and compiler correctness. In C. Beierle and L. Plümer, editors, *Logic Programming: Formal Methods and Practical Applications*, pages 20–90. Elsevier Science, North-Holland, 1995.
2. S. Dawson, C. R. Ramakrishnan, and D. S. Warren. Practical program analysis using general purpose logic programming systems — A case study. In *Proceedings of the ACM SIGPLAN PLDI*, pages 117–126, Philadelphia, May 1996. ACM Press.
3. B. Demoen and K. Sagonas. CAT: the Copying Approach to Tabling. In C. Palamidessi, H. Glaser, and K. Meinke, editors, *Principles of Declarative Programming (PLILP'98)*, number 1490 in LNCS, pages 21–35, Sept. 1998. Springer.
4. B. Demoen and K. Sagonas. Memory Management for Prolog with Tabling. In *Proceedings of ISMM'98: ACM SIGPLAN International Symposium on Memory Management*, pages 97–106, Vancouver, B.C., Canada, Oct. 1998. ACM Press.
5. B. Demoen and K. Sagonas. CHAT: the Copy-Hybrid Approach to Tabling. In G. Gupta, editor, *Practical Aspects of Declarative Languages (PADL)*, number 1551 in LNCS, pages 106–121, San Antonio, Texas, Jan. 1999. Springer.
6. J. Freire, T. Swift, and D. S. Warren. Beyond depth-first strategies: Improving tabled logic programs through alternative scheduling. *JFLP*, 1998(3), Apr. 1998.
7. G. Gupta and B. Jayaraman. Analysis of Or-parallel execution models. *ACM Trans. Prog. Lang. Syst.*, 15(4):659–680, Sept. 1993.
8. P. Kursawe. How to invent a Prolog machine. *New Gen. Comp.*, 5(1):97–114, 1987.
9. Y. S. Ramakrishna, C. R. Ramakrishnan, I. V. Ramakrishnan, S. Smolka, T. Swift, and D. S. Warren. Efficient model checking using tabled resolution. In *Proceedings of the 9th CAV*, number 1254 in LNCS, pages 143–154, July 1997. Springer.
10. D. M. Russinoff. A verified Prolog compiler for the Warren Abstract Machine. *J. of Logic Program.*, 13(4):367–412, Aug. 1992.

11. K. Sagonas and T. Swift. An abstract machine for tabled execution of fixed-order stratified logic programs. *ACM Trans. Prog. Lang. Syst.*, 20(3):586–634, May 1998.
12. K. Sagonas, T. Swift, and D. S. Warren. XSB as an efficient deductive database engine. In *Proceedings of the ACM SIGMOD'94*, pages 442–453, May 1994. ACM.
13. P. Van Roy. 1983–1993: The wonder years of sequential Prolog implementation. *J. of Logic Program.*, 19/20:385–441, May/July 1994.
14. D. H. D. Warren. An abstract Prolog instruction set. Technical Report 309, SRI International, Menlo Park, U.S.A., Oct. 1983.
15. D. S. Warren. Efficient Prolog memory management for flexible control strategies. In *Proceedings of the 1984 Symp. Logic Program.*, pages 198–202, Feb. 1984. IEEE.

Proving Failure of Queries for Definite Logic Programs Using XSB-Prolog

Nikolay Pelov and Maurice Bruynooghe

Departement Computerwetenschappen
Katholieke Universiteit Leuven
Celestijnenlaan 200A
B-3001 Heverlee, Belgium
E-mail: {pelov,maurice}@cs.kuleuven.ac.be

Abstract. Proving failure of queries for definite logic programs can be done by constructing a finite model of the program in which the query is false. A general purpose model generator for first order logic can be used for this. A recent paper presented at PLILP98 shows how the peculiarities of definite programs can be exploited to obtain a better solution. There a procedure is described which combines abduction with tabulation and uses a meta-interpreter for heuristic control of the search. The current paper shows how similar results can be obtained by direct execution under the standard tabulation of the XSB-Prolog system. The loss of control is compensated for by better intelligent backtracking and more accurate failure analysis.

1 Introduction

In [2] methods are studied for proving that a query for a definite logic program fails. The general idea underlying all methods is the generation of a finite model of the definite program in which the query is false. However the approach developed in [2] is quite different from that used in general purpose model generators for first order logic such as FINDER [10], SEM [12], and FMC$_{ATINF}$ [7]. Whereas the latter systems search for a model in the space of interpretations, the former searches in the smaller space of pre-interpretations and applies a top-down proof procedure using tabulation to verify whether the query is false in the least model of the Horn theory based on the candidate pre-interpretation. Experiments in [3], an extended version of [2], show that the abductive procedure of [2] extended with intelligent backtracking [1] outperforms FINDER and FMC$_{ATINF}$ on problems where there are a large number of different interpretations for a given pre-interpretation. The difference is not only in the number of backtracks, but also, for some problems, in time, and this notwithstanding the former is implemented as a straightforward meta-interpreter in Prolog while the latter are sophisticated implementations in a more low level language.

The current paper describes how the meta-interpreter can be replaced by a more direct implementation in XSB-Prolog [9, 4] which relies on the XSB system to perform the tabulation. This is not a straightforward task because of the intelligent backtracking and because the meta-interpreter does not follow the standard depth-first left-to-right search strategy but uses heuristics to direct the search towards early failures and selects the pre-interpretation on the fly, as components are needed by the proof procedure. To exploit the tabling system underlying XSB, one has to stick to the depth-first left-to-right execution order and one should not modify the program by creating new components of the pre-interpretation while evaluating a call to a tabled predicate.

The random selection of an initial pre-interpretation, combined with the loss of control over the search results in a system which has to explore a substantially larger part of the search space than the original system. The paper introduces two innovations to compensate for this. Firstly, it uses a variant of intelligent backtracking which is much less dependent on the random initial order of the choice points. Secondly, it introduces a more accurate failure analysis, so that smaller conflict sets are obtained and that the intelligent backtracking selects its targets with more accuracy.

The motivation for this research is in the world of planning. Planners are typically programs which search in an infinite space of candidate plans for a plan satisfying all requirements. The planner searches forever (until some resource is exhausted) when no candidate plan satisfies all requirements. Hence it is useful to have methods to show that the problem has no solution. It turns out that our approach outperforms first order model generators on planning problems.

In the next section we recall some basic notions about semantic of definite logic programs. In Section 3 we describe our approach in more detail and then in Section 4 we show the results of testing our system on different problems. The comparison not only includes the model generator FINDER [10] as in [2], and FMC_{ATINF} as in [3] but also SEM [12].

2 Preliminaries

Now we will recall some basic definitions about semantics of definite programs. Most of them are taken from [6].

A *pre-interpretation* J of a program P consists of domain $D = \{d_1, \ldots, d_m\}^1$ and for each n-ary function symbol f in P a mapping f_J from D^n to D. Following the literature on model generators, a term of the form $f(d_1, \ldots, d_n)$ where $d_1, \ldots, d_n \in D$ is called a *cell*. Given a program P and domain size m, the set of all cells is fixed. A pair $\langle c, v \rangle$ where c is a cell and $v \in D$ is the mapping of that cell is called a *component* and v the *value* of the component. A set of components defines a pre-interpretation if there is exactly one component $\langle c, v \rangle$ for each cell.

A *variable assignment* V wrt. expression E and pre-interpretation J consists of an assignment of an element in the domain D for each variable in E. A *term assignment* wrt. J and V is defined as follows: each variable is given its assignment according to V; each constant is given its assignment according to J; if $d_1, \ldots, d_n$ are the term assignments of $t_1, \ldots, t_n$ then the assignment of $f(t_1, \ldots, t_n)$ is the value of the cell $f(d_1, \ldots, d_n)$.

---

[1] We will consider only domains with finite size.

An interpretation I based on a pre-interpretation J consists of a mapping p_I from D^n to $\{false, true\}$ for every n-ary predicate p in P. An interpretation I is often defined as the set of atoms $p(d_1, \ldots, d_n)$ for which $p(d_1, \ldots, d_n)$ is mapped to true. An interpretation M is a model of a program P iff all clauses in P are true in M. For a definite program, the intersection of two models is also a model hence a definite program always has a unique least model. As a consequence, if a conjunction of atoms is false in some model then it is also false in the least model of a definite program.

Throughout the paper we will use the following simple example about even and odd numbers to show the different concepts and program transformations.

```
even(zero).
even(s(X)) :- odd(X).
odd(s(X)) :- even(X).
```

Consider a query ?- even(X),odd(X). For simplicity of the presentation we will add to the program the definite clause

```
even_odd :- even(X),odd(X).
```

and consider the query ?- even_odd. It cannot succeed as ?- even_odd is not a logical consequence of the program. The SLD proof procedure does not terminate. This is still the case when extended with tabulation as in XSB-Prolog.

We choose a domain with two elements $D = \{0, 1\}$ and consider the pre-interpretation $J = \{zero_J = 0, s_J(0) = 1, s_J(1) = 0\}$. The least model of the definite program is $\{even(0), odd(1)\}$ and the atom even_odd is false in this model.

3   The Method

Figure 1 shows the general architecture of the system. The input consists of a definite program P, a query ?-Q and domain size m. First the program and the query are transformed to P^t and ?-Q^t. The transformation replaces all functional symbols with calls to predicates defining the components of the pre-interpretation and allows the program to collect the components which were used during the evaluation of the query. Also an initial pre-interpretation J is constructed for the given domain size m. Then the query ?-Q^t is evaluated wrt. the program P^t and the current pre-interpretation J. If the query succeeds then it also returns a set of components CS which are necessary for the success of the proof. Then, based on CS, the pre-interpretation is modified and the query is run again. If we have exhausted all possible pre-interpretations for the given domain size then we can eventually increase it and run the system again. If the query ?-Q^t fails then Q^t is false in the least model based on the pre-interpretation J and we can conclude that the original query ?-Q cannot succeed.

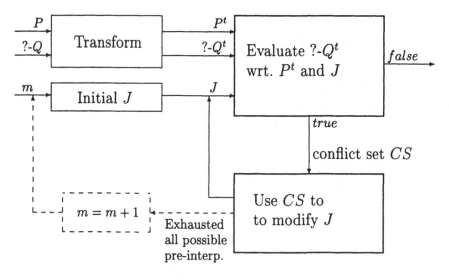

Fig. 1. System architecture

3.1 Basic Transformation

To evaluate the query in the least model based on a pre-interpretation J, we use a variant of the abstract compilation approach to program analysis used by Codish and Demoen in [5]. The pre-interpretation J of a n-ary function f is represented by a set of facts $p_f(d_1, \ldots, d_n, v)$; one fact for each cell $f(d_1, \ldots, d_n)$. In the source program, non variable terms are represented by their pre-interpretation. This is achieved by replacing a term $f(t_1, \ldots, t_n)$ by a fresh variable X and introducing a call $p_f(t_1, \ldots, t_n, X)$. This transformation is repeated for the non variable terms in $t_1, \ldots, t_n$ until all functions are eliminated. Codish and Demoen evaluate the resulting DATALOG program bottom up, obtaining the least model which expresses declarative properties of the program. In [2], one also transforms the query and using a top-down procedure with tabulation checks whether it fails. Experience showed that one typically ends up with computing the whole model of the predicates reachable from the query. So the meta-interpreter used there tables only the most general call for each predicate. As we want direct execution under XSB, our transformation has to take care that a program predicate is only called with all variables free and different, so that XSB tables only the most general call. To achieve this, a predicate $p_f(\ldots)$ which is added to compute a term t in a call is inserted after the call and a predicate which is added to compute a term in the head is inserted at the end of the clause. Finally, when a call to a program predicate contains a variable X which already occurs to the left of its position in the clause, then it is replaced by a fresh variable Y and an equality $X = Y$ is inserted after the call. The calls to the pre-interpretation are not tabled, and a call $p_f(g(\ldots), \ldots)$ is transformed in $p_g(\ldots, X), p_f(X, \ldots)$. This gives less branching than when $p_g(\dots)$ is added after $p_f(\dots)$. For our example this gives the following code:

```
even(X) :- p_zero(X).
even(Y) :- odd(X),p_s(X,Y).
odd(Y) :- even(X),p_s(X,Y).
even_odd :- even(X),odd(X1),X1=X.

p_zero(0).
p_s(0,1).
p_s(1,0).
```

In [2], values are assigned to the cells of the pre-interpretation in an abductive way, as needed by the heuristic search for a proof of the query. When a proof is found, standard backtracking occurs: the last assigned value is modified. To have direct execution under XSB, the pre-interpretation has to be fixed in advance. Obviously, it is not feasible to enumerate all possible pre-interpretations until one is found for which the query fails. The search has to be guided by the proof found so far. Failure analysis and intelligent backtracking have to be incorporated to obtain a usable system.

3.2   Failure Analysis

Elementary Failure Analysis. As the goal is to find a pre-interpretation for which the query fails, failure occurs when the query succeeds. In the more general setting of first order model generation, failure occurs when some formula gets the wrong truth value. The FINDER and FMC$_{ATINF}$ systems keep track of which cells are used in evaluating a formula and when the formula receives the wrong truth value, the set of cells used in evaluating it is used to direct the backtracking. In [3] the meta-interpreter is extended with such a failure analysis and intelligent backtracking is used to guide the search. This substantially improved the performance of the system. Incorporating these features in the current approach which relies on direct execution with XSB of the transformed query, requires special care. First let us formalize the notion of conflict set (refutation in first order model generators [7, 10]).

Definition 1 (Conflict set). *A conflict set CS of a definite program P and query Q is a finite set of components such that for any pre-interpretation J for which $CS \subseteq J$ follows that Q is true in any model of P based on J.*

The idea is that any pre-interpretation J which has the same values for all components from the conflict set CS can not be extended to an interpretation in which the query fails. Hence any candidate pre-interpretation must differ from CS in the value of at least one component. Exploiting conflict sets requires first to compute them. This can be done by adding to the program predicates an extra argument which is used to collect the components used for solving a call to this predicate. For example a call even(X) is replaced by even(X,CS) and the answer even(0) becomes even(0,[p_zero(0)]). However there is a potential problem. Also even(0,[p_zero(0),p_s(0,1),p_s(1,0)]) is an answer. Previously, the tabling system did not recognize it as a new answer and did not use it to solve calls to even/1. But as the value of the added second argument differs from that in the first answer, XSB will also use it to solve calls to $even/2$ and it will obtain a third answer. Fortunately, if the list of used components is reduced to some canonical form, then the third answer will be identical to the second and the evaluation will terminate. However, this repetition of answers with different lists of components can substantially increase the cost of the query evaluation. Fortunately the XSB system has built-in predicates to inspect and modify the tables so we can control this behavior. The idea is to replace a clause

```
p(X,CS) :- Body.
```

with a clause

```
p(X,CS) :- Body,check_return(p(X,CS)).
```

When the body of the clause succeeds, XSB will process the answer $p(X, CS)$ (add it to the table for the call to $p/2$ if it is new). Remember, that as the transformed program makes only most general calls there is only one table associated with each predicate. Using the built-ins, the predicate $check\_return/1$ looks up the previous answers in the table for $p/2$ and compares them with the candidate answer $p(X, CS)$. If there is no other answer with the same X then $check\_return/1$ and thus $p/2$ simply succeed. The interesting case is when the table already holds an answer $p(X, CS_{old})$ with a different conflict set CS_{old} (if $CS_{old} = CS$ then XSB will recognize it is a duplicate answer). Then several strategies are possible for check_return/1:

- The simplest approach is to let check_return/1 fail when the table already holds an answer with the same X.
- An alternative approach is to check whether the new conflict set CS is "better" than CS_{old}. Then the old answer is removed from the table and check_return/1 succeeds. Otherwise check_return/1 fails.
- Finally, but more expensive for the overall query evaluation, one could allow several answers, only rejecting/removing redundant ones ($p(X, CS_1)$ is redundant wrt. $p(X, CS_2)$ if $CS_1 \supseteq CS_2$).

Advanced Failure Analysis. A conflict set can be called minimal if it has no subset which is a conflict set. Obviously it is not feasible to compute minimal conflict sets. However, simply collecting the components used in a proof can be a large overestimation. For example, in our planning problems, a three argument predicate is used: one argument is the initial state, one argument is the final state and one argument is the description of the derived plan. The pre-interpretation of the terms representing the plan is completely irrelevant for the failure of the query. However the components used to compute it will be part of the conflict set.

To see how to refine our failure analysis, let us reconsider how answers are obtained. Using a slightly different notation, the base case of the *even*/1 predicate can be written as:

```
even(X) :- X=0_J.
```

This represents the basic answer, parameterized by the pre-interpretation J. Now consider the definition of the *odd*/1 predicate:

```
odd(X) :- even(Y),X=s_J(Y).
```

An answer of *odd*/1 is obtained by performing resolution with the basic answer for *even*/1, yielding:

```
odd(X) :- Y=X1,X1=0_J,X=s_J(Y).
```

This can be generalized, answers for a predicate p/n are of the form:

$$p(X_1,\dots,X_n) \leftarrow X_1 = t_{1_J},\dots,X_N = t_{n_J}, Eqs$$

with Eqs a set of equations involving $X_1,\dots,X_n$ and some local variables $Y_1,\dots,Y_n$. Under the elementary failure analysis the answer is $p(t_{1_J},\dots,t_{n_J})$ and the associated conflict set is the set of components used in computing $t_{1_J},\dots,t_{n_J}$ and the terms of Eqs.

The basis for the advanced failure analysis is the observation that the answer clauses can be simplified while preserving the solution they represent. Terms form equivalence classes under a pre-interpretations. Members of the equivalence class can be represented by the domain element which is their pre-interpretation and equalities between terms modulo equivalence class can be simplified using three of the four Martelli-Montanari simplification rules:

- $p(t_{1_J},\dots,t_{n_J}) \leftarrow X = X, Eqs$ is equivalent to
  $p(t_{1_J},\dots,t_{n_J}) \leftarrow Eqs$ (remove)
- $p(t_{1_J},\dots,t_{n_J}) \leftarrow t_J = X, Eqs$ is equivalent to
  $p(t_{1_J},\dots,t_{n_J}) \leftarrow X = t_J, Eqs$ (switch)
- $p(t_{1_J},\dots,t_{n_J}) \leftarrow X = t_J, Eqs$ is equivalent to
  $p(t_{1_J},\dots,t_{n_J})\{X/t_J\} \leftarrow Eqs\{X/t_J\}$ (substitute)

Note that $f_J(t_{1_J},\dots,t_{n_J}) = g_J(s_{1_J},\dots,s_{m_J}), Eqs$ is not equivalent to *false* and that $f_J(t_{1_J},\dots,t_{n_J}) = f_J(s_{1_J},\dots,s_{n_J}), Eqs$ is not equivalent to $t_{1_J} = s_{1_J},\dots,t_{n_J} = s_{n_J}, Eqs$, hence peel is not allowed.

So an answer can be simplified to a form

$$p(t_{1_J},\dots,t_{n_J}) \leftarrow Eqs$$

where Eqs contains equations between non variable terms and some of the t_{i_J} in the head can be variables. The pre-interpretations in the terms of Eqs decide whether Eqs is interpreted as true or false, hence the components used in interpreting the terms in Eqs form the real conflict set of the answer. However also the components used to interpret the terms t_{ij} of the head are important. When the answer is used to solve a call, they become part of new equations. Hence, with each variable we should associate a set holding the components used in evaluating the term the variable is bound to and with each answer we should associate the "real" conflict set. Moreover, the execution of the equalities $X = Y$ has to be monitored. When one of X or Y is free then unification can be performed, otherwise if X and Y have the same interpretation then the sets of components associated with X and Y have to be added to the conflict set of the answer (as before the equality fails when X and Y have a different interpretation). Note that our transformation is such that calls have fresh variables as arguments, so the equality between an argument of a call and an argument of an answer always involves a free variable and is correctly handled by standard unification. A final point is that the body of the compiled clause has to be carefully ordered: equalities on predicate calls involving a variable X should precede the interpretation of a term containing X, e.g. $p(X), Y = f_J(X)$ is a correct ordering: first the call $p/1$ binds X to a domain element and also returns the set of components CS_X used in computing that domain element. Then Y is bound to a domain element and the set of components used in computing it is $\{f_J(X)\} \cup CS_X$. Taking the above into account, the code for our example is as follows:

```
even(X,[]) :- comp(p_zero,[],X), check_return(even(X,[])).
even(X,CS) :- odd(Y,CS),comp(p_s,[Y],X), check_return(even(X,CS)).
odd(X,CS) :- even(Y,CS),comp(p_s,[Y],X), check_return(odd(X,CS)).
even_odd(CS) :-
    even(X,EvenCS),odd(Y,OddCS),
    merge(EvenCS,OddCS,CS1),unify(X,Y,CS1,CS),
    check_return(even_odd(CS)).
```

Calls to the pre-interpretation are made through an intermediate predicate comp/3 defined below. The call to combine_arg_cs/3 collects the conflict sets associated with the ground arguments of the function to be interpreted (none if the argument is a free variable) in ArgsCS and merge/3 extends ArgsCS with Comp, the consulted component of the pre-interpretation, to obtain the final conflict set ResCS.

```
comp(F,Args,R-ResCS) :-
    combine_arg_cs(Args,RealArgs,ArgsCS),
    append([F|RealArgs],[R],C),Comp =.. C,
    call(Comp),
    merge([Comp],ArgsCS,ResCS).

combine_arg_cs([],[],[]).
combine_arg_cs([A-[]|T],[A|T1],RestCS) :- !,
    combine_arg_cs(T,T1,RestCS).
combine_arg_cs([A-ACS|T],[A|T1],OutCS) :-
    combine_arg_cs(T,T1,RestCS),
    merge(ACS,RestCS,OutCS).
```

The merge/3 predicate makes the union of two sets (represented as lists) and places the result in a canonical form and unify/4 is used to monitor the unification process and can be defined by the following Prolog code:

```
unify(X,Y,S,S) :- (var(X);var(Y)), !, X=Y.
unify(X-Sx,X-Sy,Sin,Sout) :- merge(Sx,Sy,S), merge(S,Sin,Sout).
```

The first two arguments are the terms to be unified, the third is the current conflict set of the clause and the last argument is the new conflict set of the clause. The first clause handles the case that one is a free variable: unification is performed and the conflict set of the clause remains the same. The second clause handles the case that both arguments X and Y are bound to the same domain element. The set of components used in evaluating the first argument (Sx) and in evaluating the second argument (Sy) are added to Sin yielding $Sout$.

3.3 Intelligent Backtracking

Under standard backtracking, candidate pre-interpretations are enumerated according to some fixed total ordering $c_1, c_2, \ldots, c_n$ of the cells. When some partial solution $c_1 = d_1^1, c_2 = d_2^1, \ldots, c_m = d_m^1$ is rejected then the value assignment d_m^1 for the last cell c_n is modified. If no other value is left, then c_{m-1} is modified (and all domain elements become again available for c_m). The simplest use of conflict sets is based on the observation that no extension of the conflict set can be a solution, so the last element according to the total order over the cells of the conflict set is selected and the assignment to this cell is modified. However also secondary conflict sets can be derived [1]. Assume, due to different conflicts, all values for some cell c_n have been rejected. With $\{c_{i,1}, \ldots, c_{i,k_i}, c_n\}$ the conflict set which led the rejection of d_i we can formalize the knowledge in the conflict sets as:

$$c_{1,1} = d_{1,1} \wedge \ldots \wedge c_{1,k_1} = d_{1,k_1} \wedge c_n = d_1 \rightarrow false$$
$$\vdots$$
$$c_{m,1} = d_{m,1} \wedge \ldots \wedge c_{m,k_m} = d_{m,k_m} \wedge c_n = d_m \rightarrow false.$$

As we have that cell c_n must be assigned some domain element, we have $c_n = d_1 \vee \ldots \vee c_n = d_m$. Applying hyper-resolution [8], one can infer

$$c_{1,1} = d_{1,1} \wedge \ldots \wedge c_{1,k_1} = d_{1,k_1} \wedge$$
$$\vdots$$
$$c_{m,1} = d_{m,1} \wedge \ldots \wedge c_{m,k_m} = d_{m,k_m} \rightarrow false$$

which says that $\{c_{1,1}, \ldots, c_{1,k_1}, \ldots, c_{m,1}, \ldots, c_{m,k_m}\}$ is also a conflict set.

At the implementation level, an accumulated conflict set is associated with each cell and initialized as empty. When a conflict $\{c_1, \ldots, c_{n-1}, c_n\}$ is derived with c_n its last cell, then $\{c_1, \ldots, c_{n-1}\}$ is added to the accumulated conflict set of c_n. Once all assignments to a cell are exhausted, its associated conflict set holds the secondary conflict which can be used to direct further backtracking. This is the approach taken in [3] where it worked quite well, as the initial order was carefully chosen. In the current implementation, where the initial order over the cells is random, the system had to do much more search before finding a solution. Hence we adopted a variant of intelligent backtracking mentioned in [1] which leaves the cells unordered until they participate in a conflict. Under this approach, cells are split over two sets, a set with a total order (initially empty) and a set which is unordered. When a conflict is found, the cells from it which are in the unordered set (if any) are moved to the end of the ordered set. Then the last cell of the conflict set is chosen as target of the backtracking. Cells which are after the target in the total order return to the unordered set. This approach resulted in substantially better results.

3.4 Dealing with Equational Problems

There exists many problems which contain only one predicate, the equality predicate $eq/2$. They consist of a number of facts $eq(t_{i_1}, t_{i_2}) \leftarrow$ for $i = 1, \dots, m$ and a number of denials $\leftarrow eq(s_{j_1}, s_{j_2})$ for $j = 1, \dots, n$. To solve such problems, one has to add to the program the axioms for the equality theory for reflexivity, symmetry, transitivity and function substitution, the latter consists of an axiom

$$f(X_1, \dots, X_n) = f(Y_1, \dots, Y_n) \leftarrow X_1 = Y_1 \wedge \dots \wedge X_n = Y_n.$$

for each functor f/n. The least model of the standard equality theory is the identity relation over the domain of the interpretation, hence the search space can be reduced by restricting the interpretation of $eq/2$ to the identity relation.

In the abductive system of [3], this is achieved by initializing the interpretation of $eq/2$ as identity, and removing the standard equality theory (only the problem specific facts and denials remain). Backtracking is initiated as soon as either one of the denials $eq(s_{j_1}, s_{j_2})$ evaluates to true or one of the facts $eq(t_{i_1}, t_{i_2})$ results in an answer which is not in the identity relation.

With direct execution under XSB, a slightly different approach is required. Unification reduces to the identity relation, hence after compiling the terms, the call to $eq/2$ can be done by unifying the compiled terms. However, the problem is that all facts and denials need to be activated. Therefore a new predicate $p/0$ is introduced and defined as follows:

$$p \leftarrow \neg eq(t_{i_1}, t_{i_2}). \quad i = 1, \dots, m$$
$$p \leftarrow eq(s_{j_1}, s_{j_2}). \quad j = 1, \dots, n$$

Proving failure of the query $\leftarrow p$ yields the desired pre-interpretation. Indeed p is equivalent to

$$p \leftarrow \bigvee_{1 \leq i \leq m} \exists \neg eq(t_{i_1}, t_{i_2}) \vee \bigvee_{1 \leq j \leq n} \exists \, eq(s_{j_1}, s_{j_2}).$$

Hence p fails if the right-hand side is true, i.e. if

$$\bigwedge_{1 \leq i \leq m} \forall\, eq(t_{i_1}, t_{i_2}) \wedge \bigwedge_{1 \leq j \leq n} \forall\, \neg eq(s_{j_1}, s_{j_2})$$

is true. $\forall\, eq(t_{i_1}, t_{i_2})$ is equivalent with the fact $eq(t_{i_1}, t_{i_2})$ and $\forall\, \neg eq(s_{j_1}, s_{j_2})$ is equivalent to the denial $\leftarrow eq(s_{j_1}, s_{j_2})$. Thus p fails if the conjunction of the original facts and denials is true under the chosen pre-interpretation. Compilation of terms is as described in Section 3.1, i.e. a call $eq(s_{j_1}, s_{j_2})$ is replaced by a call $X_{j_1} = X_{j_2}$ preceded by the code computing the pre-interpretation of s_{j_1} and s_{j_2}. A call $\neg eq(t_{i_1}, t_{i_2})$ is handled in a similar way; the built-in $\backslash=$ (not unifiable) can be used instead of not equal. However, special care is required to ensure the arguments are ground in case t_{i_1} or t_{i_2} is a variable. Whereas the compilation leaves such variables intact, here it has to be mapped (the mapping introduces a backtrack point) to a domain element.

Similarly as in Section 3.2, conflict sets can be associated with terms for the task of advanced failure analysis. Hence a call $\neg eq(t_{i_1}, t_{i_2})$ is transformed in the sequence $interpret(t_{i_1}, X_{i_1}), interpret(t_{i_2}, X_{i_2}), disunify(X_{i_1}, X_{i_2}, S_{in}, S_{out})$ where $interpret/2$ is an abbreviation for the sequence of calls computing the pre-interpretation of the term and the associated conflict set and $disunify/4$ is defined as

```
disunify(X-Sx,Y-Sy,Sin,Sout) :-
    X\=Y,merge(Sx,Sy,S), merge(S,Sin,Sout).
```

4 Experiments

4.1 The Problems

We tested our system with a large number of different problems. Below we give a short description for each one of them and for some of them the source code is given in Appendix A.

List Manipulation. The appendlast problem uses the standard definition of the predicates append and last and the following query:

```
appendlast :- append(X, [a], Xs),last(Xs, b).
```

The reverselast problem is similar to the appendlast problem but uses the version of the predicate reverse with accumulator:

```
reverselast:- reverse(L, R, [a]), last(R, b).
```

The nreverselast problem uses the "naive" definition of reverse:

```
nreverselast :- reverse([a|X], R), last(R, b).
```

Multisets. The multiset?o are programs to check the equivalence of two multisets using a binary operator "o" to represent them. multiset3o is a problem which has a solution, thus failure cannot be proven for it.

Planning in the Blocks-World. These are simple problems for planning in the blocks-world. The theory for the blockpair problems has, besides the usual actions of the blocks-world, an action to add or remove a pair of blocks. In the blockzero problems, the extra action is to create a new block named $s(X)$ on top of a clear block X.

The queries ending in "o" use multisets based on the function o/2 and those ending in "l" use a standard list representation. Those problems which have the number 2 in their name do not collect the plan and those having 3 store the plan in the second argument. blockzero2ls[2] is a problem which has a solution.

TPTP-Problems. The rest of the examples are taken from the TPTP problem library [11]. In Table 1 in brackets are given the TPTP names for each one of them. All these problems are equational problems and are transformed in the way described in Section 3.4.

The tba problem is to prove an independence of one axiom for ternary boolean algebra.

The grp problem is to prove that some axiom is not a single axiom for group theory.

The cl3 problem is from the domain of combinatory logic and the goal is to find a set of combinators which satisfy axioms S and W and do not satisfy the weak fixed point property.

Table 1 gives some details about the properties of the problems. The column *#pred* shows the number of predicates. The column *size dom* gives the domain size for which the query has been evaluated (which is, for the failing queries, the minimum domain size for which a model proving failure exists). The column *size pre* gives the number of cells in the pre-interpretation and the next column *#pre* gives the number of all possible pre-interpretations for the given domain size. The column *size int* gives the number of atoms to be assigned a truth value in an interpretation and the last column *#int/pre* gives the number of different interpretations for a fixed pre-interpretation. For the TPTP problems this value is 1 because they have only one predicate for which the interpretation is known to be identity.

4.2 Results

The results with FMC_{ATINF} were taken from [7] or were sent to us by its author which was using a SUN 4 ELC machine. All other systems were run on SUN Sparc Ultra-2 computer. The system AB is the abductive system described in

---

[2] corresponds to blocksol in [2] and [3]

Table 1. Example properties

Example	#pred	size dom	size pre	#pre	size int	#int/pre
appendlast	2	3	12	3^{12}	13	2^{13}
reverselast	2	3	12	3^{12}	13	2^{13}
nreverselast	3	5	28	5^{28}	150	2^{150}
multiset1o	1	2	7	2^7	4	2^4
multiset2o	1	2	7	2^7	4	2^4
multiset3o	1	2	7	2^7	4	2^4
blockpair2o	3	2	19	2^{19}	12	2^{12}
blockpair3o	3	2	36	2^{36}	20	2^{20}
blockpair2l	5	2	19	2^{19}	32	2^{32}
blockpair3l	5	2	36	2^{36}	40	2^{40}
blockzero2o	3	2	19	2^{19}	12	2^{12}
blockzero3o	3	2	35	2^{35}	20	2^{20}
blockzero2l	5	2	19	2^{19}	32	2^{32}
blockzero3l	5	2	35	2^{35}	40	2^{40}
blockzero2ls	5	2	19	2^{19}	32	2^{32}
tba (BOO019-1)	1	3	32	3^{32}	9	1
grp (GRP081-1)	1	2	17	2^{17}	4	1
cl3 (COL005-1)	1	3	12	3^{12}	9	1

[3], however, running under (the slower) XSB-Prolog instead of Master Prolog for equal comparison. We used FINDER [10] version 3.0.2 and SEM [12] version 1.7 which are well known model generators implemented in C.

The system *naive* results from the direct translation of the system AB to XSB: it uses the same failure analysis, it starts from a random total order over the cells of the pre-interpretation and it uses the simplest variant of check_return which sticks to the first answer whatever the associated conflict set is. For the TPTP problems the standard equality axioms were used.

The systems *single CS* and *best CS* use a more sophisticated version of check_return which prefers the answer with the shorter conflict set, advanced failure analysis and the more sophisticated version of intelligent backtracking which leaves elements unordered until they participate in a conflict set. The system *single CS* uses the first answer to the top level query to direct the backtracking. The system *best CS* computes all answers to the top level query and then selects from them the conflict set which will add the fewest number of cells to the ordered sequence. Both systems use the technique described in Section 3.4 on the TPTP problems.

Table 2 gives the times obtained by the different systems. The time is in seconds unless followed by H, then it is in hours. A "-" means the example was not run. A "> n" means the system had still no solution after time n.

Table 3 shows the number of generated and tested pre-interpretations (number of backtracks). For the SEM system, we have modified the source code to report exactly this number. For the FINDER system we report the sum of the

Table 2. Execution times

Example	naive	single CS	best CS	AB	FINDER	SEM	FMC$_{ATINF}$
appendlast	919	0.76	1.63	1.42	0.07	0.01	45.21
reverselast	918	0.85	1.85	1.00	0.10	0.01	10.79
nreverselast	>2706	>1673	178	17.5H	> 1446	957	>900
multiseto1	0.18	0.06	0.12	0.08	0.02	0.01	-
multiseto2	0.07	0.20	0.47	0.10	0.02	0.01	0.02
multiseto3	0.94	0.54	2.77	0.28	0.03	0.01	-
blockpair2o	451	0.86	3.14	5.05	0.07	0.05	7.31
blockpair3o	>58	0.94	3.90	21.97	0.18	0.23	>900
blockpair2l	5303	1.86	7.85	3.56	0.04	0.05	204.9
blockpair3l	>222	2.05	9.70	53.88	0.12	0.18	>900
blockzero2o	7.93	7.94	4.35	2.84	0.11	0.09	-
blockzero3o	162	8.86	5.41	24.48	0.22	1.98	-
blockzero2l	18.49	2.00	20.71	5.67	0.23	0.10	-
blockzero3l	40.35	2.06	24.76	37.23	0.33	2.39	-
blockzero2ls	11.8H	648	2631	593	2287	5.05	>900
tba	>950	1331	3.65	3.29	0.03	0.03	0.06
grp	1189	1.05	5.89	13.94	0.03	0.01	-
cl3	0.13	3.85	1.63	1.03	0.02	0.03	0.04

number of *bad candidates tested* and *other backtracks*. Also in this table "-" means not run, "> n" means already n backtracks when interrupted. For the system *best CS* we give an additional column *total* which shows the total number of conflict sets obtained as "answers" to the query (divided by the number of backtracks, this gives the average number of conflict sets obtained when running the query).

4.3   Discussion

Comparing the systems *naive* and AB, we see that the straightforward transfer of AB to XSB results in a much worse behavior. Hence the heuristics used by AB to control the search have a big impact.

The effect of the advanced failure analysis is not reported separately. Its impact is only visible in the block*3? problems which compute, for the failure analysis, an irrelevant output argument. The advanced failure analysis makes these problems behave as well as the corresponding block*2? problems. Note that the AB system as well as all first order model generators behave much worse on the 3-argument problems than on the corresponding 2-argument problems. As computing some output is a natural feature of a logic program, the advanced failure analysis is an important asset of our system.

Adding more sophisticated backtracking which does not fix the order of the cells in advance yields a substantial improvement on most problems. The system *single CS* which sticks everywhere to the first conflict set is often the

Table 3. Number of backtracks

Example	naive	single CS	best CS		AB	FINDER	SEM	FMC$_{ATINF}$
	#bckt	#bckt	#bckt	total	#bckt	#bckt	#bckt	#bckt
appendlast	41045	56	27	136	43	180	27	110019
reverselast	41045	56	27	133	30	211	27	23445
nreverselast	>10000	>2000	221	2426	190170	$> 10^7$	31285086	>?
multiset1o	4	3	3	11	4	4	3	-
multiset2o	14	14	12	38	10	31	8	104
multiset3o	127	75	76	122	33	75	86	-
blockpair2o	9323	34	32	55	17	273	918	5567
blockpair3o	>3000	34	32	55	56	879	2904	>?
blockpair2l	32873	76	66	117	33	68	918	91404
blockpair3l	>6000	76	66	117	204	359	2904	>?
blockzero2o	577	241	48	148	158	823	3495	-
blockzero3o	1245	241	48	148	500	897	63032	-
blockzero2l	1145	190	181	1044	98	1131	3415	-
blockzero3l	2289	190	181	1044	380	1123	63288	-
blockzero2ls	128926	21544	20284	31969	3615	3999226	201882	-
tba	>4000	95369	41	91	72	23	5	33
grp	19996	71	138	210	361	24	14	-
cl3	5	670	93	191	41	30	3	-

fastest, although it often needs more backtracks than *best CS*. It fails only on
nreverselast which uses a 5 element domain and has a very large search space.
However, on the equality problems it becomes obvious that a good choice of
a conflict set is essential for solving such problems. In number of backtracks,
best CS compares quite well with AB. Only on blockzero2ls it needs a lot more
backtracks, while it needs a lot less on nreverselast. Perhaps on blockzero2ls,
which has no solution, it suffers from the less optimal ordering because the search
space has to be searched exhaustively.

From the model generators FINDER and SEM perform reasonably well in
terms of time and also in number of backtracks. However, the results for FINDER
were obtained only after a fine tuning of the different parameters and the representation of the problems (see [3]). The system also uses intelligent backtracking
for deriving secondary conflict sets and some other forms of failure analysis. It
has a smaller number of backtracks on the more complex planning problems
than SEM. The system SEM is the fastest in raw speed and is not so sensible to
the problem representation. Of the model generators, the system FMC$_{ATINF}$ is
the weakest on the class of problems we consider. This result contrasts with the
results in [7] where it is the best on several problems.

Compared with our system the model generators have to backtrack much
more on the planning problems and the other logic programs where they have to
explore the full space of interpretations while we look only for the least model
of the program for a given pre-interpretation (the extra cost of evaluating the

query in the least model is more than compensated for by the exponentially smaller search space). On the TPTP problems our system is doing worse which suggests that there is further room for making better use of the information in conflict sets.

5   Conclusion

In this paper we presented a method for proving failure of queries for definite logic programs based on direct execution of the abstracted program in XSB-Prolog, a standard top-down proof procedure with tabulation.

By using a better form of intelligent backtracking (proposed in [1]) which does not fix the enumeration order in advance and an improved failure analysis, we were able to compensate for the loss of flexibility which results from the direct execution of the abstracted program.

This way of intelligent backtracking could also be interesting for other systems, e.g. FMC_{ATINF} of which Peltier reports that it is quite sensitive to the initial enumeration order.

While difference in speed with the AB system are modest, the approach is still very interesting as the depth-first left-to-right execution results in a much better memory management so that larger problems can be tackled. The meta-interpreter of the AB system keeps track of the whole top-down proof tree in evaluating the query, which leads to very large memory consumption.

Interesting future work is to further investigate some control issues. One could explore whether there is a good compromise between computing only one solution to the query and computing all solutions. One could try to further improve the backtracking by developing some heuristics which order a group of new elements when they are inserted in the ordered sequence.

Acknowledgements

We want to thank Kostis Sagonas for his help with the XSB system. Maurice Bruynooghe is supported by FWO-Vlaanderen. Nikolay Pelov is supported by the GOA project LP+.

A   Code for Some of the Problems

A.1   Multiset

```
multiset1o :- sameMultiSet(a, X), sameMultiSet(X, b).
multiset2o :- sameMultiSet(o(a,o(a,emptyMultiSet)),o(X,o(emptyMultiSet,b))).
multiset3o :- sameMultiSet(o(a,o(a,o(emptyMultiSet,b))),
                 o(o(a,b),o(a,emptyMultiSet))).

sameMultiSet(X, X).
```

```
sameMultiSet(o(X, Y), o(X, Z)):- sameMultiSet(Y, Z).
sameMultiSet(o(o(X, Y), Z), U):- sameMultiSet(o(X, o(Y, Z)), U).
sameMultiSet(U, o(o(X, Y), Z)):- sameMultiSet(U, o(X, o(Y, Z))).
sameMultiSet(o(emptyMultiSet, X), Y):- sameMultiSet(X, Y).
sameMultiSet(X, o(emptyMultiSet, Y)):-sameMultiSet(X, Y).
sameMultiSet(o(X, Y), Z) :- sameMultiSet(o(Y, X), Z).
```

A.2 Planning Problems

Blocks are identified by integers represented as terms with the constant 0 and
the function $s/1$. The *actionZero*/3 predicate gives the possible actions and the
causesZero/3 predicate tries to find a plan. In both predicates the first argument
is the initial state, the last argument is the final state and the plan is collected
in the second argument.

```
blockzero3o :-
    causesZero(o(o(on(s(s(0)), s(0)), cl(s(s(0)))), em), Plan,
            o(on(s(0), 0), Z)).

causesZero(I1, void, I2):-
    sameMultiSet(I1, I2).
causesZero(I, plan(A, P), G):-
    actionZero(C, A, E),
    sameMultiSet(o(C, Z), I),
    causesZero(o(E, Z), P, G).

actionZero(holds(V), put_down(V),
        o(table(V), o(clear(V), nul))).
actionZero(o(clear(V), o(table(V), nul)), pick_up(V),
        holds(V)).
actionZero(o(holds(V), clear(W)), stack(V, W),
        o(on(V,W), o(clear(V), nul))).
actionZero(o(clear(V), o(on(V, W), nul)), unstack(V),
        o(holds(V), clear(W))).
actionZero(o(on(X, Y), o(clear(X), nul)), generate_block,
        o(on(s(X), X), o(on(X, Y), o(clear(s(X)), nul)))).
```

References

[1] M. Bruynooghe. Solving combinatorial search problems by intelligent backtrack-
    ing. *Information Processing Letters*, 12(1):36–39, Feb. 1981.
[2] M. Bruynooghe, H. Vandecasteele, D. A. de Waal, and M. Denecker. Detecting
    unsolvable queries for definitive logic programs. In C. Palamidessi, H. Glaser, and
    K. Meinke, editors, *Principles of Declarative Programming, 10th International
    Symposium*, volume 1490 of *Lecture Notes in Computer Science*, pages 118–133.
    Springer Verlag, Sept. 1998.

[3] M. Bruynooghe, H. Vandecasteele, D. A. de Waal, and M. Denecker. Detecting unsolvable queries for definitive logic programs. *Journal of Functional and Logic Programming*, 1999. To Appear.

[4] W. Chen and D. S. Warren. Tabled evaluation with delaying for general logic programs. *Journal of the ACM*, 43(1):20–74, Jan. 1996.

[5] M. Codish and B. Demoen. Analyzing logic programs using "PROP"-ositional logic programs and a magic wand. *Journal of Logic Programming*, 25(3):249–274, Dec. 1995.

[6] J. W. Lloyd. *Foundations of Logic Programming*. Springer-Verlag, second edition, 1987.

[7] N. Peltier. A new method for automated finite model building exploiting failures and symmetries. *Journal of Logic and Computation*, 8(4):511–543, 1998.

[8] J. A. Robinson. Automatic deduction with hyper-resolution. *Int. Journal of Computer Math.*, 1:227–234, 1965.

[9] K. Sagonas, T. Swift, and D. S. Warren. XSB as an efficient deductive database engine. *SIGMOD Record (ACM Special Interest Group on Management of Data)*, 23(2):442–453, June 1994.

[10] J. Slaney. Finder version 3.0 - notes and guides. Technical report, Centre for Information Science Research, Australian National University, July 1995.

[11] C. B. Suttner and G. Sutcliffe. The TPTP problem library (TPTP v2.1.0). Report AR-97-04, Fakultät für Informatik der Technischen Universität München, 1997.

[12] J. Zhang and H. Zhang. SEM: a system for enumerating models. In C. S. Mellish, editor, *Proceedings of the Fourteenth International Joint Conference on Artificial Intelligence*, pages 298–303, San Mateo, Aug. 1995. Morgan Kaufmann.

A Partial Evaluation Framework for Curry Programs*

Elvira Albert[1], María Alpuente[1], Michael Hanus[2], and Germán Vidal[1]

[1] DSIC, UPV, Camino de Vera s/n, E-46022 Valencia, Spain
{ealbert,alpuente,gvidal}@dsic.upv.es
[2] Informatik II, RWTH Aachen, D-52056, Germany
hanus@informatik.rwth-aachen.de

Abstract. In this work, we develop a partial evaluation technique for *residuating functional logic* programs, which generalize the concurrent computation models for logic programs with delays to functional logic programs. We show how to lift the nondeterministic choices from run time to specialization time. We ascertain the conditions under which the original and the transformed program have the same answer expressions for the considered class of queries as well as the same floundering behavior. All these results are relevant for program optimization in Curry, a functional logic language which is intended to become a standard in this area. Preliminary empirical evaluation of the specialized Curry programs demonstrates that our technique also works well in practice and leads to substantial performance improvements. To our knowledge, this work is the first attempt to formally define and prove correct a general scheme for the partial evaluation of functional logic programs with delays.

1   Introduction

The last few years have witnessed a maturity in the area of multiparadigm declarative languages in order to combine the most important features of functional programming (nested expressions, efficient demand-driven functional computations), logic programming (logical variables, partial data structures, constraints, built-in search), and concurrent programming (concurrent computations with synchronization on logical variables). The computation model of such integrated languages is based on a seamless combination of two different operational principles: narrowing and residuation.

The *residuation* principle is based on the idea of delaying function calls until they are ready for deterministic evaluation. Residuation preserves the deterministic nature of functions and naturally supports concurrent computations. Unfortunately, it is unable to compute solutions if arguments of functions are not sufficiently instantiated during the computation, though program analysis

---

* This work has been partially supported by CICYT TIC 98-0445-C03-01, by Acción Integrada hispano-alemana HA1997-0073, and by the German Research Council (DFG) under grant Ha 2457/1-1.

methods exist which provide sufficient criteria for the completeness of residuation [11, 19]. Residuating functional logic languages employ dynamic scheduling similarly to modern (constraint) logic programming languages, where some calls are dynamically delayed until their arguments are sufficiently instantiated to allow the call to run efficiently. Residuation is the basis for implementing many concurrent (constraint) programming languages such as Oz [32] and is also used in other multiparadigm declarative languages such as Escher [25, 26], Le Fun [2], Life [1], and NUE-Prolog [31].

On the other hand, the *narrowing* mechanism allows the instantiation of variables in expressions and then applies reduction steps to the function calls of the instantiated expression. This instantiation is usually computed by unifying a subterm of the expression with the left-hand side of some program rule. Narrowing provides completeness in the sense of logic programming —computation of all solutions— as well as functional programming —computation of values— (see [18] for a survey). To avoid unnecessary computations and to deal with infinite data structures, demand-driven generation of the search space has recently been advocated by a flurry of outside-in, lazy narrowing strategies (see, e.g., [10, 16, 28, 29]). Due to its optimality properties w.r.t. the length of derivations and the number of computed solutions, *needed narrowing* [10] is currently the best lazy narrowing strategy for functional logic programs.

Curry is a modern multiparadigm declarative language which combines functional, logic and concurrent programming styles by unifying (needed) narrowing and residuation into a single model [20, 21]. To support coroutining, the model provides for *suspension* of function calls if a *demanded* argument is not sufficiently instantiated. Similarly to recent residuation-based languages like Escher [25] or Oz [32], Curry represents (don't know) non-deterministic choices by explicit disjunctions, in contrast to narrowing which is usually defined with implicit disjunctions as in classical logic programming. The precise mechanism (narrowing or residuation) for each function is specified by *evaluation annotations*, which are similar to coroutining declarations in Prolog [30], where the programmer specifies conditions under which a call is ready for a resolution step. Deterministic functions are declared *rigid* (which forces delayed evaluation by rewriting), while non-deterministic functions are declared *flex* (which enables narrowing steps). By default, only predicates (i.e., Boolean functions) are considered flexible, while all other functions are rigid, but the user can easily provide different evaluation annotations. The computation domain considers disjunctions of (*answer* ∥ *expression*) pairs in order to reflect not only the computed values but also the different variable bindings. The following example illustrates the integrated model (the computation steps are denoted by $\xrightarrow{RN}$ as in [20]).

Example 1. Consider the following rules defining the less-or-equal function "$\leqslant$" and the addition "+" on natural numbers (built from 0 and s):

$$
\begin{array}{llll}
0 \leqslant N & \rightarrow & \text{true} & \qquad 0 + X \rightarrow X \\
s(M) \leqslant 0 & \rightarrow & \text{false} & \qquad s(X) + Y \rightarrow s(X + Y) \\
s(M) \leqslant s(N) & \rightarrow & M \leqslant N &
\end{array}
$$

where "$\leqslant$" is rigid and "$+$" is flexible. Then, the following goal is evaluated by freezing and awakening the function call to "$\leqslant$" (the subterm evaluated in the next step is underlined):[1]

$$
\begin{aligned}
\text{id} \parallel &\, X \leqslant Y \,\&\, \underline{X + 0} \doteq 0 \\
\xrightarrow{\text{RN}} &\, \{X = 0\} \parallel \underline{0 \leqslant Y} \,\&\, 0 \doteq 0 \;\lor\; \{X = s(Z)\} \parallel s(Z) \leqslant Y \,\&\, s(Z + 0) \doteq 0 \\
\xrightarrow{\text{RN}} &\, \{X = 0\} \parallel \text{true} \,\&\, 0 \doteq 0 \;\lor\; \{X = s(Z)\} \parallel s(Z) \leqslant Y \,\&\, \underline{s(Z + 0)} \doteq 0 \\
\xrightarrow{\text{RN}} &\, \{X = 0\} \parallel \text{true} \,\&\, \underline{0 \doteq 0} \\
\xrightarrow{\text{RN}} &\, \{X = 0\} \parallel \underline{\text{true} \,\&\, \text{true}} \\
\xrightarrow{\text{RN}} &\, \{X = 0\} \parallel \text{true} \,.
\end{aligned}
$$

Note that the second disjunction fails since $s(Z + 0) \doteq 0$ is unsolvable.

Partial evaluation (PE) has been established as an important research topic in both the functional [12, 22] and logic programming [15, 27] communities. Although the objectives are similar (typically, the specialization of a given program w.r.t. part of its input data), the general methods are often different due to the distinct underlying models and the different perspectives (see [6] for a detailed comparison). This separation has the negative consequence of duplicated work since developments are not shared and many similarities are overlooked.

Narrowing-driven PE [6] is the first generic algorithm for the specialization of functional logic programs. This framework provides the same potential for specialization as powerful (on-line) PE methods for logic programs (e.g., *conjunctive partial deduction* [24]) as well as functional programs (e.g., *positive supercompilation* [17]). The work in [7] formalizes an instance of the narrowing-driven PE method for inductively sequential programs based on needed narrowing. It lifts to the PE level the idea of only evaluating code when it is necessary. An attractive property of this instance is that it preserves the (inductively sequential) structure of the original program, and hence the same execution mechanism (namely, needed narrowing) can be safely used after the specialization. This property does not generally hold for other instances of the PE framework (see [7]).

The aim of this paper is to develop a partial evaluator for (kernel) Curry programs. Unfortunately, the approach of [7] is not powerful enough, since it follows the framework of [6] which does not consider the residuation principle. Hence, we generalize the original framework in order to deal with (inductively sequential) programs containing evaluation annotations for program functions. This task is difficult for several reasons. Firstly, a naïve adaptation of [7] in which floundering computations are simply stopped during PE is not adequate, since a poor specialization would be obtained in most cases and could even be unsafe in our setting (see Example 3). Thus, we introduce an extension of the standard computation model which allows us to ignore evaluation annotations during PE while still guaranteeing correctness. As a consequence, our method is less restrictive than many existing methods for (constraint) logic programs with

---

[1] Here $\&$ is the *concurrent conjunction operator*, i.e., the expression $e_1 \,\&\, e_2$ is reduced by reducing either e_1 or e_2, and $\doteq$ is the *strict* equality predicate.

delays, in which suspended expressions cannot be unfolded (e.g., [14]). Secondly, the inference of safe evaluation annotations for the partially evaluated programs is far from trivial (see Example 4). In particular, we are forced to split resultants into several auxiliary (intermediate) functions in some cases to correctly preserve the answer expressions as well as the floundering behaviour.

The main contributions of this work can be summarized as follows. We provide (total) correctness results for the transformation, including the equivalence between the original and specialized programs w.r.t. floundering-freeness. This can be used for proving completeness of residuation for the considered class of goals in the original program by analyzing the floundering behavior of the resulting program. In particular, proving floundering-freeness for the specialized program is in many cases trivial (or easier than in the original program) because partial evaluation can transform a rigid function into a flexible one (whenever the specialized call is already sufficiently instantiated), but not vice versa. Moreover, we also prove that the transformation preserves the (inductively sequential) structure of programs.

The structure of the paper is as follows. After some basic definitions in Sect. 2, in Sect. 3 we recall the formal definition of needed narrowing and residuation. A PE scheme for residuating functional logic programs is formalized in Sect. 4, together with a method to properly synthesize evaluation annotations for specialized functions. We also provide results about the structure of specialized programs and the total correctness of the transformation. Section 5 shows the practical importance of our specialization techniques by means of some examples and Sect. 6 concludes. More details and proofs of technical results can be found in [4].

2 Preliminaries

We assume familiarity with basic notions of term rewriting [13] and functional logic programming [18]. We consider a (*many-sorted*) *signature* Σ partitioned into a set C of *constructors* and a set $\mathcal{F}$ of (defined) *functions* or *operations*. We write $c/n \in C$ and $f/n \in \mathcal{F}$ for n-ary constructor and operation symbols, respectively. There is at least one sort *Bool* containing the constructors true and false. The set of *terms* and *constructor terms* with *variables* (e.g., x, y, z) from $\mathcal{X}$ are denoted by $\mathcal{T}(C \cup \mathcal{F}, \mathcal{X})$ and $\mathcal{T}(C, \mathcal{X})$, respectively. The set of variables occurring in a term t is denoted by $\mathcal{V}ar(t)$. A term t is *ground* if $\mathcal{V}ar(t) = \emptyset$. A term is *linear* if it does not contain multiple occurrences of one variable. We write $\overline{o_n}$ for the *list of objects* $o_1, \ldots, o_n$.

A *pattern* is a term of the form $f(\overline{d_n})$ where $f/n \in \mathcal{F}$ and $d_1, \ldots, d_n \in \mathcal{T}(C, \mathcal{X})$. A term is *operation-rooted* if it has an operation symbol at the root. $root(t)$ denotes the symbol at the root of the term t. A *position* p in a term t is represented by a sequence of natural numbers (Λ denotes the empty sequence, i.e., the root position). Positions are ordered by the *prefix* ordering: $u \leq v$, if there exists w such that $u.w = v$. Given a term t, we let $\mathcal{P}os(t)$ and $\mathcal{F}\mathcal{P}os(t)$ denote the set of positions and the set of nonvariable positions of t, respectively.

$t|_p$ denotes the *subterm* of t at position p, and $t[s]_p$ denotes the result of *replacing* *the subterm* $t|_p$ by the term s (see [13] for details).

We denote by $\{x_1 \mapsto t_1, \ldots, x_n \mapsto t_n\}$ the *substitution* σ with $\sigma(x_i) = t_i$ for $i = 1, \ldots, n$ (with $x_i \neq x_j$ if $i \neq j$), and $\sigma(x) = x$ for all other variables x. The set $\mathcal{D}om(\sigma) = \{x \in \mathcal{X} \mid \sigma(x) \neq x\}$ is called the *domain* of σ. A substitution σ is *(ground) constructor*, if $\sigma(x)$ is (ground) constructor for all $x \in \mathcal{D}om(\sigma)$. The identity substitution is denoted by id. Given a substitution θ and a set of variables $V \subseteq \mathcal{X}$, we denote by $\theta_{|V}$ the substitution obtained from θ by restricting its domain to V. We write $\theta = \sigma \; [V]$ if $\theta_{|V} = \sigma_{|V}$, and $\theta \leq \sigma \; [V]$ denotes the existence of a substitution γ such that $\gamma \circ \theta = \sigma \; [V]$. A term t' is an *instance* of t if there is a substitution σ with $t' = \sigma(t)$. This implies a *subsumption ordering* on terms which is defined by $t \leq t'$ iff t' is an instance of t.

A set of rewrite rules $l \to r$ such that $l \notin \mathcal{X}$, and $Var(r) \subseteq Var(l)$ is called a *term rewriting system* (TRS). The terms l and r are called the *left-hand side* (*lhs*) and the *right-hand side* (*rhs*) of the rule, respectively. A TRS $\mathcal{R}$ is left-linear if l is linear for all $l \to r \in \mathcal{R}$. A TRS is constructor–based (CB) if each lhs l is a pattern. In the remainder of this paper, a functional logic *program* is a left-linear CB-TRS. A *rewrite step* is an application of a rewrite rule to a term, i.e., $t \to_{p,R} s$ if there exists a position p in t, a rewrite rule $R = l \to r$ and a substitution σ with $t|_p = \sigma(l)$ and $s = t[\sigma(r)]_p$.

To evaluate terms containing variables, narrowing non-deterministically instantiates the variables such that a rewrite step is possible. Formally, $t \leadsto_{p,R,\sigma} t'$ is a *narrowing step* if p is a non-variable position in t and $\sigma(t) \to_{p,R} t'$. We denote by $t_0 \leadsto^*_\sigma t_n$ a sequence of narrowing steps $t_0 \leadsto_{\sigma_1} \cdots \leadsto_{\sigma_n} t_n$ with $\sigma = \sigma_n \circ \cdots \circ \sigma_1$. Due to the presence of free variables, an expression may be reduced to different values after instantiating free variables to different terms. In functional programming, one is interested in the computed *value* whereas logic programming emphasizes the different bindings (*answers*). Thus, for our integrated framework we define an *answer expression* as a pair $\sigma \, \| \, e$ consisting of a substitution σ (the answer computed so far) and an expression e. An answer expression $\sigma \, \| \, e$ is *solved* if e is a constructor term, otherwise it is *unsolved*. Since more than one answer may exist for expressions containing free variables, expressions are reduced to disjunctions of answer expressions. A *disjunctive expression* is a (multi-)set of answer expressions $\{\sigma_1 \, \| \, e_1, \ldots, \sigma_n \, \| \, e_n\}$, sometimes written as $(\sigma_1 \, \| \, e_1) \lor \ldots \lor (\sigma_n \, \| \, e_n)$. The set of all disjunctive expressions is denoted by $\mathcal{D}$.

The evaluation to ground constructor terms (and not to arbitrary expressions) is the intended semantics of functional languages and also of most functional logic languages. In particular, the equality predicate $\doteq$ used in some examples is defined (as in functional languages) as the *strict equality* on terms:

$$c \doteq c \to \texttt{true} \qquad\qquad \% \; c/0 \in \mathcal{C}$$
$$c(X_1, \ldots, X_n) \doteq c(Y_1, \ldots, Y_n) \to (X_1 \doteq Y_1) \; \& \; \ldots \; \& \; (X_n \doteq Y_n) \quad \% \; c/n \in \mathcal{C}$$

Thus we do not treat the strict equality in any special way, and it is sufficient to consider it as a Boolean function which must be reduced to the constant **true**.

3   A Unified Computation Model for FL Programs with Delays

The definition of needed narrowing [10] and its extension to concurrent programming [20] is based on definitional trees which have been introduced by Antoy [8] for the specification of efficient rewrite strategies. A definitional tree is a hierarchical structure containing all rules of a defined function. $\mathcal{T}$ is a *definitional tree with pattern* π iff the depth of $\mathcal{T}$ is finite and one of the following cases holds:

$\mathcal{T} = rule(\pi \to r)$, where $\pi \to r$ is a variant of a rule.

$\mathcal{T} = branch(\pi, o, r, \mathcal{T}_1, \ldots, \mathcal{T}_k)$, where o is an occurrence of a variable in π, $r \in \{rigid, flex\}$, $c_1, \ldots, c_k$ are different constructors of the sort of $\pi|_o$, for some $k > 0$, and, for all $i = 1, \ldots, k$, $\mathcal{T}_i$ is a definitional tree with pattern $\pi[c_i(x_1, \ldots, x_n)]_o$, where n is the arity of c_i and $x_1, \ldots, x_n$ are new variables.

A *definitional tree of an n-ary function* f is a definitional tree $\mathcal{T}$ with pattern $f(x_1, \ldots, x_n)$, where $x_1, \ldots, x_n$ are distinct variables, such that for each rule $l \to r$ with $l = f(t_1, \ldots, t_n)$ there is a node $rule(l' \to r')$ in $\mathcal{T}$ with l variant of l'. In the following, we write $pattern(\mathcal{T})$ for the pattern of a definitional tree $\mathcal{T}$. A defined function is called *inductively sequential* if it has a definitional tree. A rewrite system $\mathcal{R}$ is called *inductively sequential* if all its defined functions are inductively sequential.[2] We call a function *flexible* or *rigid* if all the branch nodes in its definitional tree are *flex* or *rigid*, respectively.

Example 2. Consider the rules defining the function "$\leqslant$" in Example 1. Then

$$branch(\text{X} \leqslant \text{Y}, 1, rigid, rule(\text{0} \leqslant \text{Y} \to \text{true}),$$
$$branch(\text{s(M)} \leqslant \text{Y}, 2, rigid, rule(\text{s(M)} \leqslant \text{0} \to \text{false}),$$
$$rule(\text{s(M)} \leqslant \text{s(N)} \to \text{M} \leqslant \text{N})))$$

is a definitional tree of $\leqslant$. It is often convenient and simplifies understanding to provide a graphic representation of definitional trees. Each inner node is marked with a pattern and the *flex/rigid* annotation, the inductive position in branches is surrounded by a box, and the leaves contain the corresponding rules. For instance, the definitional tree for the function "$\leqslant$" is illustrated in Fig. 1.

The definitional tree of a function determines the precise strategy in order to evaluate a call to this function. Informally, a rule node requires the application of this rule and a branch node requires the examination of the subterm of this function call which is specified by the position in the branch node. To provide concurrent computation threads, expressions can be combined by the *concurrent conjunction operator* &, i.e., the expression e_1 & e_2 can be reduced by reducing either e_1 or e_2. Note that we obtain the behavior of the needed narrowing strategy [10] if all functions are flexible. Moreover, functional logic languages

---

[2] Curry also supports rules with overlapping left-hand sides by providing *or* nodes in definitional trees, but we omit this feature here for simplicity.

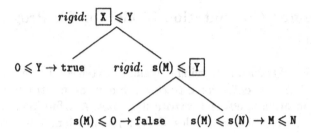

Fig. 1. Definitional tree for the function "$\leqslant$"

which are based on residuation, like Life or Escher, where functions are always deterministically evaluated or suspended and non–determinism is encoded by predicates, can be modeled with programs where all (non–Boolean) functions are rigid and all predicates (Boolean functions) are flexible.

For a precise definition of this operational semantics, it is convenient to distinguish between *complete* computation steps where one reduction has been performed and *incomplete* computation steps which are suspended due to some rigid branch.[3] Incomplete steps are called *degenerate* in [9] in the sense that some variables could have been instantiated but no subsequent reduction has been performed. We mark a substitution in an answer expression by the superscript s, i.e., $\sigma^s \circ \sigma' \parallel t$ to denote a *suspended answer expression* where the reduction part of the step has not been performed due to a suspension in a rigid branch. For convenience, we denote by σ^i a composed substitution with $\sigma = \sigma_n^s \circ \cdots \circ \sigma_1$, and by σ^c a composed substitution with $\sigma = \sigma_n \circ \cdots \circ \sigma_1$ where σ_1 does not have the form φ^s. Marks in substitutions are only a technical artifice to simplify our formulation and are simply ignored when composing and applying substitutions. $\mathcal{D}^s$ denotes the set of all disjunctive expressions where each disjunct could also be a suspended answer expression. Then the operational semantics of Curry is specified by the functions (see Fig. 2):

$$cs : \mathcal{T}(\mathcal{C} \cup \mathcal{F}, \mathcal{X}) \to \mathcal{D}^s \quad \text{and} \quad cst : \mathcal{T}(\mathcal{C} \cup \mathcal{F}, \mathcal{X}) \times DT \to \mathcal{D}^s$$

where DT stands for the set of all definitional trees. Moreover, the composition of substitutions and the replacement of subterms is extended to disjunctive expressions as follows:

$$\{\sigma_1 \parallel t_1, \ldots, \sigma_n \parallel t_n\} \circ \sigma = \{\sigma_1 \circ \sigma \parallel t_1, \ldots, \sigma_n \circ \sigma \parallel t_n\}$$
$$t[\{\sigma_1 \parallel t_1, \ldots, \sigma_n \parallel t_n\}]_o = \{\sigma_1 \parallel \sigma_1(t)[t_1]_o, \ldots, \sigma_n \parallel \sigma_n(t)[t_n]_o\}$$

As in proof procedures for logic programming, we assume that the definitional trees always contain new variables if they are used in a narrowing step. This implies that all computed substitutions are idempotent (we will implicitly assume this property in the following).

---

[3] In [20], this distinction is made by a special constant in the domain of disjunctive expressions while here we use a special mark at substitutions in answer expressions. We find this more convenient to formulate the PE method in residuating programs as will become apparent later.

Computation step for a single operation-rooted term t:

$cs(f(t_1, \ldots, t_n)) = cst(f(t_1, \ldots, t_n), \mathcal{T})$ if $\mathcal{T}$ is a definitional tree for f

$$cs(t_1 \,\&\, t_2) = \begin{cases} \text{true} & \text{if } t_1 = t_2 = \text{true} \\ (t_1 \,\&\, t_2)[cs(t_1)]_1 & \text{if } t_1 \neq \text{true and } cs(t_1) \text{ does not suspend} \\ (t_1 \,\&\, t_2)[cs(t_2)]_2 & \text{if } t_2 \neq \text{true}, cs(t_2) \text{ does not suspend,} \\ & \quad \text{and } cs(t_1) \text{ suspends} \\ id^s \,\|\, t_1 \,\&\, t_2 & \text{otherwise} \end{cases}$$

$cst(t, rule(l \to r)) = id \,\|\, \sigma(r)$ if σ is a substitution with $\sigma(l) = t$

$cst(t, branch(\pi, o, r, \mathcal{T}_1, \ldots, \mathcal{T}_k))$

$$= \begin{cases} cst(t, \mathcal{T}_i) \circ id & \text{if } t|_o = c(t_1, \ldots, t_n) \text{ and } pattern(\mathcal{T}_i)|_o = c(X_1, \ldots, X_n) \\ \emptyset & \text{if } t|_o = c(\ldots) \text{ and } pattern(\mathcal{T}_i)|_o \neq c(\ldots), i = 1, \ldots, k \\ id^s \,\|\, t & \text{if } t|_o = X \text{ and } r = rigid \\ \cup_{i=1}^k cst(\sigma_i(t), \mathcal{T}_i) \circ \sigma_i & \text{if } t|_o = X, r = flex, \text{ and } \sigma_i = \{X \mapsto pattern(\mathcal{T}_i)|_o\} \\ t[cs(t|_o)]_o \circ id & \text{if } t|_o = f(t_1, \ldots, t_n) \end{cases}$$

Derivation step for a disjunctive expression:

$(\sigma^c \,\|\, t) \vee D \xrightarrow{\text{RN}} (\sigma_1 \circ \sigma^c \,\|\, t_1) \vee \ldots \vee (\sigma_n \circ \sigma^c \,\|\, t_n) \vee D$
   if t is operation-rooted and $cs(t) = \sigma_1 \,\|\, t_1 \vee \ldots \vee \sigma_n \,\|\, t_n$

Fig. 2. Operational semantics of concurrent functional logic programming

The overall computation strategy is a transformation $\xrightarrow{\text{RN}}$ on disjunctive expressions. It takes an operation-rooted term[4] t of a non-suspended disjunct. Then the computation step $cs(t)$ stemming from t is performed, and the selected disjunct is replaced by the computed disjunction composed with the answer computed to that point. A single computation step $cs(t)$ applies a rule, if possible (first case of cst), or checks the subterm corresponding to the inductive position of the branch (second case of cst): if it is a constructor, we proceed with the corresponding subtree (if possible); if it is a function, we evaluate it by recursively applying the strategy to this subterm; if it is a variable, we suspend (in the case of a rigid branch) or nondeterministically instantiate the variable to the constructors of all children and proceed. Hence, a concurrent conjunction of two expressions proceeds by evaluating the conjunct which does not suspend. We say that a computation $D \xrightarrow{\text{RN}}{}^* D'$ flounders if every answer expression $\sigma^i \,\|\, t \in D'$ is suspended. A goal e flounders iff the computation starting from e flounders.

This strategy was first introduced in [20] and differs from lazy functional languages only in the possible instantiation of free variables and from logic languages in the lazy evaluation of nested function calls. Moreover, logic programs with coroutining (i.e., delayed predicates waiting for the instantiation of some argument) can be modeled by the use of the concurrent conjunction operator $\&$.

Note that, in each recursive step during the computation of cst, we compose the current substitution with the local substitution of this step (which can

---

[4] Here we consider only the evaluation of operation-rooted terms which is sufficient for functional logic programming where we are interested in reducing strict equalities to the constant true.

be the identity). Thus, each computation step can be represented as $cs(t) = \bigvee_{i=1}^{n} \sigma_{i,k_i} \circ \cdots \circ \sigma_{i,1} \| t_i$, where each $\sigma_{i,j}$ is either the identity or the replacement of a single variable computed in each recursive step. This is also called the *canonical representation* of a computation step. In contrast to the classical definition of narrowing (see Sect. 2), the definition of $\xrightarrow{RN}$ provides all (don't know nondeterministic) derivations at once by deriving an expression into a disjunctive expression. In order to relate $\xrightarrow{RN}$ to the classical nondeterministic narrowing relation, we also write $t \xrightarrow{RN}_\sigma t'$ if $\sigma \| t' \in cs(t)$.

The main difference with the needed narrowing strategy as introduced in [10] is the possibility that function calls may suspend and the special treatment of the concurrent conjunction & to deal with suspended evaluations. Therefore, we denote by $\xrightarrow{NN}$ and $\xrightarrow{NN}$ the relations defined similarly to $\xrightarrow{RN}$ and $\xrightarrow{RN}$ above but where the definition of $cs(t_1 \& t_2)$ is omitted and the case "$id^s \| t$ if $t|_o = X$ and $r = rigid$" is replaced by

$$cst(t, branch(\pi, o, r, \mathcal{T}_1, \ldots, \mathcal{T}_k)) = \cup_{i=1}^{k} cst(\sigma_i(t), \mathcal{T}_i) \circ \sigma_i^s$$
$$\text{if } t|_o = X, r = rigid, \text{ and } \sigma_i = \{X \mapsto pattern(\mathcal{T}_i)|_o\}.$$

The fact that $\xrightarrow{NN}$ also decorates suspended bindings with the superscript s instead of simply omitting the case "$id^s \| t$ if $t|_o = X$ and $r = rigid$" and the condition "$r = flex$" in the definition of cst (giving rise to the narrowing strategy of [10]) will become useful in the next section.

Note that the meaning of the concurrent conjunction & can be defined by the single rewrite rule $true \& true \rightarrow true$ which we assume to be implicitly added to the rewrite system when we consider needed narrowing steps. This function is inductively sequential and has the two definitional trees

$branch(X \& Y, 1, rigid, branch(true \& Y, 2, rigid, rule(true \& true \rightarrow true)))$

and

$branch(X \& Y, 2, rigid, branch(X \& true, 1, rigid, rule(true \& true \rightarrow true))).$

Now consider a term like $t_1 \& t_2$. It is obvious that a $\xrightarrow{RN}$ step where t_1 is evaluated corresponds to a needed narrowing step where the first definitional tree is taken for the root function &. Similarly, a $\xrightarrow{RN}$ step where t_2 is evaluated corresponds to a needed narrowing step with the second definitional tree for &. Thus, we obtain the following theorem which formalizes the relation between the two calculi.

Theorem 1. *Let $\mathcal{R}$ be an inductively sequential program and e a term.*

1. *If all steps in the derivation $e \xrightarrow{RN^*}_\sigma e'$ are complete, then there exists a needed narrowing derivation $e \xrightarrow{NN^*}_\sigma e'$ in $\mathcal{R}$.*

2. *If $e \xrightarrow{NN^*}_\sigma e'$ is a needed narrowing derivation for e in $\mathcal{R}$, then there exists a derivation $e \xrightarrow{RN^*}_\theta e''$ such that $\exists \varphi. \varphi(e'') \rightarrow^* e'$ and $\sigma = \varphi \circ \theta$.*

4 Partial Evaluation of Residuating Functional Logic Programs

In this section, we extend the framework of [6] (and, particularly, the instance introduced in [7]) in order to take into account delayed function calls during PE. Specialized definitions are basically produced by constructing a set of rules (called *resultants*) of the form

$$\sigma_1(s) \to t_1$$
$$\cdots$$
$$\sigma_n(s) \to t_n$$

associated to a given (partial) computation

$$id \,\|\, s \xrightarrow{\text{RN}\ +} \{\sigma_1 \,\|\, t_1 \ \vee \ \ldots \ \vee \ \sigma_n \,\|\, t_n\} \ .$$

After that, a renaming transformation is performed in order to ensure that the specialized definition is inductively sequential and also to guarantee its *independence* (in the sense of [27]).

Informally, the renaming transformation proceeds as follows. First, an *independent renaming* ρ for a set of terms S is constructed, which consists of a mapping from terms to terms such that for all $s \in S$, we have $\rho(s) = f(\overline{x_n})$, where $\overline{x_n}$ are the distinct variables in s in the order of their first occurrence and f is a *fresh* function symbol. We also let $\rho(S)$ denote the set $S' = \{\rho(s) \mid s \in S\}$. While the independent renaming suffices to rename the left-hand sides of resultants (since they are constructor instances of the specialized calls), the right-hand sides are renamed by means of the auxiliary function ren_ρ, which *recursively* replaces each call in the given expression by a call to the corresponding renamed function (according to ρ).

Unfortunately, the framework of PE above cannot simply be transferred to residuating programs, since a naïve treatment of suspended calls can give rise to resultants which do not preserve the program's behavior, as illustrated in the following examples.

Example 3. Consider again the rules defining the functions "$\leqslant$" and "$+$" of Example 1, and assume now that "$\leqslant$" is flexible and "$+$" is rigid. Given the expression $X \leqslant Y + 0$, we have the partial computation

$$id \,\|\, X \leqslant Y + 0 \xrightarrow{\text{RN}} \{X = 0\} \,\|\, \text{true} \ \vee \ \{X = s(M)\}^s \,\|\, s(M) \leqslant Y + 0$$

in which the second disjunct corresponds to an incomplete step. The associated resultants are the following:[5]

$$0 \leqslant Y + 0 \to \text{true}$$
$$s(M) \leqslant Y + 0 \to s(M) \leqslant Y + 0$$

Obviously, any specialization containing the second rule does not preserve the semantics of the original program (for the intended goals). Unfortunately, getting rid of this trivial resultant does not preserve the semantics either.

---

[5] We do not consider the renaming of resultants since it is not relevant here.

The above example reveals the need to relax the standard computation model during partial evaluation in order to "complete" the suspended steps in some suitable way. For instance, we could avoid suspensions by simply replacing $\xrightarrow{\text{RN}}$ with $\xrightarrow{\text{NN}}$ during PE. This raises the question of whether it is possible to infer safe evaluation annotations for the specialized definitions, i.e., annotations such that total correctness is entailed. The following example answers this question negatively.

Example 4. Reconsider the program and goal of Example 3, but use $\xrightarrow{\text{NN}}$ to construct the partial computation

$$\text{id} \parallel \text{X} \leqslant \text{Y} + 0 \xrightarrow{\text{NN}} \{\text{X} = 0\} \parallel \text{true} \vee \{\text{X} = \text{s(M)}, \text{Y} = 0\} \parallel \text{s(M)} \leqslant 0$$
$$\vee \{\text{X} = \text{s(M)}, \text{Y} = \text{s(Z)}\} \parallel \text{s(M)} \leqslant \text{s(Z} + 0)$$

whose associated resultants are

$$0 \leqslant \text{Y} + 0 \rightarrow \text{true}$$
$$\text{s(M)} \leqslant 0 + 0 \rightarrow \text{s(M)} \leqslant 0$$
$$\text{s(M)} \leqslant \text{s(Z)} + 0 \rightarrow \text{s(M)} \leqslant \text{s(Z} + 0)$$

Then, neither *flex* nor *rigid* is a correct annotation for the specialized rules. If we assume that they are flexible, then a goal of the form $\text{s(X)} \leqslant \text{Y} + 0$ would succeed (with answer substitution $\{\text{Y} = 0\}$) using the specialized rules whereas it suspends in the original program. On the other hand, declaring the new definition as *rigid* does not work either, since a goal $\text{X} \leqslant \text{Y} + 0$ succeeds in the original program (with answer $\{\text{X} = 0\}$), whereas it suspends using the specialized rules.

Informally, the annotation *flex* for the specialized function is not safe since the bindings for the variable Y in the lhs of the second and third resultants have been brought by the evaluation of the rigid function "+". Similarly, the annotation *rigid* does not work since (at runtime) it prevents the considered call from matching the lhs of the first resultant because the variable X was instantiated by evaluating (at PE time) the flexible function "$\leqslant$".

Our proposed solution is essentially as follows. We distinguish between two kinds of computations: those in which the initial step for the considered expression is incomplete and those which involve no kind of suspension (because they are eventually stopped before). In the latter case, we simply use the $\xrightarrow{\text{RN}}$ computation model whereas, in the former case, we proceed to complete the degenerate step by using the relaxed relation $\xrightarrow{\text{NN}}$. This allows us to infer safe evaluation annotations for specialized definitions as follows:

- We annotate as *flex* the specialized definitions which result from computations with no suspension. This is justified by the fact that all variable bindings propagated to the left-hand sides of specialized rules come from the evaluation of flexible functions (since evaluation of rigid functions causes no binding for goal variables). Thus, the handling of these specialized functions as flexible (at runtime) cannot introduce undesired bindings.

$$
\begin{aligned}
&slist(id) && = [\,] \\
&slist(\varphi_k \circ \cdots \circ \varphi_1) && = [\theta^m | slist(\varphi_k \circ \cdots \circ \varphi_{j+1})] \\
&&&\text{where } \theta = \varphi_j \circ \cdots \circ \varphi_1, m = eval(\varphi_1), \text{ and } j \text{ is the} \\
&&&\text{maximum } i \in \{1, \ldots, k\} \text{ such that } \forall p \in \{1, \ldots, i\} \\
&&&eval(\varphi_p) = eval(\varphi_1) \text{ and } eval(\varphi_{j+1}) \neq eval(\varphi_1)
\end{aligned}
$$

$$
eval(\varphi) = \begin{cases} rigid & \text{if } \varphi \text{ is marked with the superscript } s \\ flex & \text{otherwise} \end{cases}
$$

$$
\begin{aligned}
&split(l, r, [\varphi^a]) = \{\varphi^a(l) \to ren_\rho(r), \text{ with evaluation annotation } a\} \\
&split(l, r, [\varphi^a, \theta^b | tail]) = \{\varphi^a(l) \to l', \text{ with eval. annotation } a\} \cup split(l', r, [\theta^b | tail]) \\
&\qquad\qquad \text{where } l' = f(x_1, \ldots, x_n), f \in \Sigma_{\mathbf{inter}} \text{ is a fresh function} \\
&\qquad\qquad \text{symbol, and } Var(\varphi^a(l)) = \{x_1, \ldots, x_n\}.
\end{aligned}
$$

Fig. 3. Auxiliary functions for partial evaluation

– In case of a suspension, we are constrained to split resultants by introducing several intermediate functions with befitting evaluation annotations. This is necessary because the $\xrightarrow{\text{NN}}$ step can introduce bindings which come both from flexible and rigid functions (as shown in Example 4) and the splitting avoids the mixing of bindings of different nature (*flex* and *rigid*).

Formally, a partial evaluation based on the $\xrightarrow{\text{RN}}$ calculus (RNPE for short) is constructed from a set of terms S together with a set of (partial) computations for the terms in S. In the following, we denote by $\Sigma_{\mathbf{inter}}$ a set of fresh function symbols. These are the symbols which are used to construct the intermediate functions associated to the partial evaluation of suspended expressions.

Definition 1 (partial evaluation). *Let $\mathcal{R}$ be a TRS, $S = \{s_1, \ldots, s_n\}$ a finite set of terms, and $\mathcal{A}_1, \ldots, \mathcal{A}_n$ finite (partial) $\xrightarrow{\text{RN}}$ computations for $s_1, \ldots, s_n$ in $\mathcal{R}$ of the form:*

$$
\mathcal{A}_k = id \,\|\, s_k \xrightarrow{\text{RN}}^+ D_k, \quad k = 1, \ldots, n
$$

where all steps are complete, except (possibly) for the initial one. Let ρ be an independent renaming of S. Then, the set of rewrite rules $\mathcal{R}' =$

$$
\{\sigma^c(\rho(s_k)) \to ren_\rho(r) \mid \sigma^c \,\|\, r \in D_k\}_{k=1}^n \qquad\qquad (non\text{-}suspension)
$$
$$
\bigcup
$$
$$
\{split(\rho(s_k), r, slist(\theta \circ \sigma)) \mid \theta^i \,\|\, \theta^i(s_k) \in D_k, \ \theta^i(s_k) \xrightarrow{\text{NN}}_\sigma r\}_{k=1}^n \quad (suspension)
$$

is a partial evaluation of S in $\mathcal{R}$ (under ρ). The evaluation annotation for the derivations involving no suspension is flex, whereas the resultants (and their evaluation annotations) for the suspended derivations are computed by means of the auxiliary functions shown in Fig. 3. [6]

---

[6] In the definition of $slist(\sigma)$ we consider that σ is expressed in its canonical representation.

Roughly speaking, the resultants associated to (one-step) $\xrightarrow{\text{NN}}$ computations are split into a set of "intermediate" rules, one rule associated to each sequence of consecutive bindings with the same superscript mark (suspended or non-suspended). This way, the specialized rules mimic the behaviour of the original functions perfectly. Note that the intermediate rules play no particular role in the evaluation of expressions, but are only necessary to preserve the flex or rigid nature of the functions in the initial program. The following example shows the construction of a RNPE for a suspended expression.

Example 5. Let us consider the following rules:

$$
\begin{aligned}
f(a,b) &\rightarrow c \quad \% \text{ flex} \\
g(b,c) &\rightarrow b \quad \% \text{ rigid} \\
h(c) &\rightarrow c \quad \% \text{ flex}
\end{aligned}
$$

A PE for $f(X, g(Y, h(Z)))$ constructed from the (suspended) derivation

$$
f(X, g(Y, h(Z))) \; \overset{\text{RN}}{\leadsto}_{\{X \mapsto a\}^s} \; f(a, g(Y, h(Z)))
$$

proceeds as follows (here we assume that $\rho(f(X, g(Y, h(Z)))) = f'(X, Y, Z)$):

1. First, the $\xrightarrow{\text{NN}}$ step $f(a, g(Y, h(Z))) \; \overset{\text{NN}}{\leadsto}_{\{Y \mapsto b, Z \mapsto c\}} \; f(a, g(b, c))$ is computed.
2. Then, the call $slist(\{X \mapsto a, Y \mapsto b, Z \mapsto c\})$ is undertaken, which returns the set of substitutions $[\{X \mapsto a\}^{\text{flex}}, \{Y \mapsto b\}^{\text{rigid}}, \{Z \mapsto c\}^{\text{flex}}]$.
3. Finally, the computation of $split$ proceeds as follows:

$$
\begin{aligned}
&split(f'(X, Y, Z), f(a, g(b, c)), [\{X \mapsto a\}^{\text{flex}}, \{Y \mapsto b\}^{\text{rigid}}, \{Z \mapsto c\}^{\text{flex}}]) \\
&= \{f'(a, Y, Z) \rightarrow f_1'(Y, Z)\} \\
&\quad \cup split(f_1'(Y, Z), f(a, g(b, c)), [\{Y \mapsto b\}^{\text{rigid}}, \{Z \mapsto c\}^{\text{flex}}]) \\
&= \{f'(a, Y, Z) \rightarrow f_1'(Y, Z), \\
&\quad\;\; f_1'(b, Z) \rightarrow f_2'(Z)\} \\
&\quad \cup split(f_2'(Z), f(a, g(b, c)), [\{Z \mapsto c\}^{\text{flex}}]) \\
&= \{f'(a, Y, Z) \rightarrow f_1'(Y, Z), \\
&\quad\;\; f_1'(b, Z) \rightarrow f_2'(Z), \\
&\quad\;\; f_2'(c) \rightarrow ren_\rho(f(a, g(b, c)))\}
\end{aligned}
$$

where "f'" and "f_2'" are flexible, and "f_1'" is rigid.

A general requirement in the partial evaluation of lazy functional logic programs is that no constructor-rooted expression can be evaluated during PE [5, 7]. This is also true in our context, although we did not make this condition explicit in Def. 1 since the computation model is only defined for operation-rooted terms. If we consider the more general setting in which the operational semantics is also defined for constructor-rooted terms, then this condition must appear explicitly.

For the correctness of partial evaluation, a *closedness* condition is commonly required which ensures that all calls which might occur during the execution of the specialized program are covered by some program rule. The following is an easy extension of the closedness condition of [6] to the case of residuating programs. Informally, an operation-rooted term t is closed w.r.t. a set of calls S if it is an instance of a term in S and the terms in the matching substitution are recursively closed by S.

Definition 2 (closedness). *Let S be a finite set of terms. We say that a term t is S-closed if closed(S,t) holds, where the predicate closed is defined inductively as follows:*

$$closed(S,t) \Leftrightarrow \begin{cases} true & if\ t \in \mathcal{X} \\ \bigwedge_{i=1,\dots,n} closed(S,t_i) & if\ t = c(\overline{t_n}),\ c \in (\mathcal{C} \cup \{\doteq, \&\} \cup \Sigma_{\mathbf{inter}}) \\ \bigwedge_{x \mapsto t' \in \theta} closed(S,t') & if\ \exists \theta, \exists s \in S\ such\ that\ \theta(s) = t \end{cases}$$

We say that a set of terms T is S-closed, written closed(S,T), if closed(S,t) holds for all $t \in T$, and we say that a TRS $\mathcal{R}$ is S-closed if closed$(S, \mathcal{R}_{calls})$ holds. Here we denote the set of the rhs's of the rules in $\mathcal{R}$ by $\mathcal{R}_{calls}$.

Note that expressions rooted by an "intermediate" function symbol in $\Sigma_{\mathbf{inter}}$ are S-closed by definition, independently of the considered set S. This is motivated by the fact that intermediate functions are not "visible" in the specialized program (i.e., they do not belong to the set of specialized calls), but are only intended as a mechanism to preserve the floundering behaviour.

The following theorem states an important property of RNPE: if the input program is inductively sequential, then the specialized program is also inductively sequential.

Theorem 2. *Let $\mathcal{R}$ be an inductively sequential program and S a finite set of operation-rooted terms. Then each RNPE of $\mathcal{R}$ w.r.t. S is inductively sequential.*

The following result establishes the precise relation between partial evaluations based on needed narrowing (without residuation, as defined in [7]), which we call NNPE for short, and partial evaluations as defined here. Intuitively, any RNPE $\mathcal{R}'$ can be transformed into an equivalent program $\mathcal{R}''$ (w.r.t. needed narrowing) by replacing each set of rules

$$\begin{aligned} \sigma(\rho(s)) &\to f_1(\overline{x_{m_1}}) \\ \varphi_1(f_1(\overline{x_{m_1}})) &\to f_2(\overline{x_{m_2}}) \\ &\cdots \\ \varphi_k(f_k(\overline{x_{m_k}})) &\to ren_\rho(r) \end{aligned}$$

associated to a suspended expression, by the new rule

$$\theta(\rho(s)) \to ren_\rho(r), \quad with\ \theta = \varphi_k \circ \cdots \circ \varphi_1 \circ \sigma$$

and ignoring all the evaluation annotations. The program constructed in this way is a correct NNPE of $\mathcal{R}$ w.r.t. S (under ρ), as formalized in the following.

Theorem 3. *Let $\mathcal{R}$ be an inductively sequential program. Let S be a finite set of operation-rooted terms and ρ an independent renaming of S. If $\mathcal{R}'$ is a RNPE of $\mathcal{R}$ w.r.t. S (under ρ), then there exists a NNPE $\mathcal{R}''$ of $\mathcal{R}$ w.r.t. S (under ρ) such that, for all goals e, we have $e \overset{NN^*}{\leadsto}_\sigma true$ in $\mathcal{R}'$ iff $e \overset{NN^*}{\leadsto}_\sigma true$ in $\mathcal{R}''$.*

Now, we state the partial correctness of RNPE, which amounts to the full computational equivalence between the original and specialized programs when the considered goal does not flounder.

Theorem 4 (partial correctness). *Let $\mathcal{R}$ be an inductively sequential program. Let e be an equation, $V \supseteq Var(e)$ a finite set of variables, S a finite set of operation-rooted terms, and ρ an independent renaming of S. Let $\mathcal{R}'$ be a RNPE of $\mathcal{R}$ w.r.t. S (under ρ) such that $\mathcal{R}' \cup \{e'\}$ is S'-closed, where $e' = ren_\rho(e)$ and $S' = \rho(S)$.*

1. If $e \overset{RN^*}{\leadsto}_{\sigma'}$ true in $\mathcal{R}'$, then $e \overset{RN^*}{\leadsto}_\sigma t$ and $\varphi(t) \to^*$ true in $\mathcal{R}$ with $\sigma' = \varphi \circ \sigma$ $[V]$.

2. If $e \overset{RN^*}{\leadsto}_\sigma$ true in $\mathcal{R}$, then $e \overset{RN^*}{\leadsto}_{\sigma'} t$ and $\varphi(t') \to^*$ true in $\mathcal{R}'$ with $\sigma = \varphi \circ \sigma'$ $[V]$.

Loosely speaking, the previous result establishes that, if evaluation annotations are not considered (that is, no function calls are delayed), then the specialized program $\mathcal{R}'$ *is able* to produce the same answers (computed by needed narrowing) as the original one $\mathcal{R}$ (and vice versa). The preservation of floundering-freeness (i.e., absence of floundering) for the intended goals is needed to establish the total correctness of the transformation. On the other hand, it ensures that the transformation does not introduce additional floundering points, which is of crucial importance when we are using the transformation for optimizing a program. Moreover, this feature may allow us to use the transformation as a tool for proving floundering-freeness of the original program (see Example 7). In fact, if after the transformation we can state that $\mathcal{R}' \cup \{e'\}$ does not flounder, then we are also sure that $\mathcal{R} \cup \{e\}$ does not flounder either, where $e' = ren_\rho(e)$.

Unfortunately, the recursive notion of closedness introduced in Def. 2 is too weak (generous) to preserve the floundering behaviour, as illustrated by the following example.

Example 6. Let us consider the following set of rules:

$$f(X, a) \ \to \ g(X) \quad \% \ \text{flex} \qquad h(a) \ \to \ b \quad \% \ \text{rigid}$$
$$g(b) \ \to \ c \quad \% \ \text{flex}$$

A RNPE of $\{f(X, Y), h(X)\}$ under $\rho = \{f(X, Y) \mapsto f'(X, Y), h(X) \mapsto h'(X)\}$ is

$$f'(b, a) \ \to \ c \quad \% \ \text{flex}$$
$$h'(a) \ \to \ b \quad \% \ \text{rigid}$$

Now, the S-closed expression $f(h(X), X)$ has the following successful computation in the original program

$$id \ \| \ f(h(X), X) \xrightarrow{RN} \{X \mapsto a\} \ \| \ g(h(a)) \xrightarrow{RN} \{X \mapsto a\} \ \| \ g(b) \xrightarrow{RN} \{X \mapsto a\} \ \| \ c$$

whereas $\rho(f(h(X), X)) = f'(h'(X), X)$ may suspend in the specialized program, e.g., by considering the following definitional tree

$$branch(f'(X, Y), 1, flex,$$
$$branch(f'(b, Y), 2, flex,$$
$$rule(f'(b, a) \to c)))$$

for the specialized function f'.

Informally, the problem is that the recursive notion of closedness only works when the considered operational model is *compositional*, as it essentially exploits the fact that the meaning of a complex expression $f(h(X), X)$ can be retrieved from the semantics of its "unnested" constituents $f(Y, X)$ and $h(X)$ [6]. However, the $\xrightarrow{RN}$ calculus is not compositional due to the presence of delayed function calls, and hence the meaning of the call $f(h(X), X)$ (which does not flounder) cannot be obtained from the meaning of the calls $f(Y, X)$ and $h(X)$ since the second one flounders. Thus, we consider in the following a restricted notion of closedness (called *basic* closedness in [6], in symbols $closed^-$) which is defined as the recursive closedness of Def. 2 except for the case

$$closed(S, t) = \bigwedge_{x \mapsto t' \in \theta} closed(S, t') \quad \text{if } \exists \theta, \exists s \in S \text{ such that } \theta(s) = t$$

which is replaced by the more simple condition

$$closed^-(S, t) = true \quad \text{if } \exists \theta, \exists s \in S \text{ such that } \theta(s) = t \text{ and } \theta \text{ is constructor}.$$

The following result states the equivalence between the original and specialized programs w.r.t. floundering-freeness.

Theorem 5 (floundering-freeness). *Let $\mathcal{R}$ be an inductively sequential program, e an equation, S a finite set of operation-rooted terms, and ρ an independent renaming of S. Let $\mathcal{R}'$ be a RNPE of $\mathcal{R}$ w.r.t. S (under ρ) such that $\mathcal{R}' \cup \{e'\}$ is S'-closed$^-$, where $e' = ren_\rho(e)$ and $S' = \rho(S)$. Then, e flounders in $\mathcal{R}$ iff e' flounders in $\mathcal{R}'$.*

As a corollary of Theorems 4 and 5, we can establish the total correctness of the transformation.

Theorem 6 (total correctness). *Let $\mathcal{R}$ be an inductively sequential program. Let e be an equation, $V \supseteq Var(e)$ a finite set of variables, S a finite set of operation-rooted terms, and ρ an independent renaming of S. Let $\mathcal{R}'$ be a RNPE of $\mathcal{R}$ w.r.t. S (under ρ) such that $\mathcal{R}' \cup \{e'\}$ is S'-closed$^-$, where $e' = ren_\rho(e)$ and $S' = \rho(S)$.*

1. *If $e' \xrightarrow{RN^*}_{\sigma'} true$ in $\mathcal{R}'$, then $e \xrightarrow{RN^*}_\sigma true$ in $\mathcal{R}$ where $\sigma' = \sigma [V]$ (soundness)*
2. *If $e \xrightarrow{RN^*}_\sigma true$ in $\mathcal{R}$, then $e' \xrightarrow{RN^*}_{\sigma'} true$ in $\mathcal{R}'$ where $\sigma' = \sigma [V]$ (completeness)*

5   Some Experiments

The INDY system v1.8 is a rather concise implementation of a partial evaluator for functional logic programs (a detailed description of the system can be found in [3]). The partial evaluator described in Sect. 4 has been implemented in the INDY system and used to conduct some experiments (extracted from the Curry library[7]) which illustrate the advantages of the RNPE method in the context of residuating functional logic programs as well as the practicality of our approach.

---

[7] Available from URL: `http://www-i2.informatik.rwth-aachen.de/~hanus/curry`.

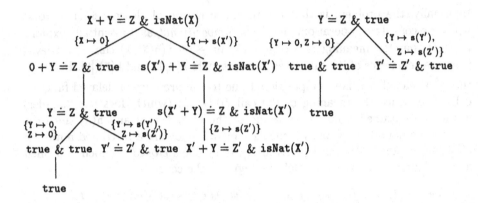

Fig. 4. Partial computations for $X + Y \doteq Z$ & $isNat(X)$ and $Y \doteq Z$ & $true$

Let us introduce an example which shows that RNPE can be used for proving floundering-freeness of a class of goals in a given program.

Example 7. Consider the following program which defines the arithmetic addition and the predicate $isNat$, which returns $true$ when the argument is a natural number:

$$0 + Y \to Y \qquad\qquad isNat(0) \to true$$
$$s(X) + Y \to s(X + Y) \qquad isNat(s(X)) \to isNat(X)$$

where "+" is rigid and "$isNat$" is flexible. Let $S = \{X + Y \doteq Z$ & $isNat(X), Y \doteq Z$ & $true\}$ and consider the independent renaming $\rho = \{X + Y \doteq Z$ & $isNat(X) \mapsto and3(X, Y, Z), Y \doteq Z$ & $true \mapsto and2(Y, Z)\}$. Now, by considering the partial computations depicted in Fig. 4,[8] the following RNPE of the program w.r.t. S (under ρ) is constructed:

$$and3(0, 0, 0) \to true \qquad\qquad and2(0, 0) \to true$$
$$and3(0, s(Y), s(Z)) \to and2(Y, Z) \qquad and2(s(X), s(Y)) \to and2(X, Y)$$
$$and3(s(X), Y, s(Z)) \to and3(X, Y, Z)$$

where both $and3$ and $and2$ are flexible functions. Then, for proving floundering-freeness it is sufficient to check that no operation symbol of the resulting partially evaluated program has a *rigid* annotation. For instance, one can easily see that the goal $X + Y = Z$ & $isNat(X)$ is floundering-free in the residual program (hence in the original), since the program has no rigid functions, while in the original program this is not immediate.

In the next example, we intend to show that RNPE can be also used to simplify the dynamic behavior of a program, thus allowing us to achieve a significant optimization.

---

[8] Here we assume that the strict equality $\doteq$ is flexible.

Example 8. Consider the classical map coloring program which assigns a color to each of four countries such that countries with a common border have different colors:

```
isColor(red)           → true
isColor(yellow)        → true
isColor(green)         → true
coloring(11,12,13,14) → isColor(11) & isColor(12)
                           & isColor(13) & isColor(14)
correct(11,12,13,14)  → diff(11,12) & diff(11,13)
                           & diff(12,14) & diff(13,14)
```

where the predefined function diff is the only rigid function (it makes use of the strict equality predicate in order to check whether its arguments are different). Now, we consider the specialization of the expression correct(11, 12, 13, 14) & coloring(11, 12, 13, 14), which gives the following specialized program:

```
and4(red, yellow, green, red)    → true
and4(red, green, yellow, red)    → true
and4(yellow, red, green, yellow) → true
and4(yellow, green, red, yellow) → true
and4(green, red, yellow, green)  → true
and4(green, yellow, red, green)  → true
```

where some potential colorings have been discarded, thus simplifying the dynamic behavior of the program and achieving a significant speedup (actually it runs 23 times faster).

Our preliminary experiments show that RNPE is able to produce significant speed-up's on several typical concurrent Curry programs. Moreover, it is a conservative extension of the previous INDY system based on needed narrowing, since RNPE boils down to NNPE when all program functions are flexible.

6   Conclusions

We have presented a general partial evaluation framework for Curry, a truly lazy functional logic language whose development is an international initiative intended to provide a standard for the area. The framework derives from that of [7] and extends it to the combination of needed narrowing and residuation. The extended framework allows us to safely deal with the evaluation annotations, which is crucial for controlling unfolding during PE as well as for correctly synthesizing evaluation annotations for the specialized functions.

Despite the practical importance of logic programs with dynamic scheduling, there has been surprisingly little work devoted to their specialization. The only transformation framework that we are aware of for logic languages with delays is that of Etalle and Gabbrielli [14], which is based on the fold/unfold approach to program transformation. It differs from our methodology, since our framework is based on the (automatic) PE approach and applies to logic languages with lazy functions. Moreover, we allow unfolding of suspended expressions at PE time, which is not the case of [14].

An interesting prospect for future work is to extend the framework to encompass the PE of non-deterministic (i.e., non-confluent) functions, which is ahead of the state of the art as we know it even for pure functional programming languages [23]. We are also considering how to discover slices of code in the residual program which are "semantically dead", according to the considered operational principle of functional logic programs with delays, since they can be safely removed without influencing the intended result.

References

1. H. Aït-Kaci. An Overview of LIFE. In J.W. Schmidt and A.A. Stogny, editors, *Proc. Workshop on Next Generation Information Systems Technology*, pages 42–58. Springer LNCS 504, 1990.
2. H. Aït-Kaci, P. Lincoln, and R. Nasr. Le Fun: Logic, equations, and Functions. In *Proc. of Fourth IEEE Int'l Symp. on Logic Programming*, pages 17–23. IEEE, New York, 1987.
3. E. Albert, M. Alpuente, M. Falaschi, and G. Vidal. INDY User's Manual. Technical Report DSIC-II/12/98, UPV, 1998. Available from URL:
   http://www.dsic.upv.es/users/elp/papers.html.
4. E. Albert, M. Alpuente, M. Hanus, and G. Vidal. Partial Evaluation of Residuating Functional Logic Programs. Technical report, DSIC, UPV, 1999. Available from URL: http://www.dsic.upv.es/users/elp/papers.html.
5. M. Alpuente, M. Falaschi, P. Julián, and G. Vidal. Specialization of Lazy Functional Logic Programs. In *Proc. of the ACM SIGPLAN Conf. on Partial Evaluation and Semantics-Based Program Manipulation, PEPM'97*, volume 32, 12 of *Sigplan Notices*, pages 151–162, New York, 1997. ACM Press.
6. M. Alpuente, M. Falaschi, and G. Vidal. Partial Evaluation of Functional Logic Programs. *ACM Transactions on Programming Languages and Systems*, 20(4):768–844, 1998.
7. M. Alpuente, M. Hanus, S. Lucas, and G. Vidal. Specialization of Functional Logic Programs Based on Needed Narrowing. In P. Lee, editor, *Proc. of the Int'l Conference on Functional Programming, ICFP'99*, Paris (France). ACM, New York, 1999.
8. S. Antoy. Definitional trees. In *Proc. of the 3rd Int'l Conference on Algebraic and Logic Programming, ALP'92*, pages 143–157. Springer LNCS 632, 1992.
9. S. Antoy. Optimal non-deterministic functional logic computations. In *Proc. of the Int'l Conference on Algebraic and Logic Programming, ALP'97*, pages 16–30. Springer LNCS 1298, 1997.
10. S. Antoy, R. Echahed, and M. Hanus. A Needed Narrowing Strategy. In *Proc. 21st ACM Symp. on Principles of Programming Languages, Portland*, pages 268–279, 1994.
11. J. Boye. Avoiding Dynamic Delays in Functional Logic Languages. In J. Penjam and M. Bruynooghe, editors, *Proc. of PLILP'93*, pages 12–27. Springer LNCS 714, 1993.
12. C. Consel and O. Danvy. Tutorial notes on Partial Evaluation. In *Proc. of 20th Annual ACM Symp. on Principles of Programming Languages*, pages 493–501. ACM, New York, 1993.

13. N. Dershowitz and J.-P. Jouannaud. Rewrite Systems. In J. van Leeuwen, editor, *Handbook of Theoretical Computer Science*, volume B: Formal Models and Semantics, pages 243–320. Elsevier, Amsterdam, 1990.
14. S. Etalle, M. Gabbrielli, and E. Marchiori. A Transformation System for CLP with Dynamic Scheduling and CCP. In *Proc. of the ACM Sigplan PEPM'97*, pages 137–150. ACM Press, New York, 1997.
15. J. Gallagher. Tutorial on Specialisation of Logic Programs. In *Proc. of Partial Evaluation and Semantics-Based Program Manipulation, Copenhagen, Denmark, June 1993*, pages 88–98. ACM, New York, 1993.
16. E. Giovannetti, G. Levi, C. Moiso, and C. Palamidessi. Kernel Leaf: A Logic plus Functional Language. *Journal of Computer and System Sciences*, 42:363–377, 1991.
17. R. Glück and M.H. Sørensen. Partial Deduction and Driving are Equivalent. In *Proc. of PLILP'94*, pages 165–181. Springer LNCS 844, 1994.
18. M. Hanus. The Integration of Functions into Logic Programming: From Theory to Practice. *Journal of Logic Programming*, 19&20:583–628, 1994.
19. M. Hanus. Analysis of Residuating Logic Programs. *Journal of Logic Programming*, 24(3):161–199, 1995.
20. M. Hanus. A unified computation model for functional and logic programming. In *Proc. of the 24th ACM Symposium on Principles of Programming Languages (Paris)*, pages 80–93. ACM, New York, 1997.
21. M. Hanus (ed.). Curry: An Integrated Functional Logic Language. Available at http://www-i2.informatik.rwth-aachen.de/~hanus/curry, 1999.
22. N.D. Jones, C.K. Gomard, and P. Sestoft. *Partial Evaluation and Automatic Program Generation*. Prentice-Hall, Englewood Cliffs, NJ, 1993.
23. Neil D. Jones. An Introduction to Partial Evaluation. *ACM Computing Surveys*, 28(3):480–503, Sept. 1996.
24. M. Leuschel, D. De Schreye, and A. de Waal. A Conceptual Embedding of Folding into Partial Deduction: Towards a Maximal Integration. In M. Maher, editor, *Proc. of JICSLP'96*, pages 319–332. The MIT Press, Cambridge, MA, 1996.
25. J.W. Lloyd. Combining Functional and Logic Programming Languages. In *Proc. of the International Logic Programming Symposium*, pages 43–57, 1994.
26. J.W. Lloyd. Declarative Programming in Escher. Technical Report CSTR-95-013, Computer Science Department, University of Bristol, 1995.
27. J.W. Lloyd and J.C. Shepherdson. Partial Evaluation in Logic Programming. *Journal of Logic Programming*, 11:217–242, 1991.
28. R. Loogen, F. López-Fraguas, and M. Rodríguez-Artalejo. A Demand Driven Computation Strategy for Lazy Narrowing. In J. Penjam and M. Bruynooghe, editors, *Proc. of PLILP'93*, pages 184–200. Springer LNCS 714, 1993.
29. J.J. Moreno-Navarro and M. Rodríguez-Artalejo. Logic Programming with Functions and Predicates: The language Babel. *Journal of Logic Programming*, 12(3):191–224, 1992.
30. L. Naish. *Negation and Control in Prolog*. Springer LNCS 238, 1987.
31. L. Naish. Adding equations to NU-Prolog. In J. Maluszyński and M. Wirsing, editors, *Proc. of the 3rd Int'l Symp. on Programming Languages Implementation and Logic Programming*, pages 15–26. Springer LNCS 528, 1991.
32. G. Smolka. The Oz Programming Model. In Jan van Leeuwen, editor, *Computer Science Today: Recent Trends and Developments*, pages 324–343. Springer LNCS 1000, 1995.

Author Index

Lecture Notes in Artificial Intelligence (LNAI)

Lecture Notes in Computer Science